PRINCIPLES OF DIRECT AND DATABASE MARKETING

We work with leading authors to develop the
strongest educational materials in marketing
bringing cutting-edge thinking and best learning
practice to a global market.

Under a range of well-known imprints including
Financial Times Prentice Hall, we craft high quality
print and electronic publications which help
readers to understand and apply their content
whether studying or at work.

To find out more about the complete range of our
publishing please visit us on the World Wide Web at:
www.pearsoned.co.uk

PRINCIPLES OF DIRECT AND DATABASE MARKETING

ALAN TAPP

THIRD EDITION

FT Prentice Hall
FINANCIAL TIMES

An imprint of **Pearson Education**
Harlow, England • London • New York • Boston • San Francisco • Toronto • Sydney • Singapore • Hong Kong
Tokyo • Seoul • Taipei • New Delhi • Cape Town • Madrid • Mexico City • Amsterdam • Munich • Paris • Milan

For Dad

Pearson Education Limited
Edinburgh Gate
Harlow
Essex CM20 2JE
England

and Associated Companies throughout the world
Visit us on the World Wide Web at
www.pearsoned.co.uk

First published in Great Britain 1998
Second edition published 2001
Third edition published 2005

© Financial Times Professional Limited 1998
© Pearson Education Limited 2001, 2005

ISBN-10: 0-273-68355-1
ISBN-13: 978-0-273-68355-1

British Library Cataloguing-in-Publication Data
A catalogue record for this book is available from the British Library

Library of Congress Cataloging-in-Publication Data
A catalog record for this book is available from the Library of Congress

10 9 8 7 6 5 4 3
09 08 07 06

Typeset by 30 in Stone Serif 9.5/13pt
Printed and bound by Ashford Colour Press, Gosport, Hants.

CONTENTS

Companion Website resources

Visit the Companion Website at www.booksites.net/tapp

For lecturers
- Complete, downloadable Instructor's Manual
- PowerPoint slides that can be downloaded and used as OHTs

PREFACE

It is now over five years since the first edition of this book was launched to an un-suspecting marketplace. Time perhaps to take a step back and ponder the place of direct and database marketing within the marketing profession. There's no doubt progress has been made: it was always the dream of old-school direct marketers that DM would be respected as a profession, and over the 1990s and the 2000s this seems to have come to pass. Most universities now offer courses in direct marketing. Some even offer entire masters programmes dedicated to the subject. Good quality graduates now aspire to places in attractive agencies in London and elsewhere. We are (almost) seen as a sexy career, which was not so a few years ago.

As direct and database marketing matures, perhaps we can assess its place in market-ing. Comparing us to other disciplines within marketing is interesting. Unlike some others, we are led by practice rather than researchers in academia. This has both strengths and weaknesses. Being practitioner-led gives us a definite 'street credibility' lacking in other branches of the profession. Students who study direct marketing know that it will lead directly to career prospects. Direct marketing practice is rooted in the success of the discipline in delivering what it says 'on the tin'. It works. The down side is that there has been a relative lack of well developed theory to underpin the profes-sion. Consumer behaviour is not as well understood as it might be, partly because the customer database concentrates on what is purchased but does not explain why. Another comparison comes through the prism of the 'is marketing an art or a science' debate. While many regard this debate as self-indulgent and unimportant, it is never-theless useful to step back occasionally and ponder what we are doing. Direct marketing, with its mix of elegant database analysis and creative communication, could be positioned as a mix between science and art. That is precisely its attraction.

A more difficult job is to predict exactly how direct and database marketing will fare over the next 20 years. On the one hand we are entitled to feel optimistic about the impact of new interactive technologies, in particular mobile devices and Internet growth. There's little doubt that direct marketing is a preeminent skill in these domains, yet the dot-com players may not necessarily define themselves as direct marketers. The same can perhaps be said about CRM. There has been an explosion in worldwide spend-ing on CRM IT since the millennium turned, and CRM is very big news indeed, attracting the attention of chief executives. Once more, direct and database marketing skills are very important, but once more there is a reluctance by CRMers to define them-selves as direct marketers. This may be because in spite of their successes, direct marketers have yet to shift themselves from their tactical backwater in marketing departments. Direct marketers are as prone as any other marketers to the charge of being over-focused on communications campaigns, and of under-achieving in creating value for customers as part of cross-functional networks.

Still, at long last, the marketing database is beginning to be deployed as a company-wide strategic tool in practise – at least by Tesco. Good for them, and if one swallow doesn't make a summer we can still take heart from their success. More will surely follow. Social changes will continue to influence marketers, and direct marketers will benefit from the increasingly complicated lives we all lead, leading to complicated segmentations – something we are very good at managing!

What about the other promised lands – relationship marketing and one-to-one marketing? The former continues to frustrate – the professional press continues to throw in thought-free references to direct marketing as a way of delivering relationship marketing, often with no evidence at all to back up these claims. It is time to get real: most direct marketing is about selling – making an offer for customers to buy – not about relationship building. Provided customers are predisposed to receiving these offers, there's nothing wrong with these approaches. Direct marketers who ignore their data and create junk mass mail need to sharpen up their act. But responsible direct marketers who segment and target should celebrate the effectiveness of their transaction marketing, not try to hide it with unnecessary 'relationship' language.

Meanwhile the 'promised land' of Don Peppers' one-to-one marketing, the 'holy grail' of DM, edges slightly closer. We now have media at our disposal (i.e. e-mail, SMS) that have such low costs for personalised communications as to make one-to-one more economically realistic. However, the sheer management effort of one-to-one remains a stumbling block.

Were it to happen, Alan Mitchell's vision of customer-led marketing would surely be the biggest leap of all for direct marketers. His book, *Right Side Up*, is a very interesting read. His thesis is that supplier-driven marketing – the current model – is inefficient because it is controlled and run by sellers for sellers, with only occasional interest taken in what customers think of it. He asks: would customers buy a firm's marketing? Probably not, is the answer. Yet, customers are desperate for help in making complex choices. Here's where a good database could act proactively on behalf of customers, not suppliers.

NEW FOR THE THIRD EDITION

You'll find plenty in this book to help you make up your mind about where and how direct and database marketing fits into marketing. In this third edition we have a new chapter (7) on relationship marketing and CRM, which includes debate about the doubts and uncertainties that some describe as a fad and others a revolution. All the latest developments in new media and the Internet, mobile marketing, interactive TV and others are discussed in detail in Chapters 8, 10 and 11.

New database software that is shaping modern direct marketing is illustrated in an updated Chapter 3. There have been some changes to the geo-demographic and lifestyle database industry: these are covered in Chapter 4. Chapters 5 and 6, covering strategic issues in detail, have been adjusted to take into account new findings on retention and loyalty models.

The book also illustrates the author's close relationship with cutting-edge direct marketing practice with a suite of up-to-date case studies from a variety of sectors. Colourful illustrations bring the stories to life: you can take your pick from Tesco, Macmillan Cancer Care, Xerox, IBM, the World Gold Council, and Vodafone, among others.

The book also boasts a new website. Visit http://www.booksite.net/tapp to find valuable teaching and learning materials, including PowerPoint slides and an instructor's manual.

Amidst the new material, the philosophy of this book remains the same: to marry sound academic principles with the reality of practice – direct marketing managers will smile in recognition of the marketing picture painted here.

ACKNOWLEDGEMENTS

I'd like to thank my wife Jane, for her good humour during the latter stages of writing. Throughout the book you will find major contributions from the excellent direct-marketing agency Harrison Troughton Wunderman. In particular, I extend my gratitude to Laura Holme, Martin Troughton, Malcolm Peters, Andy Dobson and Polly Jones. I also thank Andrew Gwynne of Vodafone for his co-operation on Chapter 14, as well as Ross Facer and Marc Farr of Experian Ltd who helped with Chapter 4. Contributions towards the case studies came from Merlin Stone and Tim Hughes of Bristol Business School. I thank Ian Ventham of the RNLI, Charlie Dawson of Duckworth Finn Grubb Waters for the Daowoo case study, and I also thank Andrew Ward of the DMA for his help with the DMA Census material. The following individuals provided valuable feedback in the pre-revision reviews:

Geoffrey Wootten – Leicester Business School, De Montfort University
Stephen Tagg – Strathclyde University
Ian Black – Strathclyde University
Sally Ann Burrows – Bradford University
Paul Brittain – Nottingham Trent University
Richard West – Haseley Consulting and Visiting Lecturer at Westminster

I also thank the publishing team at Pearson Education, in particular, Thomas Sigel, Senior Acquisitions Editor, Anita Atkinson, Senior Desk Editor, Peter Hooper, Editorial Assistant, Kate Lodge, Freelance Project Manager, and the rest of the team for helping make this third edition a reality.

How this book relates to direct marketing planning

The direct marketing planning process	Chapter
Direct marketing analysis	
■ Analysis of customers held on internal database	3
■ Analysis of external market opportunities	4
Direct marketing objective setting	5
Direct marketing strategy creation	5 and 6
How to acquire and keep customers, taking account of:	
■ segmentation	
■ targeting	
■ product/market match	
■ marketing mix	
■ positioning	
■ branding	
■ CRM	7
■ the Internet	8
Direct marketing programmes	
■ The offer	9
■ Media	10 and 11
■ Creative approach	12
Direct marketing control – testing and budgeting	13

PUBLISHER'S ACKNOWLEDGEMENTS

We are grateful to the following for permission to reproduce copyright material:

Haymarket Business Publications Limited for 'Affinity Way to do Business' by N. Denny reproduced from *Marketing Direct Magazine* June 1996 and 'IBM Case Study' reproduced from *Marketing Direct Magazine* November 1995; W.R. Swinyard for 'Segmenting According to Lifestyle Needs: Harley Davidson' published in *Journal of Targeting, Measurement and Analysis* 4 (1) 1996; Dr J Arens for 'Examining the Role of Lifestage Transitions in Modelling Consumer Behaviour' published in *Journal of Targeting And Measuremenr Analysis* 1 (4) 1993; Institute of Direct Marketing for extracts from *The Direct Marketing Guide* by R. Fairlie; Dr Tim Hughes for 'A Case Study: Insureco, From Direct Sales to Direct CRM'; British Red Cross for extracts from 'Script for Red Cross Gulf War Appeal'; Guardian Newspaper Services Limited for 'Shops on the Box' by Celia Dodd published in *The Guardian* 6 August 1998 © Guardian; The Direct Marketing Association (UK) for extracts from *The Direct Marketing Association/Royal Mail Award Winners 1999*.

Figure 1.3, Table 1.2 and Figure 10.4 adapted from *DMA Census, 2003* reproduced by permission of the Direct Marketing Association (DMA 2003); Figures 4.3 and 4.4 reproduced by permission of Experian; Figure 5.10 reproduced by permission of The Society of Motor Manufacturers and Traders Ltd.; Chapter 5, Appendix 2 'Dustcovers' advert reproduced by permission of Duckworth Finn Grubb Waters; Figure 9.3 redrawn from Finders Keepers – the basics of customer acquisition and retention in *The Practitioners Guide to Direct Marketing* edited by B. Halsey, reproduced by permission of the IDM (Holder, D. 1992); Table 10.2 based on the IDM Media/*Educator's Guide* (updated to 1996) reproduced by permission of the IDM; Figure 10.3 reproduced by kind permission of IBM and Harrison Troughton Wunderman; Figure 10.5 reproduced by kind permission of Xerox and Harrison Troughton Wunderman; Exhibit 11.4 reproduced by permission of the Labour Party; Figure 11.5 reproduced by kind permission of Xerox and Harrison Troughton Wunderman; Figure 12.3 reproduced by permission of Marketscan Ltd.; Figure 12.4 reproduced by kind permission of the RSPCA; Figure 12.5 reproduced by permission of Time Group Ltd.; Figure 12.7 (left) reproduced by permission of ITN Archive; Figure 12.7 (top, middle) reproduced by permission of Harrison Troughton Wunderman; Figure 12.7 (bottom, middle) reproduced by permission of Sky News; Figure 12.7 (right) reproduced by permission of the Financial Times; Figure 12.8 adapted from *Consumer Psychology for Marketing*, pub Routledge, reproduced by permission of Thomson Publishing Services (Foxall, G. and Goldsmith, R., 1994); Figure 12.9 reproduced by permission of Amnesty International; Figures 13.1, 13.2 and 13.3 reproduced by permission of Royal and Sun Alliance; Figure 13.5 redrawn from 'Using market research for better direct marketing' in *The Practitioners' Guide to Direct Marketing* edited by B. Halsey, reproduced by permission of the IDM and the author (Mouncey, P., 2002); Figure 13.6 reproduced by permission of the RNLI; Figures 14.3, 14.4, 14.5 and 14.6 reproduced by kind permission of Vodafone and Harrison Troughton Wunderman.

Chapter 3, Case Study, Segmentation in action, reproduced by permission of SmartFOCUS Ltd.; Chapter 9, Case Study, Club Philips 2002, reproduced by permission of Wunderman; Figure 12.7 World Gold Council – scrap metal barge, reproduced by permission of Harrison Troughton Wunderman; Chapter 10, Case Study, Xerox Win Gold – How to make direct mail interesting and Chapter 11, Case Study, Choosing Media – Xerox, reproduced by permission of Xerox and Harrison Troughton Wunderman; Chapter 12, Case Study, M&G – collective investments, reproduced by permission of M&G and Harrison Troughton Wunderman; Chapter 14, Worked Case Study: Vodafone, reproduced by permission of Vodafone and Harrison Troughton Wunderman.

Illustrations in Figures 12.12, 12.13, 12.14 and 14.6 courtesy of Ian Saunders; Percy Thrower photograph in Figure 12.12 courtesy of his three daughters, Margaret Thrower, Susan Brookes and Ann Kirkham; Emil Zatopek image in Figure 12.12 courtesy of Hulton/Getty images; Beatles fans image in Figure 12.12 courtesy of PA Photos; Tommy Cooper image in Figure 12.13 courtesy of Rex Features and John Miles for the Tommy Cooper Estate; Tony Hancock image in Figure 12.13 courtesy of TopFoto/RHR.

In some instances we have been unable to trace owners of copyright material and we would appreciate any information that would enable us to do so.

PART 1

INTRODUCING DIRECT MARKETING

1

WHAT IS DIRECT MARKETING?

Objectives

Once you have read this chapter you will:

- have a clear view of what direct marketing is;

- understand its importance in contemporary marketing;

- understand its role within the wider marketing framework.

Introduction

In this chapter direct and database marketing will be introduced. As direct marketing is a widely misunderstood area, the common areas of confusion are addressed early on, and a clear vision of direct marketing as a complete framework for a specialised form of marketing is developed. The reader will probably be familiar with typical general marketing techniques, so these are used throughout as a foil to provide a clear sense of how direct marketing differs from mainstream marketing.

Finally, the reasons for the recent explosive growth in direct marketing practice are analysed.

What is direct and database marketing?

A DISTINCT MARKETING SYSTEM

Direct marketing is a way of doing marketing. You may already be familiar with the core philosophy of marketing, summed up by Jobber (1995) as 'the achievement of corporate goals through meeting and exceeding customer needs better than competition'. This philosophy is exactly the same for direct marketing. So where does direct marketing differ from general marketing?

Direct marketing is a method of marketing based on individual customer records held on a database. These records are the basis for marketing analysis, planning, implementation of programmes, and control of all this activity.

In contrast, general marketing is structured around the creation of brands for each product, and the attainment of market share for that product. The very first marketing department, set up by Colgate Palmolive in 1938, contained that classical department structure: brand and product managers, group product managers, and so on.

In comparing these two approaches, the advantage of the direct marketing framework *is that the use of the database forces a natural focus on customers rather than products*. Modern direct marketing thinking (for example, Peppers and Rogers, 1993) holds that it is better to understand one's customers as *individuals* in more detail, than to build up product brands. Direct marketing also encourages us to think in terms of customer relationships with the company – are we talking to 'new prospects' or 'loyal, established customers'? In this respect, there is a natural alignment between direct marketing and 'relationship marketing'.

If the first tangible difference is the database, the second is that direct marketers market to customers with the aim of *attracting a direct response*. Direct Line Insurance gives you a phone number to respond to it after seeing its adverts. Direct marketers will often contact customers directly through addressable, one-to-one media. *Reader's Digest* will write to customers whose subscriptions have run out to ask them to renew, at the same time offering them an incentive to respond quickly. Direct marketers may also *distribute direct* to customers, missing out the retail link in the chain. Grattan, the mail-order company, does exactly this.

However, the problem with the previous descriptions of direct marketing is that although they are often used to explain the discipline, they don't quite get to the heart of what direct marketing is all about.

In fact, the key to modern direct marketing is the capture of individual customer details at the first sale, so that the marketer can begin a relationship with that customer, *subsequently treating them differently* over time in order to generate repeat business (*see* Fig. 1.1).

So, if someone offers you a leaflet to get money off your next cinema ticket, you join a dating agency, the charity volunteer leaves an envelope at your home for you to make a donation, or you receive a coupon through the post from Persil to redeem at your supermarket – a lot of this is described as direct marketing. But it is argued here that direct marketing in its fullest sense happens only when the customer's name, address and details are taken and the subsequent marketing to them changes as a result.

Let us consider the charity volunteer who leaves an envelope at your house for you to make a donation. The volunteer returns three days later and merely picks up your donation without noting your address, or indeed noting your contribution in any way. Although some may describe this as direct marketing, only in the most basic way (direct contact with an individual) can it be described as such.

At the other end of the scale, it could be argued that the purest form of direct marketing is that practised by business salespeople. What do good computer equipment salespeople do having made the first sale to a company? Forget all about that company until they next have a shortfall on their targets? No, they stay in constant touch, learning more and more about that company's computing needs. Then they will make the company further offers that they know will be relevant to it. Good salespeople will be constantly learning about their customers' individual needs in depth, and will adjust their own product and service offers as far as possible in order to meet customers' needs. An ongoing relationship is established between salesperson and customer, and any

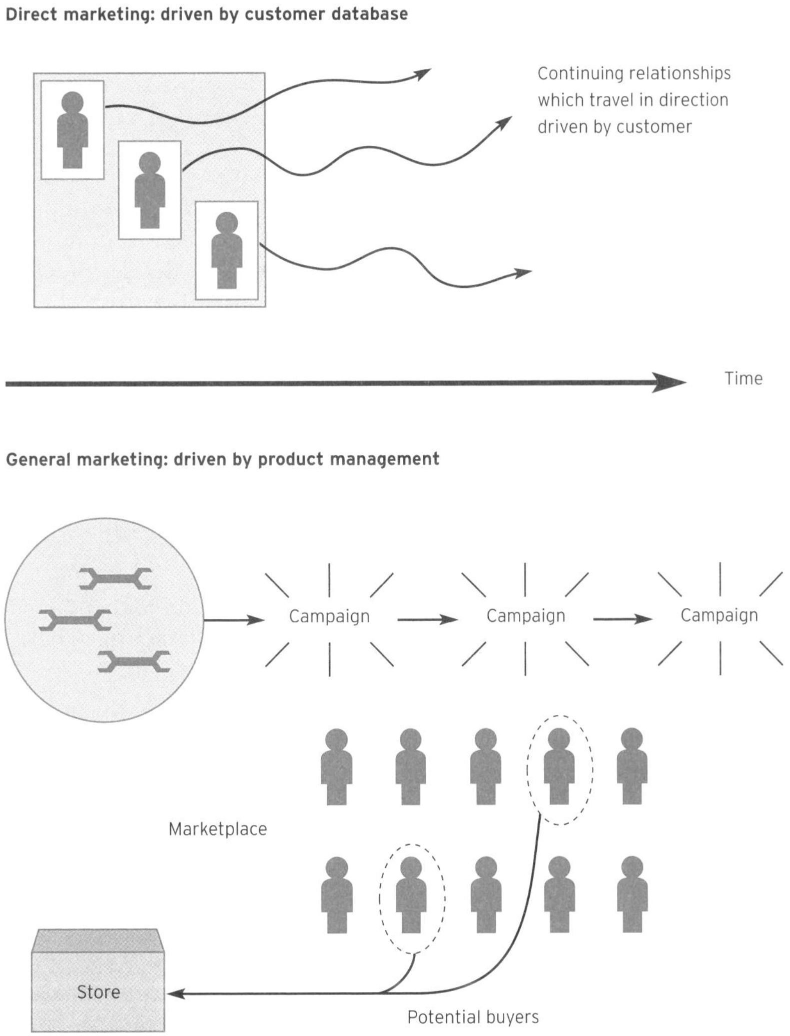

Direct marketing: driven by customer database

General marketing: driven by product management

Figure 1.1 Direct marketing: a way of doing marketing

changing needs are acknowledged and met. Direct marketing seeks to emulate the sales/customer relationship as far as possible, by gathering personal details, communicating individually, and wherever possible adjusting offers to individual taste.

RAFFLES CIGARETTES

Rothmans, the parent company of the Raffles brand of kingsize cigarettes, has undertaken a direct marketing approach in a sector dominated by classic brand marketing. It encourages smokers of competitor brands to try Raffles by incentivising trial using classic sales promotion methods - free samples in night clubs perhaps. Names and addresses are captured from trialists, and these are placed on a database. The marketing to these smokers is subsequently as much about relationship marketing as it is about 'image advertising'. They are offered the chance to join a Raffles Club, giving them rewards - anything from tee-shirts to TVs - as a way of thanking them for their loyalty.

DIRECT MARKETING: A DISCIPLINE WITHIN MARKETING

Having pointed out the distinctions that characterise direct marketing, it is important to emphasise that direct and general marketing philosophically start out from the same place. Direct marketing is a discipline within marketing and has as its goal the same aims as general marketing: that is, championing the customer as the primary focus of the business. Direct marketing's rightful place is within the marketing department, adding leverage to the overall marketing effort, and often working alongside other disciplines in an integrated fashion.

THE DISTINCTIONS BETWEEN DIRECT AND DATABASE MARKETING

At this point we can begin to address the differences between *direct* and *database* marketing. We are not quite ready for full definitions, these will be addressed a little later, but here we can introduce these terms:

■ **Database marketing.** This is using a database to hold and analyse customer information, thereby helping create strategies for marketing. There is a big overlap with 'direct marketing'.

■ **Direct marketing.** This focuses on using a database to communicate (and sometimes distribute) directly to customers so as to attract a direct response. There is a big overlap with 'database marketing'.

In the majority of practices, however, the two are brought together into a direct marketing system:

■ **Direct marketing systems.** Database and direct marketing can be brought together to provide a complete, alternative method of marketing analysis, planning, implementation and control. These words have been carefully chosen, and we will see that direct marketing systems have distinct strengths in all four of these marketing activities. This complete direct marketing process is the primary focus of this book.

The use of terms in this book

As we progress through the chapters, the slight distinctions between database and direct marketing will be drawn out. However, given the overlaps, we will avoid clumsy use of language by using the term *direct marketing* as shorthand for 'direct and database marketing' or 'direct marketing systems'.

Before we move on to full definitions, let's clear up a few misconceptions about direct marketing.

What direct marketing is *not*

The first place that a student of marketing usually encounters a mention of direct marketing is in a general marketing text book or in a marketing magazine. Unfortunately, neither source captures the entirety of direct marketing systems. Mainstream marketing texts, for example Dibb *et al.* (1994), Adcock *et al.* (1998), and Brassington and Petitt (1997) (and also marketing communications texts, e.g. Smith, 1993), tend to view direct marketing as confined to the marketing communications mix, while database applications are ignored altogether.

Meanwhile, the marketing trade press often refers to direct marketing and direct mail interchangeably. Worse, a set of euphemisms, such as 'loyalty marketing', has emerged (often used by direct marketing practitioners seeking to capitalise on emerging trends) to describe direct marketing. To cap it all, the popular press sums it all up as 'junk mail' or 'cold calling'.

The following section clears up the main misconceptions about direct marketing.

Clearing up misconceptions

Direct marketing is part of marketing communications.

This is widely believed, but unfortunately it is wholly inaccurate. The discipline of direct marketing began in mail order, which is primarily a method of *distribution* rather than communication. Direct marketing systems run through databases, the primary function of which is *analysis*, with an additional role as orchestrator of communications. Lastly, direct marketing, via database analysis, has a key role to play in *strategy creation*, as we will see.

Direct marketing is called something else.

Throughout the marketing world, across different subjects and within the academic and practitioner worlds, words are used sloppily. The word 'marketing' itself is thrown around with gay abandon by various groups to represent totally different things. How many times will you read in a marketing trade journal 'Joe Smith has been moved from advertising to a job in marketing'? Here 'marketing' presumably means what academics would call 'sales promotion', whereas some practitioners might call it 'promotion'. Then again, isn't 'promotion' one of the Four Ps, covering advertising, sales promotion, PR, and so on?

'If you would speak with me, you must define your terms...'

Voltaire

This utter confusion is, unfortunately, just as prevalent in direct marketing. You may have come across direct marketing, database marketing, direct response, relationship marketing, one-to-one marketing, data-driven marketing, loyalty marketing and interactive marketing. These are all used by direct marketing practitioners to mean much the same thing.

The only way to cope with this situation is to define each term carefully before using it.

Direct marketing equals direct mail.

Even experienced practitioners often fail to distinguish between the two terms. Direct marketing is a discipline within marketing – a system of marketing. Direct mail is merely one of the media, although a very important one, that direct marketers use. But direct marketing is also practised through the press, the telephone, and a host of other media.

Direct marketing equals junk mail.

Junk mail is direct mail which is poorly targeted, patronising, of low quality, or a mixture of all three of these. It certainly does exist, but so does a host of well-targeted, relevant and attractive direct mail programmes, which customers describe as 'letters from the company'!

Having (hopefully) dispelled some myths, we can now move towards a more rigorous definition of direct and database marketing.

Defining direct and database marketing

Direct (and database) marketing is a rather complex collection of principles and practices which together make up an entirely 'self-contained' choice for marketers. We can unravel this complexity by looking briefly at the history of definitions for direct marketing and then moving clearly towards a single definition.

Bird (1989), a practitioner of worldwide authority, originally defined direct marketing as:

any activity which creates and exploits a direct relationship between you and your customer as an individual.

This definition is widely quoted, perhaps because of its compelling simplicity and broad, inclusive nature. Bird has widened out direct marketing from being merely part of the communications mix to something which can develop *relationships* with customers.

The reader should note that other definitions of direct marketing around the world are plentiful. In contrast to the view that direct marketing is a way of doing marketing, commentators in the USA seem to agree on a definition that positions direct marketing as a part of the communications mix rather than as a strategic framework (Stone, 1996; Nash, 1995; Baier, 1985; Roberts, 1989; Katzenstein, 1992).

Some writers have split out direct and database marketing, emphasising the use of the database as an information tool for strategies, but in practice, the majority of database marketing leads to direct marketing programmes (e.g. NDL, 1996; Tapp, 1992–95). In this book, then, we will concentrate on a combined view of direct and database marketing.

For a newcomer to the discipline, the following statement best describes the typical direct-marketing process:

Direct marketing happens when individual customer details are captured and kept on a database, thus allowing that particular customer's needs to be understood. This enables any subsequent approaches to the customer to be tailored according to that customer's or the business's specific need.

This book is about direct marketing as a complete marketing system through which analysis, planning, programme activities and control are all practised. We can therefore more fully define direct marketing in the following way:

Direct marketing is a way of acquiring *and* keeping *customers by providing a* framework *for three activities:* analysis *of individual customer information,* strategy *formation, and* implementation *such that customers respond directly.*

The first part of this definition springs from Levitt's (1983) famous assertion that 'the purpose of business is to create and keep a customer'. This neatly captures the notion of direct marketing as a customer management system.

The notion of direct marketing being a framework is also very important. What this means is that all the decisions we make in general marketing – how you segment, brand, position, deliver a service, build relationships with or deliver a marketing mix to the customer – are also made within direct marketing, but start from a different place: that is, individual customer information.

With the doubts expressed in the late 1990s about the Four Ps framework, and the rise in credibility of relationship marketing techniques, it is important for us to examine the basis of direct marketing from the point of view of each paradigm.

IS DIRECT MARKETING BASED ON RELATIONSHIP MARKETING OR THE FOUR PS?

We have nearly completed our introduction to direct marketing, but there is one more thing to clear up. Modern marketing now juggles two competing philosophies. The first is the transaction approach epitomised by the 'Four Ps' of marketing: product, price, place and promotion. The second approach is known as relationship marketing, which emphasises building relationships with customers over time and the importance of bringing together customer-led quality, service and marketing within a company.

Which of these philosophies does modern direct marketing follow? If we go back to direct marketing's early development, it concentrated on prompting action from customers to make a *sale* (for example, Bird, 1989). This approach is heavily influenced by the Four Ps approach.

According to Christopher *et al.* (1991), direct marketing has developed as a powerful tool in customer loyalty strategies. Relationship marketing starts with the premise that customer retention is critical to company profitability, which is also the starting point of modern direct marketing, although subsequent relationship marketing thinking has concentrated on service and quality issues as the keys to delivering relationship strategies. Most recently, however, relationship marketers have started to integrate direct marketing into their thinking (Payne *et al.*, 1995).

In answer to our original question, we can see that direct marketing draws from both philosophies, while maintaining its own clear identity as an approach based on a customer database.

(One side issue here is that some writers (Pearson, 1994; Shani and Chalasani, 1992; and De Bonis and Nucifora, 1995) use the terms 'direct (database) marketing' and 'relationship marketing' interchangeably, and direct marketing is routinely described as relationship marketing in practitioner journals and conferences. Why this is so is not clear, because the term relationship marketing, as originally coined by Berry in 1983, clearly did not refer to direct marketing in any way at that time. We will maintain the clear distinctions between the approaches here.)

The following section begins our exploration of direct marketing in practice.

Direct marketing in practice

After comparing direct marketing to general marketing in a little more detail, we will go on to examine the various levels at which direct marketing operates in businesses.

DIRECT MARKETING COMPARED TO GENERAL MARKETING

Figure 1.2 gives a comparison between a typical direct marketing process and a typical general marketing process. It may be useful to take a look at both processes and spot the different approach taken by direct marketers.

THE SIMILARITIES AND DIFFERENCES BETWEEN DIRECT AND GENERAL MARKETING

Looking at Fig. 1.2, we can take a closer look at the ways in which direct marketing differs from the general marketing process.

Similarities

Many of the initial stages that a marketer goes through are the same for general and direct marketing. In particular, at the start of the process, *new product development* is exactly the same in both camps. Continuing through the process, much of the *strategic thinking* you need to do, for example matching your strengths with market opportunities, should be the same. *Research methods* and testing are also used by both marketing camps, although the relative emphasis is very different.

Differences

Although the process of *strategy* setting is the same, the content of that strategy is likely to be different – direct marketing gives you, the marketer, a choice of different strategies. A focus on customers rather than products; segmenting according to the value of customers to you; distributing directly to bypass retail: these are just some of the key areas.

The most obvious operational difference between the two methods is in the area of *communications*. General marketers tend to use mass media to build brands, and use sales promotions in the retail environment. Direct marketers also sometimes use some mass media when addressing new prospects, in order to get a response. They use personal media – direct mail, telemarketing – when developing a relationship with existing customers.

Figure 1.2 A comparison of direct and general marketing

Note: The following schemes inevitably contain many generalisations – neither direct nor general marketing follows the same process every time. This figure should not therefore be taken as a set of rules that are always followed: its purpose is to highlight the different patterns that direct and general marketing tend to follow.

A TYPICAL GENERAL MARKETING PROCESS

Example: The Sony Walkman

1 A new product or service is developed.
   Through superb innovation the first personal stereo is invented by Sony.

2 Marketing research is carried out.
   Sony invites consumers to give their opinions about the Walkman. Opinions are favourable.

3 The Four Ps of marketing (product, price, place and promotion) are looked at strategically.
   Sony realises that the Walkman will first be bought by innovators, but it will also have wider market appeal, especially to young people. Sony understands that it will be copied quickly by competitors. Therefore the price is set quite high initially, but to drop quickly. Sony maintains a premium position in the marketplace, in keeping with its strong corporate brand. It looks to distribute through typical high-street outlets.

4 Operational details for product, price and place are set.
   The target audience is assessed in detail. From this, product features are added, e.g. different styles of headphones, graphic equalisers etc. Typical prices for Sony Walkmans are £30–60. They are sold through Dixons and other high-street outlets.

5 The first customers are sought using promotion techniques. Advertising builds awareness, interest and brand salience.
   Sony uses corporate brand advertising on television to maintain a high profile. An emphasis on quality and reliability is highlighted.

6 Sales promotions are used to stimulate trial of the product.
   Limited use is made of these techniques by Sony until the product has been on the market for some time.

7 Customers identify themselves when they buy the product for the first time.

8 Reinforcement advertising is used to build brand loyalty. Existing customers are not identified, nor is any effort made to treat regular customers differently to new customers.

In a typical general marketing process, *brand loyalty* is achieved by:
▪ building a brand that consumers like;
▪ building customer satisfaction through excellent service when the customer is in contact with the product, service or company.

A TYPICAL DIRECT MARKETING PROCESS

Example: IBM Direct

1 A new product or service is developed, or a new channel is required.
   IBM turns to direct marketing in 1992 because its traditional markets are saturated and growth is taking place in the consumer and small-business sectors.

2 A database is built and used for analysis.
   All IBM's worldwide databases are pulled together into one and this is developed into a marketing database. It is found that IBM is confusing its customers through different brand images in different countries. This is rectified.

3 Strategy is developed. Direct marketers will plan to:
   ▪ gather information on each individual customer;
   ▪ develop customised products and communications;
   ▪ communicate directly to customers over time;
   ▪ consider direct distribution.

   IBM Direct is created, with the remit of creating leads, fulfilling orders, and customer care. An integrated approach with IBM's salesforce is developed.

Figure 1.2 Continued

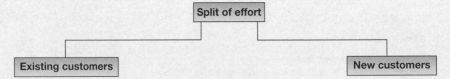

4   At this point, a clear distinction is made by direct marketers: how much can we sell to our existing customers, and therefore how many new customers do we need to acquire?

Split of effort

Existing customers

New customers

Existing customers

5   Segmentation may be carried out.
IBM Direct looks at segmenting its customers according to product category – its different customer support needs may be calculated according to this segmentation.

6   Communication with existing customers is via personal media (for example, direct mail or telephone).
IBM's database is hooked up to its telemarketing system – 250 operators dealing with inbound and outbound telephone calls to customers. Both sales and customer care are handled in one management operation.

7   The customer responds. A sale is made.
IBM Direct may generate a prospect which the salesforce will take over and look to convert to customers.

8   Sometimes the product or service is delivered direct to the customer.
IBM Direct delivers direct to the customer, bypassing retail channels.

9   This response information is added to the customer's record.

10 Market information and intelligence gathering tends to be centred around the database rather than market research, although research is sometimes used.
Both market research and data analysis are used at IBM Direct.

New customers

5   A target audience of possible customers is drawn up by profiling existing customers of other products or services.

6   Direct response media are employed to communicate the product. An incentive or sales promotion may be offered to stimulate this first purchase.
IBM's biggest asset is its brand, and this added value is used to generate responses. Mail and telephone are both used as acquisition media.

7   If a customer responds, and a sale is made, as much information as possible is gathered and stored on the database.
The new customer's name is added to the database of 600 000 contacts in 250 000 companies.

Direct marketers generate loyalty by:
■ meeting individual needs above and beyond the mass delivery of the product or service;
■ proactive service to customers using direct, two-way communication.

There are differences in the way classic and direct marketers *measure* their marketing effort. General marketers will usually use marketing research techniques to understand and predict their customers' likely behaviour. Direct marketers will analyse behaviour using their database in order to predict the best responding people and the best offers to make. They will look to market test new ideas on small samples before rolling out.

Overall, direct marketing is often more expensive, on a per-customer basis, than general marketing. The investment in direct marketing is a way of 'buying' a closer relationship with the customer: first, individual customer information, and then subsequent precision and control in customer contact.

Now that we understand how direct marketing differs from general marketing, we can examine direct marketing practice from a new angle. Let us now look at the different levels that direct marketing operates at within a business.

THE THREE LEVELS OF DIRECT MARKETING

The previous section highlighted how direct marketing can be viewed at a number of different levels, from communications to strategy setting. In fact there are three clear levels at which direct marketing can impact on a business.

Direct marketing drives the business

Example: Direct Line Insurance

Direct Line Insurance has a direct marketing strategy which drives the entire business. Everyone in the company understands that it is the customer who is the focus of their activities. As a result, the product (insurance policies) reflects what the customer wants, i.e. a competitive price, and a no-hassle claims department if the need arises. The *delivery* of the product to the customer is 100 per cent *direct*: customers are recruited via responsive TV and press adverts, and prospects are chased through direct mail that is timed to coincide with the prospects' renewal period. Once a sale is made, all details are completed using '*direct distribution*'. Direct Line has no broker network, nor is any high-street outlet used. If you have a query, you ring Direct Line, and it is sorted out over the phone. Naturally, Direct Line has a *database of existing customers* which it uses to organise direct communications aimed at *keeping customers*.

Since 1984, when it was set up, Direct Line has grown faster than any other insurance company in the UK.

The entire company is therefore run according to a direct marketing approach. This impacts on every department, not just the marketing people.

Direct marketing drives part or all of the marketing strategy

Example: British Airways

British Airways (BA), like all the major airlines, is driven by the 80/20 rule. Twenty per cent of its customers – the frequent-flyer business people – contribute 80 per cent of its profits. Not surprisingly, a great deal of BA's marketing effort goes into looking after these precious individuals. Imagine you are a frequent flyer with BA. Do you turn up at the airport two hours before the flight, queue to check in, sit around in the crowded airport lounge and then cram yourself into economy class for the flight? Forget it! You arrive half an hour before take-off at priority check-in. You are whisked through to the Executive Club members' lounge and, in these quiet, relaxing surroundings, you order yourself a free drink at the bar. You unhurriedly make your way to your business-class seat where you are pampered for the length of the trip. During the flight, you clock up Air Miles for your personal use.

All this, of course, is run through direct marketing. A direct marketing strategy is being used here: repeat customers are treated very differently to first-time or occasional customers. This is the core of any strategic direct marketing operation. Direct marketing also directs the tactical implementation: the initial recruitment of a frequent flyer is done via direct response methods to potential prospects. Once enrolled into the Executive Club (levels Blue, Silver and Gold), your details are placed on a database and continually updated depending on your involvement with BA. Communication with you to keep you informed of any offers, your latest Air Miles totals etc., is carried out through direct mail.

However, direct marketing is only part of the story for BA. Heavy expenditure is directed towards a strong brand advertising programme, and a lot of emphasis is put on overall service delivery and keeping prices as keen as possible in a highly competitive industry.

Direct marketing therefore improves the gearing on other marketing investments: it is one of the disciplines within British Airways' marketing mix.

Direct marketing is used within the communications mix.

Example: the new university sector

Some new universities, when recruiting students, rely on a mix of word-of-mouth recommendations, their prospectus – a detailed brochure distributed to schools and colleges – and luck – students sticking a pin on the map.

University marketers may not have a database of existing or past students to use for marketing purposes. Use of direct marketing may be confined to one area such as recruitment of students onto specific postgraduate courses. This could be done through direct response advertising in key press such as *The Guardian* or *Times Higher Education Supplement*. This sits alongside other elements of the communications mix, of which the major one is PR. Many new universities make heavy use of this, both proactively, with visits, open days, liaison with local events, etc., and also reactively via press editorial comment, which has a powerful effect on their public image.

In conclusion, new universities do not typically have a direct-marketing strategy, nor are their marketing operations led in any sense by direct marketing. They use direct response communications as a part of their overall communications mix.

Now that we have a clearer sense of what direct marketing is, our final task is to understand the historical development of direct marketing, putting it in context as an increasingly important discipline within marketing.

The historical growth of direct marketing

Direct marketing originated as a form of distribution from mail-order companies, publishers and book clubs (McCorkell, 1992). The mail-order discipline is in fact centuries old, although the industry as we recognise it today emerged in the latter part of the last century. It is often reported in marketing journals that the use of customer data to drive marketing is relatively new. This is not the case, however. *Reader's Digest*, for example, had been using customer databases in various forms well before the invention of computers. 'The Digest' originally used large, specialised filing cabinets to hold its customer records. By turning various handles with rods penetrating the files, lists of customers who fitted different marketing segments could be drawn out!

The expansion of direct marketing from its roots in mail order into mainstream marketing began in the USA in the 1970s. One of the few major companies to grasp direct marketing's potential at that time was American Express. However, in western Europe, very little expansion took place until the 1980s. In the UK, growth was led by financial services companies which began to make serious use of their account records (Henley Centre, 1995). British Telecom (BT) began experimenting with direct marketing, and by the late 1980s the charity sector had made huge leaps forward in its use of direct marketing, emerging as highly accomplished practitioners by the early 1990s.

The late 1990s and early 2000s have seen the coming of age of database-driven marketing. Thanks in part to cheaper, more flexible technologies, and increasingly well-educated marketing managers, there has been rapid growth in direct marketing. Industries such as airlines, hotels, car manufacturers, utilities, leisure, retail and, latterly, packaged goods have all embraced direct marketing, making it, at the time of writing, the fastest-growing marketing discipline worldwide.

REASONS FOR GROWTH

A number of sources (Henley Centre, 1995; McCorkell, 1992; DMA, 1996) have reported on the growth of direct marketing. The following factors have emerged.

Social reasons for growth

1 Fragmentation of society

Demographic changes to society have continued at an incredible pace. In particular we can witness changes from the nuclear family as being the hub of society, to a split whereby the traditional married couple with children now accounts for less than 20 per cent of households. Just as prevalent is the explosion of individualism. There has been a huge growth in lifestyle options, resulting in a more complex society.

2 Proliferation of media

Throughout Europe, satellite, cable and digital supply have changed the face of television broadcasting, resulting in rising costs for mass marketers looking to reach a large audience. The same effect can be seen within the UK in radio and magazines.

An even more profound effect is likely to arise from the arrival of new electronic media – the Internet and digital TV in particular. Both of these offer tremendous opportunities for direct marketers.

3 Greater consumer sophistication

Consumers now demand far better service than companies were allowed to get away with in the past. Part of this is the wish to be treated according to their personal circumstances. How companies communicate to their customers has also emerged as being very important.

4 Consumers want to be in control

Customers increasingly want the option of contacting organisations direct, leading to a big growth in devices such as freephone numbers and care lines.

Business reasons for growth

1 Ever more competition

The Henley Centre (1995) found that companies were worried about the increasing commoditisation of their markets. Companies see direct marketing as a way of adding value to their markets and differentiating their offerings.

2 Drive for cost-effectiveness

Coopers and Lybrand (1993) found that marketing departments were considered by senior managers to be inefficient in their spending. As we will see, direct marketing can vastly improve marketing's efficiency through its control and precision, leading to better targeting and campaign measurement.

3 Interest in customer retention and loyalty

The importance of retaining your customers is now widely accepted, while remaining a 'hot topic' within marketing. There is a growing belief (Henley Centre, 1995) that direct communications can reinforce and extend brand relationships.

While loyalty has become more important for companies, consumers have become more promiscuous, seeing little difference in competitors' product offerings (Stone and Shaw, 1988). Companies have found it more difficult to differentiate with the traditional unique selling proposition approach. Companies which offer superior service, or individualised product/service packages via database-driven marketing, are able to differentiate themselves.

4 Continuing drop in computer processing costs

Underpinning all of the preceding factors is the biggest driver of all: the relentless advance of the computer. Since the 1960s the cost of processing has halved about once every four years, on average. Because we are surrounded by this power nowadays it is difficult to appreciate sometimes just how much of a phenomenon, how much of a driver of change, this is. The author has just bought a new home PC that is *ten times as fast* and has two hundred times the memory of one bought only five years previously! Desk top PCs can now handle large customer datafiles and undertake complex calculations, selections by customer type, and so on, *in seconds*. Ten years ago this would have taken two or three weeks. This simplicity is and will be a huge driver of growth for direct marketing probably at least through the next decade.

Table 1.1: **Time and cost of one typical data processing operation**

	Time seconds	Cost £
1955	375	9.09
1960	47	1.55
1965	29	0.29
1975	4	0.12
1987	1	0.04
1993	0.1	0.01
2002	0.01	0.001

THE SPEND ON DIRECT MARKETING

The long-term prognosis remains optimistic for direct marketing. While the rate of growth has slowed, possibly due to uncertain trading conditions worldwide at the time of writing, spend on direct-marketing media and database supply remains strong, with slight growth in the UK in 2002. Compared with the shrinkage of advertising budgets this has to be seen as a good performance. The total spend on direct and database marketing in the UK in 2002 was £11.85 billion, pretty much double that of 1995. The DMA suggests that the industry is entitled to feel pleased about maintaining such a strong performance in the light of media spend showing flat growth or even decline in general advertising (*see* Fig. 1.3).

The DMA Census also suggests that there are reasons for optimism for direct marketers up to 2010 and beyond. One factor is the continued faith that marketing directors show in direct marketing when times are tough – they like the close link between spend and income, and the cost-effectiveness of this approach. One of the biggest drivers of growth of course is the proliferation of new media that will grow over the next 20 years. The Future Foundation forecasts (DMA Census, 2003) that 70 per cent of the UK population will have bought something online by 2013 (in 2003 about 20 per cent of them had bought online). This can only be good news for the industry.

Another factor driving growth is likely to be the increased spend in leisure, communications and other disposable income sectors in western markets. These are likely to begin to challenge traditional mail-order and finance markets in the coming years.

What are the most important media by spend?

While telemarketing and direct mail remain direct marketing's two most important media, growth in telephone has slowed, while the fast growers include inserts and not surprisingly 'new media' – primarily e-mail and SMS – which grew 17 per cent compared with the previous year. The significant relative decline in press compared with its position in the mid-1990s is down to the changed DMA definition of direct response press: that it must include 10 per cent of space devoted to the response element.

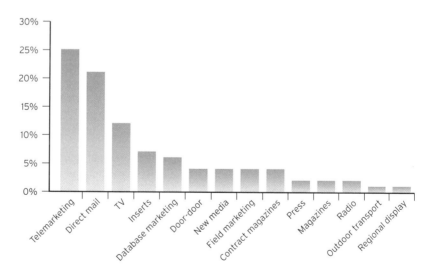

Figure 1.3 Percentage of total budget spent on UK direct media, 2002

Source: Adapted from DMA Census, 2003. Reproduced by permission of the DMA

Notes: Contract magazines are better known by consumers as loyalty magazines
Field marketing will include many activities undertaken in public spaces with the aim of identifying prospects
'Database marketing' is a figure for supplier sales only, and does not include the huge amount of in-house activity that goes on

Comparing 2002 figures for each media with those of 1995 gives interesting reading:

Table 1.2 **Media spend on direct marketing in the UK, £m**

	Direct mail	telemarketing	database marketing	press	magazines	regional	TV	door-door	inserts	radio	new med
1995	1135	1175	548	756	616	325	398	233	216	47	50
2002	2478	3036	773	294	222	144	1384	297	1145	196	525

Source: Adapted from DMA Census, 2003. Reproduced by permission of the DMA

We can see the decline in press and magazine spend, more than offset by the huge growth in the two-way direct media – mail and telephone. DRTV has also grown hugely, driven largely by the satellite channel opportunities for targeted, cheaper TV. There has also been huge growth in spend on inserts, and the growth of new media completes the overall healthy picture.

Summary to chapter

In Chapter 1 we found that direct marketing is a way of doing marketing that encompasses both principles and practical tools. The core of direct marketing is the use of a database to hold customer information on an individual level. This means marketers can treat *existing* customers in a different way to *new* prospects in order to create loyalty and profitability.

In Chapter 2 we will take a much closer look at the most important practical tool, the database.

Questions

1. Since the early 1980s direct marketing has enjoyed a period of considerable growth. Some managers believe that its ability to segment customers is direct marketing's strongest asset. Consider the relevance of this benefit, along with other benefits described in the chapter.

2. The managing director of a large, fast-moving consumer goods firm said, 'I have no need for direct marketing. Ours will always be a mass-marketing industry.' Do you think he is right? Explain your reasons.

3. What are the core tangible elements that make up direct and database marketing? Explain how they fit together.

4. What is the difference between relationship marketing and direct marketing? Explain how the two areas of marketing overlap with each other.

5. Retailers have never been so adept at meeting customers' needs as they are now. If this is so, then why is direct marketing growing so fast?

6. Explain how direct marketing can help a company develop sustainable competitive advantage. What are the keys to success?

7. The roots of direct marketing originally lay in the mail-order industry. Modern mail-order businesses will often use direct marketing to drive their business. Explain why direct marketing is so important to them.

8. You are the manager of a large, established insurance company. At present, you rely on a large pool of commissioned representatives to sell your product, but you have noticed recently that consumer opinion appears to be turning away from seeing 'financial advisors', who are generally mistrusted. One of your marketing team has written a paper advising you to look at setting up a 'direct' operation similar to that of Direct Line Insurance. What considerations should you take into account before making a decision?

References

Adcock, D., Bradfield, R., Halborg, A. and Ross, C. (1998) *Marketing Principles and Practice*, Financial Times Pitman Publishing, London.

Baier, M. (1985) *Elements of Direct Marketing*, McGraw-Hill, New York.

Bauer, C.L. and Miglautsch, J. (1992) 'A conceptual definition of direct marketing', *Journal of Direct Marketing*, vol 6, No 2, Spring 1992, pp. 7-17.

Berry, L.L. (1983) 'Relationship marketing' in Berry, L.L., Shostack, G.L. and Upah, G.D. (eds) *Emerging Perspectives on Services Marketing*, American Marketing Association, Chicago, pp. 25-8.

Bird, D. (1989) *Commonsense Direct Marketing*, Kogan Page, London.

Brassington, F. and Petitt, S. (1997) *Principles of Marketing*, Pitman Publishing, London.

Christopher, M., Payne, A. and Ballantyne, D. (1991) *Relationship Marketing*, Butterworth-Heinemann, Oxford.

Coopers and Lybrand (1993) Report on UK Marketing Departments, Coopers and Lybrand, London.

De Bonis, N. and Nucifora, A. (1995) 'Progressive databases: The underpinning for relationship micromarketing', *Journal of Database Marketing*, 2 (2).

Dibb, S., Simpkin, L., Pride, W. and Ferrell, O.C. (1994) *Marketing Concepts and Strategies*, Houghton Mifflin, Abingdon, Oxfordshire.

Direct Response magazine (1997). For database advert example *see* p. 50.

DMA Census (2003) DMA Records Centre, London.

Fletcher K., Wheeler, C. and Wright, J. (1995) 'The role and status of UK database marketing', *Quarterly Review of Marketing*, Autumn, pp. 7-14.

Henley Centre for Forecasting Ltd (1995) *Dataculture 2000*, Henley Centre, Henley, Oxfordshire.

Holder, D., Davies, D. and Stone, M. (1992) Part of IDM Diploma course material, Institute of Direct Marketing, Teddington, Richmond-upon-Thames.

Jobber, D. (1995) *Marketing, Principles and Practice*, McGraw-Hill, Maidenhead, Berkshire.

Katzenstein, H. (1992) *Direct Marketing*, Macmillan, New York.

Levitt, T. (1983) *The Marketing Imagination*, The Free Press, New York.

McCorkell, G. (1992) 'Direct Marketing – a new industry or a new idea?' in Halsey, B. (ed.) *The Practitioner's Guide to Direct Marketing*, Institute of Direct Marketing, Teddington, Richmond-upon-Thames.

Mintel (1996) 'Database marketing', Mintel Report, Aug.

Nash, E. (1995) *Direct Marketing Strategy: planning, execution*, 3rd edn, McGraw-Hill, New York.

NDL Ltd (1996) Promotional material.

Payne, A., Christopher, M., Clark, M. and Peck, M. (1995) *Relationship Marketing for Competitive Advantage*, Butterworth-Heinemann, Oxford.

Pearson, S. (1994) 'Relationship management: Generating business in the diverse markets of Europe', *European Business Journal*, **6** (4), pp. 28–38.

Peppers, D. and Rogers, M. (1993) *The One-to-One Future*, Piatkus, London.

Roberts, M.L. (1989) *Direct Marketing Management*, Prentice Hall, Upper Saddle River, New Jersey.

Schofield, A. (1995) 'The definition of direct marketing: A rejoinder to Bauer and Miglautsch', *Journal of Direct Marketing*, **9** (2).

Shani, D. and Chalasani, S. (1992) 'Exploiting niches using relationship marketing', *Journal of Services Marketing*, **6** (4).

Smith, P.R. (1993) *Marketing Communications: An integrated approach*, Kogan Page, London.

Stone, B. (1996) *Successful Direct Marketing Methods*, 5th edn, NTC Business Books, Chicago, Ill.

Stone, M. and Shaw, R. (1988) *Database Marketing*, Gower, London.

Tapp, A.J. (1992–95) Various lectures in Diploma courses, Institute of Direct Marketing, Teddington, Richmond-upon-Thames.

'Rapid Pizza'

Although most of the case studies in this book are based on real companies, 'Rapid Pizza' is a fictional company. However, the case reflects the pressures acting on commercial take-away operations.

Rapid Pizza is a medium-sized chain of pizza take-away outlets located in the Midlands. The chain is modelled on bigger, well-established names, such as Perfect Pizza. Customers can ring up and order a home-delivered pizza from a menu that is distributed to local homes. Rapid Pizza does the usual choice of popular pizzas, with no particular pretension to cater for any niche group. Its best seller is the 'Rapid Speciale', a spicy chicken-based pizza with a range of cheese toppings.

The marketing manager of Rapid Pizza, Colin McVie, has just had a conversation with an old friend, Dan Smith, who happens to be a direct marketing expert. His friend was very enthusiastic about Rapid Pizza's possible use of direct marketing, which surprised Colin, as he had not really given it much thought.

Rapid Pizza uses 'door-to-door' leafleting to distribute its promotional literature through the locality. This includes a menu, a map showing where the outlet is, and a phone number for ordering any time until midnight, seven days a week. Incentives to phone are periodically offered, again through door drops, distributed via the local freesheet. Incentives include an 'order two and get one free' offer, 'free garlic bread with any order over £10', and similar promotions.

The busiest times for the take-away business are early and late evenings, and in particular Friday and Saturday nights. Most of its customers are in their twenties or thirties, with enough expendable income to afford not to bother cooking occasionally. In order to qualify for the take-away service, customers have to live within a one-mile radius of the outlet. Each outlet caters for about 7000 households.

The main features of Colin's business are as follows:

- The top priorities for consumers are hot, tasty pizzas, fast delivery and reasonable prices.

- Some consumers are remarkably regular with their orders, wanting exactly the same items each time they phone. Some of Colin's staff have got to know the most regular customers quite well.

- When customers call in to order their pizza they leave their name and address as a natural part of the process. Their transaction details are easily taken and can be kept on a computer-based database in each outlet. At present, these transaction details are used only for accounting and stock ordering.

- Menu changes are executed quite regularly. Colin believes that these help to keep customers interested, and are an excuse to launch fresh marketing initiatives.

When Dan absorbed these details he recommended that Colin should contact a direct marketing agency and invite them to help him.

In a sense, Colin was reluctant to take his friend's advice. He had spent a lot of time and effort setting up the existing business and had an emotional commitment to keeping the status quo. Also he did not feel any particular competitive pressure. 'No one else is using direct marketing, and customers don't seem to be crying out for it. Why should we bother?' he thought to himself.

He decided to give his direct marketing friend another call and discuss it one more time.

Question

Acting as Colin's friend, explain what the benefits of direct marketing would be to his pizza operation. How would it work in practice?

THE DATABASE

Objectives

Once you have read this chapter you will:

■ know what a database is;

■ be able to picture what a database consists of;

■ know what data to hold and where to get it from;

■ be aware of some of the management issues;

■ be aware of the key legal constraints in direct marketing.

Introduction

In the introduction in Chapter 1 we saw that this book is organised around the direct market-ing planning process. Before we start on that journey, however, it is important to give a full description of the most important tool in the direct marketing armoury: the database. The purpose of this chapter is to explain what a database is. We will cover what a database looks like, what data to hold, and how to manage a database. One very important area in direct marketing is to understand the legal constraints, and we have a dedicated section on this subject at the end of the chapter.

As you might expect from the previous chapter, the various uses of database *applica-tions* are integral to direct marketing itself. Therefore, rather than discuss applications here, they are covered in detail as and when they arise throughout this book.

How this chapter is structured

In this chapter we will begin with a review of database practice. We will then address the ques-tion of exactly what a database is. The next section covers what data to hold, and is followed by a section describing typical sources of data. The intricacies of database management are then analysed and, finally, the important area of legal constraints is examined.

What is a marketing database?

A marketing database can best be pictured as an electronic version of an office filing cabinet, holding records of customers. Imagine each customer's record held on a card, detailing the customer's personal details, transactions (sales) and communication history with the particular company. The cards are held in various files according to, say, which products the customer has bought. The entire set of records is cross-referenced against the other files so that customers can be selected according to different characteristics (*see* Fig. 2.1).

From Fig. 2.1 it follows that:

■ a database is a collection of data records in a list that can be manipulated by software;

■ a data record is the entire set of information that is associated with one customer;

■ a data field is one item of data within a record: for example, a name, one line of an address, the number of a type of product bought, and so on.

This is a useful picture to hold in our minds as we move towards a full definition of marketing databases.

Definitions

There are surprisingly few definitions of marketing databases that have been proposed. Bird (1989) noted the confusion apparent amongst practitioners asked to define what a database is. Bird himself defined databases as 'lists of customers or prospects incorporating relevant information about those people', whereas Boddington (1994) said, 'A database is a record of our relationships with customers.'

Courtheux, a leading American practitioner, coined the following well-quoted definition of marketing databases (1992):

A marketing database is a comprehensive collection of interrelated data serving multiple applications, allowing timely and accurate on-demand retrieval of relevant data, and having a data management system independent of applications.

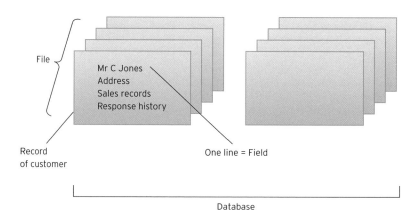

Figure 2.1 Pictorial representation of a database

Let us take a closer look at this definition:

- **Interrelated data:** Each customer record is connected to every other such that customers who have something in common can be picked out as a special list, or as part of an analysis.
- **Multiple applications:** These are the uses of the database by marketers. These uses are described throughout this book but fall under three main headings: analysis, communication and service.
- **Data management system independent of applications:** Here Courtheux is distinguishing a marketing database from the other major computer systems a company may have. The database software must not be part of the company's *transaction* systems; it should be independent of these if the database is to function properly.

An alternative, rather simpler, definition is offered here, which the reader may find helpful in understanding how the database should be viewed in the context of a direct marketing system:

> *A marketing database is a list of customers' and prospects' records that enables strategic analysis, and individual selections for communication and customer service support. The data is organised around the customer.*

THE MINIMUM REQUIREMENTS OF A MARKETING DATABASE

Data

The Practitioners' Guide to Direct Marketing (Logan, 1992) lists the following data sets as the minimum requirements of a marketing database:

- personal customer data
- purchase (transaction) data: what the customer has bought
- communication data: campaign history and responses.

Database software

Although hierarchical and network databases have played an important part in the growth of the function, the major database architecture used now is *relational*. In relational databases, data is held in the form of tables rather than records. This means that you don't have to try to anticipate all your requirements at the initial design stage, because selections and analyses are made independently of the record structure.

For marketing managers, a welcome development is the use of front-end software, which is user friendly and menu driven, such as SQL (Structured Query Language). This enables analysis to be carried out by the marketers themselves on their desktop personal computers (PCs), rather than having to ask for an analysis to be run by technicians. 'What if' analyses are now an everyday task, thanks to this interface.

Basic software functions

Database applications require the following basic software functions, according to Goldwag (1995):

■ Name and address processing: This is discussed later under 'management issues'.

■ Being able to make selections: The database must be able to generate the desired list of customers to be contacted.

■ Having analytical capability: The most basic requirement here is for simple campaign analysis. Each response is allocated to the promotion which generated it. Percentage response figures for each campaign are then output.

■ Being able to generate reports: Basic reports would include elements such as counts of customer movements in the database, or campaign reports comparing current ones with previous efforts. Goldwag made the point that business is full of useless reports. Information such as 'we had 1000 transactions yesterday' struggles for a use, whereas 'we are losing 10 000 of our database' prompts action.

The data to hold

PRINCIPLES OF DATA COLLECTION

According to Goldwag (1995), many companies are awash with unusable data. This happens for two reasons. First, data may be collected for some other reason than marketing, on another database. The information technology (IT) people will point this out and offer marketing the chance to collect this data too. Marketing says 'yes' without considering what it can be used for. This brings us nicely to the second reason for unusable data, which is that there is a tendency for marketers to ask themselves 'What data shall I collect?', rather than 'What do I need the database to do?'. The latter question should always be asked first, letting data requirements flow from these applications.

Bob Stone (1996) advises that we ask ourselves the following question: 'What data will be needed in order to carry on a meaningful dialogue with customers?' Boddington (1994) suggests the following principles should be taken into account when collecting data:

■ data should be split into 'essential now' and 'possible future use';

■ data should allow ease of sourcing and updating;

■ the cost of raw data, for example external bought-in data, must be offset against benefits.

The golden rule for data collection can be summed up as 'only hold data that is required for your strategy. If you don't use it, don't collect it.'

DATA TO HOLD

Let's take a look at the data that is typically held in a comprehensive marketing database. If we combine the suggestions from Goldwag (1995), Stone and Shaw (1988) and the Interactive and Direct Marketing Guide (2002) and then update for recent technology changes, we arrive at a typical list such as the one shown in Table 2.1. The example on the right-hand side of the table is to illustrate what a full customer record might look like. The example given may resemble a typical record from an environmental charity.

Table 2.1: **Typical customer record**

Consumer	Example: Charlotte Smythe
Name and address	Charlotte Smythe
E-mail number	Charlotte-Smythe@yourinternet.co.uk
Mobile phone number	07765 111111
House name or number Street or road Postal town Postcode	The Woodlands Princes St Dorking, Kent DS12 3AT
Sex Date of birth Married Age No. of children, ages of children	F 2/10/65 N 32 N
External data[1] Geodemographic indicator Lifestyle indicators Credit history and rating Education MPS/TPS membership[2]	 Desirable residential area, young, trendy Reads *Guardian*. Interested in current affairs Good Postgraduate level N
Communication history Campaign code number Message code Dates of contact Response Orders Returns Customer complaints	 01 03 12/12/95 Y 3 items N N
Relationship/activity data Source of recruitment[3] Account no. Product categories purchased Recency, frequency, value of purchase data Date of purchases Method of payment Date of renewal of subscriptions Loyalty programme details: points, contact, status in club, and so on	 07 Mail 12223/6789 01/04/06 Score: 67 (top third of responders) Last two years Credit card 1/4/98 N

Notes to Table 2.1
[1] External data is data purchased from a *commercial supplier* of consumer or business data. This important area of direct marketing is fully discussed in Chapter 4.
[2] There are two services, the Mailing Preference Service (MPS) and Telephone Preference Service (TPS), which the industry association (DMA) runs on behalf of the public. The MPS is a public service set up to hold records of people who do not wish to be sent direct mail. It was set up in the late 1970s and now has about 1.26 million records. (For more information visit www.mpsonline.org.uk). It is, of course, very much in companies' interests to purge their output lists of these names because they have no chance of getting any response (other than perhaps that from an irate member of the public). The TPS was set up in 1994 to hold names of people who do not wish to be telephoned by companies. Currently about 3.5 million people subscribe (for more information visit www.tpsonline.org.uk). The initiative was designed to calm fears about the spread of 'cold calling', and is considered very important for the telemarketing industry's credibility.
Source: Director of Compliance Operations, DMA, 2003.
[3] 'Source of recruitment' refers to the media/campaign used first to acquire the customer. It is often a guide to the subsequent profitability of the customer. For example, charities often find that donors recruited from TV turn out to be less profitable than those obtained by mail.

BUSINESS DATA

Business-to-business marketers would construct their data in a different way:

■ personal details:
  - job title
  - job code and description
  - fax and e-mail details
  - department

■ size of business:
  - turnover
  - no. of employees

■ nature of business (Standard Industrial Classification (SIC) sector)

Communications and activity data would be constructed in a similar way to the above example.

Data sources

PRINCIPLES

There are two main sources of data: internal and external. External data is defined as that obtained as a compiled list from outside the company: this could include outside lists, census data, and so on.

Most data is sourced internally. Merlin Stone (Stone and Shaw, 1988) makes the point that internal data sources will vary considerably between sectors, depending on whether you have direct contact with customers as a natural way of doing business.

Direct-contact businesses include examples such as retailers and sports clubs – sectors where the customer and the business have a direct interface and a data-gathering opportunity exists. In these instances, customer purchase data will be held within the company, but it may be held in an awkward form for marketing. Name and address details may not have been collected and it will be necessary to begin tracking customer communications and responses in order to build a true marketing database.

Goldwag (1995) and the Institute of Direct Marketing (1996) suggest the following sources of data:

Direct contact companies

■ online input from customer service department:
  - enquiries
  - requests for brochures, etc.;
■ responses to direct marketing prospects lists;
■ accounting records;
■ billing systems;
■ sales transactions records/order processing.

Sectors with no direct contact include packaged-goods industries that sell through retail, where no natural data-gathering opportunity is present. If a company has no direct contact with customers it could gather data in the following ways:

1 List purchase

There are over 5000 lists available in the UK, and many more in Europe. One example of these is 'lifestyle' databases. Lifestyle databases will hold lists of people according to specific products and brands bought in categories such as packaged goods, finance and leisure. For example, a national newspaper could buy a substantial list of its own readers from a lifestyle data company.

2 Data-building schemes

These might be credit schemes, club membership, or promotions. Car manufacturers looking to build up a database of their existing marque owners might run a 'phone in' free prize draw, open to existing owners only. Cigarette manufacturers, who need to get a signature of consent before they can send direct mail to an individual, often gather names face-to-face at night clubs or pubs, typically in return for free samples.

3 Introduce new contact channels

New channels that offer direct contact could be opened. Airlines could offer tickets direct over the telephone rather than through travel agents.

Indirect contact companies may also use:

- product registration documents, product warranties
- credit card details
- subscription details
- questionnaire responses
- in-store offer details
- requests for product information
- events/promotions requiring response
- established direct channels.

EXHIBIT 2.1

DATA GATHERING – THE HARD WAY

In 1996, Coventry City, a Premier League football club in England, wanted to investigate the opportunities offered by direct marketing. The club had no natural way of gathering data traditionally from the thousands of fans who regularly turned up and paid cash on the day. It decided to make a special effort to gather the data, taking advantage of the half-time break when supporters had little to do. During half time, local students were employed to distribute and collect 'voting forms' for the Coventry 'player of the year'. A free prize draw was included, and fans were invited to include their name and address.

In this way, over 1500 names were collected at one game at very low cost.

Database management issues

If we look back over the development of database marketing, we can see that it has been far from a smooth ride. Nash (1993) noted that database marketing is often 'applied backwards': in other words, the creation of the database and techniques came first, and applications later. Similarly, Stone (1997) noted that a number of UK companies built huge databases in the 1980s without having a proper idea of what they intended to use them for. For many, there was insufficient recognition of the scale of management required, or of the need for senior management commitment to ensure cross-departmental co-operation. Many of these companies were still suffering the after-effects of these problems in the late 1990s.

This chequered history highlights the need to have a clear view of database management issues. In this section, we take a more detailed look at the tasks that a large database operation demands.

Adapting a list from Goldwag (1995), we arrive at the following four main stages to database management:

1. manage the data sources
2. manage the data entry
3. manage the database
4. manage the applications.

These steps are summarised in Fig. 2.2.

MANAGE THE DATA SOURCES

In the majority of companies, data about customers rarely goes direct from the customer onto a marketing database. It may first arrive at the company via a sale made and be recorded in the sales ledger. Details are passed to accounts, and then perhaps on to billing, who send the bills out. Information goes to stock control, to let them know their stock of the product bought is reduced by one.

Into this data 'merry-go-round' comes marketing. Marketing wants the data captured to be organised around the *customer record*. It wants customer name and address, number of sales, and products bought and owned. It wants this kept on a *per-customer* basis. But sales and stock control wants the data on a *per product* basis, and in many companies it is the sales department that takes the order. Accounting wants the *revenue figures*: amount charged, and amount of cash in. Customers? Who are they?

Your last problem could be much closer to home. Within the marketing department, product managers are interested in customers – but only those who buy their particular product. As a direct marketer you are managing customers, not products, but product managers are targeted on the number of their products they sell, and may not be very co-operative about sharing their data in order to expose 'their' customers to the products the company sells.

Given the preceding competing pressures on the data flowing around the company, it is a very complicated job getting up-to-date, accurate data on to the marketing database in the form you want it.

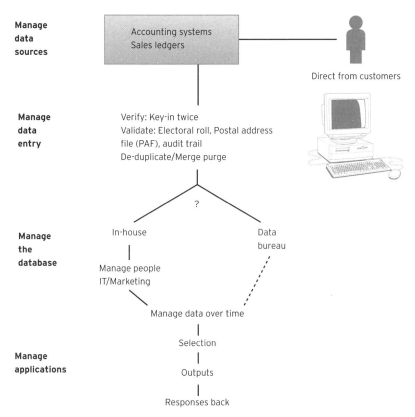

Figure 2.2 Managing the data

EXHIBIT 2.2

THE TRIALS AND TRIBULATIONS OF MARKETING DATABASES IN THE BANKING INDUSTRY

Despite spending huge amounts of money UK banks' CRM programmes are at best still in their infancy: as Emily Cubitt puts it, once you explain what CRM is to many bank customers, they may burst into tears on you.

Goodness knows CRM disciplines were desperately needed for many financial services companies. Most firms had run their operations based on accounts – products. Hence the same customer could be recorded on many different databases, with name and address information often incomplete. Purchase data was incomplete, and no record of any previous communications to the customer held.

Putting this right should not be underestimated. Lloyds and TSB are reported to still be in the process of merging data, years after the two companies merged. Abbey National is in the middle of developing a single 'customer view' across all its channels – including website, mailers, branches, and telephone. It holds a lot of customer data, but has yet to integrate it across all channels. This means a customer may be asked the same questions more than once if they use more than one channel. The Abbey is working hard to address this – they know that this service impacts on customers' trust in them as an organisation.

While banks may have moved forward in managing their data sources so that they can now move closer to a customer record rather than an account or product record, they have yet to put the data into practical use.

A cynic might ask, does it matter, given that UK banks have retention rates for their core products approaching 92 per cent? This loyalty is driven not by satisfaction but by customer inertia: to move requires a lot of effort. At the moment this is the reality in the sector – perhaps until the equivalent of easyJet enters the market and rocks the boat.

Source: Cubitt, E. (2003) 'Bank customers still crying out for service', *Precision Marketing* **15** (29), 5 February, p. 11.

Overcoming these problems is a big job. Marketing needs to isolate the data it needs from these systems and capture it on a regular basis. Woodcock (1992) suggests the following need to be in place:

■ senior management commitment to ensure co-operation across departments;

■ regular audit trails for items of data to ensure it is handled in a quality way;

■ training for front-end staff to ensure they understand the importance of capturing the data properly and keeping these standards uniformly;

■ service-level agreements between departments for delivery of data to the right standard;

■ the marketing database to update records regularly by downloading from 'live' systems during quiet periods.

MANAGE THE DATA ENTRY

Once the data has been sourced it needs to be added to the marketing database.

Stone and Shaw (1988) comment that when processing raw data into the final marketing database the key is to be structured and disciplined. The data needs to be uniform and in a useful format for the database applications.

The main steps in managing the data entry are:

1. Verification
2. Validation
3. De-duplication
4. Merge purge.

Verification

Boddington (1994) suggests that verifying that the data has been put in accurately should be standard procedure. Marketing could ask for it to be keyed in twice, and if there is a difference, letting the computer throw up the discrepancy.

Validation

Validation is checking the accuracy of personal and product data provided by the customer. This could include:

■ Checking product/source codes for invalid codes against an internal master list. Address checking can be done using the Postal Address File (PAF). This file of all UK addresses is owned and updated *daily* by The Royal Mail.

■ Carrying out audits. These involve counts of customers, and other data entries, and then comparing these counts to see that they tally.

■ Carrying out various accuracy checks (as proposed by Woodcock, 1992) such as range validation: what are the valid ranges for each field? Do any of the entries lie outside these ranges?

■ Doing a sanity check. Pull off 100 records at random and do a visual inspection. Do they look reasonable?

De-duplication

De-duplication is the act of ensuring that the database does not contain duplicate records of the same customer. In many ways de-duplication replicates what humans do in picture puzzles when we are set the problem of 'spotting the ten differences between one picture and another'. A special de-duplication programme has to be run by the computer to ensure duplicate customer records are kept to a minimum.

When adding details of a transaction to your database, it may be obvious that the new data refers to a customer already on the system. However, there are a number of problems in checking the new record against existing records:

■ Unless there is an exact match of spelling, conventional record matching will miss the match and two records for the same customer will result.

■ Different names within the same household will cause problems. Suppose the husband rang the first time and the wife the second time, about the same query? A duplicate record may be set up.

■ When a customer moves house, and then makes a further purchase, they will quote their name and order number, and new address. The database needs to be able to spot this and update the old record, not create a new one.

■ Another big problem area is that of one address divided into flats. If the database then scratched one record, one name would be buried – a mistake.

In all these cases we would want to ensure that either the new data is allocated to an existing record, or a new record is set up. De-duplication is the art and science of attempting to do this. It is not easy, and much effort is spent by database bureaus in getting this right.

Merge purge

Merge purge is similar to de-duplication, but with merge purge you are merging two files – perhaps two external, or one external and your own internal database – into one. You therefore want to make sure you do not have the same customer twice in the final file. This is sometimes difficult to do, but important, to avoid mailing the same customer twice. It is also important to make sure that *existing* customers are not mailed with an offer aimed at *new prospects*. An offer of 'How about our Gold Card at no annual fee?' would not go down too well with existing full-fee-paying customers if it were mailed to them by mistake!

Because de-duplication and merge purge are both long processes (each record on one file has to be compared to all the records on the other file), matchkey systems are used to speed up the process. A matchkey shorthand is created: the key few characters, lifted from the name, address and postcode, which define the rest of the customer record. Stone and Shaw (1988) recommend the use of 14 character matchkeys. Matchkeys are compared to see whether they are the same or different. Those that are the same may be output by the computer for visual inspection.

Another approach used is called 'Soundex' and is used for data taken down aurally. Do both records sound like each other? If so, one may be erased.

Marketing managers have to make a trade-off between the quality of data on the one hand, and cost on the other. By using bigger matchkeys (more extensive checks) they will eliminate more duplicate files, but this will take longer and cost more. It is up to the individual company to make this trade-off decision.

MANAGE THE DATABASE

Once the data has been sourced and entered, it then has to be stored on the database and managed, ready for use. The company first has to decide whether to hold the data in-house or in a bureau.

In-house or bureau?

The decision on whether to manage the marketing database in-house or make use of an expert outside supplier – a data bureau – will be affected by various factors. The best course of action is often to set up the database *initially* in a bureau. This would allow staff to gain experience while the bureau takes on the job of managing the data. A move back in-house can be contemplated later.

Table 2.2 summarises the advantages and disadvantages of in-house versus bureau management.

Table 2.2: **Advantages and disadvantages of in-house versus bureau management**

Management	Advantages	Disadvantages
In-house	A customised approach is possible Day-to-day control Data can be moved easily	High cost of development Lack of internal expertise Name and address handling is difficult
Bureau	Easier to enforce service-level agreements Share costs of hardware experience	Conflicting demands from other clients On-line access sometimes difficult High operating costs

If a decision has been made to keep the database in-house, it is probably the IT people who will manage the database on marketing's behalf. In this instance, there are typically some clashes of perspective within the company, which need to be recognised and allowed for. These can be summed up as 'people issues'.

People issues

'IT are cautious. It's their job to be cautious; they know the danger of chaos. Marketing are aggressive. It's their job to be aggressive; they know the danger of delay.'

NCH Clearing House

EXHIBIT 2.3

THE BALLOONIST

A man in a hot air balloon realised he was lost. He reduced altitude and spotted a man below. He descended a bit more and shouted 'Excuse me, can you help? I promised a friend I would meet him an hour ago, but I don't know where I am.'

The man below replied 'You're in a hot air balloon, hovering approximately 30 feet above the ground. You're between 40 and 41 degrees north, 59 and 60 degrees west.'

'You must work in IT,' said the balloonist.

'I do,' replied the man, 'How did you know that?'

'Well,' answered the balloonist, 'everything you told me is technically correct, but I've no idea what to make of your information, and the fact is I'm still lost. Frankly, you've not been much help at all. If anything, you've delayed my trip.'

The man below responded 'You must be a marketing manager.'

'I am,' replied the balloonist, 'but how did you know?'

'Well,' said the man, 'you don't know where you are or where you're going. You have risen to where you are due to a large quantity of hot air. You made a promise which you've no idea how to keep, and you expect people beneath you to solve your problems. The fact is you are in exactly the same position you were in before we met, but now, somehow, it's my fault.'

(With thanks to Mike Bartlett, an IT man.)

The human chemistry of the interface between the information technology and marketing departments is crucial to the successful integration of database marketing into the company. The differences in perspective can, however, create problems.

The marketing perspective:

As a marketer you are rightly obsessed with the customer. You understand that one of the few differentiators we have is customer information. So why doesn't the rest of the company understand? Why is it so difficult to get them to accept that this is a priority?

Marketers:

- own the objectives of the database. They want it to be up and running quickly to steal a march on their competitors;
- don't fix on the cultural 'rules'. They are there to be broken;
- are often weak on technical details;
- know the danger of delay.

The IT perspective:

IT database managers have a very different view of the world. To them, marketers are only recent arrivals on the scene, coming behind the accounting system, the billing system, the stock-control system and the sales-recording system. What does marketing do anyway? They have never understood it, and no one has bothered to tell them, so what's all the fuss about? An IT manager's job is to make sure the company's internal systems are working properly.

IT people:

- own the technical knowledge of the database and the internal systems to make it happen;

- focus on the details;
- can feel weighed down by the problems;
- need strong guidance on what data to hold and what software applications are required;
- know the danger of chaos.

The solution to conflict is understanding each other's different points of view, and understanding what each other's roles are in managing the whole picture. It is up to the marketing department to specify what it wants the database to be capable of, and then to work with IT to agree the database solution.

The next issue is the ongoing management of the data *once it is on the database*.

Data management over time

Here we are concerned with:

- keeping data up to date
- auditing
- archiving.

We will look at each of these separately.

Keeping data up to date

The problem with data is that it decays over time, and so money has to be spent keeping it up to date. In the UK, between five and ten per cent of the population move every year. People die, people change their names, get married, or change their circumstances.

The problem of changing data in business-to-business work is even more acute. Because of the rapidity with which managers change jobs, as much as *30 per cent of the data* can be out of date within a year. In the US, Stone (1996) estimates that consumer data changes by as much as 20 per cent every year. In the UK, a lifestyle database manager explained that his consumer data decays by 17 per cent every year.

Customers whose records become out of date in this way are known as 'goneaways', and are a cause of great concern to direct marketers. The last thing you would want is to waste money by mailing people who no longer live at that address, to get people's names wrong, or cause distress to relatives by mailing someone who has recently died!

To minimise these problems, the following data management procedures are recommended:

1. Verify data against the electoral roll and Postcode Address File before selections of name and address are made. This will:
   - help reduce the number of 'goneaways' mailed;
   - reduce data capture errors (like name spelt wrongly at capture) getting back to the customer.

However, the privacy laws contained within the Data Protection Act have been applied directly to the electoral roll since 2002. People are now given the opportunity to *opt out of usage* of their name in direct marketing. A growing number of people will, therefore, be unavailable for verification. Companies will have to work harder to verify their data: suppressing records that do not match the electoral roll has become something of a lazy practice – one that will probably have to change.

2. Use only recent data. What counts as recent varies between industry sectors. For example, a supermarket would count three-month-old data as getting a bit long in the tooth. A car manufacturer would see three-year-old data as usable, while 20-year-old data may be OK for a mortgage company.

3. Run off 1000 records regularly. Review common mistakes. Analyse the source of data entry: coupon, phone, in-store. Look for patterns and track down the source of the problem, then rectify it.

EXHIBIT 2.4

WHAT'S IN A NAME

Running off names is useful for idea generation as well as problem spotting. Let's say you were direct marketing manager for the Royal National Lifeboat Institution (RNLI). Look at the two names and addresses below:

Admiral R D G Harrington   Mr I Brown
The Manor   Flat 2
Abbots Lumley   Cowley Mansions
Staffordshire   Chelsea
WS12 4JG   London
                               W3 4HJ

Both the above subscribe to a computer magazine. Which one of them is more likely to donate to the RNLI? An RNLI fundraiser would quickly choose the left-hand name – it sounds older, rural, and with a naval connection – lying squarely in RNLI territory.

Auditing

Audit counts should be carried out regularly for record verification. This should include checking database records against the sources of those records, right back to the original data capture. It may be that mistakes along the way can be spotted and rectified.

EXHIBIT 2.5

SAVING THE RAINFORESTS

I had a mailer recently from my bank. It eventually reached me after being forwarded by a friend who now lives in a house I vacated over two years ago. The mailer offered me a product which I had already taken up from the bank a while back.

The overall impression was one of inefficiency and a lack of any care being taken. It is likely that proper record verification and de-duplication would have prevented the bank from wasted mailers such as this.

Archiving

In order to make decisions about how long to hold records, we need to ask ourselves this question: when does a customer become a former customer? The answer is not as straightforward as we might think. For a magazine subscription, if your customer does not renew, then yes, they are now lapsed customers. But in the case of a credit-card company, this decision is not straightforward. There are many accounts which have not been used for a while. A decision has to be made on the length of time allowed to elapse before the account is considered dormant.

Some data may be completely archived or destroyed. But marketers also need to decide when to archive customer data for active communication. The data is then kept, but used only to aid in the analysis/modelling stage.

MANAGE THE APPLICATIONS

The key area to manage is the accuracy of any data that is going to get back to the customer. There are few things more irritating to customers than seeing their name spelt wrongly, and small details like these are going to reduce the impact of the best thought-through strategies and tactics. The major areas to consider are as follows:

Selection

The selection of a customer list from the database is made on the basis of the marketing decisions made in analysis and strategy. A decision can then be made to select customers according to their characteristics on the database. This process of selection needs to be carefully monitored. Some records may need to be suppressed from the final output; for example, it is reputed that vicars are suppressed from many mailing lists because they have a higher propensity to complain than average!

EXHIBIT 2.6

HAPPY ANNIVERSARY! MISTAKES WITH DATA

A company that sells flowers once mixed up two lists: one was a list of birthdays and the other was funeral anniversaries. Unfortunately, the funeral anniversary people got a letter starting 'Happy anniversary!', while the birthday list letter began 'On this sad day ...'!

A telecommunications company launched a new product by writing to 1.7m of its customers. It needed to write to only those customers who were connected to updated equipment. By mistake, however, the list consisted of those customers not able to take up the service. When this had been discovered, the company had to write again to all these people explaining that they had been a bit hasty, and the service was not quite ready. A simple key-stroke error in the database bureau cost the company £700k.

Outputs

Outputs are those fields which are transferred from the database *to the communication material going to the customer*. For direct mail this would include address, name for the salutation (Dear Mr/s ...), and also personal data such as account information for use in the letter.

Outputting data can go spectacularly wrong! Marketers need to be careful of items such as unusual titles, decorations and qualifications. Sensitive customers can be very publicly upset if their title is used incorrectly. If no data is available on the title, then marketers need to decide defaults, for example 'Dear customer', 'Dear Ms ...', and so on.

DEAR MR DAVI...

A large British company once made a mistake when outputting data. The mistake was in the setting of fixed fields for a test mailing it was doing. Instead of allowing the usual 20 spaces for the name field, a wrongly pressed key meant only four spaces were allowed. So when customers received their mailers, their names were cut in half: instead of 'Dear Mr Bottley' the letter read 'Dear Mr Bott', and so on. Unfortunately, the chairman of the company was also mailed with his name wrongly typed. Panic ensued as executives realised they would have to own up to their mistake!

Managing campaign responses

Goldwag (1995) emphasised the need for the following in order to manage data used for campaigns:

- a code to be part of the communication (called a unique reference number, URN) for the campaign. In the event of a response, this code would tell the direct marketer which campaign generated the response;
- a response (yes/no) code placed on the database.

Goldwag suggests that this enables 'flash' figures for immediate sales to be generated, figures over time to be compared, and ultimately detailed customised reporting.

Having examined data management, we can now take a close look at legal constraints in direct marketing.

Legal constraints in direct marketing

'More regulation' came third highest on a list of company concerns in a recent poll conducted by DMA (DMA Census, 2003). Direct and database marketing is far from immune from such concerns, with the EU in particular increasing its intention on marketing activity each year. Most marketing activity in most European countries is regulated in some way. Direct marketing, because of its use of personal data, private media and extensive use of sales promotions, is particularly targeted for legal constraints. In some cases, it may even be a criminal offence to break the law with direct marketing activity; in these instances, marketers do have a significant personal as well as professional motivation to make sure they are aware of the legal framework in which they operate.

The legal framework can be divided into two areas: the law and self-regulation. Our main concern with the law is the Data Protection Act, whereas self-regulation concerns are the British Code of Advertising Practice, covering data, and the Direct Mail Services Standards Board, covering codes of practice for mailings, sales promotions, and data.

Finally, it is vital that international marketers understand the changes of regulation in each country.

THE LAW

The Data Protection Act

Fricker (1992) outlined the most important aspects of the Data Protection Act facing direct marketers. The Data Protection Act of 1984 covers, with its eight main principles, the use of information relating to individuals. Companies need to ensure that personal data is:

1. obtained and processed fairly and lawfully;
2. held only for registered purposes;
3. not used in any manner incompatible with registered purposes;
4. not excessive for those purposes;
5. accurate and where necessary kept up to date;
6. not kept longer than necessary;
7. made available to individuals on request;
8. properly protected against loss or disclosure.

Consequences of the 1998 Data Protection Act

Compared with the 1984 act, the new Act imposes the following main changes:

■ Contact names on business lists are now within scope of the legislation.

■ The definition of personal data is wider.

■ Data subjects (customers) are given the specific right to prevent, at any time, the processing of personal data relating to them for the purposes of direct marketing.

■ The onus is on the data controller (company) to let customers know of their above right, and to give them an opportunity to opt out of receiving direct marketing communications.

■ In addition, if a company rents a list, or obtains consumer data from any third party, it now has to inform data subjects of this, and again give them a chance to opt out. Confusingly, companies may be able to claim that volume of data has prevented them from informing data subjects and, if they provide the authorities with evidence of this, may be exempt from the above requirement.

■ The laws pertaining to direct marketing have now made it essential that companies clear their lists of any people who have joined the Mailing Preference Service. This strengthens the previous Act in consumers' favour.

■ The author understands that the Act also makes it an offence to telephone any person who has joined the Telephone Preference Service.

So, one of the key changes for firms is that they must now give even their own customers the chance to opt out of communications, and they must do this in an ongoing manner, not just once when they are first acquired.

Another change particularly affecting telephone agencies is that essentially direct-marketing calls are prohibited once the caller has made it clear that they do not wish to be contacted.

All regulations apply to new media such as SMS and e-mail, though this is not clear explicitly. One of the problems with e-mail, of course, is that it is probably the most 'global' medium in history – hence much of the spam comes from countries outside the EU, in particular the USA.

Note: The information provided above is not comprehensive and does not constitute legal advice. If you require legal advice on these issues you need to consult a solicitor.

(*Source*: DMA (UK) Information sheet, 1 March 2000. The author would like to thank the UK DMA for the source of this information)

In Europe, the 1995 EU directive on the Protection of Individuals' Data has led to each of the 15 states that signed up to it arguing its implications in slightly different ways. The EU directive on distance selling in 1997 also requires personal data to be regulated. The concern for direct marketers is that the current opt-out provisions may be tightened further to opt in, that is, customers couldn't be contacted at all unless they had actively agreed to be. Given that there are probably a majority of people in the 'not bothered either way' camp who by definition will not bother to opt out or opt in, this is worrying for marketers as those who do actively opt in to allow personal marketing will hence be a small number of the total market.

SELF-REGULATION

Self-regulation was considered in detail by Titford (1994) and the following comments are based on her work. However, it should be borne in mind that this work was completed before the latest changes to the Data Protection Act. The first self-regulatory code we shall consider is the British Code of Advertising Practice (BCAP).

The British Code of Advertising Practice (BCAP)

BCAP's principal rules require that consumers must be notified of intended third-party use of their details and given an opportunity to object to that additional use before the data is rented. The simplest mechanism for objections is a tick box offering an 'opt-out' option on the reply coupon.

The rules also require members to abide by the wishes of a consumer who asks for no more mailings from a company. This would be put into practice by a 'do not promote' marker on the consumer's record.

There is also an opportunity for people to opt out totally from mailings or telephone calls from companies with which they have no connection (i.e. they are not customers). By registering onto the Mailing Preference Service (MPS) or Telephone Preference Service (TPS), once the company has erased MPS or TPS records from its list, these people are not contacted.

The Direct Mail Services Standards Board (DMSSB)

The DMSSB's main function is to administer an *accreditation scheme* for all types of service supplier within the direct mail arena. If a supplier is in breach of the regulations, it may lose its recognition status. This would be made public within the industry, and would probably result in loss of business. The Royal Mail may also withdraw its Mailsort facilities from persistent offenders.

The issues covered by the regulations are focused on direct mail. This, and the telephone, are the key private media. People tend to be very sensitive to individual messages addressed to them and therefore great care is needed. The following are some examples of marketing actions with which the DMSSB would be particularly concerned:

■ misleading slogans on outer envelopes such as 'Urgent – open immediately' or 'Private and confidential' are not permissible for purely advertising literature;

■ postage and packing prices should be clearly marked;

■ claims made for any product or service must be capable of substantiation;

■ in mail order, when using advance payment, the anticipated delivery period must be stated;

■ when using premium-rate telephone numbers as response devices, the costs of calls must be clearly shown in order not to mislead respondents.

Sales promotions are heavily regulated. Typical issues affecting the direct marketer's use of sales promotions are as follows:

■ free gifts must truly be free;

■ an entrant in a prize draw must not be required to pay for a chance to enter;

■ prize draws and competitions must have the full rules printed, including closing dates, restrictions on who can enter, etc.;

■ prizes – won by a selected number of respondents – must not be confused with 'gifts' – awarded to all participants.

EUROPEAN LEGISLATION

The laws and self-regulation differ in each European country, and sales promotion laws in particular are extremely complex. At the time of writing there is a lack of uniformity, and so direct marketers wishing to target an international audience must become aware of the different rules, one country at a time.

One prime example is the area of lotteries and sales promotions (Titford, 1994). Lotteries are illegal in Belgium, unless run in association with a public authority. French law limits the value of prizes, while in Germany it is forbidden to link a competition with a requirement to purchase. In the Netherlands, it is illegal to offer 'goods' as prizes: only cash or services are acceptable.

Another area with great differences is that of data. The UK, Belgium, the Netherlands and France all have restrictions on data transfer to third countries. German data protection laws are extremely severe, allowing only three selections on personal data, making targeting very difficult.

Summary to chapter

In this chapter we found that a database is a collection of customer records that can be analysed and output for communications. The key data to hold is personal data, transaction data, and contact histories. Data sources can be internal or external, and great care needs to be taken in establishing the form in which internal data is collected. Managing the database involves managing the entire journey of the data, from its source into the database, and over time on the database, before outputting as lists or onto customer communications.

The most important legal constraints for direct marketers occur in the areas of data usage, sales promotions, and customer communications. The Data Protection Act guides the use of data through its eight principles. For international direct marketers, there are extremely complex diverse laws governing the use of sales promotions in each country.

Questions

1. Explain the role of the database in direct marketing. What are the key applications for an international airline wishing to use its customer records for marketing?

2. According to Boddington (1994), 'a database is a record of our relationships with customers'. Discuss this statement, and discuss how this philosophy guides the type of data that a company may hold on its marketing database.

3. What is the difference between a database and a list? Drayton Bird said that by understanding what a list was, marketers were some of the way to understanding a database. Do you think he's right? Explain your reasons.

4. A manufacturer of golf products was interested in mailing a list of golfers from a lifestyle database and a list of subscribers to various golf magazines, in order to build up a marketing database. What would he need to do with the data before mailing?

5. What is de-duplication and why is it so important?

6. Mr Jones recently received a mailer forwarded to him from the Royal Mail. It was from his building society, and contained an address he had vacated over two years previously. He complained to the company and was told it was a 'computer error'. Explain how the building society could have avoided this problem.

References

Bird, D. (1989) *Commonsense Direct Marketing*, Kogan Page, London.

Boddington, A. (1994) IDM Diploma course material, Institute of Direct Marketing, Teddington, Richmond-upon-Thames.

Courtheux, R. (1992) 'The absolute essentials of direct marketing', *The Database*, Institute of Direct Marketing, Teddington, Richmond-upon-Thames, video series, video 4.

DMA Census (2003) DMA Records Office, London.

Fricker, C. (1992) 'Playing by the rules: direct marketing and the law' in Halsey, B. (ed.) *The Practitioners' Guide to Direct Marketing*, Institute of Direct Marketing, Teddington, Richmond-upon-Thames.

Goldwag, W. (1995) Smith Bundy and Partners.

Institute of Direct Marketing (1996) *Educator's Guide to Direct Marketing*, Institute of Direct Marketing, Teddington, Richmond-upon-Thames.

Kotler, P. (1995) *Marketing Management: Analysis, strategy, planning and control*, 7th edn, Prentice Hall, Upper Saddle River, NJ.

Logan, R. (1992) 'Getting to know your database' in Halsey, B. (ed.) *The Practitioners' Guide to Direct Marketing*, Institute of Direct Marketing, Teddington, Richmond-upon-Thames.

McCorkell, G. (2002) *The Interactive and Direct Marketing Guide*, Institute of Direct Marketing, Teddington, Richmond-upon-Thames.

Nash, E. (1993) *Database Marketing: The ultimate selling tool*, McGraw-Hill, New York.

Stone, B. (1996) *Successful Direct Marketing Methods*, 5th edn, NTC Business Books, Chicago, Ill.

Stone, M. (1997) *IDM Newsletter*, January.

Stone, M. and Shaw, R. (1988) *Database Marketing*, Gower, London.

Titford, P. (1994) 'Self-regulation in direct marketing', *Journal of Database Marketing*, **2** (2).

Woodcock, N. (1992) Video: The absolute essentials of direct marketing, no. 4: Database, Institute of Direct Marketing, Teddington, Richmond-upon-Thames.

Northern Theatres

This case is based on a real group of theatres, whose identity has been disguised to preserve commercial confidentiality:

In the early 1990s, a group of theatre managers got together in Manchester and decided to change the face of theatre marketing for ever. Up until the 1980s, any database marketing done by theatres had been *ad hoc*, local work focusing on particular shows. Marketing had focused on posters and 'take-one' leaflets, with dubious effectiveness.

In 1988, a decision was made to pull together a network of databases into one large pool of information. This network included other leisure attractions in the area, making the entire database something over one million people.

Northern Theatres' database collected data from credit-card bookers, who made up 50 per cent of the audience. Transactions, show types, performance times and class of seat were collected, as well as personal data. Personal data collected included sex, age, name and address, and whether they were group bookers or not.

Theatre marketing runs on very tight returns on investment. For a production to break even requires a seat occupancy greater than 80 per cent, and this can only happen if the marketing is persuasive and timely. One of the key areas is segmenting the base according to show type. What the managers started to find was that some of the predictions were less obvious than they expected. For example, they expected musical attenders to be interested in forthcoming musicals. What they in fact found was more correlation between traditional musicals such as, say, 'Calamity Jane' and traditional whodunnits such as Agatha Christie.

Recently, the managers have met again and set out a number of aims for the year ahead. These include better targeting of higher value customers, and reactivation of theatre goers who have not been for a while.

Questions

1. Explain what additional data requirements you would recommend for Northern Theatres and why. Can you see any other applications for the database?

2. What problems would a theatre group have in managing the data from source (prospects and customers) through to output (communications and analysis)?

3. Where would you expect Northern Theatres to get this extra data from?

PART 2

USING DIRECT MARKETING TO ANALYSE
THE MARKETING SITUATION

THE CUSTOMER DATABASE: ANALYSIS AND APPLICATIONS

Objectives

Once you have read this chapter you will:

■ appreciate how a marketing database can help to improve customer understanding;

■ have an understanding of the techniques used to analyse customer data;

■ be better able to contribute to the process of database analysis.

Introduction

In Chapter 2 we discovered what a database was and what data to hold. In this chapter we can move the focus on to how marketers can manipulate the data in order to understand their customers better. We will review what marketers use the analysis for, and explain, in simple terms, some of the intricacies of database analytical tools.

The need for information

When a corner shopkeeper chats to one of his customers as they pop in, as well as being friendly, he is also doing a form of analysis. He is assessing the customer's needs from his shop, and if Mrs Jones makes a regular order of three boxes of eggs a week, he makes sure there are enough ordered to meet demand. Turning the focus inwards, he will understand his own strengths and limitations. He will also quickly find out if a rival opens up a new grocer's just up the road and starts to compete. In short, 'analysis' in this situation is fairly straightforward.

However, as companies have got larger, they have had more and more difficulty staying close to their customers, understanding their own capabilities, or scanning what their competitors are up to. The marketing director of a large company has no 'natural' way of staying in touch. At the same time, the demand for companies to be market focused has become imperative.

Companies try to combat these scale problems by adopting the philosophy that, if they can't stay close to each of their thousands of customers individually, at least they will try to understand them as groups of people with shared characteristics. Marketing managers view such information as increasingly vital to their business, with Fletcher *et al.* (1995), Peppers and Rogers (1993), and Peters and Waterman (1982) seeing *information* as perhaps the only remaining way of obtaining sustainable competitive advantage. Although product USPs are nearly always copied within a few months, information and the leap in market understanding that it gives remains much more difficult to copy.

In general marketing such information is typically obtained through market research, salesforce feedback, competitor monitoring, and so on. However, firms that practise direct marketing have an extra string to their bow, which can help them in understanding their customers in a more precise way. This extra string is the database.

In this chapter we will investigate the ways that marketers can use a customer database to understand their customers better, and we will clarify the particular techniques they use to turn the raw data into useful information.

How this chapter is structured

In Chapter 2 we found that companies collect many different types of data on their customers. In this chapter we are concerned with the way in which this data can be turned into management information to help marketers create more effective strategies.

There are two main subjects we need to focus on here. The first looks at the uses that marketers can make of the information that database analysis produces. These are discussed in the following section. The second area is to develop a clear understanding of the analytical *tools and techniques* themselves, which we will cover later on in this chapter.

Uses of the database

HOW DATA ANALYSIS HELPS MARKETING MANAGERS

EXHIBIT 3.1

HARD AND SOFT INFORMATION IN DIRECT MARKETING

Direct marketers have to make decisions in two broad areas. First, we have the quantitative camp: we are faced with decisions on budgets, finance, returns on your spend. This is where the database provides a great deal of leverage, helping you drive your marketing in a precise, numbers-driven way.

However, other analysis is more *qualitative* in nature. These decisions are based on 'words and pictures' rather than numbers. In particular you are looking to answer the '*Why?*' question. Your database will tell you who is remaining loyal, and *what*

products they are being loyal to. However, only market research will tell you *why* they are loyal: is it your brand strength, the appeal of your offers, or your service?

A good direct marketer will not therefore seek to use the database to replace market research. Rather, they should be used in tandem, together, to maximise the firm's understanding of customers in a cost-effective way.

The role of marketing research in campaign analysis is fully discussed in Chapter 13.

What type of information are we talking about? Table 3.1 summarises the typical approach to marketing analysis in general marketing.

Table 3.1: **The scope of marketing analysis in general marketing**

Analysis	Description
Internal information	Understanding the company's strengths and weaknesses
Marketing research	Analysing customer markets and buyer behaviour
Environmental monitoring	Scanning the wider environment for opportunities and threats
Competitor analysis	Assessing competitors in relation to your business
Measuring and forecasting markets	Predicting market demand; measuring company performance against objectives set
Market segmentation	Splitting markets into discrete groups to be treated differently
Market targeting	Selecting the best markets for the company

From Table 3.1 we can see that a marketing database can add value to analysis in two main areas. The first area is that of *measurement* and is covered in Chapter 13. The second area, which we are concentrating on here, is that of *segmentation and targeting*.

It really cannot be overstated how valuable a customer database is to a segmentation strategy. There are two reasons why a customer database is a segmenter's dream. One is the volume and type of data that is available on a good database. Instead of a few hundred sample units of researched, claimed attitude and behaviour, there are potentially hundreds of thousands or even millions of data sets which include actual behaviour, plus profile information. The second reason for the database's segmenting value is that once the segments have been created, each customer can be precisely allocated to each group, and then contacted accordingly. The core requirements of a segment – that it should be discrete, profitable and accessible – are all achieved in an *integrated* way using the database.

The single most important application of this data arguably lies in its ability to segment at the *individual level*. We can look at the data, build up a picture of who the customer is and what he or she wants from us, and create value for them accordingly. This deceptively simple use of the data leads to a one-to-one strategy (Peppers and Rogers, 1993), which is fully discussed in Chapter 5.

Customer segmentation at *group level* is an aspect of marketing that has been extensively researched and written about by marketing academics, and is very important to marketing practice. Segmentation is based on two main data types: behavioural and profile data. Various segmentation approaches have developed from this data (*see* Fig. 3.1).

A number of authors including Stone and Shaw (1988), Dupin (1992), Nash (1995), Patron (1994) and Stone (1996) have identified many such segmentation applications. In particular, database marketers have understood how *purchase (behavioural) data* allows them to segment customers according to their value to the company. Direct marketers can also use purchase data to segment according to product needs.

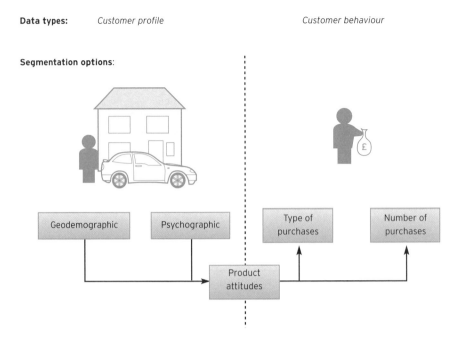

Figure 3.1 Overview of segmentation options

The second major data type, consumer characteristics data (or *profile data*, as Jobber (1995) described it), is used by direct marketers to build up 'pictures' of those customers who are *more likely to respond* to a particular campaign. McCorkell (1997) called this 'ROI-driven marketing'. Profile data is also used to target new markets more accurately, thereby lowering the costs of acquisition.

A summary of these segmentation options and their uses is given in Table 3.2.

Table 3.2: Summary of segmentation applications

1	Use purchase behaviour to segment by customer value (also, use current purchase behaviour to forecast lifetime values).
2	Use purchase behaviour to segment by product need, and to assess product/market strategy.
3	Use profile data to relate to campaign response (ROI-driven marketing).
4	Use profile data to target new customers accurately.

Having introduced segmentation as the key application of database analysis, we can now move on to discuss each of these applications in a little more detail. In order to keep an overview, you may find Fig. 3.2 helpful in keeping a visual picture of the database and what it can do.

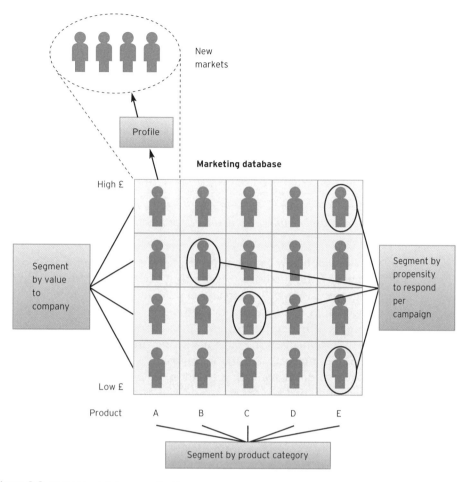

Figure 3.2 Company database applications

Segmentation applications for database marketers

USING PURCHASE DATA TO SEGMENT BY VALUE

The importance of this area to the whole of direct marketing thinking, and beyond to relationship marketing (Peppers and Rogers, 1993; Hallberg, 1996), cannot be emphasised too strongly. Hallberg summed it up in his paper 'All customers are not created equal' when he said:

> 'At the heart of the concept is the simple notion that we don't have to worry all that much about relationships with everybody. Relationships with some consumers are more important than relationships with others.'

This phenomenon is explained by applying Pareto's Principle to business. Pareto was an Italian economist who noticed that 20 per cent of the population owned 80 per cent of the land, and that this rule seemed to hold true no matter what area he studied. As a result, he created his principle, often known as the '80/20 rule', which has since been adapted for business.

Pareto's Principle applied to business

'Twenty per cent of your customers will provide you with 80 per cent of your profits.'

The actual numbers, 80 and 20, should not be taken as accurate for all businesses. This is not the case. What is crucial is that all businesses exhibit the underlying principle to some extent:

A small number of your customers provide a disproportionate amount of your profits.

If we once again compare general marketing and direct marketing, we can see the importance of this analysis. In general marketing, this attempt to split off the firm's most valuable customers and treat them differently is not done with the same precision or conviction as it is by direct marketers. The manager of a high-street store does not keep records of her customers, and so she doesn't know who the more valuable ones are. Every customer gets the same marketing effort targeted at them, and no records are kept of who is more valuable to the company.

In contrast, direct marketing spend is often deliberately spread unevenly amongst customers, such that returns are maximised. Hilton Hotels identify their biggest spending customers, who are senior businesspeople who travel frequently. Their database flags up these customers as worthy of special attention, and when they arrive at the hotel they are given priority check-in service. Their every preference, from the size of the bed to the paper they read, is logged and delivered without them needing to ask. What Hilton has done is look to improve loyalty through a strategy of superior service in which the database analysis of customer value plays a crucial part.

EXHIBIT 3.2

SEGMENTING BY VALUE: THE NSPCC

The National Society for the Prevention of Cruelty to Children (NSPCC) is one of the largest charities in the UK, and as such has a donor base of about 500 000 supporters. These are segmented according to the level of their support, and NSPCC's fundraising department is organised around these different segments. One department looks after VIP donors (over £2000 p.a.), another cares for the major donors (over £500 p.a.), while another caters for the group between £100 and £500, and so on.

Segmenting by value has enabled the NSPCC to focus on the differing needs of each group of fundraisers, and maximises their potential to give.

USING PURCHASE DATA TO SET BUDGETS

Companies can analyse their customers' purchase data in order to calculate how much each customer is likely to be ultimately worth to the company. This forecast is known as the *customer's lifetime value*. By predicting how much gross profit we will make from customers, we can then construct a budget, on a per customer basis, which clearly tells us how much we can afford to spend. This calculation is called the *allowable marketing spend per customer*, and is extremely important in direct marketing practice.

Let's say our company is in computer periphery sales. Our customers' average lifetime value is calculated at £100 gross profit per annum. Using this figure to guide us, we can arrive at an allowable marketing spend, per customer, of say £30 per year.

This is a vital application of our existing customer data. Using customer lifetime values, we can take a view of the profitability of different markets. In turn, the allowable marketing spend figure can form the basis of budget setting. Both acquisition and retention budgets can use this figure as the start point. If a target figure of sales is imposed on the marketing department, this can be converted quickly to customer numbers, and hence to a budget figure, because we have a basis for spend per customer. This budget submission is based on analysis, rooted in current customers' behaviour, not on guesswork or last year's budget. A step-by-step guide to these calculations appears on p. 60.

These calculations have a number of linkages elsewhere in this book. The strategic division of resources between acquisition and retention is discussed in Chapter 5. The use of the allowable marketing spend per customer to set budgets for tactical programmes is discussed in Chapter 13.

SEGMENTING ACCORDING TO CUSTOMER NEED

Jobber (1995) reported that segmenting by different customer needs is quite common. In general marketing, it is standard to use market research to understand the different benefits obtained by different sets of consumers from the same product.

By studying the behavioural and psychographic data held on each customer, direct marketers can offer an additional tool. As Patron (1994) pointed out, the database can help the marketer to understand the different benefits that the same product may give customers. It may be that market research will be used as an additional way of obtaining insight here, perhaps to confirm a hunch developed from the database analysis. Second, subsequent marketing can be delivered to those customers with precision.

For example, American Express ('Amex') has used advanced modelling techniques to split its customer base according to the products customers have bought with their credit or charge cards. Amex then approaches 'third parties': Shell might be interested in offering tie-in deals with big spenders on petrol, for instance. These deals would then be offered to customers with their statements.

If product information is not available, customer needs may be deduced using psychographic or demographic information. Segmentation may then follow. The Midland Bank introduced its Vector account in 1987 based on market research it had done into customer attitudes to banks. It found that customers could be divided into different psychographic segments depending on their attitudes to two variables: confidence in dealing with banks, and the extent to which they viewed banks as authority figures. Vector was aimed at people who were very confident, had low respect for authority, and viewed banks as just another retail outlet. The Vector account offered interest-free overdrafts and interest on current accounts in return for a fixed fee. The targeting of Vector could be based on psychographic profiled lists.

EXHIBIT 3.3

SEGMENTING ACCORDING TO LIFESTYLE NEEDS: HARLEY DAVIDSON

Swinyard (1996) conducted an elegant analysis of Harley Davidson motorbike owners. He analysed their responses to a series of lifestyle opinion statements, and then used cluster analysis to split up and group the riders into six segments, according to how Harley Davidson meets their needs. The following lifestyle segments provide a firm basis on which to split the existing customer database and direct the marketing of Harley accessories accordingly:

1 **Tour Gliders** Use their motorcycle for long trips. Agree with statements like: *'My bike is made for comfort rather than speed.'*
2 **Dream Riders** Now they have their Harley, but are trying to figure out what to do with it. Agree with statements like: *'Most of the time my motorbike is just parked.' 'I mainly use my bike for short trips around town.'*
3 **Hard Core** Gang bikers who like that sort of society. Agree with statements like: *'Some people would call me and my friends outlaws.' 'I think it's true that real men wear black.'*

4 **Hog Heaven** In love with the Harley mystique. Agree with statements like: *'When I ride, I feel like an old wild west cowboy.'*
5 **Zen Riders** Find spiritual solace in riding bikes. Agree with statements like: *'I like the attention I get when I am on my bike.' 'Most of the time my bike is just parked.'*
6 **Live to Ride** Passionate about motorbiking and do so rain or shine. Agree with statements like: *'I love to ride long distances; to me 500 miles is a short trip.' 'Motorcycles are a total lifestyle to me.'*

Swinyard then calculated purchase predictions of new Harleys and accessories for each segment. For example, using historical purchase data, he calculated that 'Dream Riders' and 'Zen Riders' spent much more on accessories than did 'Hog Heavens'.

He concluded that Harley Davidson riders were a much more complex set of people than the old stereotype of 'hard core outlaw gang riders' would seem to imply!

Source: Reproduced by permission from Swinyard, W.R. (1996) *Journal of Targeting Measurement and Analysis*, **4** (1), pp. 337–62.

MAXIMISING RESPONSE ON A PER-CAMPAIGN BASIS

Direct marketers use modelling techniques to identify their most 'responsive' customers. This allows us to allocate the marketing budget on a per-campaign basis such that return on investment (ROI) is maximised.

Imagine that you are running a small 'direct' operation. You have 100 customer records laid out on paper in front of you. However, you have only enough marketing budget to contact 50 of them. You need to select the 50 customers most likely to respond to your offer. If you have only 100 customers, you can look at each customer and, based on your personal knowledge of them, make a decision about who to contact.

Given the reality of thousands or even millions of customers, we clearly cannot allocate our scarce budget using personal knowledge. The answer is to use predictive statistics, described in the following section, to forecast which individual customers are most likely to respond. A new analysis may be run for each campaign, and depending on the product, the timing, and so on of each campaign, a different set of customers each time will receive the communication.

The advantage of this technique is its firm focus on profitability on a *campaign by campaign level*, as well as a strategic level: something rarely done in marketing. However, there are pitfalls. If we let the model alone decide which customers receive what communication, it is difficult to envisage a coherent set of messages, over time, going to customers.

EXHIBIT 3.4

SEGMENTING BY LIFESTAGE FOR FINANCIAL SERVICES

The principle of lifestage segmentation is that we tend to go through key life events at similar ages. Date of birth is therefore the key variable to hold on the database, and this, along with identification of life events, such as having children, allows the marketer to fit consumers to particular 'lifestage' segments. This segmentation works very well for two product areas in particular: consumer durables and financial services.

Key variables needed for lifestage segmentation are:

■ age
■ marital status
■ presence and age of youngest child at home
■ gender
■ labour force status.

The following are descriptions of typical lifestages:

Bachelor 1: young, single, not at home, age 18–35, few financial burdens, high expendible income, credit-card products, image related.

Full nest 1: age 18–35, youngest child six or under, home purchasing at peak, low expendible income, low savings, high borrowings: loans, overdrafts, mortgages.

Delayed nest: age 27–40, no kids, double income, financial position good, entertainment products: Diners Card etc., pensions, PEPS, savings products.

Older couples, retired: age 57+, no children living at home, low debts, low income, medical financial products: insurance etc., savings products.

Source: Arens, J. (1993) 'Examining the role of lifestage transitions in modelling consumer behaviour', *Journal of Targeting Measurement and Analysis*, 1 (4), pp. 345–54.

Marketers in sectors where coherent communications over time are important may therefore look to mix these 'profitability-driven' methods with 'relationship-driven' programmes.

TARGETING NEW PROSPECTS BASED ON EXISTING CUSTOMER DESCRIPTIONS: PROFILING

The database applications covered so far concentrate on existing customers – those held on the database. But is there any way that this tool can help us find new customers? Here we arrive at a second 'truism' for business in this chapter, which is as important to direct marketers as Pareto's Principle. Provided the new markets are looking for the same benefits from the product as existing markets:

your new customers will have a similar profile to your existing customers.

On giving this a moment's thought, you may not be surprised that similar types of people will like similar products, or will be attracted to similar brand images. Surprising or not, this phenomenon is absolutely crucial to direct marketers. It means that by making the effort to accurately '*profile*' our existing customers, we can then *more precisely target* new customers.

General marketers profile using market research. An aggregate profile based on customer characteristics is built up and related to media habits: TV, press readership, and so on. A media buyer is then employed to pick those media which most closely match these profiles. The problem with this approach is the imprecision of the profiling and targeting process. Rather like dropping leaflets from an aeroplane, a lot of people get the message who don't need it!

In contrast, direct marketers take advantage of the sheer volume of their data and use modelling techniques, described later in this chapter, to produce a highly accurate quantitative profile of their customers. Direct marketers can complete the precision of their marketing efforts by matching with external databases or lists, enabling a list of the most likely new market prospects for the company to be generated. This list is then marketed to directly. The use of external databases is fully discussed in Chapter 4.

Now that we know what uses direct marketers make of databases for analysis, the following section describes the techniques that make it all happen.

Analytical techniques

Table 3.3 links together the *applications* described previously with the *techniques* direct marketers use to analyse customer databases.

Table 3.3: Summary of applications and techniques in direct marketing analysis

Application	Technique
Setting budgets	Using lifetime value (LTV) analysis to set allowable marketing spend
Understanding customers' value to you	Use frequency, recency, amount, category (FRAC) analysis and LTV analysis
Understanding existing customers as individuals: what they want from you	Database overlays with external data; Profiling/modelling techniques: focus on product categories link with customer profiles; Combine with market research
Targeting your spend in order to maximise ROI per campaign	Use modelling techniques, FRAC analysis
Profiling existing customers in order to target new customers	Profiling/modelling techniques

On the right-hand side of Table 3.3 you will notice a number of technical terms. The intention of the remainder of this chapter is to introduce these techniques in a non-technical way in order to make them accessible to readers who may be unfamiliar with statistical methods. Those readers who do not enjoy numbers are urged not to skip this section, as it is the use of these methods which lies at the heart of the superior control and targeting that direct marketing can offer.

INTRODUCTION TO ANALYTICAL TECHNIQUES

The enormous amount of data that a database holds, and huge computing power, has heralded a drive towards heavy use of quantitative techniques which help in deciding where to spend one's marketing pound. Marketers' greatest concern is often with the future; in particular, who is likely to buy our products and services, and what they are likely to buy. Reflecting this, we are dealing primarily with *forecasting* techniques, known by statisticians as *predictive* techniques. However, some focus is also given to *descriptive* techniques which help us understand what our customers '*look like*'.

There are two main methods of predicting a variable (such as customer response): *time series* and *explanatory*. With time-series methods, we make predictions about future levels of customer response by projecting forwards from the trend, cycle and seasonal patterns contained in *past values* of our data. Alternatively, explanatory methods can predict customer response (the dependent variable) by identifying the factors that drive it (the independent variables), estimating their effects and projecting these forward into the future. Explanatory techniques are generally more useful than time-series ones when looking at the medium- to long-term future. On the other hand, time-series techniques are quicker and more accurate in the short term.

TIME-SERIES METHODS

Lifetime value analysis and allowable marketing spend per customer

In lifetime value analysis we are exploring the relationship between on the one hand the gross margin that we obtain from customers, and on the other hand the amount we can spend marketing to them. This spend is used to attract customers in the first place, and then to ensure they maintain or increase their value to us. The allowable marketing spend is calculated *not* as one departmental total but, more usefully, for individual customers.

First, let's understand what lifetime value is.

Explanation of lifetime values

> *Lifetime values are the sum of all future net incomes expected from a customer, translated into present-day terms.*

There are two things particularly to note about this definition. The first is net income: this is income after direct costs have been taken into account. The second is the reference to present day. This is an adjustment made to future incomes based on the principle that £10 next year is not the same as £10 today. In fact it is worth less – maybe only about £9 – depending on the 'discount rate' you set. The principle here is that money in the future is always worth less than the same amount today. To turn this economic logic on its head, another way of thinking about it is this: if you had £10 today, you could invest it and it would be worth more than £10 next year. Therefore, it is better to have £10 now than £10 next year. This adjustment figure is known as the *net present value*.

Lifetime value assessments vary according to the product sector. Dupin (1992) points out that for some sectors where revenues are stable and predictable, the calculation is simple. This is true of much of financial services. For example, a mortgage document will anticipate all the revenue received by the company over the entire lifetime of the relationship. However, other product sectors, in particular classical direct sectors such as book clubs or china collectibles, have what Stone (1996) called 'front-end' and 'back-end' revenues to consider. The front end refers to the revenue obtained from the initial sale, which may well be lower than subsequent sales because an acquisition offer was used as an enticement. The back end refers to all revenue obtained from subsequent sales, which can make the difference between loss and profit for each customer.

Calculating lifetime value and allowable marketing spend

To calculate customer lifetime values accurately, we need three key pieces of data. These are:

■ the number of years a customer buys from a company;

■ the percentage of customers remaining loyal to the company;

■ the amount spent per annum.

Stone (1996) recommends taking an historical approach to calculating lifetime values. He emphasises the need to build up a store of historical data on the above variables so that they may be more accurately predicted.

Assuming that our database contains such data, we can now press on with understanding the method used to calculate lifetime value and allowable marketing spend. This is based on work by Dupin (1992), simplified here.

There are three steps. The first step is the *calculation of lifetime revenues*, without taking into account initial recruitment costs at this stage. The second step is the *calculation of allowable marketing spend*, and the final step is the *comparison of these costs with projected revenues* to assess the validity of the investment.

Step 1: Calculation of lifetime revenues

Situation Imagine we were running a book club. We have just been tasked to recruit and retain 1000 customers. What is the lifetime value of each customer, and hence how much can we afford to spend to recruit and retain them?

Our database has tracked 1000 customers acquired five years ago. It has found that each year some customers defect or allow their membership to lapse. It has also noted that average income is £25 p.a., and non-marketing costs (production, etc.) are £12 p.a. Our database analysis reveals an average retention rate of 70 per cent per annum. A 'lifetime' length of five years is taken to simplify the calculation.

Solution To calculate lifetime values, we first set up the calculation according to Table 3.4.

Table 3.4: **Example lifetime value calculation**

	Year				
	1	2	3	4	5
Relative sales	£	£	£	£	£
per year	1	0.7	0.49	0.34	0.24
Direct income	25	17.50	12.25	8.58	6
Indirect income	3	15	10.5	7.35	5.1
Direct costs*	12	8.4	5.88	4.12	2.8
Indirect costs	1.5	1.05	0.74	0.51	0.36
Net income	14.5	23.05	16.13	11.3	7.94
Net present value per annum (NPV)	14.5	20.1	12.2	7.4	4.5
Total lifetime value (sum of NPVs) = £58.70					

* These do not include marketing costs at this stage.

Source: Dupin, D. (1992) 'Lifetime marketing: Assessing return on marketing spend, using a magazine subscription as an example', *Journal of Targeting Measurement and Analysis*, 1 (1), pp. 29–33.

Explanation of the table

Row 1: The first row represents the relative sales for all five years, expressed as a ratio of the first year. It falls away as the club loses 30 per cent of its original customers each year. Thus, if 1000 customers were recruited in year 1, then 240 of these are left by year 5.

Row 2: The second row represents direct income from subscriptions to the book club. This income falls away as per row 1.

Row 3: The third row gives the indirect income that derives from sales, and falls away in subsequent years as above. Indirect income could come from a number of sources, such as cross sales of related products, or list rental of the names generated.

Rows 4 and 5: These quantify the direct costs of supply of the product, including all direct costs of goods, plus any costs related solely to that sale. No fixed cost allocation is included, because the exercise is intended to evaluate lifetime values for marketing spend decisions only. As fixed costs would be incurred whether or not the activity goes ahead, we should not include them in an analysis of that activity's value to the company.

Row 6: This is the total net income. This is calculated by adding together rows 2 and 3 and subtracting from this total rows 4 and 5.

Row 7: This gives the final net present value of each year's income. This is calculated as follows:

$$\text{Net present value (for year } x) = \frac{\text{net income (for year } x)}{(1 + \text{DR})^x}$$

$$\text{where DR} = \text{discount rate} \quad \text{e.g.} \quad \frac{15}{100}$$

The discount rate in this example is 15 per cent. This rate is kept constant for any set of calculations. The discount rate is assumed to be the extent to which money loses its value, which changes depending on economic conditions.

Step 2: Calculation of allowable marketing spend per customer

Two separate allowable marketing spend figures need to be decided upon. The first is the amount we can spend to attract a customer for the first time. This figure may well have to be greater than the revenue from the first sale. The second is the amount we can spend on existing customers in order to keep them with us.

In the example in Table 3.4, a lifetime value of £58.70 for each customer over a five-year period sets the boundary for our *target* allowable spend. It is vital to set the allowable spend at a realistic value, but it must allow for the realities of the company's profitability expectations.

Let us set an allowable spend for recruitment at £20 per customer, and an allowable spend for retention at £3 per customer, per year. The much higher recruitment figure reflects the high costs of acquisition, something we will be discussing in greater detail in Chapter 5.

Having set this target figure, we can now set the marketing budget required to achieve the exercise – acquiring and retaining 1000 customers. First, we need to look at acquisition:

Acquisition marketing budget
= allowable recruitment spend per customer × target no. of customers
= £20 × 1000
= £20 000

(The allowable marketing spend for acquisition also allows us to calculate quickly a target response rate for a campaign. Let's say we use direct mail to attract customers from a list of prospects. £20 000 would allow us to send about 40 000 mailers (*see* Chapter 10 for costs of media). We need 1000 customers, which is a response rate of 2.5 per cent from the mailer. This is our target response rate.)

Second, we assess retention:

Retention marketing budget for years 2 to 5
= no. of customers × allowable marketing spend for retention

A total is then calculated depending on the number of customers each year.

For a customer who stays with us for all five years, we will spend the initial £20 plus £3 p.a. for four years, making a total of £32. This is the total allowable marketing spend over a customer's 'lifetime'.

Step 3: Calculation of expected return on investment

This is best done by looking at returns on investment per customer, over the expected lifetime. Subtracting the marketing spend per customer (step 2) from the lifetime value income per customer (step 1), we arrive at:

Expected return on investment per customer = 58.70 − 32 = £26.70

We can express the surplus in terms of return on investment per annum. As the expected 'lifetime' of each customer is five years, the total figure of £26.70 is divided by 5.

$$\text{Expected ROI per annum} = \frac{26.70}{5} = £5.34$$

The next technique we shall consider is FRAC scoring.

Frequency, recency, amount and category (FRAC) scoring on the database

Explanation of FRAC

FRAC is a breakdown of behavioural data on customers into its constituent parts. Frequency refers to the time elapsed between purchases. Recency is the date of the most recent purchase. Amount is the average value of that customer's purchases. Category refers to that segment which the product bought comes under.

What is FRAC scoring?

FRAC scoring is a way of assessing each customer on the database based on their purchase behaviour. The outcome of the scoring procedure is that each customer has a number, a score, attached to them. Using these scores, a prediction can be made of each customer's likelihood of responding to your next campaign. However, in addition to this tactical emphasis, FRAC can also be used as a strategic tool, to help understand the bigger picture. It is the basis on which customer segmentation by value is carried out, enabling segmentation marketing to be practised, as described earlier.

The principle behind FRAC scoring

According to Stone and Shaw (1988), FRAC scoring is one of the most valuable analyses to carry out on your database. In a nutshell, they say that this is because 'past transactions are one of the most important indicators of future transactions'.

The way in which past transactions guide future transactions depends on the market sector. In some sectors there are well-established gaps between purchases, for example the private purchase of cars. Here, a customer who has just bought a car from us is unlikely to buy another straightaway: the score may indicate a customer maximum propensity to repurchase when, say, five years have passed (five years is a typical average gap between new car purchases).

In other markets, direct marketers have found some more surprising patterns. In mail order, and other classic direct sectors, the following 'principle' seems to hold:

Your next customer is likely to be one who has just bought from you.

Whereas in financial services, a bank may find that:

A customer with many accounts is more likely to purchase further products from you than one with few or no accounts.

In general, collective direct marketing practice has revealed the following important truism:

The more your customers have spent with you, the more they are likely to spend with you in the future.

Does this sound obvious? Let's turn it on its head for a second. It can be argued that if I have bought one item from your catalogue then surely I am less likely to buy a future item than someone who hasn't bought anything? In fact this is rarely the case, and this underlies the principle that a company's existing customers are its most valuable asset, something we will discuss more in Chapters 5 and 7.

Example calculation of FRAC scoring

Stone (1996) reports a typical simple FRAC scoring method. A points system is used, with purchases broken down by quarter years. A typical formula might be as follows:

Recency points:

24 points	purchase in current quarter
12 points	purchase in last 6 months
6 points	purchase in last 9 months
3 points	purchase in last 12 months

Frequency points:

No. of points = No. of purchases $\times$ 4

Monetary points:

No. of points = 10 per cent of purchase value, with a ceiling of 9 points.

Each customer's score is then calculated and held on the database. The marketer then makes targeting selections according to these scores.

Ranking your customers

After each customer has been scored according to their FRAC data, we then organise them according to that score. Customers are divided up into cells according to their predicted response levels. Stone and Shaw (1988) report that typically ten cells, known as deciles, are used. A *gains chart*, such as that shown in Table 3.5, is then produced.

Table 3.5: **Gains chart**

Segment	Decile (%)	Score	Typical marketing decision (No. of contacts, type of media used, etc.)
1	0-10	60+	5 contacts; telephone outbound
2	11-20	54-59	|
3	21-30	48-53	|
4	31-40	42-47	|
5	41-50	36-41	|
6	51-60	30-35	|
7	61-70	24-29	|
8	71-80	18-23	|
9	81-90	12-17	|
10	91-100	6-11	1 contact; mail only

The chart in Table 3.5 is known as a gains chart because it indicates the gain that is predicted in response over the average that would have been obtained with a random targeting exercise. Customers in the first decile are much more responsive than those in the tenth decile, and allowable marketing spend can be allocated accordingly.

EXPLANATORY ANALYTICAL TECHNIQUES

In this section, we will first introduce modelling techniques, before exploring some of the more common techniques used in database analysis. We will look at cluster analysis, neural networks, regression analysis and CHAID analysis.

Modelling techniques introduced

This is a vast and complex area, and detailed coverage of all the techniques useful to direct marketers is well beyond the scope of this book. However, it is perhaps not good enough for marketers to throw up our hands and say, 'I don't understand this area. Let's leave it to the statisticians.' The best results from modelling techniques spring out of a debate between marketers and modellers, with the marketers specifying what they want out of the model, and the modellers trying to interpret these instructions. There are many objectives that a marketer can set, and there are many techniques to choose from, as we will see.

Modelling is as much an art as a science. The factors which drive, say, response to a mailer are a mix of 'orderly' and 'random' factors. It is to some extent possible to model the orderly influences on response to a mailer. However, random factors, by their very nature, are unpredictable and their effects cannot be included in a model. The marketer's intuitive understanding of the market is required to recognise when the influence of random factors, or perhaps the correlation between two or more orderly factors, is affecting the model. Very often in modelling, variables such as age and income are quite likely to be related *to each other* as well as to response to a mailer – the factor we are trying to model. Marketers need to be aware of these common problems in modelling. These can be understood and overcome by building up familiarity with both the data to be used in modelling and the limitations of modelling techniques.

The responsibilities for marketers, therefore, are to:

- specify what we want the model to do: what are the marketing objectives? These have already been established as either maximising response from our existing customers, discussed earlier, or finding new customers through profiling, discussed in Chapter 4;

- understand our data so that we know what it is we want to model;

- have sufficient understanding of modelling 'jargon' and techniques so that we can discuss these objectives with the modelling specialists and be able to interpret the outputs of the models.

To improve our understanding of what we are doing, it is useful to take a closer look at some typical customer data.

The nature of customer data

Let's examine a mythical 'Wine Direct' operation. Wine Direct is expanding, and therefore wants to target new customers as accurately as possible. Can the company use its existing data (in Table 3.6) to build up a picture of its best customers?

If we take a closer look at the data from the five customers outlined in Table 3.6, we may be able to spot how those people who have bought the most wine (high responders) are different to those who have bought less wine (low responders). The data implies that older people seem to be responding a bit better, as do those with more income and those who live in the south. However, car ownership seems unrelated, as does their liking for classical music.

As a result of this analysis, we decide to contact *new prospects* based on age, income, and where customers live. The logic we used is this:

Provided there are associations between variables, then knowledge of one variable (say, age) will help us increase the accuracy with which we predict the values of another variable (say, likelihood to respond).

Table 3.6: **Wine Direct customer data**

Customer	Cases of wine bought	Age	Income	Own a car	Classical music fan	Live in south
1	20	45	35 000	Y	N	Y
2	5	28	20 000	Y	Y	N
3	10	35	30 000	Y	Y	N
4	15	52	15 000	N	Y	Y
5	25	60	28 000	Y	Y	Y

In the example we have used, we have just built a mental 'model' of our data. Statistical modelling techniques do just the same, except that they establish the patterns in the data mathematically, using thousands of data sets rather than our five. The model establishes *associations*, or linkages, between response and other variables, that will help us predict our best future customers.

Identifying these associations lies at the heart of quantitative techniques. However, there is a difference between an *association* between variable A and variable B, and any hint that variable A may have *caused* variable B to change. This is an important distinction to make. As marketers, we are very interested in any *causal* relationship between variables because this can help us understand our customers just that little bit better. For example, if we are selling exploration holidays, it is very useful to know that our customers are mostly, say, people who are searching for some personal meaning from their holiday experience; it enables us to talk to them in their language. This psychographic variable is a probable *causal* factor in the purchase of the holiday. On the other hand, our customers may also be higher-than-average purchasers of sports cars. This variable is merely *associated* with the holiday purchase, but is unlikely to be a causal factor in its purchase.

Having made the effort to examine data in more detail, we are now ready to look at the more common explanatory techniques.

Cluster analysis

The process of clustering can be visualised by imagining a piece of paper with iron filings spread randomly all over the sheet. Each filing represents a customer, as yet not assigned to any group. Then picture what happens as a set of magnets is slowly drawn closer to the underside of the paper. The magnets represent the clustering process. As they get closer, so the filings start to separate out into groups which are pulled towards each magnet, depending on the filing's position on the paper. At the end, the original

---

EXHIBIT 3.5

QUANTITATIVE JARGON EXPLAINED

Variable A variable is simply a concept that varies; for example, age, income, response.

Dependent variable This is the variable you want to predict. In direct marketing this is often 'response', 'sales', or 'income'.

Independent variable Independent variables are other variables on the database that may be related to, and so help predict, the dependent variable. Independent variables may be 'age', 'income', 'attitudes', 'prior product purchase'.

Correlation This measures the closeness of the relationship between variables that are related to each other.

Measure of association (correlation coefficient) The correlation coefficient is a single number that expresses the strength and direction of a relationship between two variables, say age and response. It measures the extent to which the variation in an independent variable, say income, explains the variation in a dependent variable, say response to an offer of a credit card. If all responders to the offer have a high income, and all the non-responders have a low income, then income is a strong *explainer* of the variance of response to the offer. It is also said to be highly *correlated* or associated with response.

Coefficient of determination (R^2) This statistic lies between 0 and 1. It identifies what percentage of the variation in the dependent variable is explained by the overall model we have constructed. A model with an R^2 close to 1 will produce more accurate predictions than those from a model with an R^2 closer to 0.

spread of filings (customers) has been replaced by clusters, or groups, depending on the position (customer characteristics).

Cluster analysis is one of the techniques used by direct marketers to produce quantitative profiles of customers. Geodemographic profilers also use cluster analysis to manipulate the census and other data in order to profile postcode areas (*see* Chapter 4). In a nutshell, cluster analysis provides a picture of how the data clusters together.

Stone (1996) explained that the clustering process for geodemographics can be 'visualised by imagining each of thousands of postcode areas as a centroid of about 25 rays, the length of each describing the value of an independent variable (income, size of house, etc.). Cluster analysis involves the simultaneous comparison of the length of these 25 rays, pairwise, among all the postcode areas, and it brings together, as the clustering proceeds, those areas that are most alike on all dimensions.'

Cluster analysis literally tries to aggregate customers into groups. The data is analysed and customers placed in groups which have two characteristics: both the *inter-group differences* and the *intra-group similarities* are maximised. Each group or segment then contains customers which are as alike as possible to one another, and at the same time are as different as possible to customers in other groups.

Cluster analysis is often used as an *initial* exploratory technique by a database modeller. At this early stage, the important explanatory variables (those which best explain the variation in response) are not yet identified. This first stage will help the marketer understand how the mass audience splits into various segments. This is an important input into the marketing strategy: it can help us understand that we have different groups of customers who have used our business for different needs. Product development, targeting and marketing-mix decisions may all stem from this kind of analysis.

Cluster analysis does not predict how a dependent variable, say response, will vary between customers. This prediction analysis is the work of techniques such as regression and CHAID modelling.

Neural networks

The practical application of neural networks has been described in the industry as being a bit like teenagers and sex. Everybody is talking about it, but hardly anyone is actually doing it! However, neural networks are set to become a very important asset to direct marketers. On paper, they are reckoned to be potentially the most powerful of all the techniques, but results (Courtheux, 1995; Patron, 1994) seem to indicate no particular advantage in using any one modelling technique. Indeed, when considering direct marketing models, a minor advantage, if one exists, seems to lie slightly with regression techniques at the time of writing.

Patron (1994) explained that neural networks are not a statistical technique but a relatively recent development from a branch of computer science known as artificial intelligence. The technique actually simulates the way the human brain learns, memorises and reasons, although in a greatly simplified way. The internal structure of a neural network consists of cells and connections between them known as neurons. This simulates our own biological neurons/cells set-up.

Neural networks work in the following way. Imagine a baby first learning to recognise a set of keys. At first, she will not be able to understand the difference between the shape of a set of keys and, say, a pen. With correction by parents, and constant exposure to the two distinctive shapes, she gradually gets closer and closer to the perfect identification of the two shapes – a process that is characterised by certain electrical emissions through her neurons. By a process of trial and error, the end result is achieved. Neural networks replicate this pattern-recognition approach, using a computer.

To use neural networks to predict response, you have first to train the computer using 'training data'. Initially the computer will make good predictions only by chance, but as you feed into it the results, it learns more and more. When this process stops, the computer has 'learned' the way in which the variables relate to one another. The real data is now exposed to the model, and the output, in the form of scored predictions for each record, is produced.

Regression analysis

According to Patron (1994), regression is probably direct marketing modelling's most tried and trusted technique, and has been in existence for more than a century.

The way it works is as follows. We build a regression model to explain customer response using customer data from the database or independent variables. A number of variables may be causally related to customer response. Literally any variable held on the customer – geodemographic data, psychographic data, previous purchases, promotional history, and so on – may be included. There are many software packages that will compute regression models for us easily; here the reader is referred to one of the many texts specialising in this area.

Although the actual calculations are quite onerous, the basics of regression are fairly straightforward. There are six main steps that you should follow to produce a regression model for customer data.

Step 1

Graph your data and produce scatter plots to provide a visual picture of what you are dealing with.

Step 2

Identify your dependent variable (the variable you want to predict; often future response) and independent (explanatory) variables, for example customer's age or sex.

Step 3

Run the regression, easily done using standard software packages, for example SPSS.

Step 4

Check your regression statistics: 'T-ratio' and 'R-squared' coefficient. T-ratio lies astride the range –2 to +2. If $-2 \leq$ T-ratio ≤ 2, and $R^2 > 60\%$, then your model is more likely to predict the dependent variable accurately.

Step 5

Use the model to produce a prediction for *each customer* of their future response. These predictions come in the form of scores which may be attached to each customer's file. These scores are then grouped typically into deciles.

Step 6

Adjust your targeting strategy accordingly: you may want to reallocate budget to those customers with the highest scores. Typically, a gains chart similar to that described earlier for FRAC analysis can be constructed.

Interpreting the output of regression analysis

Consider the following example of regression analysis:

$$Y = a + b\,X_1 + cX_2 + dX_3 + eX_4 + u$$

where:

– response to an offer of a new credit card is the dependent variable (Y);
– 'a' is a constant;
– the independent variables from the database are age (X_1), income (X_2), car ownership (X_3), and other products bought (X_4);
– the terms b, c, d and e are the multiple regression coefficients or estimates which indicate the size and direction of the relationship between the dependent and independent variables. Computer software calculates these for us using matrix algebra;
– the function u is the *error item* which indicates the size of the random, or unforecastable, part of the variation in the dependent variable. In practical regression modelling, these random factors have some impact on the accuracy of the regression coefficients b, c, d and e. In turn, this can lower the accuracy of future predictions of response.

Having run the regression, let's assume the results obtained are as shown in Table 3.7.

Table 3.7: **Results of analysis**

Independent variables	Regression coefficients	T-ratio
Age	-0.01	-1.3
Income	0.44	3.1
Car ownership	-0.23	-4.8
Other products bought	0.39	8.1
R^2 test	0.38	

What do these results mean?

First, there is no point in interpreting the regression model if the regression test statistics (T-ratio and R^2 coefficient) are not favourable. We must therefore look at these before we make any attempt to make predictions. The T-ratio indicates whether a regression coefficient (e.g. b) for an independent variable, such as age (X_1), is important in explaining variations in the dependent variable response to a new credit card (Y). An important variable is significantly different from zero and should therefore be included in the model. As a rule of thumb, where the T-ratio lies outside the range –2 to +2 we can be confident that at least 95 times out of 100 age is an important variable in explaining the response to a new credit card. Looking at the T-ratio attached to the regression coefficient for age in Table 3.7, we see that it lies between –2 and +2. This suggests that age is *not* an important factor in explaining response to a new credit card. We should run our regression model again, this time leaving out this variable. The T-ratios for all other regression coefficients lie outside the range –2 to +2, so we leave them in the model.

The coefficient of determination (R^2) suggests that, overall, the regression model in this example, with all independent variables taken together, explains 38 per cent of the changes in response to a new credit card. This is not very high, and so we should try other customer variables in our database to attempt to increase the explanatory power of our model. Our model should explain more of the change in response before it is worth us attempting to interpret or predict customer response from it. The closer we can get to 100 per cent explanatory power, the better, although in practice anything greater than 60 per cent is considered good.

Nevertheless, the above (poor) model can still tell us a lot. The model suggests income, car ownership and other products bought are important variables in explaining response to a new credit card, as the T-ratios lie outside the range –2 to +2. Indeed the model quantifies these relationships. If customer A has an income 4.4 per cent higher than customer B, customer A's response to a new credit card is predicted as 10 per cent more likely than customer B. We can look at 'car ownership' and 'other products bought' in a similar way.

In view of the poor performance of the above model, we can construct a new model which may generate a higher R^2 value. We need to note, however, that a different model will certainly paint a different picture. Which model do we trust to give us the most accurate customer predictions? Pick the model with the highest R^2 value, but remember if the independent variables in the models are highly correlated *with one another* this will have the effect of artificially inflating the R^2 value so that the model looks better than it is. In case you are starting to give up, remember that most regression modelling problems can be overcome by following the principle of keeping the model as simple as possible, with sufficient factors to achieve a reasonable R^2 value. The proof of the pudding is in the eating: regression analysis has been used for many years by direct marketing practitioners with great success.

CHAID analysis

CHAID stands for Chi-squared Automatic Interaction Detector. This technique was developed in 1978 by Kass. It is simpler to picture than multiple regression, and so remains a popular technique, particularly when it is necessary to explain your results to senior managers.

According to Patron (1994), it is a useful exploratory technique, often used prior to regression modelling or neural network development. Table 3.8 compares regression modelling and CHAID.

Table 3.8: **Regression analysis versus CHAID**

	Regression	CHAID
Complexity	Complex	Simpler
Minimum sample size	300	1000
Software	Extra needed	No extra needed
Data type	Better with continuous	Better with categorical
Output type	Equation which allows score model	Tree segmentation
Interaction of variables	Ignores it	Detects it

Source: Portlock, W. (1992) 'An examination of regression and CHAID, and their application for direct marketing', *Journal of Targeting Measurement and Analysis*, **1** (1).

In CHAID analysis, each record is put into a discrete cell, generated by the analysis, rather than producing a score (Portlock, 1992). The essence of the technique is that the marketer first chooses the likely discriminating variables, i.e. those that best explain who responds. CHAID uses chi-squared statistics to confirm which of these variables best explains the variance in response.

Steps in CHAID analysis

Take a look at Fig. 3.3. Using the example of 'Wine Direct' and assuming the company has carried out an offer, CHAID output is constructed by using the following six-step process:

Step 1

Compare the records of 'responders' with those of 'non-responders'.

Step 2

Computer model asks, 'Which variable best explains the difference between responders and non-responders?' This is done in a systematic rather than an intuitive way.

Step 3

Split the responders' file into two cells according to the biggest difference in response between the cells.

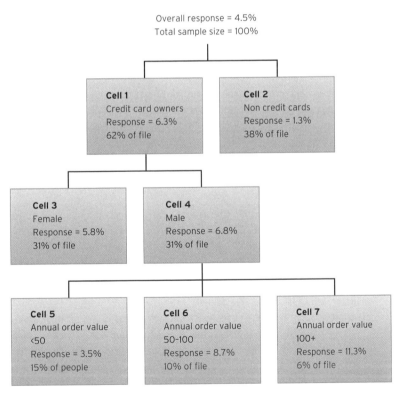

Figure 3.3 Tree segmentation for CHAID

Step 4

Model then looks at each of the segments separately to see if they can be broken down any further. Different variables may now be appropriate to segment the cells further.

Step 5

Continue process until cell sizes are too small for it to be of value to split them further.

Step 6

Output as a tree segmentation, as illustrated.

The appeal of CHAID modelling is that the output, a tree segmentation, automatically produces the desired end for the direct marketer, that is a set of customers split into segments according to their marketing potential.

Summary to chapter

One final word on modelling. Many authors have urged caution when using modelling techniques. There is a kind of aura which surrounds these techniques, because they are quite complex, but they are easily used with computers. A rather appealing 'answer' pops out at the end of the modelling process, which can be very attractive to pin your money on. However, such models are only as good as, first, the data and, second, the hard thinking that has gone into them. Care is needed.

Questions

1. Compare and contrast the analytical needs of a direct marketer in charge of a business-to-business car rental firm and a brand manager of a soft drink.

2. 'A relationship marketer would never choose which customers to communicate with based on statistical methods.' Examine this assertion and debate the extent to which marketing communications driven by forecasted responsiveness and value may damage relationships with customers.

3. A charity marketing manager is looking to understand which of her donors are the most valuable to the charity. Explain which techniques she should use to achieve this. What would she do with the information?

4. 'The only certainty with forecasts is that they will be wrong.' In what way does this statement apply to lifetime value analysis? Recommend a way of calculating a customer's lifetime value.

5. A statistician was asked to construct a regression model of a bank's data, with response to mailers as the dependent variable. The independent variables were thrown in and included age, income, household size and car ownership. However, the statistician was worried about cross-correlation, and alerted the marketing manager accordingly. What are the problems with cross-correlation in the independent variables in this case? What would you recommend is done to rectify the situation?

6. In the same bank as Question 5, a later result from the model gave a T-ratio of 0.8, and an R^2 value of 0.24. Recommend whether or not the bank should use the model to predict future responders.

7. A database owner wants to obtain a broad description of his customers to establish whether any obvious segments can be identified. Recommend to him which major technique(s) he should employ to analyse his data.

References

Arens, J. (1993) 'Examining the role of lifestage transitions in modelling consumer behaviour', *Journal of Targeting Measurement and Analysis*, 1 (4), pp. 345–54.

Courtheux, R. (1995) Workshop Masterclass, IDM Conference, 28 & 29 June, Surrey, UK.

Dupin, D. (1992) 'Lifetime marketing: Assessing return on marketing spend, using a magazine subscription as an example', *Journal of Targeting Measurement and Analysis*, 1 (1), pp. 29–33.

Fletcher, K., Wright, G. and Desai, C. (1995) 'Customer information files: The case of database marketing in the financial services industry', Proceedings of the MEG Conference, June, Bradford, Yorkshire.

Hallberg, G. (1996) 'All customers are not created equal', IDM Conference, 5 and 6 June, Surrey, UK.

Jobber, D. (1995) *Marketing, Principles and Practice*, McGraw-Hill, Maidenhead, Berkshire.

Kotler, P. (1996) *Marketing Management: Analysis, strategy, planning and control*, 9th edn, Prentice Hall, Upper Saddle River, NJ.

McCorkell, G. (1997) *Direct and Database Marketing*, Kogan Page, London.

Mitchell, A. (2002) 'Consumer power is on the cards in Tesco plan', *Marketing Week*, 25 (18) 2 May, p. 30.

Nash, E. (1993) *Database Marketing: The ultimate selling tool*, McGraw-Hill, New York.

Nash, E. (1995) *Direct Marketing: Strategy, Planning, Execution*, 3rd edn, McGraw-Hill, New York.

Patron, M. (1994) 'A comparison of four profiling techniques', *Journal of Targeting Measurement and Analysis*, 2 (3), pp. 223–32.

Peppers, D. and Rogers, M. (1993) *The One-to-One Future*, Piatkus, London.

Peters, T. and Waterman, R. (1982) *In Search of Excellence*, Harper and Row, New York.

Portlock, W. (1992) 'An examination of regression and CHAID, and their application for direct marketing', *Journal of Targeting Measurement and Analysis*, 1 (1).

Stone, B. (1996) *Successful Direct Marketing Methods*, 5th edn, NTC Business Books, Chicago, Ill.

Stone, M. and Shaw, R. (1988) *Database Marketing*, Gower, London.

Swinyard, W.R. (1996) 'The hard core and zen riders of Harley Davidson: A market-driven segmentation analysis', *Journal of Targeting Measurement and Analysis*, 4 (1), pp. 337–62.

Segmentation in action

Source: Adapted from a case study developed by SmartFOCUS Ltd. Reproduced with permission.

In the past few years software innovations have moved on to reach a key stage for direct marketers. Using software from firms such as SmartFOCUS we now have the ability to conduct relatively advanced analyses of our customer database simply and quickly. Turning such analyses into customer selections and outputs of names and addresses ready to go is then a simple matter of a couple of clicks of the mouse.

It is easy to become blasé about these software improvements, but it's important to realise that the effect of this speed and convenience has yet to be fully felt in marketing management. As you follow the example below, picture the scene for direct marketers only 10-15 years ago: they would decide on the need to analyse customer data, contact the IT department, wait two weeks for first results, after poring over these, ask for more analyses, wait another two weeks, decide to select and output customer data anyway as time was short, wait two weeks for selections, and finally move to the campaign itself . . . !

The description below illustrates how times have changed.

Example: A brand manager for a wine merchant wishes to increase sales of champagne to existing customers

Before planning the campaign, she will need to:

■ segment the customer base into those who have bought champagne and those who have not;

■ identify the appropriate target audience for the campaign.

Her experience tells her that customers who buy sparkling wine and more expensive wine, such as claret, are likely to also purchase champagne.

Therefore, it's reasonable to assume that those people who buy sparkling wine and claret but have not bought champagne would make a good target group for a campaign.

We can create a Venn diagram of these different customers, and their overlaps, by simply clicking on the customer-product list headings (see Fig. 3.4).

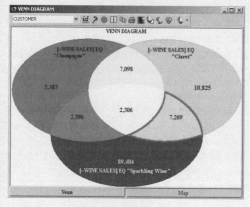

Figure 3.4 Target audience

We can see from this diagram that 7269 customers have bought sparkling wine and claret *but not* champagne. This group could be the target audience for the campaign and could be exported as a mailing segment.

This is a simple cross-sell approach, but makes no attempt to profile champagne buyers from scratch. If we wanted to do this we could examine some simple demographic data that should shed light on champagne buyers. Let us choose age, gender, home ownership and income (*see* Figs 3.5, 3.6, 3.7 and 3.8).

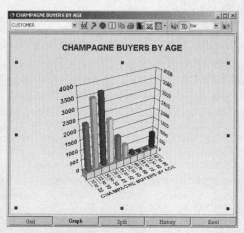

Figure 3.5 Champagne buyers by age

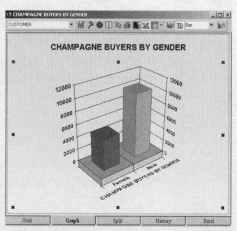

Figure 3.6 Champagne buyers by gender

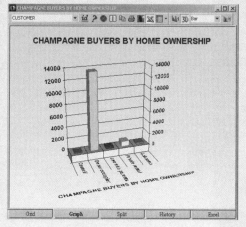

Figure 3.7 Champagne buyers by home ownership

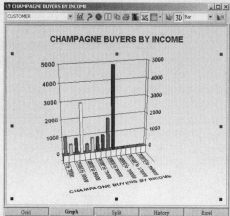

Figure 3.8 Champagne buyers by income

We have now established that, historically, most of our champagne buyers are:

■ male
■ 36 to 45
■ home owners
■ earning between £15 000 and £22 500.

What we can now do is apply these same criteria to people who have not bought champagne to give us a better target segment for the marketing campaign.

To do this, we'll create a Venn diagram of customers matching the above criteria (*see* Fig. 3.9).

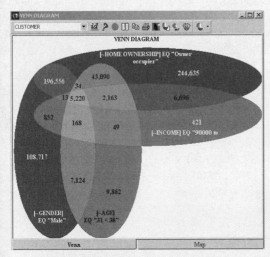

Figure 3.9 5220 customers match the profile

The final stage of this operation is to apply these criteria to customers who have *not* purchased champagne. Hence we drop the query *non-champagne buyers* onto the Venn diagram (*see* Fig. 3.10).

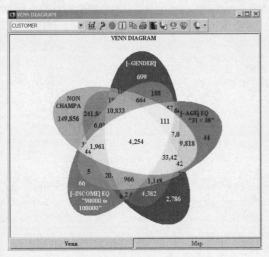

Figure 3.10 4254 customers match the profile and have not purchased champagne

We can now see that we have, in the centre segment, 4254 existing customers who match the criteria of champagne purchasers but have not bought any. By mailing this new group we can expect a higher return than the previous group of claret/sparkling wine buyers, because our target group has been profiled as very similar to champagne buyers.

So far, the brand manager has:

▪ used assumptions and experience to select a potential target audience for a cross-sell campaign;

▪ identified a more targeted audience for the campaign by analysing existing champagne customers against a series of criteria and then matching these criteria to non-champagne customers.

At this point the brand manager might export this segment for the marketing campaign, sending the output to the mailing house. However an alternative may be to refine the target audience further by using a data mining technique such as CHAID to create a propensity (or likelihood) to buy model.

Once more this is now a simple matter with software such as this. An example output (below) is quickly created. Here, CHAID is run on champagne buyers.

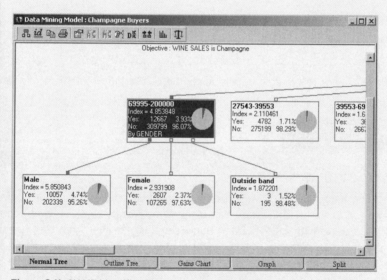

Figure 3.11 CHAID identifies high responding segments

In Fig. 3.11, CHAID has identified gender as the next most important variable, and has split the file into males and females. It anticipates a 4.74 per cent response rate from a campaign to males only, compared with 3.93 per cent for both sexes. Should you choose the both sexes option, the final stage would involve very simply calling for the names and addresses of those customers who form that very high propensity segment identified by the CHAID model, removing those who had already purchased champagne.

To summarise: with just a few clicks of the mouse, starting from scratch, we have selected a specific list of actual customers who fit our profile of high response, and we're ready to communicate with them. All in five minutes (see Fig. 3.12).

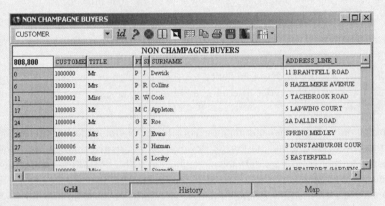

Figure 3.12 Non champagne buyers

For more information about smartFOCUS see www.smartfocus.com

Tesco Clubcard

Even if only 10 per cent of the hype is true, UK supermarket giant Tesco has still had huge success with its loyalty card Clubcard. Not many humble cards have books written about them: Tesco's direct marketing agency Evans Hunt Scott has teamed up with Clive Humby of analyst DunnHumby (now owned by Tesco) to write the story of Clubcard – such is the interest. Clubcard's fame is now such that it is probably the best known example of direct marketing in British commercial history.

Tesco Clubcard was launched in 1995 under conditions of some secrecy. After a few trials the national launch was carried out in a wave of publicity. Now, every quarter Tesco sends out a statement to its ten million regular Clubcard users, but only one in every hundred of the recipients will receive the same communication. It now mails 100 000 variants of its quarterly statement – arguably therefore getting closer all the time to the idea of 'perfect' 1–1 marketing.

The investment in Tesco Clubcard was driven not by the idea of loyalty from a discount card, but by the power of the data gathered. Not surprisingly, it is in the marketing area that the biggest benefits of the information are being felt. The principle is that Tesco is now able to understand its customers' needs in more detail and hence improve the relevance of products, sales promotions, and communications to individuals.

Tesco collects data down to single product/item level, and can therefore link individual products to individual customers. It also collects personal details such as lifestage, household details, occupation and so on, on the joining form.

Tesco quickly realised it was faced with a mountain of data, and in order to cope it has developed a hierarchy of segmentations. The top level broad segments relate household details, in particular lifestage, to broad shopping habits such as breadth and intensity of shop. So, we have 'single adults', urban professionals', 'pensioners' and so on. Shoppers have also been categorised into 'price sensitives', 'foodies', 'heavy category users', or 'loyalists' of particular brands (Mitchell, 2002). For each segment, using FRAC analysis, marketers can assess average spend, frequency of visit, lifetime value, retention rate, and similar variables, and then monitor the impact of marketing initiatives on these variables over time.

Further sub-segments could also be identified, based on shopping behaviour. These segments may be described in terms of customers' use of competitor supermarkets as well as Tesco. The lifestage data can lead to detailed tracking of, for example, families, the key target for Tesco. The focus of the analysis covers product groups as well as customer groups. In theory, therefore, Tesco could take any particular product, say milk, and assess penetration, spend and purchase frequency of any of the customer segments against this. For example, a family who fell in the 'high behaviour' category may spend, let's say, over £6 on milk in about four visits each month. Tesco could compare this data with *external market research* as well as internal profiles which would indicate potential take-up of the product. The outcome may be a list of customers whom the analysis has identified seem to be under-purchasing milk compared with a (researched) expected volume. Interestingly, Tesco has learned that it is far easier to move a top shopper to higher levels of spending than it is to get a non-shopper into the store.

The analysts have also carried out detailed cluster analyses which map out relationships between the different product groups. Therefore a cluster of a particular profile of customers who tend to purchase milk, bread and staples regularly, but only occasionally buy, say, ready meals, could be identified. This series of customer clusters, or segments, may cut across the broadscale top line segments described earlier, to provide a new focus for marketing activity.

The Clubcard is used to communicate more effectively with customers. Promotions are targeted more precisely – for example dog food is targeted at dog owners – using coupons given out at the checkout and with Clubcard statements. These are delivered at the same time to all Clubcard users, four times each year. Executives joke that it's like Christmas four times each year, such is the uplift in traffic.

Stock control, product take-up, and comparative store performance are just some of the areas where the data is helping the business. Different stores are arranged differently according to the customer data. Hence, Tesco effectively lets customers decide what each store should stock, fundamentally changing its supply chain from 'push' to 'pull'.

More recently, Tesco now offers specific details of segments of customers, minus name and addresses, plus analyses of direct marketing tests, to its suppliers – provided customers give permission of course. Manufacturers such as Kraft and P&G are keen to take advantage of such offers. This plus Tesco's sales of advertising space in its Clubcard magazine, makes the retailer a source of marketing research and a media owner, as well as a retailer. It also points to possibly increased links with suppliers in the future.

In March 2002 Tesco signed a deal with Air Miles, allowing points from Clubcard to be redeemed for air travel. It saw a 400 per cent uplift in traffic to its website and a surge in Clubcard members, illustrating the continuing power of Air Miles in attracting customers.

References

Gray, R. (2003) 'Brand benefits of loyalty initiatives', *Marketing (UK)*, 17 April.

McElhatton, N. (2002) 'Case study: Tesco', *Direct Response*, 31 August.

McKelvey, C. (2003) 'How Tesco still rules the roost', *Precision Marketing*, 20 June, **15** (36) p. 15.

Mitchell, A. (2002) 'Consumer power is on the cards in Tesco plan', *Marketing Week*, 2 May **25** (**18**) p. 30.

'Scoring Points' (2003) *Marketing (UK)*, 2 October.

Questions

1. Why is 'loyalty card' a misnomer?

2. What are the keys to Clubcard's success?

3. How has Clubcard changed Tesco's non-marketing processes?

4. Identify the different segmentation approaches adopted by Tesco. How would you describe its segmentation strategy?

CASE STUDY

Training and Enterprise Councils

Imagine you have set up a small business, let's say importing and distributing software to retailers. What are the characteristics that an outsider would notice about your business? They might find that:

■ you lack time – everything is done in a rush;

■ you focus on selling not buying, therefore you need your suppliers to deliver to you on a plate with no lapses;

■ you rely on word of mouth a lot, and relish the chance to talk to other small business people;

■ you don't consult within the company before taking decisions, everything is quick.

Small businesses therefore like direct marketing. If it can save them time, in particular from possibly unwanted sales visits, it can be an invaluable aid to their business. But they are relying on their suppliers to use direct marketing intelligently. Amongst their suppliers are the Training and Enterprise Councils or TECs.

Although primarily government funded, TECs have a surprising amount of freedom to act. They tend to be limited companies by guarantee. Their aims are to help local businesses (and hence local people) improve their competitiveness by raising the standards of business. This is done through training, education and development initiatives offered to SMEs (small and medium enterprises).

More specifically, the TECs offer:

- help in attaining the Investors in People industry award;
- National Vocational Qualifications;
- Business Link – access to experienced consultants who may be able to offer advice and help;
- access to training of all types – open learning, practical courses;
- work experience for job seekers;
- in partnership with Chambers of Commerce, membership and networking opportunities.

And so on. Asked what they do, Norfolk and Waveney TEC said they 'bring experts and potential together'. In other words, TECs are enabling organisations.

Each of the country's 81 TECs has packaged up various 'products' which they offer to small businesses at prices that are affordable. For example, a course called 'getting your Investors in People award' may be offered at £250. Of course, the TECs compete with private enterprises which are also operating in the training and consultancy markets.

In the past the TECs have tended to be 'product' driven. Most TECs have a team of salespeople who have concentrated on one of their services. Each product group has tended to be competitive with other groups within the TEC, perhaps not an ideal way of ensuring maximum success for the partnership between TECs and businesses.

More recently, TECs have started to show an interest in database and direct marketing as a way of interacting with businesses. Initially, it was thought that direct communications could just be an effective way of selling their services, and indeed this has proved to be the case. However most TECs have had the foresight to take this to the next step and begin to record their sales on a customer database. The expertise with which these are deployed varies quite considerably around the country, but it would be fair to say that many TECs still need more help in making full use of their databases.

At a recent national conference of TECs, the following ideas were raised by a consultant for TECs to consider:

- Membership schemes. Typical business associations (for example the Chartered Institute of Marketing) offer membership facilities such as regular information about their sector, chances to go to talks, networking and conferences, and training and consultancy.
- Profiling and segmentation. One experienced manager in a chamber of commerce had developed a typology of small businesses according to their attitudes and behaviour to TECs and chambers. He came up with the following segments:
  - 'sole traders' – new businesses which were just starting up;
  - 'entrepreneurs' – successful businesspeople who were looking to expand their businesses;
  - 'philanthropists' – people who wanted to give something back to the business community;
  - 'smash and grab' – businesses which spotted one course they wanted, joined for one year only and then would leave.

Other ideas included the potential for loyalty schemes. Recently, TECs had developed fairly extensive websites which the database people knew they should be integrating into their activities.

What was needed was a proper plan, a full database-driven programme that would help the TECs' customers meet their needs.

Question

Develop a strategically driven plan for how each TEC should use their marketing database to best advantage. What other segmentation possibilities are open to them? Remember that you are operating in a business-to-business market.

USING EXTERNAL DATABASES IN DIRECT MARKETING

Objectives

Once you have read this chapter you should understand:

- what external databases are;
- who operates them and what they consist of;
- what direct marketers use them for;
- the process of management that accompanies the use of external databases.

Introduction

The previous chapter concentrated on how we analyse *internal* data, on the company's own database, to understand our customers better. In this chapter, we will explore the use that direct marketers make of *external* data, held on large, commercially-owned databases. In Chapter 3 we outlined four distinct marketing analyses important to direct marketers. It is the last two of these, *segmentation by customer profile or customer need*, and *targeting new prospects based on existing customer profiles*, that external databases can particularly help with. However, external databases have a key additional benefit that lies outside their analytical capabilities. They are a valuable *source of lists* of prospects for new market development.

In this chapter we will investigate what external databases are and why they are so useful to direct marketers. The chapter is organised into three main sections as follows:

1. A short introduction describing the industry is given.

2. The uses that direct marketers make of external databases are analysed. A discussion of the advantages and pitfalls of using these products is given.

3. The products – external databases – are described in detail.

Introduction to external databases

The company's own database is an enormously powerful tool, as we saw in the last chapter. There are, however, occasions when direct marketers could use some help from outside. We may want to add to the data on our existing customers, in order to understand their personal characteristics better. If we are expanding into new markets, we will want accurate profiles of our intended targets; and best of all, we would like to have a list of *interested* individuals whom we can contact with an invitation to be a customer of ours.

It is these needs which external databases are in business to meet. External databases consist of records of individuals, available for sale to interested companies. They are split into two main areas: geodemographic and lifestyle databases.

GEODEMOGRAPHIC PRODUCTS

Every ten years in the UK, a government-run census is carried out, through which enormous amounts of (geographically-based) demographic information are gathered. This data is used by the government for a number of purposes, but is also available for purchase by interested companies. The data is only available in aggregated form, not at individual level, and so is not useful to direct marketers in its raw form.

This is where geodemographic profilers add value. Using techniques such as cluster analysis, they first place households into groups according to their common demographic characteristics: age, social class, size of house, and so on. They then take each postcode in the country, and allocate a description to that postcode according to its typical household profile. This is useful information to direct marketing clients, who will buy this data from the profiling company.

LIFESTYLE DATABASES

If you have ever completed a product registration form after buying some music equipment, or filled out a questionnaire sent to your home in return for some vouchers, you are probably recorded on a lifestyle database. These operators collect their data using these methods, and together hold millions of records of individuals and their contact details.

The data held varies from attitudinal and opinion data to lifestyle data, but the most important category is product purchase data, details of individuals' current product and brand preferences across a range of sectors of interest to direct marketers. As well as providing lists of individuals for contact, the data is also of great use as a research and segmentation tool.

A complete description of all these products is given later in this chapter, but first we will take a closer look at how direct marketers make use of this data.

What are external databases used for?

Direct marketers use external databases for two major applications: first, adding data to existing internal records in order to understand their existing customers better; second, using lists selected from the external database to contact new prospects directly. (External data is also used for retail site location analysis, but this lies outside the scope of this book.)

A well-established process is used by the database operators with their direct marketing clients to help them achieve this. We call this process *profiling*.

PROFILING USING EXTERNAL DATABASES

The following process (based on Stone, 1996) outlines how geodemographic/lifestyle operators merge their data with clients' records and what is done with this new information.

Step 1

A 'matching process' is undertaken between the client's internal database and the external geodemographic or lifestyle database. 'Matching' means letting the computer identify the common names/postcodes held on both the internal database and the external database.

If a geodemographic system is used, then postcodes are matched; however, if a lifestyle system is used, then individual names and addresses are matched.

Step 2

For lifestyle databases, typically a match of between 15 and 20 per cent of the internal database is achieved. So, for a client database of a million records, a match of 200 000 names might be available for modelling.

For geodemographic systems, a complete overlay is achieved, based on *postcode*. So, a 100 per cent match should be achieved at this level of data.

For those postcodes or individuals that are matched, *the existing customer record is then expanded to include the outside data*.

There are then two main uses for this data (*see* Fig. 4.1).

Step 3

If the data is to be used for *research/segmentation*, then the outputs are clustered descriptions of the client's customers according to their geodemographic or lifestyle attributes. Common attributes and patterns in the data are sought which reveal customer segments, or the differences between customers and non-customers.

The external database company will offer a bespoke service to clients; that is, they will go back to their *raw data*, not aggregated clusters they use to sell to new entrants, and use this raw data to build up clusters that are relevant to the client's products.

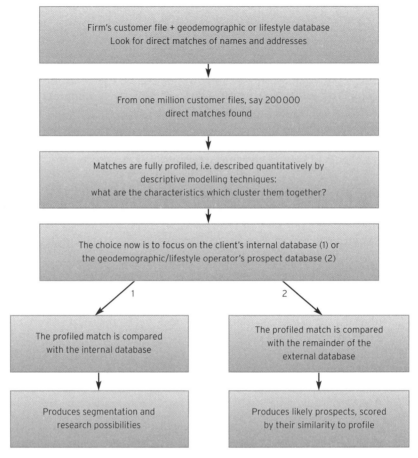

Figure 4.1 Using profiling to identify prospects on an external database

Step 4

If the output is *new market targeting* of prospects, the output is different. The variables which occur most frequently among the customers who are profiled will be used to select 'lookalikes' from the remainder of the lifestyle database, and a prospect list will be generated, ranked in order of greatest similarity to existing customers (Sleight, 1993) (*see* Fig. 4.2).

Let us now look at the two key applications of external data, starting with its use for research and segmentation.

USING EXTERNAL DATA FOR MARKET RESEARCH/SEGMENTATION

A typical situation that many firms face with customer data is that although they have the basic transaction data – what customers have bought – they may not know very much at all about the customers themselves. In particular, they may not know *why* their customers buy from them and what customers use their products for. General marketers would use market research to overcome this.

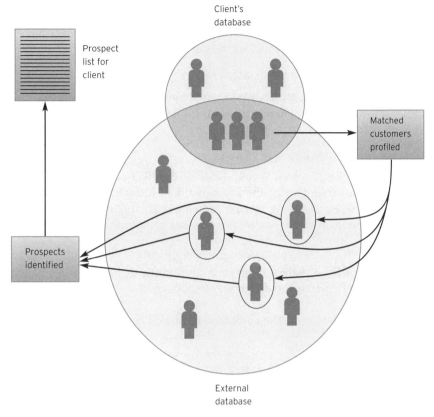

Figure 4.2 Using matching process to profile customers

However, direct marketing provides an alternative in the shape of the external database. By adding geodemographic and/or lifestyle data to our customers' records, we can understand how these attributes drive our customers' purchase behaviour. Once we have added geodemographic and lifestyle data to our internal databases, we have enhanced customer profile data which can be quantitatively analysed. We can begin to understand what might be driving our customers' behaviour.

LIFESTYLE DATA AS RESEARCH: BUITONI PASTA CLUB

Nestlé's Buitoni Pasta Club has been built up based on the development of a 75 000 user community from direct response advertising, which may eventually totally replace conventional advertising on this product. The club database was enriched through matching with lifestyle data. The lifestyle data helped to get a genuine insight into the type of people who were attracted to Buitoni pasta. One of the characteristics was that they were 'Latinophiles' – lovers of all things Italian. This sort of information was used to develop the communication vehicles and offers that sustain the Pasta Club.

Lifestyle data or market research?

Fairlie (1992) lists three advantages that lifestyle databases have over conventional market research in providing insights to customer behaviour:

1 High cost of conventional research

A typical, thorough study of a sample of, say, 300 customers may cost about £10 000, if done by a professional firm. For this price, many thousands of lifestyle records could be added to your database.

2 Limited use of market research

The Market Research Society Code of Conduct forbids the attribution of names to the data gathered. One of the key benefits of lifestyle data is the use of individual data to allow direct targeting to that individual. In this regard, market research and lifestyle questionnaires have completely opposite philosophies.

3 Follow-up

Conventional market research is more difficult to run as an ongoing exercise. Panels have to be set up and are expensive.

On the other hand, the *advantages* of market research are:

1 Accuracy of data

Market researchers argue that the anonymity that they guarantee allows them to elicit more accurate, in-depth data which gives a truer understanding of respondents' motives and deeply held beliefs. They therefore claim that their data is more accurate than lifestyle data.

EXHIBIT 4.2

WATCH OUT FOR THE SUGGERS

Sugging is Selling Under the Guise of Research. Some unscrupulous companies will approach prospects and pretend to be market research companies. They will then gather the individuals' names, addresses and details about them, relevant to the company's products. At the end of the questionnaire, they may ask, 'Are you interested in a sales call from ...'.

This activity is frowned upon by the Market Research Society, because it feels it is giving legitimate market research a bad name. It feels there is now increasing suspicion from the public, when approached by genuine researchers, that they are about to be 'sold to' and this is leading to higher refusal rates.

Clearly there is some danger that lifestyle questionnaires could be seen as Sugging. The lifestyle database operators completely refute this, and say that they make their purpose perfectly clear. Indeed, lifestyle database questionnaires do not state their purpose as market research, and make quite clear that respondents may be followed up according to the data they submit.

However, there has been some tension at times between market researchers and lifestyle database operators. Shedding some light on this, Sleight (1994) describes a caricature comparison between market researchers and lifestyle database operators: the former are regarded as 'unworldly, corduroy-wearing types', whereas the latter are 'sharpsuited salesmen'!

2 Representativeness

Lifestyle databases consist of individuals who have selected themselves by their interest in filling in the survey – arguably because they are attracted by the rewards of coupons, prize draws, and so on. Market researchers assert that this means the database is only representative of people who are interested in such rewards, and does not reflect the population as a whole.

However, both Fairlie and Sleight make the point that market research and lifestyle databases can be collaborative rather than competitive, and as we shall see later, combination products are on the increase.

In explaining how the two disciplines can collaborate, Fairlie notes that one of the hardest problems in market research is knowing in advance what questions to ask. External data can provide a vital *initial* perspective that can inform subsequently what questions to ask in research. By adding lifestyle data to our internal data, trends in lifestyle and demographics can be picked up, and theories developed as to how these characteristics impact on customer behaviour. This can save on expensive market research profiling exercises and give a sharper focus to supplementary research.

Using external data as a basis for segmentation

In Chapter 3 the use of internal database information to segment customers according to their value to us, and their product needs from us, was discussed. External databases can potentially add a lot of value to the second of these, the *analysis of customers' product needs*.

This is because product needs are often *related to*, or even *caused by*, lifestyle or demographic factors. For example, age is a key factor in driving the take-up of financial products such as mortgages, loans and pensions. Therefore, it is possible to use lifestyle and geodemographic variables, such as age, to act as 'surrogates' when segmenting according to product needs.

However, internal data is still more valuable than external data. Fairlie (1992) comments that it is unusual that generalised demographic data will significantly add to the precise, highly relevant personal data marketers have on their own customers. There is general agreement on this key principle by direct marketers:

> *It is usually the case that a company's internal data is more valuable than external data in determining customer behaviour.*

In summary, external data may sometimes be used when firms find it difficult to extract their internal data; when they want to append more data onto their own customers; and when they want to obtain a wider picture of how consumers are using competitor products as well as their own.

EXHIBIT 4.3

LIFESTYLE DATA TO DRIVE SEGMENTATION: BIKE MAGAZINE

The publisher of *Bike Magazine*, EMAP, needed to increase subscriptions and newsstand circulation of the title. *Bike Magazine* was the UK's second best-selling monthly motorcycle magazine. To help its analysis, lifestyle data was added to EMAP's existing database. To the publisher's surprise, two distinct magazine readers became apparent. The first was the typical young biker, but the second was an older, more affluent 'born again' biker who perhaps lived a conventional life with a steady job and family, but rode motorbikes as an exciting hobby to stand out from the crowd.

Subsequently, the product itself was adjusted to take into account this new segment. Targeting new customers was based on profiles of both segments, using lifestyle databases as lists (see following section).

EXTERNAL DATABASES AS LISTS OF NEW MARKET PROSPECTS

Taking the hard work out of prospecting

Rapp and Collins (1987) in their book, *Maximarketing*, described the benefit of external databases:

> *A public database has done most of the hard work for you. It has identified by name and address the people most worth bothering with, that use your product or service category, but do not use your brand; or those who have exactly the lifestyle that your product calls for.*

The use of external databases as lists enjoys an even wider application than their use for segmentation and research, according to Sleight (1994). If we compare the use of these products by direct marketers with the methods employed by general marketers to acquire new customers, we find direct marketers have major efficiency advantages, as shown in Table 4.1.

Table 4.1: Comparison of general marketing and direct marketing operations for the attraction of new markets

General	Direct
Segmentation and targeting aided by market research	Segmentation established by understanding of existing customers, overlaying external data. Profiles based on large volumes of data
Targeting operationalised by media/retail choice	Targeting achieved by exact match of accurate profiles to well-understood new market profiles
Brand building and communication to a mass audience: awareness and interest built up	Communication goes precisely to profiled prospects. Can be segmented according to type of prospect, e.g. competitor buying could be acknowledged
Sales promotion in store or in pack: mostly wasted on existing customers	Sales promotions directed to definite prospects only

Making the decision to use profiled external lists

The economics of the purchase of data to use as prospect lists are clear: it is worth doing so provided the gain in response from better targeting outweighs the costs of purchasing the external data. Here the devil is in the detail, so let us have a look at the example calculation in Exhibit 4.4.

Now that we understand the economics of prospect lists, we can analyse the extent to which our external list options can help with new market development.

EXHIBIT 4.4

EXAMPLE CALCULATION: THE COSTS VERSUS BENEFITS OF A DEMOGRAPHIC SYSTEM

Let's look at a credit-card company trying to target owners of 'gold' credit cards: they have been identified as the best prospects for a new card the company is launching.

The market size for gold cards was found to be 700 000. On matching a sample of these people to a typical geodemographic system, the company found that one group called 'ageing professionals' gave an 'index' of 300 compared with the national average of 100. In other words, the penetration of gold-card holders was three times greater in these clusters.

The company decided to mail the affinity-card offer to all households in the postcodes that fitted the 'ageing professionals' cluster description. This represented 250 000 households (hidden within which are 15 000 gold-card holders: the company's primary target). It purchased a list accordingly from a geodemographic operator and mailed its offer.

The results were as follows:

Response from gold-card holders is 5%:

    5% of 15 000 = 750 responses

Non-gold-card response is 0.5%:

    0.5% of 235 000 = 1175 responses
        Total response = 1925

Costs: 250 000 mailers @ £400 per thousand
    = £100 000
    Geodemographic list @ £150 per thousand
    = £37 500
    Total costs = £137 500

Therefore it cost the company £71 to obtain one new customer.

What would happen if the company decided not to bother with the geodemographic profiling and just mailed randomly?

Assume it mails 250 000 again, but this time randomly chosen from the electoral roll. There are 5000 gold-card holders among this random group.

This time the results were:

Response from gold-card holders is 5%:

    5% of 5000 = 250 responses

Non-gold-card response is 0.5%:

    0.5% of 245 000 = 1225 responses
        Total response = 1475

Costs: 250 000 mailers @ £400 per thousand
    = £100 000
    Electoral roll @ £75 per thousand names
    = £18 750
    Total costs = £118 750

Therefore it cost the company £80 to obtain one new customer by mailing randomly.

This is an example of the calculation that needs to be made by a marketer wishing to use geodemographic profiling for new customer acquisition.

The same calculation process can be used to estimate the return from investing in a lifestyle data list. Here, the costs per thousand names may be higher. If, say, actual gold-card carriers were requested, this list could be over £200/000 to buy. Responses would, however, be likely to be higher than those of a profiled list, which only gives a higher probability of targeting the right prospects.

Source: Adapted from Fairlie, R. (1998) *The Direct Marketing Guide*, IDM, Teddington, UK.

Prospect lists: strategic options

Ansoff's Matrix of strategic options shows a number of different ways in which lifestyle and geodemographic data can be used for market penetration, new market targeting, or new product development.

1 Lists of competitor customers based on purchase behaviour: market penetration

This category consists of prospects who are identified as known users of a direct competitor's products. These are prime prospects for brand-switching offers. Moreover, these prospects can be contacted by you without your competitors knowing what you are doing; you have the advantage of privacy.

For example, 50 local Mazda dealers used lifestyle data to write to drivers of rival BMWs, Audis and Mercedes. They also wrote to prospects who were not claimed drivers of such cars, but whose profiles fitted the behaviour.

2 Lists of prospects generated from profiles of existing customers: market penetration

This is the core business of external database operators. The majority of their revenue is obtained from clients who use the matching, profiling and targeting process described earlier. These profiles are used to identify people, or postcodes, on the external database whose descriptions match the profiles generated, the output being a list of names and addresses of prospects.

Pura Foods was looking for new customers to purchase its Light Touch sunflower oil product. The company profiled its existing customers, and used this profile to target new customers from a lifestyle database. With a mix of offers, including money-off coupons, it generated an impressive 19 per cent response from a direct-mail campaign.

Bradford and Bingley, a building society, used lifestyle profiling to help target campaigns to recruit prospects for its branch network salespeople to follow up. Its customers were found to be age 35 to 64, married, and with a known interest in financial products. Regional targeting of such prospects was carried out using, among other sources, external lists from a lifestyle database. Bradford and Bingley used such lists on a monthly basis to generate drip-feed leads for its salesforce.

3 External data used for marketing new products: new product development

When launching a new product, lists of the appropriate target market may be obtained as supplements to the internal database.

EXHIBIT 4.5

LAUNCHING A NEW PRODUCT: THE CO-OPERATIVE BANK VISA GOLD CARD

This new product was the UK's first gold card that was guaranteed free of annual charges for life. The target audience was well defined: an income above £25 000 p.a., homeowners, aged 25+ who had an existing credit card.

Four different sources were tried for a direct-mail approach.

The top-performing list gave a 7 per cent response. This mailer was rolled out to 300 000 prospects, achieving 21 000 responses.

4 A new type of customer: new market development

Although the majority of business for external databases consists of lists based on existing customer profiles, some business has also been generated from clients pursuing a new market development strategy. Here, a new profile may be built up, perhaps from market research initially, or by adapting the existing customer profile obtained from internal and external data. One such example of this approach is Croft Original (*see* Exhibit 4.6).

EXHIBIT 4.6

NEW MARKET TARGETING: CROFT ORIGINAL

Croft Original is one of the UK's leading sherry brands, holding 17 per cent of the market in 1995. Croft was looking to develop its appeal *beyond* its traditional market of people aged over 45. To begin with, Croft used NDL's lifestyle data product to build up a profile of its typical Croft customer, based on income, occupation, family life and leisure activities. This was taken as the template for a list of *younger* prospects who shared the same profile, apart from age. A list of 60 000 prospects was targeted with an offer of 'A Guide to Croft Sherry', a £2 cash-back voucher and a chance to win a Spanish holiday, with proof of purchase required to qualify for the promotion.

A 10 per cent response rate was achieved, with 32 per cent of respondents being aged 35–44, meeting the aim of reaching a new market.

Source: NDL, 1996

We now have a complete understanding of what external databases are used for by direct marketers. Our final task is to complete the description of the products themselves: who are the main players in the business, and what are their products?

External databases explained

Both geodemographic and lifestyle databases are now described under the following headings: Product overview and How the products are created.

GEODEMOGRAPHIC DATABASES

Product overview

Geodemographic products are summed up by the proverb 'Birds of a feather flock together'. The premise is that similar people have a tendency to live near one another. It is not difficult to picture this: consider two people, one very rich, the other poor. The rich person is far more likely to settle down near other people who are in a similar financial position, and the poor person likewise. What drives this is our desire to associate with people similar to ourselves. Humans have a strong basic need to form into groups, and we feel most comfortable in groups of like-minded, socially similar people. What this means is that where we live is a predictor of what we buy. As one senior practitioner of CACI puts it: 'Without ever having met or heard of somebody, we aim to predict likely spending, ownership of goods, readership, and reactions to offers – and get it right!'

Geodemographic profiling suggests there are a number of factors that will be common to neighbourhoods. One would expect that our income, the size of our families, our stage of life, and so on, could be predicted by where we live. But the profilers have found that it is also our interests, lifestyle and psychographic variables such as our social image – how we want others to see us – that are predicted by where we live. These findings are useful to direct marketers: geodemographic, attitudinal and lifestyle traits often *explain* what we buy.

But we cannot take this 'birds of a feather' premise too far. You only have to ask yourself, 'Hang on, to what extent am I like my neighbour in personality? Do we really feel the same way about things, do the same things at weekends, have the same amount of expendable income?' Probably not to the extent one might imagine on first reading the above paragraph. It is important to remember that the basis of these products is in descriptions of *groups of people*, not individuals.

Therefore, there is no guarantee that a postcode profile will be accurate for a particular household within that postcode. If we were to market to a postcode assigned 'Affluent blue collar', we would still be approaching individuals within that area who are, say, college students or unemployed older people.

Geodemographic products provide a *statistical probability* that people living in a described area are more likely than average to fit that description. In other words, in the absence of perfect information, you are better off using these products to target prospects than relying on random chance. Geodemographic operators will give you scores which reflect the extent to which the chosen postcodes fit the descriptions.

Interestingly, Fairlie (1992) commented that all of the geodemographic systems are better at locating areas of poverty than affluence, which remains the case since the 2001 census. He asserted that they are also better at broad descriptions of geographical areas (of a kind invaluable to retailers or marketers to whom geography is important) than they are at picking out individuals for new market acquisition in direct marketing. This conclusion may be disputed by the operators themselves, who will claim that many direct marketers have had great success in new prospect targeting using geodemographics.

EXHIBIT 4.7

SPARROWS OF A FEATHER...

Poorer people 'flock together' more than well-off people do. In other words, there is clearer discrimination against the average when identifying areas with low incomes than there is in high-income areas.

Geodemographic industry structure

The major players in the UK are CACI, CDMS, Experian and Infolink. The first geodemographic product released in this country was CACI's ACORN (A Classification Of Residential Neighbourhoods). To show how the industry has developed, Exhibit 4.8 gives a summary of the early history of UK geodemographics.

How the products are created

Sources of data in geodemographic systems

The core data source of all these systems is the census. Each operator then adds value to this data using sources such as the electoral roll, credit-referencing data, market research, mail-order trading data and County Court Judgments.

The 2001 UK census comes 200 years since the first census in 1801, but exactly 2000 years after a rather more famous census in Palestine!

The census consists of a questionnaire, sent to the entire population, asking for data on over 300 variables. Eighty-five per cent of this data is based on the 100 per cent sample; 15 per cent of census data is based on a 10 per cent sample (i.e. one in ten

EXHIBIT 4.8

THE HISTORY OF GEODEMOGRAPHIC PRODUCTS IN THE UK

1963	Donnelly Marketforce profiles census data at ward level – the first UK attempt at clustering areas
1970s	*Reader's Digest* uses census data for prospect modelling
1977	CACI launches ACORN
1983	PinPoint launches Pin
1985	OE McIntyre launches Superprofiles, subsequently purchased by Credit and Data

	Marketing Services (CDMS), a subsidiary of mail-order company Littlewoods
1986	Experian – a subsidiary of mail-order company Great Universal Stores launches MOSAIC
1986	PinPoint launches FinPin
1989	Infolink launches Define
1990s	Experian launches first global segmentation
2002	Experian launches the first use individual property valuation data in New Zealand

Source: Adapted from CACI company promotional materials, 2003.

households) who get a larger census to fill in. Typically, about 96 per cent of households actually return the census but the returns were lower in 2001, maybe reflecting the increasing complexity of large-scale participation exercises like this.

Contrary to popular belief, the census does not *provide* data at the individual level, although it does, as explained, *collect* data at an individual level. The latest census data is reported in units of geography called output areas comprising about 50 households, this being rather more accurate than the 1991 census.

Table 4.2 illustrates how UK postcodes are built up from the basic postcode unit, and where output areas fit into this arrangement.

Table 4.2: **How postcodes are built up**

Postal type	Example	No. in UK	No. of households in unit
Postal areas	B (Birmingham)	121	200 000
Postal district	B31	2900	8275
Postal sector	B31 4	9000	2700
Output areas	Roughly 10 postcodes	250 000	50
Postcode	B31 4AN	1.6m	15

The census data is published at output area (OA) level, but the most useful output for marketers of this sort of data is the postcode level. Therefore, one of the tasks for geodemographic operators is to represent the source data at postcode level. Fortunately, output areas are built largely from postcodes. The majority of postcodes fall within output areas – only 2 per cent falling outside the boundaries of an OA. OAs are also intended to have homogeneous populations. This has some significant implications for the creation of neighbourhood segmentation.

Experian's MOSAIC, a typical geodemographic product, uses the following census data (variables aggregated to 180 households):

age	employment type	housing tenure
marital status	travel to work	amenities
recent movers	unemployment	housing type
household composition	car ownership	socio-economic status.
household size		

At present, 'income' is inferred for an OA, using other variables as surrogates: house size, occupation types, education.

A census trial was carried out in 1996 which asked people the most important question left to marketers: 'How much do you earn?' Previously this question has been viewed as too sensitive, and geodemographic profilers have always had to infer income for an OA based on other data such as car ownership and house details. New questions asked in 2001 were about our general health, did we care for a relative, and, not without controversy, our religion. (Go to www.statistics.gov.uk for more details and lots of free information on the census.)

Creating the geodemographic product

There are two major analytical processes that need to be applied to the raw census data. First, the initial 4000 or so possible variables need to be *reduced* to the key independent variables that are seen as driving consumer behaviour. Second, the areas need to be *combined* into segments that the variables tell us will contain similar people.

According to Webber (2003) many of the analytical techniques which were used to build the 2001 MOSAIC date back to a study that was commissioned by the Heath government in 1975, to examine ways of combating inner-city deprivation in Lambeth, Birmingham and Liverpool.

Most operators use 'factor analysis' or 'principal components analysis' as a data reduction technique (although Experian claims that neural network techniques give better results in modelling geodemographic raw data than does principal components analysis). The problem with a lot of the census data is that it exhibits co-linearity; in other words, some variables are associated with each other. One can imagine that, for example, 'family size' and 'number of cars' are associated with each other. There is a need to ensure that independent variables are associated *with each other* as little as possible. Factor-analysis techniques achieve this. The data is then reduced from the original 4000 variables to between 40 and 100 variables.

To combine the records into segments that reflect the differences between areas, an exploratory, descriptive technique is needed. Cluster analysis has been found to be ideal for this job. A good segmentation is one which maximises the differences between segments, while minimising the differences between individuals within the same segment. This is exactly what cluster analysis does in a logical, quantitative way.

Geodemographic products

Each of the operators uses slightly different data, analysed using some different techniques, and hence the outputs – the products – are slightly different. However, all products consist of major clusters and sub-groupings described to give an indication of the type of people within them. To give you a flavour of these products, MOSAIC is described in Fig. 4.3. MOSAIC consists of eight major clusters, as shown in the figure.

Group A Symbols of success

Symbols of success contains people whose lives are successful by whatever yardstick society commonly uses to measure success. These are people who have rewarding careers rather than jobs, who live in the most sought after locations, who drive the more modern and expensive cars and who indulge in the most exotic leisure pursuits.

Group B Happy families

Happy families contains people whose focus is on career, home, and family. These are mainly younger age groups who are married, or at least in a permanent relationship, and are now raising children in post-war houses, often in areas of the country with rapidly growing populations. The focus of expenditure is on equipment for the home and garden, and the immediate family unit is the principal focus of leisure activities.

Group C Suburban comfort

Suburban comfort comprises people who have successfully established themselves and their families in comfortable homes in mature suburbs. Children are becoming more independent, work is becoming less of a challenge, and interest payments on homes and other loans are becoming less burdensome. With more time and money on their hands, they can relax and focus on things that they find intrinsically rewarding.

Group D Ties of community

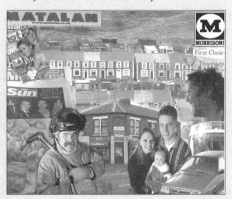

Ties of community is a group whose lives are mostly played out within the confines of close knit communities. Living mostly in older houses in inner-city neighbourhoods or small industrial towns, most of these people own their own homes, drive their own cars and hold down responsible jobs. Community norms rather than individual material ambitions shape the pattern of most residents' consumption.

Figure 4.3 New MOSAIC groups 2001-2011

Source: Reproduced by kind permission of Experian

Group E Urban intelligence

Urban intelligence contains mostly young and well-educated people who are open to new ideas and influences. Young and single, and with few encumbered by children, these people tend to be avid explorers of new ideas and fashions, cosmopolitan in their taste and liberal in their social views. While eager consumers of the media and with a sophisticated understanding of brand values, they like to be treated as individuals, and value authenticity over veneer.

Group G Municipal dependency

Municipal dependency mostly contains families on lower incomes who live on municipal council estates where few of the tenants have exercised their right to buy. Often isolated in the outer suburbs of large provincial cities, municipal dependency is characterised as much by low aspirations as by low incomes. Here people watch a lot of television and buy trusted brands from shops that focus on price rather than range or service.

Group F Welfare borderline

Welfare borderline is comprised of people who are struggling to achieve the material and personal rewards that are assumed to be open to all in an affluent society. Few hold down rewarding or well-paying jobs, and as a result most rely on the council for their accommodation, for public transport to get around, and on state benefits to fund even the bare essentials. The lack of stability in many family formations undermines social networks and leads to high levels of anti-social behaviour among local children.

Group H Blue collar enterprise

Blue collar enterprise comprises people who, though not necessarily well educated, are practical and enterprising in their orientation. Many of these people live on what were once council estates but where tenants have exercised their right to buy. They own their own cars, provide a reliable source of labour to local employers, and are streetwise consumers. Tastes are mass market rather than individualistic, and focus on providing comfort and value to family members.

Figure 4.3 Continued

You may wonder whether MOSAIC categories are over-segmenting the market – why not just have 'rich' and 'poor'? The geodemographic data sellers argue that in some product areas it is the 'clever capitalists' who represent the best market, in others it is the 'chattering classes', while the 'prosperous pensioners' and 'rising materialists' can also head the league in a number of product areas (Webber, 2003).

One of the most fascinating underpinning realities of geodemographics is that geography itself is important. Webber (2003) points out that if we take two families of matching income and age, education, employment structure and ethnicity, these two families will display very different spending patterns according to the type of neighbourhood in which they live. Put differently, a typical postman in Bradford is different to a typical postman in Bristol. This was looked at in detail by Elliston Allen as long ago as 1968: as examples he pointed out that (not surprisingly) not much Lancashire cheese is eaten in Yorkshire; that Midlanders prefer sourer beer while Londoners are more fashion conscious. Another famous example showing that neighbourhoods could be seen to be a significant discriminator was the comparison of *The Sunday Telegraph* and *The Observer* readership profiles, the latter being far more heavily skewed towards high-status inner-city neighbourhoods.

Geodemographic products are important internationally, indeed Experian's MOSAIC was first built not for the UK but for the Netherlands in 1985. This was because Experian's parent company, Great Universal Stores (GUS), wanted a marketing tool to set up an equivalent to Experian within its Dutch mail-order business Wehkamp. Since the 1986 launch of UK MOSAIC, Experian has built and updated classifications for a further nine continental European markets, and eight more countries outside Europe including the US MOSAIC and more recently Brazil and China.

There are other dimensions to geodemographic products. Experian and CACI have developed a system for calculating the age of individuals within each postcode. The systems are based on the idea that age is linked to first names. There are a lot of Chloe's and Jack's who were born in the 1990s; but not many parents call their children Violet or Herbert any more, although there are often cyclic trends, so it's important not to be too dogmatic here! CACI has identified 13 000 first names which it obtains from the electoral roll, and uses its system, MONICA, to predict age.

Building up an individual profile

Figure 4.4 shows how geodemographics can build a complete picture for any name and address. This example comes from Experian.

LIFESTYLE DATABASES

Product overview

Lifestyle databases are probably one of the most remarkable developments in marketing over the last 20 years. In the UK, anyone can now go and buy the data that reveals the products purchased, the attitudes, opinions and beliefs and the personal geodemographic data of over 15 million individuals in the country.

As Sleight (1994) reported, the market research industry has every reason to be concerned with these developments, especially when a company wants to understand simple descriptive data about its customers. It has been reported that ICD, then one of

Mrs Christine Smith, 22 Main Street, Watford, WD2 4YZ

Individual

Gender	Female
Age	26–35
Marital status	Married
Length of residence	5 years
Head of household	Yes

Family

Household composition	Family
Households with children	With children
Decision-maker type	Young couple
Lifestage	Young family

Financial

Income	£25 000–£29 999
Directorships	No
Shareholdings	None
Personal debt (CCJs)	None
Small or home office	No

Property

Property type	Numbered house
Residence type	Semi-detached
Tenure	Owner occupied

Demographic and neighbourhood

Pixel code   4348

GB household MOSAIC
Group J
Mortgaged Families
Type 43
Nestmaking Families

GB MOSAIC
Group C   Blue Collar Owners
Type 11   Lo-Rise Right to buy

London MOSAIC
Group C   Suburban Homemakers
Type 13   So So Semis

Global MOSAIC
Group B
Blue collar self-sufficiency

Factors
Percentiles
A 59 B 67 C 78 D 26 E 94

Behavioural

Touchpoint segments
Group C   Rational consumers
Type 10   Value driven switchers

Financial strategy segments
Group E   Small-time borrowing
Type 22   Wives on a budget

Financial MOSAIC
Group A
Adventurous spenders
Type 5   Mid-market borrowers

Grocery MOSAIC
Type 9   Budget shoppers

Clientele
Type 9   Round the corner regulars

Figure 4.4 Geodemographic profile
Source: Reproduced by kind permission of Experian

Purchasing propensities (person level)

Top 5 travel propensities	*Top 5 motor propensities*	*Top 5 leisure propensities*
Camping/caravanning holiday	Own private car	Lotteries
Self catering/villa/cottage holiday	Registration letter over 3 years	Pop/Rock music
Weekend/short break holiday	Next car cost £9999 or less	Give charity donations
Visited holiday camp	Next car – used	Doing pools
Fly economy class	Current car – used	Read books

Financial service propensities

Socio-cultural propensities

Top 5 propensities	*Top 10 RISC trends*	
Have personal loan	Unquestioned system	Strategic opportunism
Currently have overdraft	Hypernatural	Care for the environment
Pay bills at bank	Pleasure	Spirituality
Savings accounts: instant access	Personal expression	Integrity
Have loyalty card	Exploring human potential	Ecosystem

Notes RISC is the Paris based Institute for socio-cultural change. Combining data from the internationally renowned RISC survey with Experian's data has produced a resultant set of 36 propensity scores (or trends) that are indicative of the predominant cultures/attitudes within a household. These are useful in helping an organisation add a psychological/sociological dimension to the way in which it communicates with specific households.

Figure 4.4 Geodemographic profile (continued)

EXHIBIT 4.9

THE CHANGING FACE OF BRITAIN AND EUROPE

The 2001 census reveals how Britain has changed in just ten years. Data from the Future Foundation (*see* www.futurefoundation.co.uk) suggests these changes mirror those taking place all over Europe. Here are just some of the most important social changes:

The population has grown overall, with the fastest growth in the commuter belt around London.

More people are living alone. Of the 21.6 million households in the UK, the percentage of single-person households has risen to 30 per cent of the total. These 30 per cent are divided into retired people (usually women) who have lost a spouse, and young single people, usually men.

There's been a sharp fall in married households, from 58 per cent to just over 50 per cent.

The growth in the number of single parents is sharpest in rural areas. Note that not all single parents live in difficult conditions!

The demographic bubble of the baby-boomers moves on. Compared with ten years ago, more people are 30-60 years old and fewer people are aged 16–29.

Single-pensioner households make up 14.4 per cent of all households, but more than two-thirds of these (68.2 per cent or 2 129 000 pensioners) have no access to a car. Conversely, for pensioner-family households over three-quarters have access to at least one car. This may reflect the fact that over three-quarters of single-pensioner households comprise women (2 366 000), many of whom were brought up in an age when fewer women learned to drive.

Ownership of two cars or more within a house-hold has hugely increased, almost throughout the country. This has profound implications for lifestyles and for public policy.

Non-white population growth has been marked, even in rural areas such as Devon and Dorset which have almost completely white populace, and also in more northerly parts of Britain. Ethnic minorities now comprise 9 per cent of the UK population. Just over half the Black Caribbean group (57.8 per cent) and the Pakistani group (54.5 per cent) were born in England or Wales, underlining the interesting cul-tural differences between first- and second-generation Caribbeans and Asians living in the UK. There is growing evidence that British born Asians in particular have significant differences of outlook to their parents. In contrast, only 27.7 per cent of the Chinese group were born in England or Wales while 67.6 per cent were born in the Far East. Segregation of communities is less marked than in the US. Segregation is less likely with Afro-Caribbean communities and white people, but more likely with Asian communities (Professor Colin Clarke, Oxford University).

Most people in England and Wales describe them-selves as Christian (71.7 per cent) but Christians tend to be towards the older end of the age spectrum. Only about 8 per cent of adults regularly attend church. In answer to the religion question in 2001, 390 000 people claimed to be Jedi knights.

Sources: Office of National Statistics 2003, www.statistics.gov.uk; *The Times*, 4 August, 2003, p. 6

the lifestyle data operators, correctly predicted the result of the 1992 general election as a narrow Conservative victory. This contrasted with all the major research companies whose polls predicted a clear Labour victory only the day before the election.

According to Fairlie (1992), lifestyle databases were originally developed by con-sumer-goods manufacturers who were finding conventional advertising and market research methods either inadequate or poor value for money.

Lifestyle databases were introduced into the UK in 1983. NDL opened its London office in 1985, followed quickly by CMT, with ICD entering the market in 1988. However, it was not until the very late 1980s that NDL and CMT's databases were suffi-ciently large to be of use to marketers as lists to rent (Sleight, 1994). As we move into 2004 the UK market is now dominated by suppliers such as Claritas and Experian.

How the products are created

The whole basis of lifestyle database data is different to that of geodemographic data-bases. Lifestyle databases use data collected at *individual* level, obtained from commercially-operated surveys, or product registration forms filled in by individuals who choose to take part.

Reynolds (1993) noted that four broad categories of data are collected by lifestyle companies:

■ name and address information;

■ data relating to the purchase of products and services, known as 'lead-to-purchase' data;

■ demographic and socio-economic information;

■ values and lifestyle (VALS) information.

Clients can also add sponsored blocks of questions to the surveys, and the data obtained from these questions is confidential to that client. For example, cinemagoers can be identified by the appropriate questions, and a list of cinemagoers, with all their lifestyle information, can be built up.

EXHIBIT 4.10

LIFESTYLE DATABASES: WHAT DATA DO THEY COLLECT?

Which toothpaste do you use? What books do you buy? Have you got a video recorder? Do you eat out a lot? Do you smoke? Which brands of cigarette? Do you have a pet? What about your financial products: credit cards, PEPs, life insurance?

As an example, the 1997 ICD survey contained 207 questions in ten separate sections, ranging from mail-order purchases to health products.

VALS data

Part of the original basis of lifestyle databases was the values and lifestyle (VALS) system *originally developed by Mitchell. The question that the VALS project was trying to* answer was well summed up by Rapp and Collins (1987): 'Is there not some psychic predilection, based on a prospect's value system, that once uncovered can tell us why people choose one brand over another?'

VALS looked for correlation of product/service consumption with attitudes towards benefits sought from the service; activities, interests and opinions; and value systems subscribed to by consumers. At its simplest, one might envisage that someone who responds that they regularly go on foreign holidays would be interested in sun-cream products.

It is this correlation of psychographic data with product and service behaviour data which provides the bases for some of the lifestyle database analyses.

As we move well into the new century, the marketplace is still working to make psychographic segmentation work. There is still interest, but the real breakthrough in profitable data has yet to be made. Recently, one initiative involved a consortium of agencies, academics and clients, working on examining the decision-making processes for those people on 'the margins of response'. These are the consumers who would respond if they could 'get their bums out of their chairs' as one commentator put it. Such initiatives have yet to reach commercial fruition however.

Modern lifestyle databases: 'lead-to-purchase' data

Lifestyle operators have found that so-called 'lead-to-purchase' data is a better predictor of prospect behaviour than psychographic attributes. Lead-to-purchase data is data on consumers' *actual purchases*, past, present and future. Responders are asked questions such as 'Which of the following magazines do you subscribe to?', 'What make of car do you currently own?', and so on. In some categories, consumers are asked when they are next considering a purchase: 'When do you plan to replace your car?'

There is an increasing trend towards collecting this type of data. We saw previously that attitudinal and lifestyle data is used to create profiles of likely purchasers of a particular product; but our sun-cream supplier could, instead of relying on a list of foreign holidaymakers, home in on responders to the question: 'Do you use sun cream on your holidays?'

As a summary, we can construct a table which illustrates the hierarchy of prediction power of different data categories. Table 4.3 compares the value of data for a bank looking to maximise response from a credit-card offer.

Table 4.3: **Typical predictive power of data categories in lifestyle databases**

Data type	Description	Typical score against random mailer response (random mailer = 100)
Lead-to-purchase data	Responders have credit card	About 400
Mail order	Upmarket mail order, e.g. 'wine direct operation'; pay by credit card	About 320
Attitudinal and lifestyle	Profiled against Bank X's own customers	About 250
Demographic only	Profiled against Bank X's own customers	About 180
Entire list	No targeting	100

Notes to Table 4.3

1 The 'scores' are illustrative only and should not be used as precise 'rules'.
2 A 'super responsive' list may be created by merging, say, lead-to-purchase data and attitudinal and lifestyle data, providing profiled credit-card holders. This may have a response index of 1000+ against an indiscriminate mailer, but the total list volume is likely to be small.

The end product

The late 1990s saw a flurry of lifestyle product launches in the UK. Claritas launched the Lifestyle Universe (a list of individuals) in 1997, PSYCL£ (classifies people according to their financial behaviour) in 1998, and PRIZM (a postcode-based segmentation system) in 2000. Experian launched Pixel in early 1999, and CACI launched People UK in 1998. Some of these products are lists while others are classification vehicles that allow company databases to be segmented.

Each system has used different methods of data collection, and each has collected different data to the others. We need to remember that personal data is dynamic – constantly changing – and therefore lifestyle database operators need to spend significant amounts of money to 'stand still', that is to keep their existing data fresh. About 17 per cent of the data in any lifestyle database will become out of date within one year of gathering it, due to deaths, moving house, births, changing marital circumstances, and so on.

A summary of each major system is given in Table 4.4.

Geodemographic, lifestyle and market research companies are developing products based on merged data, known as data fusion products. These interesting products are particularly appropriate for a company wishing to improve its understanding of its marketplace for strategic marketing planning, and merit a closer look.

Data fusion

Data fusion is the combination of information on individuals or groups using data from different sources to present a more complete picture. This is a relatively new and extremely exciting development for the direct marketing industry, increasing its ability to compete with other marketing approaches. The two key areas of data fusion are combining geodemographic and lifestyle data, and combining market research databases with lifestyle data.

Table 4.4: **Major lifestyle databases**

Supplier	Product	Data	Source
Claritas	Behaviour bank	11 million consumers Lifestyle/buying behaviour	Survey of shoppers
CACI	Lifestyle	44 million people	Electoral roll; census data; investment data and lifestyle data from Experian
Experian	Canvasse	44 million people 8 million survey responders	Electoral roll; census data
Equifax	Dimensions	44 million people	Electoral roll; census data; financial data

Notes:

1 Much of the above lifestyle data is inferred using profiling techniques from source data that actually relates to individuals and comes from dedicated surveys deployed for that purpose: Claritas and Experian are the specialists here.

2 Since 2002, suppliers are having to work hard to reduce their dependence on the electoral roll – as we saw in Chapter 2 consumers can now opt out of their name being used on the roll for marketing purposes.

EXHIBIT 4.11

THE SKY'S THE LIMIT IN DIGITAL TV

Having acquired more than 5.5 million subscribers by 2001, Digital TV operator Sky had three objectives:

- looking for revenue growth through an increase in Sky subscriptions to 7 million;
- increase in revenue per subscriber including a growth in use of Sky Active, its new shopping channel opened in October 2000;
- to maintain churn – the percentage of those customers who cease service – at 10 per cent.

Understanding its existing customer-base was critical to success. Hence, Sky used a BMRB/Dunn-Humby joint venture called First T. The key product is the Target Group Index (TGI), a panel of consumer data collected over 30 years using 25 000 customers per year. This and other data such as Experian's MOSAIC were fused with the Sky database. Using this analysis it found that Sky Active customers were younger and more affluent than the rest of the Sky base. Sky also found that customers were more likely to lapse subscriptions if they were younger, with lower incomes. It also found that such customers were very offer-conscious, and looked around for deals. As a result Sky instigated a points scheme, with prizes such as trips to Alton Towers once enough points were earned. Analysis with TGI was able to highlight which customers actively read the Sky Magazine each month. It was found that greater loyalty was related to readership of the magazine. Using these methods, Sky was able to pinpoint those likely to churn ever more closely.

This careful, data-driven marketing approach has also paid dividends in recruiting new customers. Sky has learned lessons from over use of popular press such as the *Sun* in insert campaigns. While response rates were high, these new customers were the most likely to cancel their subscriptions once the initial offer ran out. Sky now uses carefully targeted lists of prospects, profiled according to its most loyal customers.

Sources: One-day conference: 'Market Research meets Database Marketing', Oct 2001, SCI, London.
Lawson, J. (2002) 'Don't touch that dial', *Direct*, March, Issue 3, p. 30

Combining geodemographic and lifestyle data

The first geo-lifestyle product in the UK was *Portrait*, a joint venture between Infolink and NDL. The data input into Portrait was as follows:

Infolink	*NDL*
Census	Income
Unemployment	Hobbies
Loans	Age
Births & deaths	Car ownership
Credit searches	Occupation
Directors	Newspapers
Electoral roll	Tenure

The output includes individual-level data which has been aggregated up to postcode level. A lifestyle profile of each postcode is created, based on a mix of actual and predicted (modelled) data. Companies whose prospects are predicted more successfully from geodemographic *and* lifestyle data should benefit from this type of product. One could envisage, say, *Virgin* PEP financial products as a good example of a geo-lifestyle sensitive product.

Figure 4.5 opposite shows how these 'virtual consumers' are built up. However, since those heady days the market has moved on to some level of maturity. Geo-lifestyle products are now developed as common practice and sold to mainstream as well as cutting-edge companies.

HOW GEO-LIFESTYLE PRODUCTS HELPED RE-ELECT THE WORLD'S MOST POWERFUL MAN

In the mid-1990s American political consultants acting for President Bill Clinton were looking for ways to improve his popularity as the US elections loomed. While looking for breakthrough ideas, they began to get increasingly interested in geo-lifestyle products. (American lifestyle categories include 'pools and patios', which describes middle-income, white suburbanite married people with kids; and 'caps and gowns', which refers to urban intellectuals living near universities. Each of these lifestyles has been identified within the American equivalent of enumeration districts known as 'census tracts'. Each is about as big as a city block.)

Clinton's advisers knew that the key to the election was swing voters, those people in the middle who tended to vote either way at different elections. What were swing voters' characteristics, and how could they be targeted? To answer this, the consultants carried out a large survey of about 10 000 people, asking questions about their lifestyle habits and enabling them to be placed into one of the lifestyle categories. Then the respondents were asked whether they preferred Clinton, Dole or were 'swingers'. From this data, those lifestyle segments corresponding to swing voters could be identified.

It turned out that a significant proportion of swing voters were campers and hikers. As a result, the President was urged to go camping and hiking for his next vacation, in spite of the fact that he allegedly disliked outdoor holidays. In the end, Clinton did venture out on a hiking trip.

Bill Clinton was re-elected in November 1996.

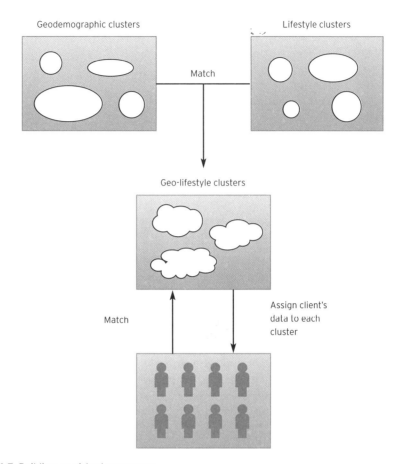

Figure 4.5 Building up virtual consumers

Combining lifestyle and market research information

The attempt to bring together the worlds of marketing research with its depth of data, and database marketing with its breadth of data, has been going on for some time now. Indeed, as far back as 1994 Sleight pointed out that various parties were looking for areas of synergy between market research and lifestyle information (Sleight, 1994). The idea is to develop 'T-cubes' of data that would greatly add to the power of the data to predict our behaviour (*see* Fig. 4.6).

The term T-cube was claimed to have been coined by Greg Ward at Taylor Nelson Sofres, a market-research firm. Research and database data is either joined (literally looking for duplicates of the same person on both datasets), or fused (linking together data profiles to create 'virtual' profiles that are claimed to predict what is actually happening). However, we need to be clear about what the database will then hold. Some of the data will be the actual, real information gathered from individuals, but other data will be inferred from the models built up by the market research. The latter represents probabilities of the individuals possessing that attribute.

Meanwhile Equifax has brought together electoral roll data, credit information, and research based information, for example Berry Consulting's FruitS financial segmenta-

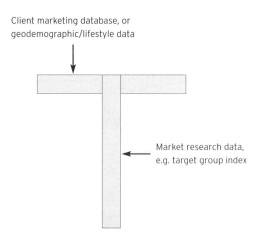

Client marketing database, or
geodemographic/lifestyle data

Market research data,
e.g. target group index

Figure 4.6 T-cube data

ARE YOU AN 'ASPIRANT MILLIONAIRE'?

Experian and market research firm MORI have combined personal data and financial buying data to create a geodemographic/lifestyle and research fusion product. One segment they identified was 'aspirant millionaires'. Banks could apply this data overlay to their data, and identify those pro- filed as aspirant millionaires. If they then found some of these people had only a current account, say, that would suggest that customer's other financial products were held with competitors. The bank could then telephone that customer to find out more.

tion onto the Dimensions database. It also linked together Dimensions with research from NOP that examined consumers' buying motives; it was then possible to model the characteristics of early adopters of new products, followers, traditionalists, and so forth.

It is still early days for these products, in spite of the industry pushing hard for their development. Clients have been relatively slow to take on board the potential of the fusion of research and database data. However, there's no doubting the potential power here. While database marketers understand what their customers are buying, how much they spend, how often they buy and so on, the fusion of marketing research gets them closer to understanding why their customers buy. The factors leading up to the decision to buy are revealed more clearly – and potentially on a mass scale. This is an exciting development for the future.

That concludes our sketch of the lifestyle data industry. We're now ready for an overview of geodemographic and lifestyle data products, and how these are changing.

Issues and trends in external data

Lifestyle versus geodemographics: which is best?

Lifestyle database suppliers are often at (very public) loggerheads with geodemographic suppliers over whose product is the 'better' offering. Table 4.5 sums up the main arguments.

Table 4.5: **Strengths and weaknesses of geodemographic versus lifestyle products**

Lifestyle strengths	Geodemographic weaknesses
Individual data	Only at OA/postcode level
Behavioural/attitudinal data as well as geodemographic data	Only geodemographic data
Income is actual not modelled	Modelled income only
Claimed update at circa 15 000 records per day	Census records decay by 12 years at end of life
Major lifestyle strength: more precision	
Lifestyle weaknesses	**Geodemographic strengths**
Partial coverage only	Census is 100% sample
Records biased to people who like incentivised surveys	No bias
Claimed behaviour anecdotes suggest quality is variable	'Official' survey more accurate?
Not based on geography	Whole basis is geographical, and therefore ideal for direct targeting
Consumers worried about data protection	
Major geodemographic strength: wider coverage and balance	

Probably the key strength of lifestyle data is that it is based on individuals, not aggregates. The key weakness lies in the data itself. First the data will be biased towards people who like filling in surveys, have got time to do so, or are attracted by the incentives to fill in. This means that profiling clients' own customers based on a sample of lifestyle survey returners may be flawed. Finally, there is the question of honesty. The entire lifestyle data industry depends on the accuracy of data filled in by the individuals themselves. However, market researchers have long known that people may distort personal data in order to present themselves in a better light. To what extent are people who own a Metro claiming that they own a more upmarket 4x4? Geodemographic operators claim that the official nature of the census improves the validity of the data. However, there is little absolute evidence for any of these claims or counter claims.

Issues in client usage of external data

Mitchell and McGoldrick (1994) conducted a delphi study into the geodemographic industry using longstanding experts from within the industry. A number of factors inhibiting the further growth of geodemographics were identified in rank order. They were:

■ lack of client understanding;

■ lack of reliable 'between census' data;

- variable and often high pricing;
- lack of industry standards;
- quality of some suppliers in the industry;
- too many different solutions.

The experts also raised concerns that the industry was too product-focused and not customer (client) focused. Key suppliers tended to be too computer-oriented and not focused on marketing applications.

On the client side, the low level of statistical and analytical techniques of marketing executives was thought to be important in inhibiting take-up. As Openshaw (1989) said, 'Geodemographics is really about response modelling, except not many clients realise it.'

The answer here may be two-fold: first, better education of clients about the products; and second, simplification of what was on offer. On the education side, many courses are now available on the use of external databases. Looking at the simplification issue, Mitchell and McGoldrick (1994) found that some companies within the industry felt that there was little to choose between the basic systems on offer.

In spite of these inhibiting factors, the panel thought the potential for growth in the industry was still very substantial. Financial services companies and retailers were seen as the two sectors with the most potential. The reasons for optimism were seen as:

- targeting systems can now be operated from desktop PCs;
- retail and FMCG goods are huge, underdeveloped markets;
- off-the-shelf database models are now available for clients;
- clients are now better educated.

One key to growth is the increasing use of PCs as the means of delivery to the client. Marketers can now do their own analysis on their desks with user friendly software. This is a major step forward from having to ask a supplier to run a particular analysis for you. Good analysis is all about trying things, seeing what results are, and re-inputting more analyses. This can now be done.

Another issue is our ability as marketers to visualise the classifications. Webber points out that 'classifications that are not capable of visualisation do not get properly understood. They fall into partial use and then disuse and fail to meet their objectives'. We must be able to picture what each group of people 'looks like' in our minds.

Moving away from the initial interest in retail location software, clients are now increasingly likely to use experts to develop their own customised database solutions, often driven by the increased interest in CRM from senior management.

Recent trends

The arguments about geodemographic versus lifestyle data may come to matter much less as the products have merged and fused together. For instance most of the innovations from Experian have been in developing individual-level targeting classifications such as Pixel.

A recent trend in product development has been the creation of classifications and lists of on-line consumers. For instance Claritas Onliners was launched in 1999 and the other major players also have products being constantly updated. Many different types of Internet users are identified with interesting names such as Virtual Virgins, Wired Living and so on. Linked to this has been the increasing demand for e-mail lists by clients. Appending e-mail lists is already being addressed in the US, and in Europe clients increasingly want e-mail addresses and mobile numbers alongside the traditional name and address.

Understanding customer channel preferences is of increasing importance to firms spending millions on CRM systems that support strategic decisions to encourage mobile or interactive TV access. One example of such a product is Experian's Touchpoint which splits consumers according to their preference for specific channels such as mail order, Internet or retail.

The business-to-business data market continues to be underserved, with relatively under-developed profiling information available. Blue Sheep offers access to 2.5 million workplaces in the UK and scores them according to their relative worth for a product or service.

Lead-to-purchase data continues to become more important to clients, with the uncertainties over psychographic data continuing. Recency of lead-to-purchase data is vital, and genuinely recent data can command a large premium. For instance, a charge of between £25 and £85 per name may be justifiable for someone who has just answered 'now' to the question 'when are you going to buy a new car?' (Reed, 2002). Since the conversion rate from test drives is around one in three, car marketers can expect to make significant margins on individuals in the market. Data such as this encourages marketers to change from a 'campaign' mindset in which, say, an entire database is targeted every quarter, to a 'one-to-one' mindset in which customers are targeted individually depending on when they want to buy. The process of talking to customers is continual and driven by customers instead of 'batch processed' and driven by the marketing department. (See Chapter 11 for more discussion of this.)

Peter Sleight (2001) recently pointed out that perhaps the most important long-term trend in the industry is the convergence of different suppliers' products. The old differences in data availability between the players has largely disappeared. Most major companies now have access to similar data sources, so any new products are quickly copied. Hence, it may well be that firms will choose their suppliers according to the quality of the service they get and the strength of their relationship with them.

Summary to chapter

This chapter described lifestyle and geodemographic databases and outlined how they can help direct marketers. Although quite different products in content, the way the data is collected, and how it is output, both product types can add to existing, internal data. Through a process of matching, then profiling using modelling techniques, external data can be a valuable research, segmentation and targeting (through subsequent list generation) tool. Companies such as Philips and Croft Original and even the President of the United States have used lifestyle and geodemographic data effectively to segment and target existing and new customers more effectively.

Questions

1. The manager of a publishing firm is looking to raise subscription numbers for her portfolio of 'house and home' and gardening magazines. What use could she make of external databases? Would the costs be worthwhile? Debate the likely returns on such an investment.

2. 'Lifestyle databases are much more useful than geodemographic products because the data is held at individual level.' Make an alternative case in favour of geodemographic products.

3. Pick any one of the case studies contained in the chapter and outline why external data was used. Were there any alternative strategies, and if so, what advantages do external databases offer?

4. There are instances when a marketer may decide to use broadscale media to attract new prospects rather than a list from an external database. Name these instances.

5. A mail-order operator wants to compare a random mailer to the electoral roll (list cost £75/000) with a targeted mailer to a profiled lifestyle data list (cost £120/000). A test of 10 000 was mailed for each. The electoral roll achieved a 1.5 per cent response, while the lifestyle list performed better, achieving 2.0 per cent. If the gross margin of his goods is £50, is it worth the marketer rolling out to the lifestyle list?

6. An external database representative giving a presentation to a client told him, 'The most valuable data you can have on your database is basic demographics – age, income, and so on.' Do you agree? If not, explain why.

References

Denny, N. (1997) 'Taking the mystery out of lifestyle data', *Marketing Direct*, Feb., pp. 46–8.
Elliston Allen, D. (1968) *British Tastes*, Hutchinson, London.
Fairlie, R. (1992) 'Making the most of geodemographic and psychographic profiles' in *Practitioners' Guide to Direct Marketing*, IDM, Teddington, Richmond-upon-Thames.
Fairlie, R. (1998) *The Direct Marketing Guide*, IDM, Teddington, Richmond-upon-Thames.
IDM Diploma of Direct Marketing material (1995) Institute of Direct Marketing, Teddington, Richmond-upon-Thames.
Mitchell, V. and McGoldrick, P. (1994) 'The role of geodemographics in segmenting and targeting consumer markets: a delphi study', *European Journal of Marketing*, **28** (5).
NDL (1996) promotional literature.
Openshaw, S. (1989) 'Making geodemographics more sophisticated', *Journal of the Market Research Society*, **31** (1), p. 111.
Rapp, S. and Collins, T. (1987) *Maximarketing*, McGraw-Hill, New York.
Reed, D. (2002) 'As large as life.' *Precision Marketing*, 21 June, p. 19.
Reynolds, J. (1993) 'Lifestyle databases, strategic marketing tools?', *Journal of Targeting, Measurement and Analysis*, **2** (1).
Sleight, P. (1993) *Targeting Customers*, NTC Publications, Henley-on-Thames, Oxfordshire.
Sleight, P. (1994) 'Can lifestyle databases and market research learn to live together?', *Journal of Database Marketing*, 1 (4).
Sleight, P. (2001) 'Slice and dice', *Database Marketing*, June, p. 39.
Stone, B. (1996) *Successful Direct Marketing Methods*, 5th edn, NTC Business Books, Chicago, Ill.
Webber, R. (2002) 'Using geodemographic and lifestyle segmentation systems', *The Interactive and Direct Marketing Guide*, IDM, Teddington, Richmond-upon-Thames.
Webber, R. (2003) Experian publicity material.

Macmillan Cancer Relief

Macmillan Cancer Relief is a UK charity helping people who are living with cancer. It provides immediate practical and emotional support which is available from the moment that cancer is diagnosed.

The charity works closely with the NHS and many other care organisations to develop and pioneer a network of services for people with cancer, working together so that standards of treatment and care can be continually improved for everyone.

Macmillan's aim is to ensure that everyone has equal and ready access to the very best information, treatment and care, and that unnecessary levels of fear can be set aside.

Every year over 200 000 people diagnosed with cancer and their families are helped by Macmillan Cancer Relief in the UK, and it is all thanks to the generosity of those people who support the charity with either monetary donations or by volunteering their time.

Macmillan Cancer Relief works with local communities throughout the UK to establish specialised cancer services including:

■ Macmillan nurses and doctors

■ information centres

■ cancer-care facilities.

Macmillan also provides practical support for patients by providing the Macmillan CancerLine and a grant scheme for patients.

Macmillan Cancer Relief is a charity funded entirely by donations from the general public so it is vitally important for the organisation to maximise the response to its mailings.

Charities have long been at the forefront of good practice in direct marketing in the UK. Many charities already segment their databases by donor value, and will run campaigns using recency, frequency, value (RFV) information they hold. However, they acknowledge that there is much to do in terms of insights into the psychology of their donors. The more they can build up pictures of their donors, the better their segmentation and targeting will be.

Liz Essex, database marketing manager at Macmillan, is a strong supporter of using geodemographics to help improve the charity's targeting. Macmillan Cancer Relief has enlisted Experian's Micromarketer software and MOSAIC geodemographic segmentation system to help deploy highly targeted and relevant direct-mail campaigns.

Macmillan has successfully piloted these systems in a recent project for London and the South East region by creating profiles of fundraisers. The charity has segmented its donors by MOSAIC geodemographic classification and 'type of donor'. It could be speculated that donor types for Macmillan could include strong links with demography, but the primary work would be to identify motives for giving: empathy, personal history, links to personal values, pity, or even some feeling of guilt, all could be drivers of giving.

Liz Essex comments: 'By having an increased insight into our donors we have a greater understanding of them as individuals and are able to more effectively tailor our future marketing strategies and campaigns. As a result of the successful pilot project, our regional partners have expressed interest in similar projects being rolled out across the country. We will be using Experian's segmentation in conjunction with Micromarketer software to visualise regions, profile and report on donors countrywide.'

Website: www.macmillan.org.uk
CancerLine: freephone 0808 808 2020 Mon-Fri 9am-6pm

Questions

1. Explain clearly why Macmillan should consider the use of geodemographic systems such as MOSAIC.

2. Access http://www.uk.experian.com/business/products/index.html. Click through to MOSAIC. Study the details of the MOSAIC system. Speculate about which MOSAIC groups might be of most relevance to charity giving. How could this help the strategy and tactics for Macmillan?

PART 3

SETTING OBJECTIVES AND STRATEGIES WITHIN DIRECT MARKETING

DIRECT MARKETING OBJECTIVES AND STRATEGIES

Objectives

Once you have read this chapter you will:

■ be able to set direct marketing objectives for any business which requires them;

■ understand the elements of direct marketing strategies;

■ be able to create direct marketing strategies when required.

Introduction

In this chapter we begin by discussing what direct marketing objectives are and how they are set. This acts as our platform for the most complex and important step in the planning process: designing the direct marketing strategy.

The remainder of the chapter will be devoted to outlining a broad framework which you will be able to use to develop direct marketing strategies. The close links that direct marketing strategy has with the overall marketing strategy will be explored. In Chapter 7 we will take a more in-depth look at the wider considerations influencing direct marketing strategy: relationship marketing, loyalty marketing and the company's marketing mix.

How this chapter is structured

This chapter takes the planning process onwards from Chapter 4, moving from analysis to objective and strategy setting. Once the analysis has been completed, and the 'Where are we now?' question has been asked, you are ready to move to objective setting, or 'Where do we want to get to?'.

Beginning with a discussion of general marketing objectives, we move on to direct marketing objectives, showing how they differ. The use of lifetime value analysis as the basis for setting 'allowable marketing spend per customer' objectives is included.

The second part of the chapter introduces direct marketing strategy, which direct marketers need to develop as their guide for subsequent tactical activities.

The key influences on direct marketing strategic philosophies are outlined before laying out a framework which direct marketers can follow to set a strategy. The final part of the chapter explores this framework in more detail.

Setting direct marketing objectives

MARKETING OBJECTIVES

The next stage in a company's planning process, after the analysis of the current situation is complete, is to set the objectives (McDonald, 1995). As a result of the analysis, we now have a clear view of the likely opportunities and threats. This enables us to set objectives which realistically represent what the company can achieve over the next planning period.

If analysis sorts out 'where we are now', objectives are a statement of 'where we want to be' by, say, this time next year.

Marketing objectives are best approached by understanding the broader context within which they are set. Objectives should be set in a hierarchical fashion; that is, the objectives of marketing, finance, and operations should all fit together so that, on meeting all of them, the corporate objectives are met. Similarly, all the different marketing function objectives should come together to achieve the prime marketing objective.

The hierarchical links described are illustrated in Fig. 5.1. Here, we can see that at the corporate level 'increasing sales' is viewed as a strategy. However, coming down to the level of the marketing function, 'increasing sales' may be delegated as an objective. Marketing objectives are therefore derived from corporate strategies.

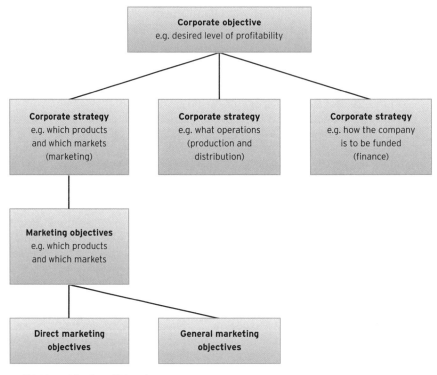

Figure 5.1 How objectives fit together

EXHIBIT 5.1

SETTING CORPORATE OBJECTIVES BASED ON RETENTION

Most corporate objectives are concerned with profitability. An alternative view of corporate-level objectives was taken by Reichheld (1996) in his work *The Loyalty Effect*. In his view, backed up by extensive work with companies across many sectors, corporate objectives should not be set around profit, but around retaining customers. He found that companies which set customer retention as their reason for existence, with profit following as a consequence of this, were extremely successful, for a number of reasons we shall explore later in this chapter.

Following Reichheld's reasoning, a typical corporate objective might therefore be 'to retain 98 per cent of our current customer base this year'.

When we come to set our marketing objectives, we have to be aware of the potential for confusion. It is tempting, when looking at the immediate marketing problems facing the company, to set marketing objectives that are too tactical. For instance, at first sight a legitimate objective might be 'to establish a database of 10 000 prospects by the end of the year', or 'to obtain 30 per cent awareness of our new product among our target market within six months'. However, it is important at this point to recall the need for the *prime marketing objective* to reflect a corporate strategy. In this instance, *marketing objectives are concerned only with markets and products*. In other words objectives may be set in terms of numbers of customers, numbers of products sold, revenue, or market share.

A useful tool to guide the setting of marketing objectives is Ansoff's (1968) Matrix (*see* Fig. 5.2). Marketing objectives (and indeed strategy) decisions can be simplified into only two decisions: which product to which market?

To summarise, then, if we follow these guidelines we may arrive at a typical marketing objective such as this: *'To sell X thousand of new product Y to market Z by the end of the financial year.'*

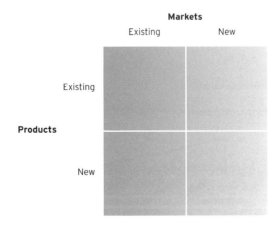

Figure 5.2 Ansoff's Matrix

DIRECT MARKETING OBJECTIVES

There are a number of considerations we need to make in order to set direct marketing objectives. We first need to link our direct marketing objectives to the overall marketing objective. We can then gain clarity of purpose by converting sales objectives to customer-based objectives. Further guidance can be given by setting allowable marketing spend and retention rate objectives. Finally, we should remind ourselves of the need to abide by the SMART discipline of objective setting. These issues are now discussed.

Linking direct marketing objectives to the overall marketing objective

Direct marketing objectives lie at the level below the overall marketing objective.

Consider a clothing company which sells through retail and mail order. Its full set of objectives might look something like those in Fig. 5.3.

As Fig. 5.3 illustrates, direct marketing needs to be positioned alongside other marketing disciplines, with the total sales, or revenues, from each discipline adding up to equal the overall marketing objective.

The emphasis on customers

Direct marketing's emphasis is on markets (customers) rather than products. As a result, direct marketing objectives are usually set in terms of numbers of customers rather than

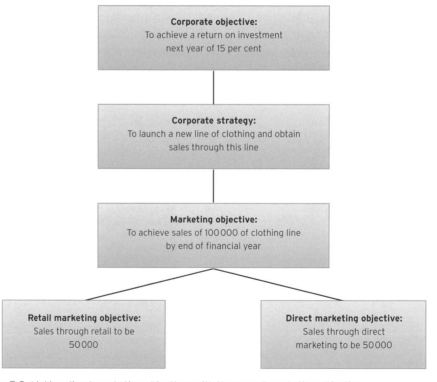

Figure 5.3 Linking direct marketing objectives with the overall marketing objective

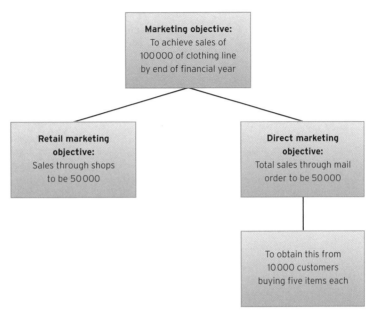

Figure 5.4 Direct marketing objectives emphasise customers

products sold. In the example shown in Fig. 5.3, we need to take the direct marketing objective a step further, as shown in Fig. 5.4.

In Fig. 5.4, we see that direct marketers have established that they need to find 10 000 customers. The next obvious question to ask is: where are these customers coming from? This is really getting into the realms of strategy, which is discussed at length in the following section and Chapter 7. But we have one more job to do yet with our customer-based objective. Let us examine Fig. 5.5; Ansoff's Matrix gives us our options.

Ansoff's Matrix shows us that we can obtain our required customers either from our *existing customer base*, or by *acquiring them* from either our competitors or totally new markets. Our final adjustment to the direct marketing objective set in Fig. 5.4 is shown in Fig. 5.6.

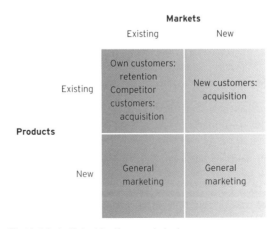

Figure 5.5 Using Ansoff's Matrix to link objectives and strategy

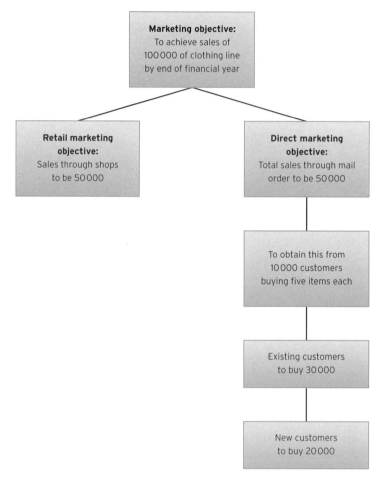

Figure 5.6 Setting direct marketing objectives for existing and new customers

Setting direct marketing objectives in this way, splitting up existing and new customers, gives clarity to the process. It guides the next step, the setting of strategy, and ensures that everyone knows the worth of existing customers, rather than concentrating too much on searching for new people.

The allowable marketing spend per customer

Direct marketing objectives can be set for more than just revenue. In Chapter 3 we found that our marketing database can help us to allocate costs precisely to each sale and to each customer. Hence, we can closely control the profitability of what we are doing. In simple terms, we can make sure that *what we spend on marketing does not exceed the worth of the customer to us*. If a customer has spent £100 with us over the last year, with a gross margin of £60, then we know that we can spend, say, £30 in retaining that customer and encouraging the same spend next year. This can and should be included in the direct marketing objectives set. Allowable spend should be set based on projected lifetime values, the calculation of which was outlined in Chapter 3.

Allowable spend objectives can be set for both existing and new customers. For example:

'To recruit 5000 new customers by the year end, at an allowable marketing spend of £30 per customer';

'To retain 90 per cent of our existing customers by the year end, at an allowable marketing spend of £10 per customer'.

These objectives give clear guidance to strategy: if your acquisition strategies are costing more than £30 per customer, and your retention more than £10, your marketing is too expensive.

It may be that you have been allocated a budget (say £100 000) and given a target of recruiting, say, 2000 customers, and told to get on with it. In this instance, your calculation is simple:

Recruit 2000 customers with £100 000.
Allowable spend per customer = 100 000/2000 = £50.

Setting SMART objectives

Finally, we should remind ourselves of the need to ensure all objectives are set in a disciplined manner. The SMART formula is well established:

Simple — Over-complex objectives only serve to confuse.

Measurable — A key advantage of direct marketing is its facility to measure precisely actual performance against a numbers-based objective.

Aspirational — The objective should motivate.

Realistic — Unrealistic objectives are demotivating.

Time-based — A time limit should be set to enable measurement criteria to be established.

EXHIBIT 5.2

AVOIDING CONFUSION BETWEEN DIRECT MARKETING OBJECTIVES AND STRATEGIES

It is easy to fall into the trap of mixing up objectives and strategies. If we decided it was necessary to build a database of 100 000 names by the end of the year, is this an objective or a strategy?

We have already seen that objectives and strategies work in a hierarchical fashion, so that one department's strategy becomes an objective for the next level down. The key is to fix onto the appropriate level at which marketing (and direct marketing) objectives should be set. McDonald (1995) believed that marketing objectives should be about *products and markets*; we have seen that direct marketing objectives, set at the same level, are often best expressed in terms of *customers*.

Therefore, building a database is *not* an appropriate top-level direct marketing objective, although it could be set for a particular department. In the above example, 'building a database' would be part of the direct marketing *strategy*, an expression (albeit a rather thin one) of *how* the objectives are to be achieved.

Creating direct marketing strategies

Before we jump straight into direct marketing strategies, it is worth our while understanding the background to modern practice in our field. Modern direct marketers see direct marketing *as a part of marketing*, adding value to other marketing tools, strategies and philosophies. Therefore, it is essential that we take a look now at the wider marketing influences on direct marketing strategy.

EXHIBIT 5.3

THE PROBLEMS WITH STRATEGY

Strategy is one of those words which has become rather overused by marketers.

You have probably seen statements described as communication strategies, media strategies, research strategies, campaign strategies, and so on and on until the original meaning of the word has got lost. In this book, the word strategy is used to mean one thing: important decisions that *guide the direction the company is taking* over the planning period.

THE MAJOR INFLUENCES ON DIRECT MARKETING STRATEGY

Classical direct marketing

Direct marketing has considerably expanded from its original roots in mail order, but many of the core principles of direct marketing strategy were established and fine-tuned by the original, highly disciplined industry. In particular, the following principles were established:

■ measurement of lifetime values and the setting of allowable marketing costs per customer to drive marketing activity;

■ the use of testing to minimise risk and to gain understanding of the relative leverage of different direct marketing elements;

■ database segmentations based on customers' responses to previous offers and the use of statistical techniques to predict responses;

■ the use of existing customer profiles to target new customers.

In summary, classical direct marketers established the principles of testing, control, targeting and continuity.

The importance of customer loyalty

In his book *The Loyalty Effect,* Reichheld (1996) outlined a study by Bain and Co. which has profound implications for businesses because it underlines the strategic importance of customer retention. Bain and Co. found that increasing customer retention by, say, 5 per cent could improve company profitability by as much as 125 per cent. We will take a close look at this work, which gives important guidance to direct marketing strategies aimed at keeping customers. It will also show us why so many of today's 'loyalty schemes' are in fact badly-flawed concepts.

Relationship marketing

Relationship marketing is an approach to marketing which emphasises a 'relationship' rather than a 'transaction' approach to business. First coined by Berry in 1983, relationship marketing concentrates on customer service, quality as the concern of all, and partnership marketing between all the business stakeholders. The emphasis on service and the focus on customer retention are two clear areas of convergence between relationship marketing and direct marketing.

The marketing mix

As direct marketing has been increasingly utilised by major players in many different sectors, so its integration with general marketing, espoused by the Four Ps mix, has become a key part of direct marketing strategy.

(General) marketing strategy has been defined by Kotler (1995) as follows:

> *Marketing strategy is the marketing logic by which the business unit expects to achieve its marketing objectives. Marketing strategy consists of making decisions on the marketing mix, marketing expenditures and marketing allocations in relation to expected environmental and competitive conditions.*

As well as the Four Ps of marketing, Kotler emphasises the importance of segmentation, positioning and branding as strategic decisions. This marketing mix approach (although being challenged by relationship marketers) remains an important element of the discussion on direct marketing strategy. Just to take pricing as an example, it is clear that direct marketers must pay attention to price as a strategic tool; indeed the ability of direct marketing to offer different prices to different segments and vary pricing over time to maximise lifetime values can be a vital corporate asset.

The product/market decision and competitive advantage

Again within general marketing, a second school of thought takes the line that marketing strategy and corporate/business strategy are closely linked. This view is summed up by Aaker (Fifield, 1992):

> *The marketing strategy concept can be encapsulated into two core elements: the product market investment decision, and the development of a sustainable competitive advantage to compete in those markets.*

This second definition is an important feed into direct marketing strategy. The product/market investment decision, which Ansoff's Matrix describes, divides markets into existing and new customers, which is the major 'scene setter' for direct marketing strategy. Porter's (1985) well-known concept of 'sustainable competitive advantage' is also important to direct marketers. Fletcher *et al.* (1995) believed that privately-held customer information, and its use, can provide sustainable competitive advantage.

Now that we have an understanding of what can influence direct marketing strategy, we are ready to tackle the subject head on.

EXHIBIT 5.4

STRATEGY TIP

Examiners often complain about the lack of thought that has gone into strategy formulation. One common fault is to mistake a marketing technique for a marketing strategy. For example, sometimes students will employ a 'strategy' of 'using direct marketing in getting new customers'. Although this may be part of a strategic approach, by itself this is not much use as a guideline for a company. Marketing strategies must clearly explain in a persuasive manner how the firm will achieve its objectives, fully acknowledging the circumstances at the time.

THE ESSENCE OF DIRECT MARKETING STRATEGY

Traditional marketing strategy emphasises a Four Ps approach, in which the emphasis is on developing something within the company that offers superior value to customers, compared with that offered by its competitors. The whole approach begins with the company's offering. Direct marketing takes a different approach, because it starts with customers, not products.

The essence of direct marketing's role in a company's strategy is the way in which *customer information*, held on the database, can be used to guide the company's actions. Because the information is held around customers, not products, the business can manage groups of, or even individual, customers over time. That said, there is evidence that this idea of customer management needs refinement: often customers like to be in control themselves, not handing it over to companies. The firm's competitive advantage then stems not from product features or brand personalities, but from information held on its customers and *the use of this information* to offer existing customers consistent, superior value.

Reichheld (1996) asserted that ultimately the key to profitability was the high retention of the firm's existing, stable, profitable customers. In view of this, perhaps the most important strategic role of direct marketing is its ability to help to achieve superior *loyalty* from customers. Given the hue and cry about loyalty over the last decade, let us be clear – the prevailing evidence is that absolute loyalty cannot be regarded as the norm in most markets. Hence, we are talking here about share of wallet – improving the amount that customers will spend with us. Direct marketing can help here: customer information helps to drive development of products and services, which are then directed to individual customers according to their needs from the company and their value to the company. It must be said that most 'loyalty marketing' remains immature and overemphasises price. But for some companies, the marketing database allows them to be quite specific. They identify those *profitable*, *but vulnerable* customers, then make quite specific efforts to keep them. The dilemma for marketers remains the same: are we wasting money with promotional efforts that aren't needed – would they have stayed anyway? Direct marketers get closer than anyone else to solving this targeting conundrum.

The relationship approach to marketing proposes the development of relationships with various groups, including customers, as key to business success in high involvement markets. There are close links between direct marketing and *relationship marketing*, as direct marketing ways of thinking and techniques also emphasise the building of relationships (Fletcher *et al.*, 1995). While relationship marketing literature develops a conceptual business strategy, it is less clear how relationship marketing is actually developed in reality. This is where direct marketing maybe enters the debate: it is a proven method of delivery for customer dialogue, and can also help deliver breakthrough levels of *service*, a key facet of relationship marketing's philosophy. We should not overclaim here though – unless the firm uses a database in an advanced manner to create a dialogue with the customer, it is stretching a point to suggest relationships are created through direct marketing.

There is more than one way of building a relationship with, and maximising the profitability of, customers. General marketers may concentrate on building brands as a way of differentiating from competitors. Direct marketers however would often focus on *segmentation*. In particular, *behavioural (value and product category) segmentations* are well supported by a database (*see* Chapters 3 and 4). Direct marketers are extremely efficient at driving the initial segmentations, guiding the marketing mix development, and then delivering the segmented offerings precisely to those who are most likely to buy. At the extreme, direct marketing can take segmentation down to the *individual* level. Mass customisation and one-to-one communications allow products and communications to be tailored according to each individual's wants (Peppers *et al.*, 1995). In his lectures, Bird (1992) once described direct marketing as potentially a 'perfect system of marketing'. If so, it is perhaps Peppers' 'one-one marketing' which is the ultimate manifestation of a truly customer-led marketing strategy, although it is probably the case that one-to-one marketing must wait for the increased use of e-mail and mobile-based media before enjoying widespread use.

The focus on customers (and sometimes relationships) does not mean that direct marketers should discard the traditional Four Ps approach. Getting an appropriate marketing mix right, so that customers feel attracted to the product and it is competitive, is still very important. For example, the root of direct marketing, mail order, is an example of a direct distribution method. Here, the 'place' element of the Four Ps approach is the remote delivery of products, providing a different shopping experience to customers.

The final perspective is the view from within the business. Here, the very cornerstone of direct marketing is the extra *control* it offers the marketer. Thanks to the precision of the database and the demand of a direct response from the customer, any returns on investment can be precisely measured. The use of individual media allows precise testing, minimising financial risks.

Let's summarise by going back to the big picture: in terms of corporate strategy, where should we locate direct and database marketing? Look at Fig. 5.7.

Figure 5.7 first divides up strategy into two key questions: where and how should we compete; second suggests the creation of differential advantage as the central requirement of strategy; and finally suggests links between this and the start point of marketing strategy – positioning. Volvo has a differential advantage in safety technology. Its positioning – the safest car in the market – naturally follows from this. The strengths of direct marketing lend themselves to it being strongly linked to market analysis and its key output – segmentation and identifying attractive markets. Then, moving to marketing delivery, direct marketing may help in building relationships, and also in delivering a Four Ps marketing mix.

There is, of course, much more to any discussion of direct marketing strategy than this summary. The next section shows how to develop a complete direct marketing strategy.

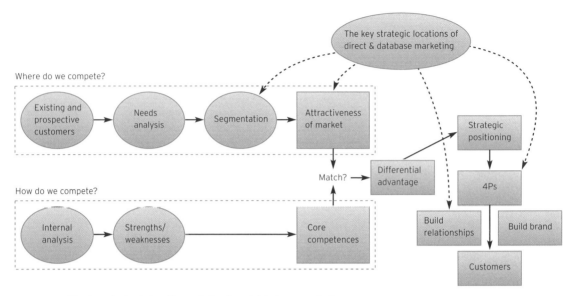

Figure 5.7 The key strategic locations of direct and database marketing

A FRAMEWORK FOR CREATING DIRECT MARKETING STRATEGIES

Now that we understand the essence of direct marketing strategy, we are ready to tackle the detailed work of creating a complete strategy. Although the final strategy statement may be only a paragraph in length, for it to be powerful it must be rooted in hard work and the consideration of all strategic issues.

To help us, what we need is a clear, simple framework which we can use as a 'map' to guide us through the decision making. Such a 'map', a framework, is shown in Fig. 5.8.

Examining the direct marketing strategic model in Fig. 5.8, we can see that we have four primary decisions to make.

We first have to decide, what will be the role of direct marketing in achieving our marketing objectives? Second, how much emphasis do we put on existing versus new customers and markets? Third, how are we going to keep our existing customers with us and maximise their profitability? Lastly, how are we going to attract new customers? In the remainder of this chapter we will take a closer look at these questions.

We will also introduce the marketing considerations – loyalty, relationship marketing, branding, and so on – which will shape our discussion of strategy. However, with these we are entering a vast and potentially complex area, so to keep things clear a fuller discussion of these considerations will be given in Chapter 6.

USING THE DIRECT MARKETING STRATEGY FRAMEWORK

'Acquire with Product. Retain with Service.'

Professor Tom O. Jones, IDM Conference, 1996

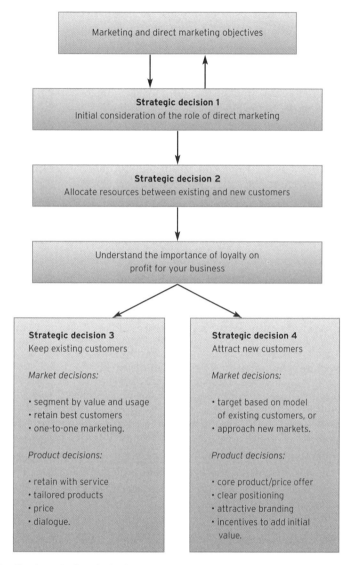

Figure 5.8 The direct marketing strategic model

Decision no. 1: the role of direct marketing

The first strategic decision to take is to consider what the role of direct marketing is in achieving our marketing objectives. (Indeed, as part of this we should decide whether or not to use direct marketing at all.) In reality, we are considering the role of direct marketing *throughout* this strategic process. However, at this early stage, the most important thing is to take a look at *macro issues*, such as industry structure, how our business is set up, and so on, and decide to what extent the *natural strengths* of direct marketing make it a viable system to use. If it is going to be well nigh impossible to build a database, for example, then there is little point giving detailed consideration to direct marketing.

First, then, we need to understand in what conditions it is favourable for direct marketing to be part of the solution for the marketing strategist. Like most strategic decisions, there are no such things as foolproof 'rules' which guarantee success in this matter. The following should therefore be seen more as an initial focus for thinking than rigid guidelines.

A marketing strategist could consider direct marketing within the strategy if one or more of the following apply:

■ the profitability of the company is heavily dependent on the loyalty of existing customers (this will only be ascertained through detailed analysis);

■ the Pareto principle applies strongly to the relationship between customers and profit (*see* Chapter 3);

■ there is scope to differentiate the product offering to different audiences;

■ the gross margin of products sold, or customers' lifetime value, is high enough to justify the costs of direct marketing (media, database, management);

■ the target audience is relatively small and/or tightly defined;

■ there is scope to gather individual customers' details and hold them on a database.

The following may also be important:

■ products in the sector are primarily sold on 'logic' rather than 'emotion';

■ control over the customer relationship is important;

■ there is an opportunity to distribute direct.

It is worth re-emphasising that the above should *not* be taken as 'rules'. There will be business situations where few or none of the above apply but direct marketing is still used successfully. Few would have expected Heinz to place over half its marketing budget into direct marketing in 1995 (or to subsequently move it back to advertising). Equally, sometimes many of the previous points may apply, but the marketing people may opt for general marketing. Many of the conditions apply to the business-to-business 'fleet' car market, but direct marketing is still used only sparingly by most car manufacturers in this area.

Having made an early exploration into the possible use of direct marketing, but keeping our options open, we move to the next level of decision making.

EXHIBIT 5.5

THE ROLE OF TESTING AND CONTROL IN COMPANY POLITICS

Testing and control are internal management issues that have a bearing on strategic decision making. If your company is risk averse, then it would want to test any initiative carefully before committing significant resources to it. If your company wants to allocate resources carefully to resulting income, the control offered by direct marketing will be attractive. Because it is driven by a database, direct marketing is often centrally run within an organisation, increasing headquarters' control over what the firm does.

These advantages of direct marketing over general marketing often underpin any strategic decision to use direct marketing.

Decision no. 2: allocating resources between existing customers and new customers

The second strategy decision for direct marketers is equally important: what should be the allocation of company resources between keeping existing customers and acquiring new customers? More particularly, how should we prioritise the following:

- defending market share by keeping our existing customers;
- improving existing customer profitability by increasing existing customers' spend;
- improving existing market share by acquiring customers from direct competitors;
- growing the market by acquiring customers from new market development?

Answering these questions requires analysis of the current situation. A number of factors specific to your company and its customers may be important. If you are just starting up a business, you obviously don't have any existing customers. Clearly then, in the first year of operation, the vast majority of your budget is allocated to new customer acquisition. Or perhaps you have a large database of existing customers but you have depressingly high levels of defection. Here, your priority is customer retention: stemming the flow.

EXHIBIT 5.6

GETTING THE ACQUISITION/RETENTION BALANCE RIGHT: THE CREDIT-CARD SECTOR

Companies which sell credit, such as American Express, know they have to strike a balance between encouraging loyal behaviour from existing customers and allocating resources to attracting prospects from competitors or new markets. To achieve these aims they may use commercial partners to attract new custom (affinity marketing). They may create a reward scheme, like Amex's Membership Miles, which rewards card spend by giving some value back to loyal customers. Inevitably, some existing customers are lost, through bad debt, defection to competitors, or just no longer needing credit. In order to keep its customer base at the same level, Amex will have to allocate resources to replace these people.

It is all a question of balance.

As we saw in Chapters 3 and 4, we can use analysis techniques to look at our database of existing customers. We need to focus on valuable, loyal customers, and look at their current and potential lifetime values and defection rates. To what extent can the marketing objectives be met by obtaining a bigger share of customers? Or by stemming the rate of defection through a commitment to loyalty? Other considerations lie outside the database analysis: if there is heavy competitor activity we may need to counteract it; any new opportunities or threats need to be dealt with.

However, a clear strategic guide has emerged to assist us in making this first key resource decision. Assuming that you are dealing with a mature business in a mature market, *your primary focus should be on keeping existing customers rather than obtaining new customers* (Reichheld, 1996). As mentioned earlier, the key research done by Bain and Co. found that loyal behaviour can be directly linked to company profitability across a convincingly wide array of sectors. This is vital for direct marketing, because it provides credibility for direct marketers' emphasis on loyalty. Database marketing techniques were developed well before Bain and Co.'s findings, but modern direct marketers have since found that these techniques have a strategic importance (in keeping customers loyal) hitherto undreamt of by the classical pioneers.

Other guidance comes from McCorkell (1997), who points out the classic direct marketer's 'numbers-driven' route. Tests can establish the lowest cost of acquiring a new customer and, similarly, how much needs to be spent to obtain a similar sale from existing customers. McCorkell proposes that the point at which funds are transferred from existing customers to new customers is when it is cheaper on a like-by-like basis to obtain sales from new customers. The strength of this approach is its foundation in financial logic. Its weakness is that it is tactical in that no account is taken of investment in existing customers, which may not pay immediate dividends but are ultimately profitable.

Decision no. 3: decide how to keep customers

Once the strategic decision between existing and new markets has been made, we are ready to move to the next level of the model – deciding how to keep our current customers with us.

Returning to Fig. 5.7 we can see that for both retention and acquisition, the strategy decisions come under two basic headings: 'product' and 'market'. The elements under each will now be briefly introduced, with a fuller discussion given in Chapter 6.

'Market' (customer) decisions

The obvious question to ask here is: which customers do we want to keep? Here is where the database marketers' ability to *segment by customer value* becomes so important. By understanding the differing value of different customers, we can separate out those who are so important to the company that it is vital they are looked after (*see* Fig. 5.9).

EXHIBIT 5.7

ISOLATING THE TOP CUSTOMERS: TESCO

Tesco, a large supermarket retailer in the UK and Europe, has been testing a programme of preferential treatment to high-spending consumers, identified from data gathered via its loyalty card. Invitations are sent offering the chance to participate in tempting new product launches of expensive wines, complimentary visits to golf ranges or the opportunity to see top hair designers. To keep customers who may spend, say, £10 000 per year with the store, this re-allocation of some value back by the store represents good business sense.

As we saw in Chapter 3, direct marketers also have the ability to segment by loyalty to the company (Reichheld, 1996), by customer needs (Jobber, 1995), by lifestyle, or by profiled likelihood of responding to the next offer (McCorkell, 1997). All these can improve the accuracy and profitability of our marketing.

The ultimate segmentation is to separate down to segments of one. Using this idea, a new way of thinking about keeping customers has emerged, dubbed one-to-one marketing by Peppers *et al.* (1995), pioneers in this area. Using a database, the firm learns over time, with the customer, how to meet customer needs more and more efficiently until the firm is regarded as being such good value for money that the idea of going somewhere else is not considered.

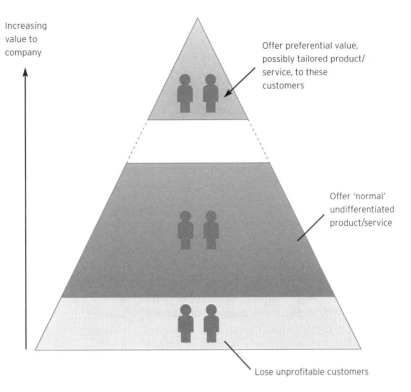

Increasing value to company

Offer preferential value, possibly tailored product/service, to these customers

Offer 'normal' undifferentiated product/service

Lose unprofitable customers

Figure 5.9 Segmenting by customer value

'Product' decisions

What can the company offer customers in order to keep as much of their spend with the firm as possible?

To achieve greater retention, direct marketers have been increasingly influenced by relationship marketing philosophies at the expense of traditional Four Ps transactional thinking. The emphasis therefore switches from product to service. In particular, the importance of delivering *superior service* has become apparent in many markets, including the hotel industry (*see* Exhibit 5.8).

EXHIBIT 5.8

TAILORED SERVICE FROM BUSINESS HOTELS

Businesspeople who travel a lot are worth an enormous amount to hotels over their lifetime. By assiduously recording these people's service needs, and making the details available to staff in live situations, these hotels can deliver a *proactive* tailored service in every aspect of hotel service delivery, from the check-in desk to the bar. Fast check-in and payment, courtesy drinks from the bar, and so on, will add to the convenience of the customers' stay and imbue them with a sense of privilege.

Another facet of relationship marketing is the opening of meaningful dialogue with customers. The dialogue can help the firm to understand individual needs better, but also can create value by delivering communications, which in itself is seen as valuable.

EXHIBIT 5.9

KEEPING CUSTOMERS WITH HIGH-VALUE COMMUNICATIONS: BENETTON *COLOURS* MAGAZINE

Cram (1994) reported on Benetton, an international clothing company, using a high-quality magazine, *Colours*, to add value to its brand. The magazine, with Benetton's unique, highly visual style, is aimed at its 14-26-year-old customer base and is distributed in six languages in 100 countries.

The other side of the value equation is price, and direct marketing systems which allow differential pricing based on spend have become very popular. These 'loyalty schemes' will be examined in more detail in Chapter 6 and Chapter 9.

Decision no. 4: how to attract new customers

The biggest strategic decisions in attracting new markets often involve the creation of attractive brands, distinctive products or innovative distribution systems. The role of direct marketing in a strategic sense is sometimes therefore quite minimal, although its role as a targeting and communications vehicle is often very important. This contrasts with the key strategic role of the database in keeping customers, as we saw in the preceding section.

Nevertheless, there are some important elements of strategy for us to consider in direct marketing acquisition, especially if we picture direct marketing as a part of the overall marketing effort. Once again, we can split our focus between market and product.

'Market' decisions

For any marketer, the core strength of direct marketing for acquiring new customers is *targeting*. Direct marketers are dealing with individuals, and they have the analysis and media tools to pinpoint prospects more precisely than general marketers. Strategically, there are a number of targeting approaches which depend on the company's strengths (does it have a database; does it have a clear idea of precisely who its new customers are likely to be?) and the marketing environment (the need to go for new types of customers, competitive activity, whether its markets are niche or mass, and so on).

Within this strategic framework, the targeting options for direct marketers are:

- asking new customers to identify themselves;
- targeting based on the principle that new customers will be similar to existing customers;
- targeting based on predicted loyalty to the company, again based on existing customer profiles;
- targeting a commercial partner's customers, known as affinity marketing.

'Product' decisions

In the acquisition of new customers, marketing practice is arguably still more influenced by the Four Ps transaction approach than by relationship marketing theory. Certainly, a look at direct marketing practice suggests that it is the *formal product* which is more important in attracting prospects than add-on service. This, however, is mentioned here more as a thought-provoker than a firm principle.

A customer seeking to buy from a supplier for the first time will seek lots of things, but some benefits may be more important on first purchase. These may include trust, *reassurance* about the quality of their purchase, being able to buy *conveniently*, or having an extra *incentive* as a temptation to purchase.

Both direct and general marketers will need to pay attention to these issues, and perhaps place them at the core of their product strategy. There are occasions where strategic advantage can be obtained by delivering these benefits more effectively through direct marketing systems.

General marketers look to imbue feelings of trust and reassurance through *building brands* which prospects will be familiar with and like, even though they have yet to purchase from that firm. Direct marketers can either *support* brands built through general marketing or take a *lead role* in building different types of brand values themselves. The links between branding and direct marketing are becoming more important, and this subject is given further attention in Chapter 7.

The use of *direct distribution* – mail order or direct delivery of service, say telephone banking – is a powerful weapon in the direct marketers' armoury when it comes to attracting new customers. The benefit they are offering is convenience. The growth of electronic media heralds the possibility of new modes of shopping by consumers who value convenience over the tangible shopping experience itself. This will offer firms the strategic advantage of bypassing retail channels, and is therefore an attractive option for FMCG sector manufacturers, among others.

Finally, a decision must be made whether or not to use *incentives* to stimulate purchase. This decision may rest on branding, pricing, competitive usage or targeting decisions, and it is with the latter that incentives used through direct marketing may well provide a huge advantage (Rapp and Collins, 1987). Instead of most of your incentives to attract new users being taken advantage of by existing customers, as happens in retail situations, incentives can be directed to the intended audience – prospects.

Summary to chapter

In this chapter we found that direct marketing objectives should be linked to the main marketing objectives, which in turn encompass separate acquisition and retention objectives.

A model of strategic decision making for direct marketers was developed.

The most important strategic roles of direct marketing were identified as a focus on customer understanding and the ability to deliver improved customer retention through powerful segmentation and targeting strategies. The service and dialogue links with relationship marketing were seen as vital in many markets. Finally, the strategic roles of direct marketing in acquiring new customers were pinpointed as efficient targeting, direct distribution, and brand building and support.

Questions

1. What are the core strengths of direct marketing over general marketing? If you were marketing director of a children's toy manufacturer, what would be your arguments for using a direct marketing system in that sector?

2. Give three reasons why a clothing company should consider distributing direct rather than through retail.

3. What are the overlaps between relationship and direct marketing? In what ways do the two approaches to marketing differ?

4. Give two differences and two similarities between direct marketing objectives and general marketing objectives.

5. Why are packaged (supermarket) goods companies less likely than business-to-business suppliers to use direct marketing?

6. 'Direct marketing's strength is its focus on customers.' Explain how this market focus influences the development of direct marketing strategy.

References

Ansoff, H.I. (1968) *Corporate Strategy*, Penguin, Harmondsworth.

Berry, L.L. (1983) 'Relationship marketing' in Berry, L.L., Shostack, G.L. and Upah, G.D. (eds) *Emerging Perspectives on Services Marketing*, American Marketing Association, Chicago, pp. 25–8.

Bird, D. (1992) *Commonsense Direct Marketing*, Kogan Page, London.

Cram, T. (1994) *The Power of Relationship Marketing*, Pitman Publishing, London.

Fifield, P. (1992) *Marketing Strategy*, Butterworth-Heinemann, Oxford.

Fletcher, K., Wheeler, C. and Wright, J. (1995) 'The role and status of UK database marketing' in Payne, A., Christopher, M., Clark, M. and Peck, H. (eds) *Relationship Marketing for Competitive Advantage*, Butterworth-Heinemann, Oxford, pp. 278–93.

Jobber, D. (1995) *Marketing: Principles and practice*, McGraw-Hill, Maidenhead, Berkshire.

Kotler, P. (1995) *Marketing Management: Analysis, strategy, planning and control*, 7th edn, Prentice Hall, Upper Saddle River, NJ.

McCorkell, G. (1997) *Direct and Database Marketing*, Kogan Page, London.

McDonald, M. (1995) *Marketing Plans: How to prepare and how to use them*, Butterworth-Heinemann, Oxford.

Peppers, D., Rogers, M. and Pine, J. (1995) 'Do you want to keep your customers forever?', *Harvard Business Review*, March–April, pp. 103–14. See also Peppers, D. and Rogers, M. (1993) *The One-to-One Future*, Piatkus, London.

Porter, M. (1985) *Competitive Advantage: Creating and Sustaining Superior Performance*, The Free Press, New York.

Rapp, S. and Collins, T. (1987) *Maximarketing*, McGraw-Hill, New York.

Reichheld, F.F. (1996) *The Loyalty Effect*, Harvard Business School Publishing, Boston, Mass.

Worked case study: Daewoo UK

This case study is based on the actual events surrounding the launch of Daewoo Cars in the UK in 1995. Many of the strategic questions you are asked to consider are parallels of those actually facing Daewoo in the late 1990s.

Setting the scene

In 1994, Daewoo launched itself into the UK car market under the strapline 'the biggest car company you've never heard of', with a small budget and just two models. Three years later, virtually everyone had heard of Daewoo, and it had exploded its one-year and three-year sales targets. Pat Farrell, Sales and Marketing Director of Daewoo, and Charlie Dawson, Deputy MD of advertising agency Duckworth Finn Grubb Waters, admitted that even they had been a little surprised by the company's performance. How had Daewoo done it?

Daewoo's background

The name Daewoo means 'the whole universe', and this was reflected in the company's business interests which extend well beyond cars into aircraft, banking, ships, textiles, computing and other areas.

The UK car market

In the UK, Daewoo's task was massive. The UK car market is highly competitive and very crowded. Daewoo set itself a target of 1 per cent market share in the *first year* of operations, the difficulty of which is appreciated when viewed in context: for instance Volvo had 2.8 per cent share after 37 years.

To make things even more challenging, Daewoo was launching with only two models, the Nexia and the Espero, based on rather outdated specifications from an historical association with General Motors. Its challenge was daunting; these two cars were competing with 42 other marques, and over 500 models in the UK at the time of their launch.

The overall picture for 1995 is outlined in Fig. 5.10. The total market size in 1995 was 1945 366 vehicles. However, the 'others' category of Fig. 5.10 was shared between a large number of manufacturers, each averaging less than 1 per cent market share.

Market structure

Before Daewoo's arrival, the UK car market had a clear structure of car manufacturers who sold the cars to dealers – the retail end of the industry. It was the dealers who owned the relationship with the customer. Although some dealers operated to very high standards, many did a less than perfect job of keeping their customer satisfied.

Car buyers have come to expect 'extras' such as electric windows, central locking, sunroofs, CD players, and so on, as standard, or as options they can choose to add to their car. Some degree of product personalisation is therefore present in most models. Daewoo, however, decided to make a virtue out of standardisation, by positioning its offering as having no hidden extras. Both its launch models were fitted with ABS brakes, side impact bars, stereo and cellular phone as standard. The prices ranged from £8500 to £11 000.

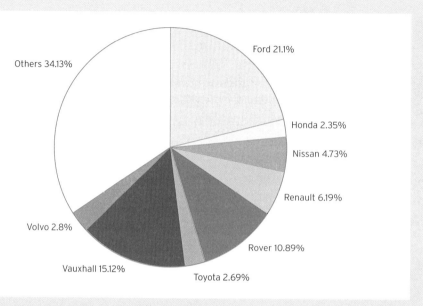

Figure 5.10 UK market shares, main players, 1995
Source: Reproduced with the permission of the Society of Motor Manufacturers and Traders Ltd

The positioning debate begins

In 1994, Pat Farrell, then the Marketing Director of Daewoo UK, sent a fax to a London-based mainstream agency, Duckworth Finn Grubb Waters (DFGW). DFGW was given just six days (in contrast to the usual six weeks) to respond to the brief asking for early strategic and creative ideas for the Daewoo UK launch. Pat's first thoughts were on a positioning of 'European cars from Korea', but the agency decided to develop the plan further. The people from DFGW knew from their own experiences as consumers that retail customers of new cars were not exactly ecstatic about their car purchase experiences. Hence the seedling idea of 'the most customer-focused car company' was born.

When DFGW gave their presentation, their ideas sparked off a discussion within Daewoo. For logistical reasons, Daewoo had already had the idea of controlling distribution to the customer direct – cutting out the dealer. It was realised that this was a tremendous opportunity to deliver a 'customer-focused' proposition in a convincing way, extremely quickly. Daewoo could become the first car company *to make service, not product*, its point of differentiation.

Marketing in the auto industry

Daewoo decided to take a look at how marketing was typically done in the car industry, and found that the weakest area was the customer interface – the dealer. Customers had low opinions of who they saw as 'sharp, suited salesmen' who would make all manner of promises in order to sell a car, then were nowhere to be seen if anything went subsequently wrong. Service levels were poor, with customers complaining of feeling helpless and unable to prevent themselves being ripped off by unscrupulous garages.

Some early market research

One of the things Daewoo was very keen to do was to talk to customers early on in the process. At the same time, the agency was aware of the biggest problem facing Daewoo's positioning strategy of the most customer-focused car company: how to make customers believe it. It knew that the more customers were told that Daewoo was customer focused, the less customers would believe it. In an innovative move, the agency suggested that a good way to begin to demonstrate customer focus was to use direct-response TV to ask customers to ring in and tell Daewoo what they wanted from a car company. This programme was to be called Daewoo Dialogue.

Meanwhile, more conventional market research was also carried out, the results of which are summarised in Appendix 1 at the end of this case study.

The first two years

Daewoo hit the UK market with a bang. Its starting point was a revolution in the way car manufacturers did business. Daewoo eliminated dealers and set up its own, centrally controlled distribution centres.

In the early days, getting the message across about Daewoo was clearly a top priority. Charlie Dawson described the process of customer purchase using a triangle diagram shown in Fig. 5.11.

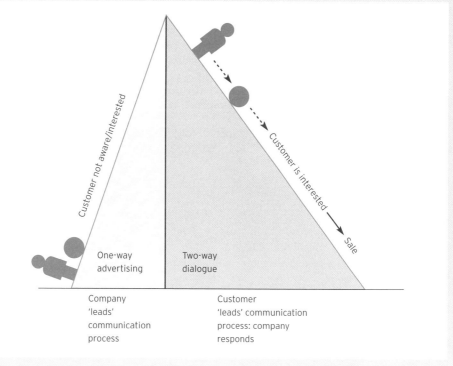

Figure 5.11 Process of customer purchase

What the triangle in Fig. 5.11 illustrates is that the hardest work for the marketer is getting the customer's initial interest. Once interest has been established, in a sense the customer leads the process towards purchase.

The challenge for Daewoo was to arouse interest with a limited budget. DFGW therefore eschewed the traditional car-advertising approach of squealing tyres, twisting roads and alpine shots, in favour of something much more forthright – service.

Early TV advertising concentrated on Daewoo's car-building credibility, and then a new phase was begun: communicating the core value of customer focus and building a database of prospects.

Then Daewoo Dialogue (described earlier) was launched. This was intended to bring a new feel to car marketing from the start. People were asked to call in and say what they wanted from a new car company. In this way, Daewoo wanted to seek ideas, but as importantly, show how it was customer led, rather than just claiming to be. Then, in an innovative move, Daewoo offered to provide 200 cars as test drives for a year, in return for driver feedback on the cars and the company's new ways of working.

The campaign was run using a DRTV approach, and telephone lines sagged under the pressure of 45 000 calls within the first hour of transmission. In fact the volume of demand was estimated as second only to the Children in Need appeal in UK DRTV history.

The result pleased the bosses in Korea. Prompted awareness of the Daewoo name went from 4 to 50 per cent, brand attributes of being 'different' and 'customer focused' grew, and a database of 180 000 names was established by the end of the campaign in February 1995.

More TV advertising was used to build awareness for the four-cornered proposition described in the following section. Again, the ads deliberately avoided the 'desert', 'top of mountain' cliché advertising that so many car manufacturers have used, and again reaction was incredibly positive (see Appendix 2 for storyboard of the advert 'Dustcovers').

Daewoo's launch year was the most successful in UK launch history. By April 1996, the end of its first full 12 months of operation, it had achieved 18 000 sales, outdoing Daewoo in all other European markets.

However, 1996 marked the end of the 'honeymoon' period when as a new company it was newsworthy and got a lot a free publicity. Pat and Charlie knew that from now on they had to generate their own 'buzz'. They kept up the momentum by continuing the Dialogue theme, and sent out a survey to responders to another TV advert calling for stories about customers' problems with their existing suppliers. This was deliberately provocative, and designed to focus on getting a response from unhappy car owners – likely Daewoo buyers.

Again response was impressive. Over 125 000 people called the hotline, and 51 000 returned a questionnaire giving feedback on the service they had received. Qualitative and quantitative results are shown in Appendices 3 and 4.

Daewoo's hassle-free buying, encouraging browsing and using fixed prices with no hidden extras, in particular, no delivery charges, no salesmen on commission, proved popular.

Scope was available for the company to capture this 'product preference' data, and some patchy data had been collected, but not as yet used. One of the reasons for this was the company's focus on service as a means of competition. Daewoo was well aware that the products themselves were not a strength.

However, Pat Farrell had always been realistic about his products, and was not too concerned by such criticism. The key was the target market at which Daewoo was aiming. Research commissioned by qualitative agency Millward Brown found that 37 per cent of car buyers regarded the car purely as a way of getting from A to B. In other words, these people did not respond to the vast majority of car advertising with its focus on specifications and performance.

The role of direct marketing

Direct marketing had evolved as a natural output of the strategy. As a mainstream agency, DFGW was unusual in having no particular interest in pushing brand advertising as the only solution. The team's opinion was that they neither knew nor cared about supposed 'differences' between brand-led and direct-response TV advertising.

In fact, their proposed use of direct-response techniques had nothing to do with database marketing. They used direct response because they saw it as the best way to *show* their commitment to customer focus, rather than merely talk about it. Customers were encouraged to respond to Daewoo's request to tell them what they wanted out of a car firm.

DFGW's philosophy was to use every advertising pound to *demonstrate* customer focus in as creative a way as possible. For example, one event was an offer of 30 cars in various showrooms for sale at 1967 prices, to highlight Daewoo's 30th Birthday in 1997. Over 23 000 phone calls were received, with over 50 000 visitors in total. In a sense, Daewoo had operated a sort of 'mass direct' approach up till now.

Research findings

Daewoo found that its early customers were very happy to be associated with the Daewoo brand. Customers reported that people came up to them and asked, 'Is it true? Do they really deliver? Daewoo customers were pleased with their self image as 'clever enough to go for the best deal, rejecting the mainstream, inferior offers'. They saw themselves as challenging, anti-establishment, and unwilling to accept any 'bullshit' from car manufacturers. In some ways, this phenomenon was similar to the impact First Direct had on the banking world.

Clearly, Daewoo customers had attitudes, opinions, and a view of themselves in common. Although relatively little 'formal' research had been done, Pat Farrell felt he knew his customer profile well. Compared with the typical new car buyer, the key attributes of the Daewoo buyer were as follows:

- Most new car buyers were over 35, but Pat's customers were probably nearer 50 or over.
- More women than average were attracted to the Daewoo offer.
- Daewoo owners saw themselves as smarter than average. They typically came from professions like teaching – possessing limited spending power, but able to 'see through' traditional marketing.
- Millward Brown's finding that '37 per cent of car buyers regard the car as primarily a way of getting from A to B' was largely agreed with by Daewoo's customers.

Recent campaigns

Later in 1996, further depth to the brand values was added with a new campaign utilising intriguing imagery unique to the car market. Symbolic brand values which built Daewoo as a brand for people wishing to be seen as smart and intelligent individuals were added to the rational, functional values of 'different' and 'customer focused' already established. Daewoo was looking for its database marketing to support these values.

The brief

Explain why Daewoo's acquisition plan was so innovative.

Imagine Pat Farrell has asked you to scope out further acquisition plans for the coming year, to build on the early successes. Produce a further acquisition direct-marketing plan for Daewoo UK, including analysis, objectives and strategies, and make explicit the role of direct marketing as a part of the marketing philosophy and mix of the company.

Appendix 1: research

Exploratory research was undertaken in which Daewoo 'listened to people's lives in relation to their cars'. An initial three-way split of needs was identified:

■ basic physical/functional needs, e.g. reliability (rational needs);

■ augmented product needs such as service extras;

■ the car as a statement of the owner's personality (emotional needs).

Daewoo also looked into the way people buy cars, exploring fresh approaches to its marketing. What it found was that, for customers buying a car, branding was very important right from the start. Because of the huge number of models from which to choose, customers used brands as a shorthand for their initial information search. They rejected models from brands they didn't like, even though a proper look may have found cars which fitted their criteria.

Having got down to a manageable choice, customers then did do a more in-depth analysis of how well various models fitted their own needs. They essentially *traded off* the various criteria functions, size, price, brand values, and so on of one car against another, *versus their personal priorities*.

Daewoo concluded that the timely flow of *persuasive* information to potential customers was crucial. Any brands not clearly understood by customers would be rejected quickly. Word of mouth was very important, as were 'chance' encounters – a ride in a friend's car, or advice from a mechanic during a service of their current vehicle. Popping a brochure through the post every now and then was simply not good enough.

Appendix 2: 'Dustcovers' advert highlighting Daewoo's customer-friendly showrooms

'Daewoo aren't just unveiling a new car, they're also unveiling a new way of buying a car ...

... the whole family will be welcome ...

... there'll be interactive displays to help you choose ...

... a café area to relax in ...

... and a kids' play area, where they can play with their cars, not with yours.

... But you won't find commissioned sales-people, just non-commissioned advisors.

(Salesman) "Hello, my name's ..." All this from a showroom? That'll be the Daewoo.'

Source: Reproduced by kind permission of Duckworth Finn Grubb Waters.

Appendix 3: customer horror stories

On asking for horror stories from car buyers, Daewoo received 51 000 replies. Here is a selection:

'On walking in I was totally ignored for half an hour. I was wearing jeans, sweatshirt and had my hair in plaits (I'm of West Indian origin). Tried to get them to sell me a standard saloon. Was told I could not buy without husband's signature. Went back two days later, smart suit, hair done up, son's toy plastic mobile phone. They were falling over themselves to help me.'

'Left car for service with a list of problems. One was wind noise coming from side door. Having left the car window open when dropping the car off, an engineer phoned me at work and asked if I had tried closing the window!'

'Car had to go into two different garages for major work which cost us £800, plus it was off the road for four weeks. However, what really summed up the whole thing was when the garage mending our car rang me and asked me "Can I borrow your tapes out of the car as you've got some really good ones?".'

Appendix 4: survey results

Early in 1996, Daewoo was inundated by 125 000 calls to its appeal for car buyers to tell them what they wanted from a car manufacturer. Some of the results are given here:

- 74% of people said they had been put off purchasing by pressure from salespeople;
- 70% felt that staff were not interested in customer care once the sale had been closed;
- 68% said they were not taken seriously when entering a showroom;
- 90% felt that number plates and delivery should be included in the price;
- 86% said the retail price of the vehicle should be the same countrywide;
- 82% would prefer a fixed price with no haggling;
- 61% of women believe the opposite sex get better treatment.

Managing acquisition and retention: BK Bank

This case is based on a real bank operating in the UK. The bank is not one of the 'big four' retailers. The name of the bank and the names of key personnel have been changed to preserve confidentiality, but the core material reflects the bank's commercial situation.

Introduction

David DeLorean sat staring out of his office window from its vantage point high up in the headquarters' building of BK Bank in Macclesfield. The view was as pretty as ever, looking out over the rolling hills as far as the Peak District in the distance, but David wasn't really taking any of it in. His thoughts were far away as he pondered the problems that had been handed to him from his superiors. As a businessman, he had grown used to pressure, but this was going to take some beating …

David DeLorean is the Direct Marketing Manager at BK Bank. The directors of BK had just had a meeting at which they had decided to reverse a key decision of three or four years ago. The meeting had concluded that BK needed to increase its revolving credit (credit card) account base urgently. Naturally, the task had fallen to him to resolve. But how …?

The credit-card business

Credit cards were introduced in the UK in 1966 when Barclaycard launched its service, although credit cards have been used in the USA for a good deal longer. Indeed, the first known credit card was introduced in stores in the USA in the early part of the twentieth century.

The early UK market was dominated by Barclaycard (card issuer) which was backed up by *'network organiser'*, Visa. Companies like Visa and Access spent a great deal of capital laying down the infrastructure of the credit-card business. They arranged deals with retailers and built up the card-processing facilities. The next chain in the business was the card issuers, such as Barclays Bank and BK Bank, which began the process of building up credit-card awareness and recruiting customers.

In the early 1980s more players, such as TSB and the building societies, entered the market.

The market soon broke into different sectors, defined by the plethora of different cards that were available. At one end, corporate clients who had high spending power were attracted by the status of 'gold' and 'platinum' cards. These charged a high fee, were exclusively marketed and were highly profitable to the issuers. Another emerging sector was that of the high-street charge cards which gave credit to regular customers of particular stores. One of the early problems encountered by these cards, however, was their impulse nature. This led to a large volume of bad debt being built up, especially among people from lower social profiles. That said, the high debt utilisation (i.e. a low number of dormant cards) made these cards a great success with card issuers.

The mid-1980s saw a new development with the arrival of *affinity cards* into the UK. These products were the result of partnerships between two businesses: the issuer (for example BK Bank) works with a well-known organisation to provide a credit card branded by that organisation. The card is then aimed at the existing customers of the partner.

There has been a steady growth in the number of these cards and now organisations as diverse as Cambridge University, charities, The Automobile Association, and many others, have affinity cards.

However, this has not been the end of the product development. The end of the 1980s saw the fall-off in growth in credit-card usage as consumers' ability to raise debt dropped off. In 1993 an attempt was made to restart market growth with the launch of 'product-based', value-added credit cards. Barclaycard launched a new type of card in partnership with Ford with which customers could get up to £2500 off a new Ford by accumulating points according to credit-card spend. A similar deal was struck between General Motors and HFC Bank, backed by Visa, giving money off new Vauxhalls.

The marketplace

The credit-card market is highly diverse, with many sectors of the population using credit cards for many reasons. However, there are two sectors in particular who contribute a major part of industry profits:

■ generally well-off sectors of the population. These people tend to be of AB social class, highly educated and they spend money reasonably freely. They will not be too upset at paying either interest or other charges;

■ less well-off people who may be working class in background and may be tempted to run up quite large credit-card bills. A subset of these consumers has been dubbed 'Essex Man' in popular culture.

The marketplace is now reaching its mature stage, with the early growth slowing down. In particular the most wealthy sectors have been exposed to a very high amount of marketing and are largely saturated. In the affinity-card sector, charities have been extensively targeted and new openings are hard to find.

BK Bank

BK Bank Limited is a wholly-owned but independent UK subsidiary of Chase Chicago, an American conglomerate which wanted to get a toehold in the UK banking sector. BK Bank is a large financial organisation with assets of over £9 billion. These assets are based on lendings to companies and individuals on a range of different products, from mortgages to lease, HP, personal loans and credit cards.

Origins

BK's traditional form of business was to provide finance through credit cards and loans. However, through the years, BK has moved into a number of new market sectors to provide finance. These include professional groups, industrial concerns, membership groups, and retailers. BK spotted these partnership opportunities very early on and was the most profitable group in its sector.

The BK business

The name BK, however, is not well known to the public, even though hundreds of thousands of them make use of its services every day through its various credit cards. The reason for this lack of awareness by British consumers is that BK does not brand its product and services itself. Rather, its products are marketed by business partners. For example, if BK and Thistle Hotels, say, were to launch a credit card, then BK would provide the card-processing facilities and the marketing know-how, but the card would be branded by Thistle Hotels with no mention of BK Bank at all. As David DeLorean described it:

'We are like a chameleon in a way. We take on the identity of whoever we happen to be in partnership with. It's a symbiotic relationship and it works very well.'

BK describes itself as a wholesaler of funds, preferring to work behind other companies' own brands. It is BK, however, that does the marketing on behalf of the business partner: BK sets out the product specification, for example the APR rate, loan facilities etc., and BK does the marketing of the cards, often acting under the name of its partner. If a customer rings in with a service issue, the BK staff who take the call take on the identity of the affinity partner. They will therefore answer the phone 'Hello, Red Cross', and so on.

Main business areas

BK Bank's main business is in loans, whether by big-ticket finance to corporate customers, or fixed and revolving accounts to consumers. A fixed-term loan is one which was traditionally offered to consumers by high-street banks. Consumers would be expected to pay back a fixed loan in instalments, to which interest was added. These loans were typically 'one-off' affairs. However, the problem with fixed-term loans was that, on average, customer turnover would be 100 per cent in six years, with less than half the customers renewing their loans or taking up another product at the end of each payment period.

The introduction of credit cards marked the start of revolving accounts. These had the advantage of allowing the customer to build up and pay off debt again and again.

Over ten years ago, BK was responsible for the launch of several large retailer credit cards now known in the market. Through this programme it has managed to recruit many tens of thousands of customers which it has retained on its database. In tandem with this, BK is an issuer of Visa cards in the UK and additionally has several large operations which are over-branded with other organisations' names: affinity cards.

Of the customers who use credit cards, about 30 per cent will build up debt and not pay it all off within a month. These are amongst the most profitable customers for BK because they pay interest on longer term debt. The bank also earns revenue through the additional charge it makes of a fixed annual fee of £12 to consumers, other customer charges (for example, late payment fees) and merchant fees (charges levied to retailers for the use of BK's credit cards).

Recent situation

In 1999 BK Bank decided to have a major review of its involvement in consumer revolving accounts. This product was making some money, but was rather slow moving compared with other parts of BK business. Costs at the time were high; marketing costs, the capital and ongoing costs of processing and customer service were all biting deep. In return, the revenue payback was quite long in coming. The conclusion of the review, after looking at the situation, was that BK should not continue to market proactively the cards to consumers.

When looked at from the point of view of the prevailing culture at BK Bank, this was not a surprising decision. BK had always gone for a strategy of steady, short-term growth across a broad range of products with no particular commitment to long-term strategy in any one area.

BK's strengths

The company has considerable resources at its disposal. Its marketing budget is fixed on a cost-justification basis and by comparison with the rest of its sector is quite large. It has its own large marketing department which is able to handle the large volumes involved. BK also has enjoyed good relations with many of the UK's top direct marketing agencies, leading to some award-winning campaigns in the past.

BK's advanced systems allow processing costs to be kept to a minimum. It has an advanced relational database which allows any customer-profiling analyses required to be done very quickly, but up till recently BK had not actually used statistical techniques to help with its marketing.

BK had the following data on most of its customers:

- name;
- address;
- transaction data including date of product purchased, which products: loans, credit cards, insurance; value of transaction;
- marketing history: what promotions had been aimed at the customer; response history;
- age, personal geodemographic details;
- what loans were used for, e.g. car purchase.

David had recently been on a direct marketing course and had picked up some basic tips on the use of modelling techniques. He knew that predictive techniques could lower the cost per response for his acquisition and retention activities. However, he needed to get a clearer picture of what could be done.

Used in tandem with the database was a sophisticated inbound and outbound telemarketing system which allowed a screen of customer information to be on every telemarketer's desk. There were over 100 personnel potentially available for a telemarketing campaign. BK Bank had established an impressive system of inbound and outbound customer contact which it used with customers who had loans (see Fig. 5.12).

Staff were well paid and well trained, backed up with good systems. This ensured the quality of customer contact was kept very high. The same outbound operatives were always used with a particular customer to ensure a genuine relationship was built up over time. Customers came to trust the advice they were given. The customer record contained details of the last three conversations they had had with BK Bank, so that service and outbound staff always knew what was going on.

BK Bank had carefully tested this relationship-building system against controls in which no contact was made, and it knew that the system paid for itself for loan products. A typical loan of £3000, paid back over five years at 18 per cent APR (Annual Percentage Rate), made a gross profit of £280 per annum. Set against this was the initial costs of acquisition. A typical mailer costing £500 per thousand would generate an average response of 0.2 per cent, although this varied dramatically depending on the affinity partner. Then there were the costs of service and outbound calling, estimated at about £120 p.a. per customer. However, David had found that under the service and telemarketing system, retention rates increased for loans (i.e. a customer with a loan renews with a new loan or takes up another product on expiry of the original loan) from under 40 per cent to nearer 60 per cent.

David's problem now was to decide whether such a system would be profitable with credit cards. The acquisition costs of credit cards were less than for loans; mailers to affinity part-

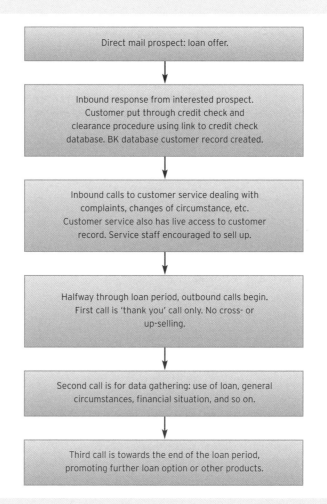

Figure 5.12 Inbound and outbound customer contact

ners' databases averaged about a 1 per cent response. However, profitability per annum was lower, at about £30 per customer.

The problem

As the fiscal year drew to a close, the marketing department at BK Bank was considering its marketing plan for the following year. David and his colleagues had for some time been increasingly concerned about the consequences of the decisions made four years earlier to slow down activity in the credit-card sector. In the meantime, BK's competitors had been far from idle. Using incentives, sales promotions, awarding larger credit limits, removing the annual fees, and promoting new uses of credit cards were just some of the tactics successfully employed to renew the momentum of the sector.

Over the last four years or so, BK Bank's recruitment of credit-card (revolving) accounts had dropped sharply compared with the mid-1990s. BK was therefore beginning to miss out on a highly profitable sector. The directors had met and hurriedly decided to restart marketing activity in the revolving-account sector. This decision was hardly surprising to David and his department; after all, the marketing department had been keeping a close eye on the credit-card marketplace for some 18 months now and could see which way the wind was blowing.

A budget of £600k had been set for marketing activity for 2004/5.

... David looked back into the office to see the team looking at him anxiously. He knew they depended on a strong strategy and plan to provide the right start to the new financial year. Fortunately, they had some plans on the table already.

BK Bank's traditional strength had always been to pick up particular niches that were too small and undeveloped for the likes of Visa and Access to bother with, but could nevertheless be highly profitable. Some ideas (which do not have to be adopted) were:

1 The previous year a staff suggestion scheme had suggested what a good idea it would be to have a credit card aimed exclusively at women. A lot of research had been done on this idea, and while not all the findings had been positive by any means, there were some possibilities to be explored.

2 David had just finished very fruitful negotiations with Toyan, a major Japanese car manufacturer with a strong UK presence, with the objective of launching a new 'product'-based credit card branded as Toyan.

The brief

Your group has been commissioned as a direct marketing agency invited to pitch for the BK Bank account in 2004/5. In your pitch include the following:

■ the key issues;

■ carefully planned, detailed marketing and direct marketing objectives;

■ an explanation of the role of direct marketing;

■ strategies for retention and revenue from existing customers and strategies for generating new prospects.

How will BK achieve competitive advantage?

Coventry City Football Club

Introduction

The ticketing manager, Jim Whelan, and the commercial manager, Ron Chippo, got their heads together and decided to approach the chairman with a plan to implement direct marketing to supporters in a more strategic manner than had been attempted to date.

It would be fair to say that up till now the use of direct marketing had been patchy.

Club structure

With some exceptions, football clubs have traditionally treated ordinary supporters as somewhat of a 'cash cow'. Senior managers in football have tended to focus their attention on sponsorship and business-to-business marketing – conference and corporate entertainment revenues – while the major supporter focus has been the short-term gains afforded from merchandising. Football clubs have never had classical marketing departments as such. They have tended to organise around ticketing – hence Coventry City had a Ticket Office Manager – and 'commercial activities', needing a 'commercial' or 'marketing' manager. Commercial activities typically include the main sponsorship deal, perimeter advertising, corporate hospitality boxes on match days, and off-field sales of the ground's facilities, conference hire, wedding hire and so on. Consequently, there is a less developed marketing approach towards ordinary supporters, and it is this that has limited the growth of database marketing. At Coventry, the commercial manager Ron was well aware that there was a cross-over between the ordinary supporter and his corporate guests, and that a database of fans would be of great use to him.

The other major business unit in football clubs is merchandising. At clubs like Manchester United, merchandising is a worldwide operation taking advantage of a global brand. In 2004, income from this source alone for Manchester United is likely to exceed £50 million. The rest of the football world is playing catch up in comparison, but even for a local club such as Coventry City, retail and merchandise is important. The retail manager at Coventry City was keen to get in on the database marketing initiatives being discussed at the club. At the moment the club has two retail outlets, one at the ground, and one in the city centre. The retail manager knew that capturing purchase data and linking it to supporters' personal details could help his operations. If only he had time to do something about it!

The second major barrier to database marketing investment was the low priority given to long-term projects. However, while it is sometimes easy to criticise, let's reflect for a moment on the frantic scramble for cash clubs need to buy and pay players and hence stay in their division. The lower divisions are littered with once highly placed clubs who have dropped into a vicious circle of lower gates meaning less money available to buy or keep the players they need to climb the table. It is this unforgiving and volatile nature of football which sometimes militates against the business side of the operation feeling that it can take a long-term approach. As a result, any new ideas had to be very thoroughly sold to the board to stand a chance, and that included direct marketing.

Current use of database marketing

The situation that Jim and Ron had inherited is represented in Fig. 5.13.

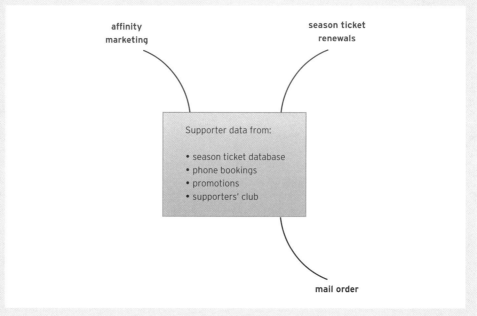

Figure 5.13 Limited direct marketing at Coventry City

A few years ago, the only 'direct marketing' from the club would have been the season ticket renewals in June and July. More recently, some affinity marketing had been started, but all on a small scale (see Chapter 6 for a section on affinity marketing). A small mail-order operation had been started by the retail manager, who used the database as a route to his customers, but with no attempt to record sales or to look at targeting.

New initiatives

At the time the future looked bright for Coventry City. The club planned to move to a state of the art stadium at the edge of the city. Holding 45 000 spectators and with a retractable pitch, the new facilities will rival any in Europe. At the moment, at Highfield Road (capacity 24 000), the club averages just over 20 000 for a home fixture. It sells out for the arrival of big draws such as Arsenal or Liverpool, but the home support shrinks a little to a core of about 16 000 for, say, Southampton on a wet Tuesday night.

The club management knew that they needed to set in place initiatives that would draw new support to fill the new stadium. The mood was favourable for expenditure on items like integrated database systems. Accordingly the club had invested in a new system called Arena which had the capability to integrate with the important functions of the club: ticketing, retail, corporate hospitality, finance and so on. The database held records of all transactions sorted by supporter name and personal details. Of course, at busy times in the shop or in the ticket office on match days it was difficult or often impossible to record details of a supporter purchasing tickets with cash. But otherwise, the club was encouraged by the amount of data it had been able to collect. A total database size of approaching 50 000 people had been accumulated.

Coventry City supporters

In conjunction with the local university (Coventry Business School), an extensive amount of market research data had been gathered about its supporters. A summary of the main findings is given in the Appendices. Some key facts were: for a typical 20 000 audience, about 11 000 were 'fanatics' who went to most or all home games. About 3–4000 were 'regulars' who went to about half the games; while about 6000 fans were 'casuals' who went to about five or fewer games per season.

'Fanatics'

Football is more than a business. As Rogan Taylor, former chair of the National Supporters' Federation, put it, 'No one has their ashes scattered down the aisle of Tesco's.' At the extreme end, some fans placed Coventry City at the very top of their priorities in life; indeed the researchers felt almost embarrassed to test their relative loyalty to the club versus their own family! A fan survey backed this up: an incredible 65 per cent of fans said that their club was very important or one of the most important things in their life.

Committed fans had multiple links with football. We were surprised about the multiplicity of associations ranging from personal friends who worked at the club, having some link with the players, or attending other local matches. Support for this 'football as lifestyle' behaviour came from the Carling survey which found that 25 per cent of Coventry fans have been to see the reserves, 14 per cent had been to see the Nationwide league that season, while 13 per cent had seen non-league action.

Given these insights, it was not surprising that there was warm support from committed supporters for increased opportunities to have contact with the club. Based around an enhanced supporters' club concept, the opportunity was for increased dialogue and improved interaction within the community. Practically everyone was eager for more information and more news than they were currently getting, and some supporters looked for increased contact with other supporters, maybe through 'supporter evenings' and so on. At present, only about 10 per cent of Coventry supporters belonged to one of the supporter club options, which indicates both the supporter club product and promotion may need addressing in order to meet the needs of these committed fans.

The special nature of loyalty

Among supporters, there were complex and sometimes contradictory sets of feelings towards loyalty and value. Some diehard fans actively defined their entire experience with Coventry City through loyalty. Unlike most business relationships, loyalty was explicit and extremely important to these fans. The link with behaviour was important for credibility among their peers: they were *required* to turn up to less exciting home games, and maybe away fixtures as well.

Other fans also *described themselves as loyal*, but, over the years, their attendance was more varied. They may have *drifted away from watching Coventry City live* and then come back. Interestingly this was behaviour they felt they needed to justify because of the peer pressure to be seen as loyal.

Casual supporters

At the other end of the scale were 'casual' supporters: those who went to an average of five or fewer games per season. For these, loyalty was not an issue they had considered. They viewed Coventry City as an entertainment option, not a lifestyle, and were therefore not subject to any pressure to attend from peers. Compared with committed fans, they tended to be more critical of the value for money they were getting. Casual supporters explained that they typically made decisions on the match day or maybe only decided to attend the game a day or two before, perhaps after driving past the ground accidently during the week. Appendix 5.5 gives some more details on 'casual' fans' attitudes.

Other segments

Coventry Business School had conducted research amongst the fans, and key segments were identified as:

■ Women. 50 years ago it was rare to see any women attending football games. The national average is now over 10 per cent, and Coventry was no exception.

■ 'Professional wanderers'. These were casual fans, with professional occupations, who had moved around the country and formed relatively weak associations with more than one club.

■ 'Repertoire fans'. 27 per cent of fans said they attended matches not involving Coventry City. This pattern was typical around many other clubs. These repertoire fans were more likely to fall into the 'casual' bracket above.

■ Match day behaviours were often different among different groups. For examples see Appendix 5.7.

■ Collectors. Many dedicated supporters we spoke to had varying degrees of *collecting behaviour*. One even wrote down transcripts of all the radio interviews involving Coventry City! The commercial opportunities were definitely there.

Possible marketing initiatives

The idea of club membership

At various points, Ron had been approached by third parties who wished to discuss initiatives with him. These people were particularly keen to act as agents in some way, middlemen who act as commercial partners between Coventry City and suppliers of goods. What these agents knew was that the relationship between a football club and its fans was a powerful one. In short, the club had immensely powerful brands, that at present were probably being under-exploited.

One way to exploit them was to develop affinity goods.

The growing role of the Internet

Coventry City's website was up and running by early 1999. It would be fair to say that the club had operated a 'follower' rather than leader strategy with its use of the Internet. Some managers at the club had seen the Net as merely another possible channel from which to make money. Others had seen the potential, however, for more strategic uses. For example, they had noted that:

- fans were heavy users of unofficial sites;

- one club executive had heard that on one Sunday a small Premier League club with a supporter gate averaging 25 000 had received over 250 000 'hits' to its website!

- international fans were heavy users of the Internet. One group of 20 Coventry City Fans who lived in Canada had organised a trip to the UK to see a game via their site;

- other clubs were looking at selling tickets over the Web. But how could they manage this facility, given that for some matches the sale of tickets needed tight control?

- merchandise was sold over the Internet;

- most of all, fans used the Internet to talk to each other. The Internet provided the ideal place for communities to establish themselves, and relationships to be built. The potential for fans to build themselves up as one voice was also greatly increased – fan power had a forum!

Other issues such as future media rights and the interest of agents in acting as middle-men between consumers and suppliers had to be considered.

The brief

The scene was set for a push to invest more in direct and database marketing. In the future, filling the new stadium was top priority, and as a result the club needed to think about acquisition and retention. This being football, loyalty was clearly important, but the club perhaps needed to be more proactive. The management at the club were very concerned to get things right. Was a points scheme a good idea? What about the Internet? The first thing to do was take a closer look at all the research the business school had produced for them. Ron and Jim opened the first of the reports.

Your task

Produce a direct marketing plan for Coventry City for the next three years, including recommendations on the club's use of the Internet.

Appendix 5.1: extracts from research carried out with season ticket and ex-season ticket holders, November 1999

'Reason ex-season ticket holders are not loyal' (tick any that apply)	Frequency
the letter from CCFC came at a time when I was short of money for just that time	20
the team performance last year put me off	18
I expected a poor team performance this year	5
I did not get round to it when CCFC sent me the renewal letter	2
I feel less loyal than I used to	5
I am watching other teams more	6
I am doing other things on a Saturday	19
I have to work on match days	16
My family commitments have increased	17
My job has changed from last year to this	16
I have less money to spend on things like this compared with last year	35
The people/person that I went to matches with does not go any more	15

I found myself not enjoying going last year	11
I would rather pay to get in match by match because my life is more complicated this year	38
season ticket price rise	37
I would rather watch football on TV	1
none of the above	3
other	25

Appendix 5.2: extracts from research carried out at an open day, June 1999

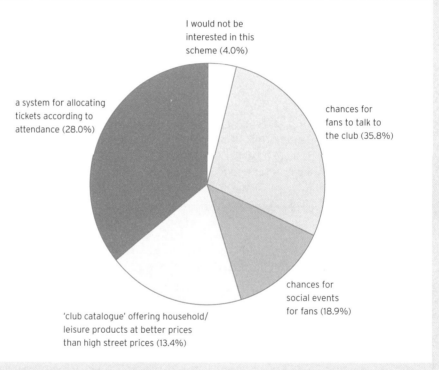

Figure 1 What the supporters would like to see in 'a membership scheme'

Appendix 5.3: The typical fan – research findings

17. Your typical fan......

■ doesn't exist!

■ a range of ages, incomes, occupations

■ but they are.....

■ more likely to be men (80%) than women

■ 50% have incomes between £10k and £30k

- but 10% have incomes >£50k
- about 40% of fans have children under 16
- about 10% of fans have children under 5
- 20% are women
- own a three-bedroom house
- have a mix of occupations with a slight C1/C2 bias but also many AB jobs
- are equally split between living in the city and living outside
- are more likely to be aged 19–34, but with plenty of fans across all age groups.

Appendix 5.4: Research carried out from segmentation of supporters study, November 1998

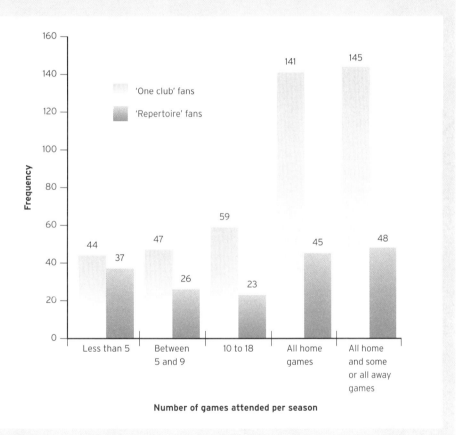

Figure 1 How repertoire fans vary versus overall attendance

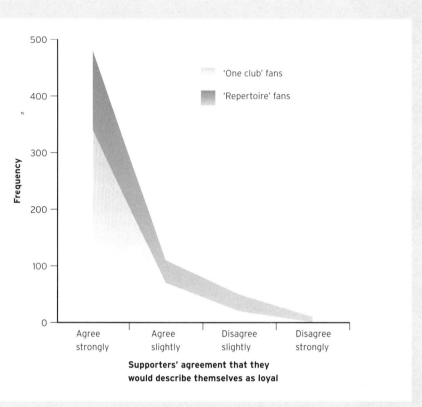

Figure 2 How repertoire fans may still describe themselves as loyal

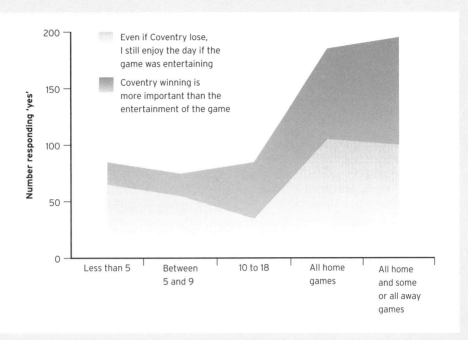

Figure 3 How attitudes towards winning and entertainment vary by supporter value to the club

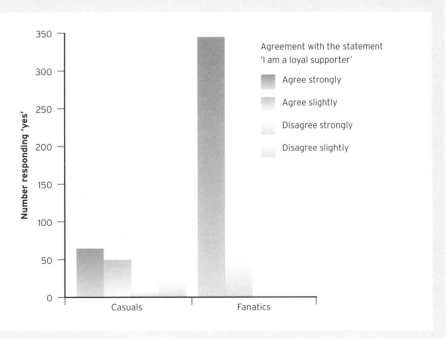

Figure 4 Showing how 'fanatics' are more attitudinally loyal than 'casuals'

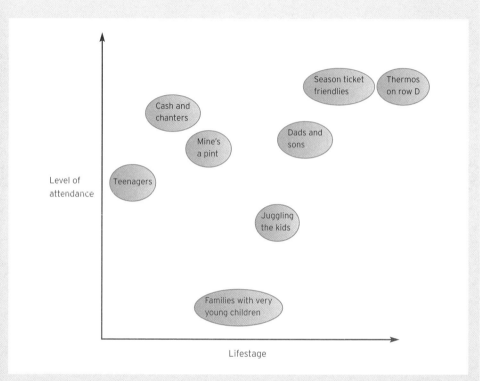

Figure 5 Behaviour-based segments mapped against level of attendance and lifestage

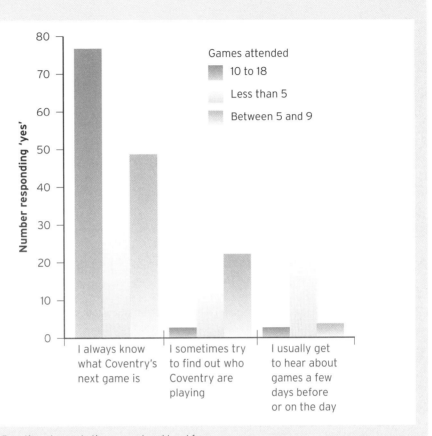

Figure 6 Reactions to marketing: casual and loyal fans

Appendix: 5.5 Casual fans: Two types of casuals

On examining the research findings in detail, *two types of casuals have emerged*. We have called these the 'carefree casuals' and the 'committed casuals'. These are defined as follows:

Carefree casuals (57% of casuals)

■ defined as those casuals who only slightly agree, or disagree, with the notion that they are loyal supporters

■ 88% of carefree casuals prefer to see an entertaining game, even if Coventry City loses

■ 50% of carefree casuals attend matches not involving Coventry City, compared with 27% of all fans

■ 88% describe watching Coventry City as just one of a number of choices for them on a Saturday

■ 63% don't know when Coventry City's next home game is

■ Summary: carefree casuals may be football lovers, but see Coventry as an entertainment option, and being Coventry City supporters is NOT part of their self image.

Committed casuals (43% of casuals)

- defined as those casuals who strongly agree that they are loyal to Coventry City
- only 26% go to non-Coventry City games
- 38% claim Coventry City winning is more important than an entertaining game (close to the % of fanatics who think the same)
- 78% of committed casuals know when Coventry City's next game is
- however, 75% still see Coventry City as one of a range of things they will consider
- Summary: committed casuals are genuine fans of Coventry City, but for them some non-football activities are of equal or greater priority (family? Playing sports/activities?). They therefore value variety and choice, and perhaps have their football support in perspective with the rest of their lives.

Appendix 5.6: The loyalty issue

When we took a closer look at how fans expressed their loyalty, we started to notice some strange contradictions. This is what we found.

27% of fans (even regular/fanatics (24%), but especially casuals (46%)) *go to competitor games*.

Of these, 68% would strongly agree that they are loyal supporters. Thus, the stereotype of the typical football fan as being a one-team person, perhaps having nothing but contempt for other teams, does not seem to be borne out by their behaviour.

In other words, when people describe themselves as loyal to one team, we should NOT take this as read. More than one in four of them will attend other matches.

Appendix 5.7: Groups distinguished by match-day behaviour

- **Mine's a pint**: people who like a drink or two either side of the game. These fans will arrive early, 'to park', will often meet casual acquaintances at the bar or maybe read the programme.

- **Juggling the kids**: families trying to fit in two or three events in the day. They may arrive at the ground at the last minute, but be high half-time spenders on snacks and so on. Families are also high spenders on merchandise.

- **'Thermos on row D'**: creatures of habit who get into the ground quite late, they are not interested in talking to anyone and may not spend much money at the ground on programmes or food.

- **Season ticket friendlies**: enjoy the social event of meeting fellow supporters by virtue of always having the same seat.

- **Loyal cash and chanters**: buy tickets with cash when they get paid and have a good shout at the game. May be 'regular' fans.

- **Dads and sons**: quiet supporters, and not part of a group. They are loyal, 'club' rather than 'football' orientated, and critical of 'disloyal' boys being Manchester United fans.

THE STRATEGIC INFLUENCES ON DIRECT MARKETING

Objectives

Once you have read this chapter you will:

- have an appreciation of the key strategic influences on direct marketing;

- be better placed to integrate direct marketing within a complete marketing framework;

- understand the key role of theories reflecting the importance of customer loyalty, the importance of relationship marketing, and the way in which direct marketing can influence the internal company environment.

Introduction

The latter part of Chapter 5 introduced direct marketing strategy and provided a model for strategic decision making in direct marketing. Within the model, we encountered a number of very important strategic elements which deserve more consideration than was possible during the introduction to the model. In this chapter we will take the opportunity to examine these elements, and their links with direct marketing, more fully.

In this chapter we will pick up from Chapter 5's discussion of strategy and also develop some new themes. We will examine three theoretical developments which have had a major influence on modern direct marketing. These are the importance of customer loyalty, the influence of relationship marketing, and the importance of database marketing in the wider business environment. However, it is also important to consider recent concerns about direct marketing's proper strategic role.

The influence of relationship marketing has become intricately tied up with direct marketing, and not always in a clear and appropriate manner. In order to deal with this important subject properly, and to fully discuss its offshoot, customer relationship management (CRM), a separate chapter (Chapter 7) is dedicated to these discussions.

The second part of this chapter deals with the specific techniques of direct marketing strategy, introduced in Chapter 5, in more detail. These are segmentation and targeting, service delivery, creating a dialogue, pricing schemes, and finally techniques for adding value to the product: positioning, branding, and incentives (see Fig. 6.1).

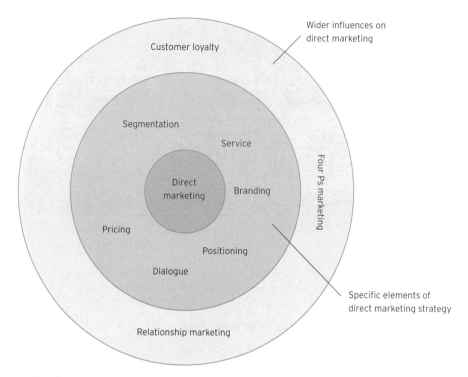

Figure 6.1 Influences on direct marketing strategy

Influences on direct marketing strategy

THE IMPORTANCE OF CUSTOMER LOYALTY

'Corporate leaders today can't understand why the troops won't rally behind a mission statement that places maximising shareholder value as the highest corporate goal.'

Frederick Reichheld (1996)

There have been a number of major corporate management trends over the last two decades which have been hailed as breakthroughs in how to do business, but have not quite lived up to their early promise. These include Total Quality Management (TQM), Business Process Re-engineering (BPR), virtual teamworking, and so on.

Throughout the 1990s, customer loyalty was another 'craze', and as we move into the mid-2000s, it remains a talking point, arousing the concerns of senior managers who unfortunately often don't act on these concerns. A recent study found that while about 80 per cent of marketing directors claimed customer loyalty was a high priority for them, only about 50 per cent said they measured loyalty, and even worse, only 30 per cent did *anything at all* about improving loyalty.

In spite of this, this book argues that customer loyalty is very important to companies and should not be seen as another 'fad'. Loyal behaviour has been directly linked to company profitability across a convincingly wide array of sectors. Indeed prioritising customer loyalty as the primary generator of profit is not new. The traditional direct marketers, mail-order companies and so on, have understood the superior profitability of existing customers, compared with new customers, for many decades.

Linking loyalty with direct marketing

An emphasis on loyalty is of great interest to direct marketers. This is because there is a *natural alignment* of direct marketing – philosophy, measures, and systems – with the notion of retaining customers. In particular, direct marketing can do the following:

1. Direct marketing can orchestrate the targeting of the most valuable customers and those who are intrinsically loyal.

2. Direct marketing can help *create* customer loyalty. It is often claimed that direct marketers can create loyalty – direct marketing initiatives, tied to price, the product, or service, can improve the value the customer gets from the company. Potentially more powerful, the customer database can orchestrate the development of one-to-one relationships which, if they come to pass, will surely have an impact on loyalty. However, the reader is cautioned: as yet there remains a paucity of evidence to back this up: it is still early days for the one-to-one concept.

3. We are on much more solid ground in asserting that direct marketing can *take advantage* of customer loyalty to maximise revenue. We can take advantage of the loyalty by understanding how to market to existing customers so that both they and the company get maximum value from the association.

4. Finally, direct marketing can measure customer retention. Both Reichheld (1996) and the relationship marketing academics (Payne, 1995) have pinpointed this as an absolutely crucial area. It is a truism in business that little gets done unless it can be measured. Customer retention is very difficult to measure, and unquestionably the most efficient tool for the job is the database. Where other systems measure customer satisfaction and use this as a surrogate for retention, a database can track customer spend over time – the only way to measure customer retention.

In order to decide the allocation of resources to customer loyalty, we need to understand how loyalty and profit are linked.

The economics of customer loyalty

The primary figure in clarifying the connection between loyalty and profit has been Reichheld (1996) whose book *The Loyalty Effect* set out clearly why loyalty is so important. The following example illustrates the point:

Example

In this example we examine the relative profitability for a company that achieves 90 per cent versus 95 per cent retention rates over seven years. The retention rate is the percentage of customers with the company at the start of the year, who remain with it at the end of the year.

The figures in Tables 6.1 and 6.2 compare the situation of 100 customers over a seven-year period. Each customer costs an average of £30 to recruit. Each customer that leaves has to be replaced, at cost to the company. Each customer is worth £10 per annum in gross margin.

If we ignore net present value calculations for the sake of simplicity, what are the comparable profit figures after seven years?

Table 6.1: **90% retention rate**

| | Year | | | | | | |
	1	2	3	4	5	6	7
100 customers' recruitment cost	3000	0	0	0	0	0	0
Replacement costs if ten leave each year		300	300	300	300	300	300
Margin @ £10 per customer per year	1000	1000	1000	1000	1000	1000	1000
Margin (cumulative)	-2000	-1300	-600	+100	+800	1500	**2200**

The final cumulative profit of 100 customers at 90 per cent retention is £2200.

Table 6.2: **95% retention rate**

| | Year | | | | | | |
	1	2	3	4	5	6	7
100 customers' recruitment cost	3000	0	0	0	0	0	0
Replacement costs if five leave each year		150	150	150	150	150	150
Margin @ £10 per customer per year	1000	1000	1000	1000	1000	1000	1000
Margin (cumulative)	-2000	-1150	-300	+650	1500	2350	**3200**

The final cumulative profit of 100 customers at 95 per cent retention is £3200.

In other words, in this example, *a five per cent increase in customer retention has led to a 45 per cent increase in cumulative profit* over the seven-year period.

Bain and Co. (Reichheld, 1996) conducted research into this effect and found that a small increase in retention rate had a hugely disproportionate effect on profit *in every sector examined*. Most spectacular of all was the credit-card industry, where a 5 per cent increase in customer retention led to a profit improvement of 125 per cent! In general, given that a typical company loses between 10–30 per cent of its customers in a year, the potential for improving profitability by focusing on loyalty is dramatic.

This example highlights the leverage that loyalty has on profitability, but it does not clearly explain *why* retaining customers is so profitable. There are a number of reasons which are important for direct marketers.

Reasons for retention leading to higher profits

1 No acquisition costs

The importance of acquisition costs on profitability is highlighted in the previous example. Whether you use direct marketing or not, acquisition costs in most businesses are high. One major financial services company found the average acquisition cost per customer for loans was £280. Acquisition costs in credit-card companies are typically £50 or more; in insurance they are often over £100. Charities now expect to lose money on fundraising activity aimed at acquiring new donors. As we saw in the example, the more we can keep customers, the less costly acquisition we need to do.

One way to visualise the importance of retention is to think of a company as a bucket with a hole in the bottom. Customers are acquired through the top of the bucket, while at the same time the company is leaking customers who defect (*see* Fig. 6.2). Let us imagine two companies, both of which acquire customers at a rate of 10 per cent per year. One loses 5 per cent of its customers per year, and the other loses 10 per cent. The company with the lower rate of loss doubles in size every 14 years. The other company has zero growth.

2 Price premium

Reichheld (1996) found that 'old' customers pay higher prices than new ones. This is partly because of the mechanic of trial discounts aimed only at new customers (discussed at length in Chapter 9). However, more fundamentally, it is because loyal customers are

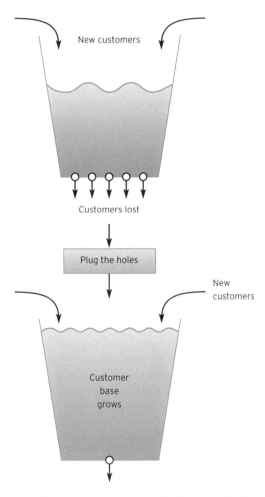

Figure 6.2 Preventing the 'leaking' of customers increases company growth

happy with the value they are getting from the company. Loyal customers ignore vouchers and coupons, and are less price sensitive on individual items than new customers.

There is an interesting irony here: many companies have 'loyalty schemes' which offer lower prices via points systems in return for loyal custom; but companies whose customers only stay with them because of the loyalty scheme don't have genuinely loyal customers. Reichheld (1996) asserted again and again in his book that companies can't *buy* loyalty. They can only earn it through consistently creating superior value for their customers.

Direct marketing can help to take advantage of the price-premium effect. Database-driven marketing allows us to know who our most loyal customers are. We can market to these customers accordingly, ensuring they receive excellent service, and avoiding offering them unnecessary discounts.

3 Referrals

Mature, satisfied customers give more referrals; that is, they recommend the company to their friends. Referred prospects in turn convert at a higher rate than prospects recruited 'cold'. Referred new customers end up staying longer, because they were originally similar types of people to existing customers anyway, and so are more likely to stay. In other words, retained customers help to lower the average acquisition cost of new customers.

Direct marketing is excellently placed to maximise this effect by using a tactic called Member Get Member (MGM), which gives a company's own customers incentives to recommend it to others.

4 Revenue growth

In most businesses, customers buy more off you when they get to know you better. In retailing, for example, as customers get to know more of your product lines, they buy more; as their trust in you increases, they buy more. Direct marketers can proactively learn with customers, anticipate their future needs and develop more products to meet them. Customers of a car dealer may start with a basic car service, but loyal customers may move to valeting, warranties, hire cars, and so on, as they get to know more of the dealer's business and learn to trust them more.

However Reichheld's work has recently been questioned by Reinartz and Kumar in a high profile *Harvard Business Review* article (2002). They found little or no evidence to suggest that customers who purchase steadily from a company over time are necessarily cheaper to serve, less price sensitive, or particularly effective at bringing in new business. Their conclusions were based on a four-year study of four different businesses in the US and Europe, and found only a moderate link between loyalty and profitability. Sometimes short-term customers were very profitable, but not worth chasing because they would not come back. Sometimes long-term customers were basically unprofitable.

It may be that Reinartz and Kumar's analysis is a more accurate reflection of business reality than Reichheld's. This is not necessarily bad news for direct marketers. Reinartz and Kumar conclude that the use of data mining on customer data is a sound approach that helps identify who is profitable and who is not. Let's take a closer look:

Table 6.3: Database marketing strategies for Reinartz and Kumar's model

Name of segment	Description	Strategy
'Strangers'	Customers who have no loyalty and bring in no profits	Identify early and don't invest anything
'Butterflies'	Customers who are profitable but disloyal	Milk them for as much as the short time they are buying from you
'True friends'	Profitable customers who are likely to be loyal	Adopt a softly-softly approach
'Barnacles'	Highly loyal but not very profitable customers	Find out whether they have the potential to spend more than they currently do

EXHIBIT 6.1

UNDERSTANDING LOYALTY

Customers can be loyal to many different things. They can be loyal to people – perhaps to a friend they make who is their contact in a business supplier, or to a friendly cashier at the bank, or to their local village shopkeeper.

They may be loyal to a brand, which in some way symbolises a group of people. Bikers who ride sports motorbikes nod to other sports bikers, although strangers, when they pass them on the road. Mini car drivers may be members of a club where they meet and socialise around their common passion.

Reichheld (1996) reports that Josiah Royce, Professor of Philosophy at Harvard University, wrote a book, *The Philosophy of Loyalty*, in 1908 in which he asserted that the highest form of loyalty is to values and principles. Reichheld holds that this is relevant to businesses too; but most companies don't earn loyalty through too much commitment to self interest. In the charity sector, there is a great deal of interest currently in developing fundraising strategies around shared values.

Reichheld believes philosophically that business loyalty is all about 'finding that elusive balance between self interest and team interest'.

The trouble with loyalty

To what extent are customers naturally loyal, and to what extent can their behaviour be changed? As long ago as 1972, work by Ehrenberg found that customers exhibited little brand loyalty across all the sectors studied, including many packaged goods categories, airlines, clothing, retail and others. An analysis of car insurance (Cram, 1994) found that 60 per cent of customers had switched companies in the preceding five years, many more than once. Of the remaining 40 per cent, many will only be 'loyal' through a lack of interest in shopping around. Hardly a ringing endorsement.

In retail the story is similar. Pressey and Matthews (2000) emphasise that despite the recent use of loyalty cards and database marketing techniques by UK retailers, most transactions are 'discrete, short-term, one-off acts'.

Customers exhibit more complex patterns of behaviour than just 'loyalty' or 'switching'. In fact customers see the whole issue of loyalty in a different way to marketers. As

McCorkell (1997) noted, 'The notion of customer loyalty is important to marketing people, but not, on the whole, to customers. Customers don't see why they should not accept a good offer from a new supplier just because they are satisfied with their present one.'

A lot of frequent-purchase behaviour (e.g. supermarket goods) is based on 'repertoire' purchasing, in that customers retain a basket of brands which they jump between in a 'polygamous' fashion. A number of reasons may account for repertoire purchasing:

■ **different brands satisfying different needs:** we may buy one brand of coffee for everyday use and quite another for a dinner party;

■ **deal switching:** some people prioritise getting a discount for their brand choice;

■ **time/convenience factors:** customers of airlines usually make their choice of carrier based on route and time. Brand loyalty is therefore low. Similarly, petrol purchases depend largely on convenience.

The clear conclusion from these different pieces of work is that exclusive brand loyalty cannot be regarded as the norm in most markets.

What are direct marketers to do with this finding? First, it is important to recognise reality, especially in the face of so much emphasis on loyalty in texts and trade press, much of which do not recognise the inherent complexities of 'loyal' customer behaviour. Second, we should recognise that striving for exclusive loyalty in some markets, for example wine purchase, is not a realistic goal; it is better to aim to be a part of customers' repertoire. Third, companies need to identify active loyals (those who have assessed other options and made an active decision to stay) and seek to keep them happy.

Most important, we can recognise that Reichheld's and Ehrenberg's findings can sit alongside each other: loyalty may not be the norm, but any improvement in retention of the right – that is profitable – customers will be extremely beneficial. Attaining loyalty is, however, hard work.

EXHIBIT 6.2

LOYALTY: WHY DON'T COMPANIES PRACTISE WHAT THEY PREACH?

Loyalty was probably the management 'buzzword' of the 1990s. However, very few companies have really believed in its principles and convincingly gone about building loyalty. In truth, most people seem to smile and agree that loyalty is important, but do they really believe, deep down, that customers can be loyal? Perhaps not. In many companies, employees do not trust their customers: the managers talk about service, but the day-to-day attitudes betray a belief that their customers are out to rip them off. These cultural attitudes are in direct conflict with a commitment to loyalty, and form a vicious circle; less loyalty means more acquisition, more acquisition means more of the 'wrong' type of customers and less trust in the system.

Investigating business priorities, the DMA Census (2003) finds that business people place 'improving customer satisfaction' and 'improving customer acquisition' as third and fourth on their priority list. But although business people may say they want more customer satisfaction, their actions often suggest otherwise. And it is argued throughout this book that it is customer retention, not customer acquisition, that is the real strength of direct marketing. Undue emphasis on the merry-go-round of customer acquisition creates problems, as customers become loyal to bribes rather than brands.

Companies such as MBNA have shown that by sharing value with your core custom you are rewarded with better loyalty and higher profits.

How can direct marketing help firms achieve customer loyalty?

In their sales pitches to clients, direct marketing agencies may claim that database-driven marketing can create loyalty. A strategy for a car manufacturer who wants to increase loyalty from consumers may be to maintain contact with the customer in between purchases. This could be done using, say, a quarterly magazine and well-timed mailings inviting the driver for a test drive of the latest range. But will this really enhance loyalty? Customer magazines have researched very well for many companies, and the trigger to come along and enjoy a test drive is an important part of the selling process; but it is hard to believe that these measures *in isolation* will cure a car company's defection problems.

Reichheld (1996) pointed out right at the beginning of his book that the creation of loyalty is a corporate, rather than a marketing, strategy. It therefore cannot be just delegated to the marketing department as a bolt-on extra, a 'campaign'. Imagine a situation where an airline with limited routes, a poor safety record, sullen service delivery, ordinary meals in flight, and so on, had a 'loyalty' pricing scheme based on Air Miles. This is not a successful recipe for customer retention. There is now substantial evidence (Pressey and Matthews, 2000; Hartley, 1997) that loyalty schemes used without a strong underpinning have little or no effect on loyalty.

According to Reichheld, and underpinned by many influential marketing strategists such as Piercy (1997) and Doyle (2002), the key to retention is *creating superior value for customers*. Loyalty is a consequence of creating value for customers, and profit is a consequence of loyalty. Reichheld found that those companies which enjoyed superior levels of loyalty had focused on people – employees and customers – not systems. In some industries where service is not a prime consideration, it may be pricing that has irresistible power over consumers' decisions.

Direct marketing's true role in creating loyalty is moulded by these wider considerations. If we accept Reichheld's logic, then direct marketers should recognise that they are part of a *corporate* effort to concentrate on creating value for customers. We will take a close look at how direct marketing can contribute to improved customer loyalty later in this chapter.

In summary, in spite of the doubts and difficulties surrounding it, improving customer loyalty remains important for businesses, and it is perhaps the most important strategic influence on direct marketing. Let us now turn to an area that more recently, is increasingly recognised as also very important: the use of database knowledge throughout the company.

The use of marketing databases in the wider company environment

In this section we take a look at how direct and database marketing can influence events in non-marketing areas of the company – outside of the marketing department. This can be illustrated in Fig. 6.3.

The marketing database can help companies whose service would otherwise be disabled by their sheer size. DeTienne and Thompson (1996) pointed out that larger companies tend to lose track of minute market information. Often this information lost

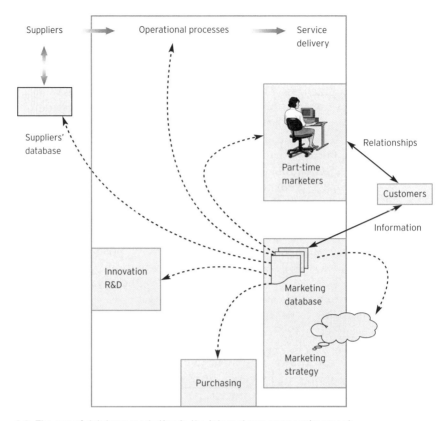

Figure 6.3 The use of database marketing in the internal company environment

includes key elements of what the customer values in his or her personal relationships with the company. However, recording personal information can help customer service people deliver the best service to customers (Gronroos, 1996; Stone and Woodcock, 1997; Bessen, 1993). This is now common business practice for service companies that make heavy use of inbound telephone channels, and in sectors such as hotels which deliver priority service to high-value customers. In all these examples, however, the marketing database is not enabling the marketing department to provide better service; rather, it is helping part-time marketers (Gummesson 1991) in the customer-facing functions give at least an impression of familiarity with the customer.

Another attribute of the marketing database is the ease with which its data and information can be accessed by the organisation as a whole (Bessen, 1993). For example Fletcher and Wright (1997) argued that DBM information could help to strengthen the supplier/buyer position by using market information to cut out inefficiency, share stock-holding with suppliers, optimise sales channels and measure supplier performance. More recently the so-called 'efficient consumer response' (Piercy, 1997) approach that describes manufacturing firms' relationships with retailers also makes use of networked databases.

This new role for database marketers, *as facilitators*, reflects the work of writers such as Gronroos (1996), Gummesson (1991) and Christopher (1996), who argue that a marketer's role is to motivate the company to adopt a greater market focus. These are just some examples of the potential of marketing databases in company-wide situations.

In summary, as DeTienne and Thompson (1996) point out, if the organisation is good at learning, the database transcends the status of a record-keeping device and becomes an implement of ever-increasing organisational knowledge. This knowledge is transferable to any part of the company, thanks to the increasing simplicity of user interfaces provided by modern technology. If an operator in the research and development arm of the company wants to see what types of customers are using what products, he or she can do so.

These developments are in fact all examples of important developments in sharing knowledge throughout the business. This quite separate area of study is known as knowledge management, and is discussed next.

EXHIBIT 6.3

USING DATA FOR COMPANY-WIDE KNOWLEDGE MANAGEMENT - TESCO CLUBCARD

UK retailer Tesco had stolen a march on its main rival, Sainsbury, through the launch of its loyalty scheme, Clubcard, in 1995. By 1997 however Sainsbury had responded with its own Reward card scheme. Tesco knew it had to work hard to maintain its lead. Its next challenge lay not with marketing communications - the card had been accepted by customers - but instead *within* the company. How could Tesco best use the data throughout the business? It identified a number of areas.

First, price. Tesco was keen to avoid a damaging price war, with Asda in particular. Yet it needed to remain competitive. It used shopping-basket analysis to identify price-sensitive customers through the clever device of homing in on Tesco value-margarine buyers. Tesco knew these buyers would be price sensitive right across the range. Special efforts were made to look after these customers.

The second area was purchasing. Purchasing from suppliers is one of the most important and powerful functions in retailing. The aim was to ensure that all the 60 000 lines on sale in an average superstore accurately reflected what customers wanted. This will of course vary geographically, and according to the social make-up of the clientele.

Third, new product development. Areas such as gourmet eating, organics, food allergy sufferers, dieters or healthy eaters provided rich pickings for the developers who, week by week, would look to innovate. Clubcard data was invaluable, not in directly answering these questions, but in setting the scene. It helped them understand better who tried what, and allowed them to build mental pictures of the lives of their customers.

Finally, competitive strategy. So far the Clubcard had primarily been used for loyalty - defence. Tesco's analysts now turned their attention to improving their market share. Clubcard allowed them to know more than either of their main rivals: the challenge now was offensive marketing.

Source: Humby, C., Hunt, T. and Phillips, T. (2003) *Scoring Points, How Tesco is Winning Customer Loyalty*, Kogan Page, London.

Knowledge management

WHAT IS KNOWLEDGE MANAGEMENT?

Perhaps triggered by the widespread adoption of business process re-engineering, which has involved shedding large numbers of middle managers, many of whom left the company taking vital knowledge with them, interest in knowledge management has exploded since the mid-1990s. Knowledge management (KM) has been widely adopted by practitioners who have led academics in developing the area. A lot of the interest in KM has been generated by the large management consultancies such as McKinsey, Ernst and Young and so on, who have used KM extensively in their own internal organisations. Bassi (1997) defined knowledge management as the process of creating, capturing, and using knowledge to enhance business performance. The dominant discourse of KM is how to better exploit the knowledge of employees through tools and methods.

The possible use of database marketing in knowledge management was first put forward by DeTienne and Thompson (1996) who pointed out that a customer database is an opportunity for organisations to mechanise the process of learning about customers. As they state: 'The usefulness of DBM for organisational learning is partly in its iterative nature.' In Chapter 13, the subject of testing in direct marketing explores this iterative learning in more detail. The point here is that iterative learning could be expanded beyond tactical promotions to a wider environment within the firm. What we will do now is to explore in more detail what knowledge management actually is, and create a picture of how database marketing could help companies improve their knowledge working.

THE NATURE OF KNOWLEDGE

Much of KM theory is based on positivism, the idea being that 'knowledge is truth', and a matter of *linking facts* to assemble ever more knowledge. In this sense a marketing database is a positivist tool, with knowledge presented in a logical manner, and the emphasis on testing and quantitative analysis. One example of this is data mining, the use of powerful analysis tools to extricate patterns from large volumes of complex data, which has become the subject of great interest by database marketers (Finerty, 1997).

An alternative view of knowledge management is that presented from a social constructivist paradigm. Here, knowledge is an everyday experience, embedded in the unwritten systems and cultures of the organisation. One illustration of this is database marketers' 'ways of thinking' about business, and their 'market sensing', i.e. a focus on managers, understanding of the market rather than on market information (Piercy, 1997). Database marketers build up their market *understanding* through examination of customer data, and through their experiences of how customers react to direct marketing initiatives.

Many writers seem to agree that knowledge is much more subtle than, say, the output of a data-mining analysis. It is more difficult to define than that: it could be the outcome of everyday experience. Some insights were that knowledge is 'messy'; it travels via language; it slips away the more it is pinned down; it does not respond to rules and systems; and the more loosely it is managed the better. It seems that attempts to 'manage' knowledge too closely will lead to problems. The big success story of database-driven knowledge management is Tesco. It seems to understand when to closely manage the analysis, and when to let it go its own way; when to go with a hunch based on experience, and when to question conventional wisdoms.

Writers have split knowledge into two types.

TACIT AND EXPLICIT KNOWLEDGE

Hansen *et al.* (1999) distinguished between *tacit* and *explicit* knowledge. Explicit knowledge is important when existing knowledge needs to be re-used to tackle problems with known solutions. Tacit knowledge is 'deep' knowledge needed for complex problems not encountered before. McAdam and McCreedy (1999) identify the distinctive characteristics of tacit and explicit knowledge. They quote Polanyi defining tacit knowledge as non-verbalised, intuitive and unarticulated. Explicit knowledge is specified as being in writing, drawings or computer records. Clearly, knowledge held on marketing databases is explicit, while much of the knowledge held by database marketers will be tacit.

Bearing all this in mind, we can now take a look at a model of how database marketing can help with the management of knowledge.

HOW DATABASE MARKETING CAN HELP WITH KNOWLEDGE MANAGEMENT

Knowledge management is about the capture or creation, codification, distribution, sharing, combination, use and finally retention of knowledge within a company. However, the emphasis in the model (*see* Fig. 6.4) is on using DBM knowledge in non-marketing environments, probably by *combining* it with local knowledge. This is illustrated in the central box of the model.

The role of database marketing – transforming knowledge

Marketing databases have a role to transform (and record) explicit knowledge. Moreover database marketers themselves may have a vital role in helping combine explicit and tacit, or tacit and tacit knowledge in order to solve complex problems, for example in a

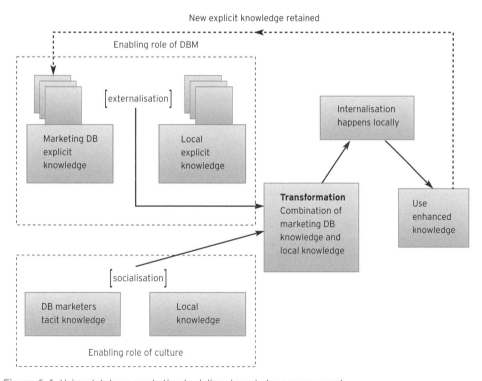

Figure 6.4 Using database marketing to deliver knowledge management

business undergoing change. Database marketers can also help by using the powerful analysis tools available (*see* Chapter 3) to transform explicit knowledge into higher forms, which (when combined in another department such as finance) may transform to *tacit* knowledge through an internalisation process.

The final element to the model is the use of the (transformed) knowledge. The temptation for database marketers has been to use the database to *record* (explicit) knowledge, yet the emphasis of the model in Fig. 6.4 reflects recent literature by emphasising the *creation* and *use* of knowledge rather than its recording. As Scarborough *et al.* (1999) put it: 'Technology should be viewed more as a means of communication and less as a means of storing knowledge.'

It is undoubtedly *usage* (*i.e. acting knowledgeably*) which appears to be the Achilles heel of knowledge management theory and practice. McAdam and McCreedy (1999) and Scarborough *et al.* (1999) see employee motivation, reward and benefits as the key elements in solving this dilemma. Meanwhile Harris (1996) sees measures of success as key to motivating managers to be market focused. Taking our cue primarily from these authors, the following initiatives may encourage the use of marketing databases across the business:

■ introducing customer-related measures of management performance;

■ using database marketing knowledge as shared currency between different departments, thereby encouraging 'shared language' and hence helping to break down barriers;

■ encouraging the use of DBM information as a powerful way of making market focus a reality.

If the steps shown in Fig. 6.4 can be implemented, then better market orientation should result. According to Kohli and Jaworski (1990) market-orientated firms will: place a priority on the collection and understanding of customer information; encourage the sharing of this information throughout the company; and place a company-wide priority to respond to these needs. Using this definition it is proposed that database marketing can improve market orientation by:

■ facilitating the collection of customer needs data across the business;

■ overcoming organisational barriers by enabling easier dissemination of customer knowledge;

■ using simple user interfaces to facilitate easy analysis and combination of customer knowledge with other knowledge centres in the firm; and

■ using knowledge-management techniques to encourage and reward the subsequent market focus.

So far in this chapter we have looked at the major strategic influences on direct marketing. Recently, however, some concerns have been raised about the lack of practice of some of these elements. The next section takes a closer look.

Recent concerns about the role of direct marketing

As we have seen, the key strategic roles of direct marketing have centred around the use of the database in driving customer management, and its role in creating and maintaining relationships, which taken to an extreme can result in one-to-one marketing (see page 186). However, recently either these concepts or direct marketing as a way of delivering them have attracted criticism.

As noted earlier, Payne (1995) argued that relationship marketing can be applied to consumer markets. However, there has been little evidence of this happening in practice. As Gronroos (1996) (among others) has pointed out, relationship marketing works only when businesses make it their primary aim to construct a mutually beneficial relationship with customers, and then allow profits to fall from this. The failure of most companies to deliver this could be linked to the lack of cost-effective relationship-building programmes using direct and database marketing. More likely, however, is the fact that companies have simply not 'put their money where their mouth is'. One example might be a bank delivering a 'relationship-building magazine' to its customers, while at the same time shutting down its rural branches in a cost-cutting measure. The company has indicated that when the chips are down it is more interested in cost efficiencies than relationship building. In summary, at present there seems little evidence linking database-driven approaches with genuine customer relationship development (Fournier *et al.*, 1998; Rosenfield, 1999; O'Malley and Tynan, 2000).

It also has to be said that the level of customer-management practice has been a disappointment. QCi's State of the Nation report (Woodcock *et al.* 2003) into global CRM highlighted the poor state of most practice in a host of direct marketing-related disciplines, including contact management, measurement, segmentation and database analysis. This is not new: Fletcher and Wright (1997) researched the use of database marketing in a strategic context and found levels of sophistication were low, while Stone and Woodcock (1997) investigated the use of DBM for customer management and found that organisational structures and cultures typically militated against good practice. Meanwhile, there are very few success stories that can be credited to one-to-one concepts (Mitchell, 1998).

At the heart of these issues is the argument about whether direct marketing is a strategic or tactical tool, and whether its home lies with transaction marketing (4Ps) or relationship marketing/customer management. At present the jury is out.

Meanwhile, the rhetoric of the business continues to hype customer management. Recent work by Gartner (2003) suggests that attempts at seller-driven 'customer management' – for instance predictive direct mail with cross-sell offers – is typically seen as intrusive, and yields are typically 2–3 per cent response at best. If, however, the marketing contact is related to a customer event, for instance moving home, customers regard such contact as much more convenient for them. Response rates may rise to values like 20 per cent. Best of all is to cross sell when the customer rings into the company on the *customer's* initiative – you may get 40 per cent responses to these approaches. These figures tell us a lot about how customers wish to be approached. They are quite happy to be approached about goods and services – but the timing has to reflect their position – do they want to buy? But the reality may be that the continued rise of direct marketing can be attributed to its ability in making old fashioned transaction marketing more efficient (see, e.g., Bouchard, 1999) by lowering the costs of going to market compared with sales force and retail/advertising models. Similarly the continued use of loyalty marketing tools such as loyalty cards probably has little to do with loyalty. Instead, such tools allow companies to target their transaction marketing more efficiently. Perhaps the best thing is for us to stay in touch with these arguments as they develop. Meanwhile, let's get on with the substance of direct marketing, and get back to what it has undeniably been good at – delivering the goods.

Delivering direct marketing strategies

Our direct marketing strategy model in Chapter 5 highlighted the importance to direct marketers of segmentation and targeting. We will therefore now consider these in more detail, before looking at how direct marketing can help to deliver more customer value.

DELIVERING SEGMENTATION AND TARGETING

Segmentation

Direct marketing has the ability to deliver *precisely defined* segmentations of existing customers, where each customer is placed in each segment with complete accuracy. This contrasts with segmentations in classical marketing, where it is educated guesswork that a customer lies in a particular segment. Because of the inevitable wastage, this raises the costs and reduces the accuracy with which classical marketing works.

The first step in our retention strategy is therefore to decide whether we should segment at all. Segmenting in order to communicate with different groups of customers in different ways, or to offer each a different product, costs money and takes a lot of effort. We have to decide whether it is worth it: will our customers value a more individual approach and be more profitable as a result? Harley Davidson found that for its motorbike business segmenting by product usage was worthwhile and has strategically gone down this route. Most retail banks in the UK, however, undertake little segmentation for much of their business; they have many managerial hurdles to overcome in order to segment with much sophistication, and in many instances they opt for a 'mass direct marketing' approach.

Probably the most powerful methods of segmentation, executed very effectively by direct marketing, are splitting by value – what customers are worth to us; splitting by need – what customers want from us; and segmenting by predicted response. All these are extensively covered in Chapter 3, so we just need to remind ourselves here of their strategic importance. The other key segmentation approach to add is segmenting by loyalty.

Segmenting by loyalty

Reichheld (1996) recommended isolating valuable customers in a slightly different way. He proposed that top priority be given to targeting those customers who are predictably loyal and stable. He found many businesses which boasted customers who were *inherently* more loyal than others. MBNA, a US credit-card provider, found that professions were the important loyalty segmenter. Teachers, accountants, nurses and engineers all showed more *innate* loyalty than the average. So did older, married people living in rural areas. These people were more attracted to familiarity and hence less deal conscious than average. MBNA, at considerable expense, targeted only affinity groups showing this innate loyalty. It has paid off: MBNA's profit levels are among the highest in the world in its sector.

Another key group may be those whose current spend with the company is modest, but whose potential is much greater. Frequent business flyers typically belong to a number of airline 'clubs' at the same time. For each airline, they may not register as a heavy spender, but their potential, if they were to focus on one carrier, is great. Using a

SEGMENTING BY LOYALTY: BUSINESS-TO-BUSINESS MARKETS

Research has found the following segments which exhibit different loyalties:

- **Programmed buyers:** small customers, less price sensitive, purchase is a routine;
- **Relationship buyers:** small, more knowledgeable, seek partnership;
- **Transaction buyers:** large customers, very knowledgeable, balance price and service;
- **Bargain hunters:** large customers, switch readily, price/service sensitive.

mixture of behavioural and profiled data, it is possible to segment and then market to these customers accordingly. For example, the high-potential frequent flyers may be offered more value in the form of better service or a one-off offer of free Air Miles.

Faced with these segmentation options, the direct marketer needs guidance. Certainly, Reichheld's loyalty-based segmentation is worth serious consideration, given his evidence of the link between loyalty and profit. However, at present, relatively few companies appear to segment in this way, possibly because loyalty is relatively difficult to measure. What we need to do is keep an overview of all the above options, and decide which is best for our situation.

Targeting

When targeting *existing* customers in order to keep them and maximise their profitability, priority segments include:

- the most valuable customers;
- the most loyal customers;
- customers with great potential for revenue growth: these may be low spenders with us, but big spenders with our competitors;
- loss-making customers: we can look for ways to make our company unattractive to these customers, edging them out of the business;
- 'segments' identified through statistics as most likely to respond to the next offer, based on their buying history or other data.

Targeting *new* customers is more problematical. Our options depend on two things: first, the market choice – are we trying to attract our competitors' customers, or are we looking for entirely new markets? Second, the extent to which we know who our prospects are – do we have a tightly defined profile? If we have a well-defined profile and are looking for prospects in our existing market, we can be much more precise in our targeting than if we were looking for poorly defined prospects in unfamiliar markets.

The top-priority categories for targeting are:

- **recently lapsed customers;**
- **former customers:** used the company in the past but are now with a competitor;
- **enquirers:** have contacted the company but are not yet customers;

- **referrals:** recommended by existing customers;
- **profiled prospects:** statistical profiles based on existing (loyal) customers;
- **'handraisers':** prospects who select themselves via the use of responsive advertising.

The lowest priority are **suspects** contacted through market research profiles, new markets and the use of responsive advertising.

Figure 6.5 shows us that our options are as follows:

- targeting prospects based on previous contact of some sort with the company;
- targeting based on the principle that new customers will be similar to existing customers;
- targeting based on *predicted loyalty* to the company, again based on existing customer profiles;
- targeting a commercial partner's customers, known as affinity marketing;
- asking new customers to identify themselves.

Targeting based on previous contact

Our top priority lies with enquirers, former customers and recent lapsers, who should all be held on the customer database. They have already shown an interest in the company and its products. Indeed, former customers and recent lapsers may not, in their minds, have lapsed at all. People drift in and out of relationships with companies, without seeing this as active switching. They may have a repertoire of brands to provide variety; they may have forgotten to renew their subscription; or a dozen other factors may have affected their status with you. The only instance in which lapsers are not your best prospects is when they have experienced dissatisfaction with your company and this has not been resolved. (In this case, they may still be top priority for contact, to try to

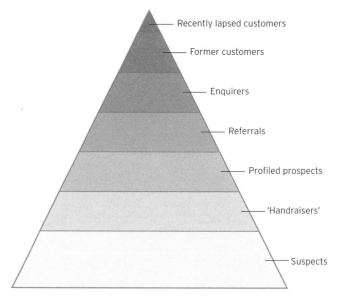

Figure 6.5 Hierarchy of acquisition targeting options

recover the situation. Relationship marketers (Payne, 1995) have pointed out the dangers of ignoring dissatisfied former customers who have a tendency to tell many others of their horror stories!) Referrals, motivated by word of mouth recommendations, are the next highest priority.

TIMING: THE UNSUNG HERO OF DIRECT MARKETING

Much of marketing these days consists of getting the right offer to the right audience but at the wrong time. Direct marketing acquisition can be accurately timed so that the offer reaches prospects when they are actively in the market.

This can be done using data collected on external databases; for example, the likely date of next car purchase can be collected. Timing to enquirers or lapsers can be even more accurate. If you ask Direct Line Insurance for a quote on car insurance and then decline to take up the offer, you are held on file as an enquirer. Exactly one year later, the company can be pretty sure you are in the market for car insurance once more, and it can time its offers very precisely.

Targeting based on profiles of existing customers

Targeting based on profiling was fully described in Chapter 4; here we can see where the technique fits strategically.

If you have a database of existing customers, the opportunity exists to build up detailed *profiles* and match these statistically with *prospect* lists. A golf supplier may find his existing customers have a high propensity to live in 'leafy suburb' geodemographic areas. The supplier can then rent a list of such prospects from a geodemographic system agency.

Targeting the most loyal customers

*'It's hard to concentrate on acquisition quality when quantity is so much easier...
Winning more and more new customers could slowly put you out of business.'*

Frederick Reichheld (1996)

Reichheld (1996) argues that the best new customers are those that are similar to your own most loyal customers. We can get help in targeting based on loyalty from Cram (1994), who, taking a relationship marketing view, suggests the following prospects as being the top priorities:

1. **Referrals:** Cram found that people who respond because of the recommendation of a friend or colleague are more likely to stay than the respondent to an advertisement.

2. **People who buy at the standard price:** These are more loyal than sales promotion respondents – 'deal conscious' consumers who are loyal to the discount, not the brand. According to Reichheld, getting these 'wrong' customers can quickly erode the efficiency and strength of the company.

3. **Risk-averse consumers:** These are more loyal than experimenters. Cautious customers are more likely to stick with you.

4. **Customers looking for high levels of service:** Cram asserted that customers who value service, and are willing to pay for it, are in turn more loyal than those who don't.

5. **Customers seeking a high level of personalisation:** Tailored service inspires loyalty. A book club that tailors its offers depending on individual tastes will attract consumers interested in that service.

EXHIBIT 6.6

TARGETING NEW CUSTOMERS: SOUTHWESTERN BELL

Cable TV is still being established in many markets worldwide. In the UK the market was opened in the early 1990s. The industry operates around the laying of cable in the ground, with the residents of each street that is laid with cable being followed up with door-to-door salespeople. Acquisition is clearly the priority in these early stages, with 70 per cent of SouthWestern Bell's budget going on acquisition in 1994, for example.

However, cabling is expensive, with infrastructure costs at £500 per subscribed house, and costs of sale another £200. With average revenues running at £15–20 per annum per house, it is therefore critical that acquisition is accurately targeted with long retention in mind. Initially, SouthWestern Bell (SWB) found that lapse rates for its services were about 5 per cent, twice those found in the US. The company was looking for improved loyalty.

SWB decided to link its acquisition to loyalty, and put in place marketing programmes which avoided marketing at all to those households where expected defections would be high. Analysis of its existing customers, in terms of their geodemographic profiles, was carried out using MOSAIC. Among others, they found a high proportion of 'prosperous pensioners' and 'singles and flat dwellers' in the profile. These were two of the highest priority groups targeted for new customer acquisition. These areas were targeted with more expensive contact strategies: mail, telesales and direct salespeople. On the other hand, lower priority areas would receive only door-drop leaflets.

Source: Coyne, A. (1994) 'A case study of data-driven marketing in the cable industry,' *Journal of Database Marketing*, **2** (1).

Affinity marketing

An entirely new method of acquisition has been developed primarily by direct marketers, known as affinity marketing. Affinity marketing is the use of a commercial partner's brand and customer base to provide a ready market for your product. Thus, a typical set-up may be a bank promoting a credit card to a charity's audience. The credit card is co-branded with the charity logo and the bank marque. In return for access to the charity list and use of the logo, the bank pays a sum to the charity each time a transaction is made, typically 0.25 per cent of the transaction.

The point of affinity marketing to acquire customers is the extra leverage that the strong branding bond your partner has with its customers can offer you. People often have a strong affinity for organisations such as their favourite charity, their university, or the football team they support. They are therefore more likely to take up offers which come from such organisations.

Strategically, affinity marketing is an important area because it raises the crucial concept of *partnerships* between *non-competing organisations* for mutual gain. Partnership marketing can be a way of overcoming the often stifling similarity of many companies to their competitors. Direct marketers can take advantage of such strategic alliances in

EXHIBIT 6.7

TO AFFINITY AND BEYOND: BENEFICIAL BANK

The name Beneficial Bank is not widely known, not even to its own customers! This is because it offers third-party affinity cards to people, and the branding on the cards is that of the affinity partner. Beneficial has teamed up with organisations such as Tottenham Hotspur, The Law Society, The Police Federation and Cambridge University.

The benefits of these tie-ups go to all parties involved. The card holder receives a Visa card with no annual fee and a highly competitive APR. For the affinity partner, Beneficial pays a one-off fee of about £5 for every member who takes up the card,

plus 25p for every £100 spent on the card. These amounts soon add up for the partner: Open University has benefited to the tune of hundreds of thousands of pounds.

The benefit to Beneficial is that it does not have to go out and find its customers – a significant saving. It saves on brand creation, incentives, prospect database costs, and so on. A recent example of the success of this method is the launch of the RSPCA platinum mastercard. This will be trialled using direct response TV, the first time this media has been used by Beneficial.

Sources: Adapted from Denny, N. (1996) 'Affinity way to do business', *Marketing Direct*, June, pp. 42-4. Reproduced from *Marketing Direct* magazine with the permission of the copyright owner, Haymarket Business Publications Ltd; and adapted from 'RSPCA tests DRTV for affinity card promotion' (2003) *Precision Marketing*, 17 January, **15** (14) p. 6.

many different ways to acquire customers. Mutual reinforcement is obtained by merging the different customer-service capabilities to add to each company's offer.

In the United States, one credit card in four is an affinity card, compared with one in 20 in the UK. Growth in Europe is a strong possibility over the next few years.

Finally, a warning about cards and their use in direct marketing. Be careful not to confuse affinity cards with co-branded loyalty cards, for example the HFC Bank/General Motors credit card. The latter also involve partnerships, but not primarily to attract new customers; rather, they are a deal for the loyal customer who benefits from points accrued through loyal spending – a General Motors customer gets points towards money off a new car, for example. Co-branded cards are fully discussed in Chapter 9.

Targeting suspects

In instances where there is little chance of using any of the previous methods of targeting, direct marketers may mimic general marketing, relying on market research to build up rough profiles of suspects. These could be:

■ competitors' customers within existing markets;

■ prospects in new markets;

■ new entrants into the market.

It is important to distinguish between these market 'pools' of prospects, because the approach – the message or the product offer – may change in each instance.

Using the targeting hierarchy to guide strategy

The targeting hierarchy gives a strong guide to our resource allocation: we should spend our targeting money from the *top down* (*see* Fig. 6.5). For example, if we have only enough budget to contact one group, then we should aim for recently lapsed customers. There would be less return in allocating spend to prospects or suspects. Once each level of potential is exhausted, any further acquisition budget is used on the next level down, until the money runs out.

Of course, this targeting 'rule' is there to aid our strategies, but it is not set in stone. We may, for other reasons, wish to expand into new markets, or learn something about the attractiveness of our products to a totally new set of customers. In this instance, we would allocate resources to targeting suspects, even though better prospects were available to us.

Targeting decisions may also depend on whether our firm is *customer* led, or *product* led. Let's take the example of the small-car market. The customer-led marketing philosophy tells us to find out people's needs first and then meet them. In this instance, we may use a list of people who have expressed the desire for a small economic car. We approach these people and obtain details of their preferences for the car, design and launch it, and precisely target our list with details of the car.

The product-led company would be research and development led, relying on good ideas internally to design a competitive car. Here, only a broad, rough idea of possible customers has been considered. It may then be best to use primarily awareness advertising and local dealers to sell the product. Here, the firm relies on customers *identifying themselves* when they show an interest.

The example used highlights two different marketing strategies, which then direct two targeting routes. The higher the commitment by the firm to being customer led, the more likely it is to target precisely; and the more precisely it targets, the more effective direct marketing is compared with general marketing.

Which is the better route? Clearly, the customer-led route more precisely follows the marketing philosophy; but it is interesting to observe that a lot of successful firms routinely use 'handraising' to identify their customers. Indeed, a swing back to the latter approach was predicted by Tyrrell (1996).

The ultimate manifestation of a segmentation and targeting approach is to drive down to a segment of one. This special case has been dubbed *one-to-one marketing* by Peppers and Rogers (1993) and is extremely important to direct marketers. In the following section we find out why.

ONE-TO-ONE MARKETING

A long time has passed now since Peppers and Rogers (1993) first wrote *One-to-One Marketing*, which outlined a new paradigm for marketing, predicting irresistible changes to the way marketing is practised worldwide. Peppers and Rogers predicted a marketing revolution based on the twin technological breakthroughs of, first, mass customisation and, second, the plethora of new electronic media which offer the opportunity for one-to-one interaction with customers. Let's have a look at the theoretical idea first, then get to what has happened in the meantime.

Mitchell (1997) made the point that mass advertising has always depended economically on the economies of scale generated by mass production – the two have had a symbiotic relationship. However, mass production economies of scale are now breaking down: car companies can make an assembly line pay with only 50 cars of one specification rolling off. The computer giant Dell can *make individually-specified orders within hours*. According to Peppers and Rogers, this means that mass advertisers will be outflanked by those companies which can make their products tailored to the individual, driven by instant, one-to-one media contact with the customer. However, the authors' one-to-one marketing takes these concepts a step further, in two main ways:

1 Learning with customers

In *One-to-One Marketing*, Peppers and Rogers give clarity to the notion of 'relationships' with customers. They propose a partnership with customers whereby customers are given incentive to share their needs, as they understand them at the time, with you. Electronic media are used to make it as easy as possible for customers to share their needs in a recordable way. With their use of the firm's products over time, more chances abound to learn more about their particular needs.

Peppers and Rogers discussed the idea of a birthday-card company which uses electronic kiosks to allow customers to design their own cards, which are then printed off instantly. A record is kept of customer designs, linked to that customer's details. Further designs are then *proactively offered* in the future when the next anniversary arrives. Customers value the convenience and are impressed with the card company's effort in getting to know them, so they buy more from that company at full price. However, the firm must make it easy for the customer to share information – hence the electronic kiosks. Overall, Peppers and Rogers describe the interaction as a partnership, not the 'stand-off' approach of much conventional marketing.

But what about the reality? Most practitioners would agree that this approach is rather different to the reality of much direct marketing as we move to the mid-2000s. In most instances, direct marketers do not address customers with one-to-one communications. At best they analyse and communicate with customers in groups.

Clearly, the one-to-one approach is potentially powerful; but how realistic is it for a company, a large bank say, with millions of customers, to treat *all* of its customers as individuals? At present, most banks are a long way from one-to-one marketing! Peppers and Rogers' solution here is to 'ring fence' your most valuable customers, 'one customer at a time', with a one-to-one approach. As this process continues down to less valuable customers, a point is reached where it does not make economic sense to attempt one-to-one marketing. At this point customers could be approached as aggregated segments (*see* Fig. 6.6).

2 Linking mass customisation with rapid one-to-one communications to create individualised products for customers

The twin logic of mass customisation and one-to-one communications using fast-response media means that customers have the ability to contact companies and say, 'I'll take that product, uniquely made the way I want it.' Motorola now makes pagers to any of over 11 million different specifications. Japanese bicycle manufacturers have similar capabilities.

According to Pine (1993), mass customisation is most important in those markets which have changing customer needs, technological advances and diminishing product life cycles. Where markets are stable and predictable, with convergent customer needs, there is less scope for this strategy.

Mass customisation can be:

■ **collaborative:** the dialogue takes place with customers before product design – the full one-to-one marketing concept. This is particularly useful for businesses whose customers cannot easily articulate what they want, and hence need the dialogue;

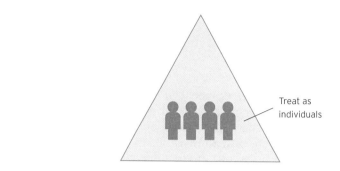

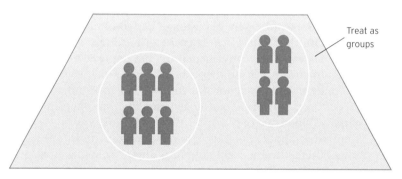

Figure 6.6 One-to-one approach to valuable customers and a mass approach to the rest

- **adaptive:** one standard product, but customisable by the users themselves, e.g. games that are programmable by customers to suit them;
- **cosmetic:** same product is presented differently with a minor amount of actual product change, such as the customer's name on the product;
- **transparent:** observation of regular customers' needs creates a customisation of service or product that is done automatically without the customer asking.

All four modes of customisation require different direct marketing approaches. What Peppers and Rogers and Pine provide is a clear call to action to direct marketers to expand their thinking outwards from *communication* and into *product* strategy, via mass customisation, an area hitherto given little attention.

Early indications are that, in general, companies have found it difficult to implement one-to-one strategies. As was mentioned, the most conspicuous success has probably been Dell Computers, which is now a world player in the computer hardware market. It is no coincidence that Dell is a major user of the Internet as a part of its business, and it may be that the future for one-to-one marketing lies in the Internet. This is more fully discussed in Chapter 8.

Having segmented and targeted our customers, our next strategic task as marketers is to maximise the value that the customers obtain from our product or service. We can now examine the product in its entirety and identify where direct marketing can deliver superior value.

ONE-TO-ONE MARKETING: A DIY COMPANY

Let's say you run a chain of DIY 'out of town' warehouse stores. You have two ways of running the company. Traditional thinking would push you to competing on market-share terms with your rivals, trying to get as many customers in as possible to buy your products. You may advertise in local press or radio. To boost sales you run incentives and broadcast these, hoping to pinch some of your competitors' customers.

Your alternative is one-to-one marketing. A customer comes in and buys some tomato seeds. He mentions that he is starting up a greenhouse in his garden. You note this onto a database with that customer's name and address, which you asked him for at the till. When a new book, *A Guide to Greenhouse Gardening*, comes out, you write to him, telling him about the book and offering it to him with a couple of packets of seeds thrown in. If he wants it, you suggest, phone in and you will send it to him. Next time he pops in you learn more about what he is doing with his garden, and again you note it.

What you are doing is learning with the customer what they want off you. You are offering them value by giving them relevant, timely information. You are making it easy for them to do business with you. You have tailored your product and your communication to that individual, in an attempt to grow your business from that one customer.

The total product/service

The 'total product' is the sum of everything a company offers to customers. For a supermarket chain this might include fast checkout facilities, bigger trolleys, cheaper price, notifying the customer of exciting new products and indeed everything else that would make a difference to the customer's experience. Within this total delivery, direct marketing may have a strategic role to play in delivering *service*, *dialogue*, *pricing* and *product value*.

DELIVERING SERVICE

Relationship marketing focuses on employee satisfaction as a major factor in service delivery. Direct marketing can link with employees in delivering *help*, *convenience* and *reassurance*. It can also be a major method of delivery of *after-sales service*.

Help, convenience and reassurance

When people are in the middle of buying a house, they are often in a state of high anxiety. Juggling suppliers, dealing with lawyers, the mortgage, the seller and the sale of their existing house is stressful. What they need above all is *help*, if possible proactively delivered by the supplier. A database can go some way to delivering this by recording progress and anticipating pressure points, thus helping the customer manage their way through.

After-sales service

Direct marketing can sometimes offer a crucial advantage here over general marketing. The following example shows how.

A customer buys, say, a second-hand car from a dealer for a few thousand pounds. A few days later the customer gets a call to ask if everything is all right with the car. At the same time, the dealer suggests the customer books in for her six-monthly service and free steam clean. In this way, the customer is well on the way to being retained for her next car purchase. Why? Because she has started a genuine relationship with the dealer which she would actively have to break in order to buy from somewhere else. It is much easier for the customer to say yes to the deal she is offered by the dealer than actively to look elsewhere. Moreover, this strategy provides sustainable competitive advantage. Only the dealer knows when the customer will need the service and what the particular needs of that customer are.

Tailored service delivery

In sectors where tailored service is important to customers, direct marketing can be absolutely fundamental to high-quality delivery. We have already looked at the way executive hotels manage their frequent customers. Such frequent visitors are highly profitable and are treated lavishly with a highly personalised service. The database orchestrates a lot of the face-to-face contact that occurs. It is the *proactive delivery of convenience* to customers that is the key to this strategy. As an aside, the customers also enjoy a feeling of exclusivity, of specialness, because they know that they are getting special treatment.

Another plank of relationship marketing that can be delivered through direct marketing is *dialogue*.

LOYALTY THROUGH REGULAR COMMUNICATIONS

Relationship marketers advocate communication that emphasises listening to and learning from the customer, rather than the 'we speak, you listen' school of marketing. Direct marketing is one way of making this happen in practice. Questionnaires can be sent out to customers asking them what they want and when they want it. Suggestions can be made on how the products can help make that particular customer's life easier, with easy telephone access provided for further dialogue.

There are many business sectors where there is little opportunity for regular contact with existing customers. Take the mortgage lenders. Once the mortgage is agreed, the house is bought and regular payments are established, there is no 'natural' occasion for any further contact between company and customer. Indeed, the better the customer, the less they will contact the company! Similarly, car manufacturers, financial services companies, utilities and car breakdown companies all have little contact with their biggest assets – their existing customers.

To overcome this, a strategy of regular communication direct to existing customers can be adopted. These companies can use direct marketing to maintain contact with customers using vehicles such as membership clubs, customer magazines, or newsletters. These vehicles need to be of high quality – they need to be of value in their own right – in order to work. It is no use bombarding customers with newsletters which are little more than glorified sales brochures. The Walt Disney Children's Club is an example of a communications vehicle which creates value for customers.

Communications to enhance loyalty has now become a mature industry. While cynics may argue that much of this activity is companies 'running to stand still' against

EXHIBIT 6.9

INTENSE COMPETITION DRIVES INVESTMENT IN IMPROVING LOYALTY USING DIRECT MARKETING

In 2003 worldwide hotel chain Marriott stepped up its drive to retain its customer base with a refreshed loyalty scheme. Currently with a membership of 18 million worldwide, Marriott wanted to emphasise the benefits of joining which include Air Miles, and rewards at Selfridges, Marks and Spencer, Hertz car rental, and more. The campaign included 2 million inserts and direct mail shots featuring a mini brochure. Marriott commented that it was looking for an approach which included 'brand planning combined with hard nosed number oriented direct marketing'.

Source: based on: 'Marriott Hotels embarks on loyalty offensive', *Precision Marketing*, 2003, 27 June, **15** (37), p. 2.

each other, provided the campaigns are well executed the evidence suggests they are still valued (Bolton, Kannan, and Bramlett 2000).

CREATING LOYALTY THROUGH PRICING STRATEGIES

'You can't buy loyalty. You can only buy the next purchase.'

Simon Roncorroni, MD, The L&R Group

'Whoever invented the term 'loyalty card' has a lot to answer for.'

Alan Mitchell

Direct marketers can tie a price-based loyalty scheme to individual spend. Rewards can be in the form of a straight price discount or can be 'points-based systems'. These are now widely known as 'loyalty schemes'. Loyalty schemes are an established, important weapon in the direct marketer's armoury, and we will take a detailed look at them in Chapter 9. However, the decision as to whether to adopt a loyalty scheme, or to look for alternative actions, is a strategic move, and as such merits some discussion here.

Loyalty schemes have for some time been criticised by a number of commentators (Dowling, 2002; Peppers and Rogers, 1993; O'Brien and Jones, 1995; Uncles, 1994). Peppers and Rogers suggested that, when used as part of an overall strategy of creating value for existing customers, they make sense, but otherwise they are essentially just another costly marketing promotion. When the airlines created frequency rewards in the form of free Air Miles, they also created a structure of preferential service in which frequent flyers benefited from upgrades, priority check-in, and so on. Car rental companies in contrast rewarded customers with free rental, followed by gifts in exchange for points, but with no service extras. What they quickly found, however, was how easily this approach was copied by competitors, and how quick customers were to switch, depending on who offered the best reward.

Uncles (1994, 1996) found that, as schemes are copied, customers realise there is no particular advantage and their behaviour is unchanged. Worse, customers become bored with all the deals, and basically filter out all loyalty-scheme messages from all the players.

Taking these perspectives on board, Lynch and Mitchell (1997) examined the use of loyalty cards in supermarkets. They questioned the effectiveness of loyalty cards in actually generating loyalty or 'relationships' towards supermarkets. By 2004, each of us,

EXHIBIT 6.10

KEEPING CUSTOMERS IN COMMODITY MARKETS

Are there any alternatives to price-led loyalty?

The problem with price-led loyalty is that when the price isn't right, customers are being trained by the deals to walk. This is very unprofitable for all concerned. The answer? This is not easy. One idea may be to use the database to identify the right customers; then look for innovative ways to share value with them. If we take car insurance, service is not a big issue in this market. So to turn away from price means creating value for customers in other ways. What about 'lock in' PEPS related to insurance payments? Or donations made direct to customers' favourite charities, based on loyal customers' no-claims records?

on average, participates in three schemes. So loyalty needs careful definition. Loyalty schemes should be used when:

- we have little choice. In some markets, such as credit cards, service issues are not as important to customers. Product/price benefits must therefore be concentrated on as ways to differentiate.

- we have the chance to reinforce brand associations (Uncles, 1996). If the loyalty scheme can reinforce the brand 'relationship' with the company, then it may be considered. American Express's Membership Miles scheme achieves this.

- we have the opportunity to meet most or all of the rules outlined by O'Brien and Jones (1995) for effective schemes. O'Brien and Jones propose five attributes that a successful scheme should have: *cash value, offer convenience, relevance, aspirational value*, and *offer choice*.

- extra value can be created outside the core programme. This could be service benefits, for example British Airways' Executive Club.

- we want to gather transaction data and this is the best way of doing it. Retailers use loyalty schemes to gather transaction data which would not otherwise be available. This data is then used to create *tailored* added value for customers, perhaps with coupon offers related directly to individuals' spend. This is often the key advantage for companies' schemes.

Verheof (2003) finds that loyalty schemes remain popular in spite of the problems. Customers are now more expert at filtering the good deals from the mundane.

EXHIBIT 6.11

THE STRATEGIC USE OF LOYALTY CARD DATA

The key player in the UK and one of the most important schemes in commercial history has been that of Tesco (see also the case study ending Chapter 3). It has revolutionised the way a multi-billion pound industry is run. Individual-level data has been systematically gathered on most of Tesco's 12 million customers, allowing the company to understand each customer's value to the company and how it may be able to increase that value, or prevent losses.

One key area has been in fighting off competition from US Giant Wal-Mart which took over Asda in 2000. While Asda's EveryDay Low Pricing strategy guides its mass discounting across a range of products, Tesco's individual data enables it to understand which price drop is valued by which customers. It therefore focuses on those customers who may be price driven rather than, say, convenience driven. The scheme is also used to analyse behaviour and segment customers, and test different promotional efforts. More strategically, it's about rearranging stores, and redirecting supply chains.

Some loyalty schemes enable a value-based segmentation to be built up, meaning firms can save money by not contacting low responsive or low value customers: instead of mailing 100 per cent of a database, just mail maybe 50 per cent.

Others enable segmentation by product need. Music retailer Tower Records recently sent thousands of e-mails to its customers, but offerings depended on that customer's particular buying pattern.

Recent linkages between data and supply chains has been made, moving database information out of the realms of marketing departments and into the genuinely strategic domain in companies. Clothing retailer Marks and Spencer analysed its customer profiles in different stores and adjusted its merchandise accordingly. It noticed huge increases in men's and women's fashion sales.

Some sectors are better than others. Credit-card firms have been noticeably less successful in using their data from loyalty schemes: special offers tend to be untargeted and rather bland, customer segmentation is undeveloped.

Sources: Marsh, H. (2001) 'Dig deeper into the database goldmine' in *Marketing Magazine*, 11 January, pp. 29–30. Mitchell, A. (2002) 'Consumer power is on the cards in Tesco plan', *Marketing Week*, 2 May p. 30.

Apart from service and pricing issues, direct marketing can help deliver a differentiated *augmented product strategy*.

THE PRODUCT

Direct marketing systems do little for core product strategies; these depend on innovative research and development, good market research, portfolio analysis, and so on. However, direct marketing is an important consideration when we focus on the extended product. Strategically, we may use direct marketing to offer *convenience through direct distribution*, *positioning and brand-related benefits*, and *incentives to trigger purchase* in getting new customers.

Convenience through direct distribution

Direct distribution, the original form of direct marketing (via mail order), is still an important tool. Direct distribution, when viewed from the customer's perspective, is a *service* issue. Customers who respond to direct offers may be attracted by the convenience of purchasing goods and services from the comfort of their own home.

Mail order was originally seen as catering for relatively downmarket sectors, but in the 1990s, new entrants such as Racing Green, Lands End and Next Directory changed the profile of the industry. Industry standards for direct delivery have been transformed. Companies typically set 48- or even 24-hour delivery promises, reflecting customer dissatisfaction with traditional mail-order performances of between 14 and 28 days. As a result, home shopping is increasing, and even conservative companies like Marks and Spencer have launched mail-order operations to complement their retail activities.

Of course there are many sectors in which most customers prefer the shopping experience of the high street. In product sectors such as fashion clothing or entertainment goods, the act of shopping itself is a big part of the satisfaction of the product. Some people want the instant satisfaction of ownership. You therefore need to make a strategic decision on whether to distribute through retail, directly, or a mixture of both.

Technological developments may provide another swing towards direct distribution. Supermarket chains have set up Internet/interactive TV-driven operations which offer direct delivery of a week's groceries for a £5 fee. Consumers may be given the trigger of their previous week's shopping list and asked if they want any changes made. The rest is automatic. The advent of Internet/interactive TV is certain to drive more business changes in this way. It can be speculated that, at some point in the near future, consumers will divide into two groups: those who like the shopping experience and don't want to pay fees for delivery; and those who want convenience and can pay for it. To compete, companies will have to run joint retail and direct distribution operations.

Positioning

Positioning is two things:

- the dimensions chosen by the company to describe the product; and
- where the product fits in the consumer's mind in relation to its competitors.

To take a simple example, BMW is positioned as a car of *engineering excellence*, and also as a *high-status* car.

Positioning is as important to direct marketing as any other type of marketing. The company and product must be positioned clearly, using direct marketing communications, if you are to succeed in attracting people to you. Direct marketing has an extra string to its bow here; it can segment your positioning dimensions to appeal to different groups. For example, a mobile-phone supplier could position its products simultaneously to young adults as status symbols, and to women with young families as security aids. The precision of direct marketing allows this to be done very efficiently.

Branding

General marketers often look to differentiate their products (especially in markets where the core products are closely matched, such as most supermarket goods) through *building a brand* which prospects will be familiar with and like, even though they have yet to purchase from that firm (Aaker, 1991).

Brands are *intangible values* added to the core product or service. The values are deliberately created and nurtured by the marketer, and exist as images held in the consumer's mind.

Direct marketers, in contrast, have not traditionally used branding techniques to the same extent, relying more on rational appeals based on products' unique selling propositions. In short, brand building came a poor second to the USP school of thought exemplified by Rosser Reeves: what is the unique selling point – why should I buy from you? These cultures stemmed from the world of mail order, where product benefits were always more important than brand symbolism. More recently, however, the idea of marrying the worlds of DM and branding has become more important as DM has become more important in sectors where branding is strong – the automotive sector for example. Pearson (1996) argued that brands can and should be built up through direct marketing. Pearson's argument is more concerned with service sectors. He asserted that modern consumers want things like help, convenience and a relationship with their supplier, and that branding these attributes as belonging to your company will build a sustainable competitive advantage.

Pearson's assertions were lent credibility by the upsurge in companies whose brands have been built by, or are related to, direct marketing. Examples include Direct Line and First Direct, to add to traditional big players worldwide such as American Express. Indeed, the word 'direct' itself has taken on positive brand values of its own, being associated with values like lower price, efficiency and convenience.

Because of these developments, brand strategy options need to be understood by the direct marketer. De Chenatony, *et al.* and Cowley (1991) outlined the branding strategic options, of which those most relevant to direct marketing are:

1 Branding as a device for recognition or shorthand

Visual brand entities can act as a shorthand for reasons to buy: quality, trust, price, value. The most important visual entities are the name and logo. Direct marketing communications usually reinforce this added value by prominent display of the brand name and logo.

2 Branding for reassurance

Imparting trust and reassurance is an essential part of marketing. People want to minimise the risk of making a purchase they will come to regret. Brands such as McDonald's reassure customers that they will receive a consistent product and service on each visit.

When recruiting customers through direct *distribution*, reassurance is particularly important. This is because consumers are buying remotely: they cannot assess the product at first hand before purchase, and they don't meet the seller face to face. The classic direct marketers, distributing direct, made an art form out of trust and reassurance by using various devices. The US mail-order outdoor clothing company L.L. Bean offers a 'no quibble' product guarantee encouraging new customers to see their purchase as very low risk.

3 Branding that communicates functional values

Functional values are the product or service benefits that are on offer. Functional branding is an important area for direct marketers, who have traditionally operated primarily on functional benefits and logical reasons to buy. Innovations, a mail-order operation, sells new products by emphasising unique selling points.

4 Branding that communicates symbolic values

Here the focus is on brand values that help the buyer express their personality. The consumer associates the brand's glamour, sexiness, high performance, youth, and so on, with themselves. Direct marketing has not traditionally been used in order to build symbolic values; this technique has been more suited to large TV advertising budgets. However, one customer value where direct marketers do make a difference is status. Companies such as American Express, BMW, and Hilton Hotels use direct marketing as a way of building and maintaining a feeling of exclusivity and privilege to both recruit and keep customers.

This is not the end of direct marketing's influence on symbolic branding, however. If we probe a little deeper, we can distinguish between using advertising to create a *communications-based brand*, and using the customer experience of the product to create an *experience-based brand*.

In instances where communications-driven brand values are very important, direct marketing usually plays a support role; its communications maintain and enhance advertising-driven values. The launch of the Audi A4 car in the UK illustrates this (McCorkell, 1997). All the Audi marketing communication, including direct response press and direct mail, contained the basic brand-building creative elements, including black and white photography, the strapline 'Vorsprung Durch Technik', and some copy featuring the advantages of the five-valve cylinder system and suspension.

With experience-based brands, direct marketers can often take more of a lead role. A prime exponent of an experience-based brand is First Direct. First Direct offers a 24-hour telephone banking operation, delivering high-quality service to its customers. The ease with which everyday transactions are conducted contrasts hugely with many retail banking operations, and as a result, First Direct's own customers are its biggest asset in spreading the news. Ninety-four per cent of First Direct's new business comes through word of mouth; over 10 000 new customers per month are joining it as a result.

EXHIBIT 6.12

BUILDING A BRAND WITH DIRECT MARKETING - GOLDFISH

The launch of Goldfish in September 1996 was a classic example of direct marketing and advertising working together to produce a strongly branded, yet cost-effective product. Launched into a hugely overcrowded sector, Goldfish stood out straight away, and the campaigns won a string of awards including the IDM Business Performance Award, and the FEDMA Best in Europe awards for 1998 and 1999. Goldfish powered from zero to a turnover of over £1.8 billion in two years, during which many of its competitors went under.

The credit-card market is typified by habit and inertia, with customers taking a low interest in the product offerings and seeing few differences between them.

The credit-card market is one of the most important for the direct-marketing sector. MBNA tops the list of spenders on direct mail, typically hitting over £50 million budgets, closely followed by Capital One and of course the traditional giants such as Barclaycard - new entrants such as Goldfish have to innovate to survive. Very few cards are up to the challenge, exceptions being the GM card launched in 1989, with its points scheme offering money off Vauxhall-brand cars.

Goldfish is owned by Centrica, which encompasses British Gas, roadside-support firm the AA and telco OneTel. The idea of the credit card was to earn points which could save money off your gas bill. Points are awarded by Goldfish on the basis of one point for every £1 spent. As well as gas-related benefits, consumers could redeem goods at Marks & Spencer, Homebase and WH Smith. More recently there are plans to extend the brand beyond finance into lifestyle services such as ticketing for events.

Looking back, the first of Goldfish's secrets of success was the name - designed to stand out as new and trendy. This then set the tone for the agency to allow its creative juices to run amok, introducing humour in particular as one of the key brand values. This mixture of wacky humour and differential service from the redemption partners proved popular from the off.

Goldfish launched on TV through a quirky campaign featuring the Scottish comedian Billy Connolly. Direct marketing programmes fed off the TV with reinforcement of the humour while also emphasising the rational benefits - a strength of media such as direct mail. Its functional benefits were always explained clearly and directly, without resorting to obscure, technical and remote language.

It's not only in the field of communications that DM has had an impact on Goldfish. Interestingly, it uses database analysis to more precisely pin down who and where its future prospects are, and this is used to guide the TV and media buying. A rare example of below-the-line running the show?

Sources: Cushing, K. (2003) 'Centrica gambles on big-bang move to HP', *Computer Weekly*, 17 June.
Kleinman, M. (2003) 'Goldfish defends shift in loyalty scheme rules', *Marketing (UK)*, 4 March.
Bashford, S. (2002) 'Goldfish restructures for "lifestyle" launches', *Marketing (UK)*, 28 February.
FEDMA, Best of Europe Awards, 1998, 1999.
Douglass, D. and May, D. (1999) 'It takes two to tango', *Admap*, June.

Using incentives

Unlike branding, the use of incentives to trigger purchase is not new to direct marketers. Incentives have been used by direct marketers in the traditional direct sectors such as mail order and publishing for a long time. For example, *Reader's Digest* has been using sweepstakes and competitions for more than 40 years. The accumulated knowledge of extensive testing has provided considerable evidence of the improved cost per sale often achieved using sales promotions (discussed in more detail in Chapter 9).

However, the long time 'love affair' that direct marketers have had with sales promotion techniques has been challenged by some practitioners (Rapp and Collins, 1987). Reichheld (1996) proposed that people recruited through powerful incentives were more likely to switch again to another competitor. Such customers were loyal to deals rather than to companies. The cellular phone industry in the US has defection rates as high as 40 per cent p.a., thanks to overuse of incentives to stimulate new custom. O'Brien and Jones (1995) raised the whole philosophy of rewarding people to switch rather than to stay loyal.

In acquisition, there are two decisions that direct marketers have to make about incentives at the strategic level:

1. For the situation at hand, should we use incentives to stimulate first-time purchase?

2. If we decide to use incentives, what strategic guidelines should govern the choice of incentive?

An examination of the advantages and disadvantages of using incentives will help to answer these questions for whatever specific situation arises.

Advantages and disadvantages of using incentives

Rapp and Collins (1987) suggested that incentives used in public media or retail environments led to high wastage because they could be used by existing customers who would have purchased anyway. In contrast, direct marketing is used to target incentives precisely, so avoiding this wastage.

Incentives are often used as tie-breakers in parity brand markets. It may be that the incentive is the only point of differentiation between suppliers. This is often the case in financial services markets, such as insurance, where brands are weak and service has not been developed such that consumers will regard it highly.

If the company has a clear cost-focus strategy, incentives can be used to draw attention to reduced prices. Similarly, if the company operates a differentiation strategy, appropriate incentives may add value. Direct marketing systems can administer complicated mechanics which tie in first-time customers to deals, locking them into future purchases (Stone, 1996). This ensures that payback on acquisition spend is reached through retained customers. An example of this might be a book club offering any three books for one pound, on the condition that the customer buys six more books at full price within a year.

One problem with using incentives as a point of difference is 'me-too-ism'. Your competitors quickly copy any successful promotion that you offer. The result is a zero-sum game, creating additional costs of doing business. Another downside is the possible damage to the brand of inappropriate incentives; many financial services' 'brands' sometimes seem to consist of free watches or alarm clocks rather than attractive brand values.

Summary to chapter

In this chapter we found that loyalty has had a major influence on direct marketing, in directing resources to retention, and in understanding how to achieve better retention levels. The increased awareness of the importance of marketers using their influence company-wide was also assessed – indicating the importance of a database as a strategic tool. The impact of a number of marketing tools in helping to deliver direct marketing strategies was assessed. Perhaps the greatest strength of direct marketing is its ability to deliver powerful segmentation and targeting strategies. It can also support service delivery, differentiate prices to different customers, and help in an augmented product strategy. The links between brand creation and direct marketing are a possible development area for the future.

Questions

1. Give an example of a sales-related objective for a retailer and an acquisition objective for a direct marketer, and explain the distinction clearly.

2. Give an example of an acquisition objective and a retention objective for an airline. How might the two objectives be clearly related to one another?

3. Both relationship marketing and the Four Ps approach to marketing have influenced direct marketing strategic approaches. Outline the key areas of direct marketing thinking affected by both paradigms, and give examples of firms following either approach in their direct marketing.

4. The Institute of Direct Marketing argues that accountability and control are two cornerstones of direct marketing. These are internal management benefits. Others argue that it is direct marketing's focus on the customer which is its best feature. Argue the merits of the various benefits direct marketing offers, focusing on the differences between direct and general marketing.

5. Why is it that it is usually more cost-effective to market to an existing customer than to acquire a new customer? Can you think of any business situations where this may not be true?

6. Tour operators selling package holidays often do very little in persuading previous customers to return for another trip. As a consultant, offer advice on customer retention and revenue maximisation strategies for a tour operator. What role would direct marketing play in such strategies?

7. A leading, upmarket credit-card brand is considering the use of incentives within a direct marketing strategy in order to acquire more new customers. Debate the pros and cons of this move.

References

Aaker, D. (1991) *Managing Brand Equity*, The Free Press, New York.

Bassi, L.J. (1997) 'Harnessing the power of intellectual capital', *Training and Development*, **51** (12), pp. 25-30.

Berry, L.L. (1983) 'Relationship marketing' in Berry, L.L., Shostack, G.L. and Upah, G.D. (eds) *Emerging Perspectives on Services Marketing*, American Marketing Association, Chicago.

Bessen, J. (1993) 'Riding the information wave', *Harvard Business Review*, September–October, pp. 150-60.

Bolton, R., Kannan, P. and Bramlett, M. (2000) 'Implications of loyalty program membership and service experiences for customer retention and value', *Journal of the Academy of Marketing Science*, **28**, Winter, pp. 95-108.

Bouchard, M. (1999) 'Why it's time to recognise DM's tangible record', *Marketing*, 5 August, p. 14.

Christopher, M. (1996) 'From brand values to customer value', *Journal of Marketing Practice: Applied Marketing Science*, **2** (1), pp. 55-66.

Cowley, D. (ed.) (1991) *Understanding Brands, by 10 People Who Do*, Kogan Page, London.

Coyne, A. (1994) 'A case study of data-driven marketing in the cable industry', *Journal of Database Marketing*, **2** (1).

Cram, T. (1994) *The Power of Relationship Marketing*, Pitman Publishing, London.

De Chenatony, L. and McDonald, M. (1992) *Creating Powerful Brands*, Butterworth-Heinemann, Oxford.

Denny, N. (1996) 'Affinity way to do business', *Marketing Direct*, June, pp. 42-44.

DeTienne, K. and Thompson, J.A. (1996) 'Database marketing and organisational learning theory: toward a research agenda', *Journal of Consumer Marketing*, **13** (5), pp. 12-34.

DMA Census (2003) Direct Marketing Association.

Dowling, G. W. (2002) 'Customer relationship management: In B2C markets, often less is more', *California Management Review*, **44**, Spring, pp. 87-104.

Doyle, P. (2002) *Marketing Management and Strategy*, FT Prentice Hall, Harlow.

Ehrenberg, A.S.C. (1972) *Repeat Buying: Theory and applications*, North Holland, London.

Finerty, L. (1997) 'Information retrieval for intranets: the case for knowledge management', *Document World*, 2 (5) pp. 32-4.

Fletcher, K. and Wright, G. (1997) 'The challenge of database marketing', *Journal of Database Marketing*, **5** (1), pp. 42-52.

Fournier, S., Dobscha, S. and Mick, D.G. (1998) 'Preventing the premature death of relationship marketing', *Harvard Business Review*, **76** (1), pp. 42-51.

Gartner Group (2003) Presentation to Relationship Marketing Colloquium, England, September.

Gronroos, C. (1996) 'Relationship marketing: strategic and tactical implications', *Management Decision*, **34** (3) (13).

Gronroos, C. (1984) *Strategic Management and Marketing in the Service Sector*, Chartwell-Bratt, Bromley, Kent.

Gummesson, E. (1996) *Why relationship marketing is a paradigm shift: some conclusions from the 30R approach*, 1st Management and Decision Internet Conference on Relationship Marketing, MCB University Press, Bradford, Yorkshire.

Gummesson, E. (1991) 'Marketing orientation revisited: the crucial role of the part-time marketer', *European Journal of Marketing*, **25** (2), pp. 60-75.

Gummesson, E. (1987) 'The new marketing: developing long-term interactive relationships', *Long Range Planning*, **20** (4), pp. 10-20.

Hansen, M.T., Nohria, N. and Tierney, T. (1999) 'What's your strategy for managing knowledge?' *Harvard Business Review*, March-April, **77** (12), p. 106.

Harris, L. (1996) 'Cultural obstacles to market orientation', *Journal of Marketing Practice: Applied Marketing Science*, **2** (4) (14).

Hartley, M. (1997) *It wouldn't stop me going somewhere else: supermarkets and their loyalty cards*, 31st Annual Conference, Academy of Marketing, 8–10 July, Manchester.

Humby, C., Hunt, T. and Phillips, T. (2003) *Scoring Points, How Tesco is Winning Customer Loyalty*, Kogan Page, London.

Kohli, A.K. and Jaworski, B.J. (1990) 'Market orientation: the construct, research propositions and managerial implications', *Journal of Marketing*, **54**, April, pp. 1–18.

Lynch, J.E. and Mitchell, P. (1997) *Supermarket loyalty cards: low involvement relationship marketing*, 31st Annual Conference, Academy of Marketing, 8–10 July, Manchester.

McAdam, R. and McCreedy, S. (1999) 'A critical review of knowledge management models', *The Learning Organisation*, **6** (3).

McCorkell, G. (1994) *The Best of Graeme McCorkell*, Institute of Direct Marketing, Teddington, Richmond-upon-Thames.

McCorkell, G. (1997) *Direct and Database Marketing*, Kogan Page, London.

Mitchell, A. (1997) *Marketing Week*, 14 March, p. 28.

Mitchell, A. (1998) 'The one–one gap', *Management Today*, July, pp. 90–1.

O'Brien, L. and Jones, C. (1995) 'Do rewards really create loyalty?', *Harvard Business Review*, May–June, pp. 75–82.

O'Malley, L. and Tynan, C. (2000) 'The utility of the relationship metaphor in consumer markets: a critical evaluation', *Journal of Marketing Management*, 15 (7), pp. 587–603.

Payne, A. (1995) *Advances in Relationship Marketing*, Butterworth-Heinemann, Oxford.

Pearson, S. (1996) *Building Brands Directly*, Macmillan, Basingstoke, Hants.

Peppers, D. and Rogers, M. (1993) *The One-to-One Future*, Piatkus, London.

Piercy, N. (1997) *Market-led Strategic Change*, Butterworth-Heinemann, Oxford.

Pine, B.J. (1993) *Mass Customisation: The new frontier in business competition*, Harvard Business School Press, Boston, Mass.

Pressey, A. and Matthews, B. (2000) 'Barriers to relationship marketing in consumer retailing', *Journal of Services Marketing*, **14** (3), pp. 272–86.

Rapp, S. and Collins, T. (1987) *Maximarketing*, McGraw-Hill, New York.

Reichheld, F.F. (1996) *The Loyalty Effect*, Harvard Business School Publishing, Boston, Mass.

Reinartz, W. and Kumar, V. (2002) 'The mismanagement of customer loyalty', *Harvard Business Review*, **80** (7), July.

Rosenfield, J. (1999) 'Whatever happened to relationship marketing? Nine big mistakes', *Direct Marketing*, **62** May (1), pp. 30–4.

Scarborough, H., Swan, J. and Preston, J. (1999) *Knowledge Management and the Learning Organisation*, Institute of Personnel and Development, London.

Stone, B. (1996) *Successful Direct Marketing Methods*, 5th edn, NTC Business Books, Chicago, Ill.

Stone, M. and Woodcock, N. (1997) 'Database marketing and customer recruitment, retention and development: what is "state of the art"? Part 1 – Strategy', *Journal of Database Marketing*, **4** (3), pp. 236–47.

Tyrell, B. (1996) 'The customer bytes back', IDM Conference, 5 June, Surrey.

Uncles, M. (1994) 'Do you or your customers need a loyalty scheme?', *Journal of Targeting, Measurement and Analysis*, **2** (4), pp. 335–50.

Uncles, M. (1996) 'Loyalty, behaviour – the direct marketing issues', Presentation to IDM Educators' Day, 30 March, Wembley, London.

Verhoef, P. (2003) 'Understanding the effect of customer relationship management efforts on customer retention and customer share development', *Journal of Marketing*, **67** (4), October.

Woodcock, N., Stone, M. and Starkey, M. (2003) 'State of the Nation 3' QCi Assessment Ltd.

BTYahoo!: Technology changing lives

This case study uses publicly available information and is based on the situation facing BT's Internet service provision and broadband delivery in 2003. The final brief as written is for educational purposes only, and does not represent any actual brief that BT has issued.

Introduction

In April 2003, chief executive, Ben Verwaayen, announced a logo to replace BT's 12-year-old piper figure. The logo, a spherical object, aimed to show BT is 'in tune with the multimedia age, as well as communicating the company's international reach', Verwaayen explained. The company probably knew that a rebranding exercise like this would lead to a lot of criticism, that it was a cosmetic surface exercise that hid a company facing the same old customer-service issues that had dogged it since privatisation nearly 20 years previously. But BT was keen to show the world that it was changing. What had changed?

BT – leaner and fitter?

In the mid-1990s BT was one of the world's largest and most powerful telecoms companies. It was well placed at home and poised to expand its international interests. However a number of environmental factors, plus its own slowness to deal with these, had left the firm in some trouble. While domestic competitors such as Mercury Communications and the cable operators, TeleWest and NTL, had largely failed to make an impact, BT was hit hard by the mobile revolution. The advent of pre-pay cheap mobile telephony left BT with a declining voice telephony market. A series of disastrous international ventures left the corporate giant with significant debts, as did the huge costs of investing in a 3G licence for its mobile offshoot Cellnet. Meanwhile the long promised revenues from Internet traffic were slow in arriving, not helped by the dot.com crash of 2001.

BT may aspire to good customer service, but, at least in terms of perception, it has a long way to go. A recent survey conducted by Internet Market Research Solutions asked respondents to name their three best and worst companies for customer service. The best were Tesco, Marks & Spencer and Asda, but BT topped the list of worst performers, followed by British Gas and NTL.

More recently BT has started to turn round its fortunes, with a more settled strategy centrally based round its position at the centre of Internet-driven growth. Broadband is perhaps its most important product for the foreseeable future. However the regulator, Oftel, has forced BT to open up its local loop – that part of its network between exchanges and customer premises – to competitors who can also offer broadband services.

BT has sold off much of its most profitable businesses to reduce its debts. The mobile arm – now O2 – went in 2002. Yell, its yellow pages service, went also in 2002. It is now leaner and, hopefully, fitter. BT is now organised around, among others, BT Retail (sells telephony direct to the consumer), BT Wholesale (sells bandwidth to other suppliers who then compete in the telephony market) and BT Openworld – a consumer-focused Internet service provider (ISP).

Verwaayen has set targets of 5 million broadband connections by 2006. He also wants these customers paying a higher average revenue per customer than current customers by getting new services from BT and other suppliers. However this is going to be far from easy.

Broadband is offered by a number of competitors, and is a commodity – the product is largely undifferentiated. Hence price is critical – and this has been BT's Achilles heel in the past. Its cost base is still relatively high, so excessive price cutting long term is not a good strategy, even if the regulator allowed it, which it wouldn't. This makes marketing all the more important.

BT marketing

It may have had a rocky ride at times with criticism of its service delivery, but BT's marketing has often been lavished with praise by critics. Since its inception as a private company, BT has spent most of its advertising budget on what it calls 'call stimulation' campaigns. Famous advertising characters like Maureen Lipman's Beattie, the Bob Hoskins character, and Buzby were created to encourage more use of the phone from under users – men, basically. More recent advertising has been about 'bringing people together' through BT's various services.

Perhaps the most important thing for the broadband and ISP marketing teams is that BT's core brand does have heritage. The awareness of the name, and trust in it to supply telecoms, remains high. However the brand does not possess caché or strong symbolism.

In the future, BT wants to surprise. This does not mean it will start to make soap operas, but it does want to make communications fun, entertaining and meaningful. It does want to be more than a set of pipes carrying data. The hard bit is making this happen.

Marketing at BT broadband

To launch broadband, BT embarked on one of the biggest awareness campaigns ever seen in the UK. It was called 'Broadband has landed' and was a TV advertising campaign worth £33 million. Its objectives at the time were to double the weekly sign-up from 12 000 to 24 000 people.

The direct marketing team wanted to support this awareness campaign, but also help educate people as there was a lot of confusion about what was in the market: prices, technology, content, and ease of use. Another factor is that fast access is not universally available – if only a few people from small towns/villages sign up then the service is not cost effective – so BT sometimes asks people to get together a group of interested customers before it will deploy the necessary exchange equipment. This lack of universal service is one of the reasons for the importance of direct marketing.

BT's agency knew that it needed to narrow down BT's 19 million customers to exactly those who were most interested in both the Internet and broadband.

Meanwhile BT's competitors NTL, Freeserve and AOL were more than happy for BT to raise awareness of broadband – which they would benefit from. That said, Telewest has stepped in to make sure customers know that BT isn't the only supplier. Telewest has 200 000 broadband customers, of which 20 000 are on its new 1mb service.

Meanwhile early market research had identified early adopters of broadband as typically 25–45 affluent males, but more recently, there have been signs of market maturity in reaching majority markets – 20 per cent of subscribers are now female and many others being online gaming addicts – presumably younger still.

Consumer behaviour on broadband

Consumer behaviour is critical. Part of the business case for broadband is that customers spend longer than hitherto on dial-up services. Some research suggests that broadband users are spending an average of nine hours per session with broadband, three times that for dial-up services.

The business case must recognise the costs of setting up content services, and the extent to which these costs can be offset by signing up more customers. The alternative is that BT should sign up more customers on the no-frills service before it introduces more content.

However, to some extent the above business case could be accused of being myopic. The likelihood is that broadband is simply too important to BT's future to be ignored. The future could be one where all our entertainment needs, plus our in-house communications, may come through whatever the next generation of broadband is. TV could well be part of the mix. Not only that, but some commentators are talking of adding to the mix of telephony, interactive TV and the Internet with another technological paradigm shift: home security, utility monitoring, automatic shopping ordering, and so on – call it 'electronic domestic help'. The point is that having missed the 'boat' so many times before, BT simply cannot afford to be caught napping this time. Broadband could be the last chance saloon for the company to secure itself at the heart of the digital revolution.

Since the launch the signs are encouraging. In late 2003, broadband was still in the middle of a 'tornado of demand' with an incredible 30 000 sign-ups per week. By September 2003 BT had over 1 million customers signed up to broadband.

Direct marketing of broadband

BT needs to be very careful with its marketing of broadband. It is not allowed by the regulator to use its own telephony customer database: this is seen as giving it an unfair advantage over its broadband competitors. Freeserve recently took it to court over its use of a bill stuffer, and although BT won, it was nevertheless a shot across the bows for BT. So, direct marketing is much more complex than just repeat mailing the BT base.

However the company has given notice of its intent to project itself as a creative company with a recent mailer to small office/homeworkers and small/medium enterprises (SMEs) that contained a creative screwed-up piece of paper asking 'How screwed up are your internet plans?' The work was designed to tackle the popular view that broadband is complicated and expensive. In another innovative piece of creativity, Proximity London has created a mailing that targets senior business people and workers within the creative service industries with the message that broadband Internet access can be 40 times faster than using a standard modem. The direct mail, to 30 000 target customers, includes a flat-pack box that opens up to build a 'swear box'. The creative idea is that the frustration of not having broadband will lead to swearing as stress increases. The mailing uses the line: 'Until you install broadband, we thought you could use this.'

BT has signalled that it wants to come out fighting with its basic broadband offer. But what should BT do in terms of content? This question led to the formation of BT Openworld.

Marketing at BT Openworld

Like most European markets, the UK Internet service provider market is hugely competitive. The biggest players are the well known AOL and Freeserve, with other players including Tiscali and Microsoft. AOL and Freeserve have spent bucket-loads of money marketing themselves. Indeed, AOL's acquisition campaigns which include free trial discs are infamous in the market place as possibly the most expensive acquisition campaign of all time.

Into this arena came BT Openworld, and although its policy from scratch was to use partners, it has understandably struggled. Openworld linked up with a number of specialists including The Online Travel Company, the gambling market with the formation of a betting channel, Classical.com, a site for classical music lovers, and Gamesdomain.co.uk, a gaming site. However in its early months the service lost money.

Recently, therefore, BT Openworld announced a permanent joint venture with specialist Internet service provider Yahoo to form a new bundled broadband product for consumers. This will be called BTYahoo! Broadband. The idea was that this would successfully compete against AOL and Freeserve by combining Yahoo's content and services, such as e-mail, into BT's digital dial-up products. BT will handle delivery, customer service and billing.

BTYahoo! Broadband appears to be positioning itself as very family friendly, perhaps in direct competition with AOL for this position. For instance, BTYahoo has tried to address the problem of junk electronic mail by becoming the first Internet service provider in Great Britain to launch a free anti-spam service for its customers. BTYahoo! Broadband comes with a range of parental controls, anti-spam and anti-virus software, as well as a facility that automatically blocks pop-up ads. It inherited 1.5 million customers from BT Openworld, of whom just 185 000 were on broadband, considerably behind AOL and Freeserve.

BTYahoo! marketing

BTYahoo! launched itself in September 2003 with a £10 million campaign. The strapline of the new service is 'The way the Internet was meant to be'. The idea for the campaign was to have West Coast US characters called Jimmy and Mikey in the net's early days, who could only imagine the possibilities afforded by today's technology.

BT Openworld customers were invited to convert to the BTYahoo! service by e-mail.

However, BT said it was still considering whether to re-brand its BT Openworld service for businesses, which has 170 000 customers, and make it part of the joint venture.

It makes a lot of sense for BT Openworld to use new technology as part of its marketing. For instance BT sent e-mails to 800 000 of its customers offering a £5 hotel voucher for an e-mail address of a friend and a further £100 for a recommendation that leads to a registration. BT Openworld has also used monetary incentives as the basis for a multichannel viral marketing campaign in an attempt to boost the acquisition rate for its Internet product Anytime.

In response Freeserve launched a £12 million campaign using its agency WWAV Rapp Collins. It used direct mail backed by DRTV and press ads, and a huge doordrop campaign. Freeserve's problem is that, following its initial 'giveaway' strategy of free sign-up, it had lots of lapsed users. The concern for them was that churn is on the increase with customers – when researched – saying they weren't sure what the right package was for them. Freeserve is setting up an advice line with trained advisers to talk consumers through what the best package for them is. There was also concern amongst Freeserve marketers that their brand name and image had lost its relevance since the firm ran with monthly subscription fees in line with its competitors.

The brief

BT had come a long way since its problems of 2001. It had a more focused strategy which centred around broadband and Internet usage. The launch of BTYahoo! signalled the firm's seriousness with this sector. However the trick now was for careful marketing that kept costs per customer down and revenue per customer as high as possible. In particular BT wanted to avoid Freeserve's problems with lapsed customers and high churn, and AOL's astronomical acquisition costs.

You have been asked by BT to advise them on their direct marketing strategy. Comment on the following:

1. The strategic acquisition-retention split and the budget split.
2. How direct marketing can help to project an invigorating brand to make the most of the link with Yahoo.
3. How direct marketing can maximise the uptake of broadband bearing in mind that you are not allowed to profile and target the BT telephony database as this is seen as anti competitive.
4. Advise BT on how it should set up its Internet service and broadband marketing databases to maximise its marketing analysis and strategy.
5. Advise BT on its marketing programmes, messages and media mix, in particular the possible use of new media to get its points across.

References

'BT goes into broadband with Yahoo' (2003) *Utility Week*, 20 June, **20** (1) p. 3.
'BT looks forward to healthy future' (2002) *Marketing (UK)*, 17 January, p. 15.
'BT wins broadband battle of the bills' (2003) *Utility Week*, **20** (5) 18 July.
'BT Openworld hires Proximity to target creative web users' (2002) *Campaign (UK)*, 5 March, (17).
'BT Openworld really delivers' (2002) *Marketing (UK)* 28 November, p. 48.
Chandiramani, R. (2003) 'BT-Yahoo! to aim £10m debut work at families', *Marketing (UK)* 9 April, p. 3.
Chandiramani, R. (2003) 'Can Freeserve give its brand meaning again?', *Marketing (UK)*, 29 May, p. 13.
'Incentive awards' (2002) *Precision Marketing*, **14** (29) p. 3, 19 April.
Mazur, Laura (2003) 'Words without deeds rightfully attract criticism', *Marketing (UK)*, 10 September.

7

RELATIONSHIP MARKETING AND CRM

Objectives

By the end of this chapter you will:

- be familiar with the concepts of relationship marketing and CRM;

- understand how these two things differ;

- understand the overlaps and also the differences between these and direct marketing;

- be aware of the practical implementation problems.

Introduction

In this chapter we continue with the theme of understanding the strategic influences on modern day direct and database marketing. Academics, commentators and writers often discuss relationship marketing as part of their assessment of what is happening in marketing practice. An even hotter topic in the first decade after 2000 has been the billions spent by firms on customer relationship management systems.

This chapter devotes itself to clarifying the extent to which relationship marketing (RM), customer relationship management (CRM), and direct marketing are intertwined. This necessitates an introduction, definition and discussion of the theory of RM and CRM. Just as important, however, will be a recognition of how practitioners have used these concepts and turned them into philosophies, strategies and activities. In fact theory and practice often diverge with relationship marketing, and this will be one of the main talking points of this chapter.

Relationship marketing

INTRODUCTION

Those of you who have embarked on a marketing career will have had plenty of contact with the use of the phrase 'relationship marketing'. One only has to read the popular marketing press to find innumerable instances of direct marketing managers describing the 'relationship building' programmes they have put into place. Usually these are replete with claims that customers have struck up relationships with the company, or the other way round. A 'dialogue' will have been built, 'two-way communications' established, and maybe even 'commitment' made.

This is the language of relationship marketing. So what is the concern? The problem here is the use of language but without very much of the substance. At a guess, a conversation with some customers of that manager might be rather revealing. 'A relationship? With my bank? Sorry. I haven't a clue what you're on about.' And so on. There are a number of issues here. One is the wanton use of language by professional marketers (and academics) that mitigates against us all being able to communicate properly with each other. Another is the attempt to dress up really quite trivial tactical campaigns under the guise of a strategy, perhaps in the hope that our efforts really will change customers' behaviour, this time. The final problem, linked to these two, is a fundamental lack of understanding of what the concept actually means.

This then is our first job here – to understand what relationship marketing is, and to clearly distinguish it from direct and database marketing.

UNDERSTANDING AND DEFINING RELATIONSHIP MARKETING

Relationship marketing is one of those areas of marketing theory that owes its development largely to academics working in competing schools of thought centred in both Europe and the USA. A rather unseemly scramble to claim first coinage of the term has ensued, but the publicity prize must go to Berry whose publication in 1983 is widely quoted when reviewing the subject. One of the most prominent Europeans has been Gummesson who in 1987 called for the 4Ps of marketing to be replaced as the dominant paradigm, arguing it is poor in theory, exaggerating some aspects such as advertising and competition, and limiting others such as inter-relationships and co-operation. The latter had been made prominent by the excellent work done by the IMP group years previously when examining business-to-business partnerships. According to exponents of relationship marketing, the use of 'hard sell' selling tactics is seen as misguided, and the customer now defines the nature of the business exchange. With increased competition, and companies realising the value of their existing customers, market leadership can no longer be maintained simply with short-term sales-oriented transactions. Customers are demanding more quality in their relationship with their sellers.

Another advocate of RM, Francis Buttle, described the transactional model as 'hit and run' marketing: get in, make the sale, and leave (1996). This traditional transactional marketing model is now seen as outdated, with relationship selling taking its place. Gummesson (1994) described transactional marketing as manipulative and exploitative of the customer's ignorance. The balance of power lies with the seller, with few mutual benefits apparently existing. In comparison to relationship selling, there is little or no after-sales service, and there is a limited commitment to meeting customers' expectations (Payne *et al.*, 1995). (Cynics of the relationship concept would probably hit back by pointing out that consumers are often quite happy to buy into so-called exploitative marketing; that most 'relationship marketers' would usually take the opportunity to exploit ignorance and make a quick buck; and that unless the product or service is of high quality, customers wouldn't buy it in the first place. These cynics are perhaps being a bit too harsh, but it may be prudent to take with a pinch of salt these claims that, after years of contempt for customers once they have sold to them, companies have completely repented and are now bending over backwards to solve our problems!)

Payne *et al.* (1995) argue that the key elements of relationship marketing are:

■ a shift in emphasis from transactions to relationships between suppliers and customers;

■ a focus on maximising the lifetime value of desirable customers and segments;

■ an emphasis on customer service as a key element in retaining customers. Providing high contact with customers and easy access back to the company are priorities;

■ quality is the concern of all rather than merely the concern of production. Quality is measured by what the customer perceives as good quality, rather than by internal measures of quality;

■ relationships are maintained with a wide set of groups, with the ultimate objective of feeding into the customer relationship. These groups could include distributors, suppliers, stakeholders, and so on.

Relationship marketing is best understood by following a story of what might happen when two businesses start to interact with each other. Imagine an IT executive meeting up with, say, a hotel manager for the first time. The hotel needs a new accounts system put in place and the manager is happy to chat it through. The dialogue begins. They have a series of meetings, phone calls, e-mails. After a while they find they have some personal things in common, both enjoying football, and this becomes infused into their business conversations. An agreement is reached about the new system, but the IT firm is let down by its suppliers, so the initial promises have to be amended. Throughout this difficult time, the IT executive keeps the hotel manager fully informed and is truthful about the delays. Both agree it is better to be 'honest in business, even if it means losing the sale'. They find they have values in common. The experience builds up trust for both parties and the hotel manager is committed to stay with the IT firm. Their interpersonal relationship improves further at Christmas when the IT firm puts on a party for its customers, and the two men get together over a few drinks.

The point of this story is to illustrate the key elements of relationship marketing: According to O'Malley and Mitussis (2002) the full extent of RM is to engage in dialogue, develop trust and demonstrate respect for customers. Another hugely important element is the actual relationship built up between two people. If a personal relationship is promised but all customers get is impersonal delivery, then 'customers will have a hard time feeling *human presence* in the relationship' (O'Malley and Mitussis, 2002). Unlike mass consumer markets, business-to-business and service markets involve exchanges where the individuals are known to each other rather than anonymous. This face-to-face element is vital for giving credence to the relationship idea.

In adding to dialogue, trust and mutual respect, Gronroos (1996), a key figure in the development of the theory of RM, would supplement 'shared ideals', 'mutual benefit', and a 'commitment to continue the relationship'. For Gronroos, relationship marketing is more than a set of activities, more even than a 'strategy' for the company. For him it is the very essence of business: a philosophy, that is deeply held by all in the company, that places a commitment to its customers higher than making a quick buck. Gronroos observed that relationship marketing is often done in a very superficial way – and implementation is often unsuccessful because the firm sees RM as a strategic option to be tested, rather than as a set of beliefs.

The fields of key account management and channel management are often the areas where relationship marketing lives and breathes most strongly. Interaction intensity, mutual disclosure of information and co-operative intention are all mentioned by Crosby *et al.* (1990). Meanwhile Selnes (1993) talks about the trust that is gained from safety, security and credibility in dealings with suppliers. Interestingly, there's been some suggestion that women are superior to men in relationship building in account management situations (Corner and Jolson, 1991). They are more likely to empathise with the customer, and more likely to disclose personal information.

Thus far we haven't mentioned where satisfaction as a crucial output of a business exchange fits into this model. Some research suggests trust and commitment, rather than satisfaction, are the key components of commercial relationships. Little and Marandi (2003) saw satisfaction as a key initial element of a customer's feelings towards their relationship partner.

EXHIBIT 7.1

KEY CONCEPTS THAT ARE PART OF COMMERCIAL RELATIONSHIPS

Satisfaction could be defined as *the feelings we get when our expectations are met or exceeded.* It seems common-sense that satisfaction must be a precursor of an ongoing relationship. Dissatisfied people *do* stay with suppliers, but only in the absence of reasonable alternatives.

However, satisfaction in itself is not enough to secure retention.

Trust is *a decision to rely on a partner in whom one has confidence.*

Commitment is *a decision to stay with a supplier in the future.*

To summarise so far we may describe RM thus:

Dialogue + mutual values + mutual interests => trust => commitment => retention (1)

This may be contrasted with a typical transaction model:

Communication of benefits => transaction => satisfaction => trust => retention (2)

Given the scepticism about relationship marketing in some quarters you may want to run with equation 2 as having more widespread application to commercial situations, especially with consumer markets. As a consumer, you might be satisfied with a wine supplier. You may trust them, feel committed to buying from them in the future. But you may still scoff at the idea that you have a relationship with them.

A business-to-business situation may be different. An acquaintance of the author who works for a large food manufacturer is trying to solve problems in supply chain with a retailer. She feels very much part of a partnership with the retailer's employees as they battle together to get this problem solved. She has a relationship with them. This story is typical of how the relationship marketing concept is frequently exhibited in channel partnerships. Relationship marketing is the 'thread that stitches all channel members together' (Bruhn, 2003). Customers become active partners with producers, wholesalers or retailers. This more involved role for the customer means that they are more proactive, and tend to feel more in control of their marketing channels. Berman (1996) goes as far as calling relationship marketing 'partnering', thus reflecting the strong mutual basis of these relationships.

The author of this book, employed by a business school, has some of his time bought out by a direct marketing agency to work on projects of mutual interest. Here individual relationships are very much at the heart of the partnership between the agency and the business school: the concept is very apt in describing what is happening with this arrangement.

THE BOUNDARY BETWEEN RELATIONSHIP MARKETING AND DIRECT MARKETING

As we have seen, the heart of relationship marketing is dialogue, human interaction, identifying mutual benefits, having shared ideals, and keeping promises. The outcomes are trust, mutual respect, and a commitment to continue the relationship. Relationship marketing hence has a clear focus on existing customers and is concerned with retention and loyalty.

As we discussed in Chapter 5, the essence of direct marketing (as it is currently *practised*) is predictive transaction marketing based on advanced segmentation approaches. However, like RM, direct marketing also has a clear focus on existing customers – to sell to them. Like RM, DM can be used to prolong and improve customer loyalty, but DM tends to rely on transaction marketing approaches – product/price packaging, pricing offers, or maybe charming customers through brand symbolism. Some direct marketers have drifted into the habit of interchangeably using the terms direct marketing and relationship marketing, as if they were the same thing. This is misleading: there is a distinct difference between, say, loyalty schemes, or lock-in cross-selling, and any genuine attempt to build partnerships or learning relationships.

Most direct marketing replicates relationship ideals only in a remote, second-hand kind of way. It is true that the act of buying and selling goods or services always involves the *keeping of a promise* in the sense that the seller promises something to the buyer in return for cash. It can be argued that 4Ps-based transaction marketing involves keeping promises just as much as relationship marketing. But until one reaches the theoretical endpoint of one-to-one marketing (creating a learning 'relationship') there is no sense in which this mass, branded, standardised delivery of service reaches a state in which it could be called a 'relationship'.

There is, however, important overlap between relationship marketing and direct marketers in one sense. Both direct and relationship marketing have at their core the idea that customer lifetime value should be valued over and above the individual transactions that take place. Both approaches emphasise the importance of this, and keeping existing customers is seen as more important than acquiring new ones.

However, can we be more specific about where the overlaps between relationship and direct marketing exist? Direct marketing systems exist primarily to transact efficiently with customers. However, there are some aspects of DM communications that can contribute in a relationship sense. These may be split into *service* and *dialogue*.

Service

There has been much work devoted to establishing the link between service and retention. Cram (1994) reported research by Rapp and Collins which illustrates the value of service in retaining customers:

Table 7.1: **Reasons why customers were lost**

Reasons	Percentage
Moved away/died	4
Relationships with other companies	5
Competitive activity	10
Product dissatisfaction	14
No contact, indifference, attitude of sales force	65

Relationship marketing advocates the provision of excellent service to customers as a critical part of improving their satisfaction with the company. Service and quality are intermixed so that quality is defined as customers' service expectation. Thus, quality is defined by the customer – if they get what they expect, that's quality (Gronroos, 1984).

Direct marketing may take a lead or support role in helping ensure customers get what they expect. The strategic advantage of using a database to drive service is that this is a proactive stance. Instead of waiting for customers to ask, and then reacting, McCorkell (1994) pointed out instances where direct marketing's predictive capabilities are invaluable in anticipating needs.

Delivering service through direct marketing systems is fully described in Chapter 6.

Dialogue

Relationship marketers argue that dialogue is central to the idea of fruitful relationship development. A two-way exchange of information needs to be constantly maintained if the relationship is to be genuine. But how can this be done with large volumes of customers? Clearly database marketing has a potential position of strength here. One way to deliver a genuine relationship through direct marketing systems may be through customer clubs.

Customer clubs

Clubs are discussed in detail in Chapter 9 but here we consider the idea that a customer club is a surrogate for a relationship between company and customer. Clubs are a good idea when the customer takes a sense of status from belonging, when they want to interact with other consumers, and when they have high involvement and interest with the product or service. In the latter two situations, it may be appropriate to instigate elements of the club that could be described as relationship marketing (Pryce, 2003). For example: a baby club set up by, say, Unilever or Procter and Gamble may move beyond information about baby products and into advice about raising children, and maybe act as a mechanism for mums to get together. This may be delivered through Internet web chat sites. A product like, say, Jaguar Cars could successfully run a club that would physically bring together customers to events and functions celebrating classic cars of the past. Such customers would quickly form relationships with each other, but would they form relationships with Jaguar? The answer is probably at least partly yes: perhaps directly with Jaguar people running the events; perhaps via e-mail with customer service representatives; and (less clearly a relationship) they may form intense affinities with the *brand* that go beyond weak associations. The author of this book would argue that 'brand liking' or even 'brand love' is more accurate than 'brand relationship' to describe these feelings. Trust, commitment, respect may well be there from customer to brand, but not in a dynamic two-way fashion – the brand doesn't 'know' the customer! Still, this is complex: the customer won't split out the above effects – to them, the brand includes the people of the company whom they have met or corresponded with.

HOW RM AND DM FIT INTO MARKETING PLANNING

Throughout this book, we have referred to the marketing planning process in an effort to provide a framework into which different elements of direct marketing can be positioned. In Chapter 1, we decided that direct and database marketing provided a process, or system, of marketing. This is worth reminding ourselves of now as we contrast direct with relationship marketing. Little and Marandi (2003) point out that relationship marketing is a strategy, i.e. a guide for the company in how to conduct itself. They pointed out that RM as a strategic guide necessarily *depends on the customer* one is having a relationship with for its direction. Therefore there is no attempt to exert an independent 'predict and control' approach that the 1950s' business managers would have wanted. With RM, the future depends on mutually agreed outcomes between the firm and customers. The predictive component of RM strategy, such as it exists at all, comes from the initial choice of customer, and the strategic emphasis placed on each customer. However, Little and Marandi report Gronroos's insight that *the essence of RM implementation lies in processes rather than in planning.* Here is the insight into where direct marketing and relationship marketing meet. Both relationship and transaction marketing could be described as *strategies*, and, if chosen, there are a variety of processes businesses could deploy to help *implement* either strategy. Direct marketing is one of these *processes of implementation*.

Different sectors, different situations

For the most part, relationship and direct approaches to marketing address different sectors, though there are overlaps. What does seem to emerge is that relationship marketing as an approach arguably has more relevance within the business-to-business and service industries, in particular with *high involvement* products, for example a business purchasing a computer system. What is less clear is the extent to which these ideas apply in *low involvement* products, such as, say, filling up the car with petrol. Focusing on the latter, it may well be the case that direct marketing techniques become relatively much more important as a way of delivering relationship marketing in 'low involvement' markets (*see* Fig. 7.1).

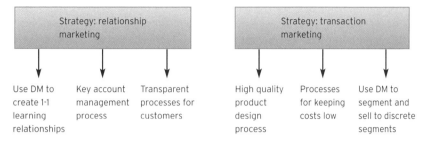

Figure 7.1 The strategic planning linkages between RM and DM

Figure 7.2 shows us the differing roles played by relationship and direct marketing depending on the sector.

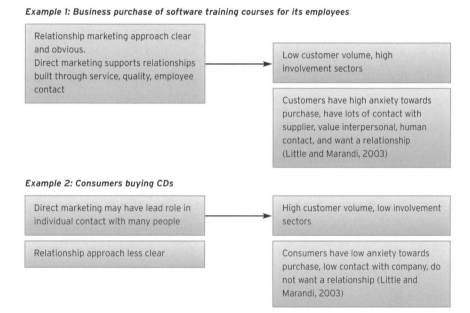

Figure 7.2 The impact of industry sector on the role of relationship and direct marketing

PARADIGM SHIFT OR HOT AIR?

By no means everyone is persuaded by the messages of relationship marketing. A leading light among the heretics is Stephen Brown who, in *Postmodern Marketing 2* (1998), started by pointing out that RM, if it exists, is a testimony to the complete failure of the original marketing concept. After all, if the original concept had delivered on its promises there would be no dissatisfied, possibly defecting, customers for us to attend to. He also points out other commentators for whom RM is problematic: Baker (1994) finds RM nothing more than an attempt to teach old dogs new tricks; yet others consider the talk of trust, commitment and partnership between typically large companies and small suppliers or even smaller consumers little more than a smoke screen for the continued coercion, exploitation and manipulation of the weak by the strong (e.g. Chen *et al.*, 1992).

In the same vein, Brown asks us to 'ponder what customer in their right mind would want to establish a relationship with a marketing organisation? Do marketers really believe that today's consumers, after having been shafted for years, have concluded that marketers have turned over a new leaf and really, really care about their customers' welfare?' Brown: 'Something tells me that consumers have probably concluded that our sobbing on their shoulders and promises to be a better boy in future are little more than pathetic attempts to elicit sympathy prior to picking their pockets... Marketers would be far better off being open about their commercial intent: we don't love you, we just want your money – and lots of it!'

Brown, S. (1998) *Postmodern Marketing 2*, ITBP, London.

Baker, M.J. (1994) 'Research myopia: Recency, relevance, reinvention and renaissance (the 4Rs of marketing?)', Department of Marketing working paper series 94/2 Glasgow, University of Strathclyde.

Chen, I.J., Calantone, R.J. and Chung, C. (1992) 'The marketing-manufacturing interface and manufacturing flexibility', *Omega* **20** (4), pp. 431–43.

CONCLUSION

Relationship marketing has strong roots. The extent to which RM happens in practise may be something we in the West are sceptical about but in Asian, South American and some European markets the building of personal relationships is a prerequisite of business-to-business marketing. So maybe our scepticism is unjustified. But just before we buy wholesale into the rhetoric of relationship marketing we must always keep one crucial question in mind: would your business relationship partner forego some short-term profit in order to maintain or strengthen the relationship they have with you? If they would then that is at least one definition of a 'true' business relationship. If they abandon the relationship the moment it no longer suits them in the short term, then one must question whether words are matched by deeds.

Transactional selling is far from ineffective. Transactional and relationship selling can co-exist, suggesting that relationship marketing should not be viewed as a replacement for transactional selling strategies, but as another perspective in marketing.

Customer relationship management (CRM)

If you read an article about customer relationship management (CRM) in the popular marketing press, you might finish it a little mystified about the difference between direct and database marketing. In fact, CRM is one of those marketing phrases that takes on a life of its own depending on the vested interests of the person writing about it. Consultants will promote it as philosophy, strategy and systems that will solve their client's headaches. Academics have had relatively little to say on the subject, but will likely focus on its relationship building aspects. Commentators in the direct marketing world often use it interchangeably with direct marketing.

CRM is important because rarely in history has so much money been spent by so many clients on improving their marketing. The sheer size of the budgets has concentrated the minds and the attention of CEOs and directors on marketing like never before. What this means is that – and this is highly significant – the size of the investment has forced senior managers to focus on what marketing departments and marketers actually do. This is both an opportunity and a threat for the marketing profession: are they up to the challenge of being in the spotlight in their lead role in ensuring returns on these huge IT spends?

EXHIBIT 7.3

HOW I.T. IS CHANGING MARKETERS' LIVES

The author was centrally involved in a recent study commissioned by the UK Chartered Institute of Marketing which investigated the impact of e-business on marketing practice. The initial flurry of excitement around the dot.com 'revolution' has been replaced by the more stolid reality of using the Internet and its associated technologies to improve the value chain of the company. The study found that marketers were reasonably innovative in taking new technology and applying it in *tactical* ways to their marketing communications campaigns: using SMS advertising was one example. However, less impressive was the marketer's strategic grasp of company-wide IT initiatives that, in theory, marketers should be heavily involved with, but in practice had largely abandoned to IT, operations, HR, or finance people. Examples of such initiatives included knowledge management systems (see Chapter 6), supply chain exchanges on the Internet, and even CRM – in theory a central domain of marketing – often now run by IT specialists. Sadly, senior managers' opinions of marketers as professionals deserving serious power within the company had not improved since the days of 'mid-life crisis' ten years ago. One quote from someone very senior in the industry aptly summarised marketers' preference for glamour rather than leadership:

> Marketers need to develop mini-entrepreneur skills – strategising, devising a business plan, making resource allocation decisions, understanding risk. In short, commercial acumen. What marketers lack are MBA graduate skills. At the moment these are in very short supply.

> Marketers should develop IT/new technology skills. We cannot influence the development and usage of IT within companies unless we know something about it.

> [Marketers should] stop wasting time hiring and firing agencies. Marketing departments are fiddling with deckchairs on the Titanic. We are playing marbles at the wrong end of the playground, while the grown ups are doing business at the other end.

Chartered Institute of Marketing (2001) 'The impact of e-business on marketing and marketers', October. Website for CIM direct purchase: http://www.connectedinmarketin.co.uk, tel. 44 (0) 1628 427427

WHAT IS CRM?

One of the most important writers and commentators on CRM is Merlin Stone. He, Woodcock, and Gamble (1999) defined CRM:

> CRM is an enterprise-wide commitment to identify your named individual customers and create a relationship between your company and these customers so long as this relationship is mutually beneficial.

A glance at academic papers or at practitioner literature will illustrate the impossibility of obtaining definitive agreement about what CRM is, but what we can do is identify its centre of gravity in terms of what it substantively consists of in the commercial world. If CRM in its totality was adopted by a firm, that firm would have in place:

■ people who regard serving the customer well as the top priority of their job and – crucially – are motivated to deliver this day after day;

■ processes that cut across traditional departmental boundaries and create ways of serving the customer better;

■ customers identified by their value to the company and prioritised accordingly (also a key part of traditional direct marketing – *see* Chapter 3);

■ a customer database that is independent of individual channels and is an integral part of live service delivery to inbound contact;

■ the database at the centre of planning and execution of direct marketing programmes for outbound contact (what much of the rest of this book is about).

So, compared with direct marketing, in its execution CRM:

■ is associated with large companies that have multiple channels and possibly multiple sources of customer data;

■ is centred around the idea of data-driven *service;*

■ focuses on *inbound* customer contact at least as much as outbound.

According to Hansotia (2002) CRM works best in sectors where:

■ there are frequent customer interactions;

■ a high level of expertise is needed to guide purchase decisions;

■ multiple products and services are purchased by customers.

So, a bank with multiple products is going to get more out of CRM than an insurance company selling only life insurance.

Customer-relationship management as a marketing idea has large overlaps with both direct marketing and relationship marketing, and we will pin down these overlaps in a moment. But what is crucial here is to recognise that CRM in practice has been driven by the supply of complex IT applications created by firms like Siebel Systems and Oracle, and by the demand for these systems by large firms. In practice, the billions of dollars spent on CRM has been driven by two things. One is the opportunity to nudge customers into ways of contacting the business that are cheaper for the firm: in some instances this may mean 'let's close down some branches and open up telephone or web channels'. Second, and linked to this, has been the desire of (usually big) firms to sort out the chaos that their basic customer contact has slipped into. A few years ago if you rang up a bank or an electricity supplier to order a new service, then walked into their retail outlet the next day, there was little hope that your order record would be known about, or that staff would be able to help you. Companies that have successfully installed CRM systems will allow 'live' processing of customer enquiries irrespective of the channel chosen by us – retail, telephone, Internet, sales force, or whatever (*see* Fig. 7.3). Given how low service standards often are in practice, this *channel free* 'customer management' may be a source of competitive advantage rather than a hygiene factor.

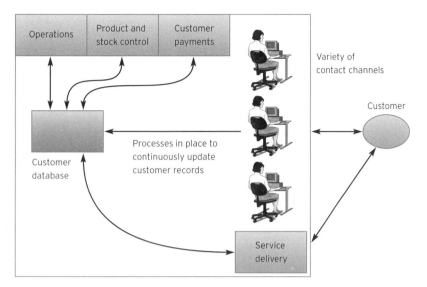

Figure 7.3 CRM in large firms

There have been many claims, usually by management accounting/consultancy firms, that CRM is a way of delivering the philosophy of market orientation (MO). MO asserts that better profits result from the whole company sensing and responding to customer needs in a dynamic way: the customer is top priority for everyone in the firm. However in reality the growth of CRM has not been driven by MO. In practice, as mentioned above, but it is worth repeating, *CRM has largely grown from a more tactical imperative – to cope with all the channels of contact that customers have been offered and now expect.* The language of vision and values that puts the customer first may have been taken up by managers, but the reality is often that internal politics still dominates and, in the worst cases, the customer is attended to *in spite of,* rather than because of, management philosophies.

WHAT IS THE DIFFERENCE BETWEEN CRM, RM AND DIRECT MARKETING?

In the light of the possible confusion between these concepts, an explanation seems in order. In short, relationship marketing is a business-wide strategy. Direct marketing is a system that allows us to implement marketing plans driven by customer data. And CRM is a system and process-driven attempt to improve contact between large firms and the customer.

The first thing to quickly say about Fig. 7.4 is not to take it at face value – it is over-simplistic. But it may be useful as a partial explanation of the key differences between the concepts.

An ideal linkage between the three concepts would be as follows. Relationship marketing is a management ethos that pervades everything the company does, and is 'top-down' from the CEO and board. In this RM-driven firm, both CRM and DM are *tools and processes* that support this ethos (and this means, for instance, not exploiting customer ignorance, but rather informing the customer when it is to their advantage to do something). CRM systems allow convenient two-way dialogue to build, and allow

Figure 7.4 CRM, RM and DM – a memory aid

tailored service at the point of delivery. DM systems may be centred around the marketing department, but are part and parcel of CRM, and support the relationship ethos through predicting customer needs and placing good service above sales.

So far so good. But we have to add one more sauce to the mix of RM, CRM and DM. We have forgotten transaction marketing.

TRANSACTION OR RELATIONSHIP MARKETING – THE TENSION IN CRM

At the heart of the confusions endemic in CRM implementation lies the transaction–relationship marketing dialectic. In other words, are we primarily interested in using CRM tools for better targeting, creating propositions, selling directly and avoiding wasting marketing budget? Or, do we want to generate a two-way dialogue, give up market power to customers, make and keep long-term commitments, and nurture that most precious of commodities, trust? In many ways this debate, yet to be resolved by academics or commentators of practice, lies at the heart of this entire book. One may summarise the present position, perhaps rather cynically, as one of talking the talk of relationships, but walking the walk of transaction marketing. And who is to say these practitioners are wrong? For all the academic work on relationship marketing, there has been little study as yet that links a genuine relationship approach with enhanced profitability.

A recent study that the author was involved with found that practitioners were by and large struggling to get past the first stages of CRM. Just aligning the channels properly so that a common view of the customer could be obtained between them was difficult work. Spotting and co-ordinating tactical *selling* initiatives was probably the next stage. As so often, *cross-sell* dominated the business case for investment. The customer who has just rung in fits the profile for a credit card, but doesn't have one. So offer them a credit card. Nothing wrong with this, but it's as yet a long way from learning and growing together, building trust, nurturing relationships.

As things stand you may be justified in asking: where is the 'R' in CRM? Most companies are probably committing 'relationship fraud' at the moment, or operating a

CSUGBR strategy: Cross Selling Under the Guise of Building Relationships. Not much seems to have changed since Gronroos said 'relationship marketing is done in a very superficial way – and implementation is unsuccessful because the firm hasn't bought into the relationship marketing philosophy of shared ideals, mutual benefit, trust, commitment and dialogue' (Gronroos, 1996).

Such a lack of authenticity can make a mockery of attempts to operate in a one-to-one marketing mode (O'Malley and Mitussis, 2002). And, according to O'Malley and Mitussis, the current CRM IT expenditure for solving the 'tricky problem of developing and enhancing consumer relationships without interpersonal interaction is highly problematic and must be questioned'. The next section discusses these issues further by investigating the current 'state of play' with CRM as it is practised.

CRM – THE STATE OF PLAY

CRM is big business. Some IT business brands, notably Siebel systems, SAP and PeopleSoft, have made global names off the back of CRM purchases by large companies. CRM has been a serious driver of hardware and software sales for big players like IBM and Oracle. Across the United States and Europe, nearly 40 per cent of the companies in sectors such as high technology, aerospace, retailing, and utilities have invested in CRM systems. Two-thirds of all US telecom operators and half or more of all US financial services, pharmaceutical, and transportation companies are either implementing or already operating them. In 2001 companies around the world spent $3.5 billion a year on CRM software, and that was only a fraction of the total; implementation, training, and integration outlays can be many times higher. All in all, a highly complex CRM installation can cost more than $100 million and take three years to complete (Giga, 2002). Agnes Nairn (2002) reported a global survey by The Data Warehousing Institute of 1670 Global CRM users that found that 'most are now adopting CRM as a mission-critical business strategy'. Even allowing for our suspicions about any group that uses the phrase 'mission critical', there's little doubt that CRM has created a lot of fuss. However Nairn, quite rightly, suggests that the case for allocating budget on CRM initiatives has yet to be proven. There is at present some concern about the wisdom of these investments: Patron (2002) reports that over 80 per cent of CRM projects fail in Europe. In many instances CRM has failed to

EXHIBIT 7.4

WHY DON'T MARKETERS STRATEGISE?

Why is it that professional marketers seem so poor at strategising? It's not as if the principles of business strategy are a great secret: there are over 50 text books in Europe alone with the words 'corporate strategy' in the title. Anyone who has an MBA will be more than familiar with Porter and Hamel. Yet this material seems to still come as a shock or as a startling revelation to marketers – year after year. The strategic process is 'unveiled', slightly altered, with new buzzwords, as a brand new panacea by management consultants, or by slick business school 'academics' selling under the guise of academia . . .

The other issue that astonishes many is just how bad many senior managers are at strategising. One presumes that the reason they rose to these senior positions can only be down to their undoubted skills at people management – lobbying, influencing, maybe making things happen by driving change. But strategy? A foreign language it seems.

yield the improvements expected in cost savings, customer-service improvements, satisfaction scores, or, ultimately, profitability. When managers were asked to assess three key functions of CRM – marketing campaign management, call-centre management, and marketing analytics – no more than 35 per cent of the respondents said that their expectations had been met in any function (International Data Corporation, 2001).

Making CRM work – the strategy gap

There is now some substance to the literature explaining how to implement CRM successfully (Gamble *et al.*, 1999, Foss and Stone, 2002).

Fletcher (2002) found that the effective use of CRM is achieved by marrying *organisational* capabilities and market contexts, rather than by uncritical adoption and development. Organisational and strategic barriers are more important than technical barriers but this is still not generally recognised. In other words too many companies have bought the technology but avoided the more difficult organisational and cultural changes needed to make the most of the technology. According to Foss and Stone (2002), *people* and *organisational* issues are the greatest contributors – and in many cases the greatest obstacles – to successful adoption of CRM practices. Often big firms fragment into departments that exist as separate silos that communicate poorly with one another.

Patron (2002) reports that CRM requires an organisational change inside the company, away from products/silos and towards customer service delivery. Organisational changes mean people having to change who they work for and where they work. This in turn means the inevitable political jockeying for position that always happens at senior levels of the firm. Cultural changes are often even more difficult. If you have worked in a large firm you will know how difficult it is to ask someone to change the way they work, the things they do on an everyday basis. O'Malley and Mitussis (2002) suggest that without a shared, culturally bound vision, the implementation of CRM systems might fail because of political infighting over the ownership of systems and data. This type of infighting has been well documented in the information systems literature.

In summary, senior managers often do not focus on the underpinning strategy behind the CRM decision or its implementation. If we list culture, strategy, organisation and technology, then the *least important* of these is technology, but this is often the element receiving most attention.

Foss and Stone (2002) cite the drivers of success as:

■ making CRM a strategic priority, driven by the CEO. Slow progress is made due to lack of commitment across the organisation;

■ an inherent customer service culture in the organisation. When ringing a firm as their customer, do you sometimes find they sound as if they don't want to hear from you, or that they are doing you a favour?;

■ keeping staff happy so that they keep customers happy;

■ collaboration across departments.

The flipside – obstacles to success – were listed as:

■ approaching CRM on a piecemeal basis rather than as an holistic investment;

■ continued emphasis on acquisition at the expense of retention. Acquisition has often – thoughtlessly – got priority because its budgets are controlled by one department –

marketing. Acquisition spend is mainly media. Retention spend on the other hand requires cross-departmental resource in people and processes and is more long term. The latter are more difficult for companies to deal with;

■ perhaps most difficult, culture change. Changing the mindset of the organisation from being, say, product-, production-, or sales-led to being customer- (service) led is a long, hard road that must be driven from the CEO downwards. To return to our earlier debate about transactions versus relationship cultures, it is often this culture change that most starkly divides: has the firm introduced CRM systems to cut channel costs, increase cross-selling, or create relationships? The CEO would probably say all three. But if a firm is not truly committed to the precursors of relationship marketing – treating customers with respect, as equal partners and sharing information – then relationship building is less likely.

Once the strategic context has been established, Fletcher also points out that good CRM requires an operational level of marketing expertise in gathering and using customer data. Here the use of customer data to understand different segments and to manage them over time profitably comes to the fore – if this sounds familiar it's because these skill sets are core to good direct and database marketing.

PUTTING CRM INTO OPERATION

This chapter has emphasised the need not to under-estimate the complexity of introducing CRM systems into large firms. There are three major stages.

The first consideration is that the channels – web, call centre, e-mail, mail, text – all have managers that guard their channels very carefully, often for good reason – security of access, etc. But these all need to be amalgamated into one customer file for CRM to stand any chance of being effective. More importantly than internal politics, the customer viewpoint has been terribly neglected when managing channels. The Future Foundation has done work on the self-service customer, the idea being that we actually want two things from company channels. First, the ability to navigate around the 'skin' of the company, hopefully getting what we want quickly and easily, without having to queue. Then, if this doesn't work, the chance to speak to someone and get help, again hopefully quite quickly and easily.

The second consideration is that in order to work well CRM systems require access to accounts data to give marketers the opportunity to share decision making on high-value customer account enquiries. Linked to this are database marketing systems, inventory systems to ensure stock is controlled, and call-centre management systems in order to ensure that customers' queries about products, support calls and the like are factored into decision making. Finally, enterprise resource planning software must also be integrated into the mix to ensure these systems talk to each other.

The third dimension of complexity is the different product lines – these need to be similarly amalgamated so that cross-sell opportunities can be identified. However in many companies each product has its own manager who often competes with other products for access to the customer. All very well in the old days of product push and market share is king, but from a customer perspective this may mean receiving competing communications – anyone for a loan and a savings plan mailer on the same day?

Figure 7.5 summarises the evolution of CRM from a channel integrator to a fully fledged supporter of relationship marketing. This summarises many of the debates we have had in this chapter.

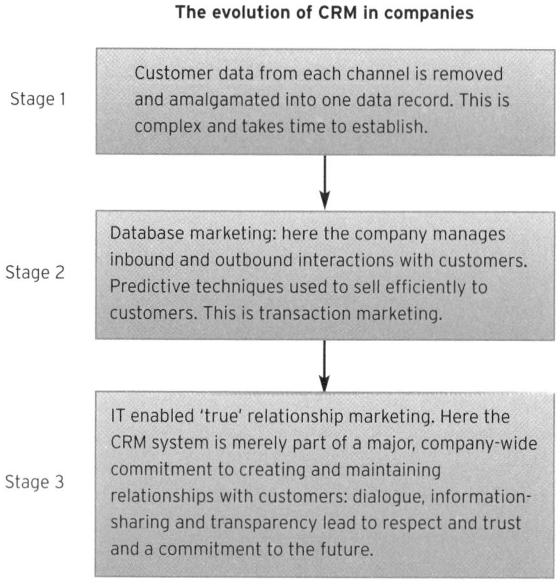

The evolution of CRM in companies

Stage 1 — Customer data from each channel is removed and amalgamated into one data record. This is complex and takes time to establish.

Stage 2 — Database marketing: here the company manages inbound and outbound interactions with customers. Predictive techniques used to sell efficiently to customers. This is transaction marketing.

Stage 3 — IT enabled 'true' relationship marketing. Here the CRM system is merely part of a major, company-wide commitment to creating and maintaining relationships with customers: dialogue, information-sharing and transparency lead to respect and trust and a commitment to the future.

Figure 7.5 The evolution of CRM in companies

Summary to chapter

To understand the state of play with CRM in business you are referred to Tim Ambler of London Business School's comment that 'most companies exist in a state of chaos and shambles'. In the author's experience, he was not exaggerating. Many commentators report that global service levels have remained static, or even declined, in the last 20 years. The theoretical principles behind managing customers and building relationships are widely available (though not necessarily widely understood) but it is the implementation of CRM that is the crucial issue. Companies have collectively spent billions of dollars worldwide on CRM IT systems. They have yet to make the leap to process and in particular culture change that will make the most of this investment: it remains to be seen whether they will. For marketers too, there is a lot at stake. As a profession, they have under-performed in terms of reaching positions at the highest level in companies. The company-wide focus on CRM represents perhaps their best, and maybe last, opportunity to make a mark on genuine value adding organisational change.

Questions

1. How are relationships and direct marketing related?
2. Think about 'relationships' you have as a consumer. How would you describe your associations?
3. What problems have big firms had implementing CRM?
4. CRM is very important to marketers as it brings marketing to the board's attention. Explain how marketers could act more strategically in future.

References

Ambler, T. (1996) *The Financial Times Guide to Marketing: from advertising to zen*, Financial Times Prentice Hall, London.

Berman, B. (1996) *Marketing Channels*, John Wiley & Sons Inc.

Berry, L.L. (1983) 'Relationship marketing' in Berry, L.L., Shostack, G.L. and Upah, G.D. (eds) *Emerging Perspectives on Services Marketing*, American Marketing Association, Chicago, pp. 25-28.

Bruhn, M. (2003) *Relationship Marketing: Management of customer relationships*, Financial Times Prentice Hall.

Buttle, F.B. (1996) *Relationship Marketing Theory and Practice*, Paul Chapman, London.

Corner, L. and Jolson, M.A. (1991) 'Perceptions of gender stereotypic behaviour: An exploratory study of women in selling', *Journal of Personal Selling and Sales Management*, XI (Winter), pp. 43-59.

Cram, T. (1994) *The Power of Relationship Marketing*, Pitman, London.

Crosby, L.A., Evans, R.K. and Cowles, D. (1990) 'Relationship quality in services selling: An interpersonal influence perspective', *Journal of Marketing*, **54**, pp. 68-81.

Ebner, M., Hu, A., Levitt, D. and McCrory, J. (2002) *McKinsey Quarterly, Special Edition: Technology* **4**, p. 49.

Fletcher, K. (2002) 'The role of CRM in changing and facilitating competitive advantage', *Journal of Database Marketing*, **9** (3), p. 203, March.

Foss, B. and Stone, M. (2002) *CRM in Financial Services*, Kogan Page, London.

Gamble, P., Stone, M. and Woodcock, N. (1999) *Up Close and Personal? Customer Relationship Marketing @ Work*, Kogan Page, London.

Giga Information Group (2002) Market Overview: *E-Business/Enterprise Software Applications in 2001 to 2005: Giga Planning Assumption*, 5 March.

Gronroos, C. (1996) 'Relationship marketing: Strategic and tactical implications', *Management Decision*, **34** (3) (13).

Gronroos, C. (1984) *Strategic Management and Marketing in the Service Sector*, Chartwell Bratt, Bromley, Kent.

Gummesson, E. (1987) 'The new marketing: Developing long-term interactive relationships', *Long Range Planning*, **20** (4) pp. 10-20.

Gummesson, E. (1994) 'Making relationship marketing operations', *International Journal of Service Industry Management*, **5**, pp. 5-20.

Hansotia, B. (2002) 'Gearing up for CRM: Antecedents to successful implementation', *Journal of Database Marketing*, **10** (2) p. 121.

International Data Corporation (2001) Demand-Side Survey: A Reality Check on CRM Software, a 2001 study of 300 companies. AMR Research.

Little, E. and Marandi, E. (2003) *Relationship Marketing Management*, Thomson, London.

McCorkell, G. (1994) *The Best of Graeme McCorkell*, Institute of Direct Marketing, Teddington.

Nairn, A. (2002) 'CRM: Helpful or full of hype?', *Journal of Database Marketing*, **9** (4) p. 376.

O'Malley, L. and Mitussis, D. (2002) 'Relationships and technology: Strategic implications', *Journal of Strategic Marketing*, **10** (3) p. 225.

Patron, M. (2002) 'If database marketing was so good, why is CRM so bad?', *Journal of Database Marketing*, **10** (2) p. 102.

Payne, A., Christopher, M. and Peck, H. (1995) *Relationship Marketing for Competitive Advantage: Winning and Keeping Customers*, Butterworth-Heinemann, Oxford.

Pryce, K. (2003) 'Consumer clubs and relationships in fmcg markets', Dissertation for Bristol Business School, UK.

Selnes, F. (1993) 'An examination of the effect of product performance on brand reputation, satisfaction and loyalty', *European Journal of Marketing*, **27**, (9) pp. 19-35.

Insureco from direct sales to direct CRM

Written by: Dr Tim Hughes, who is an expert in CRM at Bristol Business School
The author would like to thank Dr Hughes for this case study.

Insureco is a long established insurance company selling both life and general insurance products. It has a direct marketing unit with a large database of policyholders. However, the company recognised a few years ago that its direct marketing was not as effective as it could be. There was a requirement to increase average product holdings per customer. At the same time there was also a need to improve customer retention as levels of customers cancelling policies were above industry averages. The challenge for Insureco was that it had traditionally been a sales- and operations-based culture, driven by income rather than long-term profit. The efforts of the direct marketing unit had primarily been focused on direct mailings to recruit new customers.

The appointment of a customer relationship manager was an important step in changing this approach. In particular the customer relationship manager recognised that improving cross-selling and customer retention required a far greater degree of integration between marketing and the operational units dealing directly with customers. For example customer retention needs to start at the point of service: 'We don't make customers aware of the pitfalls of surrendering policies and the options open to them. We need to contact lapsers within three days of defaulting, but currently we don't, and all the customers receive the same letters. We need to change the internal culture in the service centre' (Customer Relationship Manager).

This is a common problem in organisations where customer service is based around operational centres that are driven by efficiency of processing rather than by a relationship perspective.

Following a review by the customer relationship manager a number of steps have been taken at Insureco to implement a more proactive approach to dealing with customers. A segmented marketing plan has been developed based on an understanding of the profitability of different customer segments, rather than a plan based simply on existing products that are available. Telemarketing has been integrated with direct mail activities (for instance following up direct mail with a telephone call for the best prospects). Research has been conducted into why customers cancel policies. As a result of this new customer retention initiatives in the form of proactive new customer communications (policy pack, welcome pack, newsletters) and ongoing communications (anniversary communication) have been put in place. New products have been developed specifically for achieving better retention of customers holding maturing products. A new recovery unit has been formed to contact customers surrendering policies or lapsing on payments. Finally operational units have been encouraged to focus on quality of service as well as turnaround times. The results so far have been impressive, with a significant uplift in sales to existing customers and a major improvement in customer retention. The customer relationship manager concludes that 'CRM is not rocket science, it's common sense'. However, he stresses that if marketing is separate from operations there is a danger that the operational emphasis will purely be about efficiency rather than long-term effectiveness in dealing with customers. Achieving an integrated approach is not easy.

Question

Compare and contrast the challenges and issues facing a customer relationship manager with those facing a direct marketing manager.

THE INTERNET

*The Internet brings together the convenience of a
telephone booking and the choice of a shopping centre.*

Objectives

Once you have read this chapter you will:

■ have an appreciation of the Internet as a business tool;

■ understand the important implications of the Internet for business strategy;

■ gain a clear idea of the way in which direct marketing and the Internet link together.

Introduction

It was the week of 10 March 2000 that the UK went dot.com mad. First there was the news that a number of traditional companies had been ousted from the FTSE 100 list in favour of a few Internet-based firms. Then came the launch of Lastminute.com as a public company. Within a matter of minutes frantic share buying had taken this tiny company, with its sales of £409 000 and losses of £6 million, to a paper value of £760 million, an astonishing figure. Since then, of course, the gold-rush fever that led to these speculative valuations has given way to a prolonged cold shower as the realisation dawns that the Net is not a quick route to business niches. Neither has the Internet disappeared however: as a business tool it continues to lag behind its use as an entertainment vehicle, but nevertheless it is here to stay, and will surely grow in importance.

So what is it about the Internet that sparked such a reaction? And what are the implications for direct marketing, a discipline that should surely be capitalising on its IT and direct capabilities? In this chapter we will take a close look at both the strategic and tactical issues that make the Internet such an important development for direct and traditional marketers. We begin with a description of what the Internet is, why it has grown, and what its features are that underpin its use for business. The chapter moves on to the key strategic issues - the new business models that are emerging, the links with direct marketing, and where database marketing may fit into this new world. In Chapter 10, we focus on the Internet as a medium and, using the AIMRITE model developed in that chapter, a comparative analysis of the Net as a medium in competition with direct mail and the telephone is provided.

What is the Internet?

The Internet is a collection of inter-related networks of computers that span the globe. Anyone with a PC and a modem and a telephone line can hook up via an Internet service provider (ISP).

The Internet can be thought of as a giant spider's web of data lines that link together a large proportion of the world's computers. Much larger computers called web servers are responsible for holding and sending the content, websites, onto the Internet in response to a request to see the site by ourselves. The Internet itself is laid out in a manner similar to the international road network – motorways (backbone trunk lines) serving major long-distance routes, main roads serving cities, minor roads (local lines) leading to small villages (Fig. 8.1).

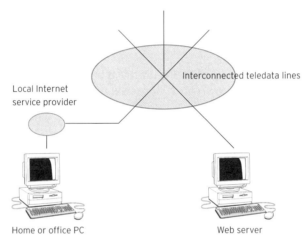

Figure 8.1 The Internet

There are two different Internet media facilities available to direct marketers: *websites*, using the World Wide Web, and *electronic mail* (e-mail).

Websites

Historians in 100 years' time will probably look back at early 2000's websites as slow, clunky and primitive, and there's little doubt that there is room for improvement. However, there has been a great deal of innovation by newcomers to business, some leading edge players such as Amazon and Dell, and most impressively by private individuals seeking to make their mark in all manner of ways. Traditional firms are catching up from a very slow start, often outdone by specialist online operators who may offer more interesting, entertaining places for us to gather information.

Websites are typically multiple electronic 'pages' of text, artwork, pictures, video and sound put together using specially created Internet languages HTML or Java. Hypertext links allow us to click from one page to another, hence affording relatively easy navigation around the site. Security buffers are now well established affording the chance to offer pay-per-view sites, or to encourage consumers to enter their details, including payment by card, and receive goods in return. These may be delivered to the customer electronically if the goods are, say, software, or delivered by traditional post.

Websites are of great potential interest to companies operating a genuine database-driven marketing strategy, because they can *capture the details of visitors to the site*. Therefore, an action initiated by a visitor can trigger return e-mails, in which the communication can be made more relevant according to which parts of the site they visited.

Electronic mail

The use of e-mail as a direct marketing medium is given full attention in Chapter 10 where it is considered alongside the other key media of direct marketing. It is worth noting here the extraordinary impact e-mail has made globally to both working and now domestic life. The low cost and convenience of the technology allows mass communication cheaply and easily. E-mail dovetails extremely well with websites, encouraging faster two-way communication between the firm and its customers.

E-mail is in some ways the electronic equivalent of direct mail, although it may best be pictured from our direct marketing point of view as sharing some qualities of direct mail, and some of the telephone. E-mail does ultimately have the potential to replace much of conventional post as it is cheaper and quicker, faster to execute and holds no 'geographical costs', costing the same to send locally or worldwide. But such a revolution, if it happens at all, is unlikely to happen for a good while – at least until the vast majority of consumers are online at home.

E-mail is being used by online marketers as an inbound channel as well as for outbound communications. It has been estimated that 60 per cent of marketers with websites encourage users to e-mail them with enquiries. E-mail is also being used as an outbound channel by direct marketers to build databases.

EXHIBIT 8.1

JARGON – WHAT YOU NEED TO KNOW

For those who aren't up on web jargon, here's your essential guide to terms relating to direct marketing:

Ad impression: a single viewing by a customer of a web page advert.

Bandwidth: the speed at which data is transferred through the Internet. A vital issue for marketers: using traditional data links, data is transferred at 56.6 kilobits per second, which for downloading pictures is very slow. Broadband (optical fibre) is now offered throughout Europe and in developed countries, and users of Broadband can expect data transfer at speeds order of magnitude faster.

Browsers: in 1993 a 23-year-old programmer called Marc Andreessen invented the first browser. This is software that we use to access the Internet, for example, Netscape or Internet Explorer.

Clickstream: the route a customer takes through a web site. This software allows web owners to track the navigation paths used by customers hence assessing the most popular pages and how the site is being used.

Cookies: websites often compile and share information on the browsing practices of net-users by means of a small electronic name-tag (a 'cookie'). Each time you visit the site, the cookie identifies you, tracks what pages you visit and the data you enter, and records where you were before and where you are heading next. Such information can be aggregated into huge direct-marketing databases, creating a composite profile of an individual web-surfer's habits, often without their knowledge. Direct-marketers can then use these data to place targeted ads in front of us as we browse. Data items that can be gathered on line very easily include: how many visitors; from which countries; when visitors accessed the site: time and date; where on the site they have been; and how many have asked for requests for information.

Disintermediation: a posh word for going direct. The removal of intermediaries. Most commonly seen by financial services companies that replace brokers and salesmen with a web site. Now common in many sectors.

e-business: web and other electronic technologies acting as an enabler for the way a company operates – supply chain, internal operations and customer links. Wider than e-commerce.

e-commerce: selling over the Internet.

Extranet: the linking of two or more intranets between partner organisations. Again private rather than public.

HTML and Java: HTML is Hyper Text Mark Up Language. HTML and Java are the software languages used to build web sites. Java is the more advanced.

HTTP: Hypertext transfer protocol. The way in which web sites are requested by a user using the domain name – the web address.

The Internet: a collection of interrelated networks of computers which span the globe. Anyone with a PC and a modem and a telephone line can hook up via an Internet service provider (ISP).

Intranet: a closed mini Internet that connects PCs within a company or organisation and allows private interaction secure from the public Internet.

IRC: Internet Relay Chat: facilitates the so-called chat rooms of the Internet. Companies are increasingly offering chat room facility for their customers as a way of creating marketing opportunities for themselves. A mother and baby club may be established by a baby product manufacturer.

ISPs: Internet service providers offer access to the web in return for a fee. The world's biggest is AOL (America On Line). The UKs biggest is Freeserve.

Opt-in email: the customer opts to receive e-mail by explicitly asking for it. Opt-out customers instruct the company not to contact them.

Paradigm shift: an entirely new technology that comes along infrequently and disrupts the norms of an industry, allowing new business models to be set up. A recent example could be 3G mobile technology.

Portals: 'portal' sites are those that are used as gateways to the Internet and include the major directories or search engines, such as Google, Yahoo! and Excite, as well as the sites run by Internet and online service providers, such as Freeserve and Virgin Net. *Destination* sites are those that Internet users go to for their content, including news, personal finance, sport, travel, community and entertainment sites. One of the biggest destination sites in Europe is the media company the BBC at www.bbc.co.uk

Search engines: a place to go if you wish to find web sites dealing with a particular subject. They use web-crawler technology called spiders that gather sites relating to key words and provide indeces that users can click through to get to the site quickly. Content providers can register with a search engine and also advertise, both for a fee.

World Wide Web: invented in the early 1990s, a newer multimedia version of the Internet. When most people talk of the Internet, they probably mean the WWW.

The growth of the Internet

The Internet has already had a massive impact on many of our lives. Radio took 38 years to acquire 50 million listeners worldwide while TV took 13 years. The Internet has achieved the same figure in just four years.

Growth in the UK is likely to follow a classical 'S shape' with a slow start, a rapid increase as the early and late majority mainstream come online (beginning about 2000), and a prob-

EXHIBIT 8.2

THE NET: FACTS AND FIGURES

■ April 2003, 54 per cent of adults in Britain had used the Internet in the last three months, an increase of five percentage points on April 2002. Sixty per cent of adults in Britain had used the Internet at some time, also an increase of five percentage points reported in April 2002.

■ 11.7 million households in the UK (47 per cent) could access the Internet from home in the first quarter of 2003, compared with 43 per cent in the same quarter of 2002.

■ Among those adults who had used the Internet in the last three months prior to interview, 85 per cent used it for e-mail, 80 per cent to find information about goods or services and 69 per cent to search for information about travel and accommodation. Almost half had used it to order tickets, goods or services (47 per cent).

■ For adults who had used the Internet, for personal and private use, in the 12 months prior to interview, the most popular purchases were travel, accommodation or holidays (54 per cent), tickets for events (41 per cent), books, magazines, e-learning or training material (40 per cent) and music or CDs (38 per cent).

■ At April 2003, 40 per cent of adults had never used the Internet. These people were asked which of four statements best described what they thought about using the Internet. Over half of non-users chose the statement 'I have not really considered using the Internet before and I am not likely to in the future.' This core group of non-Internet users represents 22 per cent of all adults.

■ A Jupiter survey from 2003 found that online buying behaviour continues to be driven largely by price across all customer segments, with only 8 per cent of online buyers surveyed saying that low price is rarely the most important factor to them when shopping on the Web. Free shipping remains the most popular online promotion; shipping costs were the reason why 51 per cent of online buyers purchased a particular item in a retail store instead of online. Retailers should focus their efforts on finding and satisfying retainable customers: those buyers for whom ease of use, customer service, brand, and reputation tend to be important.

Source: Individuals accessing the Internet – National Statistics Omnibus Survey; Access to Internet from Home – Expenditure and Food Survey (January to March 2003); www.Jupiterdirect.com

able tail off in years to come. However, worldwide hook-up could take decades, perhaps indicated by an overlapping series of S-shaped curves as countries such as China develop.

There is a growing core of research examining the Internet phenomenon from the general business perspective. Hoffman and Novak (1996) asserted that the Internet created a paradigm shift in business and fundamentally changed the relationships that exist between businesses and their customers. The geographical remoteness and community-enhancing effects of the medium support the case of a shift in paradigms. Belk *et al.* (1988) add to this by noting that many businesses are already making the transition from entities operating in the physical marketplace to those operating in the virtual marketplace.

The next section explains in more detail the different ways in which companies use the Internet as a business tool.

Table 8.1: **Worldwide Internet population 2002**

	Population	Internet population
Australia	19.5 million	10.63 million (Nielsen//netratings)
Austria	8.2 million	3.7 million
Belgium	10.3 million	3.76 million
China	1.3 billion	45.8 million
Czech Republic	10.25 million	2.7 million (GfK)
Denmark	5.4 million	3.37 million
Finland	5.2 million	2.69 million
France	59.76 million	16.97 million
Germany	83.2 million	32.1 million (Nielsen//netRatings)
Greece	10.6 million	1.4 million
Hungary	10.1 million	1.2 million
Iceland	279,000	220,000
Ireland	3.88 million	1.31 million
Italy	57.7 million	19.25 million (Nielsen//netRatings)
Japan	127 million	56 million
The Netherlands	16 million	9.73 million
Poland	39.0 million	6.4 million
Portugal	10.08 million	4.4 million
Spain	40.077 million	7.89 million
Sweden	8.9 million	6.02 million (Nielsen//netRatings)
Switzerland	7.3 million	3.85 million
United Kingdom	59.8 million	34.3 million
United States	280.5 million	165.7 million (Nielsen//netRatings)

Source: www.cyberatlas.com, 23 June 2003

How companies use the Internet

In this section we will scope out the commercial use of the Internet, focusing in particular on the new models of e-business that have recently emerged.

Given the learning curve that needs to be travelled in order to use e-commerce effectively, we would expect that the first movers in e-commerce will be those firms which have experience of computer-based systems, are used to dealing with customers at a distance and have ready-made purchasing and customer supply systems. These firms should therefore be direct marketers. Certainly in the US in the early days of Internet usage, more than half of sales in 1996/7 over the Net were CDs, books, IT software and so on that were often sold direct to customers using the telephone. However, when we examine the e-commerce breakthrough companies, there seems little doubt that traditional direct marketers are *not* the companies exploiting the full functionality of the Internet. A look at the e-commerce press reveals the entrepreneurs as those who have sprung directly from specialised e-commerce.

At one extreme, organisations may see the Net as merely another channel or medium through which they can raise a profile. Here, usage of a website would be little more than as a 'corporate brochure'. At the other extreme, some businesses are created entirely out of the opportunities afforded by the Internet, and all their operations are conducted online. The extent to which the Internet should be used as an awareness raiser, rather than as a medium for selling, is important. In turn, how far firms should go in seeking to attract informal or *ad hoc* Internet users to become regular interactors and then, if the medium is to be used for selling, how to induce them into transactions should also be examined. Armstrong and Hagel III (1996) felt that the boundaries between the browser and the purchaser are less significant on the net and thus the transition from one to the other effectively becomes more seamless. This should be borne in mind when we look at Cockburn's (1996) typology of web-based businesses. Adapting this and bringing it up to date (Chaffey, 2002), we have the following set:

- A corporate brochure/brand building site. Here no attempt at any customer dialogue is encouraged although the site may make provision for enquiries. Perhaps more innovative firms may use a website to add value to the real world brand. An example is www.Guinness.com.
- A mail-order-style direct distribution site, which uses the website for taking sales enquiries. Purchases may be confirmed online (*see for example*: www.wru.co.uk).
- A full database marketing-driven online operation, in which data from online sales are fed directly to a marketing database, which is then used for proactive marketing possibly including e-mail (*see* www.next.co.uk).
- Services-orientated relationship building websites. Not surprisingly dominated by business-to-business supplier sites. Chaffey uses the examples of professional management accountant/consultancy sites that will offer users papers and technical information that may help in their workplace. Examples include: www.accenture.com
- Dedicated e-commerce business models. Here the Internet provides the entire environment for the business, which is often an intermediary of some kind. Portals act as key points for information delivery (*see* for example www.yahoo.com or www.Lastminute.com).

EXHIBIT 8.3

PROFILE OF LASTMINUTE.COM

Lastminute.com works in a unique way. Its success is based on a simple premise: offering late details on anything from flights to concert tickets at knockdown prices. It uses a model of business that is impossible to emulate in the normal business environment. In short, its central idea is to use the 'searchability' and scope of the Web in order to access suppliers and get the best deal for consumers. It is therefore one of a new breed of intermediaries that have set up on the Internet.

The company was launched in November 1998, based on an idea of Brent Hoberman, the co-founder and managing director of Lastminute.com. He and his co-founder, Martha Lane Fox, formed the company with a relatively modest $600 000 of funding. However, the company is now well funded, having fetched about £400 million when launched on the stock market in March 2000.

Interestingly, the company has had to spend a considerable sum promoting itself using offline media such as press, posters and Underground advertising. It also used partner companies such as Freeserve, Time Out.com and Tesco.

Lastminute.com acts as a virtual marketplace by bringing together the best offers and placing them in front of customers. The key to its future success will be the speed and convenience afforded to customers, as with so many of the successful Internet companies. It takes advantage of the perishability of services by providing a 'shop window' for deals that are counting down to the time of the service itself. The value added by Lastminute.com is that it does the searching around the Web, which takes time and effort, and may also force suppliers to improve their offers, because of the transparency of the 'shop window' allowing customers to make quick comparisons.

Lastminute.com offers consumers in 11 countries last-minute opportunities for airline tickets, hotel rooms, package holidays, entertainment tickets, restaurant reservations, speciality services, gifts and auctions.

Its marketplace is clear – well-off working people who do not have time or energy to conduct detailed searches for services themselves. Hoberman explains that Lastminute.com helps make busy people's lives easier by using the Internet's unrivalled ability to bring supply and demand together.

Lastminute moved into operating profit by the third quarter of 2002. Lastminute's rosier financial position has been achieved by the nitty-gritty task of running the business efficiently. UK marketing director Carl Lyons claims it has cut the costs of acquiring a customer in the UK from £24 a year ago to £6.24 now. It has also increased the value of existing customers in partnership with Dunnhumby, the database marketing company used and majority-owned by Tesco. A weekly newsletter is e-mailed to the company's 5.6 million registered customers in 10 countries. 'We have the most sophisticated e-mail marketing set-up there is. It's complex, efficient and clever,' Lyons claims. 'We treat it more as a magazine than a sales pitch. Our products will be packaged around features such as "99 ways to feel 100 times better".'

In order to deliver a relevant, bespoke newsletter, customers are segmented according to 12 different life stages – with labels that include 'bargain-hunters' and 'Frasiers' – as well as their product purchase history, purchase value and geographical region. Using this customer understanding, Lastminute.com sent out 178 different versions of its most recent newsletter.

So what next for Lastminute.com? Hoberman has described his vision of Lastminute as: 'It's seven o'clock, your mobile phone rings and we offer you 25 per cent off at your local Italian restaurant, followed by an opera, because we know you've just come back from Italy and are feeling nostalgic.' The chances are that Lastminute will move into interactive TV but other TV specialisms such as a money channel have proved difficult to make a success, so no doubt any moves will have to be carefully planned.

Sources: Murphy, D. (2000) 'The last minute waltz', *Marketing Business*, February, pp. 22–3. Uhrenbacher, S. and Therezien, L. (2000) 'Lastminute recruits two for Euro growth', *Marketing*, 13 January, p. 9. 'Profile of Lastminute.com' (2000) *Venture Capital Journal*, Wellesley Hills, 1 May. Jardine, A. (2000) 'Lastminute wonders', *Marketing*, London, 16 March. Chandiramani, Ravi (2002) 'Winning the net survival battle', *Marketing (UK)* 15 August. City Comment (2003) *Daily Telegraph* 6 August.

Buying on the Internet has become much more an everyday thing now than it was before 2000. The Internet is proving a catalyst for new business ideas. Brockes (2000) reported that there are a small but growing number of students setting up their own businesses from their college bedrooms. For example there is Student-Net.com, an online service for students in the US (although the UK equivalent was tried and failed to survive to the writing of this third edition). Then there's CyberBritain.com, the fastest growing network in Europe, which began with a 17-year-old chief executive, Ben Cohen.

There are a variety of different models of business used by e-commerce specialists (Berryman *et al.*, 1998). They are seller-controlled sites, buyer-controlled sites, and neutral sites. Mitchell (2000) describes examples of agents of each market type in a traditional setting as:

■ *the sellers' market place* – car dealers acting on behalf of the seller;

■ *the neutral market place* – a typical supermarket retailer provides a setting which favours neither the consumer nor the supplier;

■ *the buyers' market place* – the local doctor is an agent who acts on behalf of the patient rather than the suppliers.

Online, these three models translate as follows:

SELLER-CONTROLLED SITES: EXAMPLE - WEB-BASED RETAILERS

On the face of it online retail – electronic versions of shops – looks to be a winner. Convenience for the consumer and cost savings for the business look to be an unstoppable combination. Yet it seems that the growth of Internet transactions at present is sector specific. Entertainment, finance, books and travel are some of the key growth sectors, but high street goods such as clothes and household goods have not enjoyed the same success. Virtual 'malls' such as Barclaysquare.co.uk have struggled, but the biggest crash has come from Boo.com.

EXHIBIT 8.4

IT'S BOO HOO FOR BOO

Writing in *Management Today* in November 1999, Matthew Gwyther got it spot on: 'There are anxieties, however, about Boo's ability to deliver. And when you hype to the extent that Boo has, you must deliver. Sceptics anticipate the first big-time British net flame-out. Boo's is an incredibly ambitious strategy because it is hoping for a seven-country launch, which has been postponed twice. The intricacies of selling and delivering clothes over the net are a little short of nightmarish. We wish it well.'

Gwyther's instincts were right. 'Yah Boo Sucks', 'From Boo to Bust', and 'Bang goes Boo' were just a few of the headlines in the financial pages of the weekend press in late May 2000. Boo.com had crashed.

Originally launched as a pure dot.com company selling sports clothes and trainers over the Internet, Boo.com had achieved an incredible profile in a short time. After months of hype and delay, Boo.com launched in November 1999 with £90 million of backing from investors. Launched by three photogenic young Swedish millionnaires, one of them an ex-model, and with an address in Carnaby Street, it always had news value. It launched a TV ad push, although this was criticised as gimmicky, not explaining who Boo was and what it sold.

What Boo lacked, however, was a decent business proposal. It was argued that these are the kind of products young consumers not only want to be seen to wear, *but be seen to purchase too*. Perhaps buying on the Web was too invisible for this appearance-obsessed market. Yet, even if the basic business model stood up to inspection, its delivery on the Web did not. The site's launch was delayed by five months. When it did go live, its programming was incompatible with many web browsers, to the point of being a no-go zone for iMac users, a consumer group that Boo needed to target. The site itself used flashy graphics and featured a personal shopping assistant called Miss Boo. But consumers complained it was confusing and required a high-speed connection.

What can businesses learn from this? First, spend less on advertising the brand and more on making each customer contact pleasurable and memorable, and ensuring goods are available and delivered to promise. Second, don't launch too early. Boo did the 'equivalent of Tesco opening a flagship store when the automatic doors don't work and there's a cement mixer in the vegetable aisle', as Rosier (2000) put it. Third, and most importantly, make sure business proposals are sound. What is the company's core competence? Can this be turned into an advantage that customers value? Has this been checked with the chosen market target? These strategic questions don't go away just because a company is a groovy dot.com outfit.

Sources: Gwyther, M. (1999) 'Jewels in the web', *Management Today*, London, November. Dignam, C. (2000) 'Boo's failure does not mar the whole dot.com economy', *Marketing*, London, 25 May. Rosier, B. (2000) 'What went so horribly wrong with Boo.com?', *Marketing*, London, 25 May.

EXHIBIT 8.5

HOW NOT TO RETAIL ONLINE

Visit www.webpagesthatsuck.com for examples of what not to do. Created by Vincent Flanders, this site provides a light-hearted look at typical cock-ups made by firms' websites. Flanders highlights some examples: the *Silly Flash*: 'Flash is a tool and like any tool can be used for good or evil or stupid.' *Random Mystery Meat Navigation*: 'We should all know by now that *Mystery Meat Navigation* is not for use on "real" sites. I wondered how I could make MMN even worse.

Well, how about making the links random?' *The Silly Art Fart*: 'You should be able to look at any home page and know what the site is about within 10 seconds. Without the explanatory text, you wouldn't have a clue.' The *Making it Bad*: over-use of Java design including sound files, mouse-over text, pop-up windows, flash, and everything else that irritates the user.

In summary: when designing a website, don't try too hard.

The formula for success of online retailers may include features such as a simple web home page which directs new and existing customers alike quickly around the site, a 'basket' with which the customer buys goods as they browse around the virtual store, and a secure line with which customers purchase, keying in their credit details. The retailer could run features such as an interactive online magazine for customers who have a particular interest in fashion, and various other opportunities for browsers to interact with the site.

As the World Wide Web gets more and more crowded in each category, marketing costs for retail operators will rise significantly, and have already started doing so. It is important to keep a clear view of how net-based business costs are different to high street costs. According to Ward (1999) the back-up processes that in the high street are owned by the retailer – stocking, warehousing and so on – with e-commerce are typically partnership arrangements. The web-based company providing the front end typically concentrates purely on marketing. Therefore operating costs for web businesses are lower (typically about 4 per cent, cf. 15–20 per cent for high street retailers), although distribution costs will be high if the operation is direct fulfilment. However, marketing costs may well be higher as the web business has to work hard in attracting customers to its site. The importance of branding for web-based retailers is therefore very high; in particular the importance of a 'critical mass' as Lastminute.com's MD put it. Basic awareness, particularly at this early stage in the new world of the Web, is vital. Research by Netpoll (see Ward 1999) found that after a couple of months of getting to know the Internet people settle down with 10–12 favourite sites and do not bother with much more surfing. Therefore it is likely that even e-commerce specialists will have to mix online and traditional methods of marketing – a so-called 'clicks and mortar' approach. For example football clubs have created leads in to websites, online chat facilities or electronic ticket ordering through net references in match-day programmes or via stadium advertising for example.

NEUTRAL SITES NOT CONTROLLED BY BUYER OR SELLER: EXAMPLE: THE AUCTION HOUSE

One of the first and certainly the biggest auction house is eBay, a US firm.

EBAY: THE WORLD'S BIGGEST CAR BOOT SALE

Desperate for an 'original' Buzz Lightyear? Keen to get hold of a used baby carrier at low prices? If neither of these particularly appeals, don't worry, eBay has nearly 3 million items for sale, to be captured by the highest bidder.

eBay is the world's biggest online auction house, and one of the secrets to its success is that however much you may feel that what you are selling is junk, it is always exactly what someone somewhere is looking for. The key once again lies in the unri-valled ability of the Internet to match supply with demand.

eBay charges sellers a small fee and this is its main source of income. Unlike many other Internet start-up companies it has already started to turn in a profit. In 2002, $14.8 billion-worth of merchandise sold through eBay. By comparison, Amazon.com had revenues of $3.9 billion. eBay has 60 million registered users. According to eBay, on any given day, there are more than 12 million items listed across 18 000 categories.

BUYER-CONTROLLED SITES: EXAMPLE – THE REVERSE AUCTION HOUSE

Auction houses such as QXL.com are the traditional auction model of consumers bidding against each other for a product or service.

In a reverse auction the consumer names the price they want for a particular product and sticks to it. The reverse auction house then surfs the Web and looks for the product at that price. If they find it, the consumer is contracted to buy. Perhaps the best known supplier of these services is priceline.com – a US-based organisation. However the model may not be transferable to every sector. 'Consumers are not well equipped to name their own price for a house mortgage. Nor are they going to want to name a price for a big-ticket item like a car and then be committed to buying it,' according to a Net research firm in New York (*Sunday Times*, 1999).

ALTERNATIVE VIEWS OF THE FUTURE

E-COMMERCE – THE BUBBLE ABOUT TO BURST?

According to this opinion piece, e-commerce is a 'retrogressive step dressed up as modernism'. 'If in the dark ages they'd invented the idea of shopping by staring into a glass icon and looking at foggy images of things you'd like to buy, picking them, and then waiting for a messenger to bring them to you, today we'd be excitedly welcoming the dawn of walk-in shops, where you can see the goods, feel and touch them and walk out with them.'

Morris describes e-commerce as 'no more than glorified catalogue shopping' (mail order), and extols the joys of spontaneous supermarket shopping in which the customers make any number of on-the-spot decisions about purchases based on what they pass in the aisles. Morris believes that the computer will become a place where only the basics are bought online, while we go shopping for the 'interesting stuff'.

The conclusion is that neither e-commerce nor high-street shopping will dominate. The likely end-game is a sensible, genuinely progressive amalgam of online and real shops, or 'clicks and mortar'. Then at last, as one US e-commerce expert put it, the letter 'e' can return to its rightful place as the fifth letter of the alphabet.

Source: adapted from Morris, G. (2000) 'Hall of infamy (no. 40 – e-commerce)', *Guardian*, 11 February.

Another model of business emerging is community or aggregate buying. Here, a group of consumers get together in order to increase their buying power by offering companies economies of scale.

For example, Internet start-up company Adabra offers a product for sale (let's say a video player) for a set period, say a week. The price Adabra will pay the supplier depends on the number of buyers. Adabra's website will exhibit the common high-street price for the goods, say £300. The site also displays a number of other prices, all lower than £300. Buyers log on and choose the price they would ideally like to pay. The 'gamble' they take is that if they choose too low a price, there may not be enough buyers at that low price, and Adabra will not be able to make them an offer. If enough buyers choose, say, £250, the price is forced down to this level because enough sales at this price will still be profitable to the seller, and to Adabra, which pockets the difference between the buyer's price and a price it negotiates with the supplier.

So far in this chapter we've examined the growth of the Internet and begun to look at how companies use it. One of the strategic issues raised has been the way in which the Internet encourages different types of marketplace – buyer, seller, or neutral. We are now ready to look in more detail at the distinctive features and benefits of the Internet, before turning to the impact of the Internet on direct marketing. In these sections you may like to note the emergence of the other major strategic planks of e-business: the Internet as a channel, possibly with new types of intermediaries growing in the future, and the Internet as a network that brings groups of people together.

Distinctive features and benefits of the Internet

The most radical difference (of the net) is the shift in power from the merchant to consumer.

The Economist (1997), 10 May

THE INTERNET HAS THE POWER TO CHANGE THE RULES

Bill Gates recently called the Web 'friction-free capitalism'. What did he mean by this? In traditional, non-Internet markets, there is what might be termed high 'transaction isolation'. In other words we as consumers buy without full knowledge of alternatives. Consumers often have a high inertia barrier (we are too lazy to change suppliers), so businesses can take advantage of our laziness and charge high prices knowing that we will not look around too much. In many cases big companies will exploit their power of greater distribution.

On the Internet the leverage of big companies using their distribution power does not exist. Customers are much more likely to undertake an information search for different alternatives (or use an agent to search for them: see later for a description of 'Infomediaries'), because of the ease of searching on the Web. In addition, companies themselves can benefit from the slickness of the Web to lower their own costs with suppliers, delivering a highly efficient value chain to the consumer. These efficiencies and ease of comparison means that the Internet therefore comes close to providing a 'pure' marketplace – i.e. one in which any business which provides similar content to competitors, but at a higher price, will go bust. Business guru Gary Hamel (1998) described the Internet as a 'noose for mediocrity'.

The Internet is also *quick*. This has enabled a new breed of dedicated e-commerce businesses to emerge. Companies like Lastminute.com and priceline.com rely on speed and flexibility for their operations. They use the speed of the Web to quickly establish customers' needs in, say, airline flights, and then search quickly to pull together the best last-minute deals for them. Here, the supplier uses the Net as a way of matching supply with demand in a way that is convenient for the customer, and links easy buying with the special feature of the Internet as a giant marketplace that is dynamic. Internet businesses are easily dissolved and reformed – therefore the Internet favours companies which can think and change quickly. 'Nimble businesses' will be more successful than those slow to change.

As a 'many to many' medium, the Internet enables consumers to cooperate with each other to get the best deals, something that is likely to grow considerably in the future. As we saw earlier with eBay and priceline.com, live auctions are much more likely, again utilising the ability of the Net to bring lots of suppliers and buyers together easily and quickly.

Having been introduced to the radical nature of the Internet, we are now ready to examine its individual features in more detail.

FEATURES

Customer control

If we view the Internet as a medium or channel to market, and therefore compare it to other media, the Internet has one unique characteristic: customers control when or indeed if they are exposed to the advertising/selling message. Customers also know that they can leave the site at any time and return at their own convenience, without having to make or break any social relationships with salespeople along the way. Contrast this in your mind with traditional advertising followed by a visit to, say, a high-street clothes store. In this scenario, a significant amount of control lies with the company rather than the customer.

Information flows upwards and sideways from customers as well as downwards to customers

In traditional markets, information is passed 'down' to customers from companies taking advantage of their control of the act of going to market. However, the Internet's low cost of access allows customers (or agents acting on their behalf) to take control of going to market. In addition, the Internet caters for easy 'sideways' information flows, allowing customers to talk to each other, forming communities of interest extremely quickly (Mitchell, 2000). Instead of one type of marketplace where companies tell customers what they have to sell and customers react or choose as a result, we now have three types of marketplace online as we saw earlier.

The Internet is like a flea market

If you have ever browsed amongst the antiques in a street market on a Sunday morning, you are in a flea market. One of its characteristics is that a flea market will attract casual passers-by who see the idea of casually wandering through the market as a pleasurable activity. Belk *et al.* (1988) suggested that the Internet is analogous to such an entity. In other words, individuals will generally range from passive browsers through to those who are actively searching for and seeking to buy. For Zwass (1998), the challenge for business is how to engage users by promoting the transition from non-user to passive browser and then active user of websites.

Disintermediation and reintermediation

One of the most significant impacts of the Web has been the emergence of its disintermediating and reintermediating effect. The roles of established intermediaries (such as supermarkets) are reduced or eliminated, to be replaced by new intermediaries between a business and its customers. For the firm, this has the effect of increasing the speed of products and services to the marketplace. This is something we will examine more closely later in this chapter in the section examining the links between direct marketing and the Internet.

The Internet offers freedom from economies of scale for smaller businesses

Website and e-mail facilities help to reduce the physical costs of establishing physical distribution channels for businesses (O'Connor and Galvin, 1997). For small businesses the Net offers true equality in the sense that it allows open access. As a result, the Internet site of one business cannot drown out that of another; each has a unique position and can be accessed by all net users. This is one reason why dot.com companies have experienced such phenomenal growth.

Ubiquity and omnipresence, or 'it's always there and it's all there'

The Internet is a medium and marketplace in one – it allows buyers and suppliers to come together and transact. It can be accessed at any time by the customer, so that customers know that if they want to buy an airline ticket at 10 o'clock on a Saturday night, they can do so.

Transparency

The Internet acts like a shopping centre in that customers can make price/value comparisons very quickly. Indeed, the Internet is probably superior to a shopping centre in terms of speed and convenience of making these comparisons. Everything is just a 'mouse click' away. Increasingly, in markets such as tourism customers are able to treat the Internet as a one-stop shop, in which they can gather information, make comparisons, then make a purchase all in one session. It is this ease of comparison which means that an 'average' offer will therefore not survive – as Hamel and Sampler (1998) put it: the Internet is a noose for mediocrity.

Convenience

We need to make the basic but important point that a large proportion of the population now spend some or a lot of their day in front of or near a computer. Therefore customers using the Internet have proximity to the Internet as a buying channel for much of their day. This suits the (often random) way in which people suddenly think 'Blow, I need to check my bank account', or 'Damn, I forgot to order that wine for the weekend'. For people who are 'time poor' (well-off people with busy jobs) or are less organised, and their buyer behaviour is convenience-driven, the Internet is unrivalled as a convenient channel.

Interactive capability

As Hoffman and Novak (1996) pointed out, the Internet allows a change from a one-to-many model of communication (e.g. TV advertising) to a one-to-one or even many-to-many model (e.g. interactive 'chatlines' on the Net). This allows for significant interaction between customer and firm. For example, banks may offer customers the chance to record or plan their finances, bookstores such as Amazon.com allow customers the chance to search for titles quickly, and to post their own reviews on the site. Dell Computers uses the Internet as a way of displaying help manuals.

Speed

Weiber and Kollman (1998) distinguished between traditional businesses and cyberspace business in terms of the grounds on which they compete for competitive advantage. While traditional businesses compete on cost and quality grounds, Web-based businesses can compete according to the speed with which they gather and use information, and the quality of the information they gather.

Improved service for repeat customers using the Internet linked to a marketing database

If you access the Tesco (a UK supermarket) website to take advantage of its direct delivery service, you will find that it takes a few hours to key in all your shopping when you do it for the first time. However, the next time you may find it only takes a few minutes. The database has saved your previous shopping list and now you just need to adjust your needs to suit. The service for existing customers has therefore improved markedly. The Internet helps here by providing an easy link between the customer and the company database, so enabling a personalised service to be provided.

Companies can further improve their online service to existing customers using e-mail. In this way firms can correspond outbound with existing customers in the same way as with direct mail or the telephone. An in-depth comparison of e-mail and websites with other media comes at the end of Chapter 10.

Other examples of this kind of one-to-one service come from some banks which may provide interactive online services similar to a First Direct style operation. However, in general note that as yet tailored delivery of services or products is still a rarity.

The Internet can lower the cost base of the business

Fraser *et al.* (2000) pointed out the importance of the Web to internal workings as well as customer interfaces. They felt that intranets and extranets as well as the Internet will facilitate lower costs in purchasing departments.

Fraser *et al.* addressed the fundamental question of costs and benefits of e-commerce solutions for businesses. They listed the following sources of competitive advantage for e-commerce:

1. a reduction in intermediation costs associated with wholesale and retail activities;
2. lowering of supply and logistics costs by curbing time and effort in these operations;

3. improved information gathering and processing that allow improved management of the supply chain;

4. lowering the costs of gathering customer information, allowing greater chance for effective marketing.

However, there may be a disadvantage in being the first mover in the use of e-commerce because of the high costs of establishing capital and human resources. In other words, Internet technologies have high *learning* costs. It may be that the boom in all e-commerce stocks that has marked the turn of the century will subside as many first movers do not succeed.

In summary what we call e-commerce is potentially a new paradigm or a way of doing business which generates its own rules. Direct distribution is part of this, but the real heart of it is that the Net acts as a highly efficient marketplace which dynamically brings buyers and all suppliers together. Therefore buyers and suppliers can all react to each other and the deal or offer changes depending on demand and supply. This replicates a town-centre market, but on a global scale. What seals the power of this is the convenience and control that it gives to the customer.

We can now turn to a more in-depth analysis of how database marketing techniques 'overlap' with e-commerce.

The impact of the Internet on direct and database marketing

This section discusses the impact of the Internet in changing the very heart of direct marketing concepts. As this is potentially complex, we will divide up the discussion under two headings: 'what has changed?' and 'what stays the same?'

WHAT HAS CHANGED? POWER IS SHIFTING TO CONSUMERS

In a far reaching article, Mitchell (2000) went a long way towards explaining the impact of the Internet on direct and database marketing. He pointed out the implications of the Internet's ability to transfer power from sellers to buyers. As we have seen, direct marketing strategy is predicated around the idea of customer management. Here, companies use their transaction histories with customers to understand customers' needs, predict their future needs – what they want, when they want it, how much they would be worth to the company and therefore how much discount the company could offer so that both sides win. Mitchell says that with the new world order the Internet is enabling, customers will no longer put up with being 'managed'. In this old world, the power in the relationship lay squarely with suppliers who would decide who to target, what offer to make and when to pull out of the deal if it didn't suit them and so on. In the Internet-driven marketplace, customers (via agents such as infomediaries) will have the upper hand. The infomediary is potentially the most powerful of all the new Internet models of doing business, and is discussed next.

There are a number of skills of database marketing which do not transfer well over to e-commerce. These include modelling, segmentation, targeting and so on (see Sheth and Sisodia, 1997, for more details). This is because the dominant paradigm so far has been the use of websites to attract in-bound customers rather than the use of e-mail to target customers proactively. In other words, as we said earlier, *it is the customer not the company who controls the contact*. Ironically, the importance of traditional advertising may increase as the company will have to rely on keeping its name in the customer's mind. The firm will also have to make sure its offer is competitive.

Although it is still early days, perhaps we can tentatively make some predictions about likely segmentation approaches on the Internet. For e-mail-driven proactive marketing, there is every reason to believe that transaction-based segmentations based on the customers' value to the company and needs from it should be possible. It will depend on the company's ability to link sales data from the Web traffic to a customer-based database, and secondly on customers' willingness to be targeted by e-mail.

For inbound traffic on the website, customers *will segment themselves* based on their needs and wants – all the company can do is position correctly, offer value competitively and make itself as attractive as possible.

INFOMEDIARIES

Before the Internet became established the balance of power usually lay with suppliers rather than buyers. Suppliers could use customer ignorance to exploit differences in price elasticities between different segments (Doyle, 1995). As has been argued earlier in the chapter however, the transparency and ease of switching of the Net is beginning to change these dynamics as power switches from supplier to consumer. As was also argued, with the Internet the consumer has more control. However, choice and control are double-edged swords: consumers often do not have the time, patience or perhaps ability to work out the best offer to suit them. What many of them will want is to take advantage of the better value the Net can offer them, but seek help in doing this. This opens up the field to infomediaries (Hagel and Singer, 1999, Mitchell, 2000).

Traditional intermediaries such as brokers act on behalf of the sellers rather than consumers. In contrast infomediaries will act on behalf of consumers. They take on consumers as clients and gather data about their needs across a wide variety of categories. They would also record data about purchases made through themselves and hence increase their knowledge over time about consumers, in the same way as a traditional database. Infomediaries are in a much more powerful position than traditional database marketers, however, as they can record data across competitors and across sectors, getting a holistic picture of consumers' purchases and preferences. Infomediaries may also issue smart cards and credit cards for use in the physical world, enabling more information to be gathered.

It could be predicted then that infomediaries will offer the following services:

■ lowering customers' search 'costs' – probably time;

■ finding the best value for customers;

■ shielding customers from unwanted marketing messages;

■ leveraging customers' combined buying power in a reverse auction model.

What infomediaries can also do is to get back towards Peppers' (1993) one-to-one concept (*see* Chapter 6), but this time *act on behalf of the customer*. They can gather information from customers about their preferences, and how much they have to spend. They can then react at that time to scour the Web for the best deal to meet that need, as above. But they can then do the 'database marketing' bit, which is to forecast the future needs of the customer and proactively scour the Web for deals for the customer. One example of this is Amazon.com which seems to have hit on a formula where this does work. It will use the customers' travels through its website to gather information on that individual in relation to book sales. The next time the customer accesses the site, they get information on the company's best deals for that customer. In a sector such as where new products are rife and there is a vast array of choice, this kind of marketing makes sense.

The impact of infomediaries on suppliers

If the efficiency of the process proves to be high (depending on consumer participation and the ability of infomediaries to deal with large amounts of data in an individual manner) then the costs of going to market for partner firms should also be lowered. As a channel to market, infomediaries may be attractive if they can lower the cost per sale because response will be higher than the firms would get using traditional methods. However, it may also be that firms' existing customers may be encouraged by infomediaries to shop around for deals and therefore, while acquisition costs may be lowered, retention costs may be higher, depending on the competitiveness of the supplier.

The infomediary market at present

At the time of writing, infomediation is starting to happen, but as yet is undeveloped. Companies such as populardemand.com and waysearch.com have gone bust trying. Priceline.com continues on as a reverse auction but has yet to develop in the way Mitchell suggests.

If they do take off infomediaries will thrive in complex product or service sectors, where choice is high and where detailed information is needed before making a decision. Database marketing-led infomediaries may thrive where there is a high chance of the product or service being tailored for the individual, for example health care or household services like child care.

Markets such as financial services, travel and holidays and cars are being attacked because their combination of information intensity, high search costs and pricing distortion and confusion tactics have made it difficult for customers to find the best deal at

EXHIBIT 8.8

INFOMEDIARIES: EVOLUTION NOT REVOLUTION?

It looks as though any gains infomediaries make will have to be hard earned. Duval (2002) looked at Autobytel.com which connects consumers with car dealers. The car market is a classic instance where an infomediary could potentially add value. Potential buyers submit a request for a price quote on a specific car – along with their name and contact information – which is forwarded to the dealer assigned to the area.

She found that buyers who used Autobytel saved an average of 1.2 per cent compared with those who purchased a car through conventional means, though this savings figure is higher for people who don't normally shop around. The lower prices arise because dealers have a contract with Autobytel that provides incentives to offer lower prices. In addition, Duval noted that some customers used Autobytel but made their purchase at a dealer other than the one they were referred to – and they also received lower prices. This backs up suggestions made earlier in the chapter that online consumers search around and are more educated about their purchase and, thus, better negotiators. The low cost of searching on the Internet could also expand buyers' options and make it easier to explore distant dealerships and more types of cars in search of a better deal.

Source: Duval, J. (2002) 'Test driving the Internet', *Regional Review*, 2nd Quarter, **12**, (2).

the time they need it. These are the prime sectors for early players in the infomediary business and some early players include Travelocity.com and Expedia.com. If infomediation does prove to be a powerful business model it is also possible that large powerful brands from traditional industries may enter this market. Thus the likes of IBM, BT or supermarkets like Tesco could consider themselves as players in this market.

Possible problems for the infomediary concept

Infomediaries may run up against the high costs of management time in offering customers help without charging too high a price for that help. Infomediaries based on trust may still spring up, but if the costs of proactive marketing based on predicting customers' needs is too high (as has proved to be the case with traditional one-to-one marketing) then they just become a virtual retailer pasting up what they claim will be the best offers.

The next major change to consider is the Internet's impact on loyalty.

THE REDUCED IMPORTANCE OF LOYALTY PROGRAMMES

Evans and Wurster (1997) contend that 'as it becomes easier for customers to switch from one supplier to another – something that is now commonplace on the Net – the competitive value of traditional approaches such as one-stop shopping and established relationships will drop. Cross selling will become more difficult. Competitive advantage will be determined product by product and so providers with broad product lines will lose ground to focused specialists.' If this scenario becomes reality the entire concept of customer loyalty to one company, leading to lowered costs of selling for that company, may need re-examining.

An alternative view is that, as the trend of customers buying from remote sources increases, the importance of branding may increase as trust in intangible suppliers becomes more important. However Evans and Wurster's comments about relationships may provide a stern warning to advocates of *relationship marketing* in consumer markets. It also has implications for database marketers in that it suggests that for database marketers using the Internet, the best approach may be to concentrate on exchanging information and providing value based on customer information, rather than possibly rather weak attempts at relationship building.

THE NEW ROLE OF CUSTOMER INFORMATION

Sahay *et al.* (1998) characterise the move into Internet markets as from what they describe as atom-based business (the physical world) to bit-based business (the virtual world). This will necessitate a change in emphasis towards information-based marketing (i.e. the marketing strategies and tactics are driven by customer interactions) where the interactive exchange of information, and the content, quality and speed of responses can be a source of competitive advantage. On a similar theme, Walters and Lancaster (1999) contend that 'information is the glue that holds together the structure of all businesses. A company's value chain consists of all the activities it performs to design, produce and market its product. But the value chain also includes all the information that flows within a company and its suppliers, distributors and customers.'

Walters and Lancaster make interesting points about information which are of great strategic value to direct marketers. They point out that there is a trade-off between information *reach* and *richness*. Reach is simply the number of people exchanging information. Richness refers to the amount of information going from sender to receiver, the extent of its customisation, and the extent to which interaction is possible. The idea is that, as information flows become more valuable, it is more difficult to manage these flows in a mass market. This has underpinned the difficulties that companies have had in implementing one-to-one marketing.

However, the advent of new technology should allow for an increased amount of richness at decreased cost, allowing for more reach. This has huge implications for the company's supply chain, as shown in Fig. 8.2.

The Internet allows customers to initiate the value chain process, and to infuse it with information about their needs. This supports a greater amount of mass customisation than has existed up to now.

SHOULD COMPANIES REACT TO CUSTOMERS GOING TO MARKET (REACTIVE MARKETING) OR TRY TO PREDICT CUSTOMERS' NEEDS AND BE PROACTIVE (DATABASE MARKETING)?

Mitchell (2000) discussed marketing as something that is mostly 'done' to customers in traditional markets. He points out that the Internet presents us with a new world in which customers are the 'marketers' who target companies – here companies would react to customers' approaches. This debate raises a number of profound questions. On the Internet companies may still use transaction information to do data-driven proactive marketing. The weakness of the customer management model in traditional database marketing was always that it was a set of guesses, by the company, about customer needs (timing, product) and preferences for that supplier (driven by one company when maybe the customer uses others as well). Therefore there is a lower chance of success in efficiently going to market – it is just the company 'giving itself a chance' rather than acting on firm instructions from the customer.

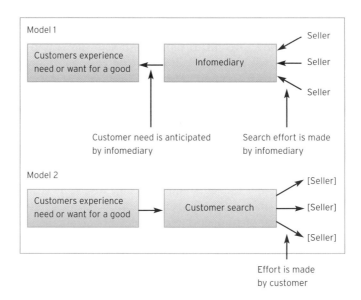

Figure 8.2 In the first model infomediaries add value by removing the effort of searching. In the second model customers do it themselves. In the first model the value chain is extended towards customers so they do less

The power of the Internet may lie in its ability to mix up reactive and proactive marketing. Take Amazon.com which lets the customer tell it when the customer is ready to enter the market for books (reactive marketing). It then proactively offers customers choices of books based on previous customer transactions (database-driven proactive marketing). Customers then take back control and complete the transaction as it suits them, without pressure. This is a powerful way of doing business.

With infomediaries, another slight variation is possible. Customers may initiate the action by contacting the infomediary, which then takes over and manages the transaction on behalf of the customer. In this sense infomediaries are practising 'customer management', but with the customers' consent and knowledge. The customer has asked to be 'managed' because they see this management as a service to them: infomediaries are carrying out a search on their behalf.

INTERACTIVE MARKETING

A number of writers have discussed the Net from the perspective of interactive marketing (Hagel (1999), Peters (1998), Spalter (1995) and Hoffman and Novak 1996)). Interactive marketing can be described as the firm and customers having multiple two-way dialogue in which both purchase and non-purchase-related information is shared. The speed, convenience and low cost of dialogue on the Internet has led to some commentators describing interactive marketing as the new marketing paradigm, superseding traditional transaction marketing or even relationship marketing. Before we get too carried away however, let's slow down just a little.

Interactive marketing's power lies in the ability of the Internet to open up access to customers eager to participate in communities of which companies may form part. As we noted earlier, Hoffman and Novak (1996) described the Internet as a many-to-many mediated environment, allowing a lot of people to talk to each other at the same time. This is distinct and different to any other medium, and replicates a group of people meeting in a traditional community. In this sense, the change to business process that the Internet brings seems to have substance. Sports websites are an example of this. Supporters have high involvement with their club and supporter 'chat lines' are extremely popular. A typical English Premier League site may get hundreds of thousands of 'hits' on the day after a game. Another example is the bookseller Amazon.com which has a facility for consumers to post their own book reviews on site. Moreover, consumers can set up their own sales of cottage industries on the Amazon website. These are innovative ideas made possible by the Internet. More profoundly, they are a symptom of the growing consumer power that the Net offers, and the need for businesses to work harder to attract custom.

EXHIBIT 8.9

INTERACTIVITY - THE CASE OF FEDERAL EXPRESS

'FedEx' is a package delivery multinational which delivers millions of packages every day. Since 1994 it has run a service online in which customers have a direct window into FedEx's package-tracking database. 12,000 customers per day click through web pages to pinpoint their parcels. That, customers feel, adds to the service and saves FedEx millions of dollars in customer service costs.

The community building attributes are one part of the Net's interactivity, but there is also the chance for more normal transactions to be interactive. In reverse auctions and standard auctions both supplier and buyer are interacting with each other in a way which is only done in a multi face to face situation, for example a traditional fruit market.

However, not all examples of interactive marketing are paradigm changes. We need to be careful not to lump in all aspects of business through the Internet as being wildly innovative, when much of it is merely replicating existing business practice, but through a new medium. Examples include sellers letting customers fill their own baskets with goods. This may well be a good, efficient use of the Internet, but as a customer/supplier way of interacting it is exactly the same as mail order shopping. Other examples of 'interactivity' are insurance companies such as Eagle Star Direct and Direct Line asking consumers for information and offering quotes for car and house insurance. While this is more interactive than using, say, direct mail (as you may get instant feedback from the supplier telling you that your order has been accepted), it is less interactive than the telephone.

Recording interactions for database marketing

Here we need to ask to what extent firms should attempt to record interactions, learn from them and then change the marketing to that individual as a result. Sceptics would argue that this is never going to be realistic as the management of such a process will be too expensive and customers do not require such minute segmentation. On the other hand, we have already seen from the work of Peppers (see Chapter 6 for a discussion of one-to-one marketing) that such ideas may have possibilities. Perhaps something in between recording all interactions and studying them, and recording none at all may lie a reasonable compromise, so that there is some sort of two-way link between customer interactions on the Net and any database marketing activity driven by it. In this instance there will be a need to distinguish transactions and non-transaction interactions, and to decide the worth of managing such data.

Now that we have examined what has changed or will change in direct marketing thinking as a result of the Internet, we can ask ourselves what will stay the same.

WHAT WILL STAY THE SAME? THE INTERNET AS A 'DIRECT CHANNEL'

Some product-based companies are using the Internet as the front end of a direct distribution operation. Here the Internet replicates a mail order style of business, and the skills of traditional direct marketing agencies will be vital (*see* Exhibit 8.10). Businesses whose service can be delivered electronically can go one step further and can distribute the product online as well. In some instances, we need to examine the motives of the companies: it may be that the customer is getting a better online service, but it is often the case that costs may be lowered, particularly for banks. *The Times* of 12 May 1999 reported that the financial services company Egg was only taking online business because 'costs for online banking are four times lower than telephone transactions and ten times lower than high street branches'.

EXHIBIT 8.10

LIFE AT THE SHARP END – FULFILLING AN ORDER EFFICIENTLY IS NOT EASY

As Laura Mazur of *Marketing Week* magazine notes, getting the idea up and running and the website designed is just the start of the battle. There are increasing signs that Web-based businesses are, not surprisingly, finding delivering on customer service promises just as difficult if not more so than their traditional counterparts.

Mazur examined a report from Ernst and Young, based on over 125 companies. Firstly companies found it very difficult to maintain consistency of service between different channels; for example, customers were accessing information on the website and then receiving a letter telling them something quite different.

More fundamental, however, were the examples of poor *fulfilment* found by Ernst and Young. Reports of the growth in online shopping were offset by others on just how unprepared many companies were for the rise in visitors to their sites. One researcher found that almost half the sites surveyed took more than five days to answer e-mail requests. Almost a fifth of suppliers failed to respond to e-mails at all, while nearly one in three charged more than the RRP for a sample product.

One of the problems is the technology itself. The speed and convenience alluded to many times in this chapter tend to raise expectations for subsequent service. But, as Mazur noted, it is not the technology that makes the relationship work, but the people in the company wanting to respond to customers' needs. Given the isolation between company and customer in a virtual market place, it is perhaps not surprising that home shopping is laden with tales of deliveries of the wrong products and late deliveries. Anecdotally, there are stories of supermarkets offering slots of delivery that are over a week later than the shopper requests.

As all traditional direct marketers know, in a 'direct company' it is the back end of operations, fulfilment, that is the hardest part of customer service to get right; it is also the most important.

EXHIBIT 8.11

IF THE WEBSITE IS THE TIP OF THE ICEBERG, WHAT LIES BELOW THE SURFACE? HOW FULFILMENT COMPANIES CAN BRING DATABASE MARKETING AND THE INTERNET TOGETHER.

Internet growth has led to a new breed of one-stop shop communication firms that help businesses deliver their Web-based operations. In October 1999 the company Dataforce launched I-Force, a new venture which offers website design, database management, and links these with payment processing, storage and packing, Parcelforce delivery and follow-up marketing using direct mail. I-Force promises to have its business customers up and running with e-commerce in just 12 weeks. Perhaps the key to the success of the operations is the efficient linking of apparently separate events like capturing and recording customer data on one hand, with picking and packing goods on the other.

Companies like Dataforce are building on the already established skills of the direct marketing supply sector, which specialises in the complicated businesses of fulfilling a customer order efficiently and in a high-quality way. This after all is the direct/database industry's core service to the customer – and, as every business studies student knows, customer service is vital to the long-term profitability of the company.

(*Source*: based on Farrelly, P. (1999) 'The nuts and bolts of net nirvana', *The Observer* Business section, 5 September, p. 9.

CAPTURING CUSTOMER INTERACTIONS AND USING THIS FOR KNOWLEDGE MANAGEMENT

The Internet has changed many things, but what is unlikely to change is the strategy of capturing customer interactions and learning from them. This may not help greatly in the company's targeting – since it is primarily the customer who targets – but it can help in areas such as supply chain management, purchasing, operations, all of which feed into a more competitive value proposition.

EXHIBIT 8.12

MERGING WEB-BASED BUSINESS AND DATABASE MARKETING

Data Factors is a company which specialises in ticketing sales for sports concerns. Established in Suffolk, it began life installing ticketing systems for Ipswich Town, the local football team. However, the company is shifting its focus and building an Internet front end to its systems so that supporters book tickets over the Web. Data Factors sees its future as an e-commerce portal advertising its clients' available tickets while allowing them to collate data about their supporters. The sports franchise then has a growing list of potential buyers of merchandise, now a lucrative part of the business of sport, and also a growing source of market information in the form of a transaction database.

(*Source*: based on Garrahan, M. (2000) 'Putting football seat sales into the back of the net', *Financial Times*, 28 January.

Mitsubishi is one example of a company using the Internet to improve its supply chain management. Mitsubishi uses a dealer extranet to give dealers access to product updates and technical bulletins and also to allow online ordering and order tracking, handing the dealer full control of the ordering process.

TESTING

Another aspect of Internet business that replicates physical marketplaces is testing. This may be relatively trivial, for instance trying new creative approaches in website design. The testing process will lack the control obtained by testing using private media – direct mail and the telephone – because different websites will have to be tried one after the other. However the speed and low costs of the Net will bring other rewards: bookseller Waterstones has used its website to explore otherwise risky new ventures in new markets at low cost. It has tested books that in a bookshop environment may be considered too risky.

EXHIBIT 8.13

HOW DIRECT SHOPPING CHANGES CONSUMER BEHAVIOUR

Helen Smith (not her real name), a teacher with two children, used to flog her way round ASDA on a Friday night. No longer. Now her 19-year-old son Rod does the shopping – without leaving his desk at work. He is part of a trial of the new Waitrose@work in which online orders are delivered to a group of shoppers who all work in the same place. The supermarket saves considerably on delivery costs and the shoppers get their shopping only hours after they ordered it. Rod is an example of what may become a social revolution – just as men who won't cook will barbecue, so men who won't shop may well be happy to order through the Net.

The large players such as Tesco and Sainsbury are offering home delivery for a £5 charge. Dave and Alison Jones use the Net for 'bulky bogstandard stuff like catfood, cereal, washing powder and wine. Shopping on the Internet is still a chore, but it's not as bad as going to the supermarket. Now it's set up it takes me about 30 minutes to update it.' It has stopped them from impulse buying. Now their store cupboard is not 'clogged full of impulse buys which they never use'.

Another online shopper had some insights: 'it changes the way you shop because you have to think in advance. It's made us keep a list on the freezer – we were never that organised before – and we've got a written catalogue at home which gets pulled out occasionally.' His partner commented: 'I suspect it works for us because we are horribly predictable.' This may be true – those people who like the chance encounters with some new and tasty foods that the supermarkets are always offering may prefer to shop in the high street.

It's not all good news stories though. One shopper got his first list wrong by about 20 per cent because of the number of confusing options in scrolling down each category list. This is a common beginner's complaint. He used his store online happily for six weeks until a major disaster put him off. 'We got stuff for newborn babies instead of our toddler. And the fish hadn't been properly wrapped so everything was ruined. I e-mailed the management about three times but nothing happened. I am totally fed up.' It looks like no matter what the new technology can do it is still the quality of customer service which is the key in keeping people loyal.

(*Source*: adapted from Dodd, C. (1998) 'Shops on the box', *Guardian*, 6 August, pp. 14–15.

Summary to chapter

In this chapter we took a close look at what is likely to be a crucial development for direct marketers in years to come. The Internet has the power to alter the entire economic structures of many businesses, to change the way businesses are created and to change consumer behaviour, permanently.

Direct marketers should understand that the Internet revolution will not be based around customer data. Instead it will be based around customers taking more control of the buying process. The new home of direct and database marketing in the future may lie with agents such as infomediaries helping customers, provided that such help is driven by customer data, in other words is proactive.

The context of data usage will also change. Transaction data will still be important but it may be that customer needs data will be expressed directly by the customer, removing the need for future purchases to be inferred from past purchases. Also, transaction data will encompass many companies rather than just one.

Strategically, developments such as the growth of infomediaries may have profound implications for database marketing – the next decade promises to be an interesting one!

Questions

1. As the marketing manager for an airline, how would you sum up the strengths and weaknesses of the following channels: travel agent, direct via a call centre and classified adverts; and the Internet?

2. Examine the following websites:

    www.etoys.com   www.ft.com   www.easyjet.com
    www.dell.com   www.tesco.co.uk   www.amazon.co.uk
    www.priceline.com   www.ford.co.uk   www.qxl.com

    Compare and contrast the features of each, and comment on how each company has used the functionality of the Internet to give themselves an advantage.

3. Click onto Amazon.com. Look at the associates and member page features. Take a close look and then ask yourself why they may doing this from a data-gathering point of view. Does this make Amazon.com an infomediary? Discuss the implications for new business models.

4. Think of a business or leisure or pastime activity in which you may be involved at the moment. Using the tips you have picked up in this chapter, construct a Web-based business idea for that sector, and then outline the features of the Net that will help your business idea. Think about services as well as products. For example a friend has moved from London to the Yorkshire Dales. He is considering setting up a website-based short-break business for busy London-based executives, providing them with a no-hassle two-day mountain-biking weekend in the Yorkshire Dales.

5. Take a look at the list of Internet features and benefits listed in the chapter. Which do you think will have the most profound effect in changing the way businesses operate? Explain why.

6. Imagine that you had decided to run a direct business online. What features would you want to include in your website to attract as many customers as possible, and maximise your revenue? Before you answer this, surf a number of Web addresses to look for ideas. Question 2 above contains a number of such sites.

References

Belk, R.W., Sherry, J.F. and Wallendorf, M.A. (1988) 'Naturalistic inquiry into buyer and seller behaviour at a swap meet', *Journal of Consumer Research*, **14** (4) pp. 449-70.
Berryman, K., Harrington, L., Layton-Rodin, D. and Rrerolle, V. (1998) 'Electronic commerce – three emerging strategies', *McKinsey Quarterly*, no 1.
Brockes, E. (2000) 'Young, gifted and very rich', *Guardian*, 8 February.
Chaffey, D. (2002) *E-business and E-commerce Management*, FT Prentice Hall, Harlow.
Dignum, C. (2000) 'Boo's failure does not mar the whole dot.com economy', *Marketing*, London, 25 May.
Dodd, C. (1998) 'Shops on the box', *Guardian*, 6 August, pp. 14-15.
Doyle, P. (1995) 'Marketing in the new millennium', *European Journal of Marketing*, **29** (13), pp. 23-41.
Evans, P.B. and Wurster, T.S. (1997) 'Strategy and the new economics of information', *Harvard Business Review*, September/October.

Farrelly, P. (1999) 'The nuts and bolts of net nirvana', *The Observer Business Section*, 5 September, p. 9.

Fraser, J., Fraser, N. and McDonald, F. (2000) 'The strategic challenge of electronic commerce', *Supply Chain Management*, 5, (1), (10).

Garrahan, M. (2000) 'Putting football seat sales into the back of the net', *Financial Times*, 28 January.

Griffith, V. (1996) 'Taking risks with d-mail', *Financial Times*, 23 May.

Gwyther, M. (1999) 'Jewels in the web', *Management Today*, London, November.

Hagel, J. (1999) 'Net gain: expanding markets through virtual communities', *Journal of Interactive Marketing*, **13**, (1), Winter.

Hagel J. and Singer, M. (1999) *'Net Worth'*, Boston, Harvard Business School Press.

Hamel, G. and Sampler, G. (1998) 'The e-corporation', *Fortune*, 7 December.

Hoffman, D. and Novak, T. (1996) 'A new marketing paradigm for electronic commerce', The Information Society.

'The rapid impact of the Internet' (2000) *Marketing Week*, 20 January, p. 40.

Internet article (1999) *Estates Gazette*, 12 June, p. 61.

Internet article (1999) *Wall Street Journal Europe*, 14 July, p. 1.

Internet article (1999) *Marketing*, 28 October, p. 13.

Internet article (1998) *Financial Times*, 5 June, p. 6.

Internet article (1999) *Marketing*, 8 April, p. 13.

Jardine, A. (2000) 'Lastminute wonders', *Marketing*, London, 16 March. Mazur, L. (2000) 'Back to basics for customer service; *Marketing Business*, February, p. 33.

Mitchell, A. (2000) 'In one to one marketing, which one comes first?', *Interactive Marketing*, pp. 354-68.

Morris, G. (2000) 'Hall of infamy (no. 40 - e-commerce)', Guardian, 11 February.

Murphy, D. (2000) 'The last minute waltz', *Marketing Business*, February, pp. 22-3.

Nagle Green, E. (2000) 'IDM Millennium lecture', London, March.

O'Connor, J. and Galvin, E. (1997) *Marketing and Information Technology*, Financial Times Pitman Publishing, London.

Peppers, D. and Rogers, M. (1993) *The One-One Future*, Piathus, USA.

Peters, L. (1998) 'The new interactive media: one-one but to whom?', *Marketing Intelligence and Planning*, **16** (1).

Rosier, B. (2000) 'What went so horribly wrong with Boo.com?', *Marketing*, London, 25 May.

Sahay, A., Gould, J. and Barwise, P. (1998) 'New interactive media: Experts' perceptions of opportunities and threats for existing businesses', *European Journal of Marketing*, **32**, 7/8, pp. 616-28.

Sheth, J.N. and Sisodia, R.J. (1997) 'Consumer behaviour in the future', *Electronic Marketing and the Future*, Peterson, R.A. (ed) Sage, California.

Spalter, M. (1995) 'Maintaining a customer focus in an interactive age', in Forrest, E. and Mizerski, R. (eds) *Interactive Marketing, the future present*, AMA Publications, ch. 12, pp. 163-187.

Sunday Times Business section, (1999) 'Online shops bring back haggling', 11 April, p. 10.

Tyrell, P. (1999) *Guardian*, 5 October 1999, p. 26.

Uhrenbacher, S. and Therezien, L. (2000) 'Lastminute recruits two for Euro growth', *Marketing*, 13 January, p. 9.

Walters, D. and Lancaster, G. (1999) 'Using the Internet as a channel for commerce', *Management Decision*, **37**, (10) (20).

Ward, M. (1999) 'Something for (virtually) nothing', *Daily Telegraph*, Connected, p. 6.

Weiber, R. and Kollman, T. (1998) 'Competitive advantages in virtual markets – perspectives of information-based marketing in cyberspace', *European Journal of Marketing*; **32** (7/8), pp. 603–15.

Zwass, V. (1998) 'Structure and macro-level impacts of electronic commerce: From technological infrastructure to electronic marketplaces', http://www.mhhe.com/business/mis/zwass/ ecpaper.html, accessed 9 April 1999.

CASE STUDY

Amazon – the online bookseller

Amazon.com opened its virtual doors in July 1995 with a mission to use the Internet to trans-form *book buying into the fastest, easiest and most enjoyable shopping experience possible.* The mail-order site, at http://www.amazon.com, allows customers to enter their credit-card number online and purchase any one of more than 1 million new and used titles.

From those heady days of the mid 1990s to today, there's little doubt that Amazon has been a success story. Its website claims that '17 million people in more than 160 countries have made [the company] the leading online shopping site'. It also claims to have the 'Earth's Biggest Selection'™ of products, including free electronic greeting cards, online auctions and millions of books, CDs, videos, DVDs, toys and games, and electronics.

Special features include a very effective search engine that enables customers to quickly find a book or CD, even if they don't know the author or artist's names. Amazon encourages customers to browse 'virtual aisles' in hundreds of product categories – everything from audiobooks, jazz, and video documentaries to coins and stamps up for auction. For those who want a shortcut, their 'essentials lists' steer customers to the 'best new and classic products'.

EXHIBIT 8.14

ONE-TO-ONE MARKETING COMES ALIVE...

One customer described his experience of using Amazon.com to the author.

He said that he had been a customer for some time and as an existing cus-tomer when he clicked onto the site he got a 'Welcome Mark' sign and 'we have some recommendations for you' page for him to click. The previous day he had been telling a friend about a new but little-known book about the Internet he wanted to take a look at. The next day he clicked on the site, and one of his recom-mendations was that very book. Not bad 'one-to-one' marketing for a company dealing with 17 million products and mil-lions of customers.

Amazon allows customers to get instant personalised recommendations based on their prior purchases the moment they log on. Customers who sign up for 'Delivers', an e-mail subscrip-tion service, will receive the latest reviews of new titles in categories that interest them. The extent to which Amazon can truly personalise this service is important: too often database marketers have claimed to personalise information but have failed to do so.

Amazon also runs a 'Special Occasion Reminder' service, reminding customers to get a gift for 'that special someone'. This mirrors exactly the kind of service that Peppers (1993) had predicted in the early 1990s, and is a classic example of how a trusted supplier can add value to customers by taking the hassle out of buying. Here, database marketing is important.

Amazon is also looking to become a 'retailer of retailers' (Mitchell, 2000). Amazon invites all visitors to its site to become an Amazon.com Associate and link their website to its own. This is an example of the sideways and upwards flows of information that Mitchell discussed. By simply linking to Amazon.com, associates can earn referral fees by having visitors click from their site through to Amazon.com to purchase items. Amazon handles all of the customer service, fulfilment, shipping and tracking of sales generated from your site. For any sales made, associates then earn referral fees from Amazon. The Associates programme, the first on the Web, started in July 1996, and has now a membership of a quarter of a million.

These formulas have undoubtedly proved to be successful. According to *The Economist* (1997) Amazon.com Inc instantly became the leading retail bookseller on the Internet, with about $16 million in revenues in 1996. *The Economist* warned, however, that other large booksellers are also planning to make use of the Internet. As it said, 'Amazon sells only in cyberspace, but it is now being joined there by invaders from the material world whose turnover makes any purely Internet business look puny.' Barnes & Noble, based in New York, is the biggest bookseller in the world, with pre-tax profits in 1996 of $81.4 million on sales of $2.45 billion. It opened for electronic business on 18 March, selling through America Online (AOL), a network with 8.5 million subscribers. *The Economist* offered some possible reasons for Amazon's early success: as it said, the mechanics of selling books online look different from those of setting up a bookshop in the shopping centre. 'Amazon's star has risen so fast (its sales have doubled each quarter) for the simple reason that it usually offers a good service. In part, this is because it has the customary skills of the nimble niche player: it is often quicker to spot trends than the big bookstores (let alone the notoriously inefficient book publishers); it also makes more effort to engage its customers (with online interviews, reviews and so on).'

It was also pointed out that Amazon has also managed to match the big chains in three crucial areas: convenience, range and price. Amazon offers 2.5 million titles, which computer users can search through 24 hours a day, then order, often at a discount to the publishers' prices, and have delivered in as little as two days. It keeps fewer than 1000 titles – just the bestsellers in its own warehouse – but it is situated near one of the warehouses of Ingram Book Company, the largest wholesaler of books in the world with 400 000 titles on hand. Ingram provided 59 per cent of the books Amazon sold in 1996. This has enabled Amazon to compete effectively with Barnes & Noble, whose massive distribution systems do not give it economies of scale in virtual marketplaces.

Amazon will not have things all its own way on the Internet however. Niche sellers such as Pandora's Books (science fiction) have set themselves up. The Internet's community-building abilities may come to the fore here, as niche customers will have much in common with each other and, via the site, the means to talk to each other. Ultimately, Amazon and its competitors will have to watch out for another Internet threat: one day, consumers may just download 'books' by computer – and print them out at home.

The dazzling array of new initiatives has not ended yet, however. *Computer Weekly* (1999) reported that Amazon has launched z-Shops, an e-commerce portal that allows anyone to set up an online store and sell directly from Amazon.com's site. 500 000 products from different vendors will be offered in a scheme similar to its 'Associates' programme.

How does Amazon promote itself? According to *Direct Marketing* magazine (1999) the Internet's top 100 e-commerce sites spent an average $8.6 million last year to build their online brands and drive additional traffic to their websites.

The size of website marketing budgets generally increased with company size; the largest companies in the group spent $21.4 million each on average. The average marketing budget among the larger consumer e-commerce firms was often over half of total revenue, an incredible figure. With some commentators forecasting a blood-bath of Internet companies in the first decade of the new millennium, these figures show the importance companies are attributing to a critical mass of brand building, customer awareness and traffic through their sites, to enable them to grow big enough to survive the first wave of industry rationalisation.

The top five marketing budgets in 1998 included Amazon.com Inc. ($133 million), ETrade Group Inc. ($71.3 million), and BarnesandNoble.com Inc. ($70.4 million). Sites are diversifying their marketing programmes, with 86 per cent now investing in conventional media buys and only 14 per cent continuing to focus their advertising dollars exclusively online. Newspapers and magazines, radio and TV are all popular media for online companies driving traffic to their sites. The results are encouraging for the marketers. While 57 per cent of Internet users still use the search engines to locate specific websites, approximately one in four have also used magazine ads and 14 per cent have used television commercials. The numbers for other off-line media are lower with approximately one in 10 (9 per cent) having found a website address through a newspaper ad and 2 per cent through a radio ad.

Amazon.com has proved to be a pioneer of making the most of the Internet's community building and interactive capabilities. One of its most celebrated innovations has been the posting of book reviews by its own customers, on its site. These have proved to be very popular, opening up to the masses a field previously restricted to the few. To make it interesting, Amazon allows customers to say pretty much anything, and awards each book up to five stars. Each book has its own page on Amazon's site and, whenever a reader submits a new review, it appears automatically. Other online bookstores, such as those operated by Barnes & Noble and Borders, provide similar features. But as the largest store, with over 80 per cent of the online market, Amazon has the most customers and attracts by far the greatest number of reviews – nearly 3 million of them to date. There are sometimes problems though (*see* Exhibit 8.15).

EXHIBIT 8.15

THE BIBLE IS 'NOT AS GOOD AS THE FILM'

Writing about customers' book reviews, *The Economist* (1999) reported on some problems that can crop up when a great deal of leeway is given to customers. As put it, 'This critical free-for-all lends itself to subversion of various subtle and not-so-subtle kinds. Thousands of reviews are submitted every day – Amazon will not say exactly how many – so it would be impractical to vet them all.

Instead, a team of editors scours the site, spot-checking that reviews conform to the company's guidelines.'

Single-word reviews, or personal attacks on the author, are not allowed. Nor are reviews that contain obscenities or give away the ending. The problem is that the reviewers are anonymous and offending reviews are removed only if

Amazon checkers notice them. This allows plenty of leeway for mischief makers to submit spoof reviews.

The Economist tracked down a story that someone had submitted a review of the Bible signed 'God'. 'It was removed – God is presumed not to use e-mail – but another review has since popped up to take its place. The Bible, it opines, is 'not as good as the film.'

There is also nothing to stop authors submitting flattering reviews of their own books. One writer was upset by bad reviews ('infantile trash', 'puerile pap'), so he submitted several anonymous ones of his own ('hilarious','fabulous') to redress the balance. His ruse succeeded until he wrote an article detailing his deception. The fake reviews were promptly removed.

Amazon.com has sometimes been a victim of its own online success. Rosenfield (1999) told the story of how Amazon had been selling book recommendations from readers to publishers. When the *New York Times* blew the whistle on this, the company had backed down and stopped the offending practice. What was the problem? Customers had seen this practice as a betrayal from a supplier that they had trusted enough to interact with in ways that went beyond just buying a book. Perhaps this is an example of relationship marketing coming alive. And when trust breaks down in a relationship, that is a serious problem. Amazon has taken the right decision in valuing that degree of trust between it and its customers higher than making money from a few reviews.

As Rosenfield noted, this story, and the story of Amazon, raises fascinating issues about how the Internet is changing business. 'The personalized, interactive, somewhat tribal relation customers have with Amazon.com made the promotions seem like betrayals. It's due to the 'social fabric' of Internet commerce. Interactivity creates involvement, which can easily become emotional involvement. The passive experience of browsing through a Barnes & Noble bookstore lacks the interactivity, and therefore the emotional charge that made Amazon customers think they had been suckered.'

As Rosenfield said, Amazon.com may be a business, but it acts like a club. Internet commerce, at least in its early stages, seems to want to be club-like. Part of this is the fact that word of mouth (generated by club-like activities) on the Internet becomes a mass medium – which can work in a powerful way to force companies to improve their act towards customers. Let Rosenfield have the last word: 'Conventional companies, abetted by conventional ad agencies, persist in pretending that the Internet is a place where you can practise business as usual. You can't. The medium is the message.'

Examining this interaction in a little more detail, there is a clever mix of reactive and proactive marketing going on here. The customers are in control – they decide whether to access the marketing message or not. The company has proactively used customer data to predict future customer needs, and has uniquely tailored that marketing to the customer. This is data driven marketing.

This suggests it is not true that the Net is 'all about putting the customer fully in charge of going to market'. Neither can traditional top-down 'customer management' work in the same way. Or can it? In reference to Exhibit 8.14, p. 252, what if Amazon.com had e-mailed Mark with its list of recommendations? In this instance the customer had not controlled the interaction, and had not signalled he was in the market for books. So maybe e-mailing is less powerful than waiting for the customer to access the website.

Questions

1. Take a close look at how Amazon.com interacts with its existing customers. How does this differ from treatment of new arrivals? In what way does it react to the customer and how is it pro-active? Discuss the strategic implications of this.
2. In what way are the customers in control of how they are marketed to? Is this different from conventional marketing?
3. What are the elements of 'interactive marketing' that rely on database marketing? To what extent do you believe it is a different way of doing marketing?
4. Discuss whether Amazon.com is an infomediary. What else would it need to do to become a true infomediary?

References

Amazon.com website (March 2000).
'Amateurs on Amazon' (1999) *The Economist* (US), 28 August, v352, i8134, p. 65.
Computer Weekly (1999) 21 October, p. 55.
The Economist (US) (1997) 29 March, v342, n8010, p. 71(2).
'Leading e-commerce sites spending big on marketing' (1999) *Direct Marketing*, September v62, i5, p. 13.
Mitchell, A. (2000) 'In one to one marketing, which one comes first?', *Interactive Marketing* pp. 354–68.
PC Week (1991) 6 November, v12, n44, p. 71.
Rosenfield, J.R. (1999) 'The Internet, Amazon.com and Book-of-the-Month Club: the old, the new, and the future view', *Direct Marketing*, June, v62, i2, pp. 44–8.

PART 4

DIRECT MARKETING IMPLEMENTATION AND CONTROL

OFFERS AND INCENTIVES IN DIRECT MARKETING

Objectives

Once you have read this chapter you will:

■ be able to define 'offers' and 'incentives';

■ understand the difference between offers and incentives;

■ appreciate the roles that different offers and incentives play in acquiring and keeping customers;

■ be able to make appropriate tactical decisions in this area.

Introduction

Chapters 5 and 6 gave us the tools we need to make the major direct marketing decisions. The next major step is to decide tactics. The individual steps we need to take in delivering direct marketing programmes are outlined in the nine-step process in Table 9.1.

From Table 9.1 we see that steps 1 to 3 have already been covered, subsumed within the analysis and strategy sections of previous chapters. There are two steps (4 and 5) still to take before moving into the communication phase. We need to use our strategic guidance to design our proposition, or offer, to customers. This will include the core product/price offering and also augmented product add-ons, including incentives.

Table 9.1: **Nine-step process for delivering direct marketing programmes**

Programme process	Chapter
1 Set objectives	5
The market	
2 Segment (based on existing customers if possible)	3
3 Decide on final target markets	5
The offer	
4 Decide product/price proposition	9
5 Decide incentive approach	9
Communication	
6 Decide media and contact over time	10 & 11
7 Decide timing issues	10 & 11
8 Develop creative platforms	12
9 Design a detailed test programme	13

EXHIBIT 9.1

THE DIFFERENCE BETWEEN STRATEGY AND TACTICS

The key elements distinguishing strategies from tactics are difficult to pin down. There is widespread disagreement among academics and confusion among practitioners about what constitutes a marketing strategy.

A pragmatic approach is offered here, as something to clarify the way in which the phrase 'marketing strategy' is used in this book.

Marketing strategies are *decisions* that are made on what products should be developed for what markets (existing and new), competitive positioning, and the marketing mix, which *provide the direction* for individual campaigns or programmes. Strategies typically have timeframes of many months and often years. Whatever the time period, it is always longer than one, single, marketing action.

For example, if we take American Express, we can see that its strategy is to differentiate itself as the charge card of exclusivity and status. It seeks to differentiate itself through its brand. A tactic may be a single mailshot to a group of prospects, which emphasises the exclusivity of the card.

Having read this chapter, you will be able to make specific tactical choices applied to your particular business problem. Direct marketing is concerned with both developing relationships and obtaining a definite response from consumers to purchase. To achieve either goal, you could decide to develop a club, to launch a 'loyalty card', or to use an 'opt-out' acquisition device. But have you made the right move? The answers to these problems are tackled in this chapter.

How this chapter is structured

In this chapter we will start by defining offers and incentives in direct marketing. Then, leaving aside offers for a moment, we will examine the case for using incentives in some detail.

The third section then brings together offers and incentives in a discussion of contact programmes to existing customers, and the final section looks at the same for attracting new customers.

Defining offers and incentives

THE PRODUCT MODEL

This well-known model is used in most general marketing texts (Dibb *et al.*, 1994) to describe what a product consists of, and is illustrated in Fig. 9.1. Take a look at the augmented product elements. It is these which direct marketers use to make offers to customers.

THE OFFER

The need to define 'the offer' becomes apparent when you hear two direct marketing practitioners talking to each other. Offer is a very common jargon word used in the world of direct marketing, and like so many other words in marketing, often seems to have more than one meaning when used by practitioners.

The offer is the proposition you make to the customer. It is what you are asking them to accept. Stone (1996) describes the offer as 'the terms promoting the product or service', which implies the price and conditions surrounding the deal. Here we can further clarify the definition of 'offer' as:

the totality of what we are offering to the customer, and what we expect back for it.

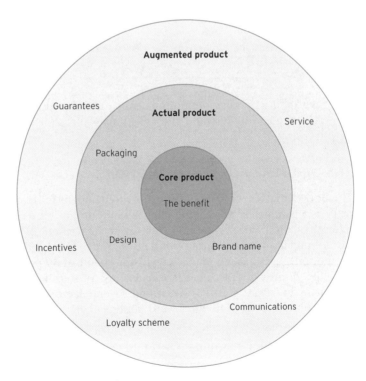

Figure 9.1 The multi-layered product

Confusingly, many practitioners refer to the incentive as the offer, while the product/price part of the message seems to be something else. Therefore we need to be careful: it is better to define the *incentive* as a *part* of the overall proposition to the customer. We can now introduce incentives.

INCENTIVES (SALES PROMOTIONS)

It is often the case in commodity markets, or those where differentiation is difficult to achieve, that a new way of standing out, or of triggering a response, is needed. In these instances, incentives (or sales promotions) can have a key role and are an important subject for us in direct marketing.

Sales promotions are defined in most marketing text books (Jobber, 1995; Dibb *et al.*, 1994) as:

> *short-term incentives which help turn consumer desire into action at the point of sale.*

Rapp and Collins (1987) coined a more colourful expression to describe sales promotions:

> *Sales promotion is the art and science of making something happen.*

Recalling that part of the direct marketing process is the need to stimulate a response (i.e. 'action'), it is not surprising that sales promotions are an important part of the direct marketer's armoury. Thus direct marketers may use simple incentives such as free gifts in return for quick response, or complex mechanics such as 'loyalty schemes', involving smart cards capturing customer transaction data.

The following section examines the case for using incentives in direct marketing.

Using incentives in direct marketing

To understand why sales promotions are so useful within the direct marketing framework, we need to understand the advantages and shortcomings of sales promotions within *general* marketing.

THE GROWTH OF SALES PROMOTIONS

The notion that sales promotions are an afterthought for companies behind advertising or PR is a completely misleading one. Sales promotions are now big business; according to Shultz (1987), sales promotions take up to 70 per cent of the marketing communications budget of many large companies. Indeed, by 1990, global expenditure on promotions had equalled media advertising spend, at 39 per cent of total global marketing expenditure. This picture is repeated across Western Europe.

Peattie and Peattie (1993) identified several factors that encourage greater use of sales promotion (in both direct and general marketing), the most relevant to direct marketing being:

■ advertising clutter: consumers becoming more immune to advertising messages;
■ micromarketing approaches: as a response to media costs and fragmenting markets, there is an increasing role for the flexibility of sales promotions, differently tailored for different markets;

- me-too-ism: a 'zero sum game' has developed in many markets, where competitors are obliged to follow suit when one player introduces an ongoing sales incentive;
- sales promotions are much easier to implement than, say, new product development or pricing changes.

THE OBJECTIVES OF SALES PROMOTIONS

Both direct and general marketers tend to use sales promotions for the same objectives (Kotler, 1995):

1 To attract new customers and to induce 'trial'. New customers can be:
   - users of another brand in the same category
   - users in different categories
   - non users
   - frequent brand switchers;

2 To reward loyal customers, by increasing the customers' time of contact with the company;

3 To increase sales among existing customers, by:
   - increasing repurchase rates of occasional users
   - trading up to higher value goods within the category
   - cross-selling.

Recently, however, a number of commentators have expressed disquiet about the effectiveness of sales promotions.

THE PROBLEMS WITH SALES PROMOTIONS IN GENERAL MARKETING

Next time you go to the supermarket, take a close look at the promotions on offer. When Heineken offers one can of lager free when you buy four, what is its objective? It is unlikely to be a reward for loyal buyers. Heineken is probably trying to attract trial from purchasers of other lagers. However, numerous studies (Smith, 1993; Rapp and Collins, 1987) have shown that most of this promotion is wasted: in fact most of the purchases are made by:

- customers who would have bought anyway;
- deal-conscious, compulsive brand switchers.

Therefore, relatively few takers of the promotion are genuine *triallists*.

Kotler (1995) noted extensive evidence of an apparent *lack of any lasting change* in consumer behaviour after the promotion has finished, although Peattie and Peattie (1993) found, when reviewing criticisms of sales promotions, that most evidence so far has centred on price promotions rather than added-value promotions.

Coming from a direct marketing perspective, Rapp and Collins (1987) and Cram (1994) provided the following list of problems associated with sales promotions used in general marketing (especially retail) situations:

- Profitability studies have found that companies using higher sales promotions/advertising ratios have lower profitability.
- A lot of sales promotion is used for the 'wrong' reasons, for example because product managers want short-term gains in market share, or that retailers expect it. Or worst of all, because 'everyone else is doing it'.

■ Consumers deliberately misredeem coupons for products other than the intended item.

■ In retail stores in the US, 60 per cent of coupons aimed at new trial are in fact redeemed by existing customers, 30 per cent by 'cheaters' who redeem one company's coupons against another's product, and 10 per cent by 'brand hoppers' (loyal to incentives, not brands) and interested triers.

■ Consumers may be educated/trained to look for the deals and to cry out when they don't get any. Anecdotally, a colleague in the business described these as 'greedy grabby' people who are out to save every penny!

■ The trade needs to be given an incentive to carry the manufacturer's brand, and tends to be hostile to many manufacturer-based promotions because they have to be administered through the trade, adding costs without improving total throughput for the retailer.

■ Consumers' price expectation will be lowered by continual price promotion. In these instances, the brand franchise is lowered because consumers frequently use price as a surrogate for quality.

A lot of these problems arise because of the highly fluid retail environment, with the resulting complete lack of ability to discriminate between existing customers and prospects. The following section explains how direct marketers overcome this.

USING SALES PROMOTIONS IN DIRECT MARKETING

Rapp and Collins (1987) point out that direct marketers can take a different approach to sales promotions. The direct marketing system *allows different customer categories to be identified, split and treated separately*. Separate treatment is the key to success.

Direct marketers can start by using external lists to identify prospects of, say, competitors' products. The sales promotion can then be exclusively targeted at the right audience, rather than wasting such promotions on existing customers. We can subsequently use our own data to highlight loyal customers who can be exclusively rewarded with price or added-value incentives to stay.

It can be seen that direct marketing brings superior targeting and control to the marketing action.

The following process can be used to construct a programme of incentives through direct marketing.

Process for delivering an incentive programme using direct marketing

When planning to use sales promotions in direct marketing, the following steps are appropriate:

Step 1

Carefully establish the objectives. The incentive may be triggering action to switch brands or buy a new product, or it may be reinforcing loyalty.

Step 2

Separate out the target markets and use private media as much as possible. This will avoid wastage. The example in Exhibit 9.2 highlights the advantages of using direct marketing.

EXHIBIT 9.2

THE ADVANTAGES OF INCENTIVES USING DIRECT MARKETING: A 'WINE DIRECT'
OPERATION VERSUS A RETAILER

Let us compare a wine retailer with our database-driven 'Wine Direct' operation. We can take a typical promotion, say a free bottle of new Romanian wine on any purchase of a box of 12. In Tables 9.2 and 9.3, each column represents differ-

ent *target markets*, while the two rows split those who are *not motivated* by the incentive from those who are. Look at the differences between the retailer's (Table 9.2) and Wine Direct's (Table 9.3) sales promotions.

Table 9.2: **Retailer's sales promotion**

	Possible new entrants into market	Loyal to competitor	Brand switcher	Loyal to company
Motivated by sales promotion	Activate?	No effect?	Activate	Waste
Not motivated	No effect	No effect	No effect	Waste

Table 9.3: **Wine Direct's sales promotion**

	Possible new entrants into market	Loyal to competitor	Brand switcher	Loyal to company
Motivated by sales promotion	Increase offer	Increase offer	Activate	Do not promote
Not motivated	No effect	No effect	No effect	Do not promote

Wine Direct uses sales promotion in a superior manner in the following ways:

■ it adjusts the promotion to its own loyal customers, thus avoiding wastage;

■ it increases the offer to audiences that are tougher to get to respond to incentives.

Step 3

Calculate the allowable marketing spend per sale (acquisition) or the lifetime value of customers (retention). Then estimate from this how much you can afford to spend on the incentive.

Our starting principle is that the more valuable the incentive is, the more response it will pull, until a point is reached where the returns will diminish and the incentive will no longer be cost-effective. This point can only be accurately determined through testing, although perhaps research could help in the decision.

To calculate the optimum budget to spend on incentives, we can use 'what if?' analysis.

Let us take the example of a direct-mail programme to 10 000 prospects (marketing cost of £5000). We want to test both a £5 and a £10 incentive. The costs of these incentives depend on response, as we only pay out to responders.

Let's say that the £5 incentive achieves a 2 per cent response, while the £10 incentive achieves a 3 per cent response. The product gross margin is £30.

To see which incentive to use, set out a table as in Table 9.4.

Table 9.4: **'What if?' analysis for incentives**

Incentive	Percentage response	Incentive costs (£)	Mailer costs (£)	Total costs (£)	Sales revenue (£)	Profit (£)
Test 1: Gift of value £5	2	1000*	5000	6000	6000	0
Test 2: Gift of value £10	3	3000	5000	8000	9000	1000

* 2% of 10 000 instances = 200, and 200 ¥ £5 = £1000

In this instance, we should choose the £10 gift, as the returns outweigh the extra costs.

By 'plugging in' other incentive costs, the necessary number of responses to reach your profitability targets can be estimated and assessed as a possible test programme.

You can see from trying out a few of these calculations that the profitability of the exercise depends on the gross margin of the product sold, and the extent to which a more valuable incentive improves the response rate.

Step 4

Choose the incentives carefully so that the brand franchise is built upon, and the positioning of the product is reflected in the promotional device. Check that you are rewarding desired behaviour rather than promiscuity.

Kotler (1995) lists a large number of different sales promotions, of which the following are suitable for direct marketers:

- price-related incentives
- free samples
- coupons: cash off the purchase of a particular brand
- premiums or gifts, either unrelated to product or related to product
- competitions
- free prize draws/lotteries
- frequency purchase schemes: now commonly known in the UK as 'loyalty schemes'
- self-liquidating premiums
- free trials
- product warranties

- third-party offers: affinity offers
- free demonstrations
- finance offers: 0% interest loans to help purchase, for example.

(Sales promotions not used by direct marketers are the retail environment specialities such as price off pack, extra pack free, bind-in offers, etc.)

To help us to choose incentives to reward loyalty, O'Brien and Jones (1995) propose five attributes that a successful scheme should have. The incentive should:

give cash value:	at least 5 per cent of product value is recommended;
offer convenience:	incentive should be offered easily within the transaction, avoiding vouchers if possible;
be relevant:	link the incentive to the product or service;
have aspirational value:	incentive should reflect the brand;
offer choice:	points systems redeemed for a choice of rewards.

Many consumers find vouchers inconvenient, or they cannot get motivated to save for rewards worth only 1 per cent of spend. Single gift incentives, such as 'free travel bags' on taking up insurance, for example, lack choice and relevance to many.

Prentice *et al.* (1975) also recommended using *consumer franchise building promotions* – those which register the brand's unique advantages or attributes in the consumer's mind (*see* Exhibit 9.3).

EXHIBIT 9.3

INCENTIVES IN DIRECT MARKETING: MARTELL COGNAC

In 1990, Martell Cognac was looking to grow its market share but suffered from low brand awareness and low comprehension of what the Martell brand stood for. Martell wanted its cognac to convey the following values: 'upmarket', 'bon viveur', 'made in France', 'aged a long time', 'prestigious', and 'smooth tasting'. Martell undertook image advertising to address this but, with limited budgets, needed its other communications to reinforce these messages as strongly as possible.

Martell decided to use direct marketing to build usage among its existing known consumers, and to encourage trial among non-users. Martell was interested in incentives as a way of conveying its brand values. It therefore put a lot of effort into testing various innovative incentives which it believed would increase purchase and improve brand saliency. These incentives were:

- a free copy of a specially written book, *The Art of Entertaining* by Miles Kington: a high-quality, witty book of high perceived value. This was sent to existing cognac drinkers who responded, in return for details of alcoholic drinks purchased. A 16 per cent response was obtained;
- American Express 'Be my guest' restaurant certificates (note the difference in positioning between these and money-off vouchers!);
- Martell Snifters in return for proof-of-purchase labels;
- a French silk scarf.

Quite apart from the extra sales achieved directly as a result of the campaign, Martell recorded large improvements in its brand saliency, from, for example, 21 per cent associating 'aged a long time' with Martell before the campaign, up to 36 per cent afterwards. The incentives had a key role to play in achieving this success.

Source: Seagram UK.

Step 5

Test different incentives against one another in small volumes to establish the most effective.

Step 6

Roll out.

Having examined incentives in detail we now need to consider both offers and incentives together as *programmes* to *existing customers*.

Programmes to existing customers

Programmes to existing customers can be split into those for which the primary objective is to help retain customers, and those which are designed to maximise the profitability of existing customers through extra sales. Figure 9.2 shows how.

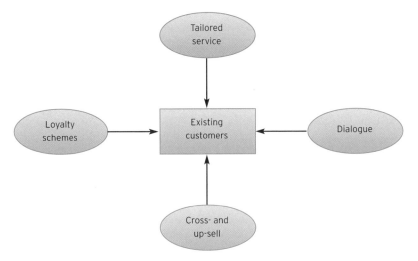

Figure 9.2 Programmes to retain and maximise profitability of existing customers

We will concentrate on these programmes. Tailored-service programmes have already been described in Chapter 6, so we will look at *dialogue*, *loyalty schemes*, and *cross-* and *up-selling*.

DIALOGUE

Direct marketing is used to provide information sheets, newsletters, product catalogues, and other vehicles which deliver help, news, information and ways of making the product more valuable to consumers. As well as creating value for existing customers, these activities can provide ways of keeping the relationship alive between purchases. A package-holiday operator could keep its name in the minds of its customers who may be a year from their next purchase.

These tactics are used widely in sectors as diverse as car manufacturers (Vauxhall provides ring-bound, high-quality folders of driver information to new car buyers) and packaged goods. In the latter sector, Persil distributed door-to-door thousands of postcards with a helpline number included. The number was little used but served as a reminder that Persil does care – positioning Unilever as more than a washing-powder supplier.

Among the 'best in the business' here are the charity fundraisers. Given that donors seldom get to see the benefits of their money directly, charities know that communicating clearly what the money is used for can be vital to ensuring donor satisfaction. Some charities see the best solution as offering a menu of communications options to the regular donor. Donors choose from magazines, reports, accounts, or updates of particular projects of interest to them.

Driven by the need to make it easy for customers, *carelines* have grown considerably in importance throughout Europe, while they have long been standard practice for US companies, from insurance to packaged supermarket goods.

Carelines are essentially reactive rather than proactive. Their objectives are to build reassurance and to provide accessibility, rather than being a major part of data-driven marketing. They can, however, be important data-gathering devices.

However, carelines are important because people who call carelines are (self-selected) high-involvement purchasers of your products. There is a high chance that they are among your most valuable customers, and making sure they are happy is then top priority. Careline interactions can be included in the customer's record and future direct marketing adjusted accordingly. For example, if a bank's careline takes a call from a customer unhappy about existing loan arrangements, it makes sense not to mail them the next day with a mass-mailed loan offer!

Outbound calling can be used to enhance the value of the core product or service. The call from American Express to confirm safe arrival of a customer's card is welcomed and valued. American Express measures this activity in terms of customer retention, and has established a positive effect. Using the telephone to foster relationships and loyalty is more crucial in business-to-business marketing. A supplier of computer training services will keep in constant touch with its customers' personnel departments to ensure high levels of satisfaction. The importance of the telephone is discussed in detail in Chapter 10.

Of particular importance in dialogue programmes are loyalty magazines.

Loyalty magazines

Loyalty magazines are a way of providing high-quality, added-value communications to existing customers, in an effort to create extra value and hence provide another reason to stay with that supplier. By 2002 loyalty magazines (contract publishing), were worth over £300 million as an industry, from a modest £50 million in 1990. This has to be one of the success stories of the loyalty industry – one cannot imagine this sort of sustained growth unless firms were at least reasonably happy with their measures.

They enjoy wide use across international markets and products from credit cards to cars, clothing to cigarettes. Firms as diverse as Barclays, Saab, Benetton, Heinz, BT, News International, Oxfam and Rothmans all use magazines. Research by the author (Tapp, 1995) in the charity sector showed 65 per cent of the top 500 charities have launched magazines to their donor base. Customers seem to welcome magazines. The Brann/Henley Centre Report 'The Loyalty Paradox' noted that 47 per cent of a consumer survey said they would be happy to receive loyalty magazines from companies they had bought from before.

Magazines achieve loyalty-related objectives by providing awareness of products and services, getting feedback from customers, helping to clean the database via customer calls, and prompting the provision of extra information to customers. Citroën's magazine, *Directions*, is an example. Citroën says that its customers are informed and entertained by the magazine, thereby feeling 'warmer' towards the company.

The key to success for these magazines is that they must be worthwhile in their own right. Some magazines have resembled a mixture of promotional product literature and company propaganda – a bad mistake. To be successful, they must be capable of competing with news-stand magazines; the acid test is whether the loyalty magazine is potentially capable of commanding a price in its own right. Sainsbury's retail magazine is bought in its stores for £1 but mailed free to high-value existing customers.

Loyalty magazines require high-quality editorial with relevant, entertaining features. In some sectors, interesting aspects of the product itself can be a major focus for the magazine; for example the AA (Automobile Association) focuses on travel and auto articles. Other sectors will probably largely ignore their product: Barclaycard's magazine or a telecommunications magazine will go for 'lifestyle' features of popular appeal. For example, a magazine from Sun Alliance Financial Services, *Foresight*, had articles on a major TV star, how to sell your home in six weeks, tips on being safer on the roads, and the chance to win an all-inclusive trip to the USA. Any mention of Sun Alliance's products was strictly 'soft sell', and occupied only a minor proportion of editorial.

Companies with tightly defined audiences find it easier to produce relevant loyalty magazines. Saab, with its high skew to AB males, can safely include articles on golf and rugby, knowing they will be well received. On the other hand, companies with loosely defined audiences may segment their magazines according to different needs.

Another important device for improving dialogue with customers is the use of clubs.

Clubs

Creating a membership scheme or club as part of the loyalty strategy was well established in direct marketing by classic direct marketers. They originally set up 'clubs' which had no fundamental basis other than to act as a type of contract, locking in cus-

EXHIBIT 9.4

LOYALTY MAGAZINES: LAND ROVER

Land Rover is a classic example of a brand for which loyalty magazines were made. There is plenty of customer interest, and plenty to write about. Land Rover understands that, although most of its customers drive about in places like Surbiton, in their heads they are crashing about off-road in somewhere like Peru. Its magazine, created with agency Craik Jones Watson, invites customers to participate in Land Rover events and off-road adventures. It runs a pro-gramme called 'A Country Affair', a series of one-day events in which customers are invited to enjoy a range of country pursuits as well as put the latest Range Rovers through their paces on and off the road. It also runs Discoverers Days – a programme of events geared to the more family/adventure-oriented owners of Discovery vehicles. Research with customers shows that the mailings achieve a high readership level and are welcomed by customers.

Source: FEDMA case study 1998.

tomers to an offer. These devices are used more for acquisition and are discussed later. In this section we will discuss clubs which have been created to help engender loyalty.

In what instances will the creation of a membership club for our existing customers be a good idea? Think for a moment about leisure or social clubs you may belong to. You may have joined because of a high level of interest in an activity, or because you feel comfortable with the type of people who have already joined. You may also enjoy the status club membership gives you, and even 'subconsciously' use membership to help define your position in society.

It is these reasons for joining which provide the clues to successful direct marketing clubs. Direct marketers should consider the tactic of creating a club to create customer value when:

1 **Customers have high involvement with the product.** Examples include Pedigree Petfoods' 'Sheba' Club, Buitoni's Pasta Lovers' Club, and Walt Disney's Children's Club. Some cat owners are quite obsessive about their pets, devoting more love and attention to them than to members of their own family. This obsession extends very naturally into the cats' welfare, including their diet – which is where Sheba, positioned as top-quality cat food, comes in. Membership of the Sheba Club entitles consumers to all manner of cat-related offers, such as personalised pet plates, books on cats, events, and so on. On informing Pedigree that their cat has died, members receive a 'mortality' mailing expressing how sorry Pedigree is that Tiddles has died and the hope that they will eventually buy another cat!

2 **Membership bestows an element of status.** Obvious examples here would be clubs run for customers of BMW, the BA Executive Club for frequent flyers, and the Hilton Hotels Executive Club. Here club membership is restricted, and customers may discreetly enjoy the exclusivity bestowed by their status as club members. Club privileges are positioned accordingly.

3 **Customers would value the association with other members.** People who own unusual or niche products often feel a strong sense of association with one another. Harley Davidson motorbike riders see their pastime, and their bikes, as a part of their identity. They define their personality through this shared interest, and product purchases are therefore made very carefully. Such products are an obvious area for direct-marketing-run clubs.

EXHIBIT 9.5

PEER ASSOCIATION: CLIMBERS

Climbing and mountaineering enthusiasts share an interest in summer and winter mountaineering, cliff climbing, sports climbing, indoor walls, and so on. Whatever the precise interest, many of these people strongly associate with a certain image and place great importance on certain products: trendy Berghaus or North Face branded clothing, and the latest rock pro-tection gear springs to mind. Though a notoriously independent and individual bunch, climbers may feel a sense of belonging through their product ownership.

Suppliers of relevant goods use direct marketing to existing clubs to capitalise on this group association, for example members of the British Mountaineering Council.

CROSS- AND UP-SELLING

Reichheld (1996) made the point that direct marketers have known for years (Holder, 1992): a firm's loyal customers are far more likely to buy its products than are new prospects. According to Holder, many sectors operate a cycle of contact programmes, shown in Fig. 9.3.

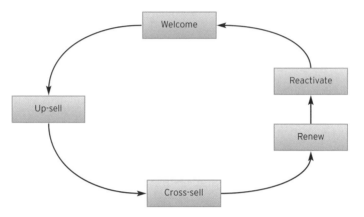

Figure 9.3 Contact cycle to increase revenue from loyal customers

Source: Holder, D. (1992) 'Finders keepers – the basics of customer acquisition and retention' in Halsey, B. (ed.) *The Practitioners' Guide to Direct Marketing*, Teddington, London.

The *welcome* stage may resist any attempt at an overt sale, but experience has shown, in sectors such as mail order, that customers often buy again just after their last purchase. Nevertheless, the primary objective of welcome mailers or calls should be service related.

If customers are satisfied with the product they first bought, they will be favourably inclined to purchase more of it, or to purchase an upgrade. Computer software consumers who enjoyed the basic product of a computer game are likely to be hot prospects for a higher-priced upgrade. This is *up-selling*.

As customers get used to your company and learn more about your offerings, the logical next step is to cross-sell. Thus a bank may interest a current account customer in a credit card or loan. For Norwich Union Life Insurance, *cross-selling* was described as a 'strategic must' (Durand, 1987). Although much cross-selling in financial sectors is often poorly targeted, it is still one step better than prospect mailing of cold lists, because at least we are selling to our existing customers.

In low-margin sectors such as packaged goods, cross-sell can be vital to the viability of a direct marketing approach: the whole basis of the direct approach is then that it makes sense to increase the share of existing customers' business rather than to attract new customers. Heinz, with its *At Home* magazine, invests heavily in cross-selling tactics, offering vouchers on new Heinz products to existing valuable customers.

Some sectors, such as subscriptions to publications, car breakdown services and car insurance, have definite *renewal* cycles, and the critical moment arrives when a customer makes an active choice to stay, lapse, or defect to competitors. Holder (1992) recommends a series of relevant communications before, during and after the renewal date. Testing has found that it is worth this level of investment in order to renew an

EXHIBIT 9.6

CROSS SELL – THE LAUNCH OF SKY ACTIVE IN 2002

Sky Active is a service of interactive games, channels, and shopping accessed by Sky viewers by pressing the red button on their remote. Sky Movies Active offers viewers a cinema-booking service, movie news and film previews. There is also the chance for viewers to air their views on a news item, vote on issues, or swap camera angles on sporting fixtures. The biggest revenue generators are betting and game playing, which viewers have shown already they find very popular and are willing to pay Sky a margin for.

The key now is to cross-sell Sky Active to the 7 million strong Sky consumer base. Sky will closely monitor the consumer behaviour of the early adopters – checking how often they switch to Sky Active, how long they stay online, what they do when they're on and so-on. The inevitable profiles will be built up, allowing Sky to understand who is interested and what they want.

Recently, Sky launched a new micro-site sky.com/skyactive to provide a focus for their marketing. They launched an aggressive online cross sell campaign, using banners, pop-ups and buttons as well as a targeted e-mail push using addresses from the Sky.com website. Sky are also communicating SkyActive through their customer magazine.

It is envisaged that the future with a merged service offering through sky.com, text and interactive TV will be upon us very soon. The present is all about learning – what works and what doesn't.

Sources: Nouchi, R. (2003) 'Sky Active prepares for a more integrated future', *Campaign (UK)*, 19 September. Carter, B., Brooks, G. (2002) 'Sky plans marketing push to attract users to Active', *New Media Age*, 17 October, p. 14.

active customer rather than reactivate a lapsed customer. At some point (this point is identified through testing) it becomes uneconomic to continue contacting people, and they then become lapsed customers.

The final stage may be to attempt to *reactivate* former customers with reminders to renew membership. These people are still better prospects than those who have never bought from you. Recalling the Rapp and Collins (1994) research (see Chapter 7), which suggests that the majority of defection comes as a result of company indifference rather than an active switch, we can see that renewal and reactivation tactics therefore have a sound theoretical foundation.

THE USE OF LOYALTY SCHEMES

There can scarcely be a soul left among us who has not encountered a loyalty scheme somewhere. Imagine a weekend trip to Paris. You take your car to the airport, picking up your petrol points on the way and using your credit card to pay, racking up credit-card points towards your next car purchase. You park in the long-term car park, promoted by its points scheme, and go to the terminal. There you pick up your daily paper, the choice dictated by your involvement in its 'Fantasy Football' loyalty competition. You jump on the plane, redeeming your Air Miles collected through your other credit card over the past year. While in Paris you stay at the hotel which attracted you as a businessperson on its prestigious 'gold card' bonus scheme, while the car you rent has a similar deal. On the way home you stop off at the supermarket to replenish supplies, participating in your eighth loyalty scheme of the weekend!

In truth, there cannot be many people who are as obsessed with loyalty schemes as our Paris tourist; if there were, their wallet or purse would be so crammed full of loyalty cards there would be no room for their money. In fact, the danger of 'loyalty overload', causing customer confusion and apathy, has led to the plethora of points schemes launched in the mid-1990s drying up considerably. At the time of writing, in the UK the biggest loyalty schemes operating are Air Miles; Tesco Clubcard and a new scheme called Nectar. This case study is examined in detail at the end of this chapter.

Early research suggested that loyalty schemes were very popular with the public (although there have been variations between countries). However, analysts such as Alan Mitchell have noted that consumers don't perceive loyalty schemes as a strong benefit, and hence increasingly, customers don't bother to participate. These problems and ways round them are discussed in detail in Chapter 6. Here we will confine ourselves to an understanding of the schemes themselves. Let us first define what these schemes are.

Loyalty schemes can be defined as:

> *Systems which persuade customers to prefer one supplier to another through 'spending-related rewards' and related marketing activities.*
>
> Andy Wood, Head of European Marketing, NCH Marketing Services Ltd

Loyalty schemes tend to be most useful in *frequent purchase markets*, and have been particularly prevalent in airlines, hotels and retail markets around the world. The core mechanic to all schemes is essentially quite simple: customers accrue 'points' or some other measured unit of value in return for spend with that company or brand. At some point, these points may be redeemable by the customer for something of value, be it money off a future purchase, gifts, cash back, or privileged services.

Loyalty schemes are also commonly found in markets where the core product is a *commodity* and companies have great difficulty differentiating themselves. Sectors such as telecommunications or car insurance are largely price led, and suppliers may attempt to keep their customers through loyalty pricing schemes, in which customers who spend more obtain volume discounts. In car insurance, the accumulated 'no claims bonus' is an example of this.

Loyalty pricing is an example of Reichheld's (1996) strategy of sharing value (or 'sharing the sweeties', as Cram (1994) put it). As you trade more efficiently with long-term customers, you can afford to charge less. Cram, however, recommends offering better value rather than straight price discounts, because the latter are so easy to copy. For example, the Heinz *At Home* direct marketing campaign offers rewards related to the product, free trials of new products, helpful hints on cooking, and so on, as incentives for heavy buyers.

Let us remember the key issues discussed in Chapter 6. These schemes do not engender loyalty by themselves; they must be *part of* a retention strategy to work. By themselves, they are only sales promotions – incentives for a particular purchase. When used properly, these schemes become an integral part of the direct marketing system: they act as the vehicle through which customer transaction data is collected. Without them, no direct marketing as such would take place. With them, the company can understand who its most and least valuable customers are, the importance of which is highlighted all through this book. Finally, these schemes combine both loyalty and sales objectives, in that they are designed to encourage customers to spend more as well as staying with one supplier.

Loyalty schemes are implemented in various ways. The original method, *proof of purchase*, has been largely replaced by *card-based schemes*. These in turn have developed

EXHIBIT 9.7

SUPERMARKET WARS: HOW CLUBCARD SAVES TESCO MONEY

British retailer Tesco uses its loyalty-card data intelligently in its ongoing battle with supermarket giant Walmart, owner of Asda. Asda will routinely discount on multiple products, in line with its low cost low price approach. For Tesco to copy directly all price drops would be very costly. Instead, it adopts a much more precise, though equally aggressive, 'rifle shot' promotion. Tesco analyses individual customers' shopping carts to determine which are the 'killer' products that drive us into stores in the first place. If any of these are threatened, Tesco will match these prices, but again only with customers it has identified as more price sensitive. Ultimately, Tesco Clubcard is a key player in the big game of minimising the profit damage of aggressive price competition. Just another example of how 'loyalty cards' have only an indirect relationship with loyalty.

into *co-branded partnership* marketing schemes. A recent variant has been the use of *competitions* as a mechanic to promote loyalty. However, some companies avoid this paraphernalia and employ loyalty pricing schemes with the data held within the company. We will now examine these different executions.

Proof-of-purchase-based loyalty schemes

The traditional mechanic, proof of purchase, is still used, especially by packaged goods manufacturers who have no way of easily using cards. In the restaurant sector, Pizza Hut has used incentives and competitions to categorise its customers by frequency and scale of patronage in order to target heavy and medium users. Heavy users are sent vouchers which must be redeemed within four weeks and are encouraged to buy special-value meals. Meanwhile, medium users have eight-week vouchers, and so on.

In markets where margins are very tight, in particular packaged goods sectors, the rewards are often self-liquidating; that is, customers are asked to pay a small fee in addition to the vouchers to receive their reward. This fee covers the company cost of the gift. For example, a premium dog-food company may offer personalised plates, leads etc. in return for both proof of purchase and a small charge. These schemes can add value to relationships while also stimulating extra sales within it – achieving the twin objectives of retention and increased sales.

Card-based schemes

The use of loyalty cards was an extremely important development in the 1990s in most developed world markets. Loyalty cards originated with the 'Divi' from the Co-op supermarket, which dates back to the last century; replacements included the famous Green Shield trading stamps and coupons. Loyalty cards are now used in a number of sectors: retail (petrol, supermarkets, DIY, some high-street sectors such as clothing and music), leisure (restaurants and pubs), business executive markets (airlines, car rental, hotels), and more recently business-to-business markets, for example the ICI bonus points scheme aimed at painters and decorators who buy Dulux paint products.

There are two types of card which run loyalty schemes: magnetic stripe and Smart cards.

THE WACKY WAREHOUSE

Allied Domecq has spotted a big gap in the market in UK pubs: catering for families with young children. It has built a series of pubs, branded Big Steak, with adjoining Wacky Warehouse play areas for children. Customers are offered the chance to join a loyalty scheme by Wacky Warehouse staff, and fill out a questionnaire asking for birthdays, anniversary dates, etc. The scheme is administered by a Gold Card which records transactions. Customers get one point for every £1 spent and £5 reward vouchers for every 100 points. Quarterly statements are sent to customers keeping them up to date. In addition, 'exclusive' special offers are run, such as vouchers offering 15 flowers free with 15 purchased for an anniversary.

Allied Domecq has combined excellent niche marketing, carefully meeting the needs of families with young children, with a loyalty scheme designed to maximise existing behaviour traits. The company knows that parents of young children will often get into routines and will return time and again: the loyalty card encourages this.

Source: Allied Domecq consumer communications.

Magnetic stripe and Smart cards

Smart cards carry computer chips within and have greater off-line functionality and data capacity than magnetic stripe cards. Customer data is held within the card, not on a database. This hands control over their own data from the company to the customer.

Magnetic stripe cards have been much cheaper (a few pence) than Smart cards but these differences are disappearing, and Smart cards are increasingly being introduced for debit and credit cards as well as loyalty cards. Magnetic stripe cards are more likely to be compatible with existing store Electronic Point of Sale (EPOS) technology, and a good database makes the need to hold the data on the card less apparent, but Smart cards are essential for coalition cards such as Nectar.

Cards are ideal for the crucial role of tracking transaction data and building the customer record.

The economics of a card-based loyalty scheme need to be carefully thought through, as it is not a cheap option. A company with a six-figure customer base would expect to pay probably £5 to £10 million in set-up costs, and then perhaps 50p per customer per year in ongoing administrative charges. Finally, there are the costs of the reward itself. This investment will only pay back if the incremental customer retention revenue achieved from the scheme outweighs these costs.

In some sectors, such as telecommunications or utilities, transaction data is automatically collected internally and cards are not necessary for loyalty schemes to be run.

AIRLINE FREQUENT-FLYER PROGRAMMES

Airlines have been described as 'a lousy business to be in'. Always operating with tight margins, the trauma of 9/11, a weakening of consumer confidence, and tough competition from low-cost carriers has served to bring many carriers to their knees. Swiss Air and Belgian Airlines effectively closed down in 2002, Northwestern Airlines filed for bankruptcy, and even mighty American Airlines was taken to the brink.

However, recent signs of recovery are beginning to show, and part of the picture has been the relaunch of frequent-flyer schemes. These began because traditional airlines have historically been starved of information about their customers because only about 15 per cent book direct. Loyalty schemes give them priceless transaction data on their most valuable customers: frequent business flyers.

Frequent-flyer programmes are now a global phenomenon. The majority of the world's major carriers, from Air Portugal to Cathay Pacific, now have well-established schemes. The biggest market is in the US, where there were 35 million estimated frequent-flying customers by 2000. The world's biggest scheme is run by American Airlines, called AAdvantage, with 26 million members worldwide including partner airline members. This scheme was launched as far back as 1981. BA's Air Miles has 2 million savers. Credit-card programmes such as the American Express Business ExtrAA corporate card, have developed partnerships with airlines, so that consumers can convert points to airline miles. The airlines have a number of partnerships with hotels and car rental firms that allow more attractive points gathering opportunities.

Source: *Potentials*, (2003) **36** (7) p. 7, July.

Cross-category promotion schemes (co-branded cards)

Most loyalty schemes are unique to one supplier in that the points earned are for purchases from that supplier, with rewards obtained within the scheme. However, cross-category promotion schemes have become popular. Here, the scheme involves a number of suppliers from different sectors. Consumers can earn points from purchases from all these suppliers, which are then redeemed for rewards in the normal way. The scheme may be set up and administered by an independent company which makes money from selling points to suppliers at a higher rate than their payout on redeemed points from consumers.

Examples of cross-category loyalty schemes include BA's Air Miles and Shell's Pluspoints. Examples of card consortia of various types include:

- General Motors/HFC Bank Visa Card: Points are collected from Visa, Esso, Comet and Best Western Hotels. They are redeemed against new car purchase;
- Tesco (UK retailer) Clubcard/Natwest Bank: Points are collected from Tesco retail store and redeemed for vouchers based on supermarket spend;
- Takashimaya (Japanese retailer)/Fujitsu, Visa, Development Bank of Singapore: This is a co-branded Visa credit card that also acts as a loyalty card. Points are redeemed for parking rights (a big deal in Japan!), delivery of purchases, and gift offers.

In theory ideas such as Shell's Smartcard are ground-breaking. Soon after its launch, Mitchell (1997) described it as developing as a brand in its own right – with its own identity, image and values – driven primarily by direct marketing. It was hoped this would be an umbrella loyalty scheme involving ten plus non-competing companies from different sectors including Hilton Hotels, Shell, and a number of retailers from wine to stationers. In fact, Shell encountered significant practical problems in making the scheme work, with players arguing over who was entitled to what. There were also problems over the branding being Shell-driven. Recently, Shell replaced Smartcard with Pluspoints – a scheme with more modest outcomes than Smartcard.

The plans for cards such as this are to tie in a large number of companies across as many sectors as possible, in particular frequent-purchase markets.

Such 'constellation brands' may be a big growth area of the future because of the added value that can be created for customers without adding costs to individual suppliers.

EXHIBIT 9.10

THE STORY OF AIR MILES

The Air Miles scheme is the product of Air Miles Travel Promotions Ltd, a company which was founded in 1988 to answer a problem facing the then British Caledonian airline company. British Caledonian, since taken over by British Airways, had many empty seats on its domestic flights within the UK, and wanted a low-cost promotion that would increase passenger volume on this margin without diluting the core business.

At the same time, other clients were looking for ways to differentiate their offerings to customers in sectors which had become increasingly commoditised; it was now a real struggle for, say, banks and petrol suppliers to position themselves as being different from other suppliers.

On 1 November 1988, Air Miles was launched in the UK. It was designed on a win-win-win philosophy. Participating clients were able to reward their loyal customers, thereby increasing their business by having the exclusive right within their category to offer Air Miles. BA, the participating airline, could fill its excess seats on flights by selling this space to Air Miles Travel Promotions (AMTP) at reduced rates. AMTP's revenue was the difference between the charges it made to participating clients and the payments it made to BA.

However, the real key to the success of this and other conventional frequent-flyer schemes is the attraction of the rewards to the consumer. Unlike some loyalty schemes, customers felt motivated to collect Air Miles for two main reasons. First, there was a substantial perceived cash value; second, there was an aspirational element and excitement to airline travel.

In the early 1990s, consumers would need to spend typically £10 on a credit card or £6 on petrol to collect one Air Mile. This meant that a free return flight from London to Paris would be possible for an average family within a few months.

In 1991, BA bought a 51 per cent share of AMTP and introduced Air Miles as the key reward in its frequent-flyer Executive Club scheme.

Although facing steep competition from company-based loyalty schemes, airline frequent-flyer schemes and other, emerging cross-category schemes, Air Miles remains highly successful. So much so that, in 1995, the *Financial Times* reported an 'illness' it called Sccams – Systematic and Compulsive Collection of Air Miles Syndrome! *Private Eye* ran a 'Great Bores of Today' article in which a party guest detailed all the different ways he could collect Air Miles. Air Miles' turnover by 1995 was a healthy £90 million.

In 2002 Air Miles reacted strongly to the launch of a rival, Nectar, by offering longer flights per set miles collected, effectively dropping its price. It has recently added BT and House of Fraser to its roster, but by far its biggest development was in resigning the Sainsbury account and signing a deal with Tesco, one of Europe's biggest retailers.

CREATING A COMPLETE PROGRAMME OF CONTACT

Taking our offers, discussed earlier, and incentives all together, we arrive at a complete programme of customer contact. The scheme in Fig. 9.4 indicates what such a programme might look like.

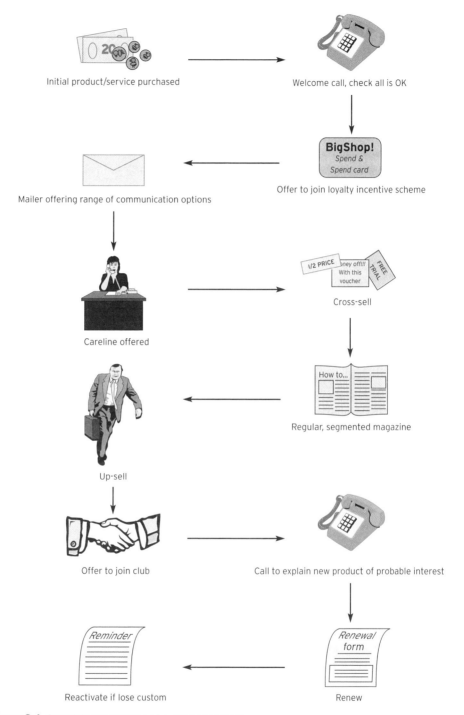

Figure 9.4 Complete programme of customer contact

Programmes of contact to attract new customers

Contact programmes to acquire customers have been used by direct marketers in traditional direct marketing sectors for a long time. Direct distribution companies such as mail order, publishing, book clubs, china collectibles, and so on, have become masters of the art of using incentives to acquire customers at the lowest possible cost per sale.

Recalling Jones's (1996) comment that firms should 'acquire with product and retain with service', there is perhaps some truth that direct marketing within the acquisition situation is often better described as 'direct selling'. Within this context, the objective of incentives within an acquisition programme becomes clearer. It is to provide that final push: to trigger a response from a customer who is interested but needs that final stimulus to act on the impulse to buy.

Thanks to extensive testing, direct marketers have built up considerable cumulative wisdom on the best ways to trigger action in a cost-effective way. To illustrate this, let us examine a typical classic direct marketing acquisition offer in detail.

THE TAPP AUDIO CLUB

As an example of the 'offer with conditions' mechanic, let us take a closer look at the specimen direct response advertisement shown in Fig. 9.5.

Headline

Take 5 ... plus your extra gift.
Save up to £80 now!

The offer

■ buy five CDs for a total of £13.99, saving up to £80;

■ send no money now; ten-day home trial money-back offer;

■ free storage unit for CDs when you join.

The condition

■ customer buys a further six CDs of their choice at the regular club price within the next two years;

■ monthly magazines and editor's recommendations are sent to the customer.

Future offers/conditions on joining

■ members can buy one CD at half price on each full price purchase;

■ other special offers and free CDs as a member;

■ gifts for replies to orders within ten days.

Imparting trust

■ the above ten-day, no quibble, money-back guarantee;

■ friendly customer service by phone;

■ Tapp company name well known;

■ states 20 years in the business, implying experience.

Take 5 ...
Plus your extra gift

- MORE CHOICE! FREE full colour monthly magazine with hundreds of titles to choose from. Order what you want when you want. You do not have to buy from every magazine.
- MORE VALUE! SAVE up to £80 NOW on this special introductory offer * That's just £13.99 for 5 CDs (plus p&p) * A free storage unit when you join * Members can buy at up to HALF PRICE every time they buy one at the Regular Club Price (normally from £11.99-£14.99) * More special offers and FREE CDs as a member.
- MORE CONVENIENCE! 10-day home trial with this introductory offer * Your favourite listening delivered to your door * No loss MONEY BACK GUARANTEE if not completely satisfied * FRIENDLY customer service just a phone call away * All we ask is that you buy a further 6 CDs of your choice at the Regular Club Price within the next 2 years, and that is all! * With over 20 years' experience, we are the BEST IN THE BUSINESS.

ROCK	POP	CLASSICAL
10001 Bryan Adams	21001 Abba	43001 Bach - Popular selection
10002 Bon Jovi	21002 The Beatles	43002 Beethoven - Popular selection
10003 Eric Clapton	21003 The Beachboys	43003 Mahler - Popular selection
10004 The Eagles	21004 Eurythmics	43004 Rachmaninov - Popular selection
10005 Queen	21005 Take That	43005 Strauss - Popular selection

Save up to £80 now!

TO THE TAPP AUDIO CLUB, FREEPOST, ANYTOWN, AN1 1NA

YES! Please accept me as a Member and send me the following 5 CDs on 10-day home trial, as well as my Member's Club Guide, Free Monthly Magazine and Gift Voucher (if replying within 10 days).

☐☐☐☐☐ ☐☐☐☐☐ ☐☐☐☐☐ ☐☐☐☐☐ ☐☐☐☐☐

I understand that you will only charge me for the price of one CD at £13.99 (plus £3.29 towards postage and packing and insurance for all 5). If not completely satisfied, I can return all 5 cassettes undamaged within 10 days of receipt, my membership will be cancelled and I will owe nothing. As a Member, I agree to buy a further 6 Regular Priced CDs of my choice within a 2-year period, at least 3 in the first year. THIS IS MY ONLY COMMITMENT. I am not obliged to order every month, and if I do not wish to receive the Editor's monthly recommendation, I will say so on the Order Forms provided. If I am replying within 10 days, the gift which I select on the voucher enclosed with my introductory selections will be sent to me as soon as you receive payment for these selections.

My favourite kind of music is: (Please tick ONE box only). Your monthly magazine includes over 200 titles with every subject catered for.

1 Chart/Pop ☐   2 Dance ☐   3 Easy Listening ☐   4 Soft rock ☐   5 Hard rock ☐
6 Soul ☐   7 Indie/Alternative ☐   8 Country & Western ☐   9 Classical ☐

MR/MRS/MISS/MS _____

ADDRESS _____

_____

POSTCODE ☐☐☐☐☐

SIGNATURE (I am over 18) _____   1000001

WE REGRET THAT THIS ORDER CANNOT BE ACCEPTED WITHOUT A SIGNATURE   TA/01/02/98

FREEPOST * SEND NO MONEY NOW * TEN DAY HOME TRIAL

Offer closes 01.02.98. All orders subject to acceptance. All titles are subject to availability. One membership per household only. Please allow up to 28 days for delivery. Offer applies to UK, Channel Isles, Eire and BFPO only. VAT, postage, packing and insurance charges quoted are based on rates at time of going to press and may vary.

The Tapp Audio Club is registered under the Data Protection Act 1994. From time to time we may pass your name and address to other companies who we believe offer products in which you may be interested. If you wish to avoid this, please write to us at the Tapp Audio Club, PO Box 000, Anytown, AN1 1NA.

Figure 9.5 Music club direct-response advertisement

As you can see, there is some complexity to the customer offer. Let us take a closer look. The following analysis highlights how the design of the offer pays back for the company while also providing instant value for the customer.

The return on investment

The economics of the use of incentives will have been carefully calculated by the company. The figures in Table 9.5 illustrate the general principle, *but are not based on actual data.*

Table 9.5: **Typical return on investment figures**

	Typical costs	Typical revenues
Five introductory CDs	£20	£14
Six subsequent CDs	£24	£78
Gifts @ £2 each	£10	
Media costs per customer (press, catalogues)	£25	
Total	£79	£92
Return =	£13	

From Table 9.5 we can see that gross margin is therefore £13 on a turnover of £92.

The five introductory CDs represent Tapp Audio's front-end revenues and costs. As we can see, the company will lose money on the initial sale, because of the high value of its incentive to join the club. It is with the sale of the six subsequent CDs, the back-end revenues, that the payback is achieved.

The key to success is that the offer demands a future obligation from customers by contracting them into future purchases. This could be:

■ customer agreement to automatic billing for a year's subscription;

■ club-style condition, e.g. 'I agree to buy six more CDs at full price over the next year'.

This example is typical of classical direct marketers in offering multiple incentives. The direct marketers' assertion that these give multiple reasons to buy is borne out by testing. They also take care to use incentives (the storage unit) that are related to the core product.

TECHNIQUES FOR ELICITING DIRECT RESPONSE

One of the most knowledgeable writers on the subject of acquisition offers is Stone (1996), who outlined many of the most common techniques used. We can now examine the most important of these.

The opt-in/out mechanic

One variant on the 'contractual' design, illustrated by the example, is the opt-out mechanic. Here a higher initial response is sought by promising no 'lock in', that is no obligation to buy in the future. The company then sends products at regular intervals to the customer; if they do *not* want these, they must act by sending back the product. This technique is often used in publishing. If the customer wants to cancel the subscription, they must write to the publisher to do so.

The success of this technique is due to the direct marketer's understanding of customer inertia. There will be a middle ground of customers who perhaps would not have made the effort to buy the products, but who also are not sufficiently motivated to cancel the subscription, being reasonably happy with the value they are receiving. These are the people who are captured by the opt-out mechanic.

The alternative is to opt in. Here customers have to act if they *do* want the product.

The question of which is better has to be carefully addressed and tested. Stone reports that opt-in offers tend to give lower initial response, because the acquisition offer is likely to be less valuable to the customer. However, retention sales are likely to be higher, because more customers with a genuine interest in the product rather than the incentive will have been attracted.

EXHIBIT 9.11

CUSTOMER INERTIA

Customer inertia does not refer to those prospects who are definitely not interested in a product: they are not going to be persuaded to change their minds. Inertia is that feeling of 'Yes I am interested in this product, and the price seems OK, but I can't be bothered to go through the hassle of purchasing it'. This is probably a feeling that affects us all at some time or another. The impact of inertia is greatest on 'non-essential' product categories such as kitchen gadgets, collectibles, fashion, encyclopedias, and so on.

Free samples

Used extensively by the packaged-goods industries, free samples can be delivered by targeted door drops. This is direct marketing if some sort of response, perhaps further information, is sought. In this way the sample offer helps to build a prospect database.

Unit of sales

In order to shift more volume, a 'two for X pounds, saving Y' may be offered. However, compared to price off, this is likely to reduce the number of customers who will respond, which may be a disadvantage if you are looking to build up your database.

Credit options

Offering payment by credit cards increases response when compared to cash demands (Stone, 1996). The ability to accept credit-card payment by phone was a major driver in the growth of direct marketing when it was introduced in the 1980s.

Free trial

Stone describes this as the 'bell-wether of mail order'. The key to this incentive is that it removes the barrier of immediate pain (having to pay!) while also providing reassurance that customers won't have to pay for a product they subsequently don't like. In any purchase made remotely, this is very attractive.

The following incentives are *related to customer knowledge.*

Member get member

> '*All things being equal, people will buy from a friend. All things being not quite so equal, people will still buy from a friend.*'
>
> Mark McCormack, CEO, IMG, 1984

'Member get member' schemes offer incentives to current customers in return for their recommendation of someone they believe will be interested in that company's products. It is based on a fundamental principle of (direct) marketing: your customers are similar people in terms of values or lifestyles; and they will know other similar people who are not yet your customers.

Member get member is most likely to work if it is part of a strategy of maximising customer satisfaction and hence loyalty. This is because only very satisfied, happy customers will recommend a supplier to friends.

Bounce backs

This is based on the notion that often the best time to sell to someone is when they have just bought from you, a phenomenon well known in the mail-order industry. The customer therefore receives a 'Thank you for purchasing ... by the way have you seen our tremendous offer running on ... ?' message.

Gifts/premiums

> '*These six books are truly, truly great novels. They are absolutely right for Dewhurst customers.*'
>
> Dewhurst Butchers' spokesperson, on the offer of free, unpublished Barbara Cartland
novels when purchasing meat products

According to Stone, gifts can make a useful secondary incentive, acting as the final push to act straightaway.

Factors which direct marketers have found to be important (McCorkell, 2002) include the following:

- Gifts should be trouble free: for example, non-electrical goods are recommended.
- Gifts should have high perceived values. It may be an advantage to make the premium unique, perhaps by branding it with your logo. Items such as sports bags or cosmetic bags have a high perceived value but low wholesale value.
- Linking the gift to your main product will help to enhance the brand image of the company/product.
- Increasingly, consumers prefer choices of premiums. Safeway's ABC loyalty card offers a catalogue of high-quality premiums. However, this makes logistics much harder to manage. You need to avoid being left with a warehouse full of unwanted cuddly toys!

In a world full of alarm clocks and calculators, one of the hardest things to do with gifts is to be distinctive. The overuse of gifts as incentives by financial services companies in the 1980s led to a number of problems for the sector. The first mistake was to use gifts as a primary differentiator between very similar offerings, promoting the gift to top spot in the advert. At the very least, this would have done little to build brand values in an already weakly branded market. Second, financial services companies all found through testing that consumer durables were their most effective premium. This led to a plethora of similar-looking offers, hence lacking any distinctiveness. Our attraction for telephone clock radios soon waned! Once the lesson had been learned, direct marketers realised that their use of gifts is subject to changing trends, and as time moves on, more imagination is required to provide value and distinctiveness.

In sectors with high margins it is perhaps easier to be imaginative. Land Rover offered picnic baskets as an incentive to attend a sales day for its new Discovery marque. However, these were offered only to carefully chosen existing customers.

One senior practitioner commented that unusual items, loosely related to the product, are very successful. A book club selling a European history set could offer a limited edition print of a painting by a classic European artist. Buyers of the product are arguably likely to value such an incentive more than another clock radio.

Competitions/prize draws

The use of competitions and prize draws in the UK is increasing. According to Peattie and Peattie (1993), this is due to the size of prizes now being offered (British Airways' 'World's greatest offer' featured £6 million worth of free flights) and the enormous success of the lottery in establishing itself quickly as a national institution. However, competitions have been a popular acquisition incentive in classic direct marketing sectors for decades. *Reader's Digest* has been using competitions to attract custom since the 1950s and has refined its methods to a high level of sophistication. For example, the use of prize draws by the *Digest* is often related to deadlines: 'Your prize will be £1000 more for every day you beat the deadline.' Stone (1996) reports D.L. Blair, a US judging agency for sweepstakes, claiming an upturn of 15 per cent at least in response rates when using prize draws with magazine subscriptions. Both Stone and McKibbin (1992) report that the most popular prizes are cash, cars and holidays, in that order.

However, some industry practitioners have commented that competitions and free prize draws related to acquiring names may improve initial responses, but poor-quality names have resulted. The *Reader's Digest* has found that using prize draws and competitions successfully takes a great deal of experience. In most sectors, competitions are perhaps best used as secondary incentives, but many classic direct marketers have led their creative with competitions. Book club offers to prospects may have 'You may already have won...' messages emblazoned across the envelope, and practitioners have had great success with such approaches.

To many marketers, this sort of approach goes against their natural instincts. How can such approaches build brand values? Why ignore the core product and concentrate on the incentive? Yet there is no doubt that such approaches have been tested and shown to obtain higher responses than other approaches, within these particular markets. In answering the critics, practitioners point out that white collar, AB marketers who find the approaches unattractive may not understand the motivations of C1/C2 subscribers.

Further insight into consumers' reactions to competitions came from a large study by Peattie and Peattie (1993) who developed an audience segmentation shown in Exhibit 9.12.

EXHIBIT 9.12

COMPETITIONS: TURNING SHOPPING INTO A TREASURE HUNT

Peattie and Peattie (1993) identified six types of consumer in relation to competitions:

1 **Non competitors:** consider competitions a waste of time.
2 **Passive competitors:** enter a competition which they qualified for as part of their normal purchases but would not switch in order to enter.
3 **Brand switchers:** switch brands from their normal purchase, within the same product category, in order to enter a competition.

4 **Product switchers:** buy a product they don't normally buy in order to enter a competition.
5 **Hoarders:** alter their buying behaviour between product and brand types, and will alter their timing of purchases to enter competitions or increase their chances of winning a competition.
6 **Dog fooders:** buy almost anything to enter a competition, regardless of core product's utility. Make excuses to buy these products. Known as hobbyist competitors. Buy any product with 'win' on the pack, including bags of Winalot – hence their name.

Direct marketers who have a high number of people from segments 4, 5 and 6 (*see* Exhibit 9.12) in their target audience will find competition-led approaches most lucrative.

EXHIBIT 9.13

ACQUISITION INCENTIVES: TRICKS OF THE TRADE

Time limits
Delay kills response. As an incentive to act immediately, you can set time limits for your offer: 'You must reply within ten days to take advantage of this unique offer.'

Quantity limits
This idea could be a 'Hurry while stocks last' message. In markets where there is an implied prestige in ownership of the product, the offer could include a deliberate quantity limit to act as an incentive in its own right. China collectibles is one such market:

'Only 500 of these beautiful hand-painted dolls have been made. You will need to act quickly.'

Guarantees
Stone (1996) recommends that guarantees should never be passed up in any direct distribution market. World-class mail-order exponents, such as L.L. Bean, a US outdoor clothing supplier, have made this into a competitive differentiator. It offers 'lifetime, no quibble, money-back guarantees' for all its lines. This represents tremendous value, in the form of peace of mind, to L.L. Bean's customers.

Summary to chapter

In this chapter we identified the difference between offers and incentives as being one of level - the incentive is part of the offer. We found that both offers and incentives are an important part of the message that customers receive from direct marketers.

The differences between the use of incentives in direct as opposed to general marketing were identified. In particular, incentives can be segmented and targeted using direct marketing, thereby avoiding wastage.

The use of activities such as magazines and loyalty schemes to help retain customers was explored. Loyalty schemes should not be relied upon without having carefully built into the business one of the routes to their success.

The well-established use of 'lock-in' offers to acquire new customers profitably was outlined, showing how initial losses are compensated by profitability over time. The success of premiums and competitions in improving response was also established.

Questions

1. What is the difference between sales promotion and direct marketing?

2. What are the major factors to consider before using incentives to tempt purchase of a product in a direct marketing context?

3. Explain the difference between opt-in and opt-out offers.

4. You are the marketing manager of a medium-sized chain of restaurants and are considering the use of a loyalty card to boost retention rates. However, there are a number of other leisure-related loyalty cards already launched, none of which seems to stand out. State the factors that you, as the manager, must take into account before making a decision, and give recommendations on the approach that would have most chance of success.

5. What is the role of a loyalty magazine in the retention strategy of a car manufacturer? Justify the expenditure versus alternative uses of the money.

6. A 'wine direct' operation is considering the use of premiums to stimulate take-up of an offer. Recommend an appropriate choice, explaining your reasoning clearly.

References

Brann/Henley Centre Report (1995) 'The loyalty paradox'.

Cram, T. (1994) *The Power of Relationship Marketing*, Pitman Publishing, London.

Denny, N. (1995) 'Bounty Bags', *Marketing Direct*, November.

Dibb, S., Simpkin, L., Pride, W. and Ferrell, O.C. (1994) *Marketing Concepts and Strategies*, Houghton Mifflin, Abingdon, Oxfordshire.

Durand, P. (1987) 'Norwich Union: Development of cross-selling in a growing file', EDMA Conference, Montreux, Switzerland.

Holder, D. (1992) 'Finders keepers - the basics of customer acquisition and retention' in Halsey, B. (ed.) *The Practitioners' Guide to Direct Marketing*, Institute of Direct Marketing, Teddington, Richmond-upon-Thames.

Jobber, D. (1995) *Marketing: Principles and Practice*, McGraw-Hill, Maidenhead, Berkshire.

Jones, T. (1996) 'Why satisfied customers defect', IDM Conference, 29 June, Surrey.

Kotler, P. (1995) *Marketing Management: Analysis, planning, implementation and control,* 7th edn, Prentice Hall, Upper Saddle River, NJ.

McKibbin, S. (1992) 'The importance of incentives in direct marketing' in Halsey, B. (ed.) *The Practitioners' Guide to Direct Marketing*, Institute of Direct Marketing, Teddington, Richmond-upon-Thames.

McCorkell, G. (2002) 'Customer incentives', *The Interactive and Direct Marketing Guide*, IDM, Teddington, Richmond-upon-Thames.

Mitchell, A. (1997) *Marketing Week*, 14 March, p. 28.

O'Brien, L. and Jones, C. (1995) 'Do rewards really create loyalty?', *Harvard Business Review*, May–June, pp. 75–82.

Peattie, K. and Peattie, S. (1993) 'Sales promotion, playing to win', *Journal of Marketing Management*, **9**, pp. 255–69.

Prentice, R., Strang, R. and Clayton, A. (1975) *The relationship between advertising and promotion in brand strategy*, Marketing Science Institute, Cambridge, Mass.

Rapp, S. and Collins, T. (1987) *Maximarketing*, McGraw-Hill, New York.

Reichheld, F.F. (1996) *The Loyalty Effect*, Harvard Business School Publishing, Boston, Mass.

Shultz, D.E. (1987) 'Above or below the line? Growth of sales promotion in the US', *International Journal of Advertising*, 6, 1, pp. 17–27.

Smith, P.R. (1993) *Marketing Communications: An integrated approach*, Kogan Page, London.

Stone, B. (1996) *Successful Direct Marketing Methods*, 5th edn, NTC Business Books, Chicago, Ill.

Tapp, A. (1995) 'Relationship fundraising techniques: Are they used and do they work?', *Journal of Database Marketing*, 2 (4).

Wade, D. (1992) 'Choosing, using and buying premium gifts' in Halsey, B. (ed.) *The Practitioners' Guide to Direct Marketing*, Institute of Direct Marketing, Teddington, Richmond-upon-Thames.

CASE STUDY

Bounty

The arrival of a new baby into a family is a life-changing event, and just one of the many things a parent has to get used to is how much they will spend on the infant. In one year, a typical parent will spend £1500 on their precious new arrival. Clearly then, this is an important and sizeable market, with around 770 000 babies born in the UK alone every year.

Companies such as Unilever, Procter and Gamble, and Nestlé are keen to show mothers how their products can help with raising the child. They also know that, once a habit of behaviour is instilled with a particular product, there is a high likelihood that mothers will stick with that product. But how do they target mothers at the right time? This is the problem that Bounty set out to solve. Bounty acts as a conduit for the product manufacturers because of the direct contact it sets up with mothers.

The key to the data gathering lies with hospitals granting Bounty access to mothers-to-be and new mothers, in return for a fee. The process starts with pregnant women who are handed *Bounty's Pregnancy Guide*, a 150-page booklet on pregnancy, containing advertisements from the above companies. Hospitals receive 30 per cent of advertising revenues. The women are encouraged to fill in a form and hand it in to the local Mothercare retail store, where they are handed their first Bounty Pack, containing free samples of baby products. Data is collected and stored at this stage.

The second phase occurs when the baby is born. Bounty representatives travel through the ward collecting data and dispensing a second bag of freebies. Again the hospital makes a charge – about 50p per mother. A baby care guide and a voucher for a third free bag, collected from Boots, the retail chemist's, are also included. Both Mothercare and Boots distribute these bags of samples free, because they benefit from the extra store traffic generated. At Boots, more data is collected, including the baby's sex and date of birth.

The value of the data gathered by Bounty is in the accuracy of targeting that it offers to manufacturers. The resulting database of mothers can be rented and mailed by interested companies, offering vouchers or frequent-purchase incentives to encourage brand switching and loyalty. Mechanisms can be set up to ensure that data on the usage of vouchers is captured.

Source: Denny, N. (1995) 'Bounty bags', *Marketing Direct*, November.

Analysis of Bounty case

Why should the likes of Unilever and Procter and Gamble pay £65 000 to place leaflets and up to £500 000 to place a sample in one of Bounty's bags? The answer is that the payback is better than would be obtained through traditional sales promotion methods. Let us look at a comparison of the use of baby product incentives through direct and traditional methods.

Traditional sales promotion methods

Here the samples would be in-store or delivered through mass media, perhaps *Mother and Baby* magazine. Costs per thousand of distribution would be lower than using Bounty's sample bags. However, wastage would be much higher because two audiences you did not want to attract would take samples:

- mothers already loyal to the firm's products;
- mothers loyal to deals rather than brands.

Vouchers could be distributed on pack, through mass media, or by door-to-door methods. Again wastage would be high because the vouchers are less likely to get to new mothers at the crucial times that they make these habit-forming decisions, but will again be used by already loyal users and deal-conscious switchers who will quickly switch away from your brand to the next incentive.

Direct marketing methods

The case study highlights the extra *costs* of using a highly targeted distribution system like Bounty's. The *payback* comes from the immense power of direct marketing when used to its full potential:

- **Targeting:** Wastage is at an absolute minimum. All sample bags will be relevant to the recipients.
- **Timing:** The samples are given at exactly the right point when the consumer is making decisions about product use and brand choice.
- **Continuity:** By collecting voucher usage data, companies can understand who is using their vouchers and how much these customers are worth to them. Ongoing incentives can be targeted accurately, with the level of the incentive set so that both company and customer benefit.

CASE STUDY

Nectar: A perfect partnership?
Can Nectar succeed where Shell Smart failed?

Written by Alan Tapp in 2003 using various referenced sources and discussions with Professor Merlin Stone of Bristol Business School. The author wishes to thank Merlin Stone for his help.

Before you read this case study you may like to access www.nectar.com and familiarise yourself with the partnership loyalty scheme.

Introduction

Shell Smart started out with high hopes in 1996. Commentators described it as one of the leading edge pieces of marketing around at the time. Shell launched its Smartcard with the idea of taking it significantly beyond a mere points scheme that bribes customers to stay. Shell's card allowed consumers to collect and redeem points with Shell plus its scheme partners, including Avis Rent-A-Car, British Gas and Hilton Hotels.

By 2001 the scheme had been reined back. What had gone wrong? Could Shell have done anything differently? The answers to these questions may become clear one day. Meanwhile partnership schemes, far from fading away, continue to grow in importance.

The launch of Nectar in 2002 raised loyalty stakes to a new high. Nectar's acquisition marketing has been excellent. When Nectar launched in the UK, it combined two existing loyalty schemes, Sainsbury's Rewards and Barclaycard Profiles. It now boasts BP petrol, Debenhams, Vodafone and Ford amongst its partners. Several more big names were expected to follow in 2004. By April 2003 the partnership had signed up over 17 million customers spread over 12.5 million households and issued more than 76 billion points.

Tesco has responded by signing up more partners for its Clubcard scheme. The 18 million members of Marriott Rewards can now earn Clubcard points on stays at any of Marriott's 2300 global hotels. The points can later be redeemed as Marriott Rewards, Clubcard points or converted to Air Miles.

The success of Nectar's marketing has shown that reports of points fatigue, at least in the UK, have been exaggerated. According to Carlson Marketing Group, 92 per cent of consumers are involved in a loyalty scheme. Of these, 78 per cent carry more than one loyalty card. Research found that 36 per cent of customers were 'much more likely' to continue to shop with a company because they were in a loyalty programme. This doesn't negate the arguments about zero sum games: the danger that everyone runs a scheme and cancels out each other's marketing.

How loyalty partnerships work – Nectar

For the scheme to work, in the long term it has to be win-win-win for all the players: consumers, the operators, Loyalty Management UK (LMUK), and the partners.

Consumers

The customer gains through getting 'something for nothing'. They would have bought the groceries anyway, and they get points as well. In a partner scheme, customers can collect points more quickly and regularly compared with single schemes, in particular through their store shopping, credit card, mobile phone and petrol. Collectors in the Nectar scheme can redeem for general rewards that include flying miles, and they need to carry fewer cards. There are plenty of redemption partners to choose from and plenty of collection partners to collect from. This is one of the successes of partnership schemes – points volumes are easy to accumulate. On the other hand they need to be because each point, arguably, isn't terribly valuable: you need to buy 500 litres of petrol to get enough free points for a McDonald's meal. This last point is subjective of course: some consumers may regard this as reasonable value. Most likely, fairly complex schemes like this tend to attract those kinds of people who can be bothered to work through the detail, and engage with the idea of collecting points here, there and everywhere. This is true of all points schemes and is a reality of the sector.

LMUK

LMUK wins by pocketing the difference between money it pays to an organisation at which a customer redeems – redemption partners – and the money it is paid when another partner – collect partners – issues points.

Collect partners

Now to the partners – take a deep breath. It is not simply the case that a customer buys at one partner and redeems at any of the others. In fact there is little cross-over between collecting and redeeming points, except at Sainsbury and Argos. When they initially signed up, customers may have been somewhat surprised that, for example, a Vodafone customer earning Nectar points cannot redeem those points for a lower phone bill. Similarly a BP customer can redeem their points at Sainsbury, but not at BP garages. Once they get used to the scheme, consumers may be happy enough with the idea of collecting points at X and getting their rewards at Y.

Let's take the example of BP and examine it in slightly more detail. BP gives its customers Nectar points which they can collect for rewards elsewhere. BP has to pay LMUK for these points. In return, BP wants to get the following:

■ BP customers to spend more of their share of fuel wallet at BP than they would otherwise have done;

■ Nectar customers who aren't currently BP customers to switch to BP, either through basic cross-sell activity by BP using the Nectar database, or more simply because competitor customers switch to BP because they are attracted to Nectar points and switch of their own accord;

■ Data-driven insights into BP customers that they wouldn't get from conventional market research, which lead to more powerful business and marketing decision making.

BP also risks losing out. It may lose out through rewarding customers for what they were doing anyway. In the case of a partner scheme like this one, the problem is enhanced when the reward is redeemed elsewhere (as opposed to with themselves in a solus scheme). Of course, some decisions (e.g. grocery shopping) are driven mainly by location, but even here customers may have two options, as catchment areas vary by time of day and day of week, and also some shopping is from work, on the way home rather than from home. In general, the more real choice or discretion the customer has, the more influential the loyalty scheme.

Redemption partners

Some firms deliver the rewards, for which they are rewarded by LMUK. The underlying economics here in some instances play out much as they do for Air Miles – yield management. Redemption partners may be airlines, holiday firms, or places to eat out that can sell excess volume cheaply. In other instances a different business case applies. For example McDonald's is a redemption partner. For 500 points you can enjoy a medium extra value meal. McDonald's presumably charges LMUK for these points, and may also gain through encouraging repeat shopping at its restaurants that it wouldn't otherwise get. Only Sainsbury and Argos are both collect partners and redemption partners.

If you're confused you're probably not alone. The consumer behaviour here is not necessarily logical. Each partner may worry about being a net loser. Some may become net contributors of value back to customers (issuing more points value than subsequently spent with their brand), others net beneficiaries (attracting more of the scheme's value to be spent with their business than they issue in points themselves).

Another motive may be the desire to cut costs. Each of Nectar's partners knows that running their own loyalty scheme (indeed their own marketing) is expensive: Tesco Clubcard is thought to cost over £100 million to run each year. This is a lot of money, even for huge companies. Nectar allows each partner to outsource a difficult and complex marketing operation. By sharing costs of customer acquisition, communications, data gathering and data analysis (so crucial to the success of Tesco Clubcard that it bought the expert firm DunnHumby), and by sharing the costs of managing each loyalty point, the partners hope to save money. Indeed, loyalty schemes are so expensive to run that unless you are the size of Tesco it is very hard to make them work without partners. This suggests partnership schemes will become more prevalent. They are already widespread in Europe: The Netherlands, for instance, has no retailers operating solus schemes.

Looking further ahead the scheme presumably gives the protagonists opportunities to cross-sell to each other's customers, and share information. By overlaying data on people with the same characteristics who shop with one partner but not with another (e.g., those who buy a lot of petrol at BP, but don't go to Sainsbury's) it is possible to establish how much they might be worth to Sainsbury's and how much it is worth spending to recruit them. LMUK chief, Keith Mills claims this is an advantage over the Tesco scheme for example – Tesco knows its own customers well but doesn't know so well those who aren't its customers.

After the honeymoon . . . the hard work begins

Partnership schemes have a chequered history. Firms such as AT&T and Shell were never able to make their schemes work because of difficulties in persuading a major grocery firm to co-operate with a petrol retailer. There are also many management difficulties. Some partners may put in more effort than others; disputes may arise over promotional affairs; spur-of-the-moment decisions to run promotions aren't possible because all parties must agree – the scheme must have rules. In short keeping all the partners happy means more management costs that could cancel out the economies of scale-cost savings.

Fundamentally proving that the schemes make money that would otherwise not accrue is hard. Tesco is fond of its statistic that Clubcard customers spend twice as much as non-Clubcard customers. It implies that Clubcard delivers more spend, but it's just as likely that the link is the other way round: high spenders like Clubcard because their discounts are higher.

Meanwhile what do customers become loyal to? Nectar or Sainsbury? Air Miles collectors like Air Miles, but not necessarily NatWest Bank. The danger for Nectar partners is that if one partner drops out of the programme and is replaced by another from the same category, consumers would drop the former. Any partner leaving would have to bear in mind that Nectar shares ownership of the data: while there's no suggestion that it may supply this to competitors, the issue of ownership remains. Finally, by entering a partnership scheme that has its own brand, the partners distance themselves from the rewards in the minds of consumers. Tesco gets all the credit for Clubcard rewards, but to what extent does Sainsbury 'take the credit' for its Nectar rewards?

Customer insight is the key

Are these schemes about loyalty? Given the criticisms about points being low priority for customers in choosing brands, this is a good question to ask. Merely offering a reward for a purchase is no more than an easily-copied sales promotion, and the majority of so-called 'loyalty' schemes are just that. The 'zero sum game' rule probably holds: competitors' points schemes cancel each other out. So, for the partners these schemes are not about points, but about customer insight. The best in the business at this is Tesco, and worth a closer look. Tesco has delivered world-class retailing through better insights into its customers, adopting the principle 'we are what we eat'. Tesco analyses its customers to measure their loyalty, their commitment to Tesco, their profitability, and their 'headroom': the difference between what they spend at Tesco and how much they could potentially spend.

Tesco has created a series of lifestyle clusters. The story of analysts of earlier schemes – indeed of check-out data - discovering lots of male shoppers with beer and nappies in the same basket bought on the way home from work is well known in the trade. The basket tells the story: harassed and tired fathers of young kids prioritising two essentials in their lives. As Hunt and Humby put it: The beer-and-nappies correlation is the 'what', the link to fatherhood is the 'why', and an insight a retailer can work with.

Analysts working on the Tesco scheme have discovered other clusters, e.g. those who like high-value pre-packaged foods; people who shop for basic ingredients and value foods; family convenience buyers, and so on. These were more useful than lifestage or recency/frequency/value approaches that had hitherto dominated. Re-running the new lifestyle clusters against old data showed the new segments to be three or four times more powerful than those based on simple lifestage.

Some of Tesco's best work has been in using Clubcard data for price-discount targeting. Price discounting is an essential and powerful tool in supermarket competition – but it's expensive. It takes a lot from the bottom line. Cutting the price of bananas is expensive - discounts are given to everyone, including many who aren't bothered about price. Could Tesco avoid discounting to those who weren't price sensitive? The hope was that Clubcard data could identify products that were signatures of people who shop *exclusively* on price. Clubcard data identified the perfect product: Tesco value brand margarine. It seems that Tesco used buyers of Tesco value brand margarine as a surrogate for price sensitive customers: they then received disproportionate discount offers to keep them at Tesco. The results were excellent. While Tesco's prices reduced by an average of 6 per cent across its entire range, its operating margins remained the same, boosted by superior loyalty amongst 'price-sensitives'.

Hunt and Humby also emphasise the importance of the names of the clusters for their marketing. While marketers often come up with names like 'young families' these do not have the power to evoke ideas in the same way as, say, 'high spending superstore families' does. You can picture the latter better – it conveys an image that allows creative thinking to solve that family's problems.

So, to what extent can partnership schemes acquire the customer insights that Tesco has successfully done? Could they even do better, as their data extends across many more categories than grocery? For example, Nectar could perhaps identify a group: males who shop for family goods in Sainsbury late in the evening, who buy lots of fuel at BP. Let's call them 'busy male executives'. Maybe Debenhams could target these people with convenience-driven upmarket gift offers at Christmas time.

This looks good on paper, but as the Tesco story illustrates, getting there isn't easy. Their analysts took years of trial and error to get the data flows and data mining right to allow these insights. It's very hard work. But at least Tesco was able to grapple with its data from close up. Can Nectar partners emulate their success when their data is held more remotely?

Using database marketing as a springboard for joint ventures

The 'holy grail' of partnership schemes may be that having arrived at a common view of the customer, and having unearthed hitherto undiscovered insights, the partners create joint ventures that offer complete solutions to the customers – a kind of 'one stop shop' that solves their consumer problems in a joined-up way. Database marketing becomes sophisticated enough to pin down who we are and what we want in a holistic way. Entire life events such as moving home, going on holiday, or changing jobs could be catered for via one joint venture. The customer wins because they have the convenience of dealing with one trusted supplier. Could it be done? Experience suggests not quite yet.

Getting the points: the secrets of success

Nectar partners know that making points schemes work is difficult. In general, people feel that they have too many different 'bits of plastic', it takes too long to collect worthwhile rewards, and redeeming points is often too complicated. So, the marketing of the schemes has to be good. So far, so good for Nectar. But the real game is going on backstage. In the final analysis, each partner is looking for the data gathered to give them that edge: marginal gains via a lot of hard work. Even the best schemes tend not to have a dramatic impact, with a 2 per cent or 3 per cent rise in sales considered a good achievement. The worry for Nectar partners is whether they give their customers 1 per cent of their margin back so they can go and spend it elsewhere.

But any loyalty scheme can fail to deliver a return on investment, as was famously the case with Safeway's ABC card launched in 1995 and discontinued in 2000. The scheme had cost £60 million a year to run. Safeway now uses the money saved to offer immediate discounts. In the end, Safeway admitted that it never properly used the data – collecting too much and being overwhelmed by it. The scheme also became too expensive for a firm of Safeway's size to absorb.

The future for schemes like Nectar is far from certain. Leaving aside cost sharing, the advantage of partnerships is to create greater possibilities - more customers and prospects, more chances to create valuable propositions with partners. The disadvantage may be management: not of the mechanics of the scheme, but of what to do with the data. Astute management from LMUK and all its partners will be needed to make a success of it.

References

Humby, C., Hunt, T. and Phillips, T. (2003) *Scoring Points: How Tesco is Winning Customer Loyalty*, Kogan Page, London.
Ingall, J. (2003) 'Is it the end of the road for loyalty?', *Admap*, January, Issue 435.
Marketing (UK) (2003) 'Tesco clubcard answers Nectar with Marriott tie', 27 February.
Stone M., Bearman, D., Butscher, S., Crick, P., Gilbert, D. and Moffett, T. (2003) 'The effect of retail customer loyalty schemes – detailed measurement or transforming marketing?', *Journal of Targeting, Analysis and Measurement for Marketing*.

CASE STUDY

CLUB PHILIPS 2002

As one of the most successful consumer electronic companies in the world, Philips has always been at the forefront in delivering the benefits of technology to consumers at home, at work or on the move. Indeed, as a heavy investor in research and development (R&D), Philips has developed many breakthrough inventions, such as the compact cassette system and laser-based optical disc systems such as CD-Audio, CD-ROM, and SACD.

Despite this, some consumers have begun to see Philips not as a high-tech innovator, but as merely a reliable producer of quality television sets, DVD players and recorders, audio systems and the like. Competitors, such as Sony and Samsung, have begun to outperform Philips in the battle to be an innovative brand.

Philips realised that it had to change this perception quickly, especially among two critical audiences: innovators or early adopters. As key influencers for the mass market, loyalty from these consumers is critical to maintain market share and take advantage of ever decreasing windows of opportunity to profit from new product launches.

Research showed that innovators and early adopters thrive on being first with information on the hottest gadgets and seek out the stories behind the development of innovative products. In addition they like to future gaze, showing a great deal of interest in the latest technology news and the future of consumer electronics itself.

Based on these insights Philips did not turn to traditional big-brand advertising to change perceptions, but instead launched a programme to inform and most importantly engage 'innovators' with the real world of Philips and consumer electronics.

Club Philips, as it was called, used e-mail-based newsletters and a dedicated website to deliver information of the depth and quality that innovators and early adopters demand. Using its rich tradition of R&D investment and its commitment to new-product development, Philips is able to draw on a wealth of material about technology and trends, giving consumers fresh, engaging and valuable insights into what makes Philips an innovative brand.

In addition, registered consumers are asked for information about existing Philips products and are invited to keep this updated in exchange for value-added services and increased levels of information. This enables Philips to measure the impact of its activity on direct sales and begin to understand real customer lifetime value.

In four European countries at the end of 2002, Club Philips generated over 50 000 registrants in the first few weeks through e-mail marketing. Research has shown that as well as changing the perceptions of registered consumers, the overall brand preference for Philips has increased in countries where Club Philips has gone live.

Philips is currently rolling out the programme to other markets and by the end of 2003 it was operational in eight countries throughout Europe.

(With thanks to Wunderman)

Question

Explain the factors that have led to the success of Club Philips.

DIRECT MARKETING MEDIA

Objectives

Once you have read this chapter you will:

■ understand and be able to apply a step-by-step guide to media decision making for direct marketing;

■ understand the main features, strengths and weaknesses of direct mail and telemarketing.

Introduction

Media decisions are very important to marketers because they are one of the biggest resource allocation decisions that we make. The question we need to answer is this: given the business situation we are in, what are the best media we should use to contact our customers or prospects?

In this chapter we will discuss in detail how to go about making these decisions. Naturally, these should be based on a good understanding of the media themselves. Therefore, the bulk of this chapter will concentrate on an analysis of the merits of each medium from a direct marketer's perspective.

How this chapter is structured

After introducing the broad range of media available to direct marketers, a decision-making framework is offered to help direct marketers choose the right media. The rest of this chapter (and most of Chapter 11) contains a detailed look at each medium, outlining the strengths and weaknesses of each. Finally, the use of media in contacting the same customer *over time* – a contact programme – is discussed.

The range of media in direct marketing

Figure 10.1 summarises the main media choices open to direct marketers. The main ones for our purposes are discussed below, but all are dealt with in depth in practitioner guides.

The most important media for direct marketers were traditionally direct mail, the telephone and press, and these are still prime choices. However, to these can be added the growing use of direct-response TV, door drops and, possibly the most significant development for direct marketing, the Internet.

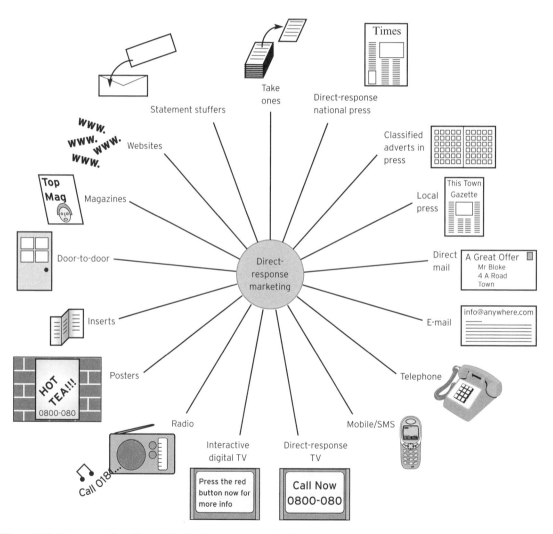

Figure 10.1 The range of media used in direct-response marketing

EXHIBIT 10.1

BETTER THE DEVIL YOU KNOW

Some businesses have a tendency to stick, out of habit, to one or two media, and they drift out of the discipline of testing. On being challenged, this routine is defended with the argument that they have found the 'best' media. On being persuaded to test, they often find that this is not the case!

The reality of business is that each situation – each campaign, each new product launch or price drop – has an element of uniqueness attached to it. The objectives of the campaign, the message that needs to be communicated, the response requirements, the handling of responses: all of these things may change slightly each time. In each case, media choices should be assessed anew.

In the next section we introduce the main factors to consider before choosing media. After this, we will take a detailed look at each medium in turn.

Factors affecting media choice

It is important to establish a way of objectively and consistently judging each medium. Direct marketing authors (Stone, 1996; Nash, 1995) have discussed each medium in terms of its strengths and weaknesses. Meanwhile, marketing communications texts (Smith, 1993) have discussed a number of issues that are important in media choice.

These can be brought together into a framework that will help us be consistent in making media choices. This framework, dubbed AIMRITE, consists of the following:

Audience: Does the medium reach the desired target audience?

Impact: Does the medium have impact; that is, does it ensure the message has a chance of getting through the clutter?

Message: Does it help to ensure the message is clearly communicated? Does it add to the message?

Response: This does not refer to the percentage response but rather, does the media make responding easy?

Internal management: Does it enhance the efficient management of the campaign?

The End result: What are the costs and projected likely revenues? Taking all the above into account and looking at typical response rates for your medium, how likely are you to hit target for the campaign?

Before discussing this framework a little more, it is worth pointing out that, in direct marketing, we can usually be quite specific about what we require. Usually, the direct marketing communications objective is to get a response of some sort. Media choice often pragmatically boils down to *that which will get the maximum desired response at minimal cost.*

Each of AIMRITE's components is now analysed in more detail.

AUDIENCE

Media choices are heavily influenced by the way the target audience is defined. If you need to target a *lifestyle* grouping, say lovers of vintage cars, you are likely to go for car magazines or direct mail to a lifestyle list. *Geographic* targeting lends itself to door drops. A pizza take-away restaurant will use door drops to make offers to its local catchment area.

Target audiences that are tightly defined can be addressed by more precise media. The most well-known audience is usually a firm's existing customers, while at the other end of the scale we have suspects – a broad category of people fitting our target description, but with no known prior contact with the company. These would be approached with very different media.

To illustrate this, let's take the example of a firm selling theatre guides to Birmingham. If the best you can do with your audience definition is 'people in Birmingham' then you are more likely to use Birmingham radio or the *Birmingham Evening Mail* as your media. If, however, you define your audience as 'people who have been to the theatre in the past year in Birmingham', then you can use direct mail to a list of such people obtained from the theatres themselves. The latter course is likely to bring an efficiency gain, not because direct mail is a 'better' medium than radio or press, but because in this particular situation the direct-mail audience is very well defined (and likely to be responsive to the offer).

The relationship between media choice and target audience in this example is summarised in Table 10.1. (Note that this target audience split is discussed fully in Chapter 6.)

Table 10.1: **Media choice according to target audience definition**

Audience type	Example	Medium
Suspects	People in Birmingham	*Birmingham Evening Mail*
Prospects	ABC1 people in well-off areas of Birmingham	Door drops to selected areas
Enquirers	Mainly existing theatre visitors	Direct mail to list of Birmingham theatre customers
Customers	Users of the guide	Direct mail to your own list

Note the way that, in Table 10.1, the size of the audience decreases as it becomes more highly defined. Media choice is likely to shift from broadscale to more highly targetable options.

Another 'audience' factor to consider is the inbuilt 'media responsiveness' of the target market. This is particularly prevalent with direct mail. Direct marketers know that certain mailing lists are more 'mailing responsive' than others. Media responsiveness is the *natural predisposition of some people to prefer to do business through one particular medium*. While some of us are very comfortable booking tickets over the phone, others will use mail. The Internet will clearly be a strong medium for those comfortable with it, whereas others will never use it. Direct marketers should take into account any information they have on the media responsiveness of their target audience.

Finally, it is worth noting that each medium will have 'black holes' of audiences which cannot be reached at all by that medium. Some people are not on the telephone, others are not on any direct-mail lists, a minority do not read any daily paper, and so on.

IMPACT

It is vital to make an initial impact on your audience. In a world where people have their senses constantly bombarded with messages of various types, they have got to notice that you are there before you can begin to persuade them to respond. A big part of impact is the creative approach, discussed in Chapter 12, but the medium also has a big role to play in getting your message through the clutter.

There are two dimensions to media impact. One is the extent to which the media can get the audience's undivided attention. Private media, such as direct mail, are more likely to achieve this than broadscale media like press advertising. The second dimension is summed up by the phrase 'The medium is the message' (*see* Exhibit 10.2).

EXHIBIT 10.2

'THE MEDIUM IS THE MESSAGE'

We have all heard this expression, but what does it mean and to what extent is it relevant to direct marketers?

If you were to consider the magazine *Vogue*, you would probably agree that the magazine itself has a strong brand identity. It is easy to picture the type of person that reads it, the articles it carries, and of course the advertisements it contains. Here the medium, in a sense, creates a halo effect around the adverts it carries. Just the fact that a company has advertised in *Vogue* carries a mes-sage to the reader. This message would be an implication of prestige, of the product being upmarket and aimed at an exclusive audience. This is what we mean by 'the medium is the message'.

There are other examples of the same principle: Channel 4 gives an image of young, trendy viewers, and advertisers sometimes take advantage of this ambience with products that fit this image: Virgin, for example, often uses Channel 4. The *Financial Times* has a businesslike, serious brand and adverts seen in the FT would benefit from this background.

MESSAGE

Once your prospect's attention has been obtained, the medium must then help you to get across the necessary information in a persuasive manner. Thus, TV has always been a compelling medium for inspiring an emotional response, because of its sound and vision qualities. Direct mail, on the other hand, is good for imparting large volumes of information about complex products such as, say, financial services. Thus, to get the best match of medium and message, we should consider both *volume* and *type* of the information we want to impart.

RESPONSE

Here we are *not* considering size of response. This factor is concerned with how much effort is required by the consumer to respond to different media.

Certain media are much easier to respond to than others. Direct marketers who use poster adverts are expecting consumers to remember a phone number until they get home or until they can get to a phone, and then still be motivated to ring it. Not easy. A well-known saying among practitioners is 'Time kills response', and if one imagines a car driver seeing a response advert on a poster, then another hour passing until he is home, it is not hard to see why posters are still a little-used direct-response medium.

The ideal response medium is one, then, which makes the act of ringing up or filling in a coupon (the two primary methods of responding) as easy and quick as possible. People are more likely to respond from the comfort of their own home, at a time when there is nothing else going on to distract them, and when very little effort is required. The telephone and direct mail, and latterly the Internet, offer the most advantages here, while at the other extreme, posters and radio present many obstacles to success.

INTERNAL MANAGEMENT

Jim has just been made marketing manager for Prestige Motorcycles. He discovers that a lot of Prestige buyers don't actually ride their motorbikes very much at all. Instead, they like to add endless accessories to them and possess them as fashion extras. Jim decides to promote a new line of silver chrome exhaust pipes, and commissions an advert to go into *Men and Motorcycles* magazine. It's time to give them a ring to place the ad. He is stunned to find a lead time of four months before the ad can be placed. All his carefully laid plans hit the dust.

This story highlights the need to get those management issues carefully understood. Which are the best media when it comes to testing different creative approaches? Which have the shortest lead times? What media are relatively easy to manage if you haven't much experience? These are some of the issues that need to be considered.

THE END RESULT

We have now pulled together the issues to consider before making that final choice in favour of a particular medium. The initial considerations are an attempt to whittle down the media to those which will get the best end result. At this final stage, our focus is on those media which we believe will give us the *highest possible response at lowest cost*.

Before committing our entire budget to one medium, we should market test different choices. This is a key process within direct marketing and is outlined in Chapter 13. However, here we are concerned with the step preceding this: which media do we put into the test process?

Experience has shown that we do need to go through the disciplined approach of AIMRITE to make the right decisions. This is because no one medium has stood out as clearly superior in fetching the highest response at lowest cost. In fact, it is a general rule that *those media which elicit a higher response also tend to be the most expensive*. For example, although telephone responses are potentially the highest of all the media, the costs are also the highest.

We can call this effect the cost/response 'rule' which offers a rough guide:

> *In general, the higher the response that a medium achieves from an audience, the more it cost to reach that audience.*

Sometimes, in a particular sector, extensive testing reveals a medium which outperforms all other media in that area. China collectibles tend to sell best using Sunday supplement press advertising, whereas charities use direct mail to recruit possible donors 'cold'. However, when totalling up all marketing activity, the average cost of getting one response is roughly similar across all media.

So what is this 'average cost' of getting one response? Here we enter a very dangerous area, because response will always depend on the specific business situation: a well thought out offer, good timing, incentives, and so on. There is therefore a huge variation around the mean response rate for a medium, even within one industry sector. A major player in the loans sector of financial services reckons on different campaigns delivering costs per response *varying from £12 to over £600*, with an *average* of £250. These 'real world' figures illustrate the dangers of generalisation by just quoting the average.

Nevertheless, it is important to press on and develop some practical 'rules of thumb', because these can be useful for media planning in the absence of more specific data. 'Official' figures are hard to come by for many media, but there are some we can use for direct mail. The Direct Mail Information Service (DMIS) surveys of companies using mail for acquisition have found average response rates of about 1 per cent. If the average cost per thousand mailers is typically about £500, and 1 per cent of 1000 is ten responses, then we can see that it typically costs £500 to obtain ten responses, or £50 per response.

With the above warnings on large variations around the mean ringing in our ears, here is a rule of thumb that can be used for planning if no other data is available:

> *A rule of thumb for quick calculations is that it costs typically about £30 to £70 to obtain one response in an acquisition programme. However, there are often exceptions to this 'rule'!*

Typical costs and response rates for the different media are compared in Table 10.2.

Table 10.2: Comparison of media costs and typical relative response rates

Medium	Cost per thousand (£)	Responses to acquisition programmes (broad averages) (%)	Targeting
Direct mail	500	1-2	High to absolute
Telemarketing outbound	6000	10-20 (retention only)	High to absolute
Press	4-20	0.01-0.1	Low to medium
Magazines	10-50	0.02-0.5	Medium
Inserts	40-70	0.1-1.0	Low to medium
Household delivery (door-to-door)	40-250	0.1-2.0	Medium to high
Direct-response TV	7-15	0.01-0.05	Low
Direct-response radio	2	0.005	Low
Websites	<£5000 to set up	?	Passive
E-mail	5-20	Low - 2%	Medium to absolute

Sources: author for 2004 updates, based on the IDM Media/*Educators' Guide* (updated to 1996).

Before we move on to the individual media in more detail, we just need to consider the different media performances when used with existing customers compared with new prospects.

MEDIA FOR ACQUISITION AND RETENTION

All media can potentially be used for acquisition, but the best media for contacting existing customers held on a database are the *individually addressable* media: direct mail, the telephone and, increasingly, the Internet.

One reason for noting this early in the chapter is to point out that a different set of standards should apply when judging media used for contacting existing customers. Responses should be much higher, results better, and the control you, as a marketer, can exert with your own database is much better than when trying to contact new customers. This is something to be aware of when comparing media performance. If someone tells you that such and such got 15 per cent response using direct mail, the first question to ask is whether this was an existing set of customers or new prospects that were mailed.

Discussion of individual media

Each of the major media used in direct communications, shown in Fig. 10.1 earlier, will now be discussed. For each medium, key qualities will be highlighted that are unique to the medium, along with a summary of relative strengths and weaknesses compared with other media.

Direct mail

INTRODUCTION

Direct mail is targeted distribution of *personally addressed* mailing packages through the postal service.

Such is the historical importance of this medium, direct mail is often mistakenly seen as synonymous with direct marketing. Although it is no longer the biggest direct marketing medium in many countries (in the US and UK alone, more marketing budget is now spent on the telephone), direct mail remains extremely important, even if its public perception with consumers is of 'junk mail'.

The difference in popularity of direct mail between consumers is mostly explained by examining the differences between acquisition and retention direct mail usage. Customers may welcome 'letters from the company' when receiving a mailer from a favoured supplier who knows their current situation and is writing to them with a relevant message. In contrast, 'junk mail' from companies mailing a prospect list arouses as much anger as ever.

Direct mail accounts for an impressive £2.47 billion of spend in the UK (2002), making it the second most important medium in spend terms. Doom-mongers of 'snail mail' may wish to note that in 2002 spend on direct mail still dwarfed that of Internet advertising, SMS and e-mail marketing *combined*. These new media will close this gap between 2003 and 2010, but fans of direct mail will also be impressed by its spend growth rate, which at the time of writing show no signs of slowing down. Growth rates have been such that total spend doubled between 1995 and 2002. This is important because direct mail has long been the target of forecasts of decline by many in the industry. Given the ruthlessness of direct response – no hiding place for poor perform-ance – we can conclude that response rates across the industry continue to hold up. Alternatively, it could be that new media have proven more difficult to use for direct marketing than was anticipated. However there is no room for complacency: UK DMIS figures show that while in 1985 83 per cent of direct mail was opened, by 2001 that had reduced to 68 per cent. This may be accounted for by the growth of over-targeting of ABC1 social groups: in 1985, these received an average of 1.5 items of direct mail per week; by 2001 this had risen to 5.9 items per week.

The following discussion outlines the circumstances in which direct mail is a sensible option.

Key AIMRITE qualities

Audience

Anyone with an address can be reached by direct mail. In the UK, that means about 26 million households and businesses. There is a large industry revolving around the pro-duction and sale of lists, catering for target audience needs. If direct mail wants to be employed as a medium but the audience is not well defined, a company can use general lists such as the electoral roll, the Public Address File which has all the UK's addresses, or as a last resort, the telephone book.

Of course, the audience is best known when they are your own customers. In this instance, mail is often used because of its addressable qualities giving it a precise target-ing ability.

When used in *acquisition*, direct mail requires a list of target prospects. These lists come in many forms, and are available to the marketer for a fee.

LISTS

Lists are big business throughout Europe, Asia and the US. In the UK, the key players in list-broking include Dudley Jenkins, Dun and Bradstreet and Zenith. But big agencies like Brann are increasingly pulling in list-broking so they have the whole offering in-house, allowing them to link list buying very closely with their data analysis team.

There are two broad types of lists in existence for both business and consumers: com-piled lists and responsive lists.

1 Compiled lists

These are lists put together deliberately by a third party, such as the ACORN geo-demo-graphic list, or a list available in the public domain, such as the telephone directory. The broad groups are:

■ electoral roll – since 2001 the public have the opportunity to opt out of their elec-toral roll details being used for commercial promotions;

- geodemographic lists;
- psychographic lists;
- geo-lifestyle lists;
- business lists such as Dun and Bradstreet or Kompass.

The cream end of the market is lifestyle data, because it involves bigger volumes and a greater understanding of data selection. Geodemographics and lifestyle databases are the subject of Chapter 4.

2 Responsive lists

These are lists put together as a by-product of someone else's business, for example mail-order buyers of catalogues, subscribers to *The Economist*, or store-card holders. These are often the most responsive lists (hence the name), because they usually contain people who have responded to direct marketing programmes. Remembering the earlier point about 'mailing responsiveness', the importance of a predisposition to do business by mail should be noted here. In the same way as retail has shopaholics, many responders to mail order may actively enjoy shopping through the post. These people are more likely than average to respond to mailers on *any* topic.

Recent changes to the list industry

As we move beyond 2003 the list industry is changing. List brokers are increasingly concerned that they are commodities that can only be differentiated on price. They are also increasingly being subsumed into data agencies that can add value by helping clients analyse their data. Hence, list brokers are repositioning themselves as 'data analysts' more and more (*see* Fig. 10.2).

What about over-use of the lists? Dudley Jenkins has a prospect tracker which records all mailings – and can go some way to acting as a check against too much from one sector. However there's still an element of turkeys voting for Christmas here. Another development is that list brokers are adding in data about responders, and doing regression analysis that can predict list responses. This again increases the pressure to over-mail responsive people.

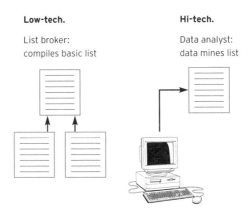

Figure 10.2 List brokers repositioning themselves

To summarise, the issue for the direct marketer is to be on their guard and to know their stuff: the list broker is *not* media neutral or even list neutral – so the client must decide.

Impact

Compared with other media, there is no doubting the impact values of direct mail. As something with the customer's address on it coming through the door in the morning, it is hard to ignore. If it is felt that cutting through competitors' clutter or noise is vital, then direct mail is likely to have a relative advantage over media like press, inserts, or broadcast media.

One downside to direct mail's impact is the poor public image that the medium is saddled with. Commonly known as 'junk mail', this term has become popular jargon, along with a set of preconceptions that the industry has great difficulty in shifting. Therefore compared with, say, a much-loved and favourite magazine, the medium of direct mail will not generate the same 'halo effect' around the message.

EXHIBIT 10.3

WHAT DO CONSUMERS SEE AS JUNK MAIL?

Research (Ian Smith, 1996) has found that in the public mind junk mail means anything they do not find interesting, in particular 'cold' mail making offers they don't find relevant. Nothing surprising there. More subtly, however, consumers don't describe mailers they find useful as either 'direct mail' or 'junk mail'. Much research will therefore fail to pick up consumers' attitudes to the totality of direct mail because consumers and practitioners do not share the same language.

Message

If segmentation is important, a key strength of direct mail is its ability to use personalised letters to carry a different message to each recipient. Potentially millions of different messages could be sent, according to each prospect or customer's situation. A conference organiser could thank a businesswoman for attending a recent event, and, based on that customer's unique history of attendance, invite her to future events. Thus, direct mail can be an important element in turning a one-to-one strategy (*see* Chapter 6) into reality.

If your message is a long or complex one, another advantage of direct mail is its flexibility for carrying a lot of information. It can arguably carry more than any other medium. The only creative boundary is what fits through a letterbox (and weighs less than 60g, if you want the lowest postage costs).

Direct marketing practitioners produce a massive range of direct mail, ranging from a simple one-page letter to packages containing 'gimmicks' that help get the message across. British Telecom used the simple approach to promote its Option 15 pricing scheme in 1992. A response device was attached at the bottom of a letter, and the only other item was a business reply envelope. A 27 per cent response from its high-value customer base was achieved.

Further up the bulk scale, there are the loyalty magazines now favoured by many companies as a prime mechanism for keeping in contact with their existing customers.

Saab has a high-quality quarterly magazine aimed at ensuring its customers are reminded of the Saab brand values in between their car purchases.

Direct mail can accommodate wide creative boundaries in order to maximise message impact. One example was highlighted by Holder (1992). He described a mailer sent by a land development group to local business directors. Selling a plot of land for hundreds of thousands of pounds, the group felt it could afford a high allowable marketing spend per response. A boxed mailer was devised with an innovative creative approach. A 'Biggles' hat, scarf and goggles were enclosed with an invite to the actual site, where the businesspeople would receive a free balloon flight. Naturally, while they were up in the balloon, their interest in the site was discussed with a company representative!

A development in the 2000s was the use of CD Rom mailers. Here, a CD Rom is sent with a letter, and the audience then receives the message in a totally different way. In spite of its expense (costs per CD Rom mailer average about £1), there is every chance that they could grow in popularity. This is because:

- the lower levels of reading and higher levels of TV viewing of today's population favour videos over reading matter;
- ownership of DVD players and PCs in the UK is the highest in Europe at over 60 per cent.

Among the organisations using video mailers in the UK are the cable telecommunications companies, which use them to recruit new customers soon after a street is cabled. The video is an excellent vehicle to highlight forthcoming attractions on cable TV, and persuasively communicates the benefits of cheaper telephone calls.

Response

Direct mail and the telephone are the two key media used for retaining existing customers. Because of the ease of response and the ability to tailor messages right down to individual level, direct mail offers very genuine opportunities to manage a dialogue with customers. One such dialogue was begun by Bradford and Bingley in 1991 (*see* Exhibit 10.4).

EXHIBIT 10.4

BUILDING UP RELATIONSHIPS THROUGH DIRECT MAIL: BRADFORD AND BINGLEY

Direct mail is an excellent medium for building up relationships with customers. Look at the ground-breaking mailers produced by Bradford and Bingley (B&B).

It all started in April 1991 when John Major, then Chancellor of the Exchequer, attacked the financial services industry, claiming that 'irresponsible mailings are tempting consumers into debt'. Bradford and Bingley decided to turn this negative publicity into a plus for them by using direct mail to forge an open and honest approach with both existing customers and prospects.

The audience was sent a questionnaire asking them a number of questions about their attitudes to mailers from B&B. Did they think they were 'junk mail' or 'useful information through the post'? What did they think of John Major's comment? And so on. The flexibility of direct mail allowed B&B to extend the questionnaire to include a request for customers' interest in loans, mortgage and PEP products, and when they would like to receive information about them.

A high percentage of B&B's audience responded, and the campaign was shortlisted for a Direct Marketing Association award.

Internal management

From the business's internal point of view, direct mail presents formidable management challenges to avoid making mistakes with the execution. The devil is in the detail. Consider the steps involved:

■ writing and communicating the brief;

■ agreeing copy and artwork;

■ printing and production;

■ organising the customer data: briefing, selection, de-duplication, and so on;

■ lasering of individual details;

■ enclosing all the mail pieces and then finally mailing.

As you can see, this is very complex and there are more hazards in its implementation than, say, in producing a press advert and placing it.

Typical *lead times*, from the marketing brief to the mailer hitting the customer's doormat, are at least six weeks and sometimes longer, and this needs to be borne in mind when choosing the medium.

On the plus side however, direct mail offers superb opportunities for *testing* of all aspects of the campaign. This could range from which list to choose to the minutiae of different creative approaches. Direct mail is an excellent medium in which to test because of the control we can exert on all the campaign variables, especially audience: we know *exactly* how many mailers are sent and who receives them. When compared with, say, press, the extra control of mail is readily apparent.

Lastly, there is the issue of *privacy* from the competition. When Coca-Cola launches a sales promotion offer in supermarkets, the effect is often deliberately masked by a counter offer introduced within days by Pepsi. Ideally, a company would like to be able to conduct many of its marketing activities without letting the opposition know what's going on. Direct mail offers the chance to do just this because it is a private medium.

The end result

The volume of mail has increased from about 1 billion delivered items in 1983 to 2.9 billion items in 1995. In spite of fears about such increases leading to an outcry about junk mail, research (Direct Mail Information Service) shows that the percentage of mail opened remains steady at an extremely healthy 85 per cent or so. In addition, unprompted recall rates for mail are much higher than those typically achieved for TV adverts.

But what do these statistics really tell us? Awareness and recall statistics should be treated with some caution, according to leading researchers like Gordon and Langmaid (1988). A better judge of the value of direct mail is the impressive bank of accumulated knowledge obtained by direct marketing practitioners over the years, based on testing direct mail against other media and comparing actual customer *behaviour*: responses. The accepted wisdom is that response rates for direct mail are typically 1–2 per cent for offers aimed at so-called 'cold lists' of prospects, but as was pointed out earlier, direct-response percentages are generalised at our peril: prospect lists can often give responses much higher or lower than this.

EXHIBIT 10.5

MILLWALL FOOTBALL CLUB

In 1991, Millwall Football Club, then in Division Two of the English football league, was in considerable financial difficulties and was keen to look at any scheme which could help it raise funds. Compared with the big clubs, Millwall had a relatively small but loyal following. How could the club capitalise on this loyalty?

The answer was the launch of the Lions' Card scheme. This scheme entitled members to discounts off season tickets, plus other benefits including, intriguingly, 'you decide where you sit'! For these privileges the fans paid £250, which would pay back for them in about seven years. What Millwall was launching was effectively a lock-in loyalty card.

Communications centred around direct mail to the existing season ticket base, backed up with posters outside the ground and adverts in the programme. The campaign cost £25 000 and generated £375 000.

Table 10.3 summarises the strengths and weaknesses of direct mail.

Table 10.3: **Strengths and weaknesses of direct mail**

Strengths	Weaknesses
Highly targetable	but you need a suitable list or database
Responsive	but expensive
Payback can be outstanding	but internal management is committing
Creative medium	but regarded as downmarket
Good for detail	but can be intrusive

EXHIBIT 10.6

IBM TIVOLI: THE INVISIBLE IT EXPERT

Tivoli is software from IBM that is designed to automatically and intelligently look after every aspect of a company's IT system. IBM simply wanted to make IT directors in three key industries aware of what Tivoli was and what it could do for them. Letting Tivoli handle your IT is basically like placing an IT expert at the very heart of your IT system. It's virtually the same as a real IT expert – except you never get to see them, they work around the clock, and they never take coffee breaks. In other words – an invisible man. Agency Harrison Troughton Wunderman's off-the-shelf software solution plays on 'Action Man' style packaging and arrives in a typical IT component's anti-static bag. So far it has generated a 1.1 per cent response rate in the financial sector and 0.5 per cent and 0.2 per cent in the public and distribution sectors respectively. Just one sale would generate revenues of between $500,000 and upwards of $5 million.

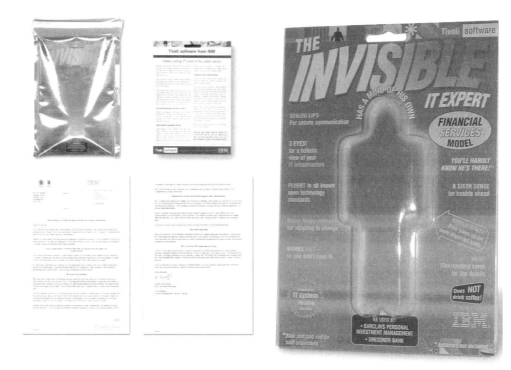

Figure 10.3 IBM 'invisible man' campaign

Source: Reproduced by kind permission of IBM and Harrison Troughton Wunderman

THE TELEPHONE IN DIRECT MARKETING

Ask a parent with teenage kids about the telephone, and you will be met with a hollow laugh: 'They come home from school and ten minutes later they are on the phone. I can't get them off the damn thing.'

The telephone is becoming a major force in our lives. The average British person now spends twenty minutes a day on it, more than triple the rate fifteen years ago. There is no reason why this figure should not continue to rise, as each succeeding generation becomes more comfortable with the phone than the last. Much of this can be attributed to the influence of mobile phones, which are discussed separately later in the chapter.

The telephone in direct marketing is used in two ways. One is to make outbound calls to customers and prospects, known as outbound telemarketing, and the other is to use the telephone to take calls from customers, known as inbound telemarketing.

Taking inbound and outbound use of the telephone together, total spend on this medium was over £3 billion in the UK in 2002, making it the most important of all direct marketing media. Most of this spend was accounted for by the salaries of teleworkers, predominantly in call centres throughout the UK and of course in Europe too. The UK is the largest call centre sector in Europe, and our love affair with the telephone looks set to continue, though it will be interesting to see what impact the Internet has on this medium. However, there are already some changes to the supply of services, with the outsourcing of telephone work to India and China being a major trend over the next decade.

Roughly two thirds of the spend is on outbound use of the telephone, but inbound telephone – inviting customers to call in if they want to buy – continues to prove very popular. For instance 84 per cent of direct response press ads have a telephone response number, though this is matched now in popularity by an e-mail address or website as in-bound media. Coupons/postal methods are declining badly in the face of these more convenient ways of buying, and now represent only niche (presumably older) markets.

OUTBOUND TELEMARKETING

Outbound telemarketing is the planned use of the telephone to make structured calls to the audience in a measurable and accountable way.

In theory at least, the telephone is the most powerful of all media in helping firms build relationships with customers. This would supplement its tactical use in helping *make a sale*. The link between the phone and relationship marketing is because of the key role of the telephone in providing *service*.

Examples of the latter may include something as simple as saying 'thank you', which although it is touted as a relationship marketing idea, was advocated by McCorkell, a leading direct marketer, back in 1989 when he said that 'the two most powerful words in advertising are not "new" and "free", they are "thank you"'.

There are increasing concerns that outbound telephone is being over-used and under-targeted, leading to an increase in complaints about 'junk calling'. This can be attributed to poor practice among utilities and financial services firms, which cold call or call their own base with trivial offers. The response has been a big jump in the public signing up to telephone preference services that bar calling.

Key AIMRITE qualities

Outbound telemarketing is probably the most powerful medium in terms of impact on the customer, potential for response, and potential for getting it disastrously wrong.

Audience

Anyone with a telephone can be called by a business, and at its simplest and crudest, the telephone book can be used as a list. This is not recommended, however (*see* 'cold calling' box). In fact, calling people who are not your own customers, without having a good reason to do so, is not seen as sound business practice by most blue-chip companies.

The telephone shares with direct mail the ability to define precisely its audience by a database or list.

Given the expense of outbound telemarketing and the sensitivity of prospects to the medium, it is not surprising that the majority of telemarketing in this country consists of calls to a firm's *existing* customers, rather than new customers. Telemarketing is primarily used to increase the profitability of existing customers, either by encouraging

EXHIBIT 10.7

COLD CALLING

You are sitting at home, settling down in front of *Coronation Street* with a bag of your favourite crisps and a cup of tea when suddenly the phone rings. Family or friends? No, it's a building society you have barely heard of, saying it has your financial details and you look like the type of person who would be interested in a loan. Reactions to this would be varied, but experience shows that many people will react strongly against using the phone in this way. Unlike other media, the telephone forces an answer from consumers, even if it is no. Not surprisingly, people resent having to say no and to explain why they are not interested, perhaps at a time when they would expect to be relaxing away from sales approaches.

Cold calling is the telephone selling of products to an untargeted list of people who have not been selected for any reason other than that they have a telephone. This is 'officially' not recommended by the industry bodies, the Institute of Direct Marketing and the Direct Marketing Association.

them to spend more by up-selling or cross-selling, or by creating value for them in some way, thereby encouraging them to stay loyal to the firm.

Outbound calling does have a place in acquisition, and this is in conjunction with other media, in particular direct mail. If you are convinced that your targeting is accurate, and you have sent a warm-up mailer with an enticing offer, it may be appropriate to make a follow-up call to increase response. Telemarketing prospects is also done in business-to-business marketing. Here, the practice of being phoned up to be sold to is much more acceptable, if not necessarily more successful, than it is at the home.

Impact

In terms of its ability to get messages through clutter, and in terms of the receivers' reaction to it as a medium, the telephone probably has the greatest impact of all media. It is very difficult to filter out telephone marketing in the way people filter out other marketing communications. Customers can screen calls using answering machines; otherwise people are forced to respond in some way (and to another human, not just to an advert). In this sense, the medium carries enormous impact, which means it is imperative it is used sensitively.

EXHIBIT 10.8

TO PHONE OR NOT TO PHONE?

The Royal National Lifeboat Institution (RNLI) uses outbound telephone calls very rarely for any fundraising activity, even to its own donors. This is because the RNLI believes that its donors, who have rather traditional, conservative views, would not take kindly to being rung up by the charity.

On the other hand, both Shelter and Amnesty International, with a much younger profile of support, make active use of telefundraising, particularly for membership renewal. Both find they get much higher responses than for mail.

Message

Compared with media such as direct mail or inserts, the telephone can only be used for relatively straightforward messages. People can only take on board limited information aurally – try listening to a lecture without overheads, for example! The telephone is often used for 'announcement' or 'urgent' top-line messages which can then be backed up later, often with direct mail, to interested parties.

One technique worth highlighting is the need to have a *reason to call*. Sudden calls out of the blue to someone about mortgages or to ask for a donation to a charity tend not to be well received unless they make sense to the recipient. So, for example, when BT made calls to its top-spending residential customers (often with bills well over £200 per quarter) the telemarketer might start by saying, 'We have noticed that your bills are very high and we were wondering if you might be interested in a scheme that could save you money?' A charity might call its supporters just after a major disaster to ask for emergency funds; charities have found that donors see this as a perfectly natural thing to do.

What does a telemarketing script look like? Exhibit 10.9 gives an example.

EXHIBIT 10.9

SCRIPT FOR RED CROSS GULF WAR APPEAL

The Red Cross launched an appeal three days after the Gulf War broke out on 15 January 1991. Its multi-media campaign consisted of direct mail to known supporters, a national press campaign and, finally, a telemessage backed up by outbound telemarketing to business leaders in major companies. The whole appeal was created and executed in a few days after the war broke out.

Outbound telemarketing script

Good Morning/Afternoon Mr/ Mrs/ Ms ...

My name is ... and I'm calling on behalf of the British Red Cross. The reason for my call is that we recently sent you a telemessage asking for your help and support. Did you receive that?

Yes – That's great. Then you will be aware that ...
No – I'm sorry about that. Let me tell you about it ...

...The war in the Gulf is causing great suffering. As you know, prisoners of war have already been taken and thousands of refugees are fleeing from the war.

They need all the help we can give them. At home and abroad the Red Cross plays a vital role. We are determined to do all we can, but we urgently need funds, which is why we have launched an appeal for £56 million and why I'm asking for your support today.

Can we count on your support at this critical time?

No – May I ask why that is? (Discuss objections – see sheet)
Yes – Will your company be making a cash donation?

Cash donations can be made by ...

Will you be dealing with this personally? (If no, get details) That's great.

Finally, thank you very much for your time and support.

Source: The British Red Cross. Reprinted with permission.

Response

Response, uniquely among media, is 100 per cent of people contacted. (There will be people who cannot be contacted because they refuse to answer, screen with an answering machine, or are not in.) Politeness usually dictates that of those contacted some sort of response will be given, even if it is to decline the offer. Uniquely, therefore, negative responses are recorded and can be probed, gathering valuable research on the campaign.

The telephone is the easiest medium to respond to, as response comes naturally as part of the call. If the offer is rejected, the caller can either try to counter objections or at least note why the offer was not accepted.

Internal management

There are many management issues to consider, and a detailed analysis is beyond the scope of this book. However, we will cover the key points which you need to factor into your media decision making, and which may prompt you into further exploration with specialist texts should you need to.

The first telemarketing decision is whether to attempt it in-house or to use a bureau. Telemarketers need a lot of *training* before they can be let loose on your precious customers, and they also need back-up systems to help them with the call. This back-up comes in the form of computer-based *scripts*, which enable the caller to 'jump around' the basic script depending on how the customer responds. Call centres tend to have teams of callers who are set demanding targets, with *incentives* on reaching these, matching the way salespeople are given incentives. Putting together all this recruitment, training and scripting, and managing everything as the calls take place, is no mean feat, and for this reason a first-time user of telemarketing is usually advised to use a specialist bureau. As time goes on, if your firm is a committed user of outbound calling, you may be tempted to bring the operation in house, thereby avoiding paying a supplier.

Many companies, particularly those in the service industry, have well-established inbound telephone operations that take in calls from customers about orders, repairs, complaints, and so on. It is tempting to use these facilities to make outbound calls but not advised. This is because very different personalities are needed for the respective operations. Outbound callers tend to be more assertive, perhaps more outgoing and extrovert whereas inbound operators are more sensitive to customers' problems, less driven by targets and goals, and more reactive as people.

One of the biggest pluses for telemarketing is that it is a fabulous medium to carry out testing. To maximise the effectiveness of your campaign it is a good idea to test the major factors – the audience, the offer, the script, time of calling, to name but a few – before rolling out the final campaign. Telemarketing is undoubtedly the most manageable medium for testing, for two reasons. The first is the high response rates, which mean only a small number of customers need to be contacted to give a valid test. This means that many tests may be carried out and the results known within a short time, often within a day. The next day's tests can be formulated accordingly, learning from the previous day. The second factor is the control that managers have over the campaign elements. The audience, offer, time of call and script can all be tightly controlled.

We should also note that the telephone is not a good medium for contacting *large volumes* of people, except in rare cases. This is partly because of the high cost per contact, and partly down to the relatively low number of contacts that an operative can make. Contacts by telephone are measured in Decision Maker Contacts (DMCs) per hour; a typical number may be about six contacts per hour, much lower than might have been supposed. Even with, say, 50 people making calls, a bureau would only expect to make about 2500 calls a day. This low number could be due to engaged lines, the person not being available/willing to take the call, and so on.

The end result

At its best, results with telemarketing can be astounding. Used appropriately, perhaps with a well thought out offer, well targeted at one's own customers, positive responses well in excess of other media can be achieved. One telecommunications company achieved 60 per cent take-up to an offer of telephone-related services. Stone (1996) claims that telephone-generated leads are *four to six* times more likely to close than mail-generated leads.

In the Red Cross Gulf War Appeal highlighted in the box earlier, the outbound calls to business directors were highly successful, generating a return of 9:1 on investment.

However, at a cost of about £6 per contact on average, high responses are needed just to break even. Even at 10 per cent response, a gross margin of £60 would then be needed on the sale in order to break even. This simple calculation shows why telemarketing is never likely to be used for single sales of low-margin goods such as FMCGs, which typically have gross margins per item of only a few pence. As a relationship-building tool, however, customer lifetime values may well justify the telephone's use for some high-value customers, even in FMCG markets.

EXHIBIT 10.10

REASSURANCE – THE TELEPHONE

The telephone is an excellent medium when the recipient is likely to require careful explanation of the campaign's messages. This was the case with the International Fund for Animal Welfare's (IFAW) programme to improve average donations and switch donors from standing order to direct debit. The telephone enabled the charity to deal with queries in a reassuring way. Only existing donors were rung up, and because of their high level of trust in this excellent charity, the anticipation was that complaints of 'junk' telemarketing would be close to zero.

This proved to be the case, with 62 per cent of those called converted to direct debit, and 45 per cent agreeing to increase their gifts. These percentages illustrate the power of the telephone in eliciting response from existing customers. As a result IFAW decided to implement an annual calling programme to its 90 000 'Champions for Animals'.

Source: Adapted from DMA case study (1999) 'Best use of DM media – telemarketing', www.dma.org.uk

---

EXHIBIT 10.11

'MARJORIE AT THE DEALERS HERE...'

Simon Roncorroni, a leading marketing practitioner, tells the story of how he bought a Citroën from his local garage, and the day after he bought it he had a phone call:

'Everything all right? Marjorie at the dealers here ...'
'While we are on, your next service is due in about six months or so. Shall we book you in now, so that you can plan around the date?'

'OK, that's all fixed up.'

Financial justification? The dealer's customer follow-up operation amounts to one woman working five hours a day (four hours making calls). She is paid cash, £25 a day. She is selling £1000 of incremental business every day.

Source: Roncorroni, S. (1992) 'Using the telephone for profit' in Halsey, B. (ed.) *Practitioners' Guide to Direct Marketing*, Institute of Direct Marketing, Teddington, UK.

Table 10.4: **Summary of the strengths and weaknesses of outbound telemarketing**

Strengths	Weaknesses
Highly specific in its targeting	but the most expensive medium
Very powerful in getting response	but potentially viewed as intrusive
Intimate	but needs close management
Immediate response	but message must be kept simple
Summary: the best relationship medium	

INBOUND TELEMARKETING

> *Inbound telemarketing is the use of paid or free telephone services to carry an invited response from other media.*

The use of inbound telephone calling is now widespread in most developed countries, ranging from carelines on supermarket goods, and customer service centres to help with repairs, through to response handling for direct marketing campaigns. The Direct Marketing Association (DMA) reported UK spending on special lines (0800, 0500, 0345, 0990) as over £400 million in 2003.

Inbound telephone service is highly valued by both consumers and business customers. A survey by Arthur Andersen found that 'efficient phone-based service staff' was rated number one by businesses asked to rank their most important factor in their suppliers. This primary importance of good interface for business customers was a key factor in the huge worldwide spend on CRM systems between 1999 and 2003.

Key AIMRITE qualities

Audience

Inbound telemarketing's audience is increasingly becoming universal. In 1970, almost no mail-order companies took orders by telephone. But by 2003, nearly all direct response was either through the telephone or through website/e-mail. Meanwhile, the use of coupons has dropped steeply.

There is only one section of society that is less likely to use the telephone than the rest and that is the retired generation. People of this generation grew up when the telephone call was a relative luxury and still limit their calling accordingly. As time moves on, and younger generations get older, this effect will lessen.

Impact

One outstanding feature of inbound telemarketing is that it is one of the few, what might be termed 'pure direct marketing' media that the public actually likes! Unlike outbound telephone promotion, which is viewed with heavy suspicion and hostility, inbound telephoning is received positively by most consumers. An 0800 number on a business's marketing communication is therefore something that has positive impact on customers.

Message

The telephone is the most interactive of all media – the only one where a true dialogue with customers can be held. Messages can therefore be as flexible as the script and/or the training of the operative will allow.

Service companies can up- or cross-sell to consumers calling about something else. People ringing in to First Direct to ask about their bank balance would be informed about First Direct's new mortgage rates and asked if they wanted to switch.

The most far-sighted companies are using inbound calls to check on overall customer satisfaction, asking callers if they have anything that needs attention.

Response

Enabling easy response is of course exactly what inbound telemarketing is all about. In the western world, consumers are used to having their lives made easier and easier, and they want convenience and minimal effort expended when they buy goods.

The other big driver of quick response, which goes hand in hand with the telephone, is the credit card, which has also been a big contributor to the growth of direct marketing.

Responses are often encouraged through the use of freephone or other special services, including the following:

- 0800 BT service / 0500 Cable: Calls are free to caller; firm pays supplier based on length of call;
- 0345 BT service / 0645 Cable: Calls are charged at local rate; firm pays supplier depending on length of call;
- 0990 BT service: Calls are charged at national rate; firm pays supplier a charge depending on call length;
- 0891 BT premium rate: Calls are charged at premium rate; firm makes profit from call charges while paying fixed fee to BT.

Telecommunications companies claim that these services improve response rates, and their widespread use probably bears this out. However, some major players, such as Direct Line, do not use freephone numbers.

Internal management

Inbound telephone marketing management is not easy. As Rapp and Collins (1987) said, 'If you are going to do it, be sure you do it well or you may offend more people than you sell to.' They recommend that managers try their lines out frequently themselves, and see how they get on.

The broad management issues are as follows:

1 Predicting call volumes

You can estimate forward trends from previous experience on the basis that 'the past is a good guide to the future'; or you can ask a consultant to estimate for you. Either way, this is critical to get right, because if you get it wrong you will lose valuable leads, and you will annoy potential customers who have been kept waiting. If you cannot handle the volumes, you can use a bureau. This is particularly recommended with direct-response TV which generates large volumes of calls in a very short time after the advert has been screened.

2 Training

The importance of front-line staff to a business's image has been well documented. Some of the top exponents of this art, such as Direct Line or First Direct, use highly trained operators who can, if necessary, work away from a script. Such people do not, of course, come cheap, and it is marketing's job to decide whether the costs are worth the payback in terms of enhanced image, differentiation from competitors through superior service, and ultimately extra revenue as a result.

3 Campaign management

The marketer needs to write the operational brief, monitor the progress of training, set out the script, define the reports that are required and project manage the campaign as a whole, so that it happens on time, on budget and on brief. One key action is to make test calls throughout the process as a quality check.

The end result

Roncorroni (1992) quotes set-up costs of £4000–£7000 and about £1 per call as typical inbound phone costs of a campaign. Although these costs have reduced a little since then, and may reduce a little more, it is still not a cheap option. The marketer's role is to justify this cost in terms of the extra revenue it will bring in. This revenue will come through:

- responses that would not otherwise have come in because customers could not be bothered to send in a coupon;

- up- or cross-selling that was carried out while the customer was on the phone about something else;

- extra loyalty generated through the service element of the call; in other words, customers who would otherwise have gone elsewhere for future business will stay with you because they liked your service.

Table 10.5 summarises the strengths and weaknesses of inbound telephone marketing.

Table 10.5: Summary of strengths and weaknesses of inbound telephone marketing

Strengths	Weaknesses
Fast and convenient for customer	but can be expensive for the company
Most customers very comfortable on the telephone	but some sectors still reluctant
Flexible: use for service and sales simultaneously	requires investment in staff training

Mobile phones and short messaging service

A keen sports follower, you're watching the world athletic championships on the TV. Your mobile alerts you: there's a text message. It's from a well-known shoe company, inviting participation in a competition. Name the winner of the 100 metres from the last three Olympics. The first correct answer back wins two holidays to the Athens Olympics. Everyone gets the message at the same time so you're under time pressure. Come on . . . Maurice Green? Linford Christie? Donovan Whatsit . . . You respond, caught up in the small excitement of the game. It's fun, and easy to respond. You're asked by the company if you wish to receive marketing from them in the future. OK, providing it's interesting. Dull shoe promotions not required. The secret is to interweave promotional material into the fabric of news, events, competitions, and so on.

This is just one version of a growing phenomenon: using short messaging service (SMS) as a direct marketing medium. In the near future the promise is of what Drayton Bird in a different context once called 'perfect marketing': real time one-to-one marketing. This works using the geographic positioning satellite facility that enables the network operator to pinpoint exactly where you are anywhere in the world. The technology is already there to, in theory, allow McDonald's to send a promotional message to any of us *as we pass within a mile of an outlet*: 'Hungry? Try our new McThai Surprise – 800 yards first left . . .' Whether this kind of marketing is desirable is another question, but this fictional example does illuminate the possibilities for time- and place-specific marketing. Speculating, one can see the growth of this sort of promotion – but personalising it so that we all receive only messages relevant to us, that is true one-to-one marketing – is likely to remain difficult. One-to-one media costs have dropped, but the management of one-to-one information and co-ordination of this into personal marketing is tricky.

EXHIBIT 10.12

GREAT MOBILE NET BORES OF TODAY

Ya the latest thing is the 'mobilemediary' it's going to reconfigure the value chain you know . . . it will serve up your wife's wish list when you are in the mall shopping for a birthday present . . . help you trade stocks when the market is plunging and you are stuck on the train . . . theme park . . . lets you know it's your turn in five minutes for the ride . . . petrol - Mobil speedpass - a digital wand that you wave in front of an electronic reader at the gas pump . . . It's less about content and more about context - hence 'contextual marketing' . . .

These are just some of the issues for debate in what promises to be a fascinating future for SMS and mobile-based marketing. Third generation digital mobile telephony – 3G – has now been launched, with the UK's first service, '3', launched by Hutchison Telecom. In effect, this means video, photography, better Internet access, all through one's handset. The technology will continue to improve – who knows whether text messaging will survive another ten years?

SMS spend was still modest at £22 million in 2002 in the UK (DMA Census, 2003), but is surely set to grow significantly in the near future. But it is likely that marketing to us via our digital mobile device – whatever form this device takes – will continue to grow. A word of caution however: Future Foundation data (DMA Census, 2003) indicates that about 10 per cent of the population is open to receiving commercial calls during business hours. This rises to about 15 per cent for SMS/text messages. This suggests that there is a market that quite likes this media for outbound commercial use, but it is still a minority – most do not want such calls.

Let's now use the AIMRITE framework to assess SMS (texting) as a media for direct marketers.

EXHIBIT 10.13

HOW GOOD IS YOUR TEEN TEXTING?

Text messages cannot exceed 160 characters. To save space, text language quickly evolved in 2001.

Translate the following:
I cnt hr u. Im @ a RS concrt!
U no I lke u really. CU l8r
Thx 4 gr8 party. BCNU soon. Wan2 do dnr 2moro? Luv *:-)

If you're having trouble, go to http://www.mobileedge.co.uk/freesms/textexplained.htm for easy-to-read translations. Text language is taken seriously by marketers wanting to communicate with the youth market. If you're MTV, then looking fuddy-duddy is not on. By the same token, the Prudential attempting to look cool is like your dad dancing at a wedding, or William Hague wearing a baseball cap at Notting Hill. According to Haig (2002) marketers for firms like The Ministry of Sound examine the language of text messages they get from their consumers carefully, and then they respond using the same language.

AUDIENCE

Mobile phones occupy an intimate place in our lives. They may be a fashion statement, a lifeline, or a crucial part of our daily social whirl. We look forward to texts from our friends, to important calls from work. Into this fabric comes the marketer – and it's easy to miss the sensitivities and end up with a clunky, clumsy promotion that serves only to irritate. It is tempting to conclude that any use of this medium should probably be to existing customers only, but clever acquisition marketing is also possible, though rarer. In fact most marketers use other media to attract 'handraisers', who respond using text. Hence, in the first instance, SMS is used as an inbound media for acquisition. It is then used as an outbound media only to those who have already responded.

Intimacy is one characteristic of mobile media, but fun and entertainment are also part of texting in particular, and it's this that marketers can turn to as a way of getting 'permission' to talk to new prospects. Whether it's Carlsberg sending m-coupons to responders of messages during the World Cup qualifiers of 2001, or The Ministry of Sound inviting clubbers to respond to a number as they queued up, marketers can take advantage of the youthful nature of the medium. Indeed age is another consideration here: when SMS took off in 2001 the users were primarily teenagers attracted by the low cost – a few pence – of sending and receiving messages from each other. Texting has since been adopted by older demographics, but amongst 40+ audiences there is still a distinct lowering of interest in this way of communicating.

Mobile media can be broadcast or narrowcast, with messages capable of being sent to millions of prospects, or a single customer. Hence this medium has greater range than most of its rivals. In practice, the strengths of mobile lend themselves to narrower targeting, with relevant messages sent to individuals who have given permission to be texted. Mass campaigns would probably be largely dismissed as spam, and may irritate or anger the recipients.

In summary, if you're marketing to 18–30-year-olds about 'fun' products then SMS could be very powerful. Reportedly the biggest text promotion of all time in the UK was the Cadbury Txt n Win sales promotion of 2001, which got four million responders. On the other hand if you're communicating with 45–55-year-olds about mortgages then SMS is less likely to be of use, but by no means should be ruled out of court altogether.

IMPACT

Our discussion earlier highlighted how intimate the mobile phone and SMS are to people. It's therefore hardly surprising that mobile messaging can rival the (landline) telephone as a medium of huge impact. Texting can rival the intrusive nature of tele-marketing, and is much cheaper, though without the forcing power of having to respond to a person. SMS also gains impact through its possible usage as a database-driven media to existing customers, hence improving the targeting of the media. Mobile also has a spontaneity and immediacy to it that land line telephony lacks. In visual/aesthetic terms SMS has to be one of the weakest media – the plain Jane of media as Haig (2002) described it. Users are limited to 160 text characters, so building strong visual brand signals is not an option here. However its low cost allows easy linkages into multi-media campaigns, particularly with press, TV, e-mail and websites. These media can off-set the low visual impact of SMS.

All this will change as we move to 3G technology which allows multi-media messaging service MMS to take over from SMS. MMS will allow the usual panoply of visual effects, graphics and so on, removing the need for text only discipline.

MESSAGE

The limited message capability clearly positions SMS as a media that needs to be used as part of a multiple media delivery. Typically SMS may be used to alert prospects to a sales promotion or event that is more fully explained elsewhere, often a website. Often directly responding will propel the customer into a series of back and forth communications with a firm, maybe allowing some kind of pseudo-dialogue to be established (but let's not overstate this: real dialogue is very rare, more commonly, consumers are nudged into pre-structured replies typically using questionnaire style approaches).

Message content is much more likely to be related to encouraging response to an event or promotion than it is to brand building or direct selling, especially in the first instance. A two or three stage campaign will progressively pinpoint those in the market to buy, and will allow more direct sales approaches to be made.

RESPONSE DEVICE

SMS will rank ahead of TV, press, or even direct mail as a medium easy to respond to, but behind telemarketing or e-mail, which is quicker and easier to type with. Marketers can encourage easy response using questionnaire devices such as asking a question and needing only a Y or N response.

INTERNAL MANAGEMENT

According to Haig (2002), 'most mobile marketers have learned that do it yourself SMS delivery is a recipe for expensive disaster'. He recommends marketers doing what they can in-house, then outsourcing more technical procedures.

Software is available that allows users to compose messages then send to prospects simultaneously. However, as always in direct marketing campaigns, handling responses is the toughest part of the operation. With large campaigns, these will come in by the thousand, requiring automated handling.

Outsourced services on offer will include the use of a text-messaging server, multiple messaging support and response handling for incoming messages.

Text-media campaigns can be created and sent within days of conception. As part of 'relationship' programmes, they can be integrated into daily activity within the marketing department. However it is likely a great deal of prior planning and trial and error will have to be experienced before this happy state of affairs is reached.

THE END RESULT

Prices quoted recently (*see* for example www.websms.com) place sending SMS messages at between two pence and six pence per message. Typically sending to a large volume of prospects may cost the marketer about £25/000 messages. Smaller volume messages may rise in cost terms to about £60/000. Response rates of 0.1 per cent would then yield a cost per response of £60. Publicly available case studies will trumpet response rates that will be much higher than this, but the reader is advised to interpret with care. That said, it may be that SMS, like e-mail, has the power to re-write the 'cost-per-response rule' proposed earlier in this chapter. An average response of say 1 per cent, similar to direct mail, is hardly out of the question. This would bring cost per responses down to less than £6, perhaps ten times cheaper than direct mail.

Websites

CHARACTERISTICS OF WEBSITES

Websites are complex media to consider. Websites themselves can act as both content of various types – entertainment, business, information – with adverts as part of this content, or as standalone commercial advertising in their own right. Both types, but the latter in particular, require ways of alerting the consumer to the existence of the site and of perhaps motivating access to the site. Hence, internet paraphernalia such as search engines, banner adverts, and hyperlinks have sprung up. These must all be seen as part of the chain of direct-marketing communications that leads the customer from search to purchase.

In some ways websites compete with the telephone, as an inbound medium in particular. As the DMA census (2003) points out, after a year of spectacular growth telephone spend is slowing, while spend on websites makes slow if steady progress. Between 30 per cent and 60 per cent of businesses use websites for marketing, depending on which country you are in (*see* Fig. 10.4).

Internet advertising spend was estimated by the DMA Census (2003) at £200 million in 2002 in the UK. Future Foundation research (DMA Census, 2003) shows that as the Internet continues to spread through populations their use of it for shopping gradually 'kicks in' from a slow start. However, shopping tends to lag well behind the use of the Internet for e-mail and general surfing: Future Foundation research shows that it takes about three years' usage before even half of Internet users use the net for shopping.

As hinted at, websites have one fundamental difference to all the other media, which is that *it is customers, not advertisers, who initiate the process of contact*. Complete control over the messages they are exposed to therefore switches to the customer. This requires a completely new way of thinking by the advertiser.

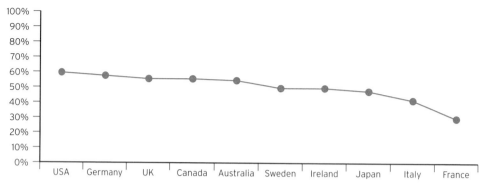

Figure 10.4 Percentage of which businesses use the Internet for marketing activity
Source: Adapted from DMA Census, 2003. Reproduced by permission of the DMA

Companies therefore need to do one of a number of things:

■ register with a 'search engine', an Internet facility which uses key words typed in by the user to search the millions of sites for ones which fit the description;

■ use hyperlinks to facilitate clickthrough from other sites to their site. This may done by establishing affiliate networks;

■ link with other companies in a 'virtual mall' – an electronic shopping centre, again reached through searching;

■ use banner advertising;

■ advertise their website through conventional media, or through electronic mail to newsgroups.

Search engines

Well known search engines include Google, AskJeeves, and Yahoo! These very popular Internet tools are used by us to find sites relating to something of interest, including commercial sites. Search engines use computer technology known as spiders to compile their indexes. The website must first be registered with the engine, and may also pay an additional fee in order to feature in the top page of the index, knowing that prospects will often go to the first likely looking site that can help them. The power and coverage of these search engines (they are typically the most visited sites on the web, and are very powerful, listing billions of websites) means that the engines can charge premiums of thousands of dollars for the most sought after listings. See www.searchenginewatch.com for more details.

Affiliate networks

These are discussed in Chapter 8 in detail, as they are of strategic importance. The highest profile example is that of Amazon which has around 300 000 affiliates: websites that provide a clickthrough facility to Amazon.com in return for a commission in the event of a purchase. The UK bookmaker William Hill pays £10–20 for a new account generated through its affiliate partners. In general rather unsophisticated promotions have

EXHIBIT 10.14

GOOGLE – THE WEB'S BIGGEST PHENOMENON?

The name Google derives from Googol – ten to the power of one hundred – referring to the incredible size and linkage of the Web. Google works with a unique software called PageRank developed by Google's founders Larry Page and Sergey Brin at Stanford University. According to the website, PageRank relies on the uniquely democratic nature of the Web by using its vast link structure as an indicator of an individual page's value. In essence, Google interprets a link from page A to page B as a vote, by page A, for page B. But, Google looks at more than the sheer volume of votes or links a page receives; it also analyses the page that casts the vote. Votes cast by pages that are themselves 'important' weigh more heavily and help to make other pages 'important'. Important, high-quality sites receive a higher PageRank, which Google remembers each time it conducts a search. Of course, important pages mean nothing if they don't match the query. So, Google combines PageRank with sophisticated text-matching techniques to find pages that are both important and relevant to the search.

See www.Google.com for more information

deployed poor targeting with the result that the affiliate sites have only the vaguest resemblance to the host site.

Banner ads

Banner adverts are paid-for adverts often placed across the top of the website – hence the term 'banner'. An interested prospect simply clicks on the banner to be whisked off to the advertiser's website where tempting offers await them. Banner ads may have nothing to do with the host website, and could simply be paid-for space hoping to catch interested people. Used in this way they are poorly targeted and will suffer low response rates.

EXHIBIT 10.15

DIFFERENT TYPES OF BANNER ADVERTS

- animated banner ads. Moving and changing images displayed in sequence to attract attention;
- interstitial pop-ups. Many people find these irritating, including the author. Interstitials pop up in between pages that the user has asked for. Often have to be manually removed;
- superstitials pop up over the top of a website that has been opened – again have to be removed by the user;
- interactive banner ads. Becoming more popular, include airlines prompting the user to enter a destination to find out the cheapest fare.

(see Chaffey *et al.*, 2003, and Rowan, 2002 for more details.)

Banner ads should follow the usual good commonsense rules of marketing communications, with good creative approaches, incentives, making sure the responses can be handled well and so on, but their big weakness is targeting. DoubleClick.net reports the latest situation (*see* Exhibit 10.16).

EXHIBIT 10.16

BANNER ADVERTISING

After its poor early performances, banner advertising is changing. More pop-ups are being used that intrude directly into the web page (though it has to be said many people find these extremely irritating – targeting is often non existent); also more banners now contain 'rich media', video and movement based, that is more eye catching. Flash and interstitials are also more common. By 2003 adverts had become much bigger, with half-page sizes much more common. One interesting trend is that the onset of rich media has meant a move away from just direct response ads towards a mixture of DM and brand building adverts being deployed. Nevertheless direct response remains crucial – the seductive nature of 'clickthrough' from the advert to the advertiser's web page remains high. Clickthrough rates from rich media sites are estimated at 1–2 per cent of web page readers, though purchase (conversion) rates will of course be much smaller again.

Measurement is slowly improving, with some firms beginning to track surfer behaviour from clickthrough to purchase more accurately.

Source: based on www.doubleclick.net, 24 July 2003

The bottom line for banner ads is that cost per thousand page impressions can range from £10–£50, while clickthrough rates are reported as 0.1–2 per cent (probably optimistic). Clickthrough rates may be one thing but purchase is quite another – of those who click through, only a low percentage would buy.

Customer behaviour with websites

It's very important that marketers develop an understanding of customer behaviour in processing websites as a medium. Branthwaite *et al.* (2000) compared the Internet to TV, outdoor and print media. They found that consumers used websites in a goal-oriented mood, whereas people were more relaxed, seeking interest or emotional gratification with other media. We tend to process TV in an episodic, superficial way, but websites are consciously, cognitively processed – words are more important than pictures. Everything is done in an active manner with website consumption, whereas outdoor and TV media are consumed passively.

The AIMRITE analysis to follow looks at how these issues affect our choice of websites as a medium.

THE INTERNET AS A MEDIUM

Key AIMRITE qualities

The most important issues when comparing the Internet with other media are:

- the Internet is electronic – the speed of data gathering, effecting transactions, is potentially faster than even the telephone;
- interactivity – the Internet probably stands somewhere between the phone and direct mail as an interactive tool. It is important to remember amid all the hype that e-mail is *not as quick, or effective*, as the telephone for use as a genuine one-to-one medium;
- unlike most media, the consumer initiates the dialogue if they are web-browsing.

We will now look at each AIMRITE element one by one, beginning with *audience*.

Audience

In the mid-1990s websites were a niche medium, attracting primarily upmarket male audiences. It had a limited coverage of just a few million users worldwide. At the time of writing, websites have already enjoyed explosive growth in audience access, with probably over 1 billion people worldwide having access at home or at work. The central position of the computer in people's lives in the 'developed world' points to a prediction of something close to saturation coverage for the Internet within a few years. The likelihood is that the only people not online will be the less privileged sections of society – in particular social classes D and E. Recent figures suggest the male/female bias is declining, as is the age factor.

In other words, as a medium, we can assume the Internet will be able to reach a wide variety of target audiences. There may be some bias towards social classes A, B, C1 and C2, and possibly younger people.

Segmentation is an interesting item of study online. Because users are in control of their access to the medium, customers segment sites, rather than the other way round.

Therefore sites will all deploy 'handraising' techniques in which they make themselves as conspicuous as possible so that users can find them. Newsgroups are effective in offering a type of *lifestyle segmentation*, and as techniques improve these will be of undoubted value to marketers.

The story is rapidly improving for existing customers of a site: firms will use cookies, usernames and passwords to identify previous browsers, then usually offer 'members only' services and so on. These may have to be paid for.

Impact

Peters (1998) points out a media attribute that she calls 'social presence'. This refers to the ability of the media to facilitate the communication's sociable, warm, personal and sensitive attributes. Channels that convey tone of voice, facial expressions and quick interactions will rank highly on the social presence scale. As you'd expect, the telephone will rank highly here, while direct mail will rate poorly. The Internet has the facility to rank very highly when the onset of video and audio interactive capability becomes more widespread for commercial use. At present most interaction is done using HTML and Java software, i.e. the program language in a sense acts as a barrier between the customer and a human representative of the firm. Nevertheless, the 'social presence' could still register from good creative approaches for both websites and e-mail.

One aspect of impact values of media is their ability to cut through the clutter of messages that prospects receive. The telephone therefore has high impact in this sense. Websites do not have the facility to create this kind of impact as it is an opt-in media.

Message

Websites are very powerful message carriers. They offer considerable, almost infinite multi-dimensional message opportunities. Full colour, illustrations or photographs, even videos, plus as much information as companies wish to add, are all possible (Dell has thousands of pages of technical information). The use of hypertext makes consumer scanning of a lot of information painless and easy. Potentially the Web is the most powerful of all media for message content but it has one weakness: the quality of the interface – the PC – is relatively low. TV watchers don't have to worry about keyboards, slow download, clunky software. In years to come, will the PC still be our favoured mode of access?

However, consumer control is a big plus. Peters (1998) reports research by Carson who found that the ability of customers to control *the pace and presentation of their contacts* via the Internet was the biggest factor on willingness to use this media. As Peters points out, consumers can also control *content* as well as contact, although it has to be said that this is not the case in the majority of commercial interactions. Controlling content means for example the use of customer bulletin boards, consumer home pages, or by supplying content that is used in the corporate website. It is interesting to note the difference in power of the Internet compared with direct mail on customer control of pace, presentation and content.

EXHIBIT 10.17

SOME THOUGHTS ON INTERNET ADVERTISING...

At the Procter & Gamble summit conference in the summer of 1998, 'Why Isn't Advertising on the Internet Working?', P&G invited competitors, consultants and Internet agencies to discuss the failure of Internet advertising. Experts pointed out that no one had coined a memorable slogan on the Internet. Even worse news: as people get more Internet-literate, they begin ignoring banner ads. The conclusion (which is pretty obvious if you understand media) was reported in multi-page stories in both the *New York Times* and the *Wall Street Journal*: the Internet is a direct-marketing medium, not an advertising medium.

Advertising is a right-brain hemisphere communications discipline. It works best on television (a right-hemisphere medium), ideally by inculcating shards of impressions into the passive brains of half-alert couch potatoes. As soon as you call for behaviour, the spell is broken.

The Internet – like direct mail – is an interactive medium, by definition left-hemisphere. The advertising industry wants the Internet to be like television, but it can't be – the wrong part of the brain is involved. It takes time to sort all of this out: cf. the McLuhan quotation. "Media are put out before they are thought out"

Source: Rosenfield, J. R. (1999) 'The Internet, Amazon.com and Book-of-the-Month Club: the old, the new, and the future view', *Direct Marketing*, June **62** (12), pp. 44–8.

Response device

Peters (1998) pointed out that there are two types of media – those which have a time lag between sending and receiving information, and those with no time lag. In fact the only truly interactive medium is the telephone, which has no time lag. But this may be closely followed by the Internet which companies may use on a 'real-time' basis, responding to requests for information, or confirming sales orders almost immediately. However, this is not the whole story. Once again, we must return to a key advantage of the Internet: *it's always available to customers*. This means that customers can conveniently plan their responses to suit themselves.

Some companies operate response facilities online. Many websites now make it possible for people to order electronically. By quoting a credit card number after choosing the order, customers complete the entire transaction without leaving their computer. However, the evidence suggests that consumers remain wary of giving their credit card details online, and so at the moment the main response vehicles are phone, mail or fax.

If and when these issues are resolved, the ability of a user to point and click if they want to order a product will make the Internet *the most powerful of all major media* from the point of view of *easy response*.

EXHIBIT 10.18

EVERYONE'S A FRUIT AND NET CASE...

In June 1997, a 15-year-old boy in Dublin was surfing the Net and came across a company offering home delivery of chocolate. A couple of minutes later he had ordered $2000 worth of Dairy Milk, Toffee Crisp and Mars Bars. Payment was online, and when asked for credit card details he just punched in the first 16 numbers that came into his head.

Four days later three huge boxes of chocolate arrived outside his front door, and the boy began to tuck in. However, the owner of the credit card, who lived in Argentina, complained, and eventually the Dublin police paid the family an uncomfortable visit.

The youngster's surfing days were temporarily over...

Internal management

Both the use of e-mail and setting up a website involve big learning curves for companies. Websites cost very little but there will be considerable hidden costs in learning how to set up and maintain them. However, once this is done, direct marketers should discover:

■ testing should be very cheap, but not necessarily as easy as with the telephone or direct mail, because of the inability to separate out target audiences;

■ lead times should be very short;

■ supplier control is high, as media ownership is not an issue at present.

In other words, from a management point of view, the Net should be very good news indeed.

The end result

The Internet has massive potential and cannot be ignored by direct marketers. Entry costs for websites and e-mail marketing are low, and ongoing costs are extremely low. The potential for direct selling, database building, and acting as a prime tool to do business, is huge.

It is very difficult to predict the impact that Web direct-response marketing will ultimately have. Nagle Green (2000) was quoted as having 'spoken to fifty marketers about how they are spending money online to generate customers'. This would include banner advertising in portal sites, and clickable links, but may not include the fixed costs of website management. These managers quoted the following average figures:

■ two cents per impression to generate awareness (an impression may be a prospect accessing a Web page which has an advert for the supplier's site);

■ 50 cents per clickthrough (those prospects who click through to the end site);

■ $5 per lead on preference (i.e. some kind of lead where the prospect has shown an interest);

■ and $80 per sale.

This last figure, though rather anecdotal, *is nevertheless highly significant.* If we compare this cost per sale figure with those of other media using the 'cost per response' rule introduced early in this chapter, we see *that yet again the average cost per response comes to somewhere around the £25–£75 area.* The developing economics of the Internet for direct sales is hugely important: if these average cost per sale figures remain steady, then websites will compete alongside other media, but are unlikely to dominate. The reader is advised to keep a close eye on developments.

There is very little research available on e-mail response rates, and few case studies have yet been built up, although this will change rapidly.

Website measurement issues

As with all forms of media, especially when they are still emerging, there are different ways of measuring performance. It is important to note that page impression figures only give advertisers part of the picture. These merely reflect the number of 'hits' which could be the same person accessing the site many times, or maybe a few casual browsers rather than serious customers. A better measure may be the number of unique users or hosts – a count of the different computers which have accessed the site. Better still would be a systematic cross reference of these with the users' figure, which will show the extent to which these sites are retaining audiences.

Table 10.6: **Summary of advantages and disadvantages of websites as a medium**

Strengths	Weaknesses
Cheap and easy to generate response	but current usage still not mainstream
Management of websites increasingly well understood	but mostly text-only creative options in reality
Very popular with customers	
E-mail very easy and convenient for both suppliers and customers	but little targeting capability at present

E-mail

CHARACTERISTICS OF E-MAIL

E-mail is huge. It's been estimated that 5–10 billion e-mails per day are sent globally – or two for everyone on the planet. On an everyday basis, e-mail has probably had a bigger impact, particularly on working life in westernised countries, than any other electronic development in the last twenty years.

E-mail has already emerged as a powerful business tool, with many firms using its flexibility and very low cost as an excellent way of keeping in touch with existing customers. E-mail marketing spend was estimated at £120 million in 2002 (DMA Census, 2003). In media spend terms this is still small beer, though one would imagine it is set to grow significantly. It may be that e-mail will replace direct mail as the favoured medium of retention marketing, particularly if a dialogue is being encouraged. For acquisition marketing e-mail looks attractive on paper but 'spamming' threatens the entire industry.

EXHIBIT 10.19

E-MAIL: SPAMMING IS LIKELY TO KILL THE GOLDEN GOOSE

Consent has long been vital with commercial e-mail. 'Spamming' is the use of technology to send the same e-mail to thousands or even millions of addresses on an e-mail list. Spamming is enabled by the very low costs of sending huge volumes of e-mail, and made possible by spider software which combs the Internet looking for e-mail addresses which are automatically added to the list. Targeting is utterly non-existent of course, response rates extremely small, but when sending millions of e-mails the cost/000 is also minute.

It has been estimated that 50 per cent of the world's e-mails are spam. Interestingly, 90 per cent of spam comes from only about 180 points of origin, mostly in the US and Africa. Exotic pornographic offers ('enlarge . . .'), financial scams ('I am transferring 20 million dollars and need you to hold it for me in your bank account . . .'), and the usual lotteries ('win a million!') seem to predominate.

However, spamming runs the risk of reprisals. 'Flaming' is the use of large files being sent back to the company from irate recipients, jamming the company's system.

Rowan 2002 has the following rules for prospective e-mailers:

■ offer an opt-out option;

■ don't solicit online with chatlines which forbid commerce;

■ don't sell e-mail addresses on to another company without opt-in permission.

Responsible companies are largely following these rules; but they cannot control the spammers. The result? Frustration and irritation will lead to a tendency to ignore or block out anything other than the personal, lowering response rates for the medium as a prospecting vehicle.

(For much more on responsible e-mailing see Rowan, 2002)

Nevertheless the e-mail industry continues to develop with established e-mail list brokers, consultants and the like giving increased structure.

AUDIENCE

E-mail has, in theory, a greater audience range than any other media, with a range from one-to-one dialogue-based communications to global mass advertising. In practice, these two extremes are used with spam at one end and good retention marketing from firms like Land Rover at the other.

However there is little scope for detailed segmentation work outside of private data held by companies. External data firms like Experian are working hard on building credible e-mail lists which they segment using other data held on that individual, but in general list-brokers have a hard job linking personal or business data to an e-mail address. This is leading to bulk e-mails to members of an interest group, say, being the norm (better than spam but still fairly hit and miss). Many e-mailers wouldn't care over much about segmentation however: the cost of sending 50,000 e-mails is similar to sending five million – everything at present encourages mass advertising rather than more 'scientific' targeting.

One important development is the use of 'viral' referral e-mails. Here, a recipient is encouraged to pass on the offer to friends who may be interested. The secret here is the convenience and ease with which we can copy mails to our address books. In this way, rapid spread of relevant offers to similar people may be effected. This particularly works if the mail contains entertainment or humour, or if it contains useful business information.

IMPACT

A strength of commercial e-mails is that they are received by the recipient alongside their personal e-mails, and hence are highly likely to be noticed.

Their weakness is that they are easily deleted without even being opened: more so even than 'junk' mail through the post.

The basic characteristics of the medium – text delivered through the PC – make this a medium of modest impact, less than TV, the telephone, or even direct mail, which has colour and tactility. However the impact of e-mail may be improved by the use of picture or video attachments, though the PC interface still makes these less appealing than their paper equivalents. For these reasons e-mail may not be used to build symbolic brand values; its strengths do however lend themselves to relationship building approaches, using its responsiveness to build dialogue.

MESSAGE

It is incredibly cheap to send extremely large volumes of information using e-mail. It's likely that the only constraining factor on message volume is the amount of information the consumer wishes to digest, rather than any media limitation. Chaffey *et al.* (2003) have compiled a commonsense list of creative recommendations for e-mailers. These include the need to grab attention in the header and early in the copy; hyperlink to websites for more information; be personalised; have a clear call-to-action, and so on. All of these ideas are based on principles that were developed for direct mail and are discussed in depth in Chapter 12.

RESPONSE DEVICE

It is very easy to respond by e-mail: this is one of the secrets of its success. Only the telephone and perhaps point and click interactive TV could claim to be easier. As a response device e-mail shares with web response the ability to offer 'delayed response' a few hours after receiving a message from a customer.

INTERNAL MANAGEMENT

Businesses need to plan for both outbound and inbound e-mail back from customers. The latter will be a minefield unless the firm has made provision to answer the queries reasonably promptly. One study done in 2002 found that only 30 per cent of e-mails were answered at all, let alone within a few hours or days. While firms preach service, they often do things to cut costs.

E-mail lends itself very well to testing, with its data driven nature allowing the set up of control cells to check and compare response rates.

THE END RESULT

E-mail marketing threatens to re-write the economic balance of marketing media – that most media deliver a similar cost per response. The potential advantages of e-mail, particularly as a retention media, are terrifying. Its cost/000 reduces significantly with bulk, but a marketer going to his own list may expect to pay about £20–£30 per thousand sent. A 1–2 per cent response rate should not be unreasonable for an offer sent to an in-house list: this leads to a cost per response of only about £1, well under the best any other media can usually manage.

This is the quiet revolution that the headlines about global spam are missing: retention-based direct mail may be under threat from easy to send e-mails. That said, maybe the two media will find ways to work together – they are complementary in many ways.

Acquisition e-mail is a different story: again very powerful in theory but in practice extremely difficult to target and currently being shouted down by the spammers. The future probably lies with in-house lists and newsletter groups, with some well-directed acquisition offers using reputable list-builders. That is, if the regulators and the consumers will let them.

EXHIBIT 10.20

THE CHANGING FACE OF E-MAIL

E-mail is rapidly changing its rather basic interface. Anderson (2003) highlighted the case of RedV, an online company that sells privacy and security software. It has moved from simple HTML e-mails that click the recipient to its website, to e-mails that contain pictures. Following good direct-marketing practice, it tested three. One displayed a picture of a man, one a picture of a woman, the third, the control, had no picture. RedV's target audience are mainly young men.

Guess which campaign did best? Some might not be surprised that most respondents clicked on the picture of the woman. The final twist however came in the conversion to sale figures: those who clicked through via the man's picture were more likely to buy. Yet again showing us the value of testing when trying to unravel how people actually do behave when responding to adverts.

Source: based on article by Heidi Anderson, www.clickz.com 17 April, 2003.

Table 10.7: **Summary of advantages and disadvantages of e-mail as a medium**

Strengths	Weaknesses
E-mail very easy and convenient for both suppliers and customers	but little targeting capability at present
Cheap to set up and on a per thousand basis	but lacks colour
Very quick to organise, personalise and send so an ideal one-to-one medium	but recipients drown in unwanted spam

Summary to chapter

In this chapter we found that media choices in direct marketing depend on a number of factors and therefore should be made carefully. These factors can be applied systematically using the AIMRITE formula.

Direct marketers have a large number of media choices, of which some of the most important are direct mail, the telephone and the Internet. In the future, it is likely the Internet will change things for direct mail and the telephone. Direct marketers may find that some traditional media will be less economic than they once were, although interestingly the early signs are that Internet costs per response are at similar levels to other media at present. Direct mail is still excellent at carrying large amounts of information, giving consumers a permanent record, and presenting messages creatively. Even with the advent of the Internet, the telephone remains the best 'relationship building' medium.

E-mail has the potential to be arguably the most powerful of all direct response media. Some direct mail usage in particular is under threat in the long term from the easier and cheaper alternative of e-mail. Hence direct marketers may find that some traditional media will be less economic than they once were. Web-based advertising – pop-ups, banners, etc. – have largely proven a disappointment with fairly low response levels recorded. Websites themselves have rapidly improved as commercial vehicles, and are popular as destinations for responders to potentially buy.

Questions

1. In what circumstances should you never use the telephone for contacting prospects? Give examples of companies or situations where this is the case.

2. Critically analyse the relative strengths and weaknesses of direct mail and e-mail.

3. A large regional car distributor with outlets in the Midlands is planning to introduce the telephone into its acquisition and retention programme. Draw up a proposal which explains:
   - how the company might benefit from some form of telemarketing;
   - the ways in which the telephone maximises short- and long-term returns;
   - what major practical difficulties will be encountered and how to overcome them.

4. 'Apart from some specialist applications, SMS will never be of much use for direct marketers.' Discuss the extent to which you agree with this statement.

5. A high-street bank has set up a major calling centre in-house, capable of taking inbound and making outbound calls. Outline how such an asset could form part of a direct marketing approach to improve relationships with customers.

6. 'Direct mail works best when integrated with other marketing media.' Evaluate this statement, outlining examples where it is and is not the case.

7. Bartlett's Office Services is a full-range supplier of office equipment. Until now it has used trade press advertising and a salesforce to operate, but is now considering the use of websites to both generate and convert leads. Using the AIMRITE formula, evaluate the effectiveness of websites for this firm.

8. Imagine you were the director of a new theatre company, and you need to acquire new customers for the start of the season. Compare and contrast the Internet as a medium with direct
mail and the telephone – what are their strengths and weaknesses using the AIMRITE formula?

References

Braithwaite, A., Wood, K. and Shilling, M. (2000) 'The medium is part of the message – the role of
media in shaping the image of a brand', ARF, ESOMAR, Conference, Rio, Brazil, 12-14 November.

Chaffey, D., Mayer, R., Johnston, K., Ellis-Chadwick, F. (2003) *Internet Marketing Strategy,
Implementation and Practice*, 2nd edn, Financial Times Prentice Hall, Harlow, England.

DMA Census (2003) Direct Marketing Association, London.

Fox, N. and Burrows, D. (2001) 'Direct marketing will knock the spots off TV advertising', *Admap*,
March, pp. 31-6.

Gordon, W. and Langmaid, R. (1988) *Qualitative Research: A practitioners' and buyers' guide*,
Gower, London.

Haig, M. (2002) *Mobile Marketing – the Message Revolution*, Kogan Page, London.

Holder, D. (1992) 'Video: The absolute essentials of direct marketing, no. 2: *Acquisition*', Institute
of Direct Marketing, Teddington, Richmond-upon-Thames.

McCorkell, G. (1994) *The Best of Graeme McCorkell*, DRM Ltd/IDM, London.

Nagle Green, E. (2000) IDM millennium lecture, London, March.

Nash, E. (1995) *Direct Marketing: Strategy, planning, execution*, 3rd edn, McGraw-Hill, New York.

Payne, A. (1995) *Advances in Relationship Marketing*, Kogan Page, London, UK.

Peters, L. (1998) 'The new interactive media: 1 to 1, but who to whom', *Marketing Intelligence and
Planning*, **16** (1).

Rapp, S. and Collins, T. (1987) *Maximarketing*, McGraw-Hill, USA.

Reed, M. (1999) 'The top sites (advertising and the Internet)', *Campaign*, Haymarket Publications,
UK, 28 May, p. 54.

Roncorroni, S. (1992) 'Using the telephone for profit' in Halsey, B. (ed.) *The Practitioners' Guide to
Direct Marketing, Institute of Direct Marketing*, Teddington, UK.

Rosenfield, J. R. (1999) 'The Internet, Amazon.com and Book-of-the-Month Club: the old, the new,
and the future view', *Direct Marketing*, June **62** (12), pp. 44-8.

Rowan, W. (2002) *Digital Marketing*, Kogan Page, London.

Smith, I., Education Director, Institute of Direct Marketing (1996) *Personal communication*,
Institute of Direct Marketing.

Smith, P. (1993) *Marketing Communications: An integrated approach*, Kogan Page, UK.

Stone, B. (1996) *Successful Direct Marketing Methods*, 5th edn, NTC Business Books, USA.

Xerox wins Gold – How to make direct mail interesting
Told by award winning agency Harrison Troughton Wunderman

The Xerox Work Centre Pro is a digital printer which needed to be launched across eight European markets. We needed to find an idea that was meaningful to all markets and able to cut through the language and culture differences. Our target was 60 834 IT managers in small- to medium-size companies. We knew they had old, out-of-date analogue copiers. We knew, therefore, that their copiers were near the end of their life and could be frustrating to use. This was the starting point for our creative. We focused upon the problem they'd been having – standing around looking after their copier when they could be doing better things.

And we dramatised this by taking a Polaroid of the worn-out carpet in front of an old printer. We sent this Polaroid to our low-end prospects. For the high-end prospects we actually sent out the carpet tile! Having dramatised the problem, the letter then explained the solution: the Xerox Work Centre Pro. These mailings generated a 12 per cent response rate. The mailings cost $436 000 to produce. Yet they generated $4 633 332 in sales. That's a return on investment of almost 11:1. The cost per lead was $60 for a machine that costs $4,400. It also won a Gold at the DMA Awards.

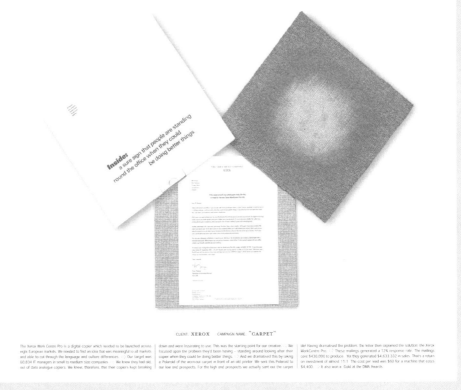

Figure 10.5 Xerox direct mail
Source: Reproduced by kind permission of Xerox and Harrison Troughton Wunderman

Question

Making business direct mail work is extremely difficult. Executives receive so much that getting a response is ever harder. Give five reasons why the Xerox Work Centre Pro copier mailer worked so well.

CASE STUDY

Dell

Dell Computers Inc. is one of the Nasdaq (stock exchange for high tech industries) success stories. Now a worldwide major player in the computer hardware market, Dell is jostling for position in terms of PC sales in the UK distribution channel. In 1998 Dell pulled in a 31 per cent share of desktop-PC sales to large organisations, ahead of IBM and only just trailing Compaq. Among smaller businesses, it achieved joint second place with Compaq, taking a 12 per cent market share.

Crucially for the future, in 1998 Dell became the first player to make selling over the Internet work. It claimed sales over the Internet of £3.7 million per day worldwide even then, an impressive figure. In 1999, Dell overtook Compaq Computers to become the UK's biggest PC seller, with 18.7 per cent of the market. *Advertising Age* (1999) reported Dell as one of the top 10 winners in the 'NetMarketing' 2000 awards.

How did Dell do it?

As *Computerworld* pointed out in 1999, Dell has made 'big bucks' ignoring the traditional PC distribution model by avoiding middlemen and selling directly to corporate customers. Dell's extraordinary success with this approach has caused the other major computer makers to sit up and take notice.

Dell's competitors

In the UK, the direct versus indirect battle rages on. The DSG, with its PC World, Currys and Dixons outlets, is by far the largest name in the high street, and is believed to account for some 40 per cent of volume sales in the 'Small Office Home Office' (SOHO) sector. However, given that second-time buyers are now thought to be in the majority, Mintel believes the direct sector, selling to consumers via mail order, will be the fastest growing over the next two years, and may quickly become the dominant channel of distribution. A number of manufacturers such as Time, Tiny and Gateway are gaining a retail presence while also maintaining their low inventory just-in-time production methods.

Littlewood (1998) reported that traditional methods of selling computer hardware primarily through 'resellers' (computer wholesalers/retailers who sell to the small and medium business sector) are being replaced by brand building or direct methods. At the forefront of the direct approach is Dell Computers, while leading the way with its brand-building approach is Compaq, although Compaq is also using direct marketing within its brand strengthening (*see* Exhibit 12.5 in Chapter 12).

The importance of branding in computer hardware

Direct marketers should not overlook the importance of branding in computer hardware. As Intel has shown, it can be a vital weapon in a product area in which customers are trusting suppliers to deliver a quality product in a high-ticket complex product sector. Increasingly, branding techniques – traditionally the forte of consumer marketing – are being used in preference to the product-specification type of selling (often led by salespeople) previously favoured by business-to-business marketers in this sector.

As Littlewood points out, computer companies' enthusiasm for branding comes as they move toward targeting their business consumers direct, which is making those in the sales channel rather anxious. For the resellers in the middle, the future seems increasingly uncertain, as the big names want direct dialogue with their customers.

Coupled with branding, direct marketing is on the increase in the business-to-business sector as it recognises the success this element of the marketing mix has enjoyed in its neighbouring consumer field. Database marketing can, if done well, both increase the volume of good leads to the sales departments and also increase directly distributed sales.

One of the keys to the rise of direct sales will be the confidence of the customer. Customers who are uncertain are more likely to purchase from a retailer or from a salesperson, because they will need the reassurance of face-to-face contact. However, IT-literate corporate clients, or second-time buyers in the small to medium-sized sector (SMEs), are more likely to buy direct. Here, Dell's low-cost business model is attractive.

Compaq is also targeting customers direct and says that it is doing so because it can then match them to the skills of the most appropriate reseller. It has also been suggested that IBM too has been gearing up for a shift in sales channels through its branding drive, a move viewed by resellers as designed to get access to customers. Commentators suggest that the reseller channel's role is likely to change to become more value-added and service-orientated.

The move towards brand building/direct operations for business-to-business hardware firms has meant a matching rise in media spending. Estimates are that IT firms are spending between 3 per cent and 5 per cent of their turnover on marketing and communications and that the figure is rising, with some companies splashing out as much as 10 per cent of their turnover on above-the-line only. The bulk of the marketing budget – between 35 per cent and 40 per cent – is probably being spent above the line, but direct marketing, which accounts for about 20 per cent, is growing.

Apple has made one of the most significant branding pushes of the IT pack recently with its 'Think Different' brand-building campaign. Alan Hely, Apple UK's marketing director, says the campaign is helping to build 'the only lifestyle brand in the industry' and says the aim is to communicate 'what Apple stands for; it's not about the product'.

IBM is also exploiting its massive brand equity (including a £1.6 billion media spend globally) with its huge above-the-line campaign positioning itself as the company that 'makes e-business a reality'. Dell, however, is eschewing the trend toward the 'corporate personality', instead focusing its efforts on the small and medium-sized enterprise sector, with '99.9 per cent of advertising in the UK directed at SMEs'. Its marketing strategy reinforces its direct-sell approach via very targeted direct mail, site visits by sales people, telesales, sales promotion and direct response advertising. It has been reported as having 30 or 40 programmes running at any one time. One Dell executive said that 'We are trying to use the products to carry the brand attributes. In the SME market, value for money is the key.'

Dell segments its customers into five sectors in the UK, according to size of company from corporate sales to the *Times* top 100 down to its consumer-only business. It tailors its marketing activities accordingly.

Dell's use of the Internet

Internet marketing now accounts for over 50 per cent of Dell's worldwide sales. Mitchell (2000) outlined two key elements to the success of Dell. First, he pointed out that with Dell the flow of information is upwards from the customer to the company, allowing something close to Pepper's ideal one-to-one scenario. The company makes computers according to customer orders – it does not keep any stock. This allows it to produce precisely what customers want, rather than nudging customers towards something that doesn't quite fit their needs. Secondly, the zero stock eliminates a whole series of costs, which fall out of the supply chain, allowing lower costs to be transferred to the customer and improving the company's competitiveness.

Apart from Dell, networking giant Cisco is the only other player doing any real e-commerce. Barriers to its take-up in the UK include the risk of conflict between manufacturers and their sales channels. But executives believe that the Net is an effective place to do business. One said that once a standard PC's price drops to £200 and Internet connection charges fall, the volume of e-commerce will go up.

'I think in the next two years we will see dramatic changes,' he says.

Questions

1. How does Dell put the customer in control of the buying process? How does the Internet help in this feature of Dell's business?
2. Compare and contrast Dell's direct approach with the brand-building approaches of Compaq and IBM.
3. How should Dell use the Internet, e-mail, direct mail and outbound telephone to best effect to support its inbound Web and telephone sales channels?
4. What are the key success factors for business-to-business direct marketing compared with consumer direct marketing?

References

Auer, J. (1999) 'Is going direct going cheaper?', *Computerworld*, 19 July.

Clancy, H. (1999) 'What does "direct" mean, anyway?', *Computer Reseller News*, Manhasset, 11 October.

'Past NM top 10 winners' (1999) *Advertising Age's Business Marketing* (Chicago), August **84** (8) p. 36.

Littlewood, F. (1998) 'Direct connections', *Marketing*, 27 August, pp. 27-9.

Mitchell, A. (2000) 'In one-to-one marketing, which one comes first?', *Interactive Marketing*, pp. 354-68.

Wasserman, T. (1999) 'IBM's magic moment', *Brandweek*, New York, 9 August.

Heinz *At Home*

In the summer of 1998, *Campaign* magazine announced that marketing executives at Heinz had withdrawn its direct marketing magazine in 1998 after deciding the Heinz brand communicated itself more readily through television and poster advertising. *Campaign* reported that Heinz believed its products would sell without the use of direct marketing and would revert to TV brand building.

Campaign, a magazine that champions brand building and advertising, suggested the following reason for the failure of the Heinz *At Home* project. Tylee (1998) reported:

> Want to know why Heinz is axing its customer magazine, *At Home?* Then try this simple test. Put your thumb across the Heinz logo on the front cover. Now imagine another name in its place. Sainsburys, Asda or Safeway perhaps. Does the magazine look a neat fit with any of those brands? If your answer is yes, you are some way to understanding why Heinz *At Home* has bitten the dust.

Tylee suggested that, while the Heinz brand oozes warmth and homely values, the magazine had struggled to sustain them, being instead a mere bolt on to the brand's distinctive multi-million pound TV advertising. Damningly, *Campaign* said that the move 'almost certainly ends Heinz's four-year flirtation with direct marketing.'

It had all started so well...

The announcement in May 1994 that Heinz was switching emphasis to an extensive direct marketing programme and dropping all product advertising in favour of 'umbrella' TV branding was much hyped at the time. It was probably the case that Heinz brought in direct marketing as an extra weapon in its armoury to match the growing power of the major retailers. Heinz had some experience of direct marketing from its US operation and a strong baby foods division which used direct marketing. A central plank of the initiative was to be Heinz *At Home* magazine, which was to be sent to customers responding to promotions: in-store campaigns, on-pack vouchers and so on. The aim was to gather customer data on an ongoing basis using the data gathered from vouchers redeemed in-store. This would help Heinz identify its most valuable customers, profile attractive prospects, target up-selling and cross-selling opportunities precisely, and improve loyalty to Heinz through the brand-building values of *At Home* magazine.

Early results looked impressive...

Richards (1995) reported that of the 3.5 million households which were mailed the first magazine in September 1994:

■ 68 per cent spontaneously recalled having received it

■ 40 per cent said they would keep it for future reference.

The number which actually took up the magazine's coupon offers or contacted its helpline was an impressive 1.5 million households. But did the activity actually result in increased sales? Heinz claims that in October 1994, a month after the first magazine went out, its soups' share increased 6.4 per cent on the month. Tomato ketchup was up 7.7 per cent and pasta meals rose by 4.9 per cent.

According to Booth (1998), by 1996 the agency had taken the scheme from a simple magazine to a highly targeted and segmented approach to customers. It whittled down the base to those customers who were genuinely responsive, and Heinz seemed happy with the return on investment the approach generated.

So why did Heinz withdraw the programme? *Campaign* offered its own analysis:

> You can see the point of a supermarket launching a magazine because it has so many products to talk to its customers about,' an agency chief who has worked on Heinz business points out. 'But Heinz makes tinned foods. There's a limit to the amount of new information it can offer – and who is bloody interested anyway?

Some commentators felt that this was an example of the customer magazine being overused as a tool. However, as *Campaign* suggested, for the right advertiser with the right product, a customer magazine is a fantastic marketing tool. Some examples of successful magazines include the AA, British Airways' *High Life*, *Saab* magazine, and in-house magazines from Tesco and Sainsbury.

One possibility is that customers get too many and suffer from magazine overload. *Campaign* again:

> Broadly speaking, a middle-class family in the UK could find itself in receipt of titles for at least one car brand, a building society, a bank, Sky's listings magazine, a supermarket, a holiday company and so on. With that kind of volume it isn't long before receiving a customer magazine stops being a bonus and becomes a chore (or a bore).

Booth (1998) quotes another agency director: 'Putting a [postage] stamp on communications to sell a 30p can of beans does not make sense.' If one estimates the net margins on a Heinz product as about 3p per item, there's no doubt the economics of direct marketing need to be worked out carefully for fmcg goods. Adding to the difficulty would be the hard work that had to go into data gathering. Customer transactions could only be recorded by Heinz using redeemed vouchers. Ironically, the supermarkets probably knew more about Heinz customers than Heinz did.

Was the magazine good enough? Tylee (1998) was sceptical:

> If 'Beans on toast with a twist' and 'Have a pizza romance' (and let's shoot whoever came up with that pun) are the two best features they can come up with, then killing off the magazine was undoubtedly a humanitarian gesture.

Questions

1. Why did Heinz UK decide to pull out of its direct marketing approach?
2. What are the key features of FMCG markets which make it so difficult for database and direct marketing to thrive?
3. Produce a cost/benefit analysis for Heinz *At Home*, estimating the costs of the campaign from the material in the case study, and the revenue benefits. Revenues were based on increased cross-selling of different goods. Assume typical margins were about 3–5p per product. Your calculation should also include revenues accrued from incremental loyalty gains: as a result of the programme, a certain percentage of customers chose Heinz rather than competitors.
4. Comment on the use of direct mail to promote fast-moving consumer goods. Outline the advantages and disadvantages versus its media competitors.
5. What do you think the major role of direct marketing is in FMCG markets?

References

Booth, E. (1998) 'Where next for fmcg loyalty?', *Marketing Direct*, July/August, p. 10.

Richards, A. (1995) 'Traditional twist to new campaign', *Marketing*, 29 June, p. 14.

Tylee, J. (1998) 'Heinz gets burnt in customer magazine market', *Campaign*, 5 June, p. 14.

ACQUISITION MEDIA

Objectives

Once you have read this chapter you will:

- understand the main features of the various acquisition media;
- understand their strengths and weaknesses.

Introduction

This chapter concentrates on support media, or media often used for prospecting competitor customers or prospecting in new markets. We will look at press, magazines, inserts, door drops, radio, and direct-response TV and new or unusual media. Each of these will be assessed using the AIMRITE formula, introduced in Chapter 10.

The chapter ends with a look at how media should be put together over time to deliver a coherent message to customers.

National press

Direct response press is space advertising in daily or Sunday papers and supplements, inviting a specific response.

The DMA definition of a direct response press advert states that it must include 10 per cent of space being devoted to the response element. Hence brand building adverts that merely contain a number or website are not counted as direct-response press. This has accounted for the relatively low figure attributed to DR press spend in recent years (DMA census, 2003). However, there has to be serious doubt about the efficacy of such a definition – many press adverts may be direct response but only use small phone numbers or web addresses. The use of coupons is, not surprisingly, declining. The '10 per cent of space' requirement accounts for the apparent decline in DR press between 1995 and 2003. The percentage of press adverts counted as direct response has declined from over 60 per cent to about 20 per cent.

At the time of writing there are more than twenty national daily and Sunday press titles in the UK and, according to BRAD, over 4500 trade, technical and professional media which carry advertisements. The national press can be very cost-effective for national advertisers. From a marketing point of view, the UK is exceptionally well served by national media, many European and Asian countries having a much more regional press.

Press advertising is extensively used by direct marketers. More than half of all press advertising is direct response, with financial services, automobile, mail order and retail all being big players. The low 'cost per thousand' of national press make it ideal for customer acquisition if the target audience is broadly defined. In addition, the broad-scale nature of the press makes it ideal for 'double duty' brand building and response advertising.

EXHIBIT 11.1

NERDY BUT NICE – ATTRACTING APPLICATION DEVELOPERS

Business press allows the advertiser to get straight to the point. In the case of an award winner from Lotus, intimacy was taken to new levels. The advert was written entirely in HTML code and was intended to raise awareness among application developers of a new aid, a constantly updated website (www.lotus-dev.net). Only the developers would get the point: if they typed in the code into their Internet browser, a colour advert appeared describing dev.net. Clicking on the advert then took you straight into the website. Between May and August 1999, over 800 members had enrolled.

Source: adapted from DMA Case Study, 1999, www.dma.org.uk

KEY AIMRITE QUALITIES

Audience

If you are looking for high volumes of exposure then the national press could be your best choice. The *Sun* is bought by 4 million people and read by about 12 million. Your advertisement therefore theoretically could be seen by about 30 per cent of UK adults, just with one placement in one title. In reality, research (Educators' Guide, 1996) suggests that fewer than this will actually notice the advert, as is discussed in the following section on Impact.

In terms of audience, the press is likely to be used in favour of other media in two situations. One is when the audience is quite broadly defined because it is not yet fully understood what type of people buy the product. For example, a new chain of hotels may enter an advert in the *Daily Mail* promoting weekend breaks. This is known as 'hand raising', when the audience identifies itself from the mass. Once customers have been identified, a description is obtained by profiling – the weekend breakers here being perhaps 'older empty nesters from cities'.

The second scenario favouring the use of the press is when the product or service has a genuinely mass audience. Household items – kitchenware for instance – may fit this category.

Impact

Compared with direct mail or the telephone, press adverts have low impact on the consumer, often being ignored altogether, or glanced at at best. As long as the advert is read by people who are in the market at that time, it does not matter that it is missed by the rest. However, most of us tend to read papers by scanning through to certain pages of editorial, often not looking at adverts at all. It is easy to see then why your message is more likely to be noticed in, say, direct mail than in the press.

The impact of the advert can be greatly enhanced by the medium surround – the editorial. This 'halo effect' can be achieved if the content of the advert relates to the editorial. A student bank account offer is more likely to be noticed opposite an article on 'What to do when entering university'.

The specific media brand also adds value to the advert. A full-page advert for a financial or business product placed in the *Financial Times* can convey a lot of credibility, just because of the medium. When the British beef crisis with BSE was at its height in 1996, McDonald's managed to look authoritative when it took out full-page national press adverts in credible papers to make an 'announcement to all its customers' explaining its position.

Message

Press adverts consist of pictures and words presented within a fixed space. Colour can be used, particularly in supplements, but otherwise the creative constraints are substantial. Much less information can be communicated compared with inserts, door drops or direct mail, although press is still better than TV, radio or the telephone at imparting volumes of information.

The major difference between press and direct mail or telephone is that the former is a public medium. This may help generate word of mouth, as you know that your friends have also had a chance to view the advert. Advertising in public confers some legitimacy on the advertiser: we associate press adverts with the company being at least pretty sizeable; also that if it's willing to advertise in public, it is probably a legal operation.

Response

Both coupon and telephone can be used as response devices. The coupon must be filled in from scratch, of course, and also clipped out of the paper, whereas direct-mail coupons may be pre-completed to minimise effort on the responder's behalf.

Internal management

Press adverts can be created and space bought very quickly. If an opportunity is spotted, say to capitalise on an unexpected news event, then a press ad can be created and placed in the *next day's* edition of a national newspaper. A mortgage broker may want to get in quickly alongside an item on an interest-rate drop. The press therefore has the potential to be the quickest of *any* medium from brief to execution.

Testing is more difficult to execute than it is with the private media: mail and telephone. Although the creative approach, the specific press title, offer and timing can all be tested, it is with rather less precision than direct mail or telephone. This is because the exact number and 'type' of audience exposed to each test cannot be completely controlled.

EXHIBIT 11.2

PRESS VARIABLES TO CONSIDER WHEN TESTING

■ **Size:** A doubling in space size usually produces less than double the responses. Often direct marketers find the optimum size may be a quarter- or half-page advert.

■ **Frequency:** Responses drop off dramatically with repetition of the ad in the same press. Direct marketers could typically expect over 80 per cent of responses from the first two insertions, with rapidly diminishing returns thereafter.

However, there is a case for running full-page ads with low frequency. Many direct marketers have found this is the best combination of the above two variables.

■ **Colour:** Colour will usually boost response, but will be slightly less cost-effective than black and white. However, colour works similarly to size, in that many direct marketers use colour but keep frequency low.

Companies test these variables to get their cost per response down, once the main media variable has been established.

Sun Alliance did just this with its new mortgage product launched in 1992. It used a series of colour adverts in quality and mid-market nationals targeting BC1s, and started its campaign in April. By the end of the summer it was using strip-shaped (like a ruler standing on end) ads only, but still using colour. The campaign generated 5000 enquiries, well above target.

Source: Halsey, B. (ed.) (1992) *The Practitioners' Guide to Direct Marketing*, Institute of Direct Marketing, Teddington, UK.
Halsey, B. (ed) (2002) *The Interactive and Direct Marketing Guide*, Institute of Direct Marketing, Teddington, UK.

The end result

Research by Lowe Howard Spink (Educators' Guide, 1996) for financial product press adverts found that 78 per cent of readers didn't even see the ads or passed them by. Of the remaining 22 per cent who glanced at the advert, only 1 per cent would be 'active shoppers'.

This low level of targeting explains why typical response rates for press adverts are very low in comparison to, say, direct mail, door drops or inserts. A press advert may only generate 0.01 to 0.05 per cent response to a typical advert. However, the media costs are low in terms of cost per thousand reached, often at well under £10 per thousand, and so the press is as competitive as the other media in terms of cost per response. The example calculation in the following box shows how to make quick calculations of cost per response.

EXHIBIT 11.3

EXAMPLE CALCULATION

A full-page advert in *The Sun* may cost £40 000. The circulation is 4.2 million.

Cost *per thousand reached* is then 40 000/4200 = £9.52 per thousand

Let's say 0.03 per cent of the audience respond. What is the cost per response?
First, calculate the number of responders:

No. of responders = 0.03% of 4.2 million = 1260 responders

As the advert cost £40 000, the cost per response is:

Cost per response = 40 000/1260 = £32 per response

The point is that, although responses are low, costs are also low when measured in cost per thousand reached. The cost per response is broadly comparable with other typical media performances.

The press, like the broadcast media discussed later, may have a *dual objective* set for its use. As well as eliciting responses, the press can be used for general marketing goals of generating awareness or building brands. This can be dubbed the 'double duty effect'.

In summary, then, the national press is a valuable part of the direct marketer's media armoury. Returns are usually adequate, and the hand-raising abilities of press advertising make further definition of your target market possible. Occasionally, returns can be spectacular (*see* Exhibit 11.4 on the Labour Party).

Table 11.1 summarises the strengths and weaknesses of the national press.

Table 11.1: **Strengths and weaknesses of the national press**

Strengths	Weaknesses
Low cost per thousand	but low response
Fast production	but low creative options
Double duty effect (brand building and response)	but lack of secrecy

EXHIBIT 11.4

RETURN ON INVESTMENT: THE LABOUR PARTY

If you can get the target audience, the medium and medium format, the offer and, crucially, the timing all just right, then press direct response can be spectacularly successful.

The Labour Party bought 20cm by two-column slots on the *Guardian's* front page for the day after the announcement of the General Election call in 1992 by the Conservatives. The headline was 'Give £30 now for a Labour victory'.

The return on investment was an incredible 14:1 for this advert.

Urgent Election Appeal

Give £30 now for a Labour victory.

The day is now drawing near when the Tories can finally be voted out of power.

The hopes of millions of people rest on a Labour victory. Only Labour can breathe new life into manufacturing industry, and use the fruits of growth to invest in the NHS, education and transport.

The Tories have reportedly raised around £20 million – much of it in massive donations from abroad – to fight their campaign. They will use that money to try and buy their way to victory. But there is something you can do to stop them.

A donation to Labour today will help us to fight Tory lies with the facts. For instance, just £30 will pay for a key poster site for a full day which will be seen by thousands of voters. It's time for a change. So please, give what you can today. And give Britain something to celebrate this election.

Neil Kinnock

YES, I want to see Labour in power. I include a cheque/postal order made payable to The Labour Party for:

☐ **£15** ☐ **£30** ☐ **£60** ☐ **£100** ☐ **Other £** _____

OR, please deduct this amount from my Labour Co-op VISA/VISA/Access/Amex/Diners card no.

Expiry date _____ / 19 ___   **G01/993**

Signed _____ Date _____

Full Name Mr/Ms _____
BLOCK CAPITALS PLEASE
Address _____

_____ Postcode _____

Send to: The Labour Party, Election Appeal Centre, FREEPOST WC5351, London WC1X 8BR. Or to make an immediate credit card donation phone 081 200 0200 now (quoting ref. G01) - lines are open 24 hours a day. **Labour**

DATA PROTECTION: Naturally, Labour will never make your name and address available to commercial organisations for their own private gain. But, if they wish to support our work, we may occasionally allow carefully-screened companies and organisations to contact you if you would prefer not to receive these communications, please tick this box ☐

The Labour Party's most successful fundraising advertisement

Source: Reproduced by kind permission of the Labour Party.

Magazines

Magazines are used for acquisition via space advertising inviting a response.

This is space advertising in magazines inviting a response. DMA figures (Census, 2003) suggest that while magazine direct-response advertising has held fairly steady, so-called 'image and response' ads have grown while 'pure' direct response ads (from say mail order firms) have declined as a percentage of the whole. This is an interesting trend which is explained by two factors: first, the growth of direct marketing in sectors such as personal care and health, and second, the movement within marketing communications towards 'brand response' marketing that mixes brand building with direct response.

Direct marketing spend on magazines was reported at £222 million in 2002, a big drop on £616 million in 1995 by the DMA, attributed to a big fall in the number of adverts carrying a response device to less than 50 per cent of the total number of adverts. Magazine readership in the UK has grown significantly over the last few years, though it remains behind that of much of Europe. Perhaps reflecting the fragmentation of society, the UK has become a nation of magazine readers to a much greater extent than ever before. There are now over 2100 consumer titles and 4500 trade and technical journals.

KEY AIMRITE QUALITIES

Audience

Whereas local press tends to target according to geography, magazines tend to separate consumers according to their *interests*. If you need to segment your audience by lifestyle, therefore, magazines are a useful channel to consider.

What's more, we can seek out some pretty unusual audiences using magazines. Your local newsagent will have the standard women's magazines, *Woman's Own*, *Cosmopolitan* (although at least 25 per cent of *Cosmo's* readership are men!), and the men's section, for example *Computer Weekly*, which, according to popular myth, is read predominantly by anorak wearers; and then there are football and car magazines of all shapes and sizes. However, lest it be thought that we are all obsessed with relationships, fashion, sport, computers and cars, there are a host of incredibly varied titles lurking beyond these – everything from *Army Quarterly and Defence Journal* to *Audiophile with HiFi Answers*, and *Potholing Weekly* to *True Romances* is out there!

Impact

As a medium, magazines offer more impact on your audience than will the press. The saying 'the medium is the message' is perhaps more apt for magazines than for most media. There are a number of reasons for this. First, the magazine brand itself may be relevant to the product you are selling, and you may gain from association with the media brand values. Second, magazine production values are higher than those of the press, with higher quality paper and full colour: this helps to heighten the impact on the reader.

Third, people exhibit a different behaviour when reading magazines. They see a magazine as a pleasure, an indulgence, and will linger over the read, in a way quite different to reading a daily paper. This again makes it more likely that adverts will be scanned.

Message

Have you ever picked up a motorbike magazine? If you are one of the majority who are not motorcycle riders, but have flicked through such a magazine, you might quickly be nonplussed by the language used within. What on earth is 'top end grunt'? Why are engines described as 'bomb proof'? (In case you're wondering, the former is engine power at high speeds, and the latter refers to reliability.)

The point is that magazine audiences are like 'clubs' in that they are talking to people with a shared interest. This shared interest leads to a sense of belonging to the group, and as a result a sense of exclusivity is encountered by anyone not in 'the club'. This extends to the language used by the club and to the products owned (Hoyer and Macinnis, 1997). In many instances, these products are the outward sign of 'membership' of the club. If Kawasaki were advertising its bikes in *Ride* magazine, it would use very different language (e.g. What torque does the bike have? How much brake horsepower?) to that used in an advert in the *Evening Standard*.

Response

Because magazines are often kept by their readers, responses can come in months, and sometimes even years, after the advert was placed, often confusing the marketer who has moved onto another campaign!

Internal management

In common with the press, testing directly against a control is difficult, although this is partially overcome by A/B split run and cross-over testing (*see* Chapter 13).

One major disadvantage of magazines for direct response is the lead times typically required to place an advertisement; three to four months is typical, and so significant forward planning is required.

The end result

Cost per thousand is higher for magazines than for the national press, but the audience tends to be better defined, leading to higher response percentages and higher quality repeat purchasers. If you are after volume, then many titles can deliver large mass audiences too: women's magazines in particular having a readership of over 500 000 in many instances.

Table 11.2 summarises the strengths and weaknesses of using magazines for direct response.

Table 11.2: **Strengths and weaknesses of magazines**

Strengths	Weaknesses
Segment audience by interest	but high cost per thousand
Medium's halo effect; colour adds to brand/message	but still has creative limitations of press
Superior targeting to press	but longer lead times

Direct-response television

Direct-response television (DRTV) is the use of commercials on local or national television to generate a direct response.

When we come to compare media, quite simply, TV is different. As Nash (1995) said, nothing else permits the advertiser to demonstrate, prove and crucially, to *dramatise,* as well as TV. Let's dwell on this for a moment. How often to you hear people say 'I saw a great press ad yesterday' or 'Have you seen this mailer? Look at that offer!' But we do talk about TV commercials. This word of mouth, this pizzazz, is a unique facet of TV adverts and, if it is important to the business problem you are considering, should be included in any decision about media.

In 1994 Merit Direct wrote in its *Guide to Direct Response TV Advertising* that 'DRTV is an idea whose time has come'. In one way they were right: it is estimated that 40–50 per cent of all TV advertising now carries a response call of some sort – usually a web address or phone number. The Ogilvy Centre for Research and Development reported that US consumers have come to expect a response number at the end of their commercials, fuelling the push for more DRTV adverts. The UK is catching up. The 2002 spend on DRTV was estimated at £1384 million by the DMA (Census, 2003).

Since 1994 in another sense however, things have not happened as predicted. Classic DRTV advertising uses a very particular style that was pioneered by book and record clubs, and mail-order firms. Long adverts concentrated on the call to action straightaway, with the telephone number to call permanently displayed, and detailed descriptions and demonstrations of the product. These adverts remain a tiny minority of the whole. Meanwhile, the direct element of mainstream ads plays second place to their brand building content.

Nevertheless the recent upsurge in interest in the UK has brought renewed optimism in the future of DRTV as a response medium. Factors compelling greater use of DRTV include:

- the fragmentation of television channels in the UK: this means that UK direct marketers can more easily reach smaller, highly defined audiences; The Henley Centre forecasts six million cabled households and four to five million satellite dishes by the end of the decade;

- an increase in advertising for high price items, such as cars or financial services, which traditionally use more direct-marketing techniques than low price-ticket items (MEAL (Media Expenditure and Analysis Ltd), 1990–2000);

- an increasing push to make image advertising more accountable: one way to achieve this is through the inclusion of a response element in the advert;

- greater acceptance of the telephone as a way of purchasing goods: Cragg (1998) reports that more than 45 per cent of a TGI (Target Group Index) sample had made calls as a result of adverts seen in newspapers and on TV in 1998. Meanwhile early fears about websites' security have largely evaporated.

- greater use of computerised call-handling systems: this has led to lowered call-handling costs.

KEY AIMRITE QUALITIES

Audience

One of the big attractions of TV for image advertisers has been the massive audience coverage that the medium offers. Although TV advertising is often expensive in terms of its production costs and prices for airtime, in terms of cost per thousand of audience reached it is very cheap. TV cost per thousand is typically between £5–£12 per thousand, which compares very favourably with all the other media, except radio.

Targeting is less well defined than for most other media. If, say, you wanted to target 18- to 35-year-old 'AB' men who were interested in computers, you might advertise in the breaks of a Formula One sports programme, but this audience would still have a lot of non AB men who were not interested in computers. Targeting can therefore only be as accurate as the accuracy with which TV programme audiences are defined. Rather like two overlapping circles, it is almost impossible to get a TV spot which exactly matches the intended audience requirements. It is this which led Lord Leverhulme, the founder of Unilever, to say, 'I know half of my advertising is wasted, but I don't know which half.' The cost per thousand of *target* audience reached is therefore higher than the paid-for figure, which represents the cost per thousand of *total* audience.

EXHIBIT 11.5

MOVING DRTV FORWARD – CABLE AND WIRELESS

Up against the might of BT, Cable and Wireless made a huge success of its move into DRTV for acquisition. Helped by a good offer of 50p cap on weekend calls and free local calls, Cable spent less than £6 million in 1999 on the campaign, but achieved more than 600 000 responses. Response rates of 0.08 per cent were achieved, which for DRTV is considered excellent. Initially off-peak slots were used, which were further refined as the programme unfolded and analysis could be done on responders. Costs per response were reduced to about £5. This campaign proved to be one of the biggest acquisition campaigns in DRTV history, and has been an oft-quoted case study by those in the industry arguing for a shift in acquisition budgets towards more DRTV.

Source: adapted from DMA case study, 1999, www.dma.org.uk

Impact

Television is unique. It can arguably generate more impact than any other medium. If we consider the effect of popular campaigns such as 'I bet he drinks Carling Black Label' or the tiger from Frosties saying 'They' re grrrrrrrrrrreat!!', what we have is adverts which permeate the public conscious in a way that is unmatched by any other medium. There is also a sense, sometimes, that what is communicated on TV is somehow 'important' or 'true', a quality which media such as direct mail do not have. It also has both sound and vision, allowing it to make a more concerted effort on our senses. To summarise, the key impact values of TV are its *ability to generate word of mouth*, *authority* and *credibility*.

In spite of these attributes, DRTV still has relatively low usage as a direct marketing medium. The reasons for this centre on the difficulties of generating action from customers. These difficulties are discussed in the Response section.

Message

Television has powers of *persuasion* arguably unmatched by any other medium. The impact values previously described, along with TV's ability to demonstrate USPs and to show the product in action, make it a highly desirable medium to use for many products. On the negative side, however, it is impossible to leave any permanent reminder of how to respond.

As Kyffin (1994) points out, DRTV comes in a number of formats. Commercials vary from pure direct sell (which was begun in the late 1940s in the States with adverts that could be 30 minutes long!) through integrated brand and direct response commercials, to primarily brand-building commercials with a response number tagged onto the end. Renault's 'Nicole' series of adverts, while primarily brand builders, have also helped build a database of responders.

Charities find that DRTV works better for those which have an emotional message to get over. Typically children's or international distress charities do very well.

Response

One reason that TV is not used more as a direct-response medium is because customers watch it in a passive state. This is that quality which one notices when entering a room full of TV watchers: everyone looks half asleep, staring without expression at the box in the corner. This relaxed state means we are not in the active mode necessary for making purchase decisions.

To maximise the chances of prodding us into action, a number of 'rules' have been recommended after extensive testing. Tests carried out, particularly in the US in the 1980s (Young, 1994), found that for *pure direct sell*:

- a 90-second minimum length was recommended;
- the response mechanism should be on screen for at least 20 seconds, with voice-overs to repeat the number;
- coverage, rather than frequency, is sought by direct-response operators. Repeat showings of the advert to the same audience bring diminishing returns;
- 80 per cent of response comes within five minutes of the commercial appearing;
- profit is measured spot by spot rather than cumulatively;
- DRTV advertisers should run long adverts in low-cost airtime to low-volume audiences with low frequency. Brand advertisers on the other hand should run short adverts in higher-cost airtime to as big an audience as possible, with high frequency for multiple exposure.

EXHIBIT 11.6

HOME SHOPPING CHANNEL

Imagine flicking through your TV channels one day and coming across one where a man and a woman are discussing the most intimate details of a new product – the Kitchen Wizard. Throughout the broadcast, the price and a telephone number for ordering are shown on the bottom of the screen. Twenty minutes later, the advert is still running, you are still captivated by the number of applications for the Kitchen Wizard, and wonder whether it would make a good present for your mum.

This is home shopping on the QVC (Quality, Value and Convenience) channel.

Home shopping is less like direct-response TV and more like an electronic catalogue; in other words, it is equivalent to mail order off the screen. There have been a number of spectacular failures of this technique in the US and experience has suggested that to be successful, home shopping channels have to conform to quite specific rules.

Launched in 1993 on BSkyB, the uptake rate (the percentage of households with access who bought something) after two years was 9 per cent, which was better than the US average of 7 per cent. Daily calling volumes are 5000–8000 calls, and repeat rates are high.

By 2001, QVC was a global success story. With sales of $3.9 billion, it had 24 million customers worldwide, concentrated in the USA, UK, Germany and Japan. It now makes extensive use of the Web and e-mail response routes to supplement the TV-led approach. QVC are also expert direct marketers, with a full transaction database, including channel preference data.

Consumers tend to be 30–45, consist of slightly more females, and are skewed slightly downmarket. The product range is primarily jewellery, home products, and collectibles.

European mail-order giants are watching QVC's progress very carefully

A number of these 'rules' have been challenged recently by new users of the technique. One of the most spectacular successes was that of Tango, which ran adverts that had 0891 response numbers up for only three or four seconds. As part of a light-hearted campaign, consumers were invited to respond if they needed help in talking about their addiction to Apple Tango. The line received over 300 000 calls to one advert alone – an astonishing response!

EXHIBIT 11.7

DRTV: TRICKS OF THE TRADE

The following 'rules' are recommended in order to minimise cost per response (see Cragg, 1998 and Kyffin, 1994):

■ Go for lower TV rating spots, i.e. lower audiences at lower cost. Your responses will be more cost effective.
■ Just before *Brookside* started on Channel 4, its audience swelled by about 300 per cent as millions of people switched to Channel 4 from ITV. If your advert is last in the commercial break on Channel 4, it is likely to be seen by far more people than at the start of the break.
■ However, advertising just as the programme starts may lower response, as scrabbling about for a pen may mean missing the start of the show!
■ Don't place your direct-response advert during *Inspector Morse*. The propensity to respond

during drama programmes is low. The best programmes to include in your schedule are those on gardening or politics. This is certainly borne out in the difference of response efficiency between daytime slots (Index: 400) and prime evening slots (Index: 50) and between satellite channels and ITV – the converse of most brand campaigns.
■ People are more responsive at the beginning and the end of the week.
■ Editorial environment can be important in the same way as it is in the press. Matching your product to the programme can improve response.
■ Bob Stone (1996) says that a pure DRTV ad of 120 seconds will outpull a 60-second advert by more than two to one.
■ Response to the ad can be increased significantly depending on how the response phone number is

displayed. Make the number as prominent as possible, keep it on screen for as long as possible, and include at least one voice-over of the number. All of this can place severe restrictions on a creative team aiming to develop ads that build the brand.

■ The best DRTV ads are those that communicate a very good reason why the consumer should respond – not just emotionally but rationally. This can result in an 'aggressive' call to action that may jar with softer brand values.

Source: Kyffin, D. (1994) *Journal of Database Marketing*, 1 (4)

Internal management

Lead times are often long. One might expect at least 12 weeks from brief to execution, with production of the advert, rather than media buying, being the main time-consuming feature. Alternatively, using existing film and buying airtime at the last minute can cut down on both costs and time. At the extreme, some charity DRTV commercials have been made in just a few days for well under £10 000, and some adverts have been bought on satellite for only a few hundred pounds, or even placed free!

The other major headache is response management. Testing on a small scale should be done first to establish the likely scale of response. It is vital to get this right because the response comes in so quickly after the advert is screened. It is quite a sight to see an inbound centre, at first quiet, suddenly burst into frantic life seconds after an advert goes on air, with lights flashing showing the level of response, and people running around to cover any extra lines.

Responses must then be allocated to each station, region, and individual spot in order to analyse return on investment.

The end result

DRTV has excellent growth potential. The US experience of TV advertising suggests that the proportion of TV advertising which contains a response element can grow considerably. There have been instances of great success in the UK with direct response. Direct Line Insurance has built up a customer base of over two million since 1984, principally using direct-response techniques in which the TV has played a major part.

TV is cheap in cost per thousand terms, but response rates are unlikely to match even the press, and typically could be about 0.01 per cent or less for a direct-sell campaign. However, this could still be profitable, depending on the gross margin of the good being sold and the lifetime value of the resulting customer.

One area of direct-sell DRTV which has seen significant growth is the use of DRTV by charities to raise funds. Charities find that DRTV works better for those campaigns which have an emotional message to get over. One such charity is the NSPCC (National Society for the Prevention of Cruelty to Children), whose DRTV story is told in Exhibit 11.9.

'Double-duty' direct response

Within DRTV, this is probably the biggest area of growth. Advertisers are increasingly looking to build brands as well as obtain responses. Here, the return on investment is in two parts: the direct revenues obtained from the immediate response, and the long-term revenues acquired from brand goodwill that the advert is helping to generate.

EXHIBIT 11.8

EXAMPLE CALCULATION FOR DRTV PROFITABILITY

ITV's regions vary in size, but let us suppose we run a daytime commercial in the Central region, which comprises 7.3 million adults, selling a product with a gross margin (before marketing costs) of £100. The costs of advertising are £7300.

Assume the daytime spot is watched by 4 per cent of adults.

Audience is then 4% of 7.3m = 292 000 viewers. Assume an excellent response level of 0.05%.

No. of responses is therefore $\frac{0.05}{100} \times 292\,000 = 146$.

The cost per response is 7300/146 = £50. Therefore, a final margin of 100 − 50 = £50 per sale, is made.

EXHIBIT 11.9

THE STORY OF 'LITTLE ELLIE'

In 1992 a little girl, known as 'Ellie', became a national star as a result of the TV commercial created by the NSPCC's agency, WWAV.

The commercial contained all the classic elements of charity fundraising and DRTV. With emotional music as the backdrop to a high-impact message describing the plight of little Ellie, abandoned by her mother over Christmas and kept locked in a room on her own, only the most hard hearted would not be moved by the advert. 'The ask', as it is known in charities, was for £15 to help save a child's life. Using the old adage that 'the ad should be as long as it takes to sell your product', tests showed that 90 seconds was the optimum length of the Little Ellie commercial.

The results? According to the Charities Aid Foundation (1994), cold recruitment of donors by charities using any medium only obtained an ROI of 0.68:1. In other words, the initial recruitment typically loses money. Against this tough background, the Little Ellie commercial achieved a return of 1.8:1 at its height, and overall across all spots did better than break even.

Little Ellie went on to win Gold in the 1992 DMA/Royal Mail awards for best DRTV ad of the year, and regularly makes even hard-bitten students give a pound or two when shown in lecture halls up and down the country!

DRTV as support

Another role for DRTV is in its support of other media. Tests by a range of firms have shown that TV can significantly improve response. The *Reader's Digest* has tested supporting its annual prize draw mailing with a ten-second TV ad and found this continuously improved response to the mailing by 25 per cent over many years.

Weight Watchers supported its mailings to past members by TV, and these mailers in turn are co-ordinated with press advertising offering free membership to new members.

Table 11.3 summarises the strengths and weaknesses of direct-response television.

Table 11.3: **Strengths and weaknesses of direct-response TV**

Strengths	Weaknesses
Massive coverage at low cost per thousand	but low response rates
High powers of persuasion and credibility	but messages must be simple
Targeting improved with channel proliferation	but still difficult to reach prime upmarket audiences cheaply
Unrivalled ability to build brands and obtain response simultaneously	

Interactive television

Launched in 1998 in the UK, interactive TV has arrived for the long term. Interactive TV (iTV) already has over 18 million subscribers in Europe capable of accessing these facilities. Both Europe and some Asian markets are ahead of the US in the use of this media. Anyone with access to digital TV channels has the capability to use interactive services, often through the remote control. Services such as voting for pop stars, or watching football matches using personally chosen camera angles are now commonplace. Here, we are primarily interested in the potential of these services for shopping. This may take place through direct advertising, where the viewer is invited to press a red button on their remote while watching a conventional advert. They are then taken through a series of steps which may lead to a product trial, or sale. Shopping is also effected through direct shopping programmes, often on shopping channels. Here, entire programmes are dedicated to the sale of weird and wonderful goods and services, presumably for people with plenty of money and also plenty of time.

As we move towards 2005 and beyond, a lot of people are getting very excited about interactive TV. On the basis that TV has been the most successful advertising medium of all time, the feeling is that iTV could do the same for direct marketing. Indeed an

---

EXHIBIT 11.10

HOW ITV COULD CHANGE DIRECT MARKETING

Traditional model	New model
TV ad awareness	iTV ad awareness
Direct mail pack – puts offer into the hands of the customer	iTV ad – delivers information to the customer
Call centre and website pick up those who you seek out and handle real-time interaction	iTV – website can handle real-time interaction

Source: Fox and Burrows, 2001.

Admap article in 2001 asked whether 'Direct marketing would knock the spots off TV advertising?' (Fox and Burrows, 2001). They propose the possibility of a revolution that would change the whole face of DM communications (*see* Exhibit 11.10).

Their feeling was that iTV could be the catalyst for the complete combination of brand building and direct response, marking the end of the current supply side split between advertising and direct marketing agencies. In theory we have a sea of eager consumers interacting with brands that interest them, taking them through the initial advert via their remote to a new world of commerce. However, be careful: over-hype is the norm with new technology (*see* Exhibit 11.11 – Your 'home shopping' in 20 years' time: lean back or lean forward?).

ITV IN PRACTICE

One of the very interesting trends is the increasing link between predictive database marketing methods and iTV. Companies such as Ford are trialling self-selected adverts from a menu of options. Delta is now testing different creative approaches to different people depending on which segment they've been allocated to on a database. Procter and Gamble is advertising different products with the same TV spot, depending on a viewing database. The future promise for lifestyle data firms such as Claritas is interesting: they may be able to offer a kind of TV audience 'to order' to advertisers looking for a market definitely interested in, say, car insurance. Only those in the market would receive the ad.

Before we all get too carried away it should be noted that early attempts to use iTV were fraught with problems. Woolworth's, a UK retailer, closed its t-commerce centre in 2002, announcing troubles with its payback on the project. Anecdotal reports from innovators at Procter and Gamble suggests that it is not easy to get success from iTV. That said, FMCG manufacturers such as P&G are, it seems, having some success from their approaches to kids – games, puzzles and so on are enticing the children into participating. Products such as Fairy are experimenting with these approaches – it seems the mums are being educated by their young children into the interactive world of digital TV. It should also be noted that there are ethical issues here – as there always are in

---

EXHIBIT 11.11

YOUR 'HOME SHOPPING' IN 20 YEARS' TIME: LEAN BACK OR LEAN FORWARD?

In many respects iTV is a direct competitor of web-based Internet marketing. The battle between TV and the personal computer to see which will be the dominant home media continues. Of course, this battle may become less coherent as time goes on and computers and TVs start to resemble one another more and more. At the time of writing, Microsoft has just released a home entertainment system which is basically a hybrid of TV and computer. It is interesting to speculate what may happen: a Gallup poll in 2001 in the UK found 37 per cent of consumers said they'd prefer using a computer for home shopping, 32 per cent said they'd prefer using a digital TV, and 22 per cent said they would use neither for their shopping. The Internet has unrivalled search capability; TV is the superior interface for entertainment. The idea of TV as a 'lean back' media and the net as a 'lean forward' media has merit. Perhaps they both have a place yet – but as part of the same machine? We are just at the beginning of this technological path.

For more information the following websites are useful:

http://www.itvmarketer.com
http://www.itvt.com/

advertising to children. Ultimately legislation may be needed to catch up with these new possibilities, and the chance for exploitation of audiences.

It must also be remembered that while iTV is of interest to direct response marketers, the case for such approaches in brand building terms is less clear. Brands are public things – shared ways in which we communicate to one another. Hence the mass advertising model has worked well in creating a common language of brands. This is in danger if advertising breaks up into micro-markets because of over-precise targeting.

Inserts

Inserts are loose-leaf, bound-in or tipped-on paper/card leaflets carried by many papers, supplements and magazines. These carry a coupon or telephone response number.

Inserts are those things that cascade out of your Sunday paper like autumn leaves when you shake it on arriving home from the newsagent. A frequent mistaken belief of newcomers to direct marketing is that inserts don't work because they just get thrown in the bin. However, the facts are somewhat different.

Inserts, along with perhaps door drops and take ones, are one of those media which would scarcely get a mention from a general marketer, but which can form an important part of the direct marketer's armoury.

Inserts work because they draw attention to themselves before the reader has had a chance to be distracted by the editorial of the paper or magazine. At the very least they will usually be glanced at before being discarded, which is more than often happens with press advertising. *Bound-in* (to the spine of the publication) or *tipped-on* (glued) inserts tend to have even more impact; standing out of the page with their physical presence, they are a natural draw to the curious eye.

Inserts cost about £50 per thousand, with about £25/000 due to the charges made by the carrying media, and another £25/000 attributed to cost of production. Spend on inserts has grown hugely over the last few years, with well over £1 billion spent in the UK in 2002 (DMA Census, 2003), making it the fourth largest medium in spend terms. This growth can be attributed in the UK market to the growth of appropriate carriers – weekend supplements, more magazine titles, growth in men's market, etc.

EXHIBIT 11.12

HOTMAIL – FROM INSERT TO ONSERT

Microsoft wanted to launch its new Internet-based free e-mail service, Hotmail, to early adopters who read computer magazines. However many PC magazines were so thick there was a danger of a press ad or even an insert simply being overlooked. That's why it chose an 'onsert', spot glued to the front cover. Under the idea 'Freedom to be who you want to be', the ad was a small card with direct response details and room to write your own e-mail address. Hotmail had a powerful USP – users could design their own e-mail address. The response rate was 1.5 per cent, with 10 000 signing up. This is ten times typical response rates achieved with this medium.

Source: Adapted from DMA case study, 1999, www.dma.org.uk

KEY AIMRITE QUALITIES

Audience

Most national dailies and Sunday newspapers will take inserts, most commonly in their magazine supplements. Most trade and technical journals will happily carry loose inserts. Most large magazine titles will also take inserts, and of course the business press and magazines will too.

Audiences are therefore defined by readership of newspapers and magazines, discussed earlier in this chapter.

Impact

Inserts tend to have higher impact than press adverts, because of the way they attract attention to themselves. The downside is that many people are irritated by inserts, regarding them as 'junk'. Any research findings that proclaim unfavourable attitudes to inserts do need to be treated with care, however. There is almost universal claimed dislike of direct mail in the UK by the public, and yet their behaviour is different: people respond, and in sufficient numbers to make mail a successful medium. The same is true of inserts.

Message

The insert has much of the flexibility of direct mail and door drops, in that different colours, shapes and sizes can be used, and there is room for a lot of information to be included. Response devices and even envelopes are often included as items within the standard insert format. These advantages give the insert superiority over the press advert or broadcast medium in terms of the volume of information that can be carried.

One variation of inserts is the use of product samples, with offers attached requiring a response. Packaged goods companies make use of this facility. Inserts can be used where colour is essential to the message but barred in the press.

Response

Responding to inserts is relatively easy. As a consumer, you are probably in the house when you read the insert, giving you chance to respond. You can save the insert until you want to get around to responding; whereas a radio ad cannot be saved! The only easier-to-respond media are the telephone (instant and verbal) and mail (personalised and therefore the response coupon is often filled in for you).

One feature of inserts is that they are sometimes kept by consumers for reference and can still pull responses months later.

Internal management

Inserts are very good for testing. Happily, a printer can cope with as many inserts as you wish to run with. An unlimited number of formats can be tested for a title, although Goodwin (1992) recommends testing only up to a maximum of six at a time, in order to control events.

One reason inserts are popular with direct marketers is their physical flexibility for use in different settings. Bird (1989) described inserts as 'the chameleon of the business, because they can be used in so many ways and can appear in so many guises'. Inserts often double up as brochures within mailers, and are also used as take ones or door drops. Needless to say, this saves on costs of creation and production, and avoids wastage.

The end result

Inserts nearly always attract more response than press advertising, although this is counterbalanced by their higher cost per thousand. The Educators' Guide (1996) reports insert costs at usually four to five times those of press ads (£50–60 per thousand against £10 per thousand for off-the-page national press), but inserts are often more than five times more responsive (typically 0.1–0.5 per cent against 0.02–0.1 per cent for press). Stone (1996) reports that a printed ad with a bind-in card will outperform the same ad without a bind-in insert by up to 600 per cent.

Many organisations base their entire acquisition media strategy around inserts. The Institute of Direct Marketing, which ought to know, uses inserts as its major medium when recruiting new students for its Diploma programme, and claims responses of over 1 per cent in relevant business media.

EXHIBIT 11.13

INSERTS CASE STUDY: CITROËN UK

In 1995, Citroën was keen to generate prospects for its full range of cars in the UK, in a bid to improve market share. Part of the overall communications strategy was a big brand-building campaign led by TV in the first six months of the year. The direct-response element was an insert campaign, aimed at gathering data from respondents about their current car ownership and intended car-purchase habits.

Citroën asked its agency to develop a new insert, which was tested using the existing insert as a control. The new insert had a creative treatment 'Skunk' in which the creative revealed, 'Roger's car didn't turn out to be quite the animal he'd expected. In fact it turned out to be a real stinker.' The copy claimed that replacing the car with a Citroën would be 'a breath of fresh air'.

The offer was a free prize draw to win a top-of-the-range Citroën Xantia, in return for information sent in on the response device.

The inserts were placed in weekend press supplements. The new insert was 36 per cent more cost-effective per response than the control, generating over 30 000 qualified responses for Citroën.

It was believed that the use of humour and a visual image uncommon in car advertising contributed to the campaign's success.

Source: Precision Marketing, 1995.

Precision Marketing reported a Sun Alliance campaign that obtained a 0.3 per cent response to its insert announcing the launch of its new mortgage product in 1992.

Table 11.4 summarises the strengths and weaknesses of using inserts for direct response.

Table 11.4: **Strengths and weaknesses of inserts**

Strengths	Weaknesses
More impact than press	but seen as 'junk'
More creative freedom than press	but production requirement means longer lead times than press
Overall: medium responsiveness at medium cost per thousand	

Household delivery/door-to-door distribution

Household delivery or door-to-door distribution is the targeted distribution of unaddressed leaflets or packages through the letterbox.

Door drops are *unaddressed* leaflets packages delivered through the letterbox. Wells (2002) describes door-to-door distribution as 'the direct marketer's secret weapon'. This is because door-to-door delivery has tended to be overlooked as part of a media mix by most companies, but for those who do use it, door dropping has tended to be very cost-effective. The media offers creative freedom delivered direct to the customer's home.

Door drops are distributed in the UK by specialist distribution companies such as Circular Distributors, the Leaflet Company or the Royal Mail's Household Delivery Service.

It is sometimes claimed that door drops offer most of direct mail's advantages but at a lower cost. With no postage to pay and no list to buy, the distribution cost can be as low as one tenth that of mailers. It is certainly true that the use of door drops is growing, and stood at £233 million (DMA Census, 1996) in 1995 in the UK, up 13 per cent on the previous year. The DMA concluded from its figures that door-to-door distribution grew faster than direct mail in the 1990s.

Nevertheless, door drops do have notable disadvantages compared with direct mail. Targeting door drops is clearly less accurate than for direct mail, being based on geodemographic (and/or lifestyle) profiles rather than individual addresses. It is this broader targeting which usually leads to lower responses than with mail. As a result, Bird (1989) recommends that only those companies which have products of fairly universal appeal should use door drops.

EXHIBIT 11.14

USING YELLOW TO STAND OUT

The land line domestic telephone market had come to be dominated by price by 1999. Telephone use being so widespread made door-to-door a natural choice of media for Cable and Wireless, particularly as it wanted to control the geographical area it advertised in. It used a strong yellow-coloured drop to stand out on the doormat.

The message made use of extensive research that found people needed clarity in a complex market. The theme was 'let's simplify things', with further messages appealing to well off people about 'being in control'. The drop acquired customers at a cost of under £7 per response, an excellent result.

Source: Adapted from DMA case study, 1999, www.dma.org.uk

KEY AIMRITE QUALITIES

Audience

If your desired target audience can be accurately described geographically, then door drops may well be your best medium. You can also target on postcode sectors that average 2500 households. However, if you want to be more precise, increasing use is being made of geodemographic and lifestyle-based targeting methods, occasionally making use of profiled areas of less than 400 households, in return for a higher fee. Individual targeting – picking discrete addresses for the drop – is not cost-effective and is therefore not offered as a service.

Door drops are used by firms for which locality is important: the local branches of services such as grocers, pizza delivery, or local hairdressers spring to mind. However, big players also use door drops in certain circumstances, for example if distributing a sample of a fairly universal product. Persil dropped 11 million samples of Persil Power washing powder when it was launched in 1995.

Cable TV and telephone companies use door drops extensively as a part of their marketing effort to sign up customers once a street has had cable installed. The initial targeting for cable companies is based on profiling their existing customers according to geodemographic characteristics, and then using companies such as CACI or Experian to help them find similar streets.

If your audience is described best in purely lifestyle terms, for example 'young women who enjoy outdoor pursuits', then door-to-door targeting is likely to be less effective. You may be better off choosing magazines, or using direct mail on rented external lists from lifestyle database companies.

Impact

Again we have a medium which would get 'a panning' in research. One can almost hear indignant citizens recounting horror stories of ever increasing 'junk' coming though their doors morning, noon and night. Naturally, they will vehemently deny *ever* having responded or made any use whatsoever of such material. Yet the fact remains that, on average, far more people respond to door-to-door leaflets than will act on a TV commercial!

People tend to notice door drops, pick them up and look at them. The 'impact' value of a door drop is therefore high.

EXHIBIT 11.15

KNOCK AND DROP

This amusing phrase refers to the practice of field-workers knocking on doors, asking a qualifying question about brand usage, and dropping a product sample or coupon accordingly (Sleight, 1993). Sometimes questionnaires are completed on product and brand usage for subsequent analysis.

These practices greatly decrease the wastage of door-drop targeting through broad geodemographic categories, but at a cost. The payoff may be worthwhile if the objective is to build a database, or if the product sample or coupon is of high value.

Message

Once again, the big advantage of this medium compared with general advertising media is its ability to carry large amounts of information. In addition, although a lot of door drops are of standard C5 brochure style, practically anything goes, provided it can be posted through a letterbox. Promotional items in the shape of the product are very popular with grocery firms (Wells, 2002).

Compared with TV, magazines or even direct mail, door drops do not imbue much natural authority. People do not say 'Well that door drop I received today said so, so it must be true'. This may be one reason why traditional brand advertisers are often reluctant to use it as a technique.

However, door-drop messages can be personal, even intimate. 'Singles clubs' tend to use door drops to recruit new members. Cards are dropped which ask people to fill in half a dozen simple questions such as 'Do you have lots of friends but no one very special?'. On returning the card, these people are then targeted directly using mail.

Door-to-door is an important medium for distributing free samples. FMCG sectors in particular make extensive use of door-drop sampling. Wells (2002) told of the story of Gillette's use of door-drop sampling to launch its Excel Sensor disposable razor. A two-day variant on the knock and drop technique was used, leading to a 42 per cent response rate. Not surprisingly, response rates to free samples are often in the 30–70 per cent range.

Response

Response devices are typically integral to the door drop, and the issues match those recorded earlier for inserts. Mailers are superior in one respect: the response device can be personalised, thereby reducing the effort customers need to make to act.

Internal management

One of the criticisms of door-to-door distribution is its reputation for variable quality control. The industry does suffer from tales of skips being found with thousands of leaflets fluttering within instead of sitting on customers' coffee tables.

EXHIBIT 11.16

BRITISH TELECOM – A CASE STUDY

British Telecom (BT) organised a door drop around the theme of the introduction of the smaller 10p coin in 1993. The line was 'The new 10p may be getting smaller, but you still get three minutes of local call time at peak rate'. The door drop had the objective of raising awareness of the low cost of local calls. A tricky issue to overcome was the need to cover the *'local call area'*, which did not tally with postcodes, the normal way of distributing door drops. The two maps had to be superimposed and a boundary set up. In the event, local paper deliverers were used to distribute the door drop alongside the free sheets. Back-checking was used by a distribution company manager to ensure the drop actually took place.

Subsequent market research found that the insert raised awareness of BT's local call charges by over 40 per cent in the Manchester test area, compared with controls.

Quality control, then, needs to be stringent, and industry suppliers will routinely use the practice of back-checking to maintain quality standards. This is where a manager will follow on behind a door drop and check with a sample of each street that they actually received the drop. The manager will obtain signatures from the sample to that effect.

These quality problems are not an issue with Royal Mail's Household Delivery Service, which also has the advantage of delivering in the morning with the post. However, its relative weakness compared with the other players is its long lead times – often a number of weeks after receipt of the order.

Apart from quality control, we need to consider testing. In fact, testing of door drops is quite easy. The target area can be split into geodemographically similar regions, and different executions of the drop tested. Alternatively, the same households can be tested at different times, allowing a suitable period to elapse between drops.

The end result

Bird (1989) reported a test carried out by the *Reader's Digest* comparing door drops with direct mail. The door drops were found to be 52 per cent less effective, which is at the top end of normal door-drop performance; a financial services client might be delighted with 0.1 per cent response.

As a rule of thumb, door drops will cost from £40–£250 per thousand, and may typically give about 0.1–1 per cent response, depending on product category, offer, and so on, provided the campaign is well thought out.

EXHIBIT 11.17

DOOR-TO-DOOR DISTRIBUTION ACROSS SECTORS

Charities

Door drops are difficult for charities to make work, because workers have found that personalisation is very important in this sector. One charity which did overcome this was the Salvation Army, which in 1991 tried door drops for the first time and achieved a return of 1.21:1 against a break-even target. The charity went out at its prime fundraising period, just before Christmas, to ABC1 households over 35 years old.

Packaged goods companies

Sampling tends to be very cost-effective using this medium. Nestlé organised a Gourmet cat and Friskies dog food sample drop to 12 million households. Occupants were screened at the time of the drop to identify dog and cat owners. The aim of the drop was trial and encouraging repeat purchase, but a major secondary objective was the gathering of millions of names from the exercise to put onto a database of dog and cat owners. Redemption of coupons is higher (at about 12 per cent) with door-dropped coupons than with those through magazines and newspapers (2–3 per cent).

Publishing

The *European* newspaper used door drops of a free sample of the *European* to 50 000 homes in affluent areas of London with an ABC1 profile and homes of over £200 000. As a result of this campaign, further refinements to the target profile were made to get tighter targeting. The estimate was that less than 10 per cent of the originally targeted homes were potential *European* readers (European context businesspeople). In the event, just under 1 per cent took up the offer of subscription at a reduced rate, compared with 3 per cent for a London City Airport sampling campaign run at the same time.

Source: Precision Marketing, 1993

Table 11.5 summarises the strengths and weaknesses of using door drops for direct response.

Table 11.5: **Strengths and weaknesses of door-to-door distribution**

Strengths	Weaknesses
Lower cost per thousand than direct mail	but lower responses
Same creative versatility as direct mail	but not personalised
High impact compared with broadscale media	but lumped with 'junk mail'
Better targeting than inserts	but lacks double-duty brand building

Direct-response radio

Direct-response radio comprises adverts placed on commercial radio stations which invite a direct response.

Radio shares a few of TV's broadcast attributes. It can generate word-of-mouth debate, and pizzazz, although not often to the degree that TV is able to. Nevertheless, this should not be underestimated: radio commercials can offer publicity and credibility, and these need to be considered as part of its set of attributes for direct-response work.

While overall radio has grown with DR spend up to £545 million in 2002 (DMA Census, 2003), since 2000 there has been a drop off of the proportion of ads carrying response mechanisms. Radio is always likely to be a support medium rather than lead medium for any DR campaign, given the difficulty of retaining the details of response numbers.

In general, there is an upward trend in the use of radio by advertisers, because:

■ it's cheap! You can reach a radio audience for about £2 per thousand, making it the cheapest of all the major media;

■ it has a higher ABC1 catchment than is typically thought. A lot of upmarket individuals listen to commercial radio on their way to and from work;

■ radio has been found to work very well with other media, increasing the response to media such as direct mail;

■ the volume of commercial radio stations available has grown tremendously; at the time of writing there are over 300 UK stations, including national coverage from Virgin, Classic FM, Talk Radio and Kiss FM. Regional stations such as Capital in London and BRMB in Birmingham have large audiences in their own right.

However, it is likely that there will always be a limited growth in direct-response radio, because of the difficulties in responding, which are discussed in the Response section.

EXHIBIT 11.18

'YEEEEEEEEEEEEEEEEEEEEESSSSSSSSSS! WE'VE SCORED!!!'

As always Vodafone was on the lookout for services it could offer to reduce the churn rate of its existing customers.

One such idea was the football text service – for 30p per message you can receive texts informing you of goals and scorers during the match.

Radio was a smart choice of medium for this service because of its symbiosis with football fans. They stay close to a radio during match days, and the creative could come alive with the excitement of a goal well portrayed by radio. Humour was well used, which in turn generated other PR. Over 6000 customers signed up in the first month of the campaign.

Source: adapted from DMA case study, 1999, www.dma.org.uk

KEY AIMRITE QUALITIES

Audience

A major characteristic of commercial radio audiences is that they are often young. Young people are typically notoriously difficult to reach through media: they are not on external lists, they don't read newspapers, they don't watch much TV. They do, however, listen to music channels on the radio, and are sympathetic to appropriately creative adverts aimed at them. Mail-order music companies, financial services, charities, and retail are all big users of direct-response radio, in order to attract the youthful audience.

Bird (1989) recommends advertising in off-peak times, on the grounds that anyone listening to radio at 2 am has nothing else to do except reply to your offer!

Local commercial radio has an audience defined primarily by geography. It therefore appeals, not surprisingly, to local businesses.

Impact

Generally, the impact of one radio advert is quite low, and is only made up for by repetition. Radio is often a background medium: one that people often listen to while doing something else.

Message

Taking in information purely aurally is harder than taking it in visually. Radio adverts should therefore be stimulating, to get our attention, and contain a simple, *short* message that is easy to internalise. As Nash (1995) said, 'broadcast is impatient'.

Repeating adverts is universal in radio, the opposite of direct-response press or TV. Repetition is cheap, and it's essential in order to get the advert noticed. The best users of the medium will, however, vary their creative to give a number of different adverts. This is recommended (Ingram, 2002) in order to avoid irritation with hearing the same advert time and again, hour after hour. In fact most stations will not let you buy spots in more than two consecutive slots to minimise irritation from repetition.

Response

If someone tells you a phone number, the chances are you will have difficulty remembering it an hour later. As Nash (1995) points out, radio is perishable. It can't be torn out or read carefully at a more convenient time.

One tactic that works well with this medium is to use it as *support* for other media, in particular websites. Raising awareness of an offer using radio, then ending with 'look out for more details in the press/mail', makes the most of radio's strengths – the publicity factor of broadcast – and minimises its main weakness – response.

If you do need to go for direct sell, then freephone numbers that are easy to remember are a great asset. An excellent example was the ingenious Guardian Direct telephone number, based on its logo, an owl. The number is 0800 28 28 20, with an owl hooting 'too-whit too-whit too-woo' in tandem with the number!

Internal management

Lead times are very short with radio – a major advantage if you are in a hurry. An ad can be created, recorded and out on air within days if necessary, although wise counsel may prevail and more time be spent, in particular to get the creative right.

Buying radio ad time is time consuming. There are 300 stations in the UK and each will have different prices. It's best to use specialist buyers.

Testing is difficult (except for tests of different areas of the country, which are easy), as most commercial radio stations are geographically based and discrete from one another. Each station therefore attracts a unique audience, not matchable with other audiences in an accurate way. Time of day and day of week are also worth testing. Peak radio listening is in the mornings, with troughs in the evenings. Weekends often attract higher percentage responses than weekdays, but from lower audiences.

The end result

Radio is excellent at getting large coverage for a business's message cheaply, and in a way which can generate word of mouth. Response rates using radio are very low compared with other media, but cost per response can be competitive. If you pay £2 per thousand of audience reach, a response of 0.001 per cent will mean you have obtained one response for £50, which is roughly on a par with typical performances of other media.

Some of the success stories of this often undervalued medium are highlighted in Exhibit 11.19.

Table 11.6 summarises the strengths and weaknesses of direct-response radio.

Table 11.6: **Strengths and weaknesses of direct-response radio**

Strengths	Weaknesses
Wide coverage cheaply obtained	but low response
Good public medium	but simple messages only
Good support medium	but needs creative to vary or risk annoyance

EXHIBIT 11.19

RADIO CAN BE SUCCESSFUL

With radio, practitioners recommend building up pictures in the listener's mind with words. One example of this was an advert by Feed the Children, an international distress agency. It interviewed one of its senior directors who had been in Rwanda in the crisis there in 1995, and used this to convey a strong 'in the front line' feel. A picture of what it was like at that time in Rwanda was quickly built up, and this was used in the 90-second radio advert.

More than £600 000 was raised, with costs being only a fraction of this figure.

The *Practitioners' Guide to Direct Marketing* (1992) reports on a radio commercial aimed at getting blood donors to respond. A test resulted in 1041 responses, compared with 79 in a control area without radio.

New or unusual media

A number of other media are in use for direct-response marketing. These include some strange alternatives, such as underground tickets, Automatic Teller Machines (ATMs), the sides of cows in fields near motorways, the back of beer mats, balloons, and so on. Just a few of the media are now discussed.

ELECTRONIC KIOSKS

Now becoming more common in the United States than in Europe, electronic kiosks were originally brought to prominence by Don Peppers as a fast way of delivering a one-to-one/mass customisation strategy (Peppers and Rogers, 1993). How do they work? One can imagine a consumer, say a mother and small child, shopping for a wedding present. Rather than standing around for a long time in the shopping complex with a tired baby, our shopper can use a kiosk linked to a large department store. The 'wedding registry' allows her to quickly and conveniently choose and purchase her present.

There are a number of advantages to both retailers and customers of kiosks. The retailer can more closely control their inventory. Kiosks allow consumers the chance to browse through the entire product line, whether or not the store carries the product. Some customers prefer to search electronically then buy face-to-face: in this sense kiosks are a mixture of 'bricks and clicks'. The trick with electronic kiosks is to become part of the fabric of everyday out-and-about shopping. If consumers can see a benefit – say saving time in searching for products – they are attracted to use this media. By entering their details, customers are potentially opening the door to more direct marketing opportunities, with their permission, of course.

Across the US, kiosks can be found in local gyms, where members can order vitamins, nutritional supplements and other fitness-related products, at cinemas, and even mundane stuff such as grocery shopping and buying fuel have been impacted by kiosks, which have been set up as automated checkout machines at many locations.

FAX MACHINES

Dowell and Associates Advertising (D&AA) used the fax very effectively as a response mechanism for a business-to-business mailer in 1995. On targeting competitors' clients with a message suggesting they should contact D&AA for better service, 60 per cent contacted the company by fax compared with 40 per cent by phone. D&AA claimed that fax was very popular because customers were often put off the phone as a way of responding, fearing the hard sell. Having a fax response sheet avoided this, while still being an immediate and convenient response device.

ON-PACK PROMOTIONS

Fast-moving consumer goods companies such as Pedigree Petfoods will offer coupons offering money off multi purchase, thereby encouraging loyalty. These are redeemable to the company direct, allowing it to collect names and addresses. A database of loyal customers is then built up.

EVENTS

Many cigarette manufacturers have representatives who give out free samples in night clubs, asking first if the recipient is a smoker. They then gather names and addresses, and signatures, which they require by law in order to mail these prospects subsequently.

SELL DURING 'HOLD' ON INBOUND TELEPHONE CALLS

According to Simon Roncorroni, a leading UK consultant, this is an undervalued opportunity in the UK. The experience of Rapp and Collins (1987) in the US supports him. For example, they report that Polaroid once generated a 16–20 per cent response from its promotions on 'hold tapes'.

Combining media to maximise efficiency: the contact strategy

Direct marketers often need to combine media in a multi-contact programme which makes sense to customers over time, rather than expecting them to plough their way through a set of unrelated campaigns. Putting together a combination of media is often known as a *contact strategy*.

Contact strategies can vary, depending on the situation, from single contact to many contacts over time. Examples are given in Figs 11.1 and 11.2.

GUIDELINES FOR CHOOSING A CONTACT STRATEGY

The *Educators' Guide to Direct Marketing* (1996) outlines the following key areas to take into account:

1 **Expense of the product.** If the product is expensive, consumers are likely to need a multiple contact approach: they are less easily parted from their money! More communication is needed.

2 **Complexity of the product.** Particularly complex products may need communication to the consumer in stages to avoid overloading them with information. It may be that multiple decisions by the consumer need to be made: in this instance, they may need to be guided through slowly. Products such as personal pensions would fit this category.

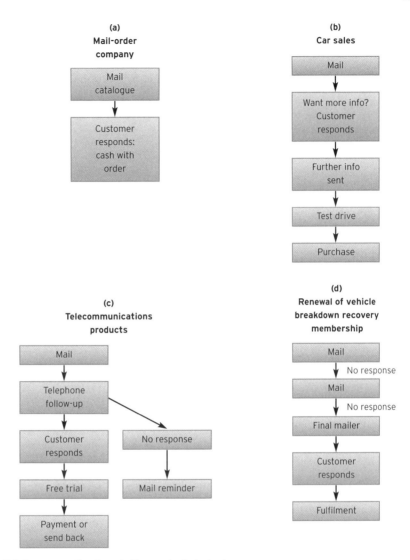

Figure 11.1 Consumer direct marketing contact strategies

3 **The need for reassurance.** Here, the remoteness of selling direct presents a problem. People need reassurance in lots of different ways: prior recommendation, well-known brands, and guarantees. Free trial offers may be the answer, adding another stage to the contact programme. Household goods, say stereo equipment, may fit here.

4 **Demonstrations.** The need for demonstrations would add to the number of required communications to the customer. If you are selling cars, for example, you will invite customers to test drive your vehicles, then perhaps follow up with more information and offers.

5 **Cost versus payback.** This should always be the final consideration. Total contact costs need to be calculated and assessed against gross margins obtained to ensure that the desired profit is made. There is a trade-off, of course: the more contacts you make, the more prospects you will convert to customers. So both costs and revenues will rise. The amount of contact needs to be fine tuned so that profits are maximised. This will usually come down to testing different approaches.

Selling photocopiers to large businesses

Figure 11.2 Business-to-business contact strategies

In addition to these five areas of consideration, there is the need to acknowledge the different contact strategy that a relationship approach would engender, compared with a traditional 'programme' approach.

Relationship approach versus campaign approach

As was discussed in detail in Chapters 5 and 7, there is a strategic decision to be made: are you better off running marketing programmes in a discrete way, with separate programme objectives through the year? Or is it a better idea to manage customers rather than campaigns, and look at each customer's marketing in relationship terms? More and more companies are starting to use the latter approach, and this does have an impact on how they conduct a dialogue with customers.

It is useful to compare both approaches, using a detailed example. Figures 11.3 and 11.4 contrast how a car manufacturer might contact its customers, depending on whether they are 'campaign' (Fig. 11.3) or 'relationship' (Fig. 11.4) oriented.

Commentators like Peppers and Rogers (1993) would argue that the relationship approach (Fig. 11.4) is superior because it is organised around customers and acknowledges their particular circumstances. For example, it acknowledges where they are on the buying cycle for the car, and each communication is likely to be much more relevant as a result.

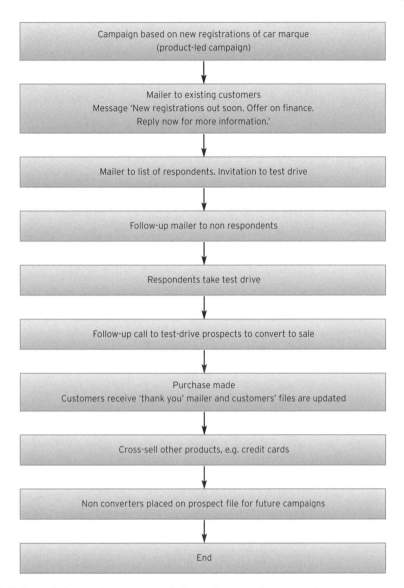

Figure 11.3 Contact strategy for a car manufacturer: the campaign approach

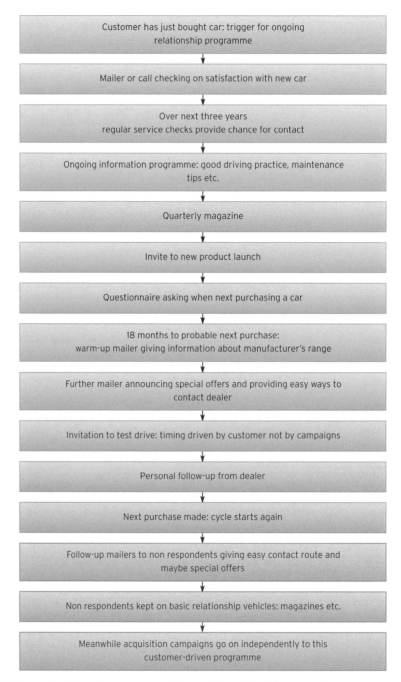

Figure 11.4 Contact strategy for a car manufacturer: the relationship approach

Summary to chapter

In this chapter we explored the press, inserts, door-to-door distribution, TV, radio and some new types of media in depth, using the AIMRITE formula introduced in Chapter 10. While press remains popular, the split in channel options is fuelling a fast growth in DRTV. Direct-response TV may well continue to grow as companies look for double-duty brand building and response generation.

Questions

1. Comfy Bedrooms is a leading manufacturer of designer bedrooms. It visits individual households and offers proposals on bedroom design. The company needs a continual feed of sales leads. What acquisition media should it consider? Use the AIMRITE formula to decide on the best candidates to test.

2. Compare and contrast the relative merits of door drops and inserts. Which would be the probable better bet for a pizza-delivery firm advertising in a small town?

3. Draw up a relationship-based contact strategy for a firm selling fax machine solutions to large businesses. Integrate your media solutions with the firm's salesforce activities.

4. Bell's Scotch Whisky has decided to start building up a database and intends using DRTV as its prime name generation medium. Outline the main benefits of DRTV to Bell's, and explain what practical considerations it needs to take in using TV to obtain response.

5. A dog-food supplier decides to use a door drop 'knock and drop' programme to distribute two million coupons nationwide. Explain what media alternatives it should have also considered, and assess whether they would be likely to achieve a better return than door drops.

References

Bilton, K. (1994) *A Guide to Direct Response Television Advertising*, Merit Direct, UK.

Bird, D. (1989) *Commonsense Direct Marketing*, Kogan Page, London.

Cockburn, C. and Wilson, T. (1996) 'Business use of the World Wide Web', *International Journal of Information Management*, **16** (2).

Cragg, P. (1998) 'Can DRTV get results and build brands', *Admap*, March.

Cross, D. (1997) article in the *Observer*, 4 May.

Davenport, H. (1996) 'Marketing on the Internet', *Journal of Targeting, Measurement and Analysis*, **4** (3), pp. 261–9.

Davis, T. (1992) Diploma lecture, Institute of Direct Marketing, Teddington, Richmond-upon-Thames.

Direct Marketing Education Programme (1995) Institute of Direct Marketing, Teddington.

DMA Census (1995, 1996, 2003) Direct Marketing Association, London.

Educators to Direct Marketing (1996) *Educators' Guide*, Institute of Direct Marketing, Teddington.

Fox, N. and Burrows, O. (2001) 'Direct marketing will knock the spots off TV advertising', Admap, March, pp. 31–6.

Goodwin, J. (1992) 'Inserts: Press advertising with direct mail appeal' in Halsey, B. (ed.) *The Practitioners' Guide to Direct Marketing*, Institute of Direct Marketing, Teddington.

Halsey, B. (ed.) (1992) *The Practitioners' Guide to Direct Marketing*, Teddington, UK.

Hoyer, W. and Macinnis, D. (1997) *Consumer Behaviour*, Houghton Mifflin, New York.

Ingram, A. (2002) 'Responsive radio', *The Interactive and Direct Marketing Guide*, IDM, Teddington, Richmond-upon-Thames.

Kyffin, D. (1994) 'The assessment of a direct response television campaign', *Journal of Database Marketing*, **1** (4).

Nash, E. (1995) *Direct Marketing: Strategy, planning, execution*, 3rd edn, McGraw-Hill, New York.

O'Connor, G. (1995) 'Delivering solutions for marketing on the Internet', *Edge work group computing report*, **6** (290), p. 10.

Ogilvy Centre for Research and Development (1993) Research paper, New York.

Peppers, D. and Rogers, M. (1993) *The One-to-One Future*, Piatkus, USA.

Rapp, S. and Collins, T. (1987) *Maximarketing*, McGraw-Hill, New York.

Sleight, P. (1993) *Targeting Customers*, NTC Publications, Henley-on-Thames, Oxfordshire, UK.

Stone, B. (1996) *Successful Direct Marketing Methods*, 5th edn, NTC Business Books, Chicago, Ill.

Tapscott, L. (1995) *The Digital Economy: Promise and peril in the age of networked intelligence*, McGraw-Hill, Maidenhead, Berkshire.

Wells, N. (2002) 'Door-to-door, now with new improved targeting', *The Interactive and Direct Marketing Guide*, IDM, Teddington, Richmond-upon-Thames.

Young, M. (1994) 'Direct response television', *Journal of Targeting, Measurement and Analysis*, **2** (2), pp. 125–38.

The Economist

Founded as far back as 1843, *The Economist* is a weekly publication of international reputation. Now owned by the Pearson Group, with markets all over the world, sales showed strong growth throughout the 1980s. By the early 1990s the only problem was the slow pace of growth in the UK, one of *The Economist's* key markets. To overcome this, it was decided to focus on increasing the number of direct subscribers, as opposed to retail buyers.

The Economist was aimed at businesspeople who wanted breadth and depth in their knowledge of world affairs. Its competitors were other business papers and international magazines such as *Time* or *Newsweek*.

The target audience of businesspeople was an important part of the publication's success. A high proportion of profits came from the magazine's own advertising revenue. The profile of the readership was:

- 90% male
- AB social class
- over 60% with university degree
- income of £20 000 plus
- a mix of older, well-established businesspeople, and younger, ambitious executives who see *The Economist* as aspirational and a reflection of their self image.

The positioning of *The Economist* was powerful: 'Reading this paper regularly can give you the edge over other businesspeople.' Brand building was considered vital and obtained a lot of support. The agency, Abbott Mead Vickers, utilised witty copy that avoided talking down to the audience, backed with the distinctive red and white artwork.

The marketing people had been using primarily direct-marketing techniques to attract new prospects. A lot of early success had been achieved with direct mail, especially with lists of top business school graduates and exchange lists with other publishers. But more recently they had resorted to less appropriate lists and had to offer greater discounts to obtain responses. As a result, acquisition costs were steadily rising and were now above the target allowable marketing spend per new customer.

There was now a need to branch out from these media, and with this brief, the marketing team prepared to put together a media test, with promising programmes to be rolled out in the next planning period.

Question

Using the AIMRITE formula, construct a media test plan, justifying each medium choice.

Choosing media - Xerox

This case study is courtesy of Xerox and Harrison Troughton Wunderman, and is an accurate portrayal of the events surrounding the launch of a new colour printer copier in 2002. However, the targets and budgets for the subsequent media campaign have been adjusted for commercial reasons.

Harrison Troughton Wunderman

Client: Xerox
Campaign name: Gavin Turk Event

The Xerox DocuColor 1632/2240 ('Carrera') launch event is a stunning example of innovative creative thinking.

In 2002, Xerox launched its new brand idea of 'Work Transformation'. The intention was to shift perceptions of Xerox from that of solely a box provider, to that of a vibrant and dynamic solutions and services-led IT organisation.

In autumn 2002, Xerox was launching 'Carrera', a high-quality range of affordable colour-printer-copiers. Extensive research had shown that high running costs presented a barrier to colour adoption in many offices. However, the Carrera range finally presented an affordable high-quality-colour machine with low running costs; an attractive prospect to many offices that had been previously unable to inject impactful colour into their business communications.

Xerox saw the launch of the DocuColor 1632/2240 as an opportunity to support the new brand idea, while creating a launch event that was bigger than a standard product launch, providing a positive brand experience as part of the total communications strategy.

Xerox was targeting businesses which needed colour copiers. In fact this represented a very wide audience, but Xerox also envisaged some sectors – design, creative and media sprang to mind – as being of particular interest for this product.

The launch theme HTW used to dramatise the creative proposition 'Quality colour at a price you can afford' was 'affordable colour'. This was an effective tool to dramatise cost effectiveness, availability to all and convey the quality-colour message.

The recommended event idea took 'affordable colour' into the world of art. The idea was to set up a Xerox Carrera printer-copier outside a prominent art gallery, and have a popular artist copy one of his paintings/drawings and sell it to the public for the price of a colour copy, roughly 10p.

Art has a perceived high value and with the creative concept, Xerox was giving it to people at a low cost, the analogy being that colour in the office had previously been a luxury and Xerox was now making it affordable.

HTW commissioned the YBA (Young British Artist) Gavin Turk, who created an original piece of artwork. Gavin Turk was a perfect fit, as he is constantly pushing the boundaries of art, and is a dynamic, driving force within the UK art scene. It was arranged that Gavin could appear at Tate Britain. There, for 45 minutes only, he used the Xerox DocuColor 2240 to make colour copies of his work and copies were good enough to be the original. Then he signed and sold them for the rough price of the colour copy – just 10p. To publicise the event, HTW created a press ad and a poster. The agency also mailed postcards to journalists, and handed them out in art student/trendy bars. Hundreds of people queued for hours (*see* Figure 11.5 on p. 380). Press photographers from the *Financial Times*, the *Daily Telegraph*, *The Times* and *The Independent* were there.

By delivering affordable art to the masses, Xerox dramatised the core benefit of the product, while supporting the current tagline of 'There's a new way to look at things' taking Xerox out of the office and onto the streets. The event itself demonstrated a practical expression of Xerox product application in a way that was fresh and exciting and this was mirrored through the event itself.

The event received press coverage in a mix of broadsheets, local press, local radio and IT publications, which included: *The Independent*, *London Evening Standard*, *Metro*, *BBC Radio London Live*, *Image Reports* and *Printing World*. The trade press, *Printing Works*, *Image Reports* etc., also covered the story.

In addition to this, the event has recently won a Cannes Gold Lion and a Campaign Direct award in the best use of outdoor category.

The brief

Xerox is very pleased with the innovative, high-profile launch of the DocuColor 1632/2240, and is now looking for direct marketing to help meet the first year targets of 25 000 copier sales. Its media budget to generate 75 000 leads is £750 000, so the media will have to work very hard.

You have been asked to help the agency choose the media strategy for Xerox. Justify your media selection for generating leads from both new and existing customers.

The client is hoping for the media selection to make the most of the creative energy established by the Gavin Turk launch campaign.

Figure 11.5 Xerox/Gavin Turk Event campaign
Source: Reproduced by kind permission of Xerox and Harrison Troughton Wunderman

12

DIRECT MARKETING CREATIVE PRACTICE

Objectives

By the end of this chapter you should understand:

■ what constitutes creative practice;

■ the origins and competing philosophies that have guided creative practice;

■ where the creative element fits into the wider direct marketing planning picture;

■ the strategic drivers of creative;

■ how to create a direct marketing advert.

Introduction

In this chapter, we start by examining the background to direct marketing creative practice, and compare the various philosophies which guide different creative approaches. We then outline where creative fits in the planning process, and show how the different marketing functions influence the creative output.

The major section of the chapter outlines how to create a direct marketing advert, based on the AIDA formula.

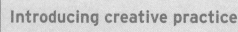

Introducing creative practice

THE POPULARITY OF CREATIVE STUDY

Direct marketers tend to pay a lot of attention to the art of creativity. There are a lot of books on the subject (some are mentioned at the end of this chapter), and training courses on creativity run by organisations such as the Institute of Direct Marketing are always popular. One reason for this fascination is the 'sexiness' of the subject – even hard-bitten business managers can be seduced by the glamour of thinking about their product in the bright lights of a Californian blockbuster advert. Advertising has been described (Martin, 1989) as 'the poetry' or 'the artistry' of marketing, although Ogilvy (1983) argued strongly that advertising has only one job: to sell. We will take a brief look at competing philosophies in the next section.

WHAT IS 'CREATIVE'?

Strangely, this question is not often addressed in texts. True to character, David Ogilvy comes up with a strong riposte to this question:

> *I have to invent a Big Idea for an advertising campaign before Tuesday. Creativity strikes me as a highfalutin word for the work I have to do between now and Tuesday. The Benton and Bowles agency holds that if it doesn't sell, it isn't creative. Amen.*

THE IMPORTANCE OF CREATIVE

Bird (1989) describes the creative contribution as the 'moment of truth' for direct-response communications. This refers to the moment when prospects or customers engage with the advert. In his view, therefore, the importance of the creative element lies in its visibility and tangibility for consumers.

However, Bird would have been the first to agree that, compared with other campaign elements – the targeting, the product, offer and incentive, and the timing – the creative element assumes *lower* importance. This has been demonstrated many times in market tests (*see* Chapter 13).

Nevertheless, creative approaches are important for another reason, which is that they can help us to understand customers better. By analysing creative in relation to corresponding behaviour, we can use it as a form of research.

Using creative as a form of research

Bill Bernbach, one of the giants of advertising history (the 'B' in DDB, the advertising agency), was asked what he thought would change in the future (Ogilvy, 1983). Referring to marketers' obsession with changing trends, he said:

> *It's fashionable to talk about changing man. A communicator must be concerned about unchanging man – what compulsions drive him, what instincts dominate his every action, even though his language too often camouflages what really motivates him. For if you know these things about a man, you can touch him at the core of his being.*

Bill Bernbach stressed that understanding customers was critical to good advertising. In direct marketing this is just as true. However, because of the body of knowledge we have built up on direct marketing creative approaches, we have generated a *feedback loop*. We can use creative tests as a driver to understand customers, as well as the other way round. In doing so, we are actually providing a key feedback loop to the beginning of the planning process – analysis – as well. In this chapter, therefore, a major role will be to gather together as much of this customer understanding as possible. This will enable us to be better informed about *how and why* direct marketing works, not just *what* works. Figure 12.1 summarises this feedback loop.

Figure 12.1 The strategic importance of creativity in direct marketing

Before examining modern creative practice, it is useful to understand the historical influences and competing philosophies of creativity.

Creative philosophies

THE ORIGINS OF CREATIVITY IN ADVERTISING

> *'The purpose of advertising is to persuade.'*
> The advertising community

In this section we will look at different creative philosophies. In order to do this we must view the entirety of advertising, and so cast our net, briefly, a little wider than direct communications.

According to American commentators on advertising (Bovee *et al.*, 1995; Martin, 1989; Rapp and Collins, 1987), the readers of this book can be divided into two camps. If you are interested in a career as a 'creative' in an advertising agency, the chances are you are a '*right-brain*' thinker. If, however, you see yourself in business, perhaps managing a marketing department, you will be a '*left-brain*' dominated person. Left-brain people are logical, persuaded by words and argument, and take a step-by-step approach to solving problems. Most of this book is written using such an approach.

Right-brain people are different. If you are right-brain dominated, you use intuition rather than logic, use emotion not reason, and are more interested in romance than rationality.

The reason for the above introduction is that this split of thinking lies at the heart of the creative debate, and to understand direct marketing creativity, we need to understand how it fits into the wider context of this fascinating creative debate that has been rumbling on now for about 100 years. This argument can be summed up as 'left brain' logical advertising versus 'right brain' emotional advertising (Rapp and Collins, 1987). What is interesting is that direct marketing has been heavily influenced by one side of the argument, whereas brand-advertising practice has chosen another route. So what are these two sides?

As long ago as 1904, John E. Kennedy described advertising as 'salesmanship in print' (Fox, 1984). He said that the best advertising *contained a logical approach*, leading prospects through reasons why they should buy the product. The opposing camp was epitomised by Cyrus Curtis, who in 1911 talked about the *atmosphere in adverts* as the key ingredient. He was backed up by Dunn, in 1918, who said, 'The psychoanalysts have found that nearly all important decisions are made in the *subconscious*.'

This argument has essentially carried on the same way to the present day. Major figures such as Rosser Reeves, the inventor of the USP concept, and advertising giant David Ogilvy have passionately, sometimes provocatively, advocated the logical approach, appealing to reason:

> '*I have never admired the "belles lettres" school of advertising. I have always thought them absurd. They did not give the reader a single fact.*'
>
> David Ogilvy, *Confessions of an Advertising Man*, 1964

Whereas other, equally eminent practitioners have advocated the opposite approach:

> '*It is not what is said but how it is said that influences us the most.*'
>
> Pierre Martineau, *Chicago Tribune*, 1957

> '*We are in the age of the eye. We have less time to read ... only the lightning strike of a picture can hit home.*'
>
> Margot Sherman, President, McCann Erickson, 1959

In summary, the left-brain enthusiasts would argue that advertising focuses on *selling* by leading the prospect through a series of reasoned, logical arguments. Unique selling points are important to help persuade the customer. Words tend to be more powerful than visual images. Functional brands, such as Intel, are built up in these ways.

The right-brain advocates will claim that people make purchase decisions on emotional grounds, although they will justify their purchases on logical grounds in research; but in fact people are ruled by their emotional subconscious, and it is this which advertising needs to play to. In this case, visual imagery is more important than words. Symbolic brands, for example Coca-Cola, are based on this premise.

EXHIBIT 12.1

LEFT-BRAIN VERSUS RIGHT-BRAIN APPEAL

Let's say you enrol on a marketing course, 'Strategic marketing: the future'. Your right-brain reasons for doing this might be the following:

■ impressing your friends;
■ getting one up on your colleagues;
■ fear of confronting a problem at work and looking for answers on the course;
■ hope: you want to move on to better things in your career;
■ getting excitement, brightening up a routine;
■ looking good back at the office as you casually drop hints of your in-depth knowledge of marketing strategy.

Whereas your left-brain reasons might be:

■ it was the cheapest course of its type;
■ it was the most convenient to get to;
■ it minimised the disruption to daily work;
■ it has the best value;
■ it has the most knowledgeable speakers.

What has made the argument even more entertaining has been the accusation from the champions of reason and logic that the 'intuition and romance' camp are more obsessed with winning awards than making sales.

Advertising: should it be entertainment as well as selling?

The following quotes summarise some of the arguments for and against the need for advertising to be entertaining:

> 'The people who know what they are doing are the direct marketing people. They know exactly what they've sold. And you don't. You don't have the faintest idea whether the advertising sells anything or not. And you don't really care. You just want to win an award at Cannes, or one of those rackets.'
>
> David Ogilvy (Martin, 1989)

> 'Our job is to kill the cleverness that makes us shine instead of the product.'
>
> Bill Bernbach, Managing Director of DDB

> 'We sell; or else.'
>
> O&M advertising agency company motto

> 'Ad writers forget they are salesmen and try to be performers. Instead of sales, they seek applause.'
>
> Claude Hopkins, 1927

> 'Advertising began as an art, and too many people want it to remain that way: a never never land where they can say 'this is right because we feel it's right''.'
>
> Rosser Reeves, *Reality in Advertising*, 1961

Martin (1989) advocated that advertisers should match entertainment with selling:

> 'Each message must indelibly lodge the brand in the viewer's memory and seed the mind with emotional reasons to buy, as well as providing entertainment.'
>
> David Martin, *Romancing the Brand*, 1989

Broadbent (1997) said:

> There is no genuine clash between selling and 'being creative'. It is only that the criteria differ. Even when brand sales get the benefit of effective advertising, this can still be done entertainingly. We cannot intrude on the public without repaying them. We must not put at risk the media audiences. 'Effective creativity' I can understand and admire. Unconnected creativity frightens me.
>
> Simon Broadbent, 'Accountability - the flaming sword', *Admap*, June, 1997

So, where does direct marketing fit into the arguments for left- versus right-brain advertising, and the need for entertainment?

THE ORIGINS OF DIRECT MARKETING CREATIVE PRACTICE

Direct marketing creative practice has traditionally been dominated by the left-brain approach. Direct marketing creative is to some extent still based on techniques developed by mail-order companies decades ago, which have always served that industry well. Rapp and Collins (1987) showed why direct marketing has historically been left-brain dominated:

■ mail-order products had to have an element of *uniqueness* about them to overcome the inertia of people at home; this led to a USP-driven approach;

■ the items were often *intangibles*, or services, which were traditionally sold in a logical way;

■ direct marketing products and services are usually relatively *high-priced items*, and it is felt that items of such value cannot be sold through emotion. Reasoned arguments are required if you want a consumer to buy a pension off you.

The culture within direct marketing remains largely driven by creative that presents logical propositions to customers (*see* for example the IDM's *Direct and Interactive* Guide, 2002) that advocate making rational arguments that inspire people to act.

In contrast, brand-building creative has predominantly been right-brain led. If we consider products such as Marlboro cigarettes, Coca-Cola, or Levi Jeans, their advertising is pure emotional symbolism. The reasons for this are:

■ brand building through imagery and association with attractive symbols is needed when you are advertising a product that is similar to others;

■ brand building is similarly important for low involvement, low price-ticket products, such as FMCGs where consumers make impulsive, subconscious decisions;

■ brand building has traditionally been used to sell tangible items such as food and clothes.

Direct marketing's stance on entertainment has been even more clear: there is no room for it in direct communications. The argument has been that even if it were required, there is simply no room for deflecting the prospect from the crux of the advert – to obtain a response.

Recent developments in the direct marketing creative approach

Developments in the 1990s suggest that direct marketing needs to embrace a wider creative influence, taking more of a generalist perspective to add to the specific direct skills already present. We may note Graeme McCorkell's (1994) observation that most of the best direct-response adverts he has ever seen were produced by *general* agency-trained creatives such as John Watson, Drayton Bird or Chris Albert. Currently the most successful agency in the UK in terms of awards won is Harrison Troughton Wunderman, which specialises in 'brand response' marketing – a marriage of brand building and direct response.

This need has arisen from the growth of direct marketing into sectors previously dominated by general marketing techniques. The car industry is a classic example of this. Cars are sold through a mixture of both symbolic branding appealing to emotional benefits, and left-brain rational argument. It follows that there is an increasing need for direct-response creative approaches to help in brand-building strategies as well as doing the job of driving sales directly.

Some argue that new thinking is needed in both direct marketing and general marketing worlds. In a brilliant piece of work, Rapp and Collins (1987) proposed an holistic solution: 'whole-brain advertising'. This approach advocates appealing to both brain centres. Part of the communication would focus on symbolism, imagery and emotion, while the rest would home in on logic, reason and argument.

EXHIBIT 12.2

WHOLE-BRAIN ADVERTISING

In the commercial break of the American Superbowl on New Year's Day, 1984, Apple Computers launched a one-minute advert introducing the Macintosh computer. Based on the George Orwell book, *1984*, this was a piece of pure right-brain symbolism, costing more per second than a Hollywood movie. Apple then ran a 30-page ad in *Newsweek*, which told prospects everything they needed to know about Macintosh computers: pure left-brain advertising.

Sales of Apple Macintosh computers rocketed.

(Rapp and Collins do not argue whole-brain advertising as a panacea for all problems. They reason that some products, say Marlboro cigarettes, should always need right-brain-only advertising, whereas others, say computer hardware accessories, should need left-brain only.)

Other leading practitioners offer a view more in line with traditional direct marketing creative practice. Nash (1995) argues that 'the direct marketing communications job is not to make an impression; it's to make a sale. Response and brand imagery are often two different beasts in an advert.' He advocates that writing a subtle headline in direct marketing means that the phones will not ring as often. One Guinness advertising campaign featuring Rutger Hauer contained surreal imagery, one headed 'It's not easy being a dolphin...' with no further explanation. (The idea was that dolphins would be unhappy because they can't drink Guinness.) Nash argued that this approach won't win you any friends in direct marketing!

Clearly then, there is no universal agreement as to the way forward. However, as direct marketing becomes a growing influence in sectors such as packaged goods, it may need to reinvent its creative approaches. The move into whole-brain advertising may be matched by a need to provide 'entertainment' as part of the communication. Martin's argument that brand advertising needs to entertain to stand out from the clutter may also stand up as an argument for direct marketing, if it wants to avoid 'junk' criticisms.

These debates will continue, but it is time to move on and examine how creative practice is derived from the elements of direct marketing strategy.

The strategic drivers of creative practice

'The stroke of creative inspiration is a rare phenomenon that comes only to those immersed in research, strategy, planning, and tactics.'

Edward Nash, 1995

EXHIBIT 12.3

REAL-WORLD PLANNING

In principle, we should always set the broad direction before we set about our creative process. But what actually happens? In reality, planning is rarely linear, in the way described in text books. A creative 'big idea' may spring forth at any point in the planning process – and if it's powerful enough, may survive through to production.

Direct marketing writers have differed in what they see as the main drivers of creativity. For instance, Nash (1995) and Bird (1989) saw *positioning* as the key strategic precursor of creative thinking. Stone (1996) cited *the product, market, medium, and budget* as essential to creative strategy. In addition to these factors, modern users of direct marketing are stressing the importance of *branding* as a strategic driver.

The creative effort should be looked upon as the *last* piece in the planning and implementation jigsaw. If the creative brief is written before decisions have been made on the other planning elements, it lacks the guidance it needs to be successful. Norman Berry, the creative director of Ogilvy and Mather Direct, once said, 'Give me the freedom of a tight brief.' He would probably have applauded this planning principle.

Figure 12.2 outlines the specific links between the elements of strategy and the creative effort.

Figure 12.2 reveals that some of the drivers are strategic: the product, the market, positioning and branding; the remainder are tactical features: the campaign budget, media choice, and the offer that will be made. Let's look at how these elements influence creative effort.

The product: An understanding of the product or service benefits is crucial to good creative practice. What is it that customers want the product to do for them? How does the product fit into their lives? The key is spending time researching the product. Ogilvy was famous for this; he once spent three weeks reading nothing but product manuals on the Rolls-Royce, before creating a classic advertisement.

The market: An intimate knowledge of your customers can greatly help in producing convincing creative material. Once you have got under the skin of your customers, you can reach out to them, knowing what to say and how to say it so that they respond to you.

Strategy

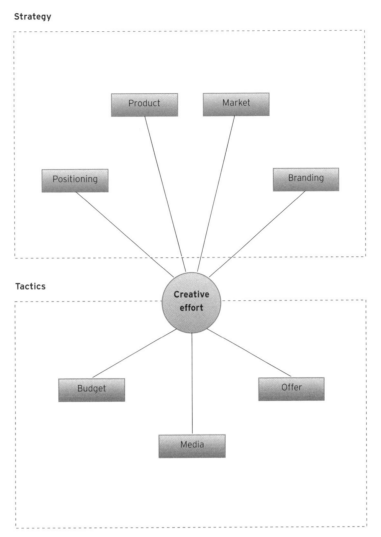

Tactics

Figure 12.2 Planning influences on the creative effort

The budget: The biggest element of the budget is usually for media spend, but creative considerations are clearly also important. Including a glossy photo of the product on expensive material will raise the 'cost per thousand' considerably. Can this be justified?

The media: The media choice has an enormous bearing on the creative, and it is essential that media choices are made before the serious creative process begins. One only has to imagine the creative necessities of, say, direct-response TV compared with those of direct mail to realise how vital it is to marry creative output with the needs of the medium.

The offer: Although arguably less critical than the choice of medium, the incentive decision is nevertheless an important part of the creative brief. The incentive is part of the message of the advert, and can also set the tone.

We will now expand on two areas which merit further attention, namely positioning and branding.

POSITIONING

We saw in Chapter 6 that positioning is two things:

■ the dimensions chosen by the marketer to describe the product;

■ where the product fits in the consumer's mind compared with its competitors.

As we observed earlier, it is the consumer who decides the hierarchy of competing products within that dimension.

The creative approach should reflect the positioning stance taken, and in particular try to emphasise:

■ the most flattering dimensions of the product;

■ the most appealing dimensions to the consumer.

Bird (1989) describes successful companies as having a clear positioning from which they rarely if ever deviate. For example, American Express has the positioning of 'the world's most prestigious financial instrument for business travel and entertainment'. This has a direct relationship with its creative line: 'Quite frankly the American Express card is not for everyone.'

Bird draws the following lessons from his experiences in creating positions:

1. Your positioning should reflect the reality of your product or service. *'The best car service in town.'* Who says?

2. Vague boasting about being the best in your category, with no back up, does not work, e.g. *'The ideal TV rental for you.'*

3. Make sure your positioning dimension is relevant. *'Our car has the safest bodywork in its class.'* No use if you are in the sports car category, whose buyers love speed and excitement, not safety.

4. Positioning may be relevant, but insufficient by itself. A successful example of this is Tango soft drinks. *'Have you been Tango'd?'* is a 'wacky' positioning which works well, but the product has other support positionings – good value for money, refreshing taste, and so on – which are vital for its success.

EXHIBIT 12.4

TYPICAL POSITIONING DIMENSIONS USED IN DIRECT MARKETING

'New!' versus *'A tradition for centuries'*

'Tough. Built to last' versus *'Easy to carry'*

'A very personal service' versus *'You won't know we are here'*

'This offer is only available to a limited few' versus *'The new product that will be all the rage'*

'This service is with you in hours' versus *'A high-quality service will be tailormade to your situation'*

Price is of course a common positioning dimension to take:

'Everyday low pricing' versus *'The very best in quality'*.

Nash (1995) developed what he termed *horizontal positioning* as a way of generating a platform for creative effort.

Horizontal positioning

Nash suggests taking the point in the consumer's buying process that they have reached and establishing that as the basis for the creative approach. Taking the example of a mobile phone:

1. Create a need: *'Hey you! You need to communicate on the move.'*

2. Fulfil a need: *'The new lightweight personal mobile for the stylish woman.'*

3. Sell competitively: *'We offer the lightest mobile phone on the market ... lowest price or your money back.'*

4. Overcome inertia: *'Suppose you broke down today ... send off now! You don't have a moment to lose.'*

BRANDING

Direct marketers have not always seen branding as an important part of their strategy. For example, *Reader's Digest* does not have a powerful corporate brand, yet it remains one of the world's most successful direct marketers. More recently, a number of direct marketing sectors have emerged to which branding is very important. These include retail, packaged goods and automobiles.

According to de Chenatony and McDonald (1992), these marketers can choose between symbolic (emotional, covert reasoning) and functional (rational, overt reasoning) brands. The creative approach must then support the chosen strategy. This is because the creative approach is important in giving brand 'clues' to prospects which are then interpreted from brand images in the consumer's mind. Thus, an exclusive brand such as American Express is unlikely to be supported by adjectives such as 'smashing', 'super' and 'unbeatable'.

All aspects of creativity – copy, illustrations, layout and production values – must support the brand strategy.

Copy

Copy is particularly important in supporting *functional* brand values.

The 'Directors at Large' direct-response press advert in Fig. 12.3 illustrates a typical business-to-business functional brand. Benefits are outlined in a logical way, with no recourse to brand symbolism.

Copy can also be used to communicate symbolic brand values. The typical American Express direct mailer conveys prestige and status to recipients, in a sense inviting them to become one of a 'chosen few'.

Figure 12.3 Direct-response press advert illustrating typical business-to-business functional brand

Reproduced by kind permission of Marketscan Ltd.

Illustrations

Illustrations are particularly important in supporting *symbolic* brands.

The RSPCA has used powerful illustrations to communicate its brand in its direct-response advertising. The RSPCA, a charity over 175 years old, has recently moved decisively to change its previously rather 'comfortable' brand into one that is much more aggressive. Its direct marketing has reflected this, with direct-response adverts and mailings (see Fig. 12.4) making strong brand statements reflecting the charity's stance over animal issues.

Figure 12.4 Examples from a fundraising appeal pack using a powerful image
Source: Reproduced by kind permission of the Royal Society for the Prevention of Cruelty to Animals

Layout/production

These elements are just as important. An example which highlights the difference between a classical direct-response approach and a more overt branding approach is that of Compaq, outlined in the case study Exhibit 12.5.

EXHIBIT 12.5

COMPAQ - A CASE STUDY

Compaq is the world's biggest personal computer manufacturer. This position has been achieved through two distribution networks: one is through IT solutions experts who sell to large corporations; and the other is through wholesalers such as PC World.

However, the new consumer and small business growth had led to the need for a different channel – direct selling. This had already been done, successfully, by companies such as Dell, Gateway and Viglen, with classical direct marketing adverts off the page selling on rational benefits. For Compaq, however, branding was a key part of its added value, and for its direct operation it was important to reflect this in the creative approach.

The two adverts shown reflect the classic direct 'straight sell' – Time Computers (Fig. 12.5); and the branded sell – Compaq (Fig. 12.6). Here, Compaq must break some of the 'rules' of direct marketing in order to accommodate its brand aims in the creative approach.

Figure 12.5 Classic direct 'straight sell' ad

Source: Reproduced by kind permission of Time Group Limited.

i want

A TOP CLASS PC ON MY DESK AS SOON AS POSSIBLE. THAT'S IN *days* NOT *weeks*. I HAVEN'T GOT TIME TO WORRY ABOUT INSTALLATION. I NEED SOMEONE TO TAKE CARE OF ALL THAT FOR ME. NATURALLY, I WANT TO ORDER IT OVER THE PHONE AND IT'S GOT TO HAVE THE LATEST SOFTWARE. I ALSO WANT A FULL ON-SITE WARRANTY BACKED-UP WITH TECHNICAL SUPPORT FROM PEOPLE WHO REALLY KNOW (AND CARE ABOUT) WHAT THEY'RE DOING. BUT I DON'T EXPECT TO PAY A PENNY TO GET

it up and running

THE NEW COMPAQ PRESARIO 2212
(HOME & OFFICE).
THE COMPLETE PC PACKAGE.

- 180 MHz PROCESSOR
- 16 MB TOTAL SYSTEM MEMORY
- 1.6 GB HARD DISK
- 8 x CD ROM DRIVE
- 14" MONITOR
- 3.5" FLOPPY DISK
- 33.6/14.4 DATA/FAX MODEM, UPGRADEABLE TO 56K*
- KEYBOARD, MOUSE, INTEGRATED SPEAKERS
- MICROSOFT® OFFICE 97 SMALL BUSINESS EDITION PRELOADED: EXCEL 97, WORD 97, SMALL BUSINESS FINANCIAL MANAGER 97, OUTLOOK™ 97, PUBLISHER 97, AUTOROUTE EXPRESS™ GREAT BRITAIN, INTERNET EXPLORER 3.0
- MULTIMEDIA BUNDLE INCLUDING ENCARTA® 97 WORLD ATLAS

- **FREE** DELIVERY TO YOUR HOME OR OFFICE WITHIN 3 WORKING DAYS**.
- **FREE** INSTALLATION (UNPACKED, SET UP AND CHECKED BY AN AUTHORISED TECHNICIAN).
- **FREE** YEAR'S ON-SITE WARRANTY.
- **FREE** ONE YEAR CUSTOMER SERVICE AND SUPPORT†.

ONLY £899 +VAT
(£1,056 INC VAT).

OR FROM ONLY £32.90 (INC VAT)
(15.9% FIXED APR) PER MONTH††.

TO PLACE YOUR ORDER
CALL US DIRECT ON:

0800 611 722

LINES OPEN 8AM – 6.30PM MONDAY TO FRIDAY.
9AM – 5.30PM SATURDAY AND SUNDAY. PLEASE QUOTE UNQ 033.

COMPAQ DELIVERS MORE

COMPAQ

ALL LOGOS AND PRODUCT NAMES ARE TRADEMARKS OF THEIR RESPECTIVE OWNERS. *UPGRADE TO 56K AVAILABLE FOR PURCHASE LATE 1997. **NORMALLY 3 WORKING DAYS (MONDAY TO SATURDAY). †CALLS CHARGED AT STANDARD NATIONAL RATE. ††FINANCE IS AVAILABLE SUBJECT TO STATUS. £32.90 INC VAT PER MONTH (15.9% FIXED APR), 36 MONTHLY PAYMENTS). £46.35 INC VAT PER MONTH (16.7% FIXED APR, 24 MONTHLY PAYMENTS). TOTAL CASH PRICE £1,056.33, TOTAL CREDIT PRICE (24 MONTHS) £1,218.03, TOTAL CREDIT PRICE (36 MONTHS) £1,290.03. WRITTEN QUOTATIONS AVAILABLE ON REQUEST. LICENCED CREDIT BROKER. PRICES CORRECT AT TIME OF GOING TO PRESS AND REFER TO SPECIFICATION DESCRIPTION ONLY. THIS OFFER IS SUBJECT TO COMPAQ TERMS AND CONDITIONS, A WRITTEN COPY IS AVAILABLE ON REQUEST. COMPAQ COMPUTER LIMITED C/O ALPERTON HOUSE, BRIDGEWATER ROAD, WEMBLEY, MIDDLESEX HA0 1EH. REG IN ENGLAND NO. 1380660. L&OIL.

Figure 12.6 Branded sell ad

Source: Compaq and Bates Worldwide

In the following section, we take a more detailed look at how to create a direct marketing advert. We will investigate the collective experience of direct marketing and see what does and does not work.

Creative execution

'I see the canvas and I begin!'

Willem de Kooning, Artist

THE DEVELOPMENT OF DIRECT MARKETING CREATIVE 'RULES'

Direct marketing's precision and control when testing allows even small changes in creative to be *accurately* related to *behaviour changes* by consumers. (This is something that brand marketers cannot do. For all the effort that goes into researching advertising effectiveness, practitioners are all too often reduced to making educated guesses about what effect their adverts have had. Not so with direct-response advertising.)

As a result, much of the myth and aura behind creative ideas has been steadily dissected by the direct marketing fraternity, and pulled together into a set of creative 'rules' which, if followed, even by a relative novice, allow the possibility of considerable success.

EXHIBIT 12.6

CREATIVE 'RULES' VERSUS ORIGINALITY

Rules

Many people ask, 'How can creative practice be set by "rules" of what to do? Surely creativity, by definition, cannot be rule bound?' Here's what David Ogilvy had to say in his brilliant book, *Ogilvy on Advertising*:

> I am sometimes attacked for imposing rules. Nothing could be further from the truth. I hate rules. All I do is report on how consumers react to creative. I may say to a copywriter, 'Research shows that commercials with celebrities are below average in persuading people to use a product. Are you sure you want to use a celebrity?'

In other words, Ogilvy believed in *guidelines* - rules that can be broken, provided there is a good reason to do so.

Originality

Respected advertisers like Bird and Ogilvy have warned against the cult of originality. Bird in particular warned against 'irrelevant originality', which wins awards and sells nothing. There are many great adverts which owe nothing to originality.

David Ogilvy started his career by copying. Later he moved on to original work. He saw no problem in admitting this in his book (Ogilvy, 1983). Ogilvy often quoted Mozart, who said:

> *I have never made the slightest effort to compose anything original.*

The agency HTW recently worked on a brief for the World Gold Council. Here is what happened:

Martin Troughton and his team were presenting to the Foreign and Colonial board. By chance the board also contained the chairwoman of the World Gold Council. The WGC exists to ensure the price of gold remains buoyant by lobbying governments. She explained to Martin that WGC had a problem. Gordon Brown, UK Chancellor, wanted to shift the reserves from gold to currency (Dollars, Euros and Yen). Could they change his mind?

↓

So she gave the agency £100 000 with a brief to make things 'uncomfortable' for the Chancellor and raise awareness of the sell off. They decided to use direct response press adverts but needed a strong idea.

↓

The creatives sat down and kicked around ideas. Gold itself . . . it's very heavy, it looks distinctive. Very unlike paper money. The team wanted to generate anger: why swap gold for mere paper? This thinking led to the headline:

↓

'If you can tell the difference between Gold and Paper tell us'

↓

The call to respond generated 70 000 protestors. MPs were written to, a petition was delivered to Downing Street. One week before the sell off the WGC came back to Martin: do us a poster outside the Houses of Parliament please. The team checked: no poster allowed! What could they do?

↓

There was a river . . . Someone suggested a barge flowing past Parliament. The barge reminded the team of scrap metal . . . that's it! We'll do a 'Gordon Brown scrap metal sell off' stunt! Production bought a load of junk metal for £600, hired a barge, painted the scrap using gold spray and gold wrapping paper. They hired a PR firm to tip off the press. This is what happened:

↓

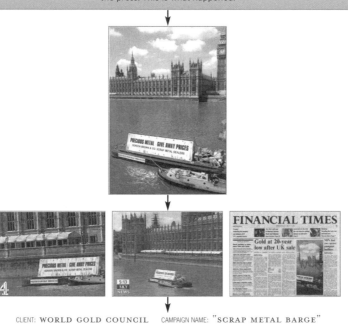

CLIENT: WORLD GOLD COUNCIL   CAMPAIGN NAME: "SCRAP METAL BARGE"

The World Gold Council approached us to organise opposition to Chancellor Gordon Brown's plans to sell off half the UK's gold reserves. At the time, public awareness was minimal. So we created an old scrap metal barge and piled it high with gold painted scrap – cars, fridges, bikes etc. Then we erected the 96 sheet poster you see in the photograph. At noon (when the first sale began) we moored it outside the House of Commons. The barge appeared on the Channel 4 news that evening. It also featured on the hour, every hour on Sky News throughout the day. The following day it appeared in national and international papers. In combination with a small budget press campaign it generated over 70,000 responses and an estimated £800,000 worth of publicity. All for just £7,000.

Figure 12.7 World Gold Council – scrap-metal barge
Source: Reproduced by permission of ITN Archive (left); Harrison Troughton Wunderman (top, middle); Sky News (bottom middle); Financial Times (right)

There are almost as many formulas for helping you to dream up a new idea as there are direct marketing writers. Most of them seem to agree on the main issue, however, although Ogilvy (1983) probably put it most forcefully. He and the others were quick to extinguish the romantic notion that brilliant ideas will effortlessly fall into a creative's mind as if by an act of God. Their view is summed up by the old adage:

'Genius is 99 per cent perspiration, 1 per cent inspiration.'

Thomas Edison

The 'perspiration' in advertising is the hard work of researching the product and the market exhaustively. World-class creatives see the client's creative brief as only the first step in acquiring knowledge on the marketing problem.

Bird (1989) proposed a three-step process for producing creative ideas (*see* Exhibit 12.7).

EXHIBIT 12.7

WHERE IDEAS COME FROM

Drayton Bird offers the following advice in his book, *Commonsense Direct Marketing*:

1 **Master your subject.** Become thoroughly familiar with your product/service and customers. Find out the truth about your marketing situation. 'Your imagination will never dream up anything to beat the truth.'
2 **The inner game.** Once the ideas are in, let your subconscious take over. 'Don't try to force ideas and they will pop out, probably while you are doing something else.'
3 **Use sounding boards.** When you have an idea, expose it to your colleagues, however painful this might be. The chances are they will see things you can't, maybe because you have got too close to the problem.

Bird's final piece of advice on this subject is salutary: *'Lead an interesting life! Don't be dull!'*

On a similar note, Nash (1995) offered three secrets of advertising. They are 'research, research and research'. He explained that meaty copy – lots of anecdotes and examples, intimate details about the service or product which are more convincing than bland claims – is good copy. He then suggested that after the hard work of research, you should do the following: think, 'dump' (that is, get everything in your head down onto paper), write up and, finally, 'make it sing!'. Don't say a book is entertaining; give an example of the humour. Don't talk of the need for strategy; give a strategy.

The process of creating an advert is greatly helped by the use of one of the available frameworks. The most important of these frameworks is the *AIDA model*, which we will follow in detail a little later. First we can cover *practitioner frameworks* and the *consumer buying process*.

PRACTITIONER FRAMEWORKS

There are plenty of alternative frameworks offering a structure for creating a direct-response advert. These have been mainly conjured up by practitioners, and although they may not have any particular academic basis, they are based on a lifetime's practice of advert creation and testing. It is therefore well worthwhile repeating two such frameworks here, outlined in the following exhibits. They are Nash's Five Ss, and Stone's seven-step formula for copywriting.

EXHIBIT 12.8

STONE'S SEVEN-STEP FORMULA FOR GOOD COPYWRITING

1 Promise your biggest benefit in your headline.
2 In the copy, immediately enlarge on your most important benefit.
3 Tell readers specifically what they are going to get.
4 Back up your statements with proof and endorsements.
5 Tell readers what they might lose if they don't act.
6 Rephrase your prominent benefits in your closing offer.
7 Incite action. Now.

EXHIBIT 12.9

NASH'S FIVE Ss FOR A DIRECT MARKETING ADVERTISEMENT

Stop 'em: Give a headline or picture that people notice.

Show 'em: Use visual images to communicate powerfully.

Seduce 'em: Appeal to higher psychological needs than just the basic product needs: emotion, self image, changing the world.

Satisfy 'em: Show how the product fulfils their needs.

Sell 'em: Ask for the order.

THE CONSUMER BUYING PROCESS

From an academic standpoint, what we need is a theoretical framework that allows us to understand what the job of a direct-response advert is. Consumer behaviour models were divided by Foxall and Goldsmith (1994) into *high-involvement* purchases and *low-involvement* purchases. It can be argued that we are concerned more here with high-involvement models because most direct marketing is concerned with higher price-ticket purchases, in which the consumer goes through a significant decision-making process. There are three comprehensive models of consumer decision making (Nicosia, 1966; Howard and Sheth, 1969; and Engel *et al.*, 1968) which Foxall distilled into the model shown in Fig. 12.8.

This is a useful basic framework to explain how the prospect interacts with the advert. One criticism of this framework, outlined by Foxall himself, is that it assumes too rational a consumer. As we saw earlier, consumers make decisions on emotional grounds as well as rational grounds, and the detailed discussion on creative guidelines that follows takes full account of this.

THE AWARENESS, INTEREST, DESIRE, ACTION (AIDA) MODEL

(Direct) marketers have used the well-known AIDA model as perhaps the simplest way of helping explain how (direct-response) adverts work (Smith, 1993). First constructed in 1928, The Awareness, Interest, Desire and Action model is still popular as a way of

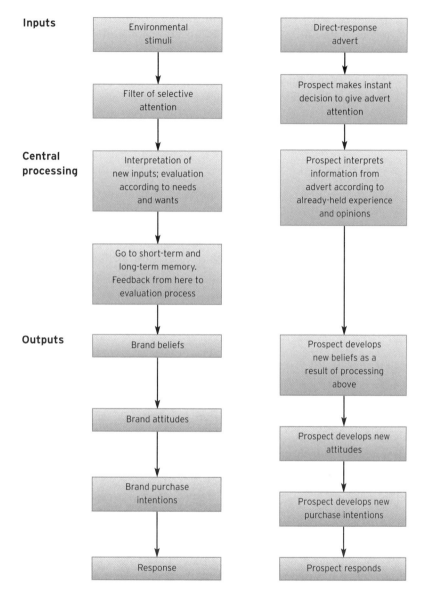

Figure 12.8 A model of consumer decision making

Source: Adapted from Foxall, G. and Goldsmith, R. (1994) *Consumer Psychology for Marketing*, Routledge, London. Reprinted with permission.

explaining how we notice, internalise and respond to advertising. It is particularly important to help explain direct-response advertising, because direct response is primarily about getting the prospect from awareness through to action (response) *all within the one advert*.

Taking each of the headings in turn, the following section describes the key elements of creative that take the prospect from awareness to action. It is important to understand the limitations of this approach before we proceed, however.

In line with Foxall and Goldsmith's comments on consumer decision-making processes, the AIDA framework is probably most realistic when applied to high-involvement products such as financial services, holidays or cars. It may be less relevant to impulse purchases.

Most of the following guidelines refer to the written media: mail, press, inserts and door drops. Many of the principles outlined are also relevant to the broadscale media and the telephone, but guidelines will vary. For more information, you are referred to one of the specialist creative texts suggested in the reference section.

Awareness

The moment of truth is nearly at hand. Your mailer lands on the mat. Your full-page press ad lies there on page 7, between the feature on cooking and the TV guide. Your insert falls out onto the hallway floor. The first crucial question is: will it get the audience's attention? To some extent this depends on the medium, the offer, and so on, but the chances of you succeeding also lie with the quality of your creative.

EXHIBIT 12.10

GETTING ATTENTION: TRICKS OF THE TRADE

■ In direct mail, outer envelope messages get attention by playing on curiosity: 'You start telling a story, then just when it gets interesting you … (please see inside)'. According to Bird, envelope messages work because they encourage those who are interested to get into the envelope right away. It puts off uninterested people, which does not matter.

■ 'Eye camera' tests have shown the eye settles around the middle of the page. Ogilvy advises that you put the headline under the picture, not above it. This will lift response.

■ Attention-getting devices are sometimes used. Tricks like plastic cards with the consumer's name on can increase response by as much as 70 per cent, according to Bird. He reported a very successful mailer in which a plastic frog which hopped out with a message: 'Hop it! Act now!' was used to get the attention of businesspeople.

The job can be likened to a person in a crowd trying to attract someone's attention some way away. This may explain why the two key tools used to attract attention in all written direct marketing media are the *headline* and the *picture*. Research done by using cameras to follow readers' eye movements has shown that the eye is attracted to an advert by these two main elements.

Headlines

When writing a direct-response press advert, what is the role of the headline? Given that the average broadsheet paper has 350 headlines, the primary job of the headline is to stop the reader from moving on. A similar role for headlines can also be envisaged in other media: direct mail, door drops or inserts.

Halsey (1992), in a review of creative in direct marketing, outlined self interest, news, and curiosity as the three core platforms for headline writing. The following issues need to be thought through carefully before writing a headline:

- **Maximise your chances of hitting the right audience:** Bob Stone underscored the pragmatism of direct response with his principle that out of 100 potential readers or viewers of the advert, only a very few are prime prospects to buy. Therefore, although it is tempting to write a highly creative headline that may catch the eye of many readers, it is better to make sure that you definitely catch the prime prospects by laying out clearly what it is you have to sell.

- **Promise a benefit:** Stone revealed more details of typical benefits, emotional and rational, which may appeal to the self interest of readers. He outlined two kinds of benefits. First, the obvious type related to the product; for example, Stephen Hawking's book, *A Brief History of Time*, is a quick way to satisfy one's curiosity about how the universe is formed. Second, we should consider a deeper benefit, related to possible emotional reasons for purchase; for example, Hawking's book will enable the buyer to sound well educated in front of his/her friends.

The following examples are based on Stone's ideas. Suppose we are selling a recruitment agency service. We could concentrate on the following benefits:

- **Health:** *'Is your current job making you ill?'*

- **Money:** *'You're undervalued at work, right? Up your salary by £10K...'*

- **Security:** *'These days it's hard to feel safe, but 80 per cent of our clients feel more secure in the post we found them.'*

- **Pride:** *'Do you yearn for the job that will make your friends look at you with envy?'*

- **Enjoyment:** *'You spend half your life there. So for God's sake enjoy it. Get a new job with...'*

- **Excitement:** *'Remember the last time you woke up with that thrill of wondering what the day at work will bring. You can't? Maybe we can help...'*

Finally, Ogilvy offers the following advice for writing winning headlines:

1. Offer helpful information: *'How to win friends and influence people.'*

2. Specify your audience in the headline or picture: *'Do you live in a detached house?'*

3. Be specific: Not *'Save money with us'* but *'Save £2.31 every time you buy a pair of shoes'*. It's more credible.

EXHIBIT 12.11

SOUNDBITE HEADLINES

'I want to be tough on crime; tough on the causes of crime.'

Why do soundbites work? Why use little jokes or plays on words as a headline or strapline? Because soundbites or straplines are retained in our short-term memory very easily and are associated there with other chunks of information in the mind,

forming weakly held beliefs about a brand. When it comes to purchase we then recall these feelings and they can have a big say in the product choice.

In direct-response adverts leading straight to purchase, it may not be necessary to use sound-bites, since we are trying to convince the prospect to act straightaway.

Illustrations

In the past, direct marketers have used visuals much less than have brand advertisers. As Stone points out, however, nowadays this may be a mistake in many markets. He found that the 'rules of the game' for direct mail changed considerably in the 1990s, as direct marketing communication's role in the marketing mix expanded. He identified two key changes:

1 **Copy has become shorter and better.** The 'TV generation' is less inclined to stay with a company if it doesn't get its message across very quickly.

2 **More visuals are being used.** There are three benefits to advertisers of using illustrations. First, brand advertisers have known for a long time that *pictures can communicate more quickly and possibly more forcefully than copy*. Direct marketers in recent years have increased their use of pictures quite considerably.

Second, illustrations are crucial as attention getters within a direct-response advert because, compared to copy, *visuals are easy to look at and take in*. Taking direct mail as an example, research has found that many readers will look at the picture on a brochure before picking up the letter.

Third, a number of writers (Nash, 1995; Bird, 1989; and Jones, 1992) have emphasised the importance of visuals in *communicating the positioning* of the product or service. This is explained in Exhibit 12.12.

EXHIBIT 12.12

SEMIOTICS: THE HIDDEN SCIENCE OF SIGNS

A product can be quickly repositioned, moving it upmarket or downmarket, without changing any of the words, by the use of simple visual signs.

Typefaces are important. Ogilvy used a classic serif typeface in his advert for Rolls-Royce to convey elegance and a sense of history.

Production values such as the thickness of paper, and the use of models or actors in photos, will all make a huge difference. It is easy to see that using Jeremy Paxman, 'Newsnight' presenter, rather than, for example, a game-show host, will change the position of a brand upmarket.

All these apparently minor changes are very important because people want to buy products that reflect their self image, and the picture gives hugely powerful clues to people about whether the product is 'for them'.

Naturally, words can also be used powerfully to change a product's position. If we change 'Now's your chance to win!' to 'By an act of serendipity, an opportunity befalls you', we have altered the whole feel of the advert.

Exhibit 12.13 outlines a number of art directors' 'tricks of the trade'.

Interest

Most people who glance at an advert in the press do not go on to read the body copy. The average readership of body copy in magazines is about 5 per cent. In daily newspapers it is even lower at about 1 per cent. Even with direct mail, a lot of prospects will glance at the contents of the mailer and then discard it.

EXHIBIT 12.13

TRICKS OF THE TRADE: ART DIRECTION

Nash (1995) recommended choosing models who are a little thinner, wealthier, younger or wiser looking than the target audience. People want to see themselves represented by what they want to be, not the reality of what they actually are. If you are marketing to retired people, use models who are 55–65, not over 65.

Cycles seem to exist in advertising art direction and copy. Look at the mailers you get from a particular sector, or look at TV adverts. It is clear that a lot of copycatting goes on!

Ogilvy (1983) offered the following guidelines for print advertising, which still seem to be relevant today:

- Pictures which arouse curiosity are the most powerful. Ogilvy described this as 'story appeal'. Faces and eyes in particular attract attention. A lot of children's charities use children's 'big eyes' in attracting attention.
- People want to see people with whom they can identify and to whom they can aspire. If you put a man in the picture, women may ignore it, and vice versa.
- Of all illustrative forms, cartoons will attract the most attention; but direct-response marketers have found that photographs pull the biggest response.

However, this does not matter as long as the highest possible number of good prospects have noticed the advert. Unlike brand advertisers, direct marketers don't need to appeal to a mass audience, just those who are considering purchasing in their product sector.

At the 'interest' stage, the prospects are looking at your advert with their curiosity aroused. They are looking for something of interest. The next requirement of the advert is to foster that interest by building on the primary benefit you presented in the headline or picture.

What has to be borne in mind here is that the reader/viewer is always looking for a reason to stop reading and move on to something else. It is an effort to read; your prospect will constantly evaluate whether it is worth it. The job of the copy is to keep them reading through to the end by making it very difficult not to read on.

There are a number of ways of creating and keeping the reader's interest:

Artwork/ layout

- Lead the reader naturally from the headline/picture to the copy, building up interest.
- Dropped capitals make entering the copy easier on the eye.
- Use a short first paragraph. It's less intimidating.

Copy

1. Help the reader into your advert with bullets, arrowheads or asterisks.
2. Highlight key phrases with italics or bold type.
3. According to Bird, busy layouts outpull neat ones. They seem to add interest.
4. Write short sentences and short paragraphs. Use simple words.
5. Ogilvy advises copywriters to stay away from bragging with unsubstantiated 'our product is the best' copy. In his view, such claims are very unconvincing.
6. Give people reasons to buy; cut off their reasons not to buy. Lead them through the argument so that by the end they have no choice but to buy.
7. Expand on the product benefits. The more you can present the better.

EXHIBIT 12.14

APPEALING TO THE AUDIENCE'S NEEDS

Here are just some benefits that can be high-lighted: independence, importance, fame, wealth, popularity, sex and romance, love and affection, not being lonely, excitement, variety, happiness, helping others, making progress, security, having a change, fitting in, gaining respect, pride in performance, feeling good through looking good, enjoyment of humour, feeling smarter, getting 'one over', being energetic, aesthetic pleasures such as food or art.

8. Present your message as news. Presenting something as news appeals to our sense of curiosity. We also have a desire to keep up to date. News feeds both these elements of psychology.

9. Tell a story. Charities often use this technique to highlight the human interest in what they are doing. Amnesty International has won a number of awards with its powerful, shocking and compelling copy detailing atrocities throughout the world (*see* Fig. 12.9). This brands Amnesty as a serious organisation confronting these issues head on.

10. Personalise your copy. At a fairly trivial level, personalisation works because we like seeing our own name. It makes us feel special. However, personalisation can be taken well beyond just merging the name and address of the individual into a standard letter. True personalisation means tailoring the message to include details unique to that individual. This would reflect a 'one-to-one strategy', as outlined in Chapter 6.

EXHIBIT 12.15

PRACTITIONERS' VIEWS ON LONG VERSUS SHORT COPY

'Good copy takes you by the hand and leads you gently from where you are to where the advertiser wants you to be.'

Victor Schwab

Ogilvy (1983) always maintained that long copy worked better in direct-response press ads. Nash (1995). however, took the view that short copy is better. He quoted Victor Schwab: 'Tell me quick and tell me true, or else my love, to hell with you.' Nash asserted that the old style '49 reasons why you should buy this product' approaches no longer work.

Bird (1989), a believer in long copy, felt that persuasion rarely came through brevity.

Stone (1996) asserted that modern times demand shorter copy because the amount that people read has lessened.

McCorkell (1994) took the commonsense view that if marketers can still edit their copy without detracting from the power of the sales message, then it is too long!

You always meant to join us. How many deaths ago was that?

Burmese soldier in a pose familiar to democracy supporters.

mountainsides to fall to their deaths.

Amnesty International has produced report after report on Burma. We campaign for an end to forced portering and for the release of more than a thousand people who are in prison for daring to call for democracy.

To date the Burmese generals refuse to allow Amnesty International into the country. We need to pile the pressure onto them, and to do this we need the support of everyone who gives a damn. Do you?

Please don't turn away again.

This advertisement was going to open with the words: "We don't mean to make you feel guilty." But it's not true. We do.

Feeling guilty proves that you care. That you value justice and freedom and basic human rights. That you're not one of those who can watch people's agony on TV while wondering what's on the other channel.

You care. That makes you very special. We *need* you. Please act on your best instincts. Do *something* to help.

Joining us isn't the only way you can help, but it's one of the most effective.

For thirty five years we have campaigned tirelessly against human rights abuse all over the world. There are many examples of how the intervention of Amnesty International has helped free people from jail, save them from torture or from being killed.

What is Amnesty International but people just like you? People who on their own can do little, but by joining together can help thousands.

We need you because despite everything we're doing, it still isn't enough.

We know it's not enough because the killings, torture and imprisonment haven't stopped. Until they do, neither can we.

Please take this opportunity to join us or make a donation to help our work. Make today the day. Make this the moment. Pick up your pen and fill in the coupon. Or pick up the phone. Do it now. Do it for the sake of the suffering people in Burma whose acts of principle and courage deserve more than our complicit silence.

Most of all, do it for yourself.

Did you see John Pilger's shocking documentary about Burma, where thousands have been killed for daring to call for democracy, where the woman who won an election was held under house arrest for years, where children are forced to labour for the army and you can be clapped in manacles and chains for singing a song about freedom? Can you see such things and not want to help?

Amnesty International, working worldwide for the release of prisoners of conscience, fair trials for political prisoners and an end to torture, extra-judicial executions, "disappearances" and the death penalty.

Earlier this week, millions of TV viewers saw John Pilger's terrifying film about Burma, which for 34 years has been ruled by generals who renamed the country Myanmar, closed it off to the outside world and imprisoned, tortured or killed anyone who disagreed with them.

With our own eyes we saw the evidence.

We watched young Burmese students calling for a 'democracy' which most of us take for granted, being shot down, running away through the streets and falling, drenched in blood.

"Keep filming till they shoot us."

We saw these things because Burmese people risked their lives to film them secretly.

We heard the voices of cameramen who had been warned that they would be shot if they kept on filming. As the soldiers raise their guns one cameraman asks the other:

'What shall we do?'

'Keep on filming till they shoot us.'

We saw brave Aung San Suu Kyi, who won a democratic election with 82% of the seats, who was confined under arrest in her house by the generals who lost.

We saw how the generals imprison any who dare to express a desire for freedom –

by singing a song, or writing a poem.

We saw these 'criminals' bound in chains and manacles and compelled to labour.

We watched a small boy, forced to work long hours each day, crying as a barrowload of cement collapsed on top of him.

The horrors you didn't see.

If you were moved by John Pilger's film, you should know that, harrowing as it was, it was just a snapshot of the fear that rules Burma. Amnesty International has been watching Burma for years.

One of the things the film couldn't show was the horrific human processions that wind through Burma's mountains: thousands of people, Burmese villagers who have been forced at gunpoint by the army to work as porters, carrying heavy loads along steep trails with little food or rest.

The sick, old, mentally ill – none are spared. If they fall they are left to die by the wayside. One man was hacked to death with a hoe. Many are just shot and kicked over

---

I want to be a member of Amnesty International. Here's my annual subscription fee:
£21 Individual ☐ £27 Family ☐ £7.50 Student ☐ Under 22 ☐ Claimant ☐ Senior Citizen ☐
I wish to donate £500 ☐ £250 ☐ £100 ☐ £50 ☐ £25 ☐ £10 ☐ Other _____
Please charge my Access/Visa/Mastercard Number: ☐☐☐☐
Total: _____
Signed: _____ Card valid from ☐☐-☐☐ Expiry ☐☐-☐☐
If you are paying by credit card please give the address where you receive your card statement bill.
Mr/Mrs _____ Address _____
Postcode _____
If you do not want to receive information about mailings from sympathetic organisations please tick this box ☐
To join or make a donation please call **0345 611116**. Calls are charged at local rates.
TO: DEPT. AA, AMNESTY INTERNATIONAL UK, FREEPOST, LONDON EC1B 1HE.

AMNESTY INTERNATIONAL

Figure 12.9 Amnesty advert using hard-hitting copy

Source: Reproduced by kind permission of Amnesty International

Involvement devices

Involvement devices include scratch-off cards, toys, quizzes, stickers, half- completed elements which the reader completes, and 'highlight' devices like coins or bits of product.

Involvement devices are commonly associated with traditional direct marketing sectors such as book clubs, subscriptions, collectibles, weight watchers, and so on. These 'direct marketing led' companies have ruthlessly tested the use of involvement devices in their campaigns, and the results speak for themselves. Involvement devices in these markets raise response. As Drayton Bird puts it, 'Why are they used? Because they work!'

However, there is a lot of resistance to the use of involvement devices among sectors like financial services companies, car companies, and so on. This resistance is largely down to perceptions among marketers that such devices will damage their brands because of a perceived downmarket image. Traditional direct marketers argue that this premise is unproven.

So should mainstream market sectors make more use of involvement devices than they do at present? Prima facie, these devices do not fit very well with a serious brand/product category. However, there are increasing examples of strongly branded companies using involvement devices successfully, as Tango has shown with its 'helpline' for consumers. This 'fun' approach has worked very well; after one ad, Tango generated over 300 000 calls to this 'helpline'!

Mark Fiddes (1996), a leading direct marketing creative who has worked on Tango campaigns, feels that involving consumers in the brand is a very important part of the future. To him, it represents a new direction from traditional 'we talk, you listen' mass communication.

Finally, let us note that toys, quizzes and stickers are commonly used in business-to-business mailers, often aimed at *senior* managers ... with great success!

Practitioners have claimed a variety of psychological drivers underpinning the success of involvement devices. Some examples are:

■ **Scratch-off cards, executive toys:** '*Within every person there is a child, and that child likes to play*' (Nash, 1995).

■ **Quizzes:** Practitioners claim that these work because we love the chance to test or show off our knowledge, even to ourselves.

■ **Completion:** It is felt that some people have a compulsive desire to obtain order. Picture yourself in front of a jigsaw, nearly complete with one piece lying close by waiting to be placed. How many could resist completing the jigsaw? There is a great deal of pleasure, aesthetic satisfaction, in completion.

■ **Making choices:** Many people enjoy making choices, especially when they feel they are getting a bargain. This is the basis for the 'which three books do you want for a pound?' type of offer.

■ **Lots of pieces in an envelope** have consistently worked well in many traditional direct marketing sectors. Why is this? According to Bird it is because 'one piece in an envelope means one chance to make a sale; eight pieces means eight chances'. Here Bird is reinforcing John E. Kennedy's comment (1904) that advertising is 'salesmanship in print'.

According to Nash, involvement devices work because they hold interest long enough to keep the prospect interested until the whole message is got over. Bird notes that the devices work by locking in already interested people towards responding. Bird quotes research which said that each piece in a mailer is looked at for about

3 seconds before being discarded. Consumers filmed opening mailers showed they spent longer on multi element packs than packs with little in them.

■ **The use of coins:** Bird described one of the most famous mailers of all time: the 'two pennies' letter of the *Reader's Digest*, first used in the 1950s. Copy, lying between the two pennies, advised the consumer to keep one and spend the other on the *Reader's Digest*. Coins are still used by the *Digest* today.

Desire/conviction

At the interest stage, the prospect is still hedging his/her bets. The frame of mind is one of appraisal, which tends to be made on a logical, calculating basis.

Desire is different. Here, your prospect has started to have some *emotional feeling* for the product or service. S/he starts to *imagine* what it is like to own or experience what you are selling; s/he pictures this happening. With desire, emotion takes over from logic and the powerful motivations leading towards a sale are in place.

The point of good creative is that it triggers and then fosters these emotional feelings. Emotional benefits are linked with the product: looking good, arousing envy in your friends, being successful, having control, and so on.

The flip side of accentuating positive benefits is the reassurance required that the buying decision will be a good one. Here, *conviction* is the required emotion for your prospect. You must convince them that they have nothing to fear, that you are trustworthy, that your product will be what you say it is in the advert. Above all, you must convince them that they are getting value for money.

Desire and conviction are built using the following techniques:

1 **Testimonials:** Ogilvy quoted James Webb Young, one of the best copywriters in history: 'Everybody in advertising has the same problem: to be believed.'

2 **Description:** Bird extolled the use of words in such a way as to arouse desire: 'thick cream on scrumptious puddings'. This is also true of the incentive: 'Imagine winning a holiday in the Caribbean. Feel the tension release as the warm sand trickles between your toes, you hear the clink of the ice in your drink and the sea gently slides its way up the shore.'

3 **Tone:** Bird advised making sure that the tone is appropriate; don't overstate by using 'fantastic, tremendous, superb' and so on *ad nauseum*.

4 **Illustrations/pictures:** To trigger emotional feelings, pictures are often very powerful. Here the role of the art director is key. The art director helps to identify pictorial ways of communicating themes related to emotions, fantasy and self image. People want to be able to associate the product with themselves.

A lot of emotional messages have much more credibility with people if they are communicated visually rather than in the written word. For example, a picture of the use of perfume making a model feel younger and sexier would be completely natural. However, imagine a headline explaining that you can feel sexier with perfume. This would be ridiculous.

An important part of arousing desire is ensuring the product fits in with the self image of the buyer. The most powerful way of doing this is through pictures. Mail-order companies know that the choice of models in their catalogues is critical to sales; consumers want to identify with the models.

5 **Building credibility and trust:** Well-known powerful brands such as British Airways should not have any trouble obtaining trust from prospects. A small mail-order operation asking for cash with order is in a very different situation. It may use:

■ testimonials from peers who have endorsed the product;

■ famous personalities who have bought the product to endorse it;

■ the fact that it has advertised publicly, 'As advertised on TV', in its merchandising.

Action

There are two creative strands to generating action. One is to emphasise the need to act straightaway; the other is to minimise the effort required.

Encouraging immediacy

You have the reader's attention. You stimulated their interest through well worked copy and layout. You triggered their desire with pictures showing the emotional benefits of your product. You must now seize the moment! You must inspire action. Many authors (e.g. Nash, 1995) report an old saying in direct marketing: 'Delay kills response.' If your prospect puts down the advert maybe to look at it another time, the chances are the sale is lost. Direct marketers use various creative techniques which maximise the sense that time is short:

■ creative exhortations to be urgent, strongly allied to an offer which rewards urgency: for example, 'Limited edition product', or 'Free gift if you reply in ten days';

■ creative approaches which emphasise the urgent need for the product: 'Act now to avoid paying/discomfort/loss later' approaches may be appropriate for products such as antifreeze, roof coating, or children's school clothes;

■ simply telling the consumer what you want them to do in clear terms: Nash describes this as 'command terminology'; e.g. 'Send it now', 'Act straightaway', and so on;

■ a sense of immediacy, conveyed by techniques like sending a fax, enclosing faxes or telegrams, using handwritten notes or half-cut photos: these techniques utilise 'calculated crudity' (Nash, 1995), which work because the more finished the advert, the more permanent it looks, and the less immediate. A balance between good production values and conveying urgency often needs to be struck. These techniques are often used by the charity sector;

■ setting a deadline: this is usually done in conjunction with an offer: 'Offer closes in ten days. Hurry!'

Minimising effort: making it easy to respond

Your prospect is now convinced of the need to act quickly. They decide to respond now. They reach for the pen. It doesn't work. They have run out of envelopes. Your ad is put aside 'until later'. Even at this late stage you have probably lost the sale, because you did not *make it easy* for them.

Direct marketers are past masters at making it easy for customers to respond. Consumers increasingly look for more convenient ways of living their lives; this is one of the main reasons for the growth of direct marketing. Given that buying is a function of reward divided by effort, marketers should minimise the effort involved in purchase.

Thirty years ago, buyer and seller would have exchanged polite, courteous and well-written letters acknowledging the sale. No longer!

Direct marketers make it easy for consumers to respond using the following devices:

1 The telephone and credit card. These have had a massive influence in driving the growth of direct marketing. Most mail-order companies now offer telephone alternatives for ordering, and the trend towards the use of the telephone increases. Stating in the advert that credit cards are accepted, and using the credit-card logos, VISA, Access, and so on, will raise response. Credit cards are extremely popular, and the brand names will enhance the credibility of the advert. Freephone numbers are worth prominent display; they enhance credibility and are popular. Forte Hotels used 0800 40 40 40 in its direct-response TV adverts.

2 The response coupon or order form. The creative dimensions of the response coupon have been extensively tested. The following techniques will increase response:

- the coupon should be as large as possible;
- space to fill in name and address details should be clearly laid out and easy to fill in;
- coupons with the prospect's name pre filled in can be used with direct mail; all the prospect has to do is sign;
- using yes/no coupons gives prospects boxes to tick even if they don't want to buy. Nash believes they work because some people need to be forced to make up their minds;
- the process of making purchases from catalogues should be simplified for consumers. An astute direct marketer can ease the process of calculating how much to pay by precompleting the calculations for common combinations, or packaging products together with an easy 'tick box' option on the form.

3 Enclosing reply envelopes. These are now standard for direct mail. The author once conducted a direct-mail campaign in which the business reply envelope (BRE) was accidentally left out of the pack! Response was about ten percentage points below the level of the other tests.

PUTTING IT ALL TOGETHER: LAYOUT

Nash (1995) outlined what he called the Five Cs of layout:

1 Concentration: A small-space ad with one large element in it will get more attention than a large-space ad with no large element in it. For example, a small press ad with a bold headline 'How to be happier' will be more eye-catching than a large article next to it without a headline.

2 Cohesion: Each element of the advertisement – the headline, picture, caption, body copy and coupon – should lead to each other rather than to the outside of the ad.

3 Convention: As children we are taught that certain shapes have certain meanings; for example, a pencil is always recognised by its shape. These conventions are locked in our minds very strongly, and if a picture goes against these conventions we get confused. Devices such as reversed-out copy, white on black, will lower response because we are not used to reading this way. Similarly, typewriter typefaces or handwritten signatures

EXHIBIT 12.16

THE SECRETS OF TYPEFACE

Nash, Stone, Bird and Ogilvy have all emphasised the importance of typeface in direct-response adverts. The following guidelines are offered:

■ Sans serif is associated with modernity, but ... sans serif is difficult to read for long passages of text. Serifs, the little 'feet' at the edge of the letter characters, keep the eye moving horizontally along the line of type.

■ Times Roman is associated with books and papers and so suggests reliability, authority and credibility.

■ *Typeface at an angle gives an impression of speed.*

■ **A bold typeface conveys loudness.**

■ 𝕲𝖔𝖙𝖍𝖎𝖈 𝖎𝖒𝖕𝖑𝖎𝖊𝖘 𝖙𝖗𝖆𝖉𝖎𝖙𝖎𝖔𝖓𝖆𝖑.

■ CAPITALS ARE MORE DIFFICULT TO READ. This is because they have no ascenders or descenders to help reading and tend to be read letter by letter.

■ Small type on coupons inspires distrust.

■ **Reversed-out type is tiring on the eye in any great volume.**

■ Type set at funny angles, over pictures, or in large columns across the page is more difficult to read.

look like convention, and this is why they are a good idea. Contrary to popular belief, handwritten-style signatures are not used because they fool readers into believing they have had a letter personally signed by the chairperson. They are used because that is what convention demands.

4 Contrast: The first law of layout is *to be noticed*. Your ad must stand out from its environment. However, a balance needs to be struck between getting noticed and swamping the sales message. The best way to get noticed is through some creative way of enhancing the benefits of your product. One radio advertisement, sponsored by the government, used long periods of *silence*, punctuated by a voice explaining how much the advert cost per second, to dramatise how money was wasted through heat loss in buildings! This ad worked because of the contrast it created with adverts played before and after.

5 Convection: Flow, or convect, the reader from one element to the other, from the headline to the coupon. Ogilvy, a master of print advertising, recommended the following ways of keeping the reader moving through the advert:

■ use columns of 35 to 45 characters;
■ use drop capitals to start your body copy;
■ captions are widely read – use them;
■ subheadings which break up the body copy are a good idea;
■ direct the reader to the coupon at every opportunity. Nash recommends that when writing an advert you should start with the coupon.

Summary to chapter

In this chapter we found that there is a strong basis in classic creative direct response from the 'left-brain' school of advertising. There are signs that this is changing to include some brand-building techniques, as the two objectives of branding and response merge in certain sectors.

Direct marketers have been able to test different creative approaches, and the cumulative wisdom from these tests has led to a number of 'rules' or guidance for maximising response. By following the AIDA model of consumer behaviour, the novice direct marketer gives him or herself the best chance of success.

Questions

1. You are shown a press advert and asked to identify it as either a brand-building advert, a direct-response ad, or a mixture of the two. What clues would you use from the advert itself to help you identify its objectives?

2. Picking any Sunday colour supplement, go through the magazine and identify the objectives, target audience and creative principles of the direct-response adverts contained within.

3. Define positioning and branding, and explain why they are so important in creative considerations.

4. Outline what creative principles an international distress charity should take into account before mailing prospective donors.

5. In what instances is it acceptable, if any, to break the direct marketing 'rules' of collective wisdom gathered in this chapter?

6. You have been asked to put together a creative execution of a direct-response ad for Stilton blue cheese, a relatively expensive cheese sometimes eaten on special occasions. Explain how you would approach the problem and what creative factors you would take into account.

References

Bird, D. (1989) *Commonsense Direct Marketing*, Kogan Page, London.

Bovee, C., Thill, J., Dovell, G. and Wood, M. (1995) *Advertising Excellence*, McGraw-Hill, New York.

de Chenatony, L. and McDonald, M. (1992) *Creating Powerful Brands*, Butterworth-Heinemann, Oxford.

Fiddes, M. (1996) Personal communication to the author.

Fox, S. (1984) *The Mirror Makers*, Morrow and Co., New York.

Foxall, G. and Goldsmith, R. (1994) *Consumer Psychology for Marketing*, Routledge, London.

Halsey, B. (ed.) (1992) *The Practitioners' Guide to Direct Marketing*, Teddington, UK.

Jones, C. (1992) 'A visual language – the role of art direction in print' in Halsey, B. (ed.) *The Practitioners' Guide to Direct Marketing*, Institute of Direct Marketing, Teddington, Richmond-upon-Thames.

Martin, D. (1989) *Romancing the Brand*, Amacom, USA.

McCorkell, G. (1994) *The Best of Graeme McCorkell*, DRM, London.

Nash, E. (1995) *Direct Marketing: Strategy, planning, execution*, McGraw-Hill, New York.

Ogilvy, D. (1964) *Confessions of an Advertising Man*, Longman, Harlow, Essex.

Ogilvy, D. (1983) *Ogilvy on Advertising*, Crown, USA.

Rapp, S. and Collins, T. (1987) *Maximarketing*, McGraw-Hill, New York.

Reeves, R. (1961) *Reality in Advertising*, Knopf, New York.

Smith, P. (1993) *Marketing Communications: An integrated approach*, Kogan Page, London.

Stone, B. (1996) *Successful Direct Marketing Methods*, NTC Business Books, Chicago, Ill.

The English Cricket Board

The brief

While the attendences of international one-day and test-match fixtures was as high as ever, the ordinary county cricket scene in England was not well supported. The profile of cricket followers was older than that of its much bigger rival, soccer. The brief from the English Cricket Board was for the direct-response advertising to help whip up some appeal across a broader age range, while still fulfilling its primary role of pulling in response for tickets.

Figure 12.10 Advert using humour to appeal to broader age range

Source: The English Cricket Board and Bates Direct.

The solution

The agency, Bates Communications, decided to take an irreverent, humorous approach to the forthcoming test series between Australia and England. The picture and copy (in Fig. 12.10) refer to the fact that some of the original white settlers in Australia were convicted British criminals carrying out penal service. The campaign attracted good publicity, with the *Daily Mirror* describing it as a 'provocative' campaign, and also attracting quotes from Australian cricketers.

Questions

1. From the brief, and referring to the classical direct marketing 'rules' in the chapter, critically analyse the off-the-page advert. In what ways does it differ from a classical direct-response advert?
2. Given the brief, produce your own version of the advert.

CASE STUDY

Friends of the Earth

Friends of the Earth is one of the highest profile charities in the UK. Barely a week passes without its name appearing in connection with its key campaigns including 'industry and pollution', biodiversity and habitat, and biotechnology. In 2000, the hottest issue was probably the tests on GM modified foodstuffs, something that did not appear popular with much of the general public. 'We are here to transform society, and have a track record going back 30 years' said Steven Montgomery, development manager. Founded in 1971, FoE strives to offer a 'better future' through campaigning, research and education.

As ever, fundraising is important. The direct marketing team looks after more than 100 000 supporters, and has its own mailing house in Luton. The fundraising mix is typical of sophisticated charities: members get a quarterly magazine, *Earthmatters*, and regular mailings containing appeals to fund specific campaigns. The typical FoE supporter is aged 35–55, well educated, geographically biased to London and the South East. 55 per cent of them are female. This profile is similar to the typical charity giver, with the exception of age: FoE supporters are younger than other donors. Not surprisingly, ideology is very important to FoE donors. They are committed enough about a better world to support their ideals through hard cash.

Montgomery and his team were particularly concerned to develop what they called 'major donors'. They trawled the database and came up with more than 800 names who had given more than £250 per year. The decision was made to contact these people in an effort to increase the average donation by a considerable amount. Issue-specific appeals would be the focus, with the first three being toxic pollution, food and climate change. Future plans for Major Donors included invitations to special meetings and evenings to see behind the scenes, and find out where their money was going.

Before that, however, plans were being laid for the all-important direct-mail campaigns to the 800 key supporters. A powerful creative approach was needed. Montgomery had good resources available to him. What should he do?

(Based on information in Booth, E. (1999) 'Back to the planet', *Marketing Direct*, October, pp. 39–40.)

Extract from 'Mailing do's and don't's' (*Marketing Direct*, November 1999, p. 42)

■ Don't forget to keep your mailing simple and single minded if you want a good response.
■ Don't forget who your customers really are and what they want from you.
■ Avoid the three Gs in copy: grovelling, grammar-ridden, gobbledegook.

In other words, get straight to the point, don't feel the need to stick to formal grammar, and avoid jargon.

■ Think about the medium – direct mail is tactile.

Question

Outline the key messages of the Friends of the Earth campaigns. Make creative recommenda-tions for the copy tone of voice, artwork and layout. Your creative solution should consider key messages, audience, the outcomes desired, brand values of FoE and any other considerations you think are important.

CASE STUDY

M&G - collective investments

Source: Harrison Troughton Wunderman

It pays to tell the whole truth

Summary of entry

In Autumn 2001, M&G was a declining brand with poor fund performance and dwindling responses to advertising. It was also approaching a third consecutive year of stockmarket decline and tough competition. With this backdrop direct marketing had to achieve increased sales targets with reduced marketing budgets.

Planning identified a distinct target market, an original approach and, through research, helped hone the executions to increase their relevance and potency.

The subsequent campaign featured long, straightforward and informative copy, and boldly relaunched the ailing M&G brand in time for the crucial ISA selling season. This season is like Christmas for retailers – January to April accounts for 50 per cent of total ISA sales.

The campaign actually acquired customers at a time when the ISA market, as a whole, was down an alarming 30 per cent.

In fact, the results were excellent. Compared with the previous year, 2001, media spend was down 31 per cent, yet responses were up 32 per cent and cost per enquiry was down 53 per cent. This successfully converted to sales seeing the cost of acquiring new customers, as a percentage of sales, falling by 35 per cent. Also 19 per cent less people redeemed their investments despite fears of a continued downturn. The campaign was also effective in seeing positive shifts in brand awareness versus the competition.

Background

We found in our analysis that much of the communication from financial services companies was very similar and tended to be grouped in two camps – either large headlines highlighting past performance rates or dramatisations about realising dreams.

In terms of branding the most prominent companies simply relied upon a mnemonic (a planet – Jupiter, a solar system – New Star, a mountain – Fidelity, a woman in widows weeds – Scottish Widows) to maintain recognition. They relied on the thought that recognition leads straight to purchase. However, this approach made it difficult for consumers to differentiate one message from another. This lack of differentiation in the market was also very much evidenced when you looked at brand awareness figures of the major players. In particular for M&G there was confusion with Legal & General advertising (see Fig. 12.11). If you covered the logos of both providers on their advertising it was near impossible to differentiate one ad from another.

Figure 12.11

M&G knew that just following the crowd with a big media budget was no guarantee of improving awareness levels. In fact in 2001 when expenditure was raised by 48 per cent, against the previous year, spontaneous awareness actually dropped by 9 per cent.

In addition, all this competitive marketing took place against a backdrop of two years of successive falls in the FTSE and a general mistrust of financial institutions. This mistrust was due to several reasons; corporate accounting fiascos like Enron, recent scandals in the financial services industry – including the Equitable Life collapse, pensions and endowments mis-selling – and general overclaims made in advertising and marketing material. It was not surprising, therefore, that consumers treated the advertising with much cynicism and distrust.

As a result of this, M&G embarked on a large research project to understand what qualities consumers really wanted from an investment company.

To supplement M&G's existing research, additional qualitative and quantitative studies were conducted. This bespoke research encompassed insights and views from consumers, intermediaries and staff.

It is important to note that while the main task of this project was to focus on direct customers we also had to consider the effect intermediaries opinions can have – mostly IFAs (Independent Financial Advisers), as many of our target consumers have a relationship with financial services companies through one.

Defining and refining the target audience

Investment products, by their very nature, rely on consumers having 'spare cash' to invest, so it's quite easy to define the target market by levels of assets or income. The first definition of the target group to emerge, therefore, was 'mass affluents' – those with assets of £30K-£200K and/or an income of £30K-£100K. These people represented only 8.4 per cent of the adult population but were worth some £500 billion and expected to grow 50 per cent in numbers by 2004.

While this target was very useful in quantifying the size of the market it didn't give us any insights into lifestyle trends, or the mindset of this group, that would be essential in developing compelling communications. It also, as was discovered, included a wide range of demographics that would have made it difficult to focus on a single proposition and creative approach.

Specifically, 'mass affluents' included large numbers of people who during the best years of the 'nineties had, through a combination of high salaries, good bonuses, property and inheritance, amassed serious amounts of capital. Many of them were under 40, however, and as previous research had shown, they were a hard nut to crack when it came to long-term financial planning. In fact, a frightening statistic highlighted this; 35 per cent of under 35-year-old ABs had no pension provision whatsoever.

The key targets with the most capital were identified as those over 45. They take investing seriously and invest large amounts. Having money put aside for a 'rainy day' is important to this generation. Crucially, every year their children are gaining independence, or have left home, and their mortgages are either paid off or are very small, therefore they have the greatest motivation and ability to invest. This group also formed a major part of the M&G existing customer base.

This was the first insight and we dubbed this core group the 'Affluent silvers'. They accounted for about 80 per cent of the UK financial wealth.

Most importantly, they were identified from research to be consistently more money-management minded than younger people, more financially astute and confident, and, known to prefer informative advertising.

In addition to the quantitative facts, we added the following qualitative observations as important 'colour' to the creative brief. This gave the creative teams a real understanding of the target's mindset and feelings towards marketing:

They are time-rich and therefore more analytical and less impulsive in the way they digest information – investigating is a popular pastime. They feel they are consistently ignored by the media and popular culture and irritated by often being portrayed as dotty eccentrics, despite the fact that they are young at heart. They do not regard old values as old-fashioned.

Towards a strategy

Before looking at M&G's position in the market, and any relative strengths and weaknesses, it was important to identify what values the ideal investment company was expected to have. The study of consumer and IFA needs led to a summary of five values that both audiences appeared to desire and share in common:

An investment brand should be/have . . .

Expert

Informative

Straightforward

Integrity

Durable

Subsequently, using the same research, we probed people's perceptions of the M&G brand in order to analyse these versus the 'ideal' values (above).

The M&G brand was seen to have two strong qualities over and above the competition; having *integrity* and being *durable* – both consumers and IFAs felt M&G was trustworthy, valued the fact that it had been established a long time and had been through both 'bull' and 'bear' markets. These formed the foundation of the strategy.

We were also mindful of them wanting expertise and an informative and straightforward manner from an investment company.

So to take this to a logical conclusion it was decided that:

Brand benefit = TRUST

Consumers will trust product offerings, or advice given, from durable companies that are regarded as having integrity.

Key strategic insights

'Trust' is fine for a brand benefit but we were very wary of it becoming a proposition for any communication. The very phrase 'you can trust me' was likely to evoke cynicism and with some people a reaction of 'walk-the-walk don't talk-the-talk'.

The next insight was that consumers were looking for an institution that told the truth, a company that gave the real facts and treated the potential or existing customer like a grown-up. This, it was felt, would attract the more mature investor that we had identified; but above all it would make M&G stand out completely.

This insight was based on more than simply the financial market. We felt very strongly that consumers were fed up of hype and 'spin' in all areas of their life from 'builders' promises' to politics. For instance, most of the consumers interviewed believed that politicians would happily substitute the truth with any excuse to get them out of a problem or win a vote.

We felt the time was right for a marketing campaign in which exaggeration and hype were refreshingly absent.

Again, however, the campaign should not talk about how M&G always told the truth, or indeed even mention the word at all. It should demonstrate its transparency through the content of the information that it offered through facts, bold opinions and not hiding things in the small print.

The culmination of research, planning and agency discussion led to the brand idea:

The truth about investing as we see it.

Developing the campaign

With the brand idea as our focus we developed brand response and product advertising, Fulfilment and direct mail all aimed at meeting the tough sales targets set.

Brand response advertising

From the brand idea a brand response advertising campaign was developed that explained M&G's point of view and offered guidance through the difficult economic times people were experiencing (*see* Fig. 12.12).

The long, straightforward and informative copy, served to demonstrate M&G's depth of knowledge on market issues. We took previously impenetrable subjects, like ISAs and bonds, explained them in full and demystified all the financial jargon that normally accompanied them. Moreover, the ads were written for the 'affluent silver' market who, as we knew, were willing and able to absorb lengthy information. Only towards the end of the copy did we mention M&G products, and then it was more of a suggestion than a hard sell.

Likewise the visuals of the 'right' heroes of yesteryear, used to highlight aspects of the communication, were chosen to appeal to this age group i.e. using a gardening analogy, watering little and often, to illustrate the benefits of drip feeding your investments. Consumer research was very valuable at this stage, hence the use of Percy Thrower (not Alan Titchmarsh), Bobby Moore (not David Beckham) and Emil Zatopek (not Colin Jackson).

In fact, one of the research concepts featured Tony Hancock. The agency regarded Hancock as a comic genius. The 'affluent silvers' saw him as depressing and having ideas above his station. Just like that, Hancock was replaced with Tommy Cooper.

This turned a poster and a press ad, which would have both been utterly rejected by the target audience, into a marketing success (*see* Fig. 12.13).

Figure 12.12 Full-page brand response ads that appeared in national daily and weekend papers Jan-Mar 2002

Original concept

Final ad

Figure 12.13

Media choice

For the brand response advertising, in a quest to really stand out and take the high ground, we looked for alternatives to the traditional money sections where all the competition advertised.

We opted for colour pages in main news sections of national newspapers. In addition, we kicked off the campaign with 48-sheet cross-track posters, for railways and tube stations, where we could impart detailed information when the target would have time to digest it.

In addition to using different media from the competition, to increase stand-out, we decided to break the campaign in January before the traditional ISA advertising season.

Each ad/poster featured a telephone number that was specific to each execution, and for press ads each coupon had a code that represented the specific insertion. This enabled us to track the campaign by execution and by medium.

This inputted into the M&G lead management system and provided a fresh injection of new prospects (see lead management system below).

Product advertising

We followed the brand response campaign with product ads, which explained how specific M&G products worked, what the customer could expect from them and how they could be bought as an ISA. These were written for both the consumer and IFA audience – appearing in the national newspapers' financial sections, the 'pinks' and the IFA trade press.

IFA advertising for Managed Growth Fund   Consumer advertising for Corporate Bond Fund

Figure 12.14

Fulfilment

The call to action in posters and press was for the *M&G Guide to Investing* which maintained the clear and simple explanatory style of the advertising, and the frames of reference that were particularly relevant to the 'affluent silvers'. The guide helped investors make choices about asset classes and investment products, and generally demystified the whole investment marketplace.

Latterly, a bespoke piece was written and produced as a fulfilment to bond product advertising entitled *Spin Free Guide to Bonds*. This turned out to be as popular with IFAs as consumers, because it provided them with a sales aid when recommending bond products to their clients.

Direct mail

Again the tone was empathetic. While other investment houses were urging the public to make their ISA decision, M&G was acknowledging how difficult that decision was and urging them to have a cup of tea and take their time. As the ISA cut-off date grew closer, the relaxing cup of tea gave way to a quick cup of instant coffee and a more urgent call to action.

Lead management system

Prospects from all direct marketing activity were invited to contact M&G via telephone, coupon or the website. Responses were closely tracked and related back to campaign codes on specific press insertions or mail packs. This enabled us to constantly monitor cost per response on both an execution and medium level, and adapt the media schedule and execution lay-down accordingly.

Requests for information were promptly fulfilled with bespoke information packs as outlined above. Each lead received a follow-up outbound telemarketing call shortly after.

All converters subsequently entered the customer marketing programme so that M&G could include them in retention and cross/up sell activities.

Warm prospects were retained for future direct mail opportunities.

Results

Overall effectiveness of the 2002 M&G ISA campaign has been assessed at two levels:

1 M&G spend, performance and cost per enquiry – 2002 vs 2001.
2 Performance against the market – market share and awareness.

M&G spend, performance and cost per enquiry

In short, compared with the key ISA selling season of the previous year (Jan to April 2001), the 2002 campaign was a tremendous success.

■ *More response*. Response rates were up 32.5 per cent. In February response actually increased by over 100 per cent vs 2001.

■ *Less money*. Media spend was down 31.7 per cent.

■ *Better efficiency*. Cost per enquiry was down 53.9 per cent. For March, the peak ISA selling month, cost per enquiry fell by 75.6 per cent. Overall, the acquisition costs as a percentage of sales were down 35 per cent.

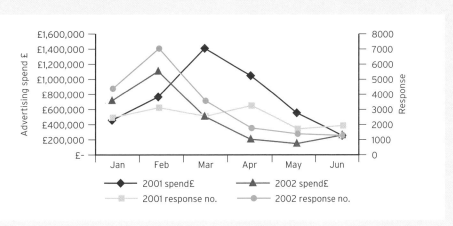

Figure 12.15 M&G advertising spend versus response – total brand and acquisition

All of this was achieved in a rapidly shrinking market. Over the period in question, direct industry business was down over 30 per cent and IFA industry business was down 30 per cent.

Redemptions

Moreover, we were hanging on to our customers a lot better than before. Even in times of poor performance and crumbling consumer confidence, M&G's redemptions were actually 19 per cent down versus 2001. This was a real contrast to the competition when the market was seeing redemptions up between 20–25 per cent. It came as a surprise and a positive benefit from the campaign.

Direct sales

Total sales January to April 2002 increased 15.3 per cent and ISA sales increased 19 per cent vs. 2001. Sales through the internet channel increased by 38 per cent. In addition, M&G's share of new business generated by direct sales increased by 33 per cent at the height of the press campaign (March 02).

All forms of media contributed to this overall success. For example, to achieve payback the February 'Cup of Tea' direct-mail pack had to get 0.28 per cent of people to buy an M&G investment product. In fact, 2.7 per cent of people mailed actually bought an M&G product. This outperformed our breakeven by 864 per cent.

Performance against market

Brand awareness

The ads generated the greatest prompted brand awareness over our key competitors during the advertising period. In fact, our advertising outperformed Fidelity, a leading competitor, despite our spend being 15 per cent lower.

Figure 12.16 Prompted brand awareness
Source: Marketminder

Market share

Finally, by the end of April 2002, the total market share (IFA and direct sales) was up 14.3 per cent on 2001.

Specifically, ISA/PEP market share was up 24.8 per cent on 2001.

TESTING, BUDGETING AND RESEARCH IN DIRECT MARKETING

Objectives

Once you have read this chapter you should:

■ be able to set up a direct marketing test programme and interpret its results;

■ be able to structure a direct marketing budget and use it to aid decision making;

■ appreciate how research and direct marketing can work together.

Introduction

There are three distinct techniques that direct marketers use to control their activities. They are setting a budget which includes target responses, testing to maximise return on spend, and market research to understand the qualitative impact of campaigns. The actual measurement of the campaigns themselves is based on direct response, not surprisingly, and these results, fed into the budget, give a precise, accurate measure of success or otherwise. There is no hiding place for direct marketers!

This chapter will exhibit why direct marketing measurement exhibits clear superiority over general marketing's equivalent. The problem in general marketing is the lack of precision in relating spend to revenue. On increasing its advertising, a packaged goods supplier notices its sales rise. But how does it know the improvement was down to advertising? At the same time as the adverts were being shown, perhaps other competitors put their prices up; maybe footfall through the retail outlets rose, or its salespeople completed some breakthrough contracts to increase distribution.

The key to direct marketing's control lies with its ability to connect any spend precisely to corresponding revenues. Direct marketers can focus on an identified group of customers on their database, and track exactly how much is spent on them over the year, and how much revenue they generate for the company. Return on marketing investment is easily and accurately calculated, as we will see.

How this chapter is structured

This chapter covers three topics. The first is testing; we will look at what testing is, what we should test, and how to do so. The second section brings testing and budgeting together, showing how to set overall marketing budgets and then how to set out a series of tests for programme budgeting. Finally, we take a look at how market research can help with direct marketing analysis and campaign planning.

Testing

'By his actions shall you know him.'

Testing is more than just an operational detail in direct marketing. It is a crucial advantage which direct marketing has in comparison with general marketing. A key aspect of business and marketing strategies is assessing and understanding the risks inherent in any particular chosen route. All other things being equal, the strategist should choose the least risky option. The point about direct marketing is that it is strategically a low-risk option to take. This is because the unrivalled testability of its direct communications means that the success or failure of its campaigns is predictable, allowing returns to be maximised. The initial capital investment in a database, however, is a higher risk enterprise, in which returns are unlikely to break even inside three years (Shaw and Stone, 1988).

In this section, we cover the operational details of testing. The structure will be:

- what testing is: a definition;
- why we test;
- justifying testing financially;
- what variables to test;
- how to design a test programme;
- the effect of sample size on the accuracy of the roll-out predictions.

WHAT IS TESTING?

Testing is the marketers' word for what scientists call experiments. The method has been used for as long as science has been practised, which says something about its validity.

The mechanics of a basic test are extremely simple. A test of a campaign is run concurrently against a control campaign. The test will have all elements kept the same as those of the control, apart from the element under investigation. For example, let us say a bank is offering a new credit card to its customers and wants to test different offers.

The 'control' elements could be:

Audience:	random sample of bank's database
Offer:	new credit card with no annual fee in first year
Timing:	May
Creative:	simple mailer with no brochure, reply envelope and response device

while the 'test' elements are:

Audience:	as above
Offer:	new credit card with annual fee at £12 charged
Timing:	as above
Creative:	as above.

As you can see, the golden rule is to vary only one element at a time. This way any differences in percentage response can be attributed to the element being varied: in the above case, the annual fee waiver.

We are now ready for a formal definition of testing.

Definition

Testing is the small-scale measurement of the performance of individual campaign elements in order to maximise returns on rolled-out full marketing campaigns.

Let us expand a little on this definition.

Small scale

Typically a full, roll-out campaign may involve expenditure of hundreds of thousands of pounds in order to reach many thousands of potential customers. A direct marketing test, usually carried out before the full roll out, typically consists of a mailer to 5000 customers costing, say, £10 000 including all fixed costs.

Measurement

The most important performance measure is the response to the campaign, measured as a percentage. The other critically important performance measure that is used, directly related to response, is profitability. More secondary objectives would include awareness, percentage of mailers read, change in attitudes to the product, and so on.

However, a key strategic performance measure for direct marketers is customer retention (*see* Exhibit 13.1).

EXHIBIT 13.1

MEASURING CUSTOMER RETENTION

To obtain the simplest measure of retention, a company needs to record the number of customers left at the year end, and express this as a percentage of the customers held at the start of the year.

Reichheld (1996) felt that measurement of retention was the most fundamental barrier to corporations adopting a company-wide loyalty strategy. He found that some companies *with much higher than average profitabilities* in their sector, e.g. Toyota's Lexus, or MBNA in credit cards, had retention as their *prime* measure, ahead of market share, revenue or even profit.

The most effective tool for measurement is to use a database, which measures actual rather than claimed behaviour. Some classical direct marketing companies have built in retention measures as the prime performance measure, including Land's End and L.L. Bean, the US-based mail-order specialists.

These companies measure retention in terms of the originally recruited customer cohort. The first measure is the number recruited in year zero. Defections are then tracked and any losses allocated to other customers from the same pool.

Maximising returns on roll out

The idea with testing is to make the individual elements of the campaign as effective as possible so that when large expenditure is committed to the roll out, returns are maximised.

Individual marketing elements

What should we test? This is discussed later, after we have understood all the benefits of testing.

THE BENEFITS OF TESTING FOR DIRECT MARKETERS

We have already covered the primary reason for testing: that is to minimise financial risk. As well as this, there are other, secondary reasons for testing. They are:

■ protecting existing customers from unsuccessful campaigns: by using only small samples with each test, you can treat the bulk of your customers to a proven offer;

■ stimulating creativity: there is a fascination for the creative team in designing a new treatment to beat the current control; testing provides healthy internal competition;

■ helping us to understand customers better: testing can work alongside research in helping to understand customer behaviour. Testing provides a real environment in which to validate claimed behaviour in research. The two do not always tally!

Doing without testing

Some marketers believe they can put together the 'optimum' campaign based solely on intuition and experience, and without the need for prior market testing. This has been proven time and again to be a fallacy. The combined collective experience of the direct marketing industry has been that testing is the only sure, systematic way of maximising campaign profitability.

However, let's call the practitioners' bluff and try to beat the testing 'system'. Take a look at the six creative approaches in Figs 13.1–13.3 (a) and (b) for car insurance. Using your skill and judgement, try to pick the two which gained the greatest response.

(a)

Grab a bumper 20% off motor insurance.

Call The Insurance Service and you could look forward to cheaper motor insurance and a host of benefits.

- Friendly, efficient staff
- Free loan car
- Easy ways to pay
- 24hr windscreen replacement
- £50,000 of free legal expenses insurance in the first year

Full details supplied with your quotation

FREE £20 M&S VOUCHER
when you take out your first policy with us.

0800 989898

CALL FREE AND QUOTE REF:-W01

Mon to Fri 8am - 8.30pm Sat 9am - 4pm

For your benefit we record or listen to telephone calls to ensure high levels of customer service are maintained.

The Insurance Service
a member of the
♔ Royal Insurance
group of companies

The Insurance Service plc. Registered in England & Wales no. 2145778. All offers are subject to change. Offer only available in mainland Britain.

(b)

How much could you save
on motor insurance?
(If you don't call you'll never find out)

FREE M&S VOUCHERS
FREE LEGAL COVER

Receive £20 worth of Marks & Spencer vouchers when you first take out a policy with us

All first year policy holders are entitled to £50,000 worth of Legal Expense Cover, Free of charge

The Insurance Service
a member of the Royal & SunAlliance Group

0800 989898

Opening hours: 8am - 8.30pm Monday to Friday, 9am - 4.30pm Saturday
CALL FREE AND QUOTE REF: EXA 908

For your benefit we record or listen to telephone calls. If you would prefer not to receive information on other Group services, please make us aware when you call. Checks may be made with a licensed credit referencing agency for risk rating purposes.

Figure 13.1 Direct-response ads for the insurance service

Source: Reproduced by kind permission of Royal and Sun Alliance

(a)

BUYING CAR INSURANCE

CUTTING YOUR PREMIUMS DOESN'T HAVE TO MEAN CUTTING YOUR COVER

When car insurance is due for renewal, nobody wants to pay more than they really have to. Royal & Sun Alliance – one of the UK's leading direct insurers recognise this, so they have developed a superbly priced package for drivers with good records.

They treat each customer individually, taking into account their driving history, and rewarding them with savings and discounts It's little wonder their customers make an average saving of £50 when they join – just by making one free phone call!

Royal & Sun Alliance also recognise that lower priced car insurance is of no use without adequate cover which is why their policy includes immediate authorisation of repairs at their network of Quality Assured Recommended Repairers, a free courtesy car whilst yours is being repaired and 24 hour windscreen repair and replacement.

Not only that but customers get a discount of £25 when they insure a second car and up to 30% off Green Flag National Breakdown cover.

With savings like this, can you afford not to give them a call?

'Money saved, a courteous service...and a courtesy car!'

Maurice Pack-Davison called Royal & Sun Alliance and saved over £100. "What's more, the service was efficient and friendly - especially after someone ran into the back of me. Within 24 hours Royal & Sun Alliance had arranged for my car to go to one of their Quality Assured Recommended Repairers

and gave me a courtesy car. One week later my car was back as good as new!

ROYAL & SUNALLIANCE

£20 M&S VOUCHER FREE
WHEN YOU TAKE OUT A MOTOR POLICY

0800 300220

CALL NOW & QUOTE | MLA 938

Lines are open Mon–Fri, 8am to 9pm, Sat 9am to 5pm

For your benefit we may record or listen to telephone calls. Offer only applies to Mainland Britain. If you would prefer not to receive information on other group services, please make us aware when you call. Checks may be made with a licensed credit referencing agency for risk rating purposes. Offer subject to normal underwriting criteria.

(b)

Cut your motor premiums without cutting cover

Most of us recognise that buying motor cover direct can provide substantial savings, but it pays to look really closely at what you actually get for your money.

Using The Insurance Service as an example, some people have saved as much as £100 on their premiums, yet also received additional features like free legal cover up to £50,000 in their first year and a discount of up to 30% with Green Flag National Breakdown.

But what would happen if someone ran in to you?

The Insurance Service's Claims Action Line operate one of the fastest, friendliest services around. If you have an accident their Recommended Prime Repairers can be given instant permission to begin work on your car and you could have the use of a free courtesy car while yours is being repaired.

Can you afford not to give them a call?

"I got £100 worth of savings and complete peace of mind"

Susan Harding, a housewife from Whitchurch, Shropshire drives an E reg Rover. She was surprised at the savings The Insurance Service offered. "I was delighted to find that including the Green Flag National Breakdown discount, I saved nearly £100. Plus, if I'm on holiday in the UK and I have an accident, they'll recommend a quality garage and supply me with a courtesy car whilst mine is being repaired."

Call now for a free motor insurance quote

0800 98 98 98

Quote ref: MIR 919

Monday to Friday 8am - 8.30pm   Saturday 9am - 4.30pm

FREE £20 M&S VOUCHER WHEN YOU TAKE OUT YOUR FIRST POLICY

The Insurance Service
a member of the Royal & SunAlliance Group

For your benefit we record or listen to telephone calls. If you would prefer not to receive information on other Group services, please make us aware when you call. Checks may be made with a licensed credit referencing agency for risk rating purposes.

Figure 13.2 Direct-response ads for the insurance service

Source: Reproduced by kind permission of Royal and Sun Alliance

(a)

(b)

Figure 13.3 Direct-response ads for the insurance service

Source: Reproduced by kind permission of Royal and Sun Alliance

If you chose Fig. 13.2 as the 'winning' adverts, well done – you get the star prize! In descending response order, the adverts were ranked as follows:

Fig. 13.2 (b)
Fig. 13.2 (a)
Fig. 13.1 (b)
Fig. 13.3 (b)
Fig. 13.3 (a)
Fig. 13.1 (a)

Although you may have been successful this time, you would probably agree that it is extremely difficult to pick the winners consistently for a number of programmes over time. This is why we test.

EXHIBIT 13.2

GARDENERS' WORLD

A garden tools manufacturer wanted to test whether using male or female models in his catalogue would affect response. To his surprise, response jumped some 20 per cent when female models were illustrated with the implements, even though many of them were heavy and difficult to handle. He was unable to explain why. This is an example of testing showing what happens, and that such results are often hard to predict. Here the role of research would be to explain why it happened.

Source: Halsey, B. (ed.) (1992) *The Practitioners' Guide to Direct Marketing*, IDM, Teddington.

However, testing costs money and also takes up a lot of time and management effort. The question of how much to test and how much to leave to management judgement is still a difficult one to answer. Some clarity can be obtained by taking a look at the following financial justification.

JUSTIFYING TESTING FINANCIALLY

The mathematics of testing can be illustrated using the following example.

A children's toy manufacturer has a number of possible products it could lead with as a special offer in its next catalogue, aimed at upmarket young families. Its total database is 600 000 households. It decides to test each product idea before rolling out. Each test is to 5000 customers. The tests are:

Test A: board games   Test C: computer games
Test B: outdoor garden toys   Test D: children's books.

1. Costs are:

Fixed costs per campaign = £2000
Variable costs per catalogue = £1000 per thousand

∴ Total marketing costs per test = £7000.

2. The response rates obtained from the tests were as follows:

Test A: 7%
Test B: 8%
Test C: 5%
Test D: 4%

The gross margin on each purchase averages £20 for all the products.

3. Financial returns per test were as shown in Table 13.1.

Table 13.1: **Financial returns per test**

	Test A	Test B	Test C	Test D
No. mailed	5000	5000	5000	5000
No. of responses	350	400	250	200
Test gross margin	£7000	£8000	£5000	£4000
Costs of marketing	£7000	£7000	£7000	£7000
Net margin	0	£1000	(£2000)	(£3000)
Overall net tests margin = (£4000)				

4. The manufacturer rolls out with the outdoor garden toys (Test B) as the special offer.

Roll out
No. mailed = 600 000 – tests = 580 000
No. of responses = 46 400
Total margin = £928 000
Total marketing costs = £582 000
Net return on roll out = £346 000
Overall return on test plus roll out = £342 000

5. What would be the alternative if the test had not taken place? This depends of course on which product had been chosen for the roll out. Let us assume that product A (board games) was chosen.

Roll out on product A:
No. mailed = 600 000
No. of responses = 42 000
Gross margin = £840 000
Total marketing costs = £602 000
Net return = £238 000

Clearly, even though the tests lost a small amount of money, they were well worth doing, unless the company is lucky enough to guess right with its campaign elements.

Having established the need to test, we are now ready to tackle what variables we should be concentrating on. What exactly should direct marketers be testing?

TEST VARIABLES: WHAT WE NEED TO TEST

We can test just about anything. However, it is important to test only those variables that matter.

'Test the Big Things.'

Bob Stone

What are the most important elements to test? In the 1980s, a very large test was put together by Stewart Pearson, a senior practitioner in the UK. Pearson wanted to understand which elements of direct marketing had the biggest impact on response. He put together an enormous matrix of 57 variables, all within one broad product/market area. He varied the media, the offer (the price, incentives, etc.), the timing, and the creative treatments.

His results, shown in Table 13.2, were a critical lesson for direct marketers.

Table 13.2: **Varying elements to test impact**

Element	Percentage impact – extent to which the best test outperforms the worst test
Media/audience	600% (i.e. the best medium gave a response six times higher than the worst medium, with other elements held constant)
Offer	200%
Timing	100%
Creative	33%

Source: Pearson, S., Personal communication

What does Table 13.2 tell us? First, it says that the target audience is the most important thing to get right, for any given product. As we saw in the strategy section earlier, the product market investment decision is the most important strategic decision a marketer makes, so this result here is perhaps not surprising.

Everything else is less important, with the creative element (often the most tested) being the least important. This does not mean creative differences are not worth explor-

EXHIBIT 13.3

THE DIFFICULTY OF RESEARCHING CREATIVE APPROACHES

A large utility company wanted to test various creative treatments for a direct-mail campaign to its highest value customers, offering them 10 per cent off their bills if they joined its pricing scheme. The main difference in the packages was the outer envelope which had a number of treatments:

■ the blank control

■ a large 'Save 10% off your bills' message

■ a perforated cut at one end of the envelope suggesting you 'Cut 10% off your bill'.

Inside each was copy relating to the envelope theme. The blank control had a very simple letter with no brochure.

In *research*, the large 'Save 10%' treatment was the clear winner. However, the *test results* showed a clear win for the control pack, which got a 20 per cent better response than the others. This example highlights the difficulties of researching creative, which works as much on a subconscious level as a conscious rational level. It is primarily the latter which the research would have picked up, leading to an erroneous conclusion.

ing; a third gain in percentage response can still be critical. But it is necessary to get the importance of the creative element in perspective, compared to other elements of the direct marketing mix.

Pearson's results will not hold exactly true for every situation; they are only guidelines. However, they do lead us to a more profound conclusion. As a marketer, what you say and who you say it to is more important than how you say it. This is particularly important because, in marketing, we often seem to concentrate on the latter at the expense of the former.

TESTING WITH DIFFERENT MEDIA

There is a lot of detail behind the design of a complex test programme, which is outside the scope of this book. The reader is referred to the *Practitioners' Guide to Direct Marketing* (1992) for more information. What we will do here is to touch on the different ways that testing is carried out in different media.

Direct mail

As outlined previously, just about any element of direct mail is easy to test, because the marketer controls every aspect of the campaign, including the exact time that the mailer is released.

Telemarketing

Telemarketing is extremely easy to test, and this is a powerful part of the telemarketer's armoury. Indeed, testing in telemarketing is easier than in direct mail. At the start of an evening's calls, the operatives can be asked to promote a particular product. Because response is instantaneous and high, it may only take 100 calls before a good indication is obtained of the success of that offer. On the same evening, a new offer can be tried and its results compared. Script changes are also commonly tested.

Press and inserts

Inserts and press space are both testable, although not as easily as the above media.

- **Split-run testing:** This is employed for inserts. Here a number of different options (often up to eight) can be tested by interleaving in the print run, allowing the same title to run with different tests and a control. By coding the response device, or using different phone numbers, responses can be tracked back accordingly.
- **A/B splits:** Many publications allow for each alternative copy of the print run to contain either advert A or advert B. Typically, creative changes or, say, colour versus black and white are tested in this way.
- **Cross-over testing:** This is best described through an example, shown in Table 13.3.

In Table 13.3, the first issue of press 1 is compared with the second issue of press 2, and vice versa, and then a comparison is also made between creative approaches. In this way, a comparison is possible between the creative and also the press title. The flaw is that not all other variables are held constant: a second issue has had to be used. There is, however, no better way.

Table 13.3: **Cross-over testing**

| | Press 1 | | Press 2 | |
	Creative	Response	Creative	Response
First issue	A	400	B	200
Second issue	B	250	A	300

Other media

Testing on DRTV is possible, though not easy to achieve without disturbing external variables, rather like press testing described earlier.

New electronic media such as the Internet will provide excellent possibilities for testing offers, creative formats, and so on.

We have seen how test results are used to *predict* what would happen in a roll out. However, to what extent can we be sure that on rolling out we would obtain the same result as the test? Because we only used a sample to test, there is a degree of *uncertainty* in the prediction which we need to take account of. The following section shows how.

CALCULATING UNCERTAINTY IN ROLL-OUT PREDICTIONS

The level of uncertainty in our test results depends primarily on the sample size of the test. The smaller the test, the more uncertain we are of its applicability to the entire database. Having said that, direct marketers want to use as small a test sample size as possible, because testing costs money. What is the minimum test size we can use?

The answer depends on how certain we want to be that the test results represent the whole customer base. The relationship between certainty and sample size can be obtained from a few simple statistics.

The following worked example explains what direct marketers need to do to calculate test sample sizes.

Let us say we test an offer of a free CD on joining a music club. We obtain a response of 2.5 per cent. Our break even for roll out is 2.3 per cent. Can we confidently roll out, being certain the roll out will achieve a response of 2.5 per cent?

If we were to run the same test to another 5000 people within the same target market, would we get exactly the same result? What would your instincts tell you? The answer is that it is possible we would get the same result, but we would not be surprised if the results were slightly different, say 2.4 per cent. If we were to run the test eight times to different samples of the same group, one might envisage the following results:

Test 1:   2.5%
Test 2:   2.4%
Test 3:   2.6%
Test 4:   2.5%
Test 5:   2.7%
Test 6:   2.3%
Test 7:   2.6%
Test 8:   2.8%

We have obtained a variation in test results, with an average of 2.55 per cent. We can say that, of our test results so far, the likelihood is that the full roll out will lie between 2.3 per cent and 2.8 per cent. This bracket within which the roll-out result would be likely to fall can be estimated using statistics. The lower and upper figures (2.3, 2.8) are called the limits of error. The *limits of error* give us a range within which we would expect the roll-out result to lie.

There is one more expression of our uncertainty we need to include. This arises from the fact that, although we believe that the true roll-out response lies within the limits of error calculated, we cannot be 100 per cent certain that it lies therein. There is a small possibility that the rest of the customer base would give a result outside this range. Statistics allow us to calculate how confident we can be that our result will lie within our limits of error. We use *confidence levels* to express this part of our uncertainty. By far the most often-used level is the 95 per cent confidence level. So, in our example, we could say that we are 95 per cent confident that the roll-out response lies between 2.3 per cent and 2.8 per cent. In other words, we can say that 95 times out of 100, our roll-out figure should lie between 2.3 per cent and 2.8 per cent.

To summarise, we want to express our level of uncertainty: it is possible that the roll-out result will be different to the test result. There are two aspects to expressing this uncertainty: limits of error and confidence levels. We will complete the picture now by showing how to relate these measures to the test sample size.

Relating sample size to uncertainty

Provided we fix our level of confidence (nearly always set at 95 per cent), the level of uncertainty in a sample result depends on two things. They are:

- the sample size
- the response percentage.

However, uncertainty is particularly sensitive to sample size, and so it is this which the direct marketer needs to concentrate on to control the predictability of the test. Note that the size of the *roll-out population*, perhaps surprisingly, is not a factor in uncertainty.

Suppose we tested a sample of 5000 people. The response obtained is 2.5 per cent. What are the limits of error associated with this result?

The formula for calculation is:

$$\text{Limits of error, } L = k \sqrt{\frac{R(100-R)}{n}}$$

where

k = constant depending on confidence level chosen (k = 1.96 for 95% confidence levels)
R = response percentage obtained for the test
n = sample size

For our example,

$$L = 1.96 \times \sqrt{\frac{2.5\,(100-2.5)}{5000}}$$

$$L = 0.43$$

It is always best to write out in full what this result actually means to us: We can be 95 per cent confident that the roll out will be 2.5 ± 0.43 per cent. Put another way, we are 95 per cent confident that the roll-out response will be between 2.07 per cent and 2.93 per cent.

How is this useful to us? Bearing in mind that the break even was 2.3 per cent, we can see that this test result leaves us in a quandary. It is possible that the full roll out will yield a response as low as 2.07 per cent, placing us in a loss-making situation. The answer is to test again with a bigger sample size, thereby obtaining a prediction with a smaller limit of error.

Budgeting for direct marketing programmes

In this section, we approach budgeting at two levels. The first is the high-level planning budget that may be set for the year's activities – a strategic budgeting exercise. The second is the individual programme budget, created to manage a discrete activity.

SETTING TOTAL MARKETING BUDGETS

Setting the overall budget is a fairly simple process, utilising the concepts of lifetime value and allowable marketing spend which we introduced in Chapter 3. Ideally the key input that dictates the budget is an accurate target/objective-setting process.

Figure 13.4 shows how the overall yearly budget may be calculated.

Having constructed the total marketing budget, our next task is to divide this into individual programme budgets as efficiently as possible. To do this we use the following seven-step process.

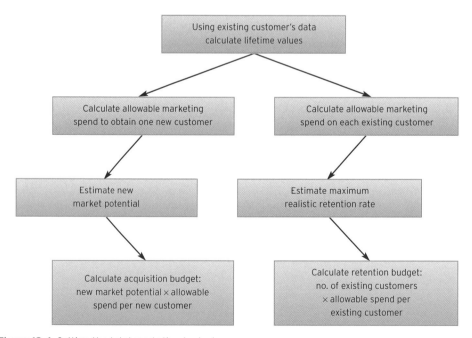

Figure 13.4 Setting the total marketing budget

The seven-step process to constructing a programme budget

Let us say our first programme has a target of acquiring 2000 new customers buying computer accessories. From the lifetime value calculations, the allowable marketing spend has been set at £50 per customer. Our programme budget is therefore £100 000 for the programme (2000 × £50).

The gross margin of each sale is £20. This is less than the targeted spend of £50, but the assumption here is that these customers are highly profitable later on in their 'lifetime' with the company. (In fact this mirrors many actual direct marketing situations.)

The seven-step process enables you to:

■ draw up a test budget to meet the targets set;

■ calculate *target* response rates;

■ undertake 'what if?' analyses with different tests;

■ calculate the percentage of the programme budget to be spent on testing;

■ input the actual test results and calculate the best options for roll out;

■ plan the final roll out and predicted return.

Step 1: Decide what you want to test

Our first step is to draw up a list of tests depending on our need for more knowledge. Let's say we wanted to test media types. A typical list of media types (we won't go as far as actual titles here) for our example might be as follows:

■ direct mail to existing customers

■ direct mail using lifestyle lists

■ direct mail using mail-order lists

■ telephone marketing to existing customers

■ computer magazines

■ direct-response television during computer programmes

■ direct-response radio.

Step 2: Calculate your total test budget

This depends on how much testing you wish to do before moving on to the campaign roll out. If you are following a well-understood direct marketing campaign, you may only be carrying out one or two tests to look for small improvements. If, however, you are trying something totally new, you have a significant learning curve. In this instance, the test budget can often be as much as 30 per cent of total budget.

To estimate total costs for our test we need to decide its size in terms of audience, and then multiply this by the cost per thousand for each medium. Table 13.4 lists typical test cell sizes for different media.

Using the test sizes in Table 13.4 we can calculate the costs of testing, as shown in Table 13.5.

Therefore we are spending 30.5 per cent of our total budget on testing.

Table 13.4: **Typical test cell sizes for media**

Medium	Test cell size
Direct mail	5000 customers
Telephone	1000 customers
Inserts	50 000 customers
Press or magazine advertisement	say 200 000
DRTV/radio	say 500 000

Table 13.5: **Calculation of the total costs of testing**

Medium	Cost/ 000 (£)	Size of audience	Total cost (£)
Direct mail to existing customers	400	5 000	2 000
Direct mail using lifestyle lists	500	5 000	2 500
Direct mail using mail-order lists	500	5 000	2 500
Telephone marketing to existing customers	6000	1 000	6 000
Computer magazines advertisement	50	200 000	10 000
DRTV during computer programs	10	500 000	5 000
DR radio	5	500 000	2 500
Total costs			£30 500

Step 3: Calculate the number of responses required to achieve target

Our target is to spend less than £50 per customer. If we divide the total costs (from Table 13.5) for each medium by £50 we obtain our target recruitment per medium, as shown in Table 13.6.

Table 13.6: **Calculation of no. of responses required to hit target**

Medium	Total cost (£)	No. of customers needed to hit target
Direct mail to existing customers	2 000	40
Direct mail using lifestyle lists	2 500	50
Direct mail using mail-order lists	2 500	50
Telephone marketing to existing customers	6 000	120
Computer magazines advertisement	10 000	200
DRTV during computer programs	5 000	100
DR radio	2 500	50

Step 4: Calculate estimated target response rates

$$\text{Target response rate} = \frac{\text{No. of customers needed to hit target}}{\text{total size of audience}} \times 100\,\%$$

We can therefore work out the target response rate for each medium, as shown in Table 13.7.

Table 13.7: **Calculation of estimated target response rates**

Medium	Size of audience	No. of customers needed to hit target	Target response rate (%)
Direct mail to existing customers	5 000	40	0.8
Direct mail using lifestyle lists	5 000	50	1.0
Direct mail using mail-order lists	5 000	50	1.0
Telephone marketing to existing customers	1 000	120	12.0
Computer magazines advertisement	200 000	200	0.1
DRTV during computer programs	500 000	100	0.02
DR radio	500 000	50	0.01

Step 5: Decide which tests to implement

Assess the response rates in Table 13.7 in terms of previous experience. Decide which tests actually to run with. In the case of the media tests in the example, we would use the AIMRITE formula outlined in Chapter 10 to evaluate the validity of our test choices. Are there any other media that should be tested in place of our choices?

Let's say we decide that the list of media in Table 13.7 is our final test choice.

Step 6: Identify test winners

When the actual test results come in, calculate the return on investment. This is done by multiplying the actual number of responses by £20 (margin per sale), which gives the total margin. The net profit is then total gross margin minus total marketing (in this case media) costs. Table 13.8 shows these calculations.

Step 7: Roll out the test winners to the full audience

Our final step is to roll out to the full audience using the best media. We start with the test medium showing the best *percentage return on marketing investment*, calculated by dividing net profit by marketing costs (expressed as a percentage). When that medium is used up, move down to the second best, and so on, until our budget is exhausted.

In the example, we have £100 000 minus our test budget of £30 500 = £69 500 to apply to the roll out. The best medium is direct mail to existing customers (with a 75 per cent return on marketing investment); the only other profitable medium is DRTV (with a 20 per cent return). Therefore the roll-out in this example might look like Table 13.9.

Table 13.8: **Calculation of net profit margin**

Medium	Total media cost (£)	Actual response rate (%)	Actual no. of customers	Total gross margin (£)	Net profit margin (£)
Direct mail to existing customers	2 000	3.5	175	3 500	1 500
Direct mail using lifestyle lists	2 500	2.0	100	2 000	(500)
Direct mail using mail-order lists	2 500	1.5	75	1 500	(1 000)
Telephone marketing to existing customers	6 000	25	250	5 000	(1 000)
Computer magazines advertisement	10 000	0.20	400	8 000	(2 000)
DRTV during computer programs	5 000	0.06	300	6 000	1 000
DR radio	2 500	0.025	125	2 500	0
Total	£30 500			£28 500	(£2 000)

Table 13.9: **Calculation of total gross margin for roll out of best medium**

Winning medium	Maximum quantity	Maximum quantity minus test quantity (actual roll out)	Roll-out costs (£)	Percentage response (%)	Total gross margin*(£)
Direct mail to existing customers	100 000	95 000	38 000	3.5	66 500

*Total gross margin = actual roll-out quantity × percentage response × margin per sale (£20)

The budget left after this roll out is £31 500 (£69 500 – £38 000). This dictates the roll out to the other remaining test success: DRTV (*see* Table 13.10).

Table 13.10: **Calculation of roll out using remaining medium**

Medium	Budget left (£)	Roll-out quantity*	Percentage response	Total gross margin (£)
DRTV during computer programs	31 500	3.15m	0.06	37 800

*Here, the roll-out quantity is dictated by the budget remaining.

Thus from Tables 13.9 and 13.10, the gross margin from roll outs using these two media is £104 300 (£66 500 + £37 800). Deduct from this the costs of the tests from Table 13.8 and we arrive at an overall gross profit of £102 300.

By inputting the 'actuals' into these calculations, valuable clarity can be gained for the next round of budgeting decisions. This is why direct marketing can exhibit such tight control over its returns on marketing investment.

Market research in direct marketing

In 1992, Mouncey remarked in the *Practitioners' Guide to Direct Marketing* that research had traditionally been under-used by direct marketers. He felt that this was due to the historical development of direct marketing from small entrepreneurial companies who had little interest in market research. The mindset that developed meant that there was little interest in understanding consumer behaviour, that market research was viewed as an expense not an investment, and that testing was viewed as a complete alternative to research.

Within the last few years, however, the picture has changed. Market research is being used increasingly within direct marketing. Writing again in 2002, Mouncey suggested this is because:

■ current and future growth in direct marketing is now largely through major corporations, who have a well-established culture of market research use;

■ the value of market research in adding to the knowledge base that testing provides is being increasingly acknowledged.

Market research has a number of roles in direct marketing which mirror its traditional strengths in general marketing. These include understanding customers and their needs, assisting in product or offer development, providing stimulation for creative development, and assessing the effects of direct marketing campaigns on customers (Webb, 1992).

However, we can sum up the core advantage that market research has over testing more succinctly. Although testing can tell us what consumers' behaviour is, and how much they will respond or stay with us, only market research can tell us *why* they do so. It is vitally important to answer the 'why' question in order to analyse accurately and develop effective strategies for the future.

We need to focus on two main areas of work that can be assisted by market research. The first of these is database analysis, and the second is campaign planning and development.

DATABASE ANALYSIS

We saw in Chapter 3 how the database can be used to analyse our markets. Market research and the database can be used very effectively in tandem, drawing from the complementary skills of each technique.

In general marketing, a large part of the market research budget is used in *descriptive* research. Descriptive research takes a snapshot picture of the marketplace, providing marketers with data on customer profiles, product preferences and underlying attitudes which may underpin their purchases. Most of this research is quantitative, and is concerned with measurement: the number of customers who fit a certain profile, and so on.

These analyses are familiar territory to direct marketers, but we use a database rather than descriptive market research as our analytical tool. The database offers the advantage of looking at populations rather than samples, and behavioural data (what customers actually purchased) rather than claimed behaviour from research surveys.

Another advantage is the vast numbers that can be used for quantitative analysis. Techniques such as cluster and factor analysis, correspondence techniques, and so on, are far more effective with large volumes of data. Databases offer tens or hundreds of thousands of customers; market research typically makes do with samples of a few hundred.

However, market research can provide tailor-made *causal* studies which look specifically to understand what the dependent factors are for customer purchase. This can be better than the database equivalent, which is applying techniques such as regression analysis to data which *may not have been collected for that specific analytical purpose.* Customer databases contain data from a variety of sources, which is there primarily to help in understanding individual customers' value to the company and their needs from that company. We may know that someone plays golf and is wealthy; we may have other lifestyle data about him, but none of this may be related to his psychological drive to buy other golf products, even if regression analysis suggests a correlation. This is where carefully done causal market research can provide an advantage.

Perhaps the greatest value market research can add to direct marketers is in the use of *qualitative* research in an *exploratory* role to increase understanding of marketing situations. Imagine a scenario where a company is faced with a sudden, unexpected increase in customer defections. It is obviously necessary to understand quickly what is going on. Exploratory market research using qualitative techniques such as in-depth interviews and focus groups is an excellent way of increasing our understanding of what drives customers in our market. Although experienced direct marketers of, say, china collectibles (porcelain dolls, decorative plates, and so on) know what makes their customers tick, how does a new entrant operate? What is it that drives someone to spend hundreds of pounds every year collecting china dolls? Answers to questions such as this are best obtained through carefully executed in-depth interviews, group discussions and other qualitative techniques.

To summarise, when analysing markets in order to develop strategies, direct marketers traditionally use databases to replace a lot of measurement work that quantitative research performs in general marketing. Probably the most valuable role for market research in direct marketing is in the use of qualitative research to increase our understanding of our marketing situation.

CAMPAIGN PLANNING AND DEVELOPMENT

Let us take the example of a new product launch through direct marketing. Mouncey (2002) proposes a six-step model which illustrates the role of market research. This is shown in Fig. 13.5.

Each step in Fig. 13.5 can be summed up as follows:

Step 1: Use the database to select samples for market research to test the initial product concepts.

Step 2: Use postal quantitative research to forecast demand, obtaining a low-cost measure of intended take-up. This early forecast enables test product and pricing issues to be solved before test costs are incurred. Postal research replicates the direct-response technique of the direct marketing exercise itself.

Step 3: Use knowledge from database analysis and qualitative research to develop communications material.

Step 4: Move to test: lists/media and product offers are vital to test at this stage.

Step 5: Roll out.

Step 6: Use the database to carry out response analysis, and back up with qualitative and/or quantitative research to understand consumer attitudes to the campaign.

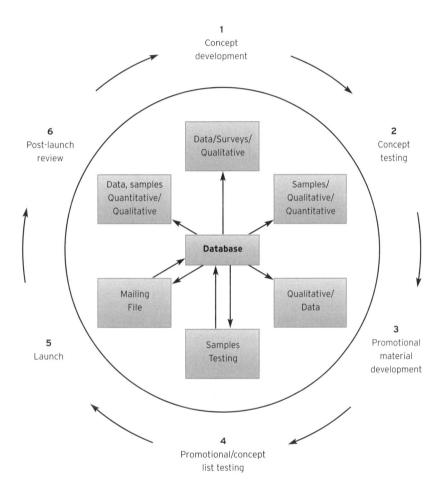

Figure 13.5 Six-step model illustrating role of market research

Source: After Mouncey, P. (2002) 'Using market research for better direct marketing' in Halsey, B. (ed) *The Practitioners' Guide to Direct Marketing*, IDM, Teddington, UK. Reproduced with permission.

Summary to chapter

In this chapter the use of testing in direct marketing was attributed to the close control direct marketers can exert over the various campaign elements. By only varying one factor at a time, marketers can learn a great deal about how to maximise response, while keeping risks of big losses to a minimum. The accepted wisdom is that the audience and the product offering have the biggest impact on response, while the creative element has the least.

Because direct marketers can directly relate costs to revenues, highly accurate cost/revenue budgets can be produced. These can be integrated with testing using the process given, and a full top-level and individual programme budget can be drawn up to be used for 'what if?' analysis.

Questions

1. Why is testing so important to managers, and why is direct marketing better suited to testing than conventional marketing?

2. John Brown Supplies sells office equipment to small and medium businesses in its locality. Each sale averages a gross margin of £30, and next year's budget is £100 000. Use the seven-step process of budgeting outlined in the chapter to draw up a 'break even' test budget, drawing on cost assumptions from Chapters 9 and 10 if necessary.

3. Most mail-order operations make very little use of market research as a tool to help them, preferring to rely on testing instead. If you were addressing them as a market researcher, what benefits of market research could you point out to them?

4. City Products is a mobile phone retailer in London. It wants to test an offer to its own database using direct mail, and has calculated its break-even response rate to be 3.0 per cent. Previous results indicate that this test result should be about 3.5 per cent. Given that it wants to ensure any roll out is in profit, what size sample should the company use for the test?

5. Merchants Financial Services has a customer base of 500 000 existing customers. In September, the marketing manager will mail the complete file but wants to test two new formats, two new creative approaches and two new incentives against the existing control mailer. The cell size in each case will be 10 000. Devise a matrix which makes optimum use of the minimum number of customers for the tests.

6. A university wants to recruit students for the next academic year, and wants to use press advertising for the first time to achieve this. The marketing manager decides to test two creative approaches in an A/B split of the Guardian education section. She does not see the need for any other tests. What comments would you make about her testing priorities?

References

Fairlie, R. (2002) 'Testing, testing, testing' in *The Interactive and Direct Marketing Guide*, IDM, Teddington, Richmond-upon-Thames.

Halsey, B. (ed.) (1992) *The Practitioners' Guide to Direct Marketing*, IDM, Teddington.

Mouncey, P. (1992) 'Using market research for better direct marketing' in Halsey, B. (ed.) *The Practitioners' Guide to Direct Marketing*, IDM, Teddington, Richmond-upon-Thames.

Mouncey, P. (2002) 'Useful market research techniques for interactive and direct marketing' in *The Interactive and Direct Marketing Guide*, IDM, Teddington, Richmond-upon-Thames.

Reichheld, F.F. (1996) *The Loyalty Effect*, Harvard Business School Publishing, Boston, Mass.

Shaw, R. and Stone, M. (1988) *Database Marketing,* Gower, London.

Webb, J. (1992) *Understanding and Designing Market Research*, Dryden Press, Orlando, Florida.

The Royal National Lifeboat Institution

Setting the scene

'It's almost unbelievable isn't it? Over 75 per cent of our income comes from people who have never set foot in a boat in their lives.'

This comment by one of the fundraising team really summed up a worry for the fundraising department of the Royal National Lifeboat Institution (RNLI). Its traditional donor base (recruited and supported by direct marketing methods) often lived many miles from the sea. With their help, the RNLI had grown to be one of the five biggest charities in the UK, able to offer a complete sea rescue service for Britain and Ireland's 5000 miles of coastline. However, this comfortable picture hid looming threats to income: the age of the RNLI's core supporter base indicated a decline in volume, threatening the long-term financial base of the charity itself. What were the fundraising team to do about it?

The Royal National Lifeboat Institution

In 1824, The National Institution for the Preservation of Life from Shipwreck was founded by Sir William Hillary as a voluntarily supported organisation. The folklore of the charity includes the famous story from this time of Grace Darling, a young girl who, on her own, rescued a foundering ship in stormy weather. In 1854 the organisation was renamed The Royal National Lifeboat Institution, which remains unchanged to this day.

The RNLI is a registered charity whose mission is simple, but powerfully expressed: 'to save lives at sea.' It has a legal responsibility to the governments of the UK and Ireland to provide a statutory 24-hour emergency service, to cover search and rescue requirements up to 50 miles out from the coast in all conditions.

Things have changed a lot for the RNLI since those early days. In 1995, RNLI lifeboats were launched 7382 times, with a staggering 52 launches *every day*, on average, during August. Over the last ten years, calls on lifeboats have increased by nearly 50 per cent. This is mainly due to the numbers of people using the water vastly increasing. There has been an increase in the number of 'beach rescues', and also rescues to pleasure craft, commercial power and sail, as well as surfers and swimmers. On average, every day, a lifeboat is launched 16 times in the UK and four lives are saved each day.

This rescue service costs a great deal of money. The RNLI now uses the most modern rescue equipment, including 11 different types of lifeboat, ranging from the 50-foot-long Severn class of boat with a crew of six, capable of 25 knots, to the 16-foot D-class inflatable boat, which operates with a crew of three. Each D-class now costs over £11 000 to buy and more to run each year. This modern fleet is required to ensure that the RNLI's future commitment to reach any point 50 miles off the coast within two-and-a-half hours is met.

With over 400 lifeboats operating in 219 lifeboat stations, the RNLI costs £70 million to run annually, or £194 000 per day. Its fundraising budget is about £7 million p.a. Running costs are used for:

- operational costs
- a new lifeboat building programme

- training crews (vital)

- back up and administration (less than 4 per cent of revenue).

RNLI funds are raised entirely through voluntary contributions, unlike some charities which get state support as well.

The RNLI's supporters

The RNLI has a quarter of a million members and donors, and about 40 000 volunteers who raise money through community fundraising activities. Only about 70 000 of the members are seagoers – about a quarter of the membership base. The RNLI's income currently comes primarily from 'middle Britain' supporters with traditional values.

Middle Britain supporters: a profile

Middle Britain supporters donate because they admire the bravery and self-sacrifice of the RNLI's volunteer crews, who risk their lives to save the lives of others. These donors typically hold 'conservative', traditional values of honour and chivalry, and are attracted to the qualities of bravery and calmness under pressure that are attributed to the RNLI crews. An example of the material that has worked well with this audience is shown in Fig. 13.6.

Over two-thirds of the database are over 65 years old, and 75 per cent are male. They may typically read the *Daily Telegraph* and have some prior connection with the navy, civil service, or similar organisation with traditional values.

However, this membership is facing slow decline. There are a number of reasons for this. The 'middle Britain' and war-time generation – the core demography of the members – is in decline. Another problem is that the RNLI is increasingly in direct competition with other charities for donors' income.

Most of the RNLI's income is from legacies: in 1992 about 70 per cent of its funds came from those who left something to the RNLI in their will. This figure has now declined to 60 per cent and may continue to fall. The reason for this appears to be the increasing costs of long-term elderly care which is depleting retired people's life-savings at an alarming rate. The Henley Centre's research in this area suggests that legacy income to charities may continue to decline for the next 15 years. However, legacies are still tremendously important to the RNLI. Sixty per cent of its income comes from only about 2000 people who leave money in their wills.

Of the five million people who use the sea, only a tiny percentage support the charity that could save their lives. Only about 2.5 per cent (50 000) of the two million boat owners regularly support the RNLI.

There has also been little growth in the number of younger supporters – a worrying trend with such an old base of donors. The problem here is that the RNLI has a low level of saliency among younger people. The values of the RNLI had their strongest resonance among a society with traditional values. There was also a relationship between the RNLI and Britain as a symbol of civilisation, via the Empire, around the world. With the decline of British influence, young people do not identify with this sense of national pride, and the RNLI has suffered; it is no longer something younger people feel *proud of*.

The RNLI's appeal to their donors has been the courage and bravery of the crews. These volunteers go out in any weather, at any time of the day or night, and stay out until the job is done. The RNLI's core message to donors was, 'They'll face 30-foot waves, blizzards, force 9 gales and sub-zero temperatures. All we ask of you is £...'

He'll face 30ft. waves, blizzards, force 9 gales and sub-zero temperatures.

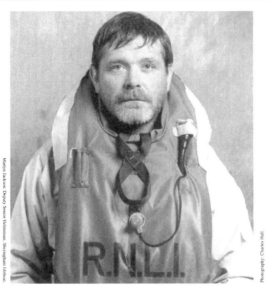

All we ask of you is £15.

- -

To: The Director, RNLI, FREEPOST, West Quay Road, Poole, Dorset BH15 1XF.   SG7/35

☐ I enclose my gift of   ☐ £15   or ☐ £_____

☐ I wish to join the RNLI as a member. My first annual donation is:

£_____ for Shoreline membership (min £15 p.a.)

£_____ for Joint Shoreline membership
(Husband & Wife – min £26 p.a.)

£_____ for Governorship (min £50 p.a.)

£_____ for Joint Governorship
(Husband & Wife – min £90 p.a.)

£_____ for Life Governorship (once-only
payment – min £1,000)

£_____ for Storm Force membership (under 16's –
min £5 p.a.) Please attach name, date of birth & sex of child.

Mr/Mrs/Miss/Ms _____

Address _____

_____

_____

Postcode _____

Lifeboats
Royal National Lifeboat Institution

The RNLI never releases its supporters' names and addresses to other organisations. We may occasionally send information on other, different ways to support the RNLI. If you do not wish to receive this information, please tick the box. ☐ 07

Reg. Charity No. 209603

Figure 13.6 Classic insert used to recruit traditional support

Source: Reproduced by kind permission of the Royal National Lifeboat Institution.

The problem for the RNLI's fundraisers now was to retain their traditional values in fundraising while changing their approach so as to appeal to seagoers. A meeting within the RNLI had yielded some early thoughts about how to achieve this. They felt that seagoers would still relate to the image of the lifeboat helmsman, but would have a more pragmatic view of him and what he and his crew does. The question was: what values should the helmsman project?

Charity fundraising generally

Charity fundraising is very different to commercial marketing. When someone gives to a charity, they are receiving something back, but establishing exactly what is often not easy. For 'inner-directed' people, it may be a satisfaction that they have helped make the world a better place, that by supporting the charity they have done something concrete to uphold their own beliefs and values.

'Outer-directed' people may get satisfaction in expressing their giving as part of their personality. They will associate with the brand values of the charity by giving, and will want to show others that this association says something about them. Thus by giving to, say, Greenpeace, they are identifying with Greenpeace's values of defiance, youthfulness, non violence, and so on.

Others may give for other reasons. Some will give because they get a direct benefit from the charitable service, or they know someone who has benefited.

Although some charities have a big retail presence, the importance of repeat donations from a relatively small number of big givers means that direct marketing is a critical part of the charity fundraising mix. The large charities all have databases of many hundreds of thousands of donors, some of whom give thousands of pounds a year in support. Recruitment is achieved through a variety of methods, of which direct mail has traditionally been the key medium. However, intense competition has led to an overuse of 'cold' direct mail, now regarded by many recipients as 'junk'.

Many charities swap lists in an effort to recruit more donors, although the RNLI has refused to do this. The RNLI will also limit the use of the telephone to its donor base, whose age and values make them highly sensitive to privacy issues and less comfortable with the phone than young people.

Most recruitment is done at a loss: the Charity Aid Foundation's figures found that the average return on investment for acquisition activities is about 0.7:1. Break even on acquisition is considered good. The money is made from repeat donations, perhaps through automatic schemes like direct debit. In contrast to their public image, charities are now very professional outfits, and maximising returns through statistical modelling of their donor base, or using relationship-building techniques to build closer links, are very important activities.

Some charities have found that offering tangible benefits works well for them. The Royal Society for the Protection of Birds offers a range of 'products' (which may include information, access to sites, certificates, car stickers, and so on) which donors or members can opt for in return for guaranteed donations of various sizes. Others set up special clubs or membership schemes for committed givers, in which they may be invited to special events, to receive privileged information, or to see the results of their donations. Action Aid's Sponsor a Child campaign is a long-running example of this.

More recently, growth in donations has come through partnership projects with corporate partners. These could take the form of allowing access by the corporate partner to the donor file for marketing initiatives, or a PR-style connection in which the corporate partner gains from association with the charity. In return, the charity may get help with its own donor recruitment, or direct donations may be made by the partner.

A paper by Saxton (1996) on charity fundraising strategies outlined the primary choices taken by the larger charities. He detailed the following five choices:

1 **Donation-led strategy:** The most commonly used strategy (often inappropriately), the core elements are the need for a large number of new recruits, a heavy frequency of subsequent appeals and high supporter attrition rate. Average lifetime values are low. This approach depends on a constant supply of motivating new stories or topics to provide new stimulus to donate.

2 **The intimacy strategy:** A limited number of new supporters is recruited, but each is carefully nurtured to maximise lifetime value. Communications are carefully put together in such a way as to create a feeling of closeness. This strategy is often suited to major donor departments of large charities.

3 **Audience-led strategy:** A specific audience is taken and a close and lasting relationship is sought, often through membership. The group can be based on attitude and lifestyle. More donations and better relationships are then sought through offers which are carefully put together to take account of the sensibilities of the group. In many ways, the RNLI's approach to its traditional base fits into this strategy.

4 **Product-led strategy:** Here the donor is offered a clear product, such as membership. The Royal Society for the Protection of Birds organises its fundraising clearly around its membership scheme which offers assorted benefits.

5 **Multi-product strategy:** This is a mix of donation-led and product-led strategies. An array of catalogues, appeals, newsletters, and different opt-in membership schemes are communicated to the donor.

Offshore

To counteract the slow but radical changes in its membership profile, a firm policy decision was made to recruit and retain more *seagoing* members. This was to be achieved through the launch of 'Offshore', a new grade of membership especially for sea users. This scheme was to offer a variety of marine-related benefits.

The team at the RNLI wanted to get over a feeling of belonging: that for seagoers, the RNLI is *their* charity. There could also, with some justification, be grounds for marketing 'Offshore' as a thing of duty, or personal responsibility. If anyone should support the RNLI, seagoers should; it is they and they alone who benefit. Why should they rely on the support of others without giving themselves? However, the team knew that attempts to instil feelings of guilt could backfire. Good fundraising was all about arousing such strong feelings of empathy with the cause that instant action was the result. However, such feelings had to be built around values and beliefs if they were to remain beyond a one-off donation.

One possibility was to promote 'Offshore' as the sea equivalent of car breakdown insurance. Whether or not this was a good idea for a charity had yet to be discussed.

Seagoers: A profile

The segment of seagoers defined within the charity as top priority were those who use the sea for pleasure purposes. These were mainly owners of pleasure craft – weekend sailors, and so on – but also users of other craft such as windsurfers and surfers. Sailing is not a cheap sport, and so the profile of seagoers is accordingly quite upmarket. It is also rather younger than the RNLI's core support.

Seagoers' attitude to the RNLI was rather different to that of traditional supporters. Clearly, the RNLI is more relevant to them: they viewed it as a background presence, always there, and the ultimate safety line, but didn't have high everyday awareness of it. They respected the RNLI's abilities – for example, seamanship, knowledge of sea safety and their experience of rescues were all acknowledged, but remained very much in the background of sailors' lives. 'Yachties' in particular were difficult to approach. They were notoriously independent, free-spirited people who disliked being pressured into anything. They were extremely proud of their seamanship, and some saw the RNLI as being only for 'incompetent' inexperienced sailors, although this was not the case.

RNLI research showed that seagoers were always interested in the latest sea safety information, and had a need for all kinds of sea-related products, from sailing accessories and clothing to boat fashion goods.

Official surveys found that seagoers:

■ were younger than traditional supporters: 66 per cent were under 44;

■ were affluent: 63 per cent had a combined income of £25 000 or above;

■ comprised more women than traditional supporters: 32 per cent of seagoers were women.

The surveys also suggested that seagoers were likely to be style conscious, aspirational, self-interested and less altruistic than traditional supporters. They are more aware of marketing techniques, and so would assess approaches rationally rather than emotionally.

Programme issues

An initial analysis document drawn up by the fundraising team revealed the following issues to consider:

■ There was a need to get past the 'taken for granted, always there' state that all rescue services suffer from.

■ There was a need to remind seagoers that the sea is an unpredictable place.

■ A new proposition, repositioned brand values, and a different tone of voice was needed in order to account for the differences between seagoers and middle Britain donors. However, it was important to remember that any material produced for 'Offshore' may be seen by traditional supporters, and they should not feel alienated or 'short changed' by this alternative scheme.

■ At the same time, current brand values needed to be upheld for middle Britain support, but adjusted in tone for seagoers' support, while maintaining a credible overall image. This was a considerable challenge, but could not be ignored by the fundraisers.

■ The team stressed the need to keep recruitment costs as low as possible. It needed to find ways to spread the message and attract supporters at an average of less than £50 per new supporter.

■ 'Offshore' was to be offered to prospects at £40 per annum, i.e. probably making an *initial* loss on the first year's income. However, surveys found that seagoers had suggested a fee of only about £23, on average, for such a package. There is therefore a strong need to offer a package that is perceived as good value for money, but which also puts the correct value on the RNLI's service.

■ The RNLI had given a presentation to some potential business partners. The RNLI was looking for help in promoting the scheme, and in return it would ensure the assisting company would benefit by association with RNLI's powerful brand values.

■ The fundraising team was investigating the possibility of using volunteers to help with the recruitment of 'Offshore' members, but as yet had not developed detailed plans.

■ Various lists of seagoers were available, ranging from subscribers to sailing-related magazines, to the possibility of sponsored questions on lifestyle databases (estimated quote was £1500 per question, plus £100 per thousand names obtained).

■ Seagoers read a wide variety of publications ranging from *Motor Boats Monthly* to *Yachting Life*.

■ The RNLI maintained a strong presence each year at the London International Boat Show, and also ran an RNLI day each year in which fundraising opportunities were maximised. The RNLI was due to celebrate its 175th anniversary in 1999, another major fundraising opportunity.

The task

The RNLI team had a number of planning and implementation issues still to resolve:

1 Formalising objectives and strategies. The key target is to recruit 50 000 Offshore members within three years.

2 The launch of 'Offshore' such that 60 per cent of seagoers are aware of the scheme within six months of launch.

3 A set of programmes to recruit and retain Offshore members, such that each member is recruited at an average of less than £50 each, and gives a return of at least £40 per annum for at least five years.

Questions

With the help of Appendices 13.1–13.3, provide a detailed action plan for the launch and delivery of 'Offshore', giving details of marketing programmes which will deliver the required targets. Your plan should include:

1. A description of what programmes will be delivered to whom and when, with justification. In particular:
   ■ target audiences
   ■ product/price offers
   ■ incentives
   ■ media
   ■ tests
   ■ required target response rates.

2. Decisions on other marketing mix elements and an explanation of how they integrate with direct marketing.

Appendix 13.1: Membership rates and grades

Name	Aimed at	Rate
Stormforce	Junior members	£3
Shoreline	Traditional supporter	£15 (in line with World Wildlife Fund, National Trust)
Offshore	Seagoers	£40
Governors	Major donors	£50–£100
Life governors	Major donors	£1000 one-off payment

Appendix 13.2: Headings from previous RNLI creative briefs to its direct marketing agency, Burnett Associates

A GUIDE FOR TONE AND APPROACH

TARGET AUDIENCE

TONE

AIMS

PROPOSITION

Appendix 13.3: List of questions in survey of yacht club members to be carried out within three months of the brief

General

How long have you been sailing?

How often do you sail?

For what purposes do you sail:

■ work

■ cruising

■ racing

■ other?

Which publications do you read regularly (if any):

■ *Motor Boats Monthly*

■ *Practical Boat Owner*

■ *RYA News*

■ *The Lifeboat*

- *Yachting Monthly*
- *Yachting World*
- *Yachts and Yachting?*

Have you heard of the RNLI?
Do you support the RNLI?
If so, how?

Offshore
[Opportunity for six questions about Offshore to be included.]

Other charities
Do you regularly support other charities?
In what way?

About yourself
Gender
Age
Occupation
Income
Marital status

Reference

Saxton, J. (1996) 'Five direct marketing strategies for non-profit organisations', *Journal of Non Profit and Voluntary Sector Marketing*, 1 (4).

14

WORKED CASE STUDY: VODAFONE

This detailed case study was written after extensive consultation with Vodafone and Harrison Troughton Wunderman. Permission has been granted by Vodafone to tell this story which is based on the realities confronting the company since the turn of the millennium. However, where appropriate, facts and figures have been changed to preserve issues of commercial confidentiality. In particular, confidential database details and budgets have been changed.

This case study would not have been possible without the help of key individuals. Special thanks to Andrew Gwynne of Vodafone, and Martin Troughton and Polly Jones of Harrison Troughton Wunderman.

Since its beginnings, Vodafone, like the other network operators in the mobile phone market, has been aggressively focused on acquisition. Since their introduction as a consumer item in the mid-1980s, mobile phone sales have followed a classic 'S' shaped curve, which reached its peak in the late 1990s to early 2000s (*see* Fig. 14.1).

Mobile phones have been a worldwide phenomenon. This is a story of how technological breakthroughs have driven enormous social changes: we all take for granted now the benefit of instant communicability anywhere, but ten years ago this was a luxury. The early handsets were large and cumbersome, and this was a significant factor in slow

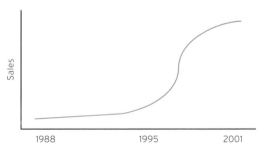

Figure 14.1 Vodafone's mobile phone sales – late 1990s to early 2000s

early growth. But by the mid- to late-1990s the handsets were small and attractive, and the network operators had achieved nearly 100 per cent coverage of the land. In the late 1990s the onset of pre-pay options triggered a dramatic upturn in sales in what Geoffrey Moore, an IT guru, calls a 'tornado of demand'. By 2003 over 77 per cent of the UK were signed up to a network. Mobile phones impact on every aspect of life, being indispensable items for teenagers and their social lives, for anxious parents ensuring their kids can get in touch, for small and big business alike to check on messages, and for hosts of, as yet undiscovered, applications.

With third generation UMTS (Universal Mobile Telecommunication System) technology now available, the speeds of data transfer have enabled a broadband style of 'always on' data transfer capability that enables video downloads in acceptably fast times. This service was launched in the UK in 2003, led by Hutchison Telecom's '3' company. It is hoped that 3G will emulate the success of the existing 2.5G: picture messaging has been one of the success stories here.

Market structure

These technological advances have also contributed to the increasing complexity of the market structure. The strict demarcation between the network operators and the handset suppliers has broken down. In fact there are two types of network operator in the mobile market:

■ 'real' network operators which provide UK-wide mobile phone coverage through a network of masts. Primary players are Vodafone, T-Mobile, Orange, O2;

■ 'virtual' network operators which buy airtime and connection from a real fixed-line or mobile network owner and rebrand and repackage it for specific market segments, for example Virgin Mobile, Value Telecom.

The story of Vodafone

On 1 January 1985 Vodafone made the UK's first mobile call. Vodafone is the world's biggest mobile network operator. It has over 13 million customers in the UK, this being a market share of approximately 32 per cent by revenue. It now have a customer base of over 100 million and interests in network operators across 28 countries. It is said that about 1 in 100 people worldwide have a Vodafone mobile, making over 100 million calls daily.

Vodafone has a strong visual identity based on the colour red and the Vodafone red-and-white 'quotation mark' logo. With a turnover of over £4 billion, and a healthy operating margin of typically over 20 per cent, Vodafone UK is in strong financial shape to face the challenges of the next few years.

Vodafone's major UK competitors: Orange, O2, T-Mobile, Virgin Mobile and 3

O2 (formerly BT Cellnet) launched in January 1985, and in the first year 25 000 customers joined the Cellnet network. For the first time in 1988, Cellnet connected 100 000 customers in a year. In 1992 Cellnet launched the UK market's first consumer tariff package and by 1994 Cellnet had achieved one million customers. Cellnet launched GSM Digital service and launched the UK's first mobile two-way digital fax and data service. However the Cellnet brand ran into difficulties, and was replaced by O2 when BT sold off Cellnet in 2001.

O2 wanted to contrast itself to the functional branding, with a concentration on handsets and price tariffs, it felt favoured by T-Mobile and Vodafone. So, when O2 launched in early 2002 with a £130 million pan-European campaign it announced its intention to build a symbolic brand more in line with that of Orange.

Table 14.1: **Market shares in the UK - 2002**

O2	24
Vodafone	27
Orange	27
Virgin Mobile	23

O2 has a turnover of just under £3 billion and an operating margin of typically 7–10 per cent.

While Orange won a host of awards for its early brand-building efforts with its famous strap line 'The future's bright, the future's Orange', it has done rather less well since. Orange was accused by some as still trying to reassure customers when they no longer need reassuring. Orange has recently launched a rival to 'Vodafone live!' – called 'Orange World'. However the success of 'Vodafone live!' means Orange has some catching up to do. Orange also communicates regularly with its customers via the *Orange* magazine, which acts as a channel for educating customers on new voice and data services available from Orange, and also mails one-off promotions. In 2002 the company discontinued its 'equity' loyalty point system due to lack of customer interest, but offered equity point holders compensation vouchers.

T-Mobile is owned by Deutsche Telekom, the fourth largest telecommunications company worldwide. T-Mobile (formerly One2One) was originally launched on 7 September 1993 – the UK's first fully digital mobile communications network. Today over 9 million people use the One2One network. The network covers over 99 per cent of the UK population and handles around 260 million calls a week. The company changed its name from One2One to T-Mobile on 18 April 2002. For its relaunch as T-Mobile the advertising campaigns featured Andre Agassi and Steffi Graf as 'ambassadors' for the T-Mobile brand. T-Mobile launched its new brand with a multimedia campaign in March 2002 with the strapline 'Get more', positioning the network as offering more to customers than its rivals offer.

Virgin Mobile is now established as the most successful virtual network operator in the world, and is the UK's fifth major operator in this area. Since its launch in November 1999 it had attracted 3.1 million customers to November 2003, making it one of the fastest growing mobile phone companies in history.

Virgin Mobile is a 50:50 joint venture company between Sir Richard Branson's Virgin Group and Deutsche Telekom's T-Mobile, and is the UK's first mobile virtual operator. Virgin pays wholesale prices for the use of the network of (former) operator 'One-One'. (Another new player is Tesco which does the same with O2's network.)

It was the first operator to scrap peak rate calls, introducing a daily discounting tariff. The Virgin brand is very powerful as a symbol, rightly or wrongly, of being 'on the customer's side'. Hence this is definitely a threat to the big players including Vodafone. The original four players have been criticised by some commentators for weak brand building, which some say has allowed new entrants like Virgin and Tesco into the market.

New technology – the launch of 3G

The lessons from the past suggested that new technology has to be customer focused to succeed. With the failure of the first WAP launch, the network operators and the handset manufacturers have learnt the lesson that mobile phone users are not interested in technology for its own sake. The big difference between the '2.5G' phones and the old WAP phones was the new emphasis on fun and entertainment – most of the content services are aimed at younger users who are most likely to upgrade their phones every year to keep pace with the latest models. 2.5 G – the technology behind 'Vodafone live!' – has succeeded. The question with 3G was whether, even if the services were what people want, they can be persuaded to pay for them. The first player in 3G was Hutchison with the launch of 3. It had signed up 150 000 customers in its first three months of launch in 2003. This was well below its first year target, with criticism coming that its technology was basically not yet ready. Handsets were too clumsy and the promised high quality video had yet to deliver.

Vodafone – from acquisition to retention

By late 2003 it had been clear for some time that the market was in transformation. No longer were there unlimited supplies of new customers to sign up, in fact these had significantly reduced. The priority for all the networks has therefore moved from acquiring customers to retaining them. The key measure is churn – the rate of customer turnover. Through the last few years Orange has claimed to have the lowest overall churn rate in the industry, while Vodafone's has been close to the industry average of 28 per cent.

Retention was an issue for both contract and pre-pay customers. The industry had yet to make a success of loyalty schemes. Vodafone had operated a scheme of collection of BA Miles between 1996 and 2002. While the scheme had a small number of loyal, dedicated collectors, it was not seen as relevant to the product or the brand by the majority of Vodafone's customers and was discontinued at the end of 2002. The blow was softened by offering high-value customers who collected BA miles a free business equipment offer, but it was clear that some rethinking was needed to refresh the strategic commitment to retention. More recently, Vodafone has signed up as one of the partners for the Nectar loyalty scheme. Vodafone will give customers two Nectar points for every £1 they spend on calls, text messages, picture messages, ringtones and games. The task was to integrate Nectar into a successful retention strategy – points on their own are never enough.

Vodafone realised that in order to reduce its unacceptably high levels of churn, it had to first understand the things that led customers to leave, and then secondly to use this knowledge proactively. Price, new products, branding, and service delivery were all potentially important. The role of direct marketing was yet to be fully developed however. Thanks to good teamwork between Vodafone and the award winning agency Harrison Troughton Wunderman, Vodafone could see the potential of direct marketing. What was needed now was a strategic plan.

Understanding the retention problem

As with all telecommunications sectors, in the mobile business there is a strong momentum towards price as the major driver of choice. Business and domestic customers now see little difference between network quality amongst the suppliers. As a result, all the operators have introduced price schemes that can quickly become a maze of complexity. Cynics have argued that the strategy is deliberate price confusion, making comparisons so difficult that customers simply give up on the detail and take whatever seems an attractive deal on the surface. Hence the importance of sales promotion driven marketing.

Part of the problem was that all this skirmishing between the operators on price deals simply alerted customers about price as an issue all the more. This was a particular problem as customers approached the end of their contract period. Vodafone knew that the point of maximum danger was about a month before the contract ran out.

It was less clear what role customer service played. Of course service was important, in the sense that if a customer contacted Vodafone with a request or with a problem to be solved, then they expected to be acknowledged that they were known, that their problem was understood, and that it would be 'owned' by the company. As a minimum, customers expect that if they rang Vodafone the next day, they would not have to start from scratch explaining what their problem was.

To address this was as difficult for Vodafone as it was for all large service companies. CRM was a major issue. One competitor, Orange, had built a strong reputation for the quality of its customer service. Orange has five communication centres offering telephone and e-mail response to customer queries. It was important for the CRM system to be linked to the proactive database-driven contact planned for by the direct marketers. If a customer has contacted the firm and made his or her needs explicit and clear, they want this reflected in any subsequent communications. So, someone who has expressed an interest in data transfer may expect contact about new developments. In contrast, a retired gentleman who has bought a phone and then rung Vodafone to ask how to switch it on, would expect simple help. Vodafone has recently appointed a new director of CRM, responsible for increasing its focus on its existing customers. The new director will look to further improve Vodafone's data capabilities for direct marketing.

Meanwhile Vodafone has been addressing its data capabilities. Vodafone information systems could now identify account holders (pay the bills) and end users (everyday users of the phone). They now held behavioural data that could identify calling habits. How long users phoned for, how many times they phoned, calling destinations, use of SMS and data transmission, use of voicemail, and so on, were all analysable to an individual level. Quick decisions were required about whether to overlay the data with geodemographic and lifestyle products, and also business data.

Although Vodafone had yet to build up a complete picture of its customer base, it recognised that segmentation strategies were now becoming critical with the new focus on existing customers. The data made segmentation theoretically possible in terms of customer value, loyalty, likelihood of switching behaviour, product usage including innovativeness, as well as the more traditional geodemographic and lifestyle methods. For the first time, predictive modelling was being used to estimate future lifetime values for individual customers based on a host of variables including recency, frequency and value data from the past, switching history, and product data. Further back, customer history data was also important: for instance it was known that many of the recently acquired customers were previous users from other networks. This meant they had switched networks at least once, and were high risk to do so again.

Increasing average revenue per user

The other, linked, issue that was now uppermost in the operators' minds was average revenue per user (ARPU). Network operators began reducing subsidies on pre-pay handsets in late 2001 as they saw the effect that high numbers of pre-pay customers was having on their ARPU. This contributed to the downturn in pre-pay sales. By 2002 the four major network operators had introduced new pay-monthly tariffs which offered much better value than in previous years, with more generous allowances of free call minutes and text messages, cheaper rates for calling other mobile networks and flat rates for calls made at peak times of day. Independent retailers as well as major specialist chains such as The Carphone Warehouse had reported an increasing proportion of pay-monthly contracts as a result.

Nevertheless, while the capabilities of the phones had increased dramatically, customers had yet to catch up in usage of these extra services. Much of the industry marketing in this area had suffered from an over-focus on the technology itself, with meaningless acronyms like WAP being bandied about. There was an urgent need for a more customer focused approach.

Vodafone's extensive products and services in 2003 included:

- an extensive array of handsets, sold in conjunction with original equipment manufacturers. High value handsets include the Sony Ericsson T68i. Standard handsets offered through Vodafone include the Samsung A-300;
- ringtones;
- a range of answering and messaging services, including voicemail – an automatic answering machine service;
- 'Vodafone live!': This is Vodafone's primary 2.5G offer to customers, and has proved very successful. Picture messaging, gaming capability, access to e-mail, news and

entertainment services are all included. Football highlights are also about to be offered on a pay-per-view basis offering video highlights of goals and interviews from top premier league clubs. However the quality of video services will improve significantly with the launch of 3G services;

■ 'new WAP' services. Vodafone's website describes wireless application protocol as the technology that enables a slimmed-down version of the Internet to appear on the screen of a mobile phone. It's useful for travel information, sports headlines and e-mail – in fact, anything where customers need concise information within seconds. However this service is rarely promoted now as it has been largely superseded by 'Vodafone live!';

■ GPRS services. The website again: 'GPRS, or General Packet Radio Service, is a new way of sending and receiving information using a mobile phone. With a GPRS phone you can be always connected to Internet services, whereas with non-GPRS phones you have to log-in every time you want to access information. The introduction of GPRS means that accessing services like the Internet, WAP or your company's Intranet, is quicker, easier and better value for money.' Vodafone's new BlackBerry product allows people to keep in touch with calendars and e-mails while on the move. Aimed at the business audience, this was an innovation that had yet to reach mainstream audiences.

■ personal digital assistants: 'PDAs, or handheld PCs, offer pocket-sized computing to anyone who needs their diary, address book, e-mail and important files wherever they go. Most PDAs can be synchronised with a laptop or desktop PC, allowing you to carry essential information with you when you leave your home or office. However, to make the most of a PDA, you also need access to the Internet wherever you are, so that you can check your e-mail and browse the Internet when you're on the move.' (*See* Fig. 14.2.)

■ texting services or SMS: 'Text messaging is the best way to keep in touch when it's difficult to talk. Whether you're in a noisy bar, on a crowded train, in a meeting or just don't want to be overheard, Vodafone text messaging lets you send a message of up to 160 characters straight to another mobile phone. You simply type the message using the keypad of your mobile. Some mobiles have a built-in dictionary that pre-

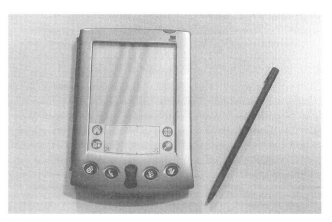

Figure 14.2 A typical PDA

dicts the word you're typing, which can help you send messages even faster. Receiving standard text messages from other mobiles is completely free. Sending text messages is charged according to your price plan – they're 12p each (inc. VAT) in the UK on most Vodafone pay monthly plans, although they can be as low as 6p (inc. VAT) on some price plans that include a monthly text message allowance';

■ a great variety of payment options and methods. For example M-Pay. 'Vodafone m-pay bill is a new way to buy low cost items online by charging them to your mobile phone. Anyone can use it – all you need is a Vodafone mobile phone. Whatever you want to buy, from games and ringtones to business news and birthday e-cards, you can pay quickly and easily using Vodafone m-pay bill.'

(For the latest Vodafone products and services go to http://www.vodafone.co.uk)

Understanding the problem – ARPU

At the heart of the problem is the complexity of the services on offer. 'No-one gives you a lecture about how to use the phone' complained Vodafone's marketing team. 'You just buy it and off you go.' This could get worse before it gets better with the new video services. The gap between the early adopters (those who are experienced with the new technologies) and mainstreamers (those who are content to use the phone for voice only) is widening. Somehow Vodafone in common with the other operators had to first excite the mainstreamers about the possibilities of the new services, and secondly persuade them over the learning curve of how to actually use them.

One example of this has been Vodafone turning its efforts toward an older audience with a £4 million campaign that contrasted with the network's youth-focused 'Vodafone live!' ads fronted by David Beckham. The TV and outdoor ads were designed to encourage people aged 35-plus to use their mobile spontaneously. Apparently over 35s are less likely to keep their mobile on and turn to it as a way of passing the time. They are also much less likely to have personalised voicemails or send text messages.

Towards a direct-marketing strategy

Vodafone's director of marketing sat down with the team from his specialist direct marketing agency Harrison Troughton Wunderman. He had heard all the hype about data driven one-to-one marketing, predicting individual customer's needs precisely based on their data, and communicating with them uniquely. Fair enough: thanks to the efforts of the CRM team, the capability was there for the future. But, at present, he needed to understand how to weave in this capability into the things Vodafone did already.

There were a number of things to throw into the mix. Customers already received what Vodafone called 'administrative' communications, such as bills and contracts. There were always opportunities for 'bill stuffers' or similar, which could be included in these mailings. A recent example was the questionnaire/bounceback campaign to business customers (*see* Fig. 14.3).

Campaign Name: *Questionnaire/Bounceback*
Live Date: *June/September 2002*
Author: *Jenny Poulter*

Objectives
- Update customer data.
- Determine customer product requirements, by size and nature of company.
- Project learnings across customer base and use to develop targeted programme of product-based communications.
- Respond to individual's stated requirements with relevant product information.

Targeting
- 64 000 OMBs/SOHOs business customers – decision makers.
- Selected by current usage – from users of basic products (e.g. Voicemail) to e.g. GPRS users.

Structure
- Mail OCR-scannable questionnaire, attached personalised letter and RPE.
- Collect and scan responses.
- SMS thanking responders.
- Mail bounceback multi-product brochure to responders – with personalised letter directing customers to the pages on which the products for which they declared an interest are featured (restricted by budget to this format).

Idea
- Questionnaire was branded 'How are you' (in line with Vodafone's overall branding) as we are asking customers for information about themselves.
- £5 credit offer on questionnaire to encourage response.
- 'Bounceback' – a very generic multi-product guide explaining how to use mobiles to boost customer's business.

Creative
- Proposition: 'Vodafone would like your help to improve its service offering to you'.
- Outer line questionnaire: 'Is your mobile doing enough for your business?'
- Outer line on bounceback: 'Thanks for your company' – acknowledges response. A5 brochure, with section for each product. Cover = drag queen, in showbusiness-y dress, in an 'I'm the business' pose. Headline = 'I'm the business'.

Projected return
- Questionnaire not a direct return driver – primarily an information-gathering exercise.
- However, expected (but undefined) positive spin-offs in customer satisfaction and product take up/ARPU for customers who are sent questionnaire.
- Bounceback: aim for 12 per cent of all customers to start using or significantly increase their usage of any of the services in the booklet.

Results
- 8.6 per cent response rate on questionnaire.
- Bounceback: no response could be recorded – as generic publication for other uses.

Learnings and recommendations
- Analysis of results has been useful in determing and reassured NBA decision making. Also helpful in building up better picture of business customers.
- Clear picture of preferences (for Vodafone services) by size of company and overall.
- Restricted by Vodafone database – low population of company type/size data prevents results being properly applied to base.
- Results skewed because mailing decision maker not end-user – inadequate data.
- Product questions were structured around Vodafone propositions. In some cases, could have been misleading – direct questions may have improved accuracy.
- Company data distorted, probably as not enough categories given (restricted by Vodafone industry from database).

Figure 14.3 The questionnaire/bounceback campaign to business customers
Source: Reproduced by kind permission of Vodafone and Harrison Troughton Wunderman.

Figure 14.3 Continued

New product developments were clearly important. The style and capability of the phones, driven by technological improvements, were in constant flux. The opportunities to offer upgrades and new styles were always there, but needed to be organised into a plan. When should these upgrades be offered? Should special offers be part of the marketing approach? While this was tempting to retain customers, it had to be offset against the need to increase average revenue per user. Dropping the price of the phones seemed contrary to this. More detailed analysis of customer segments and decisions about precise targeting were needed. In May 2002 Vodafone had sent the innovative Q1 upgrades mailer to business customers at the end of their contracts (*see* Fig. 14.4).

Campaign Name: *Q1 upgrades*
Live Date: *May 2002*
Author: *Kylie Framp*

Objectives
■ Upgrade 6 per cent of the target audience (10 per cent response rate with 60 per cent conversion rate).
■ Reduce churn as a result of customers signing a new 12-month contract when they upgrade.

Targeting
■ 24 000 Vodafone business customers who are at the end of their contracts.
■ Split by customer value, i.e. high-value customers offered a better upgrade deal (in terms of price) than low value customers.

Structure
■ Phased DM over two weeks to the account holders (not the end user).

Idea
■ Vodafone are offering businesses the latest GPRS mobile phones on the market. By upgrading to these handsets, customers can work more efficiently. With faster Internet access they will be able to send and receive information whilst out of the office – saving time and increasing productivity.

Creative
Proposition: 'Get more business done when you upgrade to the fastest handsets on the market.'
■ The customer receives a small white box with the headline reading 'Something to help you keep up with your new mobile'. They then open it to find a sachet of energy sweets inside.
■ A personalised letter is enclosed detailing the handset upgrade offer.

Projected return
■ Average response rate of 10 per cent across all cells.
■ Churn to decrease.

Results
■ Pack well received at Vodafone.
■ Pack used again for Q3 upgrade mailings.

Learnings and recommendations
■ There was concern that some customers may complain about the danger to children receiving sweets in the mail – it was ensured that the pack reflected these concerns and this was also checked off by the legal department.

Figure 14.4 The Q1 upgrades mailer
Source: Reproduced by kind permission of Vodafone and Harrison Troughton Wunderman.

Figure 14.4 Continued

It was also clear that customers themselves created marketing opportunities through their behavioural signals. Given the range of products and services now available it was tempting to create multi-item brochures and market these to everyone as often as possible. This 'mass' approach has the merit of marketing simplicity but this was misleading: the last thing customers wanted was to be swamped with detail about complex products and services, much of which wasn't relevant to them. They were looking for the company to understand their lives in terms of how they used their mobile phones – and then to help with solutions. Vodafone could see that the database could trigger individually-driven marketing (*see* Fig. 14.5 and Fig. 14.6).

Campaign Name: ***Wicked Welcomes NBA***
Live Date: ***August 2002***
Author: ***Nicola Jones***

Objectives
■ To encourage the uptake of Wicked Welcomes to customers.
■ Achieve 200 000 Wicked Welcomes users.

Targeting
■ Vodafone pay as you talk and contract customers with a slight bias towards pay-as-you-talk customers.
■ Customers who already have shown an interest in logos and ringtones.
■ Under 25s who see their phone as a fashion accessory.

Structure
■ Direct mail.

Idea
■ Get someone famous to answer your phone.

Creative
■ Proposition: 'Would you like someone famous to answer your phone?'
■ Postcard with a picture of a Michael Caine look-a-like on the front.
■ Headline on front: 'Oi! Not a lot of people know this . . .'
■ Headline on reverse: '. . . but did you know Vodafone has over 100 Wicked Welcomes to choose from?'

Projected return
■

Results
■ Anecdotally, the feedback has been that the product has not preformed as well as initially hoped.

Figure 14.5 Individually-driven marketing
Source: Reproduced by kind permission of Vodafone and Harrison Troughton Wunderman.

Figure 14.5 Continued

Campaign Name:	NBA5 – international roaming DM
Live Date:	November 2002
Author:	Jenny Poulter

Objectives
- Communicate new flat rate roaming charges in Europe, as well as benefits of international call saver.
- For business customers, increase roaming awareness, usage and revenue.
- Provide a device for customers to keep which details roaming-call costs.

Targeting
- 7000 business customers a month, not currently using international roaming.

Structure
- A mailing as part of Vodafone's programme of communications to move business customers' up the product ladder', i.e. towards using more complicated (and often data-rich) services, in order to increase ARPU. Once a customer has started using a new service, they will then be sent a communication about the 'next best' service in this 'product ladder'.
- DM pack
- Primary call to action is for customers to take phone with them when they go abroad.
- Also secondary CTA – call Vodafone with any problems/queries.

Idea
- Customers' chief concern in using their mobiles abroad is that they'll be landed with a large and unexpected bill on their return. Especially pertinent for small businesses with low margins. To remove this fear, and make it easier to understand call charges, need is to communicate that Vodafone have introduced two flat rates for calling from abroad. A £5 incentive to be used to encourage customers to try using their mobiles while abroad.

Creative
- **Proposition: 'With Vodafone's flat rate roaming-call charges, you'll always know the cost of a call.'**
- Outer line, 'Important numbers to remember when you're abroad.'
- Letter with tipped on red Z-card (for customers to keep), with front reading, '75p per minute' (gold networks) and '99p per minute' (silver networks). The headline underneath reads, '(Vodafone's new flat rates for Europe are all you need to know to make business travel easier.)'.
- Z-card opens up to show map of Europe with cost of calling each country marked. Back of Z-card shows other useful info, e.g. numbers of international airports.

Projected return
- 7 per cent of audience to start using or significantly increase roaming calls each month.

Results
- The piece was well received internally at Vodafone. It has been deemed an important activity which should be continued.

Learnings and recommendations
- This was the third concept presented for this brief. This was partly because the limited budget restricted the 'keepsake' part of the mailing. This third concept was the simplest, which seems to be the best solution in this case.

Figure 14.6 Individually-driven marketing
Source: Reproduced by kind permission of Vodafone and Harrison Troughton Wunderman.

April 2003

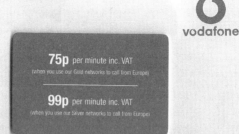

(Vodafone's new flat rates for Europe are all you need to know to make business travel easier.)

Dear Mr Sample

The next time you take off for a business trip to Europe, be sure to pack your Vodafone mobile as well as your toothbrush. These days you'll find it's just as easy to use.

There are just two flat rates when you're calling from any of 32 European countries to the UK: 75p per minute inc. VAT (64p exc. VAT) when you use our Gold networks and 99p per minute inc. VAT (84p exc. VAT) on our Silver networks (you'll find full details in the easy-to-follow guide attached above).

In other words, you'll not only be able to keep track of your business, but keep track of your spending as well.

There are a few other important numbers you might find worth remembering, too. For a start, you can use your Vodafone mobile on over 320 networks in over 140 countries around the world. So even if you're travelling outside Europe, chances are you'll be able to use your phone – which means you won't have to pay high hotel tariffs. Neither will you have to waste time trying to find a payphone (and then seeing if it takes coins or a phonecard, and then trying to work out the Latvian for 'excuse me I can't get this phone to work, can you help me, please?').

See for yourself how easy it is and get £5.00 worth of free international calls.

Here's another number to remember. Simply call us on **08700 736 436*** to try out our new flat rates the next time you go to Europe, and we'll credit £5.00 worth of free international roaming calls to your mobile 07777 777 777 on your next Vodafone bill.

I hope all this makes it easier for you to get more from your Vodafone mobile. If you have any questions, just call us on the number above.

Yours sincerely

Helen Keays

Helen Keays
Customer Development Director

* Calls charged at your telephone provider's published rate. Lines are open 8.00am – 8.00pm Monday to Friday, 9.00am – 6.00pm Saturday.
  Calls may be monitored or recorded for training, security and other purposes permissible by law.

Vodafone Limited
Vodafone House, The Connection, Newbury, Berkshire, RG14 2FN, England.   08/VC500006/07777777777/0000027/123456/01

Registered Office: Vodafone House, The Connection, Newbury, Berkshire, RG14 2FN, England. Registered in England no. 1471587.

Figure 14.6 Continued

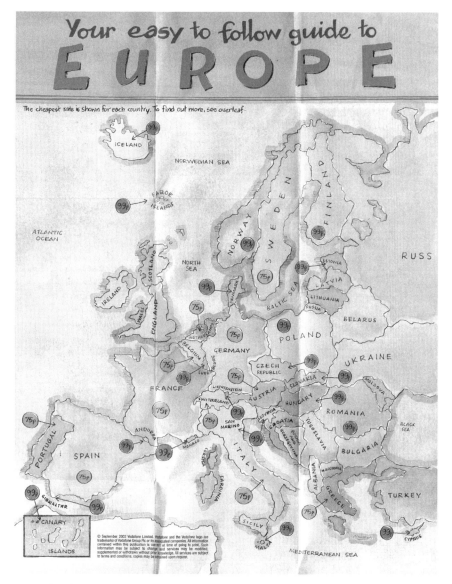

Figure 14.6 Continued

Figure 14.6 Continued

The brief

Before answering the brief you are directed to access the following websites:

www.o2.co.uk

www.virginmobile.com

www.vodafone.co.uk

www.orange.co.uk

www.t-mobile.com

and analyse the product offerings and price tariffs. Note the complexity of what is offered and the difficulties of comparison of prices.

You have just joined HTW and have been drafted on to the Vodafone team. They have asked you to get involved in drawing up next year's direct-marketing plan. Create a detailed direct-marketing strategy and set of programmes that will achieve the following:

■ reduce churn rates across the board by 10 per cent;

■ increase average revenue per user from £270 p.a. to £290 p.a.

In your answer include analysis, objectives and strategies, and make explicit the role of direct marketing as a part of the marketing philosophy and mix of the company.

You have been given a budget of £15 million and will be expected to break even on direct product/service sales from that activity, before taking into account reduced churn or increase in average revenue per user. Once these are taken into account, the final ROI should be of the order of 3:1.

Make recommendations for a three-year time period ahead.

ANSWERING A DIRECT MARKETING CASE STUDY

The purpose of this section is not to spoil the Vodafone case study by seeking to give a 'chapter and verse' answer to it. Rather it is to give readers an insight into what a tutor might want from their submission, based on the experience of many hours spent marking student submissions at undergraduate, postgraduate and diploma level.

The case asks for a one-year plan. Although there are many ways of setting out a plan, the broad headings of McDonald's well known planning process will be used here. We will therefore use this as our framework, within which some hints are offered for a typical answer. Some specific hints about the Vodafone case are given later on.

EXECUTIVE SUMMARY

This should summarise:

- the paper's objectives
- its methodology
- the findings of its analysis
- recommendations.

STAGE 1: ANALYSIS

The usual output here would be a *prioritised* SWOT and PEST analysis, covering *only* those issues which are important to the planning period, and emphasising those over which Vodafone has control. Further analysis would lead to a succinct 'key issues' list which should inform the subsequent stages. These 'issues' should be the main informer of the strategy because they imply that the company cannot ignore them.

STAGE 2: OBJECTIVES

Objectives should be SMART: Simple, Measurable, Aspirational yet Realistic and Time-based. While marketing objectives should be about *products and markets*, direct marketing objectives can give clarity to the business if they are specified in terms of target numbers of customers to be acquired and retained, and relating budget to target with an *'average spend per customer'* objective.

STAGE 3: STRATEGY

Often the most difficult stage to produce a credible answer. The CIM approach for general marketing (rather than direct) situations is to use Ansoff's matrix headings as triggers for strategy. However, students may be advised to follow the direct marketing strategy process outlined in Chapter 5, with the following key elements:

- the role of direct marketing as a part of the overall marketing approach;

- deciding the split between acquisition of new markets and retention of existing customers;

- the acquisition strategy: targeting decisions on new or similar markets; the product/price offer; positioning and branding issues; communications mix;

- the retention strategy: segmenting the database by value/need; targeting according to objectives set; retaining through price/service/dialogue/one-to-one approach.

How the company is to achieve competitive advantage should be clearly outlined. It may also be that wider marketing/business issues should be considered. Distribution, market research, customer service, new product development, and so on, may all be strategically vital to consider for the direct marketing plan.

It is worth re-emphasising here that strategies are *guides* that give the broad direction which tactical activities should follow.

STAGE 4: TACTICS

Here, a full programme of activities, based on the strategy, should be outlined. Target audiences, product/price offers, incentives, timings, and communication issues – media, message, contact strategies, creative (if asked for), and tests to be carried out – are all required here. Core tactical decisions on media, incentives and creative approach should all be justified.

STAGE 5: BUDGET

Broad costings for each programme should be given and a test and roll-out budget calculated as shown in Chapter 13. The ratio of testing to roll-out spend should be justified. The budget should clearly relate costs to revenues, showing what response rates are required to break even or hit target. Sample costs per response for each programme should be outlined. A commentary on the likelihood of hitting each programme target should be offered.

Any programmes not related to customer contact (e.g. operational improvements) should still have incremental revenue calculations estimated, with justification.

AVOIDING TYPICAL ERRORS

The following is a summary of typical examiners' comments on submissions which have received low marks:

- Executive summaries are often just verbal contents pages.

- SWOTS/PESTS are not prioritised, full of generalisations and containing issues outside the control of the company concerned.

- The remainder of the plan then ignores any SWOT/PEST or key issue output.

- Objectives are too broad, not related to budgets available. Average allowable marketing costs per customer are not calculated.

- Sometimes objectives and strategies are badly mixed up. Although one person's objective is another's strategy, depending on the level of the business they are at, there should still be no confusion because the writer adopts a particular level of the business in their answer. If this is at marketing director/marketing manager level, then 'to build a database' is *not* an objective; rather it is an element of strategy.

■ Direct marketing strategies are very formula driven, with no appreciation of the choices available. They are over focused on communications, revolving around media choices and offers which should be in the tactics section. Little appreciation is shown of how direct marketing has been used to add value to the business in a strategic way. Too many platitudes about competitive advantage, relationship building and targeting are given without any careful consideration of choice.

■ Tactical decisions are not justified, and just presented in a descriptive way.

■ Budgets are superficial lists of costings, with no attempt to link to projected revenues and response rates required to hit target.

HINTS FOR THE VODAFONE CASE STUDY

The intention here is not to provide a complete prescription, but to give some broad guidance for students attempting an answer. The following narrative is in no way designed to constitute a complete or definitive answer.

By reading between the lines a little here, you will see that direct marketing is in some ways yet to fully develop in the mobile sector as a whole.

Relatively few figures were given in the case. However, budgets should be estimated from previous years' figures, taking into account market opportunities. Objectives in terms of numbers of customers acquired and retained should be set, ensuring the marketing spend per customer is realistic.

The key area for your consideration is retention. It is a good idea to take a step back: in the industry as a whole, possibly only Orange has created a corporate brand that has been a successful attractor of custom. Much more important has been price: but here you are cautioned against over-aggressive discounting which would be unprofitable for the firm. The trick is to use price as a much more precise weapon – who needs to be targeted from price offers? Where is it profitable for the firm to do so?

All these options and more should be considered. A careful answer would look for a realistic role for direct marketing, in some ways playing a support role in up-selling new products and services, but taking a lead role in retention.

Acquisition strategies may also be mentioned and should be realistic: there is almost total saturation in the market, so much new custom will come from either new entrants – kids – or from competitor customers switching. Bear in mind that if you aggressively discount to attract – what are these new customers going to be loyal to? You, or the deal? Is there a better way?

INDEX